Scholars of Tort Law

Edited by
James Goudkamp
and
Donal Nolan

•HART•
OXFORD • LONDON • NEW YORK • NEW DELHI • SYDNEY

HART PUBLISHING

Bloomsbury Publishing Plc

Kemp House, Chawley Park, Cumnor Hill, Oxford, OX2 9PH, UK

HART PUBLISHING, the Hart/Stag logo, BLOOMSBURY and the Diana logo are trademarks of Bloomsbury Publishing Plc

First published in Great Britain 2019

A catalogue record for this book is available from the British Library.

Library of Congress Cataloging-in-Publication data

Names: Goudkamp, James, 1980- editor. | Nolan, Donal, editor.

Title: Scholars of tort law / edited by James Goudkamp, Donal Nolan.

Description: Oxford [UK] ; Chicago, Illinois : Hart Publishing, 2019. | Includes bibliographical references and index.

Identifiers: LCCN 2019021088 (print) | LCCN 2019021905 (ebook) | ISBN 9781509910588 (EPub) | ISBN 9781509910571 (hardback)

Subjects: LCSH: Torts. | BISAC: LAW / Torts.

Classification: LCC K923 (ebook) | LCC K923 .S35 2019 (print) | DDC 346.03—dc23

LC record available at https://lccn.loc.gov/2019021088

ISBN: HB: 978-1-50991-057-1
ePDF: 978-1-50991-059-5
ePub: 978-1-50991-058-8

Typeset by Compuscript Ltd, Shannon
Printed and bound in Great Britain by CPI Group (UK) Ltd, Croydon CR0 4YY

FSC www.fsc.org MIX Paper from responsible sources FSC® C013604

In Memoriam

Patrick Atiyah (1931–2018)

Preface

THIS VOLUME IS intended to be the first of several concerned with scholars of private law who have played a significant role in defining the field in which they worked. We have incurred several significant debts of gratitude in relation to this project. Kit Barker and David Ibbetson acted as referees in connection with funding applications. Keble College supported the project by way of a research grant. Worcester College provided the venue for the workshop at which drafts of the essays that comprise this volume were delivered and discussed. The Oxford Law Faculty gave generous support in the form of grants from its Research Support Fund. Bill Asquith of Hart Publishing received our publishing proposal enthusiastically and Hart gave the project its backing from beginning to end, and contributed to the costs of the workshop. Invaluable editorial and research assistance in connection with the production of this book was provided by Leo Boonzaier, Václav Janeček, Mariam Kamil, Eleni Katsampouka, Ndjodi Ndeunyema and Scarlett Ying.

We were fortunate to have present at the workshop the following observers, whose contributions enriched the debates: Jacob Eisler, John Gardner, Václav Janeček, Eleni Katsampouka and William Twining.

Sadly, Patrick Atiyah, one of the scholars whose work is celebrated in this volume – and the only such scholar to have been alive when the project was conceived – passed away on 30 March 2018, just a few days before the workshop took place. In these circumstances, we have chosen to dedicate this book to his memory.

James Goudkamp
Donal Nolan
Oxford
26 January 2019

Table of Contents

Contributors

Guido Calabresi is Senior Judge of the US Court of Appeals for the Second Circuit, and Sterling Professor Emeritus and Professorial Lecturer at the Yale University Law School.

Peter Cane is a Senior Research Fellow at Christ's College, Cambridge, and an Emeritus Distinguished Professor at the Australian National University.

Paula Giliker is Professor of Comparative Law at the University of Bristol.

John CP Goldberg is Carter Professor of General Jurisprudence at Harvard Law School.

James Goudkamp is Professor of the Law of Obligations at the University of Oxford and a Fellow and Tutor in Law at Keble College, Oxford.

Michael D Green is Williams Professor of Law at Wake Forest University School of Law.

Mark Lunney is Professor of Law at the University of New England and Visiting Professor at the Dickson Poon School of Law, King's College London, and the Faculty of Laws, University College London.

Paul Mitchell is Professor of Laws at University College London.

Donal Nolan is Professor of Private Law at the University of Oxford and the Francis Reynolds and Clarendon Fellow and Tutor in Law at Worcester College, Oxford.

Christopher J Robinette is Professor of Law at Widener University Commonwealth Law School.

Jenny Steele is Professor of Law at the University of York.

Robert Stevens is the Herbert Smith Freehills Professor of English Private Law at the University of Oxford.

Benjamin C Zipursky is the James H Quinn '49 Chair in Legal Ethics and Professor of Law at Fordham University.

Table of Cases

Table of Legislation

Australia

European Union

France

New Zealand

United Kingdom

United States

1

Pioneers, Consolidators and Iconoclasts: The Story of Tort Scholarship

JAMES GOUDKAMP AND DONAL NOLAN

I. INTRODUCTION

COMMON LAW SCHOLARSHIP is overwhelmingly focused on judicial decisions, with the result that the writings of even highly influential legal scholars have, by comparison, rarely been the subjects of scrutiny in their own right. This represents a serious gap in our understanding of the common law and its development. The purpose of the current volume is to begin the process of redressing this imbalance, by considering the role played by leading scholars of tort law from across the common law world in the development of the subject.[1] The focus of the contributions is on the nature of the work produced by each of the scholars in question, important influences on them and the influence which they in turn had on thinking about tort law.

The process of subjecting tort law scholarship to sustained analysis provides new insights into the intellectual development of tort law and reveals the central role played by scholars in this regard. The book also serves to emphasise the importance of legal scholarship to the development of the common law more generally. As Patrick Atiyah – one of the scholars whose work is considered in this collection – wrote in 1987:

> [L]egal theory, and the work of academics, has in truth played a much larger role in the development of our law than has generally been acknowledged, and … a great many fields of our law have been profoundly influenced by academic writing and

[1] Although we are not aware of any previous projects of this kind in the common law world, we note the recent publication in English translation of a major collection of essays on 37 scholars who were influential in the development of German private law in the twentieth century: S Grundmann and K Riesenhuber (eds), *German Private Law Scholarship in the 20th Century* (Cambridge, Intersentia, 2018).

> theory … [T]here is a more general case for thinking that legal writing, and particularly academic writing, is in the long perspective of history, an important part of the law itself … [I]t seems certain that we have greatly underestimated the influence of academics on the development of the law in the past.[2]

Furthermore, as Susan Bartie has argued,[3] the study of our predecessors is of considerable potential benefit to the enterprise of legal scholarship itself. As well as contextualising earlier work of relevance to present controversies, studies of past scholars can serve as a challenge to current notions of academic standing, and 'may sow the seeds of a stronger intellectual tradition' by encouraging 'scholars to recognise their potential and the possibilities that this engenders'.[4]

Several preliminary observations are in order. One is that the collection is limited to the common law world.[5] In the tort context, it will be seen that the intellectual connections within that world are strong. Beyond it, they inevitably weaken. Those weaker connections are important, and much studied by comparative lawyers, but our enterprise is deliberately a different one from theirs.[6] Another point is that we included in the project only scholars who were deceased or, if alive, no longer research active.[7] While the echoes of the former English convention against judicial citation of living scholars are unfortunate, we proceeded in this way because we considered it important that the contribution of each scholar be assessed in the light of the entirety of his work. Finally, these limitations resulted in a lack of diversity in the scholars under scrutiny, to which the possessive pronoun used in the previous sentence attests. It should be emphasised that once the decision was made to restrict the field in these ways, the lack of diversity was inevitable. We were therefore faced with the options of abandoning the endeavour, or producing a volume that would highlight the extent to which common law tort scholarship was, until recent decades, almost entirely the preserve of men. While we stand by the choice we made between those alternatives, we recognise that others may take a different view. In any event, we regret the absence of women's voices in the story that is told in this book.

Opinions may also differ on our choice of scholars. We should start by making it clear that we did not unilaterally decide which scholars should be

[2] PS Atiyah, *Pragmatism and Theory in English Law* (London, Stevens & Sons, 1987) 166, 179–80.

[3] S Bartie, 'Histories of Legal Scholars: The Power of Possibility' (2014) 34 *LS* 305.

[4] ibid 327.

[5] Although Peter Cane's more general chapter in this volume (P Cane, 'Law, Fact and Process in Common Law Tort Scholarship') engages with the civil law tradition at some length.

[6] We should mention here that two of the scholars under consideration – John Fleming and Tony Weir – were also comparative lawyers of great distinction. The extent to which their comparative work influenced their tort scholarship is an interesting issue, which we unfortunately do not have the space to address.

[7] The only scholar who was alive at the time when the collection was planned, Patrick Atiyah, sadly passed away on 30 March 2018.

discussed; that decision was made in close consultation with the contributors. And while we would readily accept that in some instances the reputation and influence of a scholar essentially compelled his inclusion, in other instances a case could of course be made for X rather than Y and so on. We make two points in anticipation of such objections. One is that it seemed important to us that our contributors be given the freedom to write about the scholar (or, in one case, scholars) in whom they themselves were interested. And the other is that, since there is no objective criterion by which the importance of a legal scholar can be measured, such objections can always be put forward, no matter which choices have been made. We are in any case satisfied that the selection of scholars studied in this volume is effective in demonstrating the influences that tort scholars had on their discipline and on each other, especially when supplemented by previous work on the intellectual history of the subject that has highlighted the contributions of some – though by no means all – of the more significant tort scholars not considered here.[8]

One other important preliminary point that we wish to make about this project is that when assessing and analysing past scholarly work in a particular field it is of course difficult, if not impossible, to set aside one's own views on the area in question. It was therefore inevitable that our contributors – all of them scholars of contemporary tort law – would be tempted to use their discussion of past scholarship to fight the intellectual battles of the present. We leave it to the reader to decide to what extent they succeeded in resisting that temptation (or, indeed, whether they sought to resist it at all). Nevertheless, we wish to emphasise at the outset the supreme importance of avoiding anachronism, and of evaluating the contributions of the scholars under consideration in the light of the existing tort scholarship in their day, and the intellectual culture in which they worked. It hardly needs to be said that a perception or understanding which may seem obvious to us now would not always have seemed so. And it follows that in assessing the contributions of our predecessors a degree of humility is appropriate, not least in the hope that those who follow us will in turn prove merciful when faced with the missteps and mistakes of our own era.

The discussion that follows in this overview chapter divides the scholars considered in this volume into three categories: *pioneers* (Cooley, Holmes and Pollock); *consolidators* (Salmond, Bohlen, Winfield, Prosser and Fleming) and *iconoclasts* (Green, James, Atiyah and Weir). Any such taxonomy is naturally problematic, and we employ it – and its constituent categories – only in the

[8] We draw attention to three previous publications in particular: RB Brown, 'Cecil A Wright and the Foundations of Canadian Tort Law Scholarship' (2001) 64 *Saskatchewan Law Review* 169 (highlighting the work of Cecil Wright); GE White, *Tort Law in America: An Intellectual History*, expanded edn (New York, OUP, 2003) (highlighting the work of, among others, James Barr Ames, Joseph Beale, Fowler Harper, Page and Robert Keeton, Warren Seavey, Jeremiah Smith and John Wade); and M Lunney, 'Legal Émigrés and the Development of Australian Tort Law' (2012) 36 *Melbourne University Law Review* 494 (highlighting the work of Wolfgang Friedmann).

loosest of senses, and with appropriate circumspection. We also recognise that while, in our view at least, some of the scholars fit relatively easily into one or other of these categories (say, Prosser and Green), in other cases the classification of a scholar is less obvious (say, Salmond and Fleming). Nevertheless, we hope to show that the threefold taxonomy is revealing, and that it can be used to identify commonalities between the scholars within each category, and recurrent distinctions between the different categories of scholar. Furthermore, in the final part of the chapter, we supplement the discussion of the three categories of scholar with some thematic observations about tort scholarship more generally.

The framing of our discussion by reference to three categories of scholar gives rise to a difficulty that should be acknowledged at the outset. This is that, although naturally the pioneers came first, the other two categories are not chronologically distinct, with the result that consolidators were influenced by iconoclasts and vice versa. It follows that while we discuss the scholars in each category in date of birth order (the criterion used to order the other chapters in the volume), in some cases the treatment of a particular scholar must inevitably anticipate material in a later part of the chapter.

II. PIONEERS

A. The Origins of the Subject

The scope of this volume rests on an important distinction between the study of causes of action, cases and so on that are now treated as part of tort law, and 'tort law' as a subject of study in its own right. This is because we consciously chose to limit the project to consideration of scholars of tort law *as a subject*, and not to include in it writers whose work pre-dated the recognition of tort as a distinct legal category. (That is why there is no chapter in this book on, for example, Bracton, nor on Blackstone.) And it raises the question of when 'tort law' as such was first the subject of scholarly attention.[9]

Happily, there is a general consensus that the recognition of tort as a distinct legal category dates back to the second half of the nineteenth century.[10] Indeed the evidence to this effect is overwhelming. The first significant[11] English-language work on the subject was published in 1859 by the American Francis Hilliard,[12] and this was followed a year later by Thomas Addison's *Treatise on*

[9] Regarding the origins of tort law as a subject, see generally, White, *Tort Law in America: An Intellectual History* (n 8) ch 1.

[10] See, eg, ibid 3 ('Torts was not considered a discrete branch of law until the late nineteenth century'); and Atiyah, *Pragmatism and Theory in English Law* (n 2) 176.

[11] Percy Winfield identifies one earlier English work, from 1720, but little more seems to be known of it: see PH Winfield, *The Province of the Law of Tort* (Cambridge, CUP, 1931) 8.

[12] F Hilliard, *The Law of Tort or Private Wrongs* (Boston, Little, Brown & Co, 1859).

the Law of Torts in England.[13] Other American treatises followed Hilliard's, and the first case book on the subject was published in 1874.[14] A flurry of books on tort were also published in England towards the close of the nineteenth century.[15] The subject's arrival was also proclaimed by the curricula of the universities: the first torts class was taught at Harvard in 1870, and tort made its first appearance as an examination paper in Cambridge in 1890, and in Oxford in 1905.

Nor is the explanation for the timing of tort's recognition as a distinct category in common law systems hard to find. The forms of action 'had militated against abstraction to principle',[16] and their demise 'cleared the way for more systematic exposition and analysis of decisional law with, at most, only subsidiary reference to the process and procedures that produced it'.[17] In England, the final nail in the coffin of the formulary system was the Judicature Act 1875, but that legislation marked the culmination of a long process of decline, one mirrored in developments on the other side of the Atlantic.[18] From the collapse of the writ system emerged a reimagined legal landscape, populated by new categories, or subjects, such as contract and tort. And while the cases were the bricks and mortar of the new superstructure, its architects were the scholars who wrote the books that both created and reflected the nascent taxonomy.[19] The dawn of the modern expository tradition went hand in hand with the advent of common law scholarship as a profession, of the schools of the common law in which the new professionals worked[20] and of the scholarly journals in which they published.[21] It is in this context that the contribution of the pioneers of tort scholarship must be evaluated.

B. Cooley and Holmes

John Goldberg and Benjamin Zipursky (chapter 2) identify Thomas McIntyre Cooley and Oliver Wendell Holmes Jr as pioneers of the serious scholarly study of tort law in the US, and investigate why, in their view, Holmes's legacy has been so much more prominent than Cooley's. Holmes stands out among the scholars considered in this collection for never having written a book specifically on

[13] T Addison, *A Treatise on the Law of Torts or Wrongs and their Remedies* (London, Stevens & Sons, 1860).

[14] JB Ames, *A Selection of Cases on the Law of Torts* (Cambridge, MA, Harvard Law Review Publishing Association, 1874).

[15] Atiyah, *Pragmatism and Theory in English Law* (n 2) 176.

[16] N Duxbury, *Frederick Pollock and the English Juristic Tradition* (Oxford, OUP, 2004) 234.

[17] Cane, ch 13 of this volume, p 374.

[18] See White, *Tort Law in America: An Intellectual History* (n 8) 8–12.

[19] For the metaphor, see Atiyah, *Pragmatism and Theory in English Law* (n 2) 173.

[20] The Oxford Honour School of Jurisprudence dates, for example, from 1870, and the final iteration of the Cambridge Law Tripos from 1875.

[21] The *Law Quarterly Review* was founded in 1885, and the *Harvard Law Review* in 1887.

tort – his influential theory of tort law (the first put forward by an Anglophone writer[22]) is instead to be found in periodical writings[23] and lectures III and IV of *The Common Law*.[24] But despite this, some of his theoretical insights have resonated into the modern era: the idea of tort law as striking a balance between security and freedom, the objective approach to fault, and the threefold division of tortious liability into liability for intentional conduct, liability for negligence and strict liability, a classification that has dominated, in particular, American thinking about tort law ever since.

As the foregoing suggests, Holmes's focus was almost entirely on defendants (and potential defendants). The centrality of the defendant to Holmes's conception of tort law laid the intellectual foundation for much that followed, including the rise of the fault principle, which soon came to dominate tort law throughout the common law world, and, in more recent times, the resurgence of deterrence-based theories under the guise of 'economic analysis'. By contrast, Holmes had relatively little to say about plaintiffs. As Atiyah pointed out, there was 'absolutely no hint in *The Common Law* that Holmes identified the possible importance, for instance, of the distinctions between bodily injury, property damage and pecuniary loss', since to have done so would have 'run counter to his fundamental objective of restating the principles of tort law by reference to the nature of the defendant's conduct'.[25] Underpinning Holmes's theory was a 'moral vision', albeit one that rested not on the 'personal morality of each individual' but on the standards of the community at large.[26] Hence the persistent focus on the question of whether the defendant's conduct conformed to an objective standard of behaviour, whether set by the legislature, the judge or the jury.

Compared with Holmes's relatively abstract and, in its way, revolutionary theory, Cooley's treatment of tort in his treatise of 1880 was more granular, and represented less of a break from earlier modes of thought.[27] Whereas Holmes organised the subject around different types of conduct, and focused attention firmly on the position of the defendant, Cooley's classification of wrongs centred on the interest of the plaintiff affected by that conduct. This was closer to the formulary system and (as befitted the compiler of an American edition of the *Commentaries*[28]) to Blackstone's thinking. As for the substance of what

[22] W Cornish et al, *The Oxford History of the Laws of England: Volume XII* (Oxford, OUP, 2010) 891.

[23] See particularly 'The Theory of Torts' (1873) 7 *American Law Review* 652.

[24] OW Holmes, *The Common Law* (Boston, MA, Little Brown, 1881).

[25] PS Atiyah, 'The Legacy of Holmes through English Eyes' (1983) 63 *Boston University Law Review* 341, 362.

[26] Cornish et al, *The Oxford History of the Laws of England: Volume XII* (n 22) 891.

[27] TM Cooley, *A Treatise on the Law of Torts, or, the Wrongs Which Arise Independent of Contract* (Chicago, IL, Callaghan, 1879).

[28] W Blackstone, *Commentaries on the Laws of England*, TM Cooley ed (Chicago, IL, Callaghan, 1871).

was going on in tort cases, Holmes's starting point was that *losses* should lie where they fell unless there was a good enough reason to shift them, while Cooley conceived of such cases as involving redress for *wrongs*. This tension between a 'loss view' and a 'rights/wrongs view' of the subject continues to divide tort lawyers to this day.[29] Goldberg and Zipursky argue that the two men's very different approaches to the new subject reflected their divergent thinking about law in general. Holmes, they say, was concerned with the identification through 'inductive and empirical analysis [of] law's general principles', while Cooley considered that legal insight came 'from immersing oneself in the details of doctrine, understood to reflect inherited wisdom and, more importantly, ordinary morality'.[30] As is so often the case, these differences of mindset manifested themselves not only in the substance of the two scholars' writings on tort, but also in the form that those writings took.

C. Pollock

Sir Frederick Pollock is generally considered to be the pioneer of the serious scholarly study of tort in England.[31] Along with his treatise on contract, his 1887 treatise on tort[32] was described after his death as having 'inaugurated a new era in the literature of English law',[33] while Pollock himself has been said to signal 'the beginning of a change from one juristic era to another'.[34] In assessing his legacy as a tort scholar, it is important to emphasise the novelty of the enterprise that he was undertaking. For not only was Pollock writing *about* tort, he was in a very real sense *creating it* as a category within English legal thought.[35] As his intellectual biographer, Neil Duxbury, says:

> [Pollock's] treatise on torts was both a study of principles and an effort to establish a body of law – to show, that is, that there really is a unified Law of Torts rather than just a haphazard collection of rules about different kinds of torts.[36]

[29] See R Stevens, *Torts and Rights* (Oxford, OUP, 2007) ch 1.

[30] Goldberg and Zipursky, ch 2 of this volume, p 47.

[31] The earlier treatise by Addison was described by William Holdsworth as 'not a wholly satisfactory book when it was first published', since it merely collected the relevant decisions and did not 'bring out clearly the underlying principles' (WS Holdsworth, *A History of English Law* (London, Methuen & Co, 1965) vol XV, 300). Holdsworth points out that later editors of the work accepted this, and credited Pollock and the authors of *Clerk and Lindsell* with the first proper elucidation of this branch of English law. See also CHS Fifoot, *Judge and Jurist in the Reign of Victoria* (London, Stevens & Sons, 1959) 47 (Addison 'made no attempt to generalise').

[32] F Pollock, *The Law of Torts* (London, Stevens & Sons, 1887).

[33] Lord Wright, 'In Memoriam: Sir Frederick Pollock' (1937) 53 *LQR* 151, 162. Fifoot (*Judge and Jurist in the Reign of Victoria* (n 31) 52) described the treatise as 'the first English book devoted to a scholarly and systematic examination of torts'.

[34] Duxbury, *Frederick Pollock and the English Juristic Tradition* (n 16) 280.

[35] For the equivalent claim about Holmes in the American context, see TC Grey, 'Accidental Torts' (2001) 54 *Vanderbilt Law Review* 1225, 1227.

[36] Duxbury, *Frederick Pollock and the English Juristic Tradition* (n 16) 225.

The nature of the challenge that Pollock set himself in his treatise is apparent from the opening page, where he says that he has sought to 'fix the contents and boundaries of the subject'.[37] In the spirit of legal science,[38] he sought also to create 'a formal, logical system of rules, teased out of the historical material of the common law'.[39] These were not easy tasks. The demise of the forms of action meant that substantive doctrine could now replace the older learning focused on process and procedure, but where was the doctrine to come from? Pollock turned to Blackstone, and to the US. His intellectual debt to Holmes is well-documented, but it seems that Cooley was also a major influence on his thinking,[40] and while Pollock's overall schema has been described by Duxbury as 'an amalgamation of Blackstone, Cooley, and Holmes',[41] its threefold foundation seems closer to Cooley's approach than to Holmes's. Pollock also departed from Holmes in basing the law of torts firmly on a moral foundation. Then again, Pollock's inductive methodology was more Holmesian, and less grounded in the detail of the positive law than Cooley's. Like Holmes, Pollock saw the function of the jurist as identifying the *principles* that could be inferred from the case law, and these were set at a very high level of abstraction. Indeed, Pollock even discerned in the vast mass of decided cases one overarching general principle of tort liability, that it was a wrong 'to do wilful harm to one's neighbour without lawful justification or excuse',[42] a principle which – as Robert Stevens demonstrates in his chapter on Pollock (chapter 3) – was highly tendentious when first put forward, and impossible to reconcile with important decisions of the courts in the years that followed its promulgation. Pollock also emulated Holmes by downplaying strict liability and promoting the fault principle.

Pollock was, as all scholars are, a creature of his time, and his approach to the task of systematising the law of tort was in keeping with the tradition of the treatise writers of the late nineteenth century, as encapsulated in this quotation from Brian Simpson:

> [T]he treatise writers of the nineteenth century, insofar as they consciously embraced a theory of law, inherited and claimed to express the belief that private law consisted essentially of a latent scheme of principles whose workings could be seen in and illustrated by the decisions of the courts, where they were developed and applied. The text writer sought to expound these principles in a rational, coherent manner, as was appropriate to a science.[43]

[37] Pollock, *The Law of Torts* (n 32) 1.

[38] On Pollock's 'scientific' presuppositions, see M Lobban, 'English Jurisprudence and Tort Theory' in M Lobban and J Moses (eds), *The Impact of Ideas on Legal Development* (Cambridge, CUP, 2012) 130–31.

[39] M Lobban and J Moses, 'Introduction' in Lobban and Moses (eds), *The Impact of Ideas on Legal Development* (n 38) 10.

[40] Duxbury, *Frederick Pollock and the English Juristic Tradition* (n 16) 237.

[41] ibid 239.

[42] Pollock, *The Law of Torts* (n 32) 21.

[43] AWB Simpson, 'The Rise and Fall of the Legal Treatise: Legal Principles and the Forms of Legal Literature' (1981) 48 *University of Chicago Law Review* 632, 666. See also White, *Tort Law*

At the same time, however, Pollock was also a pragmatist in the English tradition, whose view of the common law was that it was *reasonable* rather than *rational*.[44] Hence his scepticism about 'fashionable economic theories' that were not grounded in the raw material of the common law itself,[45] and his view that the reconciliation of 'the just freedom of new kinds of collective action with the ancient and just independence of the individual citizen' would be founded, not on theoretical insights from other disciplines but from 'knowledge of the world, and on broad considerations of policy', or in other words what he called '[n]atural law'.[46] This grounded approach, which elevates common sense and tradition over rationality and theory, was also discernible in the work of Pollock's successors – men like Salmond and Winfield – and remains characteristic of much English tort scholarship to this day.

D. Pioneers in General

Whatever the perceived merits or demerits of their writings, Cooley, Holmes and Pollock clearly deserve a place in the pantheon of tort scholarship. As Simpson says, 'in treatise writing, as in mountaineering, a special significance is rightly accorded to those who achieve first and thereby demonstrate that the feat is in fact possible'.[47] According to G Edward White, the contribution of these and other pioneers was

> to isolate Torts as a distinct field of study, to supply that field with an overarching theoretical perspective, and to transform its existing rules and maxims into doctrines consistent, where possible, with that perspective.[48]

The result was that by the start of the twentieth century, tort jurisprudence had developed a 'discernible philosophical identity'.[49] As that summation of their achievement suggests, a central characteristic of the two most influential

in America: An Intellectual History (n 8) 34 ('The aim of the great scientific treatises was to produce, out of the chaos of a constantly growing body of case law, syntheses that made [the field of study] orderly and manageable').

[44] See Duxbury, *Frederick Pollock and the English Juristic Tradition* (n 16) 231 ('[t]o claim, as Pollock did, that the common law is founded on reason is not the same as claiming that it is rational, or even potentially rational'). On the tension between rationality and irrationality in the common law's intellectual tradition, see D Sugarman, 'Legal Theory, the Common Law Mind and the Making of the Textbook Tradition' in W Twining (ed), *Legal Theory and the Common Law* (Oxford, Basil Blackwell, 1986).

[45] F Pollock, *The Genius of the Common Law* (New York, Columbia UP, 1912) 108.

[46] F Pollock, *The Expansion of the Common Law* (London, Stevens & Sons, 1904) 131–32.

[47] Simpson, 'The Rise and Fall of the Legal Treatise: Legal Principles and the Forms of Legal Literature' (n 43) 652.

[48] White, *Tort Law in America: An Intellectual History* (n 8) 38.

[49] ibid 39.

of our three pioneers – Holmes and Pollock – was their attachment to broad principles: no liability without fault, as judged by an objective standard; general liability for harm done wilfully without justification, etc. '[T]he thrust of their methodology', White says of them and their contemporaries, was 'toward … generalized intellectual frameworks'.[50] Another prominent feature of the work of the pioneers is their interest in classification, with all favouring one or other tripartite division of the subject.[51] While later writers could afford to take a more relaxed approach to taxonomical questions[52] and to focus their energy on the substance of the law, the pioneers had no choice but to take it seriously, since one of their central tasks was to map the new legal landscape. Conversely, however, Holmes and Pollock appear not to have felt constrained, as some of their scholarly descendants were, by the demands of established audiences of students and practitioners (indeed, the pioneers seem not to have been particularly concerned about their 'audience' at all). As a result their writings are less tied to authority than those of the twentieth-century consolidators, such as Percy Winfield and William Prosser.[53] This attitude towards case law is exemplified by Pollock's stubborn refusal to abandon his general liability principle in the teeth of inconsistent authority at the highest level. The tension between the supposedly universal and timeless principles set out in his treatise and the messy dynamism of the case law points to a dilemma faced by many of the early conceptualists, which was the capacity of the principles they claimed to discern in the cases to adapt as the case law developed.[54] Pollock for one never resolved that dilemma, with the result that his treatise aged rapidly, and survived its author by only a couple of decades.

Whereas the influence of later scholars is often thought to be observable in specific aspects of the modern law, and their impact traceable to particular moments in the law's development, in the case of the pioneers it seems to operate on a broader plane. Rather than being associated with, say, the move from fault-based liability to strict liability for defective products, the legacy of the pioneers instead lies deeper down, in the assumptions that drove the law's subsequent development and the presuppositions that underlay later scholarship. As Atiyah wrote of Holmes, he 'helped to shape the way in which lawyers viewed

[50] ibid 68.

[51] See WL Prosser, *Handbook of the Law of Torts* (St Paul, MN, West Publishing, 1941) 34 ('[b]y some odd coincidence, the classifications [of the law of torts] usually have gone by threes'). For a prominent example of a threefold classification to rival that of Holmes, see JH Wigmore, 'The Tripartite Division of Torts' (1894) 8 *Harvard Law Review* 200.

[52] Prosser, for example, remarked that apart from 'mere convenience in discussion', there was 'of course no inherent merit' in any of the classifications that had been promulgated (Prosser, *Handbook of the Law of Torts* (n 51)).

[53] Of Holmes, it has been said that 'his boldest claims' about tort were 'unaccompanied by extensive documentation' (GE White, *Justice Oliver Wendell Holmes: Law and the Inner Self* (New York, OUP, 1993) 163). Similarly, Pollock's general liability principle 'was not to be found in any express authority' (Cornish et al, *The Oxford History of the Laws of England: Volume XII* (n 22) 891).

[54] See White, *Tort Law in America: An Intellectual History* (n 8) 74.

the law of torts'.[55] The complete dominance of Holmes's threefold classification in subsequent American tort scholarship – which can be contrasted with the range of approaches found in the Commonwealth – is a good example of this kind of influence, as is the constraining effect that Holmes's writings had on the theoretical parameters within which his successors operated.[56] Holmes's thinking has also been said to have paved the way for legal realism,[57] a movement of huge significance for common law tort scholarship, and similar claims have been made about Holmes and the rise of economic analysis of law, the dominant approach to tort scholarship in the US in recent decades, if less influential than realism beyond American shores.

As for Pollock, although his general liability principle has not survived into the modern era, its progeny may have done. One apparent legacy of Pollock's principle, for example, is the tendency of many English and Commonwealth scholars to refer to the 'law of *tort*', a designation less often used in the US; another is the idea of a tort of negligence, and the decision of the House of Lords in *Donoghue v Stevenson*[58] that confirmed its existence. Pollock's influence may also be observable in modern thinking about the place of the law of tort within private law. Of particular interest here is his insistence on the clear separation between tort and property, as when he wrote – in connection with the obstruction of light – of 'the risk of digressing from the law of Torts into the law of Easements'.[59] Although the implication that tort and property are mutually exclusive categories is a troublesome one, the separation between the two is now deeply embedded in the common law mindset.[60]

III. CONSOLIDATORS

A. Salmond

Sir John Salmond could easily be classified as a pioneer rather than a consolidator. His famous textbook on the law of torts was published in 1907,[61] still

[55] Atiyah, 'The Legacy of Holmes through English Eyes' (n 25) 352.

[56] See PJ Kelley, 'The First Restatement of Torts: Reform by Descriptive Theory' (2007) 32 *Southern Illinois University Law Journal* 93, 131.

[57] Lobban and Moses, 'Introduction' (n 39) 132.

[58] *Donoghue v Stevenson* [1932] AC 562 (HL).

[59] Pollock, *The Law of Torts* (n 32) 336 (cited by Duxbury, *Frederick Pollock and the English Juristic Tradition* (n 16) 241).

[60] For a brief discussion of the issue, highlighting the problems this can cause, see D Nolan, '"A Tort Against Land": Private Nuisance as a Property Tort' in D Nolan and A Robertson, *Rights and Private Law* (Oxford, Hart Publishing, 2012) 486–87.

[61] J Salmond, *The Law of Torts* (London, Stevens and Haynes, 1907). Sugarman, 'Legal Theory, the Common Law Mind and the Making of the Textbook Tradition' (n 44) describes the period 1850–1907 as 'the classical period of modern legal education and thought'. The fact that Salmond's text was published right at the end of that period is suggestive of the transitional nature of his scholarship.

relatively early in the short life of the subject. And he also shared one of the characteristics of the pioneers discussed previously, in that he was not a career academic.[62] After writing his textbook, Salmond spent the remainder of his life in legal practice in New Zealand, first as Solicitor-General and later as a judge of the Supreme Court. Nevertheless, Salmond's categorisation as a consolidator seems to us to be justified. After all, his textbook post-dated the most important tort works of the three pioneers by two decades or more, and the task that he faced was very different from theirs, since by the time of its writing tort already had an established position in the thinking of common lawyers and in the curricula of the leading Anglophone universities. We shall also see that there are clear similarities between Salmond's approach to that task and the approaches of later consolidators, such as Winfield and Prosser.

Salmond is a typical consolidator in being associated with a leading text on the law of tort, but unusual in not having published a great deal else on the subject. His reputation as a tort scholar therefore rests almost entirely on that work, and the extent of that reputation is a testament to its significance. If Pollock's book had been a treatise in the nineteenth-century mould, Salmond's was a twentieth-century 'textbook', and a highly successful one at that: it dominated the market for three decades, was hugely influential in the courts, and under a series of editors ran to 21 editions, the last of them published more than 70 years after Salmond's death. In part, the success of the book was down to the lack of serious competition, but that was certainly not the whole story. As Mark Lunney emphasises in his chapter on Salmond (chapter 4), a key reason for the book's popularity was that the author kept his intended audience of students and practitioners in mind, and gave them the work of 'practical utility' that they each, in their own ways, wanted.[63]

Two further points should be made about Salmond's tort scholarship. One is that, although he was an adoptive New Zealander, nobody reading his book would have had any inkling of this. It was a thoroughly 'English' treatment of the subject, even though its author lived on the other side of the world.[64] And the other point is that although Salmond was influenced by Holmes and Pollock, and shared their preference for fault-based liability, his basic approach to the law of torts departed fundamentally from theirs. For while Holmes and Pollock had been concerned to try to distil from the body of the case law a small number of overarching principles, Salmond preferred – doubtless with one eye on his readership – to stay close to the cases and to shy

[62] Cooley and Holmes spent the bulk of their careers on the bench, and while Pollock did hold the Chair of Jurisprudence at Oxford for much of his life, his centre of operations was legal London, and he operated in a sort of shadowland between the academy and profession.

[63] See Salmond, *The Law of Torts* (n 61) v.

[64] See P Mitchell, *A History of Tort Law 1900–1950* (Cambridge, CUP, 2015) 19 ('it is fortunate that Salmond signed off the preface to the first edition 'Wellington, New Zealand', as it would have been otherwise impossible to tell whether the book had been written in Northamptonshire or North Island').

away from generalisations. Far from the law of torts instantiating a general principle that it was wrongful intentionally or negligently to cause harm to others without justification or excuse, as Pollock maintained, Salmond wrote in the second edition of his book that it consisted of 'a number of specific rules prohibiting certain kinds of harmful activity, and leaving all the residue outside the sphere of legal responsibility',[65] an 'anti-reductionist' approach[66] reminiscent of Cooley.

As a result, Salmond and his legacy served as a counterweight to Pollock's influence in the first half of the twentieth century. That this is so is particularly apparent from the so-called 'tort or torts' debate that raged among English tort scholars in the early decades of the twentieth century, and which amounted to an (ultimately unsuccessful) attempt by Pollock and his protégé Winfield to defend the general liability principle against a critique which was spearheaded by Salmond, and based on the incompatibility between the principle and the positive law.[67] The triumph of Salmond's take on the subject was only partial, however, for his refusal to acknowledge negligence as a stand-alone cause of action put him on the wrong side of history, as the decision in *Donoghue v Stevenson* demonstrated. Indeed, the rise of negligence suggests that in the end the 'tort or torts' debate – understood as a contest between generality and particularity – played out to a draw, with the particularised nominate torts ultimately coming to co-exist with a more generalised fault-based liability principle in the form of the '*über*-tort'[68] of negligence. Although his impact was most obvious at the fine-grained level at which he preferred to operate, Salmond's effective articulation of particularism gives his work a broader significance in the history of English tort scholarship.

B. Bohlen

Christopher Robinette describes Francis Bohlen as 'the dominant torts figure in the United States in the first several decades of the twentieth century'.[69] Like Salmond, Bohlen avoided generalisation and abstraction: his particular talent, it has been said, 'was to focus his brilliant mind on a particularly confused, discrete area of tort law and come up with a creative theory to clarify and resolve the problem'.[70] Hence his reputation was built not on the back of a grand theory but on a popular student casebook,[71] a raft of law review articles on a

[65] J Salmond, *The Law of Torts*, 2nd edn (London, Stevens and Haynes, 1910) 9.
[66] See Goldberg and Zipursky, ch 2 of this volume, p 54.
[67] For a summary of the debate, see Mitchell, *A History of Tort Law 1900–1950* (n 64) ch 2.
[68] Stevens, *Torts and Rights* (n 29) 295.
[69] Robinette, ch 8 of this volume, p 236.
[70] Kelley, 'The First Restatement of Torts: Reform by Descriptive Theory' (n 56) 124.
[71] FH Bohlen, *Cases on Torts* (Indianapolis, IN, Bobbs-Merrill, 1915) and subsequent editions.

diversity of topics[72] and above all on his role as the reporter for the first *Restatement of Torts.*[73] It is that final role that justifies Bohlen's categorisation as a consolidator. The American Law Institute (ALI) had been established in 1923 with the avowed aim of bringing order and predictability to American law by distilling the voluminous case law of the multiplicity of state jurisdictions into sets of black-letter propositions on particular subjects, supported by extensive commentary and notes.[74] Although the reporters produced the drafts of these 'Restatements', they had to be agreed by the membership of the ALI – a diverse group of judges, practitioners and academics – with the result that the final text was not the work of a single scholar but embodied the 'composite thought'[75] of the Institute. In the case of tort, the process took well over a decade, and the result was described by Prosser as 'the most complete and thorough consideration' that tort law had ever received.[76] Furthermore, as Michael Green points out in his chapter on Bohlen (chapter 5),[77] the torts *Restatements* have been the most influential *Restatements* of all.

Typically for a consolidator, Bohlen was a pragmatist, who charted a difficult course between the conceptual purity of the 'scientific' approach to tort and the doctrine-scepticism of the increasingly influential legal realists. In White's words:

> [Bohlen] remained unconvinced that a Realist theoretical perspective should fully supplant the perspective developed by nineteenth-century conceptualists ... [but at the same time he] believed in the primacy of social change, in the necessity of tort doctrines to accommodate themselves to changed conditions, in the futility of static classification systems, and in the value, in an increasingly interdependent universe, of elite policymakers serving as an active force on behalf of progress.[78]

Bohlen's age, background and personality militated against his conversion to the realist cause, and may in part explain the mutual antipathy between Bohlen and the realist tort scholar Leon Green. But Bohlen's conceptualism was sufficiently progressive and flexible to enable him to maintain his scholarly standing and influence amid the realist maelstrom of the 1930s. As Michael Green says, he 'successfully negotiated the transition away from legal formalism'.[79] That same flexibility also served Bohlen well in his job of *Restatement* reporter, where compromises were required for consensus to be built around an agreed

[72] For some of the most important of these, see FH Bohlen, *Studies in the Law of Torts* (Indianapolis, IN, Bobbs-Merrill, 1926).

[73] *Restatement of Torts* (Philadelphia, PA, American Law Institute, 1934).

[74] For a brief but characteristically engaging summary of the thinking behind the ALI and its *Restatements*, see B Cardozo, *The Growth of the Law* (New Haven, Yale UP, 1924) ch 1.

[75] ibid 9.

[76] Prosser, *Handbook of the Law of Torts* (n 51) 24.

[77] Green, ch 5 of this volume, p 137.

[78] White, *Tort Law in America: An Intellectual History* (n 8) 78.

[79] Green, ch 5 of this volume, p 163.

final text. Bohlen's ability to strike a workable compromise between doctrinal and functional approaches served as an inspiration for later North American scholars, such as Fowler Harper, Prosser and the Canadian Cecil Wright, all of whom were heavily influenced by Bohlen and his work. As for his broader legacy, the *Restatement* and its successors came to symbolise an American doctrinalist tradition in tort law scholarship that survived in the face of the realist and post-realist critique of conceptual analysis. Although not always accorded sufficient recognition by the American legal academy, the gravitas and sophistication of this tradition was much admired elsewhere, and helped to maintain the intellectual connection not only with the Commonwealth, but with the more conceptualist civil law systems as well.

C. Winfield

The most significant of the scholars of English tort law to follow Salmond was Sir Percy Winfield; indeed, Donal Nolan argues in his chapter on Winfield (chapter 6) that he is arguably the most successful such scholar in the subject's history. If Winfield's vision of tort law was closer to Pollock's, his approach to scholarship was more reminiscent of Salmond's. Although he wrote many influential articles, and a significant monograph on the place of tort within the legal landscape,[80] Winfield is best remembered, like Salmond, for a work aimed at students and practitioners, his 1937 *Text-Book of the Law of Tort*.[81] Furthermore, Winfield was keen – as Salmond had been – to keep his intended audiences on board, and similarly mindful of the need to stick closely to the decided cases.

Winfield's pragmatism ran deeper than Pollock's, and extended to all aspects of his scholarly activity. Hence while Pollock had stubbornly stuck to his general liability principle through thick and thin, Winfield demonstrated more flexibility, and eventually conceded ground to those, such as Salmond, who argued that the principle was inconsistent with the cases. Similarly, while Pollock had perceived the law of tort as concerned with the enforcement of moral duties, Winfield believed that the common law reflected the ethics and the morality of the community it served, and not some 'ideal ethical standard'.[82] Winfield's tort scholarship was, above all, animated by the simple but powerful idea that the law should meet the needs of the community it served. While Pollock's principles had seemed both eternal and universal, Winfield readily accepted that the law of tort should evolve in response to new social phenomena or changes in popular attitudes, and that legal rules might need to be tailored to better fit different common law communities,

[80] Winfield, *The Province of the Law of Tort* (n 11).
[81] PH Winfield, *Text-Book of the Law of Tort* (London, Sweet & Maxwell, 1937).
[82] PH Winfield, 'Ethics in English Case Law' (1931) 45 *Harvard Law Review* 112, 132.

with different cultural norms. This made him (like Bohlen[83]) simultaneously both a conservative and a progressive.

Two other features of Winfield's scholarship that Nolan highlights are his deep historical learning, and his intellectual open-mindedness. Winfield was perhaps the last Commonwealth tort scholar who managed seamlessly to blend historical analysis with exposition of the current law in a manner that would scarcely be possible today. As for his open-mindedness, at a time when American and English legal scholarship were rapidly growing apart, Winfield sought valiantly to bridge the gap, publishing in American journals, and consistently drawing the attention of his English and colonial readers to developments in the US, such as Bohlen's *Restatement*. There were, however, some matters in respect of which Winfield was immune to transatlantic influence. While fully cognisant of the work of realist tort scholars such as Leon Green and Fleming James, Winfield seems to have been entirely unmoved by their arguments for a more functional, policy-oriented tort law. Although progressive in his attitudes, at heart Winfield was a conservative with a deep respect for the common law and its doctrinal framework, and the editions of his textbook that he authored betray not even a hint of the realist-inspired revolution that had taken American tort scholarship by storm during his lifetime. But despite the fact that changing fashions had made such an approach seem outmoded by the time of his death in 1953, Winfield's textbook has nevertheless survived into the present century,[84] a fitting testament to the enduring quality and influence of his scholarship.

D. Prosser

If Winfield is perhaps the most influential twentieth-century English tort scholar, then in the US the equivalent accolade must surely be bestowed on William Prosser. Like Bohlen, Prosser wrote a popular casebook (indeed *the* most popular, even today),[85] a considerable number of high-profile articles on discrete topics, and was a reporter for a torts *Restatement* (the second, which was completed by John Wade after Prosser's resignation in 1970).[86] But to top all of that Prosser also authored four editions of by far the most influential book in the history of American tort law, his *Handbook of the Law of Torts*.[87]

[83] See White, *Tort Law in America: An Intellectual History* (n 8) 83.

[84] WE Peel and J Goudkamp, *Winfield & Jolowicz on Tort*, 19th edn (London, Sweet & Maxwell, 2014).

[85] CJ Robinette, 'The Prosser Letters: 1917–1948' (2016) 101 *Iowa Law Review* 1143, 1144. The first edition was YB Smith and WL Prosser, *Cases and Materials on Torts* (Brooklyn, NY, Foundation Press, 1952). So far the book has run to 13 editions.

[86] *Restatement (Second) of Torts* (Philadelphia, PA, American Law Institute, 1977).

[87] Prosser, *Handbook of the Law of Torts* (n 51) and three subsequent editions. In a survey conducted at the end of the last century, the fifth edition of Prosser's work (WP Keeton et al,

Not bad for a man who had scored a measly 59 in Torts before dropping out of Harvard Law School.[88] A consummate consolidator blessed with a photographic memory,[89] Prosser's reputation and scholarly impact derived not from original thinking, but from his 'combining an unusual gift of synthesis with high literary artistry and, perhaps most important of all, an unfailing perception of contemporary legal values'.[90] The result was that he managed to pull off the challenging feat of reducing 'tort law to manageable proportions while not underemphasizing its diversity and capacity for change'.[91]

When evaluating Prosser's legacy the sheer scale of his scholarly undertakings should be borne in mind. Although the second *Restatement* was built on the foundations of the first, in tort terms a great deal of water had gone over a great many dams[92] in the decades between the two, and its four volumes included nearly one thousand black-letter provisions. As for the *Handbook*, in a spoof review of the first edition Prosser attributed to Warren Seavey – the chair of the meeting of the fictional 'National Union of Torts Scholars' ('more popularly known by its initials'[93]) at which the book was discussed – the telling observation that the title of the book, which ran to over 1,300 pages, was 'something of a misnomer, as the book was not very well adapted to carrying in the hand without imminent peril to the feet'.[94] By the third edition Prosser was citing no fewer than 22,000 cases.[95] To consolidate mid-twentieth-century American tort law was no walk in the park.

Like other consolidators, Prosser thought carefully about his audiences.[96] Since the *Handbook* was supposed to be a work for students, its author kept the main text reasonably succinct, but he consciously extended the appeal of the work to judges and practitioners through the voluminous footnotes, which probably account for more than half of the work's length.[97] A superb writer, with an engaging and accessible style, Prosser was the 'master synthesizer of

Prosser and Keeton on the Law of Torts (St Paul, MN, West Publishing, 1984) was the runner-up for the title of most-cited legal treatise in the US published since 1978: FR Shapiro, 'The Most-Cited Legal Books Published since 1978' (2000) 29 *Journal of Legal Studies* 397, 404 (Table 2).

[88] See Robinette, 'The Prosser Letters: 1917–1948' (n 85) 1166.

[89] KS Abraham and GE White, 'Prosser and his Influence' (2013) 6 *Journal of Tort Law* 27, 35.

[90] JG Fleming, 'Prosser on Torts (3rd edition)' (1964) 52 *California Law Review* 1068, 1068 (review).

[91] White, *Tort Law in America: An Intellectual History* (n 8) 113.

[92] See Prosser, *Handbook of the Law of Torts* (n 51) vii.

[93] WL Prosser, 'Handbook of the Law of Torts' (1941) 4 *Louisiana Law Review* 156, 156 (review).

[94] ibid.

[95] Fleming, 'Prosser on Torts (3rd edition)' (n 90) 1070.

[96] Indeed, by the time that he wrote his *Handbook*, it seems that Prosser had become a student of the genre (see CJ Robinette, 'The Prosser Notebook: Classroom as Biography and Intellectual History' [2010] *University of Illinois Law Review* 577, 595).

[97] See Prosser, *Handbook of the Law of Torts* (n 51) vii. On the appeal of extensive footnotes packed with citations to practising lawyers, see A Fernandez and MD Dubber, 'Introduction: Putting the Legal Treatise in its Place' in A Fernandez and MD Dubber (eds), *Law Books in Action: Essays on the Anglo-American Legal Treatise* (Oxford, Hart Publishing, 2012) 10–11.

American tort law',[98] who excelled at 'joining the dots' so as to provide his readers with clear and precise doctrinal overviews of topics that had hitherto defied lucid exposition.[99] And another explanation for his success was his talent for spotting trends, and responding to them in such a way as to reinforce and intensify them, a quality that gave him the appearance of a mover and shaker, and one in tune with the times.[100]

More than anything else, however, the roots of Prosser's success lay in his ability to strike a balance between conceptual and functional approaches, by fusing doctrine with policy to produce rules that were (in his words) 'sufficiently flexible to allow for the particular circumstances, and yet so rigid that lawyers may predict what the decision may be, and men may guide their conduct by that prediction'.[101] Prosser was too wedded to doctrine and the traditional superstructure of private law to be described as a realist, but his methodology was 'congenial to realism',[102] and he shared with Leon Green a desire to demystify and where possible simplify the subject.[103] He also acknowledged the role of social policy in tort law, and was – as Robinette explains in his chapter on Prosser (chapter 7) – broadly pro-plaintiff, but his detached attitude was worlds away from the zealous instrumentalism of Fleming James. For James, liability insurance was *the* central driver for the development of accident law; for Prosser it was no more than a makeweight. This 'consensus' approach was in keeping with the 'dominant thrust of post-war legal thought', namely 'derivative and incorporative', and tending towards the modification rather than the rejection of previous assumptions.[104] For present-day conceptualists, this makes Prosser an ambivalent figure. Was his influence a malign one, sanitising and popularising realism so as to embed it into mainstream tort law and scholarship? Or was his the finger in the dyke, preserving the viability of doctrinal analysis by doing just enough to adapt it to the new thinking, and hence enabling its survival?[105] Perhaps there can never be a clear answer to that question, but either way the magnitude of Prosser's influence is not in doubt.

[98] WS Malone, 'Prosser on Torts (Second edition)' (1955) 43 *California Law Review* 740, 741 (review).

[99] For discussion of Prosser's style, see Abraham and White, 'Prosser and his Influence' (n 89) 46–49.

[100] The classic three examples of this phenomenon are the move to strict products liability, the division of the vague right of privacy into four separate causes of action, and the recognition of the tort of intentional infliction of emotional distress (for details, see Robinette, 'The Prosser Letters: 1917–1948' (n 85) 1145). For a critical appraisal of Prosser's role in the development of strict product liability, see GL Priest, 'The Invention of Enterprise Liability: A Critical History of the Intellectual Foundations of Modern Tort Law' (1985) 14 *Journal of Legal Studies* 461.

[101] Prosser, *Handbook of the Law of Torts* (n 51) 18.

[102] White, *Tort Law in America: An Intellectual History* (n 8) 155.

[103] Hence Prosser's treatment of both duty and proximate cause in negligence closely mirrored Green's: see ibid 260–61.

[104] ibid 140.

[105] For support for this interpretation, see ibid ch 5, and also Abraham and White, 'Prosser and his Influence' (n 89).

E. Fleming

Moving from Prosser to John Fleming, we need cross not an ocean but only a corridor, since the two men were colleagues in Berkeley in the early 1960s. But if Prosser was American through and through, for Fleming southern California was the end of a long road. Born in Germany, a schoolboy, student and young academic in England, and then a pioneering figure in the post-war Australian legal academy,[106] Fleming's globe-trotting was echoed in the jurisdictional ambiguity of his tort scholarship – the 'law of everywhere and nowhere' – and in his eminence as a comparative lawyer. To pigeon-hole Fleming is impossible, but despite an agonistic streak emphasised by Paul Mitchell in his chapter on Fleming,[107] he seems to us to be most appropriately classified as a consolidator, if in some respects an unusual one.

Like Salmond, Winfield and Prosser, Fleming's reputation as a tort scholar owes much to a single book, his magisterial *The Law of Torts*, first published in 1957 and running to nine editions under his pen. Although Fleming also published two shorter books on tort law,[108] and many influential articles, book chapters and case notes, his name is inextricably associated with that remarkable work, which Basil Markesinis described as 'his classic textbook (or, more accurately, short treatise)'.[109] The self-correction is telling, for *The Law of Torts* was not a textbook in the traditional vein; as Cane points out in his intellectual history of the work, it was a book '*about* tort law, not a book *of* tort law'.[110] Along with its cross-jurisdictional nature – albeit with Australian law as its '*point d'appui*'[111] – this made the book unsuitable for students and practitioners of a less ambitious bent. In Mitchell's words, it was 'not for children'.[112] Instead the natural audiences for the book were other scholars, and the appellate judiciary, with Fleming operating 'as a sort of *amicus curiae*' for the Commonwealth's higher courts, making his 'knowledge and expertise … widely available to judges through his writings'.[113]

The result was that Fleming was an unusual consolidator, consciously liberating himself from the need to placate the traditional readerships of tort texts, and exploiting the freedom this gave him to present what he saw as the 'best law' to an elite international caste of jurists and judges more in need of ideas than exposition.[114] At the same time, there is a similarity here with

[106] See Lunney, 'Legal Émigrés and the Development of Australian Tort Law' (n 8).
[107] Mitchell, ch 10 of this volume.
[108] JG Fleming, *An Introduction to the Law of Torts* (Oxford, OUP, 1967); JG Fleming, *The American Tort Process* (Oxford, OUP, 1988).
[109] BS Markesinis, '*The Law of Torts*, 7th edition. *The American Tort Process*' [1989] *CLJ* 134, 134 (review).
[110] P Cane, 'Fleming on Torts: A Short Intellectual History' (1998) 6 *Torts Law Journal* 216, 228.
[111] JG Fleming, *The Law of Torts*, 3rd edn (Sydney, Law Book Co, 1965) vi.
[112] Mitchell, ch 10 of this volume, p 289.
[113] Cane, 'Fleming on Torts: A Short Intellectual History' (n 110) 232.
[114] ibid *passim*.

Prosser, Fleming's 'intellectual hero'.[115] For where Prosser tried to glean general propositions from the mass of precedent produced by the multitude of US jurisdictions, Fleming sought to weave the cases[116] of a number of leading jurisdictions into a tapestry of Commonwealth tort law.[117] And in both instances the multi-jurisdictional nature of their work weakened the binds of precedent, giving them more scope to steer the law in the direction they thought appropriate. To pull this off required mastery of the art of synthesis, but here Fleming was more than a match for Prosser. A combination of encyclopaedic knowledge and a unique style – an uncanny ability to say as much as possible in as few words as possible – enabled him to write a 'highly compact book',[118] a multiple-jurisdiction treatise of a similar length to the single-jurisdiction textbooks of Salmond and Winfield.

Like Salmond, writing about English law in New Zealand, Fleming had an 'ambivalent sense of place',[119] updating a work on Australian tort law from the far side of the Pacific. This ambivalence ran deep. On the one hand, Fleming was truly a scholar of 'Commonwealth' tort law, equally at ease with the tort law of all the major Commonwealth jurisdictions, and beloved of apex courts in Australia,[120] Canada, New Zealand and the UK. On the other hand, it is important to remember that Fleming spent the bulk of his career in the US, and that he was profoundly influenced by the leading American figures of the previous generation, including Green, James and Prosser, whose works were referenced liberally in *The Law of Torts*. A realist at heart, Fleming had a 'presentist' mindset,[121] was sceptical of concepts and verbal formulae,[122] and believed in the role of tort law as a response to social problems generated by modern conditions.[123] He was also, as Mitchell explains, a critic of the bipolar

[115] ibid 221. See, eg, Fleming's laudatory review of the third edition of *Prosser on Torts*, cited above, text to n 90.

[116] Statutes were a problem for Fleming's approach, as Cane points out (Cane, 'Fleming on Torts: A Short Intellectual History' (n 110) 235–36). It is therefore fitting that the last edition of *The Law of Torts* written by Fleming was published in 1998, just before the Australian legislatures passed a raft of civil liability legislation (see, eg, the Civil Liability Act 2002 (NSW)) that both transformed and fragmented Australian tort law.

[117] For the metaphor, see Cane, 'Fleming on Torts: A Short Intellectual History' (n 110) 217.

[118] See ibid 239.

[119] See Mitchell, *A History of Tort Law 1900–1950* (n 64) 19 (discussing Salmond).

[120] According to Michael Kirby, 'Fleming's writing ... came to have an unequalled influence on the opinions of the Justices of the High Court of Australia writing, as they often must, upon problems of tort law' (MD Kirby, 'Comparativism, Realism and the Economic Factors: Fleming's Legacies' in NJ Mullany and AM Linden (eds), *Torts Tomorrow: A Tribute to John Fleming* (Sydney, LBC Information Services, 1998) 2).

[121] On 'presentism', see White, *Tort Law in America: An Intellectual History* (n 8) 65–67.

[122] See, eg, JG Fleming, 'Remoteness and Duty: The Control Devices in Liability for Negligence' (1953) 31 *Canadian Bar Review* 471, 472–73 ('mechanistic mumbo-jumbo'). Fleming's anti-formalism is emphasised by Mitchell, who refers to Fleming's 'fundamental scepticism about judicial language' (Mitchell, ch 10 of this volume, p 300).

[123] For particularly clear evidence of this, see Fleming, *An Introduction to the Law of Torts* (n 108) ch 1 ('The Task of Tort Law'). The title of Fleming's monograph on *The American Tort Process* (n 108) is also a nod to the realist emphasis on the processes from which legal outcomes emerged.

focus of traditional tort law, who was fascinated by the third-party interests in tort suits that had been emphasised by Green.[124] Though in some respects intellectually detached from his adoptive home (and of greater influence beyond its borders than within them[125]), Fleming is therefore a central figure in the overall history of common law tort scholarship, a connecting thread – as Winfield had been – between the US and the Commonwealth at a time when the gulf between the two was wider than ever before.

F. Consolidators in General

Some clear similarities are observable in the tort scholars we have classified as consolidators. With the exception of Salmond (in many ways a transitional figure), they were all career academics. All but Bohlen are associated with canonical texts, so much so that the scholar and the book became quite literally synonymous: *Salmond*, *Winfield*, *Prosser*, *Fleming*. Their scholarly methodologies were also constant, a point that White makes about Prosser[126] but which is clearly true also of, say, Winfield, who consistently blended historical analysis with exposition of the current law and suggestions for reform. The role of the consolidator is a time-consuming one, and another theme of the chapters on these scholars is their remarkable work ethic: Winfield's long days in the Squire Law Library in Cambridge; Prosser labouring through the Minnesota night on his *magnum opus*, the light in his office 'giving way only to dawn'.[127]

Three further similarities should be highlighted. First, the consolidators were audience-focused, since they had to keep their readerly constituencies happy. For traditional textbook (or 'hornbook') writers such as Salmond, Winfield and Prosser, this meant students of course, but also (as all three understood) legal practitioners. Bohlen and Fleming may have had a different audience, to some extent – the success of both the *Restatement* and *The Law of Torts* was closely bound up with their appeal to judges, particularly appellate judges[128] – but they were nevertheless driven by the same desire to give that audience what it wanted

[124] See, eg, L Green, 'Tort Law: Public Law in Disguise' (1959–1960) 38 *Texas Law Review* 1 and 257.

[125] That said, Fleming's impact in the US should not be under-estimated. Although, surprisingly, he is not mentioned in White, *Tort Law in America: An Intellectual History* (n 8), James Goudkamp's citation analysis in his chapter in this volume shows that Fleming is cited far more often in American law reviews than any other twentieth-century Commonwealth tort scholar (Goudkamp, ch 11 of this volume, Table 11.2). Fleming's influence on American courts (particularly the Supreme Court of his home state of California) was also considerable.

[126] White, *Tort Law in America: An Intellectual History* (n 8) 177.

[127] DW Louisell, 'William Lloyd Prosser: The Myth and the Man' (1963) 51 *California Law Review* 263, 263.

[128] The question of Fleming's intended audience is a difficult one, and it may have changed over time, as he realised how appealing his style of scholarship was to the appellate judiciary. At the time of the first edition of *The Law of Torts* he seems to have had the more traditional student/practitioner audiences in mind: see Lunney, 'Legal Émigrés and the Development of Australian Tort Law' (n 8) 517.

(and in Bohlen's case by the more pressing need to get his drafts through the ALI's approval process). The need to keep their audiences on board also had a conservative effect on the consolidators, discouraging them from adopting new language or new taxonomies that might alienate their readerships.[129]

The second similarity is closely linked to the first. One senses when reading about the consolidators that all were, in their different ways, treading what Nolan calls 'an intellectual tightrope'.[130] Salmond was faced with a tension between *principled* and *practical* exposition (or 'prescription and description'),[131] Bohlen with the challenge of finding a *via media* between legal science and legal realism, and Prosser with the need to satisfy the competing demands of doctrinalism and functionalism. And while Winfield was a scientifically-minded progressive operating in a deeply conservative – and at times even reactionary – academic culture, Fleming 'was tentatively testing how far he could go'[132] in seeking to persuade traditionally minded Commonwealth tort lawyers to think about their subject in new ways.

Finally, a characteristic of the consolidators that differentiates them from the pioneers is their practical mindset and their scepticism of theory. Nolan argues that Winfield's pragmatism and the fact that he kept his 'feet on the ground' is central to understanding his scholarly success, and the same traits are visible in the other consolidators, all of whose scholarship was rooted not in ideas but in the detail of the case law. Robinette makes the point, for example, that Prosser was profoundly anti-theoretical and deprecated the other-worldliness of legal academics oblivious to the fact that 'a lot of low-browed individuals are shaking their fists under each other's noses down in the District Court'.[133] Similarly, Cane argues that Fleming was not interested in 'large issues', and that he 'wanted to influence and persuade at the level of what to do about tort law, not at the level of how to think about it'.[134] Like Winfield and Prosser, Fleming was in other words an activist scholar,[135] more interested in bringing about legal change than in changing lawyers' thinking. The consolidators also tended to take a no-nonsense approach to the overall organisation of the subject, and did not get hung up on matters of taxonomy.[136]

[129] See, eg, Winfield, *The Province of the Law of Tort* (n 11) 32; Prosser, *Handbook of the Law of Torts* (n 51) 35; and Fleming, *The Law of Torts* (n 111) 16.

[130] Nolan, ch 6 of this volume, p 187.

[131] See Lunney, ch 4 of this volume, pp 127, 131.

[132] See M Lunney, 'Legal Émigrés and the Development of Australian Tort Law' (n 8) 518.

[133] See Robinette, 'The Prosser Letters: 1917–1948' (n 85) 1179, quoting a letter from Prosser to his mother shortly after he began working as an academic in 1930.

[134] Cane, 'Fleming on Torts: A Short Intellectual History' (n 110) 234.

[135] ibid 229.

[136] See, eg, Prosser, *Handbook of the Law of Torts* (n 51) 34–35. See also Nolan, ch 6 of this volume, pp 180–81, discussing Winfield; and Cane's comment that Fleming seems to have had 'very little interest in the overall structure of the subject' (Cane, 'Fleming on Torts: A Short Intellectual History' (n 110) 233).

The practical attitude of the consolidators may explain why they tended to be derivative, rather than original, thinkers, and why they were at their best not on more abstract or general questions but when struggling with more specific problems arising in particular areas, what Cane calls 'the fine-grain of tort law'.[137] As a result, their influence came not – as with, say, Holmes – from a handful of 'big ideas', but from the accumulated impact of their writings on a host of different topics, ranging across the entirety of the subject. It is perhaps this, above all, that explains the extraordinary success of the consolidators and the continuing significance of their scholarship.

IV. ICONOCLASTS

A. Green

Leon Green's classification as an iconoclast is unlikely to be contested. Green's work is characterised by a radicalism quite unlike anything previously seen in common law tort scholarship. A realist, Green rejected the legal scientists' elevation of tort doctrine into a discrete, eternal and self-sufficient system of norms, instead arguing that tort law should be responsive to changing social realities and that tort lawyers should switch their focus from doctrine, concepts and verbal formulae to process, the facts of the case and the policies driving the law's development. And 'unlike Bohlen, who believed that broad principles underlay tort law … Green rejected the view that there was a unified body of tort law'.[138]

Legal realism is easily caricatured, and Jenny Steele's sympathetic portrait of Green in this volume (chapter 7) serves as a powerful corrective to perspectives that gloss over the complexities of the realist approach. In particular, Steele is anxious to emphasise that Green's iconoclasm was far from nihilistic. His relentless assaults on the superstructure built by the nineteenth-century pioneers were instead motivated by his profound faith in the power of the common law to regenerate itself in the face of new societal challenges, a power that could be freely exercised, he believed, only if the restraining chains of legal formalism were smashed to pieces.

Realism can be understood as a product of the American pragmatic tradition, and the practical streak that runs through Green's scholarship – the emphasis on the particular rather than the abstract, and on the 'law in action' rather than the 'law in books' – reflected his early career as a trial lawyer in Texas. Green's pragmatism was also apparent in his decision to abandon classificatory orthodoxy in his casebook and instead organise it around 'functional'

[137] Cane, 'Fleming on Torts: A Short Intellectual History' (n 110) 238.
[138] Brown, 'Cecil A Wright and the Foundations of Canadian Tort Law Scholarship' (n 8) 187.

categories of social circumstance, such as 'automobile traffic' and 'manufacturers and dealers',[139] and in his avowed aim of demystifying and simplifying tort law and its doctrines, as exemplified by his campaign to rid negligence law of what he saw as the smokescreen of 'proximate cause'. It is observable, too, in his seminal work on the role of the jury in the American tort process, and on the impact of the judge/jury relation on the development of doctrines such as the duty of care.[140]

Green's granular, fact-sensitive approach was antithetical to grand designs, and as Steele says, '[he] had no blueprint for the development of the law'.[141] In this latter respect, he is a very different figure from James, another realist, but one driven by the single goal of making tort law a more effective mechanism for spreading accident losses. A true common lawyer, Green was instead 'convinced of the factual integrity and autonomy' of the individual case,[142] and of the ability of the judges to reach the right decision if left to their own devices. Of all the scholars whose work is discussed in this book, Green was probably the most sceptical of the legal academic project as initiated by the pioneers and carried forward by the consolidators. That scepticism is apparent in his disdain for Bohlen's *Restatement*,[143] which he perceived as a usurpation of the tasks that rightfully belonged to the participants in the legal process. But despite his antipathy to academic theorising, the influence of Green and other realists on subsequent tort scholarship was immense. By the late twentieth century an approach to tort law that was revolutionary half a century earlier had become entirely orthodox, and not only in America but across the Commonwealth as well.

B. James

If Green was a methodological subversive, the radicalism of Fleming James – 'the dominant [American] tort scholar of the 1940s and 1950s in terms of the volume, scope, and influence of his ideas'[144] – was directed more at the substance of the law.[145] As Guido Calabresi explains in his chapter on James (chapter 10), his project was a simple one: to transform tort law into as effective a mechanism at spreading losses as it was possible for it to be.

[139] L Green, *The Judicial Process in Tort Cases* (St Paul, MN, West Publishing, 1931).

[140] See Steele, ch 7 of this volume, p 204.

[141] ibid p 205 fn 11.

[142] White, *Tort Law in America: An Intellectual History* (n 8) 75.

[143] See L Green, 'The Torts Restatement' (1935) 29 *Illinois Law Review* 582.

[144] Priest, 'The Invention of Enterprise Liability: A Critical History of the Intellectual Foundations of Modern Tort Law' (n 100) 470.

[145] In this, the two men epitomised two distinct strands in realist thought: on these two strands, see White, *Tort Law in America: An Intellectual History* (n 8) 71.

James's 'radical single-mindedness' in pursuing that goal is striking,[146] and Calabresi speculates that it may be connected to his background as the son of a Protestant missionary.[147] As to why James set himself the goal that he did, the explanation for that seems tolerably clear: James's early career as a defence lawyer for the New Haven Railroad during the Great Depression. Having seen first-hand the devastating personal consequences of accidents in a society that lacked a proper system of social insurance, James became convinced that only tort law was capable of alleviating the plight of accident victims and their families, and that the more effective tort was at loss-spreading, the greater its beneficial impact would be. Regardless of one's feelings about his tort scholarship, it is hard not to admire James's humanitarian impulse, and the dedication to which it drove him.

It is worth pausing here to emphasise the degree to which James's way of thinking about tort law – which came to dominate tort scholarship from the 1950s onwards – was a product of a particular characteristic of early twentieth-century progressive thought, namely the 'discovery' of new social problems, coupled with 'a confidence in the possibility of their being solved by governmental institutions'.[148] There was, after all, nothing new about accidental personal injury and death – even if exaggeration of the novelty of the issue as a by-product of the 'machine age' and so forth was a *leitmotif* of modernist tort scholars such as Fleming. What had changed was the perception of it as a *problem to be solved* by a process of 'social engineering'. Here, the contrast with the ethos of the nineteenth-century pioneers, who had not conceived of tort actions primarily in terms of compensation – recall Holmes's emphasis on *defendants* – was indeed stark. As White says, the conception of tort law as a compensation system was 'a distinctly twentieth-century phenomenon, brought about by an altered view of the social consequences of injuries'.[149]

The central focus of James's scholarship on the law's capacity to effect positive social change lends it a different flavour from Green's, but his iconoclasm was no less pronounced.[150] Profoundly instrumentalist in outlook, James simply

[146] Priest, 'The Invention of Enterprise Liability: A Critical History of the Intellectual Foundations of Modern Tort Law' (n 100) 470. See also ibid at 474 (referring to the 'unrelenting character of his criticism of the fault system'); and PS Atiyah, 'American Tort Law in Crisis' (1987) 7 *OJLS* 279, 290 (referring to the 'single-minded fervour that shone through [James's] writings').

[147] James was born in Shanghai in 1904.

[148] White, *Tort Law in America: An Intellectual History* (n 8) 69.

[149] ibid 62. It might be thought appropriate to add 'and the rise of liability insurance', but in fact that phenomenon is perhaps best understood as itself a product of this altered ethos of injury, albeit one that in turn reinforced the new thinking. The result was 'a marvellously circular argument' (ibid 149).

[150] See Priest, 'The Invention of Enterprise Liability: A Critical History of the Intellectual Foundations of Modern Tort Law' (n 100) 480–81, who argues that James's scholarly contemporaries, though persuaded by him to think in terms of risk distribution, were reluctant to commit fully to his radical and single-minded approach.

brushed aside inconvenient doctrines if these reduced the utility of tort law as a loss-spreading mechanism. Hence it is that in James's work we see the first serious challenge to the Holmesian ethos of tort law, and to the fault principle in particular.[151] Since the purpose of tort law was to compensate the injured, not to deter, nor to admonish the blameworthy, the whole edifice of fault-based liability should be swept away. For James, the downside risk of this was low, since he did not consider that tort law contributed a great deal to accident prevention. In the context of accidental injury real fault (in the sense of moral culpability) was rare, and the deterrence potential of liability was very limited.[152] Though James was less radical than Green when it came to questions of method,[153] the intellectual connections between the two men were strong.[154] Green had taught James at Yale, and the realist undermining of doctrine and concepts paved the way for an instrumentalism in which those doctrines could be manipulated – or, where necessary, dispensed with – so as to enable tort law better to perform its role as a mechanism of social engineering. Without the pioneering work of Green and other methodological realists, James's doctrinal opportunism would have been inconceivable.[155]

Since the loss-spreading potential of tort law derived from the usually significantly superior ability of defendants to absorb and pass on the costs of accidents, James's scholarship is inextricably connected with the rise of liability insurance in the first half of the twentieth century, an association epitomised by his seminal 1948 article 'Accident Liability Reconsidered: The Impact of Liability Insurance'.[156] His instrumentalist outlook also explains the centrality of policy in his writing, and the emphasis in his work on insights from other disciplines and reliance on non-legal materials to illuminate legal questions (his co-authored casebook with Harry Shulman was entitled *Cases and Materials on Torts*,[157] and included a wide range of such writings). In all these respects and others, James left a deep imprint on tort scholarship, readily observable up to the present day.

[151] See Atiyah, 'The Legacy of Holmes through English Eyes' (n 25) 362 (arguing that the increasing association between tort and insurance – an association that James was of course instrumental in promoting – 'has helped to destroy the fundamental theoretical structure of tort law that Holmes laboured to create').

[152] See Priest, 'The Invention of Enterprise Liability: A Critical History of the Intellectual Foundations of Modern Tort Law' (n 100) 471–72, 477.

[153] See White, *Tort Law in America: An Intellectual History* (n 8) 89–90.

[154] See F James, 'To Leon Green' (1978) 56 *Texas Law Review* 535.

[155] The connection between the two strands of realism in the tort context is illuminated in JCP Goldberg, 'Unloved: Tort in the Modern Legal Academy' (2002) 55 *Vanderbilt Law Review* 1501, 1510–11.

[156] F James, 'Accident Liability Reconsidered: The Impact of Liability Insurance' (1948) 57 *Yale Law Journal* 549.

[157] H Shulman and F James, *Cases and Materials on Torts* (Chicago, IL, Foundation Press, 1942).

C. Atiyah

That imprint is particularly obvious in the tort writings of Patrick Atiyah. One of the foremost English jurists of the twentieth century, Atiyah's interests and influence extended far beyond tort law to encompass contract law and theory, intellectual history, legal and moral philosophy and legal method. As a tort scholar, Atiyah's reputation derives primarily from three sources: his weighty early monograph on vicarious liability;[158] *Accidents, Compensation and the Law*, his seminal study of the tort system and other accident compensation mechanisms;[159] and, right at the end of his career, *The Damages Lottery*,[160] a polemic against the operation of tort law in the personal injury context.

Atiyah's iconoclasm is self-evident,[161] and it manifested itself both in his method and in the substance of his analysis. Whereas Green had organised his casebook on tort according to the factual context out of which the decision arose, in *Accidents, Compensation and the Law* Atiyah went one step further, and replaced tort itself as an organising category with a new one based on a social problem: compensation for loss caused by accidents. This new category overlapped with the old one, but much of tort law was missing – anything that did not relate to personal injury, for a start – and Atiyah's holistic approach encompassed much more besides, including the everyday operation of the tort system, along with alternative compensation mechanisms such as social security, criminal injuries compensation and first-party insurance. Atiyah's normative stance was also more radical than James's, since while James believed in the capacity of tort law to adapt so as better to achieve the goal of loss-spreading,[162] Atiyah was an abolitionist who took the instrumentalist critique of the fault principle to its logical conclusion. Although the rise of liability insurance had transformed tort law from a system of interpersonal justice into an accident compensation mechanism, he argued, its inability to shake off its origins fatally undermined its ability to perform its modern role. The only solution was therefore to get rid of it entirely, at least in the case of negligently inflicted personal injury. As James Goudkamp points out in his chapter on Atiyah (chapter 11), he was perfectly consistent in holding to this position throughout his career. All that changed was his view as to what should replace tort law: in the 1970s, a no-fault compensation scheme, run by the government; in the 1990s, first-party

[158] PS Atiyah, *Vicarious Liability in the Law of Torts* (London, Butterworths, 1967).

[159] PS Atiyah, *Accidents, Compensation and the Law* (London, Weidenfeld & Nicolson, 1970) and two subsequent editions authored by him.

[160] PS Atiyah, *The Damages Lottery* (Oxford, Hart Publishing, 1997).

[161] See, eg, the title of his last chapter in an edited collection, which presaged the argument of *The Damages Lottery*: PS Atiyah, 'Personal Injuries in the Twenty-First Century: Thinking the Unthinkable' in P Birks (ed), *Wrongs and Remedies in the Twenty-First Century* (Oxford, Clarendon Press, 1996).

[162] Even if he saw it as only a half-way house on the way to a comprehensive scheme of social insurance for accidents (see Calabresi, ch 9 of this volume, p 266).

insurance, a free-market solution. A political pragmatist, he simply tailored his analysis to the dominant ideology of the time.

Like Fleming, Atiyah was a Commonwealth tort scholar whose thinking owed a great deal to the American realists, most obviously Green and James – as Goudkamp demonstrates, his focus on the social impact of tort law is observable even in his early book on vicarious liability. But Atiyah's tort scholarship was also rooted in the social conditions of post-war Britain, with its extensive welfare protection and universal healthcare. This meant that while realists like James had seen tort law as a potential solution to the social problem of accident costs (a form of '(decentralized) social insurance'[163]), Atiyah saw it as an obstacle in the path of progress, a throwback that should be supplanted by its more efficient competitors as a compensation system. In this, Atiyah was very much a man of his time. By 1970, when *Accidents, Compensation and the Law* was published, tort law was widely perceived to be a dying subject in the Commonwealth.[164] This perception operated on two levels. Most obviously, it was assumed that tort liability itself would be replaced – as indeed it substantially was in New Zealand – by no-fault compensation, at least in the personal injury cases that dominated the subject in practice. But the survival of the subject *as a legal category* was also endangered by the rise of the realist-inspired law-in-context movement, which sought to break up the old conceptual categories and to repackage their subject-matter under new headings in a reimagined pedagogical landscape.[165] Hence in the case of tort, the intentional torts might go into a course on civil liberties, defamation into media law, nuisance into planning law and so on, with the rump of the subject dominated by negligence and essentially amounting to 'accident law'. Since Atiyah's tort scholarship can best be understood in terms of this two-pronged attack on tort itself – *Accidents, Compensation and the Law* was the first volume to be published in the famous 'Law and Context' series – he was in a sense the ultimate tort iconoclast. And even though the subject survived, Atiyah's relentless assaults on it had shaken tort lawyers out of their complacency and forced them to seek to justify its continued existence in the modern age.

D. Weir

The continuities that are clearly visible in the intellectual progression from Green through James to Atiyah come to an abrupt halt when we switch our focus to Tony Weir. A common law conservative, Weir's view of the subject is

[163] James, 'Accident Liability Reconsidered: The Impact of Liability Insurance' (n 156) 550.

[164] Indeed, the point had been made by Fleming as early as 1958 (see JG Fleming, 'Ready for the Plaintiff' (1958) 46 *California Law Review* 137, 138 (review)).

[165] See, generally, W Twining, 'Reflections on Law in Context' in P Cane and J Stapleton (eds), *Essays for Patrick Atiyah* (Oxford, Clarendon Press, 1991).

much closer to that of early English doctrinalists, such as Pollock, Salmond and Winfield, than it is to that of the American realists and their Commonwealth disciples. And yet at the same time he was a profoundly iconoclastic scholar, a contrarian with a polemical style not dissimilar to that of Green and (latterly) of Atiyah.

One consequence of Weir's contrarianism is that it is much easier to say what he was against than what he was for. And, as Paula Giliker shows in her chapter on Weir (chapter 12), he was *against* a lot of things: the European Union, the European Court of Human Rights, the Law Commission,[166] the 'compensation culture', private law theory,[167] economists[168] and economic analysis of law, just for starters. Weir was also against the post-realist orthodoxy that saw tort cases in terms of competing interests and social policies, and against the push towards no-fault compensation in the 1970s.[169] Like creating a photograph out of a negative, we can use Weir's antipathies to build a picture of what he did believe in. He believed in the common law, which he thought threatened by creeping Europeanisation and misguided legislative reforms. And as a Scot working in England, and a renowned comparativist and translator, he believed in the importance of local difference and legal tradition, and loathed what he saw as the reductionism of projects seeking to harmonise European private law. He also believed in law as an autonomous discipline, decrying what he called the 'trahison des clercs'[170] of those who would sell it out to economists or philosophers, and in the importance of principle, which he defended in the face of the dominance of policy analysis in contemporary tort discourse. Finally, he believed in individual responsibility, and that tort law should roughly accord with the common-sense perceptions of ordinary people. This gave Weir's scholarship a populist, often pro-defendant edge,[171] which was in stark contrast to the prevailing academic mindset in favour of expanding liability, and which found an intriguing parallel in Atiyah's *The Damages Lottery*.

In addition to a wide range of original and insightful articles and book chapters on a cross-cutting array of topics, an introductory book in the Clarendon Law Series[172] and a short volume on the *Economic Torts*,[173] Weir published 10 editions of his *Casebook on Tort*,[174] and over 50 case notes. Most of his notes

[166] See, eg, T Weir, *A Casebook on Tort*, 10th edn (London, Sweet & Maxwell, 2004) vii.

[167] See Weir's scathing review of a collection of theoretical essays compiled by Ernest Weinrib: T Weir, '*Tort Law. Contract Law*' [1992] *CLJ* 388 (review).

[168] '[A]n adult does not abdicate his senses – until he becomes an economist' (T Weir, '*Tort Law and Economic Interests*' [1991] *CLJ* 551, 553 (review)).

[169] See, eg, T Weir, *A Casebook on Tort*, 4th edn (London, Sweet & Maxwell, 1979) 3.

[170] Weir, *A Casebook on Tort*, 10th edn (n 166) 7.

[171] As epitomised by his note on *Revill v Newbery* [1996] QB 567 (CA), where a pensioner was found liable in negligence for accidentally shooting a man who was breaking into his allotment shed (see T Weir, 'Swag for the Injured Burglar' [1996] *CLJ* 182).

[172] T Weir, *An Introduction to Tort Law*, 2nd edn (Oxford, OUP, 2006).

[173] T Weir, *Economic Torts* (Oxford, OUP, 1997).

[174] T Weir, *A Casebook on Tort* (London, Sweet & Maxwell, 1967) and nine subsequent editions.

were published in the *Cambridge Law Journal*, which until recently gave authors only a thousand words or so to summarise the decision and to comment on it. As Giliker demonstrates, Weir was from the start a master of this miniaturist form,[175] capable of conveying to the reader more meaning in those few words than lesser writers could manage in articles of ten or twenty thousand. This ability was also apparent from his *Casebook*, as in this memorable synopsis of the House of Lords' decision in *White v Jones*:[176]

> While Lord Goff opted for a pocket of liability, regardless of principle, Lord Browne-Wilkinson produced a principle out of his pocket and Lord Mustill found the pocket irreconcilable with any principle.[177]

The emphasis on case commentary in Weir's tort scholarship may have limited his broader influence, but it also played to his strengths as a critic, capable of concisely conveying the essence of the decision while simultaneously delivering a razor-sharp evaluation of it in a series of often devastating one-liners. Of all the scholars considered in this collection, it is probably fair to say that Weir is the only one whose work is worth reading for its wit and brilliance (in both senses) alone.

E. Iconoclasts in General

The iconoclasts are distinguishable from the consolidators in that they tend not to be associated with a single expository text, but to have established their reputations primarily through other scholarly forms, such as casebooks, monographs, articles and even (in Weir's case) the humble case note. This is surely no accident. Whereas the textbook writer must tread carefully to attract and retain the broad readership essential to the success of the enterprise, the iconoclasts' chosen modes of publication gave them a much freer rein. Furthermore, the textbook is by nature a conservative medium, requiring its author to present the entirety of the law in a comprehensive and systematic manner. In a monograph, or an article, it is much easier for an iconoclast to break away from established modes of thought, to pose fresh questions, or to approach issues from a radically new perspective. And since the primary audience for this kind of writing is other scholars, it is unsurprising that the influence of, say, Green was most immediately obvious in the work of later academics, even if in time – and with the aid

[175] See D Johnston, 'A Case, a Statute and Some Thoughts on the Proper Role of Policy' (2013) 87 *Tulane Law Review* 887, 888. After Weir's death, his Cambridge colleagues published a collection of his *CLJ* notes (C Bernard et al (eds), *Tony Weir on the Case* (Oxford, Hart Publishing, 2012)).
[176] *White v Jones* [1995] 2 AC 207 (HL).
[177] Weir, *A Casebook on Tort*, 10th edn (n 166) 71.

of consolidators like Prosser and Fleming – it also passed into the consciousness of students and legal practitioners.[178]

A second point to note about the iconoclasts is that far from treading a tightrope, as the consolidators did, they went out of their way to provoke and sometimes even to shock. On occasion, this meant adopting a polemical style in the hope of eliciting a reaction from the reader, as in much of the work of Green, some of the work of Weir[179] and Atiyah's *The Damages Lottery* (an unusual work of legal scholarship in its being aimed at the general public[180]). In her chapter on Green, Steele highlights Bohlen's comment that in his writing, words are often used 'not so much to define thoughts as to evoke emotional reactions',[181] and the telling comparison that Bohlen drew between Green's book *Judge and Jury* and modern art. And indeed, Steele's description of Green's language as 'vibrant' and 'simple, direct, and colourful'[182] brings to mind the work of the modernist painters of his time, reacting, as he was, against the staid conventions of an earlier age.

A third distinction between three of the iconoclasts – Green, James and Atiyah – and the consolidators is that their scholarship concentrated on one particular aspect of the law of tort, namely the cause of action for negligence, with particular reference to personal injury. As Carol Harlow has pointed out, such an approach tempts us 'to equate negligence with civil liability and tort law with accident compensation'.[183] This narrowing of the field of study was a consequence of the realists' conception of tort law in terms of its potential as a solution to the social problem of accidents and their consequences. Intriguingly, however, a similar emphasis on negligence and accidents at the expense of the remainder of tort law is observable in the work of many contemporary North-American tort theorists, despite their rejection of the realist

[178] George Priest has suggested (Priest, 'The Invention of Enterprise Liability: A Critical History of the Intellectual Foundations of Modern Tort Law' (n 100) 483) that James recognised the limitations of the law review article in directly effecting legal change, and that this may explain his switch of focus in the late 1940s to the preparation of his famous treatise, co-authored with Fowler Harper (see FV Harper and F James, *The Law of Torts* (Boston, MA, Little Brown, 1956). Whether or not this is true, Priest argues (ibid 501) that the clothing of James's loss distribution agenda in the authoritative form of a treatise contributed substantially to his influence in the American courts in the 1960s.

[179] A notable instance is T Weir, 'Governmental Liability in Tort' [1989] *Public Law* 40, an article that at times descends into a rant against a 'wondrously unstoical and whingeing society' (at 51).

[180] See Goudkamp, ch 11 of this volume, pp 322–23. There is little evidence that the work in fact reached a wider readership, but this was not perhaps Atiyah's fault. In the UK, 'very few law books by academics, however well written, reach a general audience' (W Twining et al, 'The Role of Academics in the Legal System' in M Tushnet and P Cane (eds), *The Oxford Handbook of Legal Studies* (Oxford, OUP, 2005) 928).

[181] F Bohlen, 'Judge and Jury' (1932) 80 *University of Pennsylvania Law Review* 781, 781 (review).

[182] Steele, ch 7 of this volume, p 207.

[183] C Harlow, 'A Treatise for Our Times?' (1984) 47 *MLR* 487, 492 (review).

emphasis on social policy in favour of approaches based on interpersonal justice arguments.[184] By contrast, as a conservative doctrinalist, sceptical of both policy and theory, Weir shared the consolidators' interest in the entirety of the subject as traditionally conceived.[185] Hence his book on the economic torts,[186] which was certainly not a topic that was likely to have animated James, for example.

Having pointed out some differences between the iconoclasts and the consolidators, we should also highlight a similarity, which is their shared antipathy to theory. Both Green and James were, as we have seen, pragmatists in the American tradition, empiricists interested in the nuts and bolts of tort litigation in practice, dismissive of abstract principle, and 'dubious about … appeals to moral values or norms'.[187] Similarly, Goudkamp points out that although Atiyah was a distinguished theorist in the field of contract, he 'shunned and, indeed, was derisory of' the efforts to theorise tort law in economic or moral terms that began to emerge in the US from the 1970s onwards.[188] As for Weir, theorising and philosophising about tort law was one of his pet hates, as he made abundantly clear in the preface to his introductory book on tort in the Clarendon Law Series:

> The Dean of an American Law School once asked me over lunch 'And what is your normative theory of tort?' It was rather a poor lunch and, as I thought, a very stupid question. Tort is what is in the tort books, and the only thing holding it together is their binding … In any event, before producing a 'normative theory' or even discussing the purpose of 'tort', it is surely desirable to become familiar with what that ragbag actually contains: otherwise we shall be like adolescents spending all night discussing the meaning of life – before, perhaps instead of, experiencing it.[189]

It was, at any rate, not a question that was likely to have been posed by Dean Green or Dean Prosser. While a connection can be made in this regard between the consolidators and the iconoclasts, it should not be pushed too hard. Although both types of scholar had a practical edge that reacted against abstract theorising, in other respects their pragmatisms were very different, since while the iconoclasts took a practical view of the law and its operation and impact, the pragmatism of the consolidators is most obvious in their approach to the scholarly enterprise itself. Bohlen's flexibility, Winfield's common sense and Prosser's detachment contrast sharply with Green's doggedness and the missionary zeal of James. (In this respect, Weir is again an exception, his instincts and approach reminiscent of his fellow Cantabrigian Winfield.)

[184] A point made by Cane, 'Fleming on Torts: A Short Intellectual History' (n 110) 225.

[185] Cf J Fleming, 'Once More – Economic Loss' (1992) 12 *OJLS* 558, 558 (referring to 'traditional tort scholars accustomed to view the subject primarily through the lens of personal injuries').

[186] T Weir, *Economic Torts* (Oxford, Clarendon Press, 1997).

[187] White, *Tort Law in America: An Intellectual History* (n 8) 69 (discussing realists in general). In Prosser's spoof review of his own *Handbook* he attributed to James the comment that 'a few more years in a law office would do the writer [ie, Prosser] the world of good' (Prosser (n 93) 164).

[188] Goudkamp, ch 11 of this volume, p 313.

[189] Weir, *An Introduction to Tort Law* (n 172) ix.

V. PLACE, PUBLICATIONS AND PROSE

There is insufficient space for us to consider all the general themes that run through the essays in this collection, and we have in any case already touched upon a number of these, including pragmatism and theory, the question of scholarly audiences, and the complex relationship between the scholars under scrutiny and the constitution and conception of the subject they studied. Nevertheless, in this part of the chapter we wish to highlight three refrains that recur throughout the remainder of the book, namely the importance of place, of publications and of prose.

A. Place

It would not be difficult to write an entire chapter on the significance of place in common law tort scholarship. Here we must content ourselves with a few observations, mere signposts to aid the reader's navigation.

In jurisdictional terms, the most important intellectual fault-line is unquestionably between the US and the rest, though the depth of the rift has varied over time. The scholarly world of the tort pioneers was immeasurably smaller than that of their successors, and the closeness of the connections that resulted is epitomised by the transatlantic friendship of Holmes and Pollock. In an early example of the profound influence of American tort scholars on their counterparts elsewhere – a persistent theme of this collection – Pollock dedicated his treatise to Holmes, writing in the letter of dedication that the book was an attempt 'to turn to practical account' the lessons of a visit to the Harvard Law School three years earlier.[190] As Stevens points out, the substance of the treatise reflected Pollock's affinity with the US, 'with American cases interspersed with the English, on the assumption that the common law formed a seamless whole'.[191]

That assumption, always questionable, began to wear very thin as the twentieth century wore on. Institutional variation increasingly drove a wedge between the US and the remainder of the common law world. Just as the realists were drawing attention to the importance of the jury in American tort law and process, the civil jury was in terminal decline elsewhere (with the exception of the Australian state of Victoria).[192] Consequently, the division of tasks between judge and jury, so essential to an understanding of the dynamic of

[190] Pollock, *The Law of Torts* (n 32) vi.

[191] Stevens, ch 3 of this volume, p 78.

[192] On the decline of the civil jury in England, see D Ibbetson, *A Historical Introduction to the Law of Obligations* (Oxford, OUP, 1999) 188–91. Ibbetson argues that it was largely obsolete by the time *Donoghue v Stevenson* [1932] AC 562 (HL) was decided. Green's *Judge and Jury* (Kansas City, MO, Vernon Lawbook Co, 1930) had been published in the US only shortly earlier.

American negligence law, lost most of its significance in other common law systems. Fleming, one of the few scholars equally at home with American and Commonwealth tort law, would later write of them that while '[t]he dish, so to speak, may consist of the same basic ingredients', it was 'metamorphosed by the manner of its cooking'.[193]

In the 1930s and 1940s, scholars such as Winfield and Prosser struggled to maintain the connection between the two systems. Unusually for an English scholar of his (or, for that matter, any other) generation, Winfield published a good deal in American law reviews, and continually emphasised to his more insular contemporaries the value to be derived from American law and scholarship. As for Prosser, he began his torts class in Minnesota in 1938 with a survey of the English texts (describing *Salmond* as the best of the bunch),[194] and when his own *Handbook* appeared three years later, it was replete with references to English cases and the writings of English authors. Nevertheless, the gulf continued to widen in subsequent decades, though the influence of American thinking could clearly be seen in the work of Commonwealth scholars such as John Fleming in Australia, Cecil Wright in Canada and Harry Street in England. (Wright is a particularly interesting figure in this connection, profoundly influenced by Americans such as Bohlen, Green, Prosser and Roscoe Pound, and severely critical of what he saw as the deadening conservatism of English tort scholarship.[195])

Another story, that of England and her 'legal satellites', is if anything even more complex and multifaceted. Along with the English language, the common law has been one of the most enduring legacies of British colonialism. One consequence of this is that the deep structures of private law – including the law of tort – are surprisingly similar across the Commonwealth, from Antigua to Auckland, and from Mumbai to Mombasa. And the effects of Empire and its aftermath are everywhere observable in the history of tort scholarship. Pollock's pioneering treatise, for example, arose out of a project to codify the law of tort in India, while Winfield's monograph *The Province of the Law of Tort* was based on lectures he gave in Calcutta in 1930 (Pollock having lectured in the same series some 37 years previously). Furthermore, as Lunney emphasises, Salmond was 'an Englishman abroad', a scholar writing about English law for an English audience, but from the other side of the world, in Wellington, New Zealand.

In the post-war years, when the Empire had morphed into the Commonwealth, the connections stayed strong, even as the law itself began to fragment.[196]

[193] Fleming, *The American Tort Process* (n 108) v.

[194] See Robinette, 'The Prosser Notebook: Classroom as Biography and Intellectual History' (n 96) 598.

[195] See Brown, 'Cecil A Wright and the Foundations of Canadian Tort Law Scholarship' (n 8) *passim*.

[196] For discussion see J Goudkamp and J Murphy, 'Divergent Evolution in the Law of Torts: Jurisdictional Isolation, Jurisprudential Divergence and Explanatory Theories' in A Robertson and

A key personality in that narrative is Fleming, who we have seen was truly a scholar of *Commonwealth* tort law from the 1950s through to the 1990s. The timing was no accident. Fleming's endeavour would not have been a rewarding one in earlier times, when Britain's dominance – epitomised by the Privy Council's status as the ultimate appellate court of the colonies, coupled with the principle that the common law should be the same across the Empire[197] – resulted in a high degree of legal uniformity. And in the present century the different jurisdictions have diverged to such an extent that the very idea of a 'Commonwealth' tort law is increasingly questionable. But in the second half of the twentieth century, the opportunity arose for a scholar to supplant the Privy Council's traditional centripetal role – if only, this time, by persuasion – and Fleming was the perfect man for the job.[198] The fact that his book, which purported to be about Australian law, should end up being be so influential in Canada was no coincidence.

Finally, place also had an effect both on the form that scholarship took and on the expository tradition itself. In the US, the use of the case method of instruction puts the casebook centre stage in pedagogical writings, whereas in England the textbook has traditionally reigned supreme. Furthermore, as we have seen, the American tort scholar concerned with description rather than prescription faced a distinctive challenge in the form of the multiple jurisdictions that combine to produce 'American' tort law. Meeting that challenge required a very particular skill set, and the resulting output was itself quite distinct from the single-jurisdiction texts produced by consolidators in England and elsewhere: 'less dogmatic' and more discursive in tone.[199] The multi-jurisdictional nature of American expository scholarship also manifested itself in the large-scale treatise, a form with 'no real parallel at all' in the rest of the common law world.[200] The only Commonwealth scholar to take and comprehensively implement an explicitly multi jurisdictional approach was Fleming, whose unique work *The Law of Torts*, though notionally focused on Australian law, was really a study of tort law in several Commonwealth jurisdictions, and (for that and other reasons) fell somewhere between a textbook and a concise treatise.

M Tilbury (eds), *The Common Law of Obligations: Divergence and Unity* (Oxford, Hart Publishing, 2015).

[197] In *Trimble v Hill* (1879) 5 App Cas 342 (PC), the Privy Council said (at 345) that 'it is of the utmost importance that in all parts of the Empire where English law prevails, the interpretation of that law by the Courts should be as nearly as possible the same'.

[198] For a premonition of this aspect of Fleming's enterprise, see AT Denning, '*Winfield on Tort*' [1955] *CLJ* 113, 113 (review), arguing that now that appeals to the Privy Council had largely been abolished, 'the textbooks must provide the links to keep the [Commonwealth legal] system together'. This was just two years before the publication of Fleming's *The Law of Torts*.

[199] PS Atiyah and RS Summers, *Form and Substance in Anglo-American Law* (Oxford, Clarendon Press, 1987) 396.

[200] ibid. See also the discussion of American legal literature, and in particular the multi-volume treatise, in Atiyah, 'American Tort Law in Crisis' (n 146) 280–84.

B. Publications

The importance of a scholar's chosen form or forms of publication should not be under-estimated.[201] The most classical form employed by the legal scholar is the treatise, and we have seen how the arrival of common law scholarship as a significant phenomenon was inextricably linked to the publication of the great nineteenth-century treatises. Indeed, it is only when tort treatises began to be written that tort came to be seen as a legal subject in its own right. 'Tort law' and the tort treatise – the subject and its study – are thus literally inseparable. Once the subject had established its place in the common law imagination, it soon found its way into the curricula of the law schools, and this in turn created the demand for the student text: the textbook/hornbook and (particularly in the US) the casebook. This largely spelt the demise of the treatise, at least in England, where it was overtaken by the textbook as well as by the more detailed practitioners' books, such as *Clerk & Lindsell*,[202] which were typically lacking in the scientific ambitions of the earlier genre.

If the nineteenth-century treatise was a sort of 'proto-code', as Brian Simpson argued,[203] then the closest we come to such a thing in twentieth-century tort scholarship is the American *Restatement*. Directed primarily at the courts – as opposed to students or legal practitioners – Benjamin Cardozo envisaged the *Restatements* as 'something less than a code and something more than a treatise'.[204] They were of course a distinctly American phenomenon, a response to the felt need for something to hold together – even if only loosely – the law of the multiple jurisdictions, and thereby to hold on to the idea of an American *common* law in the face of the federal courts' unwillingness to perform this role.[205] The unique mission of the *Restatements* conferred on them a unique status within the common law expository tradition, as what Nils Jansen calls 'the main reference text[s] of the [American] *ius commune*'.[206]

As for the textbook, or hornbook, while many such works were (and are) largely devoid of scholarly ambition, the best of them came to achieve canonical status, and to establish the reputations of their authors in the tort pantheon. It was characteristic of the most successful examples of this form that they

[201] On the importance of form in legal scholarship, see N Jansen, *The Making of Legal Authority: Non-legislative Codifications in Historical and Comparative Perspective* (Oxford, OUP, 2010) 107–08.

[202] *Clerk & Lindsell on Torts*, 22nd edn (London, Sweet & Maxwell, 2017).

[203] Simpson, 'The Rise and Fall of the Legal Treatise: Legal Principles and the Forms of Legal Literature' (n 43). On the connection between treatises and codification, see also A Braun, 'The English Codification Debate and the Role of Jurists in the Development of Legal Doctrines' in Lobban and Moses (eds), *The Impact of Ideas on Legal Development* (n 38) 215–19.

[204] Cardozo, *The Growth of the Law* (n 74) 9. This was before any *Restatement* had actually been promulgated.

[205] See Cane, ch 13 of this volume, p 370.

[206] Jansen, *The Making of Legal Authority: Non-legislative Codifications in Historical and Comparative Perspective* (n 201) 56.

purported to provide a comprehensive exposition of the entirety of the subject, and that they not only appealed to their primary audience of students, but were extensively used by practitioners and judges as well. It was also characteristic of such works that they were carried on by other scholars after the deaths of their original authors, so that *Salmond* became *Salmond & Heuston*, *Winfield* became *Winfield & Jolowicz*, *Prosser* became *Prosser & Keeton* and so on. The duration of this form of scholarly immortality varied, and much depended not only on the adaptability of the *Ur*-text, but also on the skill of the subsequent editor or editors in ensuring the work's continued utility.[207] And the more idiosyncratic the original scholar, the less likely his work was to survive (it would, for example, be a brave soul who would seek to perpetuate Weir's *Casebook*). Though the textbook route to scholarly stardom was a long and arduous one, the fruits of success were sweet. While the pioneers and iconoclasts may have had a greater impact on 'deep thinking' about the subject, it was the consolidators associated with the classic texts who became the closest a tort scholar can become to a 'household name', their works forever associated with their subject in the minds of successive generations of students and lawyers, and their citations ratcheting up year on year in the courts. The success and influence of those works provides compelling evidence for Jansen's claim that the form of the publication 'is an important factor contributing to its authority in legal discourse'.[208]

Other forms of scholarship were of course also important. Casebooks coloured the perceptions of the countless students who passed through American law schools, and in Australia and Canada it was the arrival of casebooks, not textbooks, that signified the recognition of a distinctive, indigenous law of tort in the 1950s.[209] In England, by contrast, casebooks historically played a subsidiary role, augmenting or supplementing the textbooks, and their impact was therefore more limited. Monographs tended not to be cited as much by the courts as treatises and textbooks, but the more practitioner friendly ones, such as Atiyah's *Vicarious Liability in the Law of Torts*, were an exception, while those directed at an academic audience were capable of shaping the thinking of later generations of scholars. As for law review articles, these sometimes fulfilled a similar role to that of the legal monograph – especially in the US, where the

[207] See Nolan's discussion of the likely reasons for the survival of Winfield's textbook (Nolan, ch 6 of this volume, pp 181–82).

[208] Jansen, *The Making of Legal Authority: Non-legislative Codifications in Historical and Comparative Perspective* (n 201) 108. See also Priest's suggestion (Priest, 'The Invention of Enterprise Liability: A Critical History of the Intellectual Foundations of Modern Tort Law' (n 100)) that the clothing of Fleming James's loss distribution agenda in the authoritative form of his co-authored treatise with Fowler Harper may have contributed substantially to the American courts' adoption of strict products liability in the 1960s.

[209] See CA Wright, *Cases on the Law of Torts* (Toronto, Butterworths, 1954) and WL Morison, *Cases on Torts* (Sydney, Law Book Co, 1955). The first work on tort law in New Zealand was, however, a textbook (AG Davis, *The Law of Torts in New Zealand* (Wellington, Butterworths, 1951)). Excepting Fleming's *The Law of Torts* (not, as we have seen, a traditional textbook), the first textbooks on Australian and Canadian tort law did not appear until the 1970s.

latter was a relative rarity – but throughout the common law world much of the periodical literature had considerable wider influence, both on the courts and on the students whose reading lists it peppered. And even that most humble mode of legal academic publication, the case note, could affect perceptions or persuade a court to alter the path of the law's development, particularly in the hands of a master of the form such as Pollock or Weir.

C. Prose

Readers of this collection will continually be reminded of the importance of a scholar's prose. A scholar's style of course reflects his or her personality, and even the nature of his or her scholarship – contrast, for example, Winfield's use of homely metaphor with Green's flights of verbal fancy. And yet perhaps the most important message about style that emerges from this book is its significance to scholarly success and influence. Legal scholars are after all *writers*, and, like a poet or novelist, the tools of their trade are the pen, the typewriter and the word-processor. Legal scholarship is ultimately words, and the choice of words matters. Style can be at least as important as substance.

The importance of style to scholarly accomplishment is particularly apparent in the case of the consolidators. A textbook writer, after all, needs to attract and retain readers in a competitive marketplace. As Lunney explains, Salmond's ability to encapsulate a sophisticated idea in a neat verbal formula – as exemplified by the so-called 'Salmond test' in the law of vicarious liability[210] – was a trait that endeared him to students, practitioners and judges. And Nolan also emphasises the importance of its attractive style in establishing Winfield's textbook as the leader in its field, while what Fleming called his 'felicity of style and humor'[211] is a consistent theme of the secondary scholarship that has been published about Prosser in recent decades.[212] Similar praise has been heaped on the 'clean, vigorous and searching' writing of Fleming himself.[213] Indeed, on any assessment, Fleming's prose was highly distinctive, and was one other way in which his work *The Law of Torts* stood apart.

Style was perhaps less central to the influence of the pioneers and the iconoclasts. The natural advantage of coming first ensured the pioneers their place in the history of the subject, even if (as in Pollock's case) their writing left a lot to be desired. And even an early consolidator like Bohlen could get away with leaden prose: after all, his *Restatement* had no competitors. As for the iconoclasts, to the extent that their primary audience was other scholars, style

[210] See Lunney, ch 4 of this volume, p 125.

[211] Fleming, 'Prosser on Torts (3rd edition)' (n 90) 1068.

[212] See, eg, White, *Tort Law in America: An Intellectual History* (n 8) 156 (one of the explanations of Prosser's success was that his writing 'was clear, light, and eminently readable').

[213] MA Millner, '*The Law of Torts*' (1957) 74 *South African Law Journal* 469, 474 (review).

may have mattered less than it did to consolidators whose success depended on their broader appeal. But the audiences for the iconoclasts' work varied, and no matter how powerful the idea, the force and clarity of its expression mattered. Green was a consummate wordsmith, as Steele emphasises, and few legal scholars can match Weir's sparkling prose and acerbic wit.

VI. CONCLUSION

It will, we think, be difficult after reading this book to escape the conclusion that scholars of tort law have played a significant role in the development of the subject since its arrival on the scene in the late nineteenth century. Each of the three categories of scholar we have identified has played a different part in the story of tort law. The pioneers established tort as a legal subject and at the same time set the intellectual parameters within which later scholarship was conducted. The consolidators synthesised the extensive case law on the subject, and wrote the canonical tort texts that shaped the thinking of generations of students and practitioners. And the iconoclasts successfully undermined the received thinking about tort law and transformed its intellectual foundations, with profound consequences for the scholarship and practice of tort law in the modern era.

We have emphasised throughout this chapter the difficulty of measuring scholarly influence in law. We are also acutely aware of the impossibility of distinguishing when a scholar's thinking has shaped general attitudes, and when general attitudes are manifested in the scholar's thinking.[214] Nevertheless, we are convinced that Atiyah was right to argue that scholars have played a much greater role in the development of the common law than has generally been acknowledged. In many instances, scholarly influence is both specific and obvious, as with, for example, the American courts' adoption of strict products liability in the 1960s.[215] But 'the impact of juristic speculation is subtle',[216] and most of the time scholarly influence is no doubt more general and less susceptible to direct observation. Time and again, we suspect, the writings of the tort scholars considered here, and of many others, were (in Lunney's words) 'read and used by students, practitioners and judges in learning, arguing and adjudicating on tort law'.[217] And nor should it be forgotten that the influence of jurists

[214] See further White, *Tort Law in America: An Intellectual History* (n 8) xix.

[215] As to the significance of legal scholarship in this development, see Priest, 'The Invention of Enterprise Liability: A Critical History of the Intellectual Foundations of Modern Tort Law' (n 100), who argues (at 517) that the true foundation for the strict liability standard [laid down in § 402A of the *Restatement (Second) of Torts*] was … the accumulated effect of thirty years of scholarship'.

[216] Duxbury, *Frederick Pollock and the English Juristic Tradition* (n 16) 282.

[217] Lunney, ch 4 of this volume, p 131. It goes without saying that the citation of scholarly works by judges is a wholly inadequate measure of their influence. As Duxbury points out, citations to a scholarly work 'are not necessarily indicative of its influence, just as absence of citation to

can derive not only from their published writings, but also from their work for law reform bodies,[218] their responses to law reform proposals, and their informal contacts with policy-makers and judges.

In his more general chapter on tort scholarship in this collection (chapter 13), Peter Cane echoes Leon Green's scepticism about the role of the legal academic in the common law world. According to Cane, 'under the common law model, "jurists" have no distinctive niche in the legal ecosystem'.[219] Like Green, Cane focuses, as common lawyers are wont to do, mainly on the process of adjudication, and concludes from what he argues to be the marginal role of jurists in that process that theirs is a marginal role in the common law ecosystem more generally. Conversely, it can be argued that in the codeless world of the common law it is the scholar who must synthesise and order the multitude of precedents generated by the decisions of the courts, and who bears the primary responsibility for abstracting from those decisions more general principles and organising them into a system of norms understood to govern a particular topic or subject. As we have seen, this is a particularly important task in the US, where scholars are the only participants in the legal system capable of pulling together the threads of the many distinct jurisdictions into something resembling an American common law. Add to this the universal role of the jurist as expositor of the law to future generations of practitioners and judges,[220] as well as the evidence from this collection and elsewhere[221] that more academically-oriented scholarship is capable of affecting deep thinking – prevailing intellectual assumptions and attitudes – across the legal system, and there are strong grounds on which to contest the scepticism that continues to surround the common law scholar and his or her role.

One final thought is that in the century-and-a-half of its existence, tort law scholarship has undergone several paradigm shifts. In the early days of the

[such a] work does not compel the conclusion that it had no influence' (N Duxbury, *Jurists and Judges: An Essay on Influence* (Oxford, Hart Publishing, 2001) 1). For a discussion of the use of tort scholarship by the House of Lords, see K Stanton, 'Uses of Scholarship by the House of Lords in Tort Cases' in J Lee (ed), *From House of Lords to Supreme Court* (Oxford, Hart Publishing, 2011). Stanton's chapter does include a citation analysis, in which consolidators such as Fleming and Salmond perform particularly strongly.

[218] 'In the areas of public policy and law reform, legal scholars almost certainly have more direct influence through membership of Law Commissions, public committees, or activist pressure groups than through their published writings' (Twining et al, 'The Role of Academics in the Legal System' (n 180) 928). On the role of English tort scholars in the early work of the Law Revision Committee, see Mitchell, *A History of Tort Law 1900–1950* (n 64) Pt II.

[219] Cane, ch 13 of this volume, p 382.

[220] See Harlow, 'A Treatise for Our Times?' (n 183) 489, referring to the way in which '[s]tudents absorb texts and become the practitioners who rely on the same texts to index their legal reasoning'. For a possible example of a scholar influencing a judge's reasoning in a case through university lectures delivered decades earlier, see P Mitchell, '*Hedley Byrne & Co Ltd v Heller & Partners Ltd* (1963)' in C Mitchell and P Mitchell (eds), *Landmark Cases in the Law of Tort* (Oxford, Hart Publishing, 2010) 195–96.

[221] See, eg, White, *Tort Law in America: An Intellectual History* (n 8) *passim*.

pioneers, tort law was closely connected to criminal law, with the focus primarily on defendants, and the central concern the culpability of their conduct. By the middle of the twentieth century, attention had shifted to claimants, and the desirability of spreading accident losses through stricter forms of liability, backed up by third-party insurance. Towards century's end, however, defendant-focused approaches were once again in the ascendant, at least in the US, with the rise of deterrence-based theories based on economic analysis.[222] At the same time, other theorists began to reject instrumentalist approaches, instead conceiving of tort law in terms of rights, wrongs and interpersonal justice, and arguing that the focus should not be on one party to the effective exclusion of the other, but on the interaction between the two.[223] Contemporary debates across the common law world show that battle continues to rage between these very different conceptions of tort law. But no matter whose vision of the subject ultimately wins out, experience suggests that theirs is unlikely to be the final word. On the contrary, the story of tort scholarship looks set to continue its halting course for decades and centuries to come.

[222] See, eg, RA Posner, 'A Theory of Negligence' (1972) 1 *Journal of Legal Studies* 29.
[223] See, eg, GP Fletcher, 'Fairness and Utility in Tort Theory' (1972) 85 *Harvard Law Review* 537; and EJ Weinrib, *The Idea of Private Law* (Cambridge, MA, Harvard UP, 1995).

2

Thomas McIntyre Cooley (1824–1898) and Oliver Wendell Holmes (1841–1935): The Arc of American Tort Theory

JOHN CP GOLDBERG AND BENJAMIN C ZIPURSKY*

I. INTRODUCTION

TORT LAW HAS been around for a long time. What is now called 'tort theory' emerged only in the late nineteenth century. Two figures, separated by an ocean yet conjoined by a lifetime of correspondence, loom large in this development. Indeed, if one were to play the parlour game of identifying the founding fathers of modern tort theory, Sir Frederick Pollock and Oliver Wendell Holmes, Jr would be plausible choices.

While this chapter will attend to Holmes's views of tort law, it approaches his work through a different and more parochial pairing.[1] Specifically, it compares his work with that of his most formidable American predecessor: Thomas McIntyre Cooley. A member of the Michigan Supreme Court from 1864 to 1885, Cooley gained national renown for his treatise on constitutional law.[2] More relevantly for present purposes, in 1879 he published one of American law's first comprehensive torts treatises.[3]

* For very helpful feedback on this chapter, our thanks to John Manning, Henry Smith, Mark Tushnet and the participants in the April 2018 Scholars of Tort Law workshop held at Worcester College, University of Oxford.

[1] It is more 'parochial' in that our focus will be on two American scholars and on American tort theory. However, as we note in section IV, the divide between the two men can be found in, and has implications for, tort theory outside of the US.

[2] TM Cooley, *A Treatise on the Constitutional Limitations Which Rest Upon the Legislative Power of the States of the American Union* (Boston, MA, Little, Brown and Co, 1868).

[3] TM Cooley, *A Treatise on the Law of Torts or the Wrongs Which Arise Independent of Contract* (Chicago, IL, Callaghan and Co, 1879). The first edition of the *Treatise* received a second printing in 1880. Cooley published a second edition of the *Treatise* in 1888. Posthumous third and fourth editions were published, respectively, in 1906 and 1932. A one-volume revised edition was also published in 1930.

In the late 1800s, Cooley was, according to one learned commentator, 'the most respected lawyer in America and among the most widely respected persons in American public life'.[4] Yet, in one of history's endless supply of ironies, Cooley's corpus would soon be dismissed for being *Lochner*-ian,[5] even as the work of Holmes – who was probably more sympathetic to laissez faire and Darwinism than Cooley[6] – was being embraced as the path to legal progress.[7]

Reasons abound for considering Cooley and Holmes together. Both were academically minded judges on state high courts that fed on a steady diet of tort cases. Both insisted that a separation of law and morals was necessary to achieve an understanding of tort law. And both saw the judicial role as requiring lawyerly craft and policy-sensitive reasoning. True, Cooley saw himself more as a lawyer than a grand theorist. This is not to say, however, that he lacked a vision. As we shall explain, one can find in his treatise a general conception of both tort law and scholarship. In the end, a deep divide separated these two great jurists – one of both temperament and substance. Cooley, true to the common law tradition, held a 'wrongs-and-redress' view of tort law. With typical bravado, Holmes developed a distinctive 'loss-based' view.

The Cooley-Holmes divide in tort theory is not merely a matter of historical interest. An aim of this chapter is to inquire how Holmes's approach has come to claim a larger market share among American tort scholars than Cooley's. We shall also suggest – contrary to conventional academic wisdom in the US – that torts scholars would do better to follow Cooley.

II. COOLEY AND HOLMES

We begin with brief biographical sketches. Thomas Cooley was born in 1824 in Attica, a small town in western New York State located about 40 miles

[4] PD Carrington, 'Law as "The Common Thoughts of Men": The Law-Teaching and Judging of Thomas McIntyre Cooley' (1997) 49 *Stanford Law Review* 495.

[5] *Lochner v New York* 198 US 45 (1905) (striking down maximum-hours legislation for bakers as violating the right to freedom of contract guaranteed by the Due Process clause of the Fourteenth Amendment); Carrington, 'Law as "The Common Thoughts of Men": The Law-Teaching and Judging of Thomas McIntyre Cooley' (n 4) 524; PD Carrington, 'The Constitutional Law Scholarship of Thomas McIntyre Cooley' (1997) 61 *American Journal Legal History* 368, 369. The feature of Holmes's jurisprudence that endeared him to New Deal-era progressives – namely, his resistance to hard-look judicial review of social welfare legislation – may have been a feature of Cooley's jurisprudence as well: ibid 375–76.

[6] Indicative of Holmes's Darwinian outlook is *Buck v Bell* 274 US 200, 207 (1927) (Holmes J) (observing that '[t]hree generations of imbeciles are enough' in the course of upholding a state's right to sterilise a woman it deemed mentally incompetent).

[7] Holmes carefully cultivated his reputation with the leading lights of younger generations, especially Felix Frankfurter: B Snyder, 'The House that Built Holmes' (2012) 30 *Law and History Review* 661. Our focus is on Cooley's writings about tort law. Others have discussed his views of constitutional and administrative law: Carrington, 'Law as "The Common Thoughts of Men": The Law-Teaching and Judging of Thomas McIntyre Cooley' (n 4); AR Jones, *The Constitutional Conservatism of Thomas McIntyre Cooley* (New York, Garland, 1987).

from Lake Erie. The area was at the time experiencing a frontier boom that coincided with the building of the Erie Canal, and it was also a hotbed of religious revivalism.[8] Thomas was the tenth of 15 children, and lived in modest though not dire circumstances on a 100-acre farm owned and operated by his father.[9]

At 19, Cooley headed west to make a life for himself in Michigan.[10] Studious from an early age, he learned law working in a small law office and was admitted to the Bar in 1846.[11] For about a decade, he maintained a modest practice while also reading widely in history, literature and political philosophy, editing local newspapers, publishing poetry and essays on political topics, and participating in local politics.[12] As a Jacksonian Democrat, Cooley believed that governments too frequently pursued policies favouring special interests (through public works projects, charters, monopolies and 'class legislation'). He was thus committed to limited government and notions of self-reliance and self-improvement. At the same time, he insisted on a right to free public education for men of all economic classes so that each might have a fair opportunity to succeed.[13]

In 1857, the Michigan legislature tasked Cooley with compiling the state's laws. Soon thereafter, he was named a reporter to the Supreme Court of Michigan and appointed as one of three faculty members in the newly minted law department at the University of Michigan.[14] In 1864, he was elected to the Michigan Supreme Court, on which he sat until 1885, and for which he served as Chief Justice. While on the Court, he published treatises on constitutional, tax and tort law, and an edition of Blackstone's *Commentaries*. Although Cooley was a plausible candidate for a seat on the US Supreme Court, his political independence alienated those who would have needed to support his nomination.[15] In 1887, President Grover Cleveland appointed him to the Interstate Commerce Commission (ICC). Cooley stepped down from the ICC in 1891 and died in 1898.

[8] Jones, *The Constitutional Conservatism of Thomas McIntyre Cooley* (n 7) 6–7, 11–17. Jones suggests that Cooley was sceptical of religious fervour, and of the mixing of politics and religion, favouring instead a form of Presbyterianism that emphasised individual industry and responsibility, frugality, and reliance on reason to identify right and to control one's passions: ibid 15–16.

[9] ibid 7–8.

[10] ibid 26.

[11] ibid 33.

[12] ibid 35–39, 48–49. Cooley was affiliated with the 'Free Soil' party during its brief existence. It opposed the expansion of slavery not on the moral grounds advocated by abolitionists, but primarily out of concern that a slave-based economy would make it impossible for 'ordinary' free men to earn a living and own property.

[13] ibid 40–51.

[14] Cooley remained on the Michigan faculty until 1884. In part because he was the only member of the law department who resided in Ann Arbor, Cooley served as de facto Dean for most of this time. Sometime between 1872 and 1875, the formal title was conferred on him. E Gaspar Brown, *Legal Education at Michigan, 1859–1959* (Ann Arbor, MI, The University of Michigan, 1959) 31–40.

[15] Jones, *The Constitutional Conservatism of Thomas McIntyre Cooley* (n 7) 215–16.

Roughly a generation later, Oliver Wendell Holmes, Jr emerged out of quite different circumstances. Born in 1841, he grew up in Boston at a time when that city was poised to emerge as the intellectual hub of the nation.[16] His grandfather on his mother's side had been a justice on the Massachusetts Supreme Judicial Court, and his father and namesake was a prominent physician and medical researcher, as well as a poet and an essayist. The last pastime made the elder Holmes something of a celebrity.[17] His mother Amelia was a committed abolitionist.[18]

The younger Holmes grew up in rarified air. His family moved in the same circles as Ralph Waldo Emerson and Henry Wadsworth Longfellow, and Holmes himself maintained lifelong friendships with Henry James, Jr and William James.[19] Befitting his station, he attended Harvard College, already by then filled with young elites destined for the professions.[20] Later he, along with William James, Charles Sanders Pierce, Nicholas St John Green and others, formed a discussion group – the ironically named 'Metaphysical Club' – that contributed to the emergence of American pragmatism as a school of thought.[21]

After college, Holmes volunteered to serve in the Northern Army in the US Civil War. During three eventful years of service, he was wounded multiple times, nearly died from dysentery and witnessed first-hand the myriad horrors of war.[22] The experience probably traumatised him, and seems to have left him with a darkly romantic ethical perspective: like a soldier who charges into battle not knowing if any worthy cause is really being served, a man should throw himself into his chosen profession without supposing that, by doing so, he will accomplish anything of significance.[23] Holmes subscribed to a comparably dark Darwinian conception of politics as a relentless power struggle among competing groups, with the victors, in the ordinary case, imposing their will on the vanquished.[24]

After concluding his military service, Holmes attended Harvard Law School for one year, clerked briefly in a law office, then practised in Boston for 15 years, primarily in admiralty and commercial law. Throughout this period (1864–82), he regularly travelled to England, where he moved in elite circles and established close relationships with prominent English jurists.[25] He also managed to find

[16] GE White, *Justice Oliver Wendell Holmes: Law and the Inner Self* (Oxford, OUP, 1993) 20.

[17] ibid 9, 17.

[18] ibid 15.

[19] ibid 35.

[20] ibid 29, 87, 91–92.

[21] ibid 92; L Menand, *The Metaphysical Club: A Story of Ideas in America* (New York, Farrar, Straus and Giroux, 2001).

[22] White, *Justice Oliver Wendell Holmes: Law and the Inner Self* (n 16) 49–65.

[23] ibid 82–83. White plausibly traces these ideas to the Puritan notion of a 'calling', to which Holmes would have been exposed in his youth. Probably implicit in this notion was the assumption that such a life was available only to men of a certain background and education (hence our use of masculine pronouns in the text to convey what we take to have been Holmes's outlook): ibid 23.

[24] ibid 290–91.

[25] ibid 96–102.

time to write *The Common Law*, published in 1881. The following year, Holmes was appointed to the Massachusetts Supreme Judicial Court, on which he served for two decades, including as Chief Justice. In 1902, Theodore Roosevelt appointed him to the US Supreme Court. He remained there until 1932, retiring at the age of 90 and dying two years later. As a Supreme Court Justice, Holmes offered a vision of American constitutional law largely consistent with his Darwinism. The US Constitution, he reasoned, sets basic ground rules for the political struggle; it should not be read to enshrine the principles of any of the warring factions.[26]

Cooley's and Holmes's different sensibilities about law (and life more generally) no doubt are attributable in part to their different backgrounds and early experiences. Indeed, Cooley himself seems to have appreciated that he was coming from a different place than Holmes, both biographically and intellectually. As Paul Carrington has documented, in 1886, Harvard University awarded Cooley an honorary doctorate, which gave Cooley occasion to speak at a dinner attended by Holmes (and CC Langdell).[27] In his remarks, Cooley emphasised the importance for jurists of intellectual humility, and of the law's staying in touch with commonplace notions of morality (that is, citizens' own sense of what they owe one another).[28] This was very much a common lawyer's mindset. And, as Cooley probably recognised, it was not Holmes's.[29] Shuttling between Boston and London, and writing at the cutting edge of philosophy and jurisprudence, Holmes gave far more credence to theory and to expertise, whether economic, historical or legal. To understand law, and particular areas of law, it was, he thought, necessary and desirable to identify law's general principles through inductive, empirical analysis.[30] A good judge would be guided by these principles, while remaining open to carving out policy-based exceptions as needed.

Cooley supposed that, in law at least, insight comes from immersing oneself in the details of doctrine, understood to reflect inherited wisdom and, more importantly, ordinary morality (albeit modified to fit the domain of law). In this regard, at least, Cooley was heir to Coke and Blackstone, whereas Holmes followed Hobbes and Bentham. With these differences in mind, it is hardly surprising to learn that Cooley wrote practitioner- and student-oriented treatises, while Holmes wrote in a more recognisably academic vein.

[26] Such, at least, seems to have been the view expressed in his famous *Lochner* dissent, as well as in his opinions on the right of free speech.

[27] Carrington, 'Law as "The Common Thoughts of Men": The Law-Teaching and Judging of Thomas McIntyre Cooley' (n 4) 495, 498–99.

[28] ibid 499.

[29] ibid 520–32 (contrasting Cooley's and Holmes's general orientations toward law).

[30] OW Holmes, 'The Path of the Law' (1897) 10 *Harvard Law Review* 457, 471–72 (claiming to have identified an emerging general principle of tort liability and describing how a 'very eminent English judge' rejected it for being prescriptive rather than descriptive).

III. WRONGS AND REDRESS v RESPONSIBILITY FOR LOSSES

We turn from biography to tort law and theory. Treatises specifically devoted to the subject of torts were new to the second half of the nineteenth century. Cooley and Melville Bigelow published theirs within a year of each other, having been preceded among US scholars only by Francis Hilliard.[31] As the extended title of Cooley's work indicates – *A Treatise on the Law of Torts or the Wrongs Which Arise Independent of Contract* – what made the subject new was *not* that post-Bellum courts had suddenly fashioned a hitherto unknown body of doctrine. Rather, the civil side of the common law was being reorganised, and more fully elaborated, around the distinction between contract (roughly, civilly actionable wrongs involving the failure to perform a duty one has agreed to perform) and tort (roughly, civilly actionable wrongs involving the failure to heed a legally-defined duty to refrain from injuring another). In essence, the task was to take Blackstone's familiar category of 'private wrongs',[32] to isolate the tort component of that broader category and to give it a more detailed treatment than Blackstone had.[33]

Cooley's treatise offers about what one would expect to find in this genre of writing: it is filled with discussions of cases and doctrines. Yet it begins with more than 100 pages of what would now be considered tort theory. Those familiar with his constitutional law treatise will not be surprised to learn that the initial framework sketched in these pages is quite sophisticated. Cooley did not write in the grand and arresting manner of Holmes. By the same token, he perhaps proceeded with greater analytical precision and theoretical restraint.

For present purposes, the opening portion of the treatise is usefully divided into two components: one substantive and one jurisprudential. In this section, we attend primarily to Cooley's substantive views. We take up jurisprudence more fully in section IV.

As his title indicates, Cooley thought of torts as *wrongs*. The first chapter of the treatise – 'The General Nature of Legal Wrongs' – thus aims to identify what makes torts a distinctive species of the genus 'wrongs'. As we have noted,

[31] MM Bigelow, *Elements of the Law of Torts: For the Use of Students* (Boston, MA, Little, Brown and Co, 1878); F Hilliard, *The Law of Torts or Private Wrongs* (Boston, MA, Little, Brown and Co, 1859).

[32] W Blackstone, *Commentaries on the Law of England* (Oxford, Clarendon Press, 1765–69) (on private wrongs). Prior American legal commentators, including Nathan Dane and Zephaniah Swift, had likewise imported into American law Blackstone's notion of private wrongs. See further, JCP Goldberg, 'Two Conceptions of Tort Damages: Fair v Full Compensation' (2006) 55 *DePaul Law Review* 435.

[33] Like all well-educated nineteenth-century American lawyers, Cooley knew his Blackstone. But his familiarity went beyond mere consumption. As noted, he published and edited an annotated version of the *Commentaries*: T Cooley (ed), *Commentaries on the Laws of England* (Chicago, IL, Callaghan and Co, 1870).

Cooley deemed torts to differ categorically from the class of wrongs known as breaches of contract.[34] At the same time, torts also shared an important feature with that class. Both were on the civil side of the civil–criminal divide, and thus both were 'private' rather than 'public' wrongs.[35]

In contrast to public wrongs, private wrongs necessarily involve interferences with individual rights. In torts, as in contracts, right and wrong are two sides of the same coin. According to Cooley, every tort implicates a claim-right and hence a duty – the rights in question are entitlements that others refrain from acting in certain ways upon right holders. When others fail to so refrain, they necessarily breach their duties and violate a rightholder's right, which is to say that they commit wrongs. In Cooley's language:

> When, therefore, the law of the land undertakes to declare and protect rights, and establishes a standard of conduct for that purpose, the acts or omissions which disturb or impede the enjoyment of such rights may be treated as legal wrongs or torts, but none others can be.[36]

Unsurprisingly, given his analytic linkage of wrongs to rights, Cooley's second chapter is titled 'General Classification of Legal Rights'. Consistently with the integrated approach to rights and duties just described, his analysis of rights goes hand in hand with his recognition of different wrongs. He defines a person's legal right to reputation, for example, as a right that requires others not make false statements about him of a sort that tend to lower a person's standing.[37]

The chapter's list of rights is in some ways familiar, including as it does the rights to life and reputation, as well as a right 'to be let alone' – understood as a right to be free from physical molestations or attempted molestations[38] – and a right to 'acquire, own and enjoy property'.[39] Interestingly, the chapter is broader than it needs to be to ground a tort theory, for there is also a substantial discussion of rights that do not figure (or do not figure centrally) in tort actions, including rights to religious liberty and to 'select and follow any lawful employment', as well as rights to participate in government.[40] Cooley also includes a broad discussion of family rights, including a right to marry, and a quite starkly described asymmetrical set of rights between husband and wife – a husband's right to services and a wife's right to support.[41]

[34] Cooley, *A Treatise on the Law of Torts or the Wrongs Which Arise Independent of Contract* (n 3) 2.
[35] ibid 6.
[36] ibid 4.
[37] ibid 30.
[38] ibid 29.
[39] ibid 36. Cooley deems property ownership a 'civil' rather than a 'personal' right, perhaps in part to emphasise that the latter is legitimately subject to various forms of state regulation.
[40] ibid 33–44.
[41] ibid 38–44.

It is critical to appreciate that Cooley took himself to be describing rights actually recognised in American law (and the law of comparable jurisdictions). Although Cooley may not have been sceptical of the idea of pre-legal, natural rights, he made clear that any such rights were not the concern of a legal treatise. A minor child, he explained, might have a natural right that his father protect him from being beaten by a stranger. Yet, while a father who neglects this obligation 'may have demonstrated how lamentably he is wanting in natural feeling, … he has violated no positive command of the law', and hence cannot be deemed to have committed a tort.[42] The right–duty pairings of tort law, in Cooley's view, existed only by virtue of judicial or legislative adoption of legal rules specifying those rights and duties.

Having laid out the sense in which torts are wrongs, the treatise in its third chapter ('Civil Injuries; Their Elements, and the Remedies for their Commission') explains another fundamental feature of tort law, namely, that it provides persons who have been legally wronged with a right of redress. The first several pages of the chapter discuss a variety of self-help remedies for certain legal wrongs. These discussions, however, turn out to be a preliminary to the main theme of the chapter:

> The cases which are above mentioned are in the main to be regarded as cases in which the individual is permitted to act on his own behalf, in order that he may prevent a mischief already begun from becoming more serious. … But to obtain redress for any wrong done him he must invoke the assistance of the law.
>
> … [T]he principal remedy, and for the most part the only remedy which the law can give for a wrong, is an award of money estimated as an equivalent for the damage suffered.[43]

Cooley offers the same thought in asserting that where there is a legally recognised individual right, 'the remedy must follow, of course'.[44] For the law to recognise a private wrong (and hence a right against being acted upon in a certain way) yet at the same time to deny right holders the power to sue for the wrong, would be for it to deny them equal treatment to which they are entitled, putting them 'out of the protection of the law'.[45]

Chapter 3 – and the lead-in to the doctrinal chapters that form the body of the treatise – also provides a more precise account of tortious conduct that, again, places rights and wrongs front and centre. First, Cooley emphasises that

[42] ibid 40. See also ibid 6, fn 1 (observing that talk of a government's duty to 'recognize' natural rights is unhelpful because such rights cannot be described at the level of specificity required to resolve actual disputes).

[43] ibid 60.

[44] ibid 19. Although Cooley describes as a 'truism' the maxim holding that 'wherever there is a right there is a remedy', he does not mean what contemporary jurists mean when they say such things. His point is *not* that legal remedies determine legal rights. Rather, it is that when the law confers rights, it always contemplates their enforcement, and that, likewise, whenever the law does not confer rights, it means to deny redress, even to those who have been harmed by another.

[45] ibid 35.

torts are by definition *injurious* wrongs: 'It is said by the authorities that it is the conjunction of damage and wrong that creates a tort, and there is no tort if either damage or wrong is wanting.'[46] Crucially, the reference to 'damage' in this statement refers *not* to tangible harms or losses (what Holmes would later call 'temporal harm'), but instead to the violation of a legally recognised right. This much is made clear in Cooley's acknowledgement that, while there are many torts that involve tangible harms (such as a broken limb or damaged property), there are also torts for which damage may be 'implied or presumed'.[47]

Although today the phrase 'implied or presumed' might be understood in an epistemological or evidentiary sense, that is not how Cooley meant it. Discussing the tort of trespass to land, the treatise notes that courts will recognise a valid trespass action even if there was *not in fact* any actual harm to the land. While the reasons for presuming damage in such a case are pragmatic, it is important to see precisely the sense in which they are pragmatic: 'Subject every man to the necessity of pointing out in what manner a trespass had caused him a pecuniary injury, and for many of the most vexatious there might be no redress and for the rights invaded no protection.'[48] The need for 'implied' or 'presumed' damage is not to ensure nominal conformity to a rule stating that actual damage or loss is required to generate a tort cause of action. Cooley supposes no such rule. Rather, damage is presumed in order to vindicate and protect the legal right in question. On this account, the dog is the rights invasion and the tail is the concept of presumed damage.

Cooley also explores with some subtlety a related feature of tortious wrongdoing – one that has tripped up legions of subsequent commentators. In tort, the term 'wrong' has a double meaning. Consider negligence. Negligence always involves a wrong *at the level of conduct*; that is, a failure to act in a manner that meets the legal standard of ordinary care. But the wrong of negligence – the entire tort requires not only conduct lacking ordinary care but an injury proximately caused by such conduct. There is a wrong in the first sense even before there is any injury, but there is a wrong in the second sense only when there is an injury. Cooley's analysis on this point anticipates by over a century a line of thought we have developed in our own work: there are no *inchoate torts*.[49] The wrongfulness of a tort resides not just in the defendant's sub-standard conduct but also in the realisation of that conduct in the right sort of setback to the plaintiff. To be a tort, the wrong must involve an injuring of the plaintiff (although, again, the injury need not take the form of a breaking of bones or a destruction of property).

[46] ibid 62.
[47] ibid.
[48] ibid 64.
[49] JCP Goldberg and BC Zipursky, 'Tort Law and Moral Luck' (2007) 92 *Cornell Law Review* 1123; JCP Goldberg and BC Zipursky, 'Unrealized Torts' (2006) 88 *Virginia Law Review* 1625; A Ripstein and BC Zipursky, 'Corrective Justice in an Age of Mass Torts' in G Postema (ed), *Philosophy and the Law of Torts* (Cambridge, CUP, 2002).

Some additional features of Cooley's tort theory deserve mention in this initial summary, even though they take us beyond his substantive views to issues of jurisprudence and political theory. As we have already suggested, Cooley was at least in one important respect a legal positivist. In particular, he clearly and emphatically announced his acceptance of a version of what has come to be called 'the separation thesis':

> An act or omission may be wrong in morals, or it may be wrong in law. It is scarcely necessary to say that the two things are not interchangeable. No government has undertaken to give redress whenever an act was found to be wrong, judged by the standard of strict morality; nor is it likely that any government ever will.[50]

To this he added, 'But while it is true that many things wrong in morals may not be wrong in law, it is equally true that some things that constitute wrongs in law may not be wrongs in morals.'[51]

Cooley's 'positivism' is in turn connected to a political-theoretic vision that draws on the social contract tradition. (He even alludes briefly to a hypothetical state of nature to explain why there must be law.) Because his tort theory is so explicitly rights-based, and because he connects his jurisprudential starting point to his theory of legal rights, it is worth quoting at some length:

> A legal right is something which the law secures to its possessor by requiring others to observe it, and to abstain from its violation. … In the domain of speculation or morals a right may be whatever ought to be respected; but in law that only is a right which can be defended before legal tribunals. Protection in rights gives to a man his liberty, but the same protection sets bounds to and constitutes a limitation upon the liberty of every other person, and the maximum of benefit of which government is capable is attained when individual rights are clearly and accurately defined by impartial laws, which impose on no one any greater restraint than is found essential for securing equivalent rights to all others, and which furnish for the rights of all an adequate and an equal protection.[52]

For Cooley, the government's legitimacy depends on its protection of individual rights, and tort law is a critical means of providing such protection.

With these introductory remarks complete, the treatise digs into the details of tort law. In doing so, it acknowledges that the law's metes and bounds are unclear, especially given variations among the laws of the different American states. Yet obviously Cooley thought there was enough commonality to offer generally applicable descriptions of the various torts – assault, battery and false imprisonment; fraud, libel and slander; negligence, nuisance and trespass; etc – as well as the affirmative defences applicable to them. In the treatise, a lawyer or judge would thus find a good deal of guidance on what sort of injurious

[50] Cooley, *A Treatise on the Law of Torts or the Wrongs Which Arise Independent of Contract* (n 3) 3.

[51] ibid 4.

[52] ibid 5–6.

interactions amount to torts, though of course particular cases would raise questions for juries (on such issues as whether the defendant acted with the requisite intent or failed to exercise due care), and courts would still be left to fill gaps in the law to ensure that it operated fairly and in a manner responsive to new conditions.

Here, then, is a thumbnail sketch of Cooley on Torts. Because Holmes's tort theory has received substantially more attention, it can be presented with somewhat greater concision.

The Common Law hit bookstores within two years of Cooley's treatise.[53] Yet it seems to belong to a different era. Not satisfied with cataloguing the pattern of wrongs, rights, duties and remedies recognised in case law, Holmes offered sweeping historical claims about the development of common law from which he extracted a general theory of tort and indeed of common law as a whole. In his mind, lawyerly habits of mind had bred confusion in several ways – *by mistaking form for substance* (for example, falsely inferring from the sparseness of the old writ of trespass that liability under the writ was substantively strict); *by mistaking taxonomy for analysis* (for example, by vastly overstating the substantive differences among different torts); and *by mistaking law for morality* (for example, by falsely supposing that moral wrongdoing or blameworthiness is required for tort liability). The trick was to get outside of the lawyerly mindset by viewing judges for what they 'really' are – power-wielding government officials – and then by isolating the distinctive terms on which judges exercise their power when they impose tort liability.

From this vantage point, Holmes purported to find a deep unity in tort law. In modern times, judges hearing tort suits are overseeing a qualified or limited scheme of indemnification – one suited to the liberal, individualist ethos of their time. 'The business of the law of torts', Holmes explained, 'is to fix the dividing line between those cases in which a man is liable for harm which he has done, and those in which he is not.'[54] It would be illiberal for judges to force individuals to indemnify others' losses strictly, that is, merely on the basis of causation. On the other hand, it would be inappropriately moralistic, and insufficiently protective of individual's legitimate holdings, for judges to require proof of blameworthy conduct as a condition of indemnification. This is why modern courts had more or less self-consciously settled on a middle ground – the failure to take certain steps to avoid causing objectively foreseeable harm – as the basis for all, or almost all, tort liability.[55] In negligence cases, the trigger of

[53] OW Holmes, Jr, *The Common Law* (Boston, MA, Belknap Press, 1881). This is not to say that Holmes has been consistently well understood by those who claim to follow him.

[54] ibid 73.

[55] Courts sometimes purported to require proof of other kinds of misconduct – involving 'intent' or 'malice', for example. However, Holmes argued, their use of these words was misleading. In the course of deploying ordinary language to resolve particular cases, judges (perhaps only semi-consciously) had conferred new, technical meanings on these terms. See ibid 118–30.

liability was, of course, the failure to take precautions that a prudent person would take. For 'intentional' torts such as fraud, liability would attach when the circumstances were such that the defendant could and should have foreseen that his conduct would in fact cause a loss to the plaintiff, yet the defendant nonetheless proceeded to cause the loss. Strict liability – an outlier, according to Holmes – still required the defendant to have been a position to foresee harm to the plaintiff, but for policy reasons shifted the risk of accidental loss to the defendant.

It is unsurprising that, to many modern eyes, Holmes's emphasis on foreseeability and fault suggest a deterrence-oriented perspective on tort law: unsurprising but still mistaken. To Holmes, tort was a law of indemnification or compensation, not deterrence. Indeed, its focus on indemnification – rather than Blackstone's and Cooley's distinction between 'public' and 'private' wrongs – is what, in Holmes's mind, fundamentally distinguished tort from crime.

Holmes thought criminal and tort law both incorporated objective, fault-based standards of liability and did so for the same basic reason. The function of these standards, on his view, was to provide citizens with a safe harbour to which, as members of a liberal society, they were entitled – that is, a fair chance to avoid being subjected to state power.[56] Subject to this fundamental constraint, crime and tort pursued different objectives. Court-ordered criminal punishments for faulty conduct promised deterrence; court-ordered damages payments for losses resulting from faulty conduct allowed for indemnification.[57] As noted, Holmes did not think that tort law was an insurance scheme, much less a system for redistributing wealth (the classical liberal's bogey of 'taking from *A* and giving to *B*'). Rather, tort law's fault constraint tied indemnification to a notion of personal responsibility suitable to a modern polity. *A* would be required by a court to pay for *B*'s losses only if *A* caused those losses after failing (for whatever reason) to avail himself of the fair opportunity given him by the state to avoid causing them.

The contrast between Cooley's and Holmes's understandings of tort law is in some respects subtle. Both aimed to account for roughly the same body of rules and doctrines: neither regarded his approach as laying the groundwork for radical rethinking of the contours of tort liability. Yet their accounts also differ dramatically: Holmes obviously aimed for a hyper-parsimonious or reductive account; Cooley's was anti-reductionist. Again, this is not to say that Cooley lacked a general view of the subject. To assert that negligence, battery and libel are all private wrongs is to say something significant about them, even though it rejects the notion that they all amount to pretty much the same thing.

In addition to differing over their ambitions for tort theory, the two men held different views on the question of whether tort law involves wrongfulness. One of Holmes's central aspirations for *The Common Law* was the articulation of

[56] ibid 130.
[57] ibid 44, 130.

what he took to be a business-like, pragmatic and 'demoralised' understanding of law. He thought that modern law, befitting the rationalism of its time, had evolved to the point that its rules no longer embodied ancient or Christian notions of wrongdoing as sinful or blameworthy conduct. His point was not that morality had 'died', or that modern law operated on terms that flouted or undermined morality. Rather, it was that determinations of criminal and civil liability in particular cases were no longer rooted in moral judgements but were instead made by reference to legal standards that routinely departed from the requirements of morality. In particular, the standard set by the prudent person was 'objective' in ways that allowed liability to be imposed even in the absence of anything that could count as morally wrongful conduct by the defendant. This was by design. In a modern legal system, Holmes argued, tort liability is neither understood nor justified as accountability for wicked or blameworthy conduct (though such conduct often would give rise to liability). Its point, again, is to enable certain persons who have suffered losses at the hands of others to transfer those losses.

For Cooley, tort law was not fundamentally about loss-shifting but about redress for wrongs; it is therefore unsurprising that he posited a closer connection between tort law and ordinary morality. Cooley agreed with Holmes that legal standards did not merely mimic or track moral standards. Indeed, he was perhaps among the first modern scholars to place great emphasis on the gaps between moral wrongs and legal wrongs. Yet, for Cooley, part of what it meant to call judge-made law 'common law' was to accept that its standards draw from, and should draw from, common or ordinary standards of conduct. Otherwise, law would take on the cast of an alien, imposed order, and would lose much of its efficacy and legitimacy.[58]

The difference between Holmes's loss-based and Cooley's wrongs-based approach can also be seen in their respective treatment of those torts for which proof of tangible harm or loss is not required. We noted above the traditional rule (still observed), according to which a plaintiff can recover on a claim for trespass to land without proving any tangible damage. While Cooley deemed mere entry or seizure – the rights-invasion itself – to be the injury that completes the tort, this was not an option for Holmes, precisely because *loss-shifting*, not redress for wrongs or rights invasions, is what he took tort law to be about. (If there has been no loss, there is nothing to indemnify.) To his mind, it thus made no sense that that there would be tort liability absent a loss:

> Consider, too, what the defendant's liability amounts to, if the act, whether an entry upon land or a conversion of chattels, has been unattended by damage to the property, and the thing has come back to the hands of the true owner. The sum recovered is merely nominal, and the payment is nothing more than the formal acknowledgment of the owner's title; which, considering the effect of prescription and statutes of

[58] Cooley, *A Treatise on the Law of Torts or the Wrongs Which Arise Independent of Contract* (n 3) 3.

> limitation upon repeated acts of dominion, is no more than right. All semblance of injustice disappears when the defendant is allowed to avoid the costs of an action by tender or otherwise.[59]

Aside from the question of whether Holmes is here being true to doctrine, it is plain that he thinks that there is no genuine tort liability in the case of a harmless trespass, because there is no loss that can be shifted from the plaintiff to the defendant. Yet Holmes (like Cooley) was not a formalist; indeed, he characteristically offered narrower, functionalistic explanations of parts of tort doctrine that did not quite fit his broader, also functionally explained, framework. Our point here is that Holmes's treatment of trespass to land displays that actual harm and actual loss really were central to his idea of what constitutes a tort, a view that contrasts sharply with Cooley's notion that rights invasions, not losses, are at the heart of tort law.

IV. TWO LEGACIES

Versions of Cooley's and Holmes's respective understandings of tort law are still with us today. In the twentieth century, Cooley's wrongs-and-redress approach was developed and espoused most forcefully by Benjamin Cardozo. This was no coincidence. We know from Andrew Kaufman's comprehensive biography that when Cardozo entered Columbia Law School in the Fall of 1889, he was met with lectures on Blackstone's *Commentaries*.[60] We also know that he took a separate short course near the end of his first year, entitled 'Redress of Private Wrongs by Courts'.[61] Then, in the Fall of his second year, he spent a month in Professor George Chase's torts class, the assigned text for which was the 1888 second edition of Cooley's treatise.[62]

Cardozo seems to have continued to rely on Cooley's work once on the bench. For example, at a key juncture in his opinion for the New York Court of Appeals in *Palsgraf v Long Island Railroad* – an opinion that, as we have explained elsewhere, is unusually explicit in its invocation of a wrongs-and-redress approach to tort law – Cardozo quotes a 1903 Maryland decision that he perhaps first found in Cooley's treatise: 'In every instance, before negligence can be predicated of a given act, back of the act must be sought and found a duty to the individual complaining, the observance of which would have averted or avoided the injury.'[63] A string citation containing an explicit reference to Cooley and his treatise follows this quotation.

[59] Holmes, *The Common Law* (n 53) 90 (footnote omitted).

[60] A Kaufman, *Cardozo* (Cambridge, MA, Harvard University Press, 1998) 44. At this time, courses were taught sequentially rather than simultaneously.

[61] ibid 45.

[62] ibid 47.

[63] *Palsgraf v Long Island Railroad Co* 162 NE 99, 100 (NY 1928) (quoting *West Virginia Central & Pittsburg Railway Co v State* 54 A 669, 671–72 (Md Ct App 1903)). In support of our speculation

Our civil recourse theory of tort is a direct descendant of the work of Blackstone, Cooley and Cardozo.[64] As did they, we maintain that torts are injurious wrongs – not just in name, but in substance. Tort law sets rules as to how each of us is required to interact (or avoid interacting) with others; of what counts, in the eyes of the law, as one person wrongfully injuring another. While torts are legally recognised injurious wrongs, they are also, in our view as in Cooley's, tethered to positive morality. This is why novice law students tend not to experience tort law as a Bizarro World of unrecognisable rules, principles and norms. Beneath the colourful facts that make for compelling teaching cases, and beneath the courts' use of technical legal language, are (mostly) conventional judgments about when one person can be deemed to have wrongfully injured another. This is so even when tort law arguably goes further than ordinary morality by defining wrongful conduct on 'strict' or unforgiving terms.[65]

Likewise, we have taken inspiration from the notion that torts, by virtue of being wrongs that are always rights violations, go hand in glove with private rights of action. To be the victim of a tort is to be entitled to respond, civilly, to the wrongdoer – for every wrong a remedy. While Holmes and Holmesians (among others) dismiss this way of thinking as valorising primitive notions of vengeance, their criticism misses the mark. There is a spectrum of responses to wrongdoing that ranges from a polite request for an apology to enraged axe-wielding. Consistent with the notion of *civil* recourse, tort law requires victims to present their demands to courts, which must validate them in accordance with

that Cardozo found *West Virginia Central* through Cooley's treatise, we note that the precise passage from the Maryland court's opinion that Cardozo's opinion quotes is found on the second page of the Treatise's exposition of the tort of negligence, which page, as indicated in the text above, is also cited in *Palsgraf* after the citation of *West Virginia Central* itself. (As Cooley died in 1898, the treatise's quotation of *West Virginia Central* was added by John Lewis, the editor of the third edition.) TM Cooley, *A Treatise on the Law of Torts or the Wrongs Which Arise Independent of Contract*, 3rd edn (Chicago, IL, Callaghan and Company, 1906).

Another passage from Cooley's treatment of negligence suggests that Cardozo's approach to *Palsgraf* owed something to the sources from which Cardozo learned torts: 'a duty owing to everybody can never become the foundation of an action until some individual is placed in position which gives him particular occasion to insist on its performance: it then becomes a duty to him personally'. TM Cooley, *A Treatise on the Law of Torts or the Wrongs Which Arise Independent of Contract*, 2nd edn (Chicago, IL, Callaghan and Co, 1888) 792. This passage was retained in the third edition of the treatise, and appears on the page immediately following the page that cites *West Virginia Central*. TM Cooley, *A Treatise on the Law of Torts or the Wrongs Which Arise Independent of Contract*, 3rd edn (Chicago, IL, Callaghan & Co, 1906) 1412.

Shortly after Cardozo's graduation, his torts professor, George Chase, who by then had left Columbia to help found New York Law School, published a torts casebook: G Chase, *Leading Cases Upon the Law of Torts* (St Paul, MN, West, 1892). The initial section of the book reproduces opinions said to be illustrative of tort law's 'general principles'. Chase formulated the first of those principles as follows: 'No tort committed, unless a legal right or legal duty is violated' (ibid 1).

[64] Ronald Dworkin's early writings, though focused on jurisprudence, constitutional law and political theory rather than tort per se, were in the same tradition. See JCP Goldberg, 'In Memoriam: Ronald Dworkin' (2013) 127 *Harvard Law Review* 494, 495–97. In later work, his writings on tort law took on a somewhat Holmesian cast.

[65] JCP Goldberg and BC Zipursky, 'The Strict Liability in Fault and the Fault in Strict Liability' (2016) 85 *Fordham Law Review* 743.

an elaborate scheme of procedural, evidentiary and substantive rules. Moreover, as Cooley noted long ago, remedial rules for the most part limit the sort of response a victim can obtain to money damages. For these and other reasons, tort occupies a point on the spectrum that is so distant from the axe-wielding end as not to count as vengeance in a meaningful sense.[66]

While traces of Cooley's ideas are still to be found, his footprints in the legal academy are faint as compared with Holmes's. William Prosser, a policy-oriented doctrinalist, and Richard Posner, a pioneer of the economic approach to tort law, were equally inspired by Holmes's brass-tacks sensibilities, although each took them in a Utilitarian-inspired direction that Holmes himself did not.[67] For both, Holmesian 'pragmatism' meant leaving behind the notion that tort law calls on judges to make nuanced judgments about when individuals can fairly be held responsible for another's losses. As state actors, judges bear a power and responsibility to legislate or regulate in the name of the public good. Accordingly, the judicial focus should be less on questions of individual responsibility and more on whether the imposition of liability in the case before them stands to make a net contribution to social welfare, either by delivering compensation to the injured (Prosser) or by deterring conduct that society should want deterred (Posner). Other leading modern theorists, including Fleming James, Jr and Guido Calabresi, were or are of a similarly Holmesian mindset, even though they too adopted Holmesian methods to support conclusions that Holmes himself did not (in particular, a broad embrace of strict liability).

We do not mean to suggest that the Cooley–Holmes divide is unique to tort theory in the US. Along with Robert Stevens, we have wondered whether the non-contractual aspect of the law of obligations in civil law systems, like that in France, is best characterised as a Holmesian loss-based scheme even though, just across the Channel, tort law is a Cooleyite, rights-based system.[68] Moreover, in a variety of common law jurisdictions, including the UK, Canada and Australia, torts scholarship comes in many flavours, and includes the work of important and influential scholars who take a loss-based approach. Some, like Tony Honoré, are non-instrumentalist loss-based theorists.[69] Others, including Patrick Atiyah, argue that tort liability has little or nothing to do with notions of individual responsibility, and is instead a (poorly designed) insurance scheme.[70] Others still, such as Peter Cane, offer a capacious, pluralistic understanding of the notion(s) of 'responsibility' at work in tort law that includes, but is not

[66] Tort law comes closest to vengeance in authorising punitive damages awards. Even here it is not really close. In the rare cases where the relevant legal standard is met, jurors retain complete discretion to decline to award punitive damages. Moreover, such awards are now in the US subject to significant substantive constitutional limits.

[67] JCP Goldberg and BC Zipursky, 'The Moral of *MacPherson*' (1998) 147 *University of Pennsylvania Law Review* 1733, 1756–57.

[68] R Stevens, *Torts and Rights* (Oxford, OUP, 2007) 342–45.

[69] T Honoré, *Responsibility and Fault* (Oxford, Hart Publishing, 1999) 14–40.

[70] PS Atiyah, 'Personal Injuries in the Twenty-First Century: Thinking the Unthinkable' in P Birks (ed), *Wrongs and Remedies in the Twenty-First Century* (Oxford, Clarendon Press, 1996).

limited to, loss-shifting principles.[71] Our hope, therefore, is that by focusing on two figures who set the stage for modern American theory, we shall shed light on tort theorising more generally.

V. POLITICS AND POSITIVISM

Holmes is winning, and by a lot. Yet the Holmesian ascendancy is not in all respects easy to explain. While Holmes perhaps never quite matched Posner's audacious willingness to sheer off a moose's antlers and call it a horse, his academic writings in no way offered a faithful depiction of the law he purported to interpret. His core claim – that tort law had largely coalesced around a single notion of wrongfulness (the failure to take steps to prevent foreseeable losses) – was untenable when he made it and has remained untenable since. In terms of fealty to law, the general picture offered in Cooley's treatise is vastly superior. This pattern still holds. As we have demonstrated in our work, wrongs-and-redress theories offer more compelling interpretive accounts not only of the doctrines on which moderns love to focus – such as the rules of negligence law or punitive damages – but also of the many torts they tend to ignore or downplay, including, for example, libel and fraud.

In sum, American tort scholars, including Holmes and his many eminent successors, have gone badly astray in their efforts to understand tort law, and have done so even though there is a perfectly respectable line of 'indigenous' scholarship that would have pointed them in the right direction. Why? There is no shortage of explanations – or putative explanations – to which Holmesians have explicitly or implicitly appealed. We here review two familiar explanation clusters. In the next section we argue that, while each identifies a plausible set of concerns about Cooleyite, wrongs-and-redress approaches to torts, each is best understood as requiring the clarification and refinement of wrongs-and-redress theory, rather than the abandonment of it. In flooding the American legal academy with cynical acid, Holmes-inspired tort theory is threatening to burn through the very idea of a common law of torts.

A. Politics: Courts and Rights

In his lifetime, Cooley was more famous for his writings on constitutional law than tort law. As political winds changed, Cooley's emphasis on the wisdom of constitutional limits on legislative power would be held against him.

The Progressive and New Deal eras saw the rise of salutary legislative efforts to protect some of society's vulnerable members. At the state and federal level, statutes aimed to provide safer working conditions, to guarantee a living wage

[71] P Cane, *Responsibility in Law and Morality* (Oxford, Hart Publishing, 2002).

to labourers, to kick-start a depressed economy and to provide something of a social safety net. Some courts, particularly federal courts, were prone to deem these laws ultra vires or to violate rights supposedly guaranteed by the Due Process Clause of the federal Constitution's Fourteenth Amendment (especially the right to freedom of contract). The Supreme Court's 1905 *Lochner* decision,[72] striking down a maximum-hour law for bakers, famously emerged as the emblem of the regressive doctrine of economic substantive due process. In this environment, a scholar like Cooley – who had made a point of claiming that limitations on legislative power are what made American constitutionalism superior to its British parent, and who had insisted that there were indeed substantive guarantees in the Due Process clause – was almost destined to be dismissed as a defender of the callous philosophy of laissez faire.[73]

Holmes, of course, was a member of the Supreme Court at the time of *Lochner* and famously dissented, thereby all but guaranteeing that he would end up on the right side of twentieth-century history. That he himself had little sympathy for progressive causes in some ways helped his legacy. Young progressives delighted in being able to trot out as an apostle of 'judicial restraint' a grizzled Civil War veteran who, given his age and life circumstances, should have been (and was) a fan of the rugged individualist philosophy that seemed to undergird decisions such as *Lochner*. For his part, Holmes was equally delighted to gain the national stature for which he had long strived.

Related to this cleavage over *constitutional* rights was a deeper conflict over how to think about the place of rights – and hence of duties and wrongs – in adjudication more generally. Cooley, again following the common law tradition, posited that 'the definition of rights and the providing of adequate security for their enjoyment' is the 'chief business' of government. To repeat a quotation offered earlier, Cooley deemed a government good if it is one in which 'individual rights are clearly and accurately defined by impartial laws, which impose on no one any greater restraint than is found essential for securing equivalent rights to all others, and which furnish for the rights of all an adequate and equal protection.'[74] As noted in section III, the rights he had in mind were, for the most part, the familiar list of 'liberal' rights – rights to life, liberty, property, reputation and family, as well as religious liberty and political participation.

A particular conception of the judicial role followed from this larger perspective. The point of having courts that hear and resolve criminal and civil

[72] 198 US 45 (1905).

[73] A Jones, 'Thomas M Cooley and "Laissez-Faire Constitutionalism": A Reconsideration' (1967) 53 *Journal of American History* 751 (citing criticisms of Cooley to this effect).

[74] Cooley, *A Treatise on the Law of Torts or the Wrongs Which Arise Independent of Contract* (n 3) 5–6. This is not to say that Cooley was committed to a narrow 'night-watchman' version of liberalism. To identify the ultimate aim of government as the achievement and maintenance of a scheme of equal rights is hardly to deny that various forms of affirmative government intervention and support might be necessary to achieve that scheme. This is why, for example, Cooley thought government was obligated to provide free public education.

complaints 'is to prevent the commission of wrongs; to compel redress to those who have suffered them, and to inflict punishment in proper cases on those guilty of their commission.'[75] To say this is just to say that courts are in the business of identifying, protecting and vindicating individual rights. The identification of legal wrongs, and the provision of redress to victims of wrongs, was essential to this enterprise, because '[a] legal right is something which the law secures to its possessor by requiring others to observe it, and to abstain from its violation.'[76]

So tort law, on Cooley's view, was judge-made law concerned to establish, protect and vindicate individual rights within an overall scheme of law that aspired to ensure the equal rights of each. A crucial feature of this enterprise is the articulation by courts of (what today are commonly called) 'primary rules' – rules of conduct. In tort law, each such rule directs an actor to refrain from interfering with another in a certain manner, or to assist another in avoiding such interference. As Cooley explained, no tort occurs absent the proper combination of 'something which for any reason the party ought not to do or to permit' and a 'distinct invasion of right' that gives rise to actual losses or to 'implied or presumed' losses.[77] Because tort law's rules of conduct have this form, they always generate duty–right pairings. For example, the rule that long ago emerged out of decisions resolving disputes concerning the seizure by one person of another's personal property is the rule that one must not intentionally take control over a thing possessed by another. This rule of conduct, built into the tort of conversion, in turn generates correlative duties and rights: non-possessors have a duty to refrain from intentionally destroying or taking control of a thing possessed by another, and possessors have a right that others not intentionally destroy or seize their things.[78]

The primary concern of Cooley's Torts treatise was to present these myriad rules in a systematic manner, while also acknowledging when they were ambiguous, apparently in conflict with one another, or seemingly unable to operate in a manner consistent with the overall enterprise of providing a law of wrongs and redress. As the length of his treatise attests, it is no simple matter to come to terms with this body of law: there is a lot of material to master. And some of it might seem puzzling or counter-intuitive. Consider, for example, the aspect of the no-conversion rule that deems an *innocent* seizure of another's property to count as a wrong and a rights violation. To commit conversion, one needs

[75] ibid 1. There is a reference to 'punishment' in this sentence because Cooley is here discussing wrongs generally, including crimes, not just torts and breaches of contract. He later makes clear that punishment is the state's response to public wrongs: ibid 7.

[76] ibid 5.

[77] ibid 62–63.

[78] Courts on this view are also required to fashion rules pertaining to procedure, evidence and remedy. These rules determine the terms on which a person is allowed to proceed in her effort to prove that a right against being injured conferred on her by tort law has been violated (and its corresponding duty breached), such that she is entitled to the court's assistance in demanding and obtaining redress for the rights violation from the rights violator.

only intentionally to seize something that is the personal property of another. One does not need to intend, know or *even have reason to know* that one is dispossessing another.[79] While this aspect of tort law is perfectly defensible, it is striking, and a certain mental agility is required to be able to grasp why or on what grounds it is defensible.

So, even on a traditional Cooleyite view – or perhaps it is better to say *especially* on such a view – tort law is complex. It covers a lot of ground substantively (encompassing all the different right–duty pairings one finds in all the different torts) and doctrinally, in its meshing of substantive law with procedural, evidentiary and remedial law. And yet Holmesians would argue that the elaborateness of tort law, on this understanding, masks a problematically *narrow* account of the place of courts in the US legal system. On a Cooleyite approach, they would say, there is a lot of tort law, but the law – and the judicial role – is characterised in ways that actually disable courts from addressing issues they ought to address in ways in which they ought to address them.

To fast-forward from Cooley's time to ours, consider a problem faced by modern societies: drunk driving. Tort law, on a traditional understanding, has something to say about this phenomenon. One who injures another while driving drunk might find himself paying both compensatory and punitive damages to his victim. However, if one shifts the focus from one-off instances to 'root causes', tort law, on a traditional understanding, may have less to say, and it may have less to say precisely because of its focus on duties and rights, and wrongs and redress. Behind many drunk-driving accidents lurks an alcohol provider, whether in the form of a commercial establishment such as a bar or restaurant, or in the form of a person who hosts a party. If we really want to make a dent in drunk driving, some say, courts should be able to render decisions that will induce these background actors to take steps to solve the problem at the wholesale level.

An effort to justify the imposition of tort liability on these sorts of actors is challenging from within a Cooleyite framework. While it is not impossible to imagine courts imposing liability on social hosts for injuries caused by drunk driving, courts in the US and elsewhere have been reluctant to do so in the absence of applicable legislation.[80] In part they have worried that the recognition of liability would involve a misattribution of responsibility within a body of law whose point is to articulate wrongs and provide victims with the ability to obtain redress. For example, the intervening and more immediately

[79] Cooley, *A Treatise on the Law of Torts or the Wrongs Which Arise Independent of Contract* (n 3) 438–39 ('if one goes upon the land of another to take away his own sheep, and by mistake takes some which do not belong to him, his mistake cannot excuse the trespass. So, if one is sent to take property, and does so in good faith, believing it to belong to his employer, this is trespass in him if the belief proves unfounded') (footnotes omitted).

[80] JCP Goldberg and BC Zipursky, 'Intervening Wrongdoing in Tort: The *Restatement (Third)*'s Unfortunate Embrace of Negligent Enabling' (2009) 44 *Wake Forest Law Review* 1211, 1225–29 (discussing US and Canadian case law).

harm-inflicting conduct of the drunk driver seems to render inapt a description of the social host as having injured, in a 'doing-unto' manner, the driver's victim. And, while one might more cogently assert that the host *failed adequately to protect the victim* from being injured by the drunk driver, this description, to be a basis for liability, would cast social hosts in the role of 'minders' of their adult social guests – hosts would now be legally required to take steps to block guests from leaving their residences whenever they suspect, or should suspect, their guests of being unfit to drive because of intoxication. Putting people in charge of others in this way sits badly with custom. It also sits badly with the idea of treating competent adults as responsible agents. And so it is that the effort, from within a Cooleyite framework, to make a case for social host liability is tenuous.

To the modern Holmesian, this discussion of the 'limitations' of a Cooleyite approach to the imposition of liability on background actors reveals a general problem in wrongs-and-redress approaches to tort law. A loss-based approach, by contrast, offers greater flexibility and hence greater regulatory potential. If judges (or at least high court judges) conclude that holding social hosts liable to drunk-driving victims is an effective strategy for reducing these unwelcome events, they have done all they need to do to justify the adoption of rules imposing liability on these actors for these losses. The same would be true if they concluded that liability would enable victims to gain access to needed compensation they could not otherwise obtain. Freed from having to justify liability as redress for something that can cogently be described as the defendant's having wronged the plaintiff, or having violated the plaintiff's legally recognised right that the defendant take care to prevent her from being injured by a third party, judges under a loss-based approach can wield tort law as a policy tool capable of addressing a wide array of social ills, including newly emerging problems.

In sum – on the line of argument under review in this subsection – Cooley's politics, and his relatedly 'limited' notion of judicial competence, have counted against the adoption of his understanding of tort law. Just as a Cooleyite understanding of constitutional law had to be rejected on the ground that it would prevent the state from doing things it ought to do for the public good, so must a Cooleyite understanding of tort law be rejected on the ground that it precludes tort law from fulfilling its progressive potential. Conversely, just as Holmesian constitutional jurisprudence allowed for the modern regulatory and welfare state, so a loss-based model of torts allows for new, welfare-enhancing forms of liability. Twentieth-century tort scholars saw this difference, the story goes, and adopted loss-based models for political reasons that remain sound today.

B. Jurisprudence and Legal Reasoning

Another familiar cluster of justifications that are thought to favour Holmesian, loss-shifting conceptions of tort law focuses on the jurisprudence that undergirds them. Simply put, Cooleyite approaches are said to carry with them philosophical baggage that Holmesian approaches do not, and for that reason the latter are to be preferred despite their interpretive deficiencies.

It was very much part of the common law tradition to emphasise the complementarity of natural and positive law, of moral and legal right, and of law and customary practices.[81] In this tradition, the key figure is the lawyer in the role of legal counsellor and as judge. Employing the distinctive mode of practical reason known as legal reasoning, lawyers could be counted on deftly to navigate back and forth across these divides, stitching and re-stitching the law so as to maintain a complex, evolving yet harmonious system of rules that, while not entailed by the abstract principles of natural law, nonetheless is consistent with them. Judges, on this view, bear a special responsibility and ability to shape the law in a manner that would protect traditionally recognised rights. In thus securing their freedom, the law also earns the people's allegiance. Common lawyers did not deny the existence of erroneous judicial decisions, nor the need for legislation to reform or fill gaps in the common law. Nonetheless they embraced a generally optimistic picture of the common law's contribution to a just polity.

Of course it was just these features of the common law mind that drove rationalist critics such as Bentham to distraction. By treating positive law as grounded in, and consonant with, natural law, Blackstone and his ilk had deliberately blurred the line between is and ought. To think clearly about law (according to Bentham) required an appreciation that, strictly speaking, the only real rights are rights granted by positive law. Relatedly, Bentham rejected the idea that legal reasoning – the teasing out, application and revision of quasi-moral 'principles' embedded in case law – is a distinctive (and distinctively valuable) form of reasoning. The idea of the 'artificial reason' of the law was a fantasy invented by lawyers and judges to bolster their power and status. Law requires the same reasoning as any other practical discipline, and there is no basis for supposing that lawyers and judges were especially to be trusted to engage in it.

A quick look at Cooley's treatise reveals clear evidence of a common law mindset.[82] As we noted in section III, he thought of tort law as a fulfilment, in part, of government's obligation to establish courts charged with preventing wrongs (ie, protecting rights) and providing redress for wrongs that are committed. In applying and developing this body of law, judges contributed to the equal protection of basic rights. Because these rights had been customarily embraced by Americans, courts were to go about their rights-protective and rights-vindication functions through constructive interpretation – that is, by identifying and harmonising the 'principles' already embedded in case law and

[81] JCP Goldberg, 'The Constitutional Status of Tort Law: Due Process and the Right to a Law for the Redress of Wrongs' (2005) 115 *Yale Law Journal* 524, 532–37.

[82] Jones, 'Thomas M Cooley and "Laissez-Faire Constitutionalism": A Reconsideration' (n 73) 757–58 (discussing Cooley's embrace of common law constitutionalism).

common usage.[83] To be sure, in the course of refining and applying the common law, courts would have occasion to revise it, but they would do so in an incremental manner, thus maintaining its general coherence, as well as its connection to custom and habit. This connection was crucial. Legal rules that are recognisable to the populace, Cooley emphasised, are rules that can be administered without excessive reliance on force to ensure compliance, and tend not to be experienced as onerous by those who live under them.[84]

Holmes did not display Bentham's deep antipathy for 'Judge & Co', and he had little patience for the Benthamite notion that progressive law reform could be guided by the principle of utility. Nonetheless, Holmes agreed with Bentham that judges must not be mistaken for wise men or moral philosophers. Judges are government officials who wield power through the application and the making of legal rules. In doing so, they bring to bear their legal training, along with a set of broad policy orientations reflective of prevailing sentiments among those of their caste. Deciding cases, on this view, involves grasping and applying legal concepts and, on some occasions, making judgments about which case outcomes or rules mesh well with the prevailing ethos.

Holmes's 'jobbist' view of adjudication informed not only his scholarship, but also his judicial decisions. As Tom Grey famously noted, Holmes's opinions for the Massachusetts Supreme Judicial Court tended overwhelmingly to be short and spare statements and applications of legal rules, indicating that, for the most part, he was something of a 'formalist' about adjudication.[85] Even his more dramatic opinions, including his famous *Lochner* dissent, can be said to display the same jurisprudential commitments. After all, his dissent argued that the majority had gone astray because it had read a controversial, 'thick' political morality into the Due Process clause of the Fourteenth Amendment. Had it instead just stuck to the law – to the actual Constitution – it would have found much less substantive content in it, thus giving legislatures greater leeway to legislate, wisely or unwisely.

The same commitments arguably were on display in Holmes's famous rejection of the notion of a general, national common law, understood as a 'brooding omnipresence' awaiting discovery by state and federal judges.[86] Here Holmes quite clearly disparaged the Blackstonian inclination to commingle morality, law and custom. In deciding common law cases whose outcomes are not clearly dictated by precedent, courts might claim to 'discover' rules in tradition,

[83] Cooley, *A Treatise on the Law of Torts or the Wrongs Which Arise Independent of Contract* (n 3) 14–15.

[84] ibid 15. In confirmation of his generally Blackstonian outlook on law, Cooley concludes the opening chapter of his treatise by quoting from Bentham's critique of the common law, then dismissing it on the ground that Bentham's preferred alternative – a code system – would end up reproducing the common law system in the form of judicial glosses on the code: ibid 17–19.

[85] TC Grey, 'Molecular Motions: The Holmesian Judge in Theory and Practice' (1995) 37 *William and Mary Law Review* 19.

[86] *Southern Pac Co v Jensen* 244 US 205, 222 (1917) ('[t]he common law is not a brooding omnipresence in the sky, but the articulate voice of some sovereign or quasi sovereign that can be identified').

custom, ordinary morality or the like. But, whether they knew or admitted it or not, they were legislating. Indeed, Holmes hoped that by debunking common law mythology, he would encourage judges to legislate (when legislation was called for) with increasing self-consciousness, such that they would forthrightly reason instrumentally from desired policy goals to legal rules.[87]

On questions about the nature of law and legal reasoning, Holmes is generally thought to have been pointing in the right direction and Cooley the wrong one. An approach that cleanly separates positive law from natural law or custom, and that treats legal reasoning as distinct from moral reasoning, is one that takes the law and judges for what they really are – appliers and makers of legal rules. Loss-based views of tort were, in Holmes's case, closely connected to his demoralised jurisprudence. That they are so connected counts in their favour. By contrast, it is thought to be a mark against wrongs-and-redress views that they partake of a Cooleyite common law mindset.

VI. COOLEY REVISITED

There is something to the foregoing efforts to justify the Holmesian ascendancy. This is why Holmes-inspired views have gripped so many thoughtful American torts scholars. Under closer scrutiny, however, both the 'political' and the 'jurisprudential' grounds for rejecting Cooleyite tort theory collapse.

A. Politics Revisited

As other scholars have demonstrated, it is probably erroneous to suppose that Cooley himself subscribed to the particular version of substantive due process on display in *Lochner*. In fact, he worried throughout his career about the need to prevent law from becoming the handmaiden of powerful business interests. This was very much the central point of his treatise and its emphasis on the unconstitutionality of 'partial' or 'class' legislation that doled out benefits to railroads and other special interests. Moreover, he seems to have thought that courts should be cautious in how they go about enforcing these limitations on legislative action.[88]

Still, Cooley did embrace some version of substantive due process. More broadly, he had at least some of the individualistic instincts that formed part

[87] Holmes, *The Common Law* (n 53).

[88] Jones, 'Thomas M Cooley and "Laissez-Faire Constitutionalism": A Reconsideration' (n 73) 762. At the end of his professional life, Cooley sat as a commissioner on the first federal regulatory body – the ICC – and from that perch acted in a manner that demonstrated an appreciation of the need and the potential for administrative regulation of the powerful railroad industry: see A Jones, 'Thomas M Cooley and the Interstate Commerce Commission: Continuity and Change in the Doctrine of Equal Rights' (1966) 81 *Political Science Quarterly* 602.

of the *Lochnerian* philosophy. Most notoriously, in his capacity as judge and commentator, he embraced and applied rules that imposed on employers only modest obligations to ensure their workers' safety. Employees, he reasoned, assume the risks of injury 'incident to' particular jobs – that is, well-known or obvious dangers attending certain employments or tasks. Moreover, employees injured as the result of a fellow employee's negligence could not take advantage of the doctrine of *respondeat superior*. Different courts offered broader and narrower renditions of this 'fellow servant rule', and Cooley defended a broad version.[89] Near the time of Cooley's death, his court was identified by one author as being particularly worker-unfriendly in its application of negligence law.[90]

By modern lights, and perhaps even the lights of his day, Cooley was thus conservative in the sense of being individualistic. Still, this hardly provides a reason to favour Holmesian theory. Indeed, there is something deeply odd about celebrating Holmes as the font of progressivism, not only in constitutional law, but also in tort law. After all, Holmes's insistence on fault as the basis for tort liability was part of an effort to ward off forms of liability through which 'the state would make itself a mutual insurance company against accidents, and distribute the burden of its citizens' mishaps among all its members.'[91] More to the point, it seems likely that Holmes's views of individual responsibility were not much different from Cooley's, including with respect to doctrines such as the fellow servant rule.[92] Neither Cooleyite nor Holmesian views can claim an original progressive pedigree.

More fundamentally, as we demonstrated 20 years ago in our first jointly-authored article, the tarring of 'rights-talk' and 'duty-talk' as inherently regressive modes of analysis is simply unwarranted.[93] Cardozo, after all, was among the liberal progressives who helped undo *Lochner*'s doctrine of economic due process. Yet he was also the author of *Palko v Connecticut*,[94] which offered an alternative, historically sensitive and progressive version of substantive due process. And it is barely an overstatement to assert that an insistence on the lack of an inherent association between rights and regressive politics has been the project of American constitutional theory since the early 1970s.

[89] TM Cooley, 'The Cases in which the Master is Liable for Injuries to Servants in His Employ' (1876) 2 *Southern Law Review* 108–12. In fairness to Cooley, the remainder of the article identifies various scenarios in which employees *could* recover from employers for injuries resulting from employer negligence.

[90] CB Labatt, 'The Right of Employers to Carry on Their Business with Extra-Hazardous Appliances' (1898) 32 *American Law Review* 515.

[91] Holmes, *The Common Law* (n 53) 88.

[92] White, *Justice Oliver Wendell Holmes: Law and the Inner Self* (n 16) 266–68 (discussing some of Holmes's opinions for the Massachusetts Supreme Judicial Court concerning employer liability for employee injuries).

[93] Goldberg and Zipursky, 'The Moral of *MacPherson*' (n 67).

[94] *Palko v Connecticut* 302 US 319 (1937) (holding that the Due Process clause identifies judicially enforceable rights that are 'of the very essence of a scheme of ordered liberty').

The analogous point holds true for tort theory. There is nothing about the treatment of torts as wrongs, or tort claims as rights of action enjoyed by victims of wrongs, that links tort law to any particular political position. This was, of course, the most profound message of *MacPherson v Buick*.[95] To say, with Cardozo (and Cooley), that negligence consists of a breach of a duty of care owed by the defendant to a person such as the plaintiff is miles from saying that a duty of care exists only if there is privity of contract between careless manufacturer and injured consumer. The latter is a substantive (and narrow) claim about the content of the duty of care. The former is a structural claim about the nature of the wrong of negligence. To say that it is structural is not to say that it is empty. (Indeed, it is this structure that Cardozo would – rightly, and in a manner perfectly consistently with *MacPherson* – invoke years later as the basis for denying Mrs Palsgraf's claim.) It is instead to say that it is capacious, and can thus readily permit, where standard modes of legal reasoning permit, a ruling that manufacturers owe anyone who might foreseeably be injured by their carelessly made products a duty to exercise due care in the manufacturing process.

As to social host liability and like-minded progressive agendas to cure social problems through tort liability, our response is mixed. First, there are many ways in which a rights-based framework is *more* powerful than a loss-based framework. Consider, for example, the role of tort law in bringing to light clergy sexual abuse. Plainly, it is judges' and jurors' understanding of the wrongs committed against child congregants and the violation of their rights that has driven this litigation. Moreover, tort liability up the hierarchical chain easily flowed from right-and-duty based understandings of certain church leaders' gross violations of their responsibilities. Rights-and-redress were core to this progressive development. As to other and in many ways broader landmark developments of tort law – for example products liability law – we have argued elsewhere that a wrongs-and-redress framework not only accommodates, but actually undergirds a progressive approach.

With respect to liability for those who supply alcohol to a person who later injures another as a result of drunk driving, the implications of a wrongs-and-redress view are more complicated. There is nothing in such a view that would deny the propriety of statutory liability for commercial entities that are in other ways highly regulated, and that is, of course, what Dram Shop Acts do. Similarly, to the extent that minors are legislatively prohibited from consuming alcohol and adults are legislatively prohibited from providing it to them, liability in the case of a host who makes alcohol available to a minor guest fits comfortably within a Cooleyite approach. Judicially imposed social host liability with respect to adult guests is, however, too great a stretch, at least in our current culture. It forces courts to undertake an aggressive reconstruction of social norms concerning attributions of responsibility. We do not doubt that liability of this sort is within the competence of a legislature (though we note

[95] *MacPherson v Buick* 111 NE 1050 (NY 1916).

that legislatures emphatically have not followed this route). Nor do we reject outright the possibility that there is sometimes virtue in a judge's pushing the boundaries of his or her judicial competence. It is far from clear, however, that these cases are the right ones for such boundary pushing.

Separate and apart from the 'benefits' of a wrongs-and-redress approach to tort are the 'costs' of adopting a Holmesian, loss-based approach. One such cost is that political winds are apt to change, sometimes quickly. To view judges as government officials or policymakers, and tort law as regulation, is thus to render tort more vulnerable to such changes. Indeed, the great success in the US of the liability-restrictive tort reform movement is largely an outgrowth of the success of the Holmesian model.

The largest cost, in our view, is more insidious still. It resides in the diminished capacity of tort law to provide meaningful guidance to legal actors. That capacity, as Cooley emphasised, depends on maintaining at most a modest gap between accepted norms of conduct and the body of rules contained in tort law. In explaining the value of a judiciary committed to incrementalism (with the awareness of a legislature ready to act abruptly), Cooley sounds a bit like Cass Sunstein:

> A large share of the value of any law consists in the habitual reception and the spontaneous obedience which the people are expected to give to it, and which they will give when they have become accustomed to and understand its obligations. The people then may be said to be their own policemen; they habitually restrain their actions within the limits of the law, instead of waiting the compulsion of legal process. A violent change must break up, for the time being, this spontaneous observance, and some degree of embarrassment is always to be anticipated before that which is new and strange becomes habitually accepted, and its advantages appreciated, and before that which remains of the old is adjusted to it.
>
> For this reason an imperfect law let alone may be much more conducive to the peace of society and the happiness of the people than a better law often tampered with. But there are always some particulars in which improvements by judicial decisions is impossible, and where legislation alone is adequate to the purpose.[96]

B. Jurisprudence Revisited

In order to respond to a critical argument, one must first adduce what the argument is. Yet it is hard to put one's finger on the 'jurisprudential' arguments favouring a Holmesian over a Cooleyite approach. The most obvious characterisations of these arguments lead to weak versions of the critique – so weak that, if we were to adopt them, we would be accused of having set up a strawperson.

For example, if we were to say it is the positivist critique of natural law that leads to the rejection of Cooley's approach, we would be attributing to

[96] Cooley, *A Treatise on the Law of Torts or the Wrongs Which Arise Independent of Contract* (n 3) 15.

Holmesians an obviously unsound argument. As mentioned in section III, Cooley *was* a legal positivist. Over and over again, he cites to the work of John Austin, and he plainly states that law is one thing and morality another. Presaging the likes of Joseph Raz, he repeatedly emphasises the importance of having in law something that is institutionally entrenched, clearly discernible and easily enforceable. And he plainly rejects the claim that putative law that fails to conform to morality is invalid.

We are similarly at risk if we label the jurisprudential critique 'realist' or 'anti-formalist', because Cooley was remarkably candid about the lawmaking role of judges in certain tort cases. After referring to the roots of the common law in the Magna Carta, Cooley states that its efficacy and legitimacy 'depend very largely on a species of judicial legislation which from time to time, as new conditions were found to exist, has endeavoured to fit and conform the old law to them'.[97] Noting candidly that the phrase 'judicial legislation' seems in itself a 'contradiction', and recognising (dialectically) the argument that judicial legislation might seem a 'usurpation' of the power of another department of government, he nonetheless explains why it is a 'necessary condition of any steady improvement in the law, and, therefore, deserving of no censure'.[98] Indeed, Cooley opens his treatise by stating that increasing modernisation in commerce and social relations creates a need for new tort law:

> In the more advanced society [the judge's] attention is invited to invasions of copyrights and patents, to frauds accomplished by new and peculiar methods, to questions in the law of common carriers, which are intimately connected with the new improvements in methods of transportation, and to a variety of wrongs that are new, because the conditions from which they spring, or which give occasion to them, are new.[99]

Any remaining attraction to the erroneous view that Cooley was a formalist should be removed by a glance at his critique of the common law rule against imposing liability on tortfeasors whose tortious conduct results in the death of the victim, and his approval of the wrongful death statutes that remedied this deficiency in the common law.[100]

We find a stopping place in our search for a cogent challenge only when we turn, as we have in the past, to Holmes's much-admired lecture, *The Path of the Law*.[101] Holmes's critics have made mincemeat of the affirmative semantic account of legal rights and duties offered there. It is simply not sustainable to argue, as he did, that statements about legal duties are nothing but predictions of what courts will do, and so forth. Holmes's great strength, however, was criticism, not construction. And he was plainly warranted in warning graduating law students that it is perilous to confuse the question of a legal duty with

[97] ibid 11.
[98] ibid 11–12.
[99] ibid 2.
[100] ibid 26–29.
[101] Holmes, *The Common Law* (n 30).

a moral duty, just as he was warranted in asserting that legal rights and duties, so called, are largely defined institutionally. Lawyers and judges must apprise themselves of what the law books say and what other courts will likely do. But the crucial premise in this part of *The Path of the Law* is largely suppressed. It is not that the institutional takes precedence over the pre-institutional (which, presumably, would not be doubted by students who have just spent years studying law). Rather, it is that duty-like and right-like concepts will not help in understanding the institutional. In other words, it is the Benthamite proposition that duty–right concepts, detached from their welfare-based implications and prior to their embodiment in a particular law or legal rule, are fundamentally incoherent and therefore incapable of sustaining legitimate and cogent normative reasoning. One might call this view 'conceptual moral scepticism'.

Conceptual moral scepticism lay at the core of Holmes's rejection of the sort of tort theory Cooley held, and it has played the key role pushing Holmesian tort theory over Cooleyite tort theory in modern times. (In our tort-theoretic work, we have taken Cardozo as the chief antagonist of this view, since Cardozo was anything but a conceptual moral sceptic.) As to conceptual moral scepticism – whether under this label or others we have used, such as 'duty-skepticism', 'brass-tacks pragmatism' and 'reductive instrumentalism' – we have argued that it is wholly indefensible in tort theory and more generally. First, it rests entirely on crude epistemological and semantic views that were discarded long ago. Second, it is internally unstable, indefensibly privileging and relying on the subset of moral concepts that invoke welfarist notions. Third, its tenability as a mode of legal reasoning is usually tied to its ability to capture and make sense of doctrine, yet it does no such thing.

In short, there is a philosophical naiveté about Holmesian conceptual moral scepticism that is little short of breathtaking. We have voiced and continue to voice dismay at such naiveté not because we think everyone needs to be a moral philosopher. On the contrary, our dismay stems from the fact that pretty much the only thing conceptual moral scepticism ever had going for it was its supposedly rigorous philosophical foundation. But there is no such foundation – it is a house of cards. Considerations of jurisprudence thus provide no basis for favouring Holmes over Cooley. Quite the opposite.

VII. CONCLUSION

With a zeal for Cooley that no doubt manifests some self-servingness, we have argued that bad reasons have led American scholars to favour Holmes's arresting but ultimately misguided loss-based conception of torts over Cooley's traditional wrongs-and-redress approach. To counter the perception of self-servingness, we think at least one anti-Cooleyite concession is in order. It connects and thereby strengthens the political and positivistic critiques – each quite weak on its own.

In law, right–duty concepts make sense in part because they draw some of their content and much of their structure from concepts with which one becomes familiar in less institutionalised settings, particularly from moral and political concepts that are already somewhat socially entrenched. This means that legal reasoning in torts that utilises such concepts will have a sort of drag on it. Customs and social norms and entrenched beliefs about moral and political principles carry weight, even if, as Cooley and Cardozo both emphasised, revision is possible and often appropriate. In an era where background notions of rights and duties are especially tilted in one political direction (and it could be any such direction), those pushing for changes that point tort law in a different political direction will indeed have reason to be somewhat wary of right–duty reasoning of the type characteristic of the common law, especially when it is applied by judges in a wooden manner.

The Holmesian turn in early twentieth-century American tort theory arguably stemmed from this particular conjunction of political and jurisprudential concerns. The worry was that right–duty reasoning, at least when deployed by an elite and complacent judiciary, was likely to push in a libertarian direction, because notions of individual rights to property and contract at the time were taken to be paradigmatic of the very idea of a right, and could easily be cast in terms that are overblown. This was a legitimate worry, and indeed Cooley's own proclivities (although typically exaggerated) provided some support for the idea that rights talk, at least in the US context, has a modest natural affinity with laissez faire. Holmes's charisma, and the lure of a kind of objectivist, empiricist pragmatism, mixed with these understandable anxieties about traditional modes of political and legal discourse to create a potent glow for a form of tort theory that simply abandoned concepts of rights, wrongs and duties. We have maintained all along that a Cardozoan pragmatism offers a more thoughtful take on rights and duties, and has always been a better direction to take. In the early twentieth century, however, the choice between these two paths was hardly obvious.

Today, we are in a very different place, as we have been for half a century. Those who think about wrongs in tort cases are often thinking about the wrongs committed by multinational companies seeking profits, sometimes at the expense of consumers or the public good. Those who think about rights are typically thinking about equality and the physical, mental and dignitary rights of the vulnerable. In short, the core notions of right and duty that suffuse moral and political thinking today are hardly those of the nineteenth-century libertarian. It is therefore no surprise that today in the US, conservative critics of tort law happily embrace Holmesian, loss-based tort theory. Wrongs-based and rights-based thinking – if it has a political tendency today – pulls 'left'. That is why modern tort reformers do not talk about rights and duties but about efficiency and public policy. Yet the American legal academy, or much of it, still has not caught on. They remain captive to the old trope – never fundamentally correct on its own, but perceptive at a particular point in history – that rights and duties are a trap for would-be progressives.

Neither Cooley nor Holmes generated a tort theory based on political aspirations. Both were actually interested in explaining how tort law worked and how it fit together, and both wanted judges to be able to grasp the law in order to move it forward in a pragmatic manner. Ironically, it was Holmes, not Cooley, who came to the task with a set of jurisprudential premises that skewed his account. The challenge of squeezing a law of wrongs and rights into a framework without deontic concepts made for very engaging reading. But it did little, and has done little, to make sense of tort law, and today it leaves tort law more vulnerable to ill-advised and irresponsible reform.

3

Professor Sir Frederick Pollock (1845–1937): Jurist as Mayfly

ROBERT STEVENS

I. INTRODUCTION

NOBODY READS POLLOCK anymore. Nor should they. The first, and most obvious, reason is that he is outdated. Most of Pollock's work, in particular his textbooks on contract, torts and the law of partnership, is descriptive. He is a collator, gathering together the decisions and statutes. The facts have now changed. The facts of the posited law are not the same as they were in 1929 when Pollock produced his last and thirteenth edition of his torts textbook, let alone compared with 1887 when he published the first. The main use of his texts, finding out what are the relevant authorities on, say, the tort of deceit, is now fulfilled by more modern texts.

Second, he was a truly terrible writer. A flavour of this is given from his letter to Oliver Wendell Holmes that serves as the preface to the early editions of his torts text:

> It may seem a mere artifice, but the assurance of your sympathy will enable me to speak more freely and naturally, even in print, than if my words were directly addressed to the profession at large. Nay more, I would fain sum up in this slight token the brotherhood that subsists, and we trust ever shall, between all true followers of the Common Law here and on your side of the water; and give it to be understood, for my own part, how much my work owes to you and to others in America, mostly citizens of your own Commonwealth, of whom some are known to me only by their published writing, some by commerce of letters; there are some also, fewer than I could wish, whom I have had the happiness of meeting face to face.
>
> When I came into your jurisdiction, it was from the Province of Quebec, a part of Her Majesty's dominions which is governed, as you know, by its old French law, lately repaired and beautified in a sort of Revised Version of the Code Napoléon. This, I doubt not, is an excellent thing in its place.
>
> ...

> You will recognize in my armoury some weapons of your own forging, and if they are ineffective, I must have handled them worse than I am willing, in any reasonable terms of humility, to suppose.[1]

And so it goes on. It may be that we can, to an extent, forgive this sickly, pretentious, verbose, common law romanticism as a product of its Victorian age. His correspondent, Holmes, is however, still very readable today, and I often find myself quoting his epigrammatic writing. The blame cannot wholly be put upon the era.

Third, and most importantly, he was not very good. Pollock has been the subject of a brilliant intellectual biography by Professor Neil Duxbury, *Frederick Pollock and the English Juristic Tradition*.[2] On one level this is deserving. Pollock's biography and publications are extremely impressive. He was, without doubt, one of the most important figures of his age. In England, he was in the same group as Maine, Maitland, Anson, Dicey, Holland and Sir James Fitzjames Stephen. They, however, may all still be read, if not necessarily with profit then with pleasure, in a way that in my judgement Pollock cannot. No doubt his work, in particular his textbooks, were much used by practitioners and judges, although it is difficult to measure the extent of the usage due to the judicial convention that applied before the 1960s against citing the work of living scholars.

He is difficult to assess in other ways. As Duxbury states, 'one usually has to dig deep to find his opinions'.[3] This makes him an elusive figure to write about. Once we have engaged in the digging, however, we can see that his normative pre-suppositions, such as they were, were largely wrong.

I shall seek to show that Pollock's influence within the law of torts has been both a profound and a malign one (much the same claim for the same kind of reasons can be made about his work on contract). Within the law of torts this was because of his attempt to overlay the traditional understanding of the subject with a re-ordering of it suggested by Holmes (who was an original thinker). The chaotic result has lived on in more modern textbooks, causing confusion within the law itself.

II. BIOGRAPHICAL SKETCH

Pollock was born in 1845, the son of Sir William Frederick Pollock and grandson of Sir (Jonathan) Frederick Pollock who was Lord Chief Baron of the Exchequer. He was educated at Eton, and then Trinity College Cambridge. He won the

[1] F Pollock, *The Law of Torts: A Treatise on the Principles of Obligations Arising from Civil Wrongs in the Common Law* (London, Stevens & Sons, 1887) v–vii.

[2] N Duxbury, *Frederick Pollock and the English Juristic Tradition* (Oxford, OUP, 2004).

[3] ibid xi.

first chancellor's medal in 1867, and was elected a fellow of the College the following year. He was called to the bar in Lincoln's Inn in 1871.

After a brief period as Professor of Jurisprudence at University College London, from 1883 to 1903 he was the Corpus Professor of Jurisprudence at Oxford (with a fellowship at Corpus Christi). It would, however, be a mistake to think of him as a legal academic in the modern sense. He was never resident in Oxford and was, at most, a semi-detached member of the faculty who made virtually no impact through the education of the young. Being employed as a professor of *jurisprudence* did not fit with his strengths. Although he wrote a well-regarded book on Spinoza, when it came to the philosophy of law he made no contribution at all (in this respect and others he resembled his successor Arthur Goodhart).

Nor, however, was he primarily a practitioner. He almost never appeared in court, and although he did some advisory work, this was not the main source of his income.

Pollock's career was instead one that has not existed before or since: a legal man of letters. He lived by his editorial and published work. He was the founding editor of the *Law Quarterly Review* in 1885, serving until 1919. In this role he was exceptionally active, publishing articles and numerous notes on cases. Any piece from that period that is unattributed is by him. He was chief editor of the Law Reports for an even more astonishing period, from 1895 to 1935, leaving this position at the age of 90. This was a very influential role, determining which cases were sufficiently important to merit reporting.

In 1876 he published *Principles of Contract at Law and in Equity*, and in 1877 *A Digest of the Law of Partnership*. His work on partnership was to become the Partnership Act 1890. These volumes were followed in 1887 by *The Law of Torts*.[4] This seems to have been inspired by the work he was commissioned to do five years earlier on a Code of Civil Wrongs for India, which was never taken up and forms a rather forlorn appendix to the work.[5] The structure of that draft code also forms the structure for his book. His torts text went through 13 editions in his lifetime, his contract work, although beginning life a decade earlier, nine. This difference may have reflected demand. His contract text faced stiffer competition – from (the far clearer) Anson's *Principles of the Law of Contract* (the first edition of which appeared in 1879) – than did his torts text, at least until the publication of Salmond in 1907 (by which time Pollock had had 20 years in which to become the market leader). The torts text had two editions after his death, the last in 1951, both by PA Landon,[6] who was primarily a criminal law academic.

[4] Pollock, *The Law of Torts: A Treatise on the Principles of Obligations Arising from Civil Wrongs in the Common Law* (n 1). All references are to the first edition, save where otherwise indicated.

[5] An equivalent of the Indian Contracts Act 1872 (still in force today) that had been drafted by Sir James Fitzjames Stephen.

[6] Philip Aislabie Landon (1888–1961) was a Fellow of Trinity College Oxford, and its Bursar 1921–51.

Pollock also produced a large number of works addressed to a more academic audience (as opposed to practising lawyers), some more concerned with politics than law: *Essays in Jurisprudence and Ethics* (1882); *English Opportunities and Duties in the Historical and Comparative Study of Law* (1883); *An Introduction to the History of the Science of Politics* (1890); *Oxford Lectures and other Discussions* (1890); *The Expansion of the Common Law* (1904); and *The Genius of the Common Law* (1912). His more political and historical work has aged the least well. Few now can stomach accounts of 'our lady' the common law and her 'knights'.

If anything is read today with Pollock's name on the cover it is probably Pollock and Maitland's *History of the Law of England before the time of Edward I* (1895).[7] However, Pollock wrote very little of that work, and his name appeared on the cover in order to help sales in the United States (US).[8] Maitland had rushed to finish the book to prevent Pollock's writing any more of it.[9]

He had a lifelong affinity with the US, and in particular with Harvard Law School. He was a correspondent with both Langdell and Ames, entering into a debate as to the nature of the contractual doctrine of consideration with the latter. His most famous correspondent was his friend Oliver Wendell Holmes, with whom he carried on a 58-year correspondence that was subsequently published. His torts text reflects this affinity, with American cases interspersed with the English, on the assumption that the common law formed a seamless whole.[10]

Pollock married Georgina Harriet Deffell in 1873, and had a son and a daughter. He died in 1937, aged 91, two years after Holmes, who had been four years his senior.

This is a great life well lived in the law. A range of accomplishments it is unlikely we shall ever see again, with a degree of influence on the law that it is difficult to imagine anyone obtaining, other than a senior judge of longstanding.

III. HOLMES

As we shall see, Holmes was not the central influence on Pollock's views on the law of contract (which creates a strange dissonance when we compare

[7] The only thing written by Pollock that I read as a student nearly 30 years ago was F Pollock and RS Wright, *An Essay on Possession in the Common Law* (Oxford, Clarendon Press, 1888) written with the judge RS Wright. No student would read this now.

[8] SFC Milsom, 'FW Maitland' (1982) 66 *Proceedings of the British Academy* 265.

[9] ibid 265, 277.

[10] The first case discussed in the book is the decision in *Vandenburgh v Traux* 4 Denio 464 (NY Sup Ct 1847), a decision of the Supreme Court of New York: Pollock, *The Law of Torts: A Treatise on the Principles of Obligations Arising from Civil Wrongs in the Common Law* (n 1) 33. By contrast, some of the standard English cases that we would now expect to be included, such as *Baker v Bolton* (1808) 1 Camp 493, 170 ER 1033; *Cattle v Stockton Waterworks Co* (1874–1875) LR 10 QB 453 (QBD); or *Simpson and Company v Thompson* (1877) 3 App Cas 279 (HL), were omitted.

his contract text with that on torts). Pollock took two ideas from Holmes, both of which were to have a longstanding, and wholly malign, impact upon our understanding of the law of torts.

The first was the 'prediction' theory of law. Holmes expressed this as follows: 'The only question for the lawyer is, how will the judges act?'[11] In Pollock's words, the science of law as with other sciences is to 'predict', specifically within law the prediction of 'the decisions of courts of justice'.[12]

Within private law this places civil recourse, one party successfully suing another and getting judgment in his favour, at its heart. This civil recourse view of private law is encouraged by the way in which we are taught in common law systems since the time of Langdell. The case-law method teaches us that what matters is the outcome of litigated cases, and the reasons given by the judges for those outcomes.

Within private law in general, and the law of torts in particular, this leads us into thinking of the law in terms of liability formulae: 'If X, Y and Z are proven, judge will give order A.' As what the claimant is most commonly claiming is compensation for loss suffered, the law of torts is then flattened into a series of liability rules, with the compensation of loss the gist.

The second idea was Holmes's tripartite division of the law of torts first set out in his article 'The Theory of Torts'.[13] Here he suggested that torts fell into three categories: first, claims where culpability is an essential element; second, at the other extreme, claims of strict liability; and, third, in the halfway group 'lie the great mass of cases in which negligence has become an essential element'.[14] This division of the law of torts is based upon degrees of moral culpability, not the individual rights the violation of which constitutes a civil wrong.

IV. POLLOCK

The subtitle of Pollock's torts book, 'A Treatise on the Principles of Obligations Arising from Civil Wrongs', raises false hopes.[15] The concept of a civil wrong plays almost no role in his work. So we are told in his initial attempt at definition that '*Tort* is nothing but the French equivalent of our English word *wrong*',

[11] Holmes first expressed this theory in a review of *The Law Magazine and Review*, 'Book Notices' (1871–1872) 6 *American Law Review* 723, 724. It is most famously found in his address 'The Path of Law' (1897) 10 *Harvard Law Review* 457.

[12] F Pollock, *Essays in Jurisprudence and Ethics* (London, Macmillan and Company, 1882) 237.

[13] OW Holmes 'The Theory of Torts' (1873) 7 *American Law Review* 652, 652–63. Approved by Pollock in a letter to Holmes on 3 July 1874 (MDW Howe (ed), *Holmes-Pollock Letters: The Correspondence of Mr Justice Holmes and Sir Frederick Pollock 1874–1932* (Cambridge, MA, Harvard University Press, 1941) vol 1, 4; Duxbury, *Frederick Pollock and the English Juristic Tradition* (n 2) 238.

[14] OW Holmes, 'The Theory of Torts' (1873) 7 *American Law Review* 652, 653.

[15] The subtitle was probably chosen so as to accord with the Indian Civil Wrongs Bill that he had been commissioned to draft.

but then that '[i]n common speech everything is a wrong, or wrongful, which is thought to do violence to any right'.[16] This, he says, tells us nothing useful, as '[m]anslaying, false witness, breach of covenant, are wrongs in this sense. But thus we should include all breaches of all duties, and therefore should not even be on the road to any distinction that could serve as the base of a legal classification'.[17] The idea of a civil wrong, dismissed as too broad, plays no further role in the analysis.

Pollock's reference to 'false witness' indicates a failure to distinguish between duties of virtue and duties of right. Further, he made no attempt to distinguish between breaches of public duties (mainly crimes) and the violations of private rights (mainly torts). He saw the distinction between torts and crimes in Holmesian terms: which kind of court had jurisdiction to hear the claim.[18] Similarly, the distinction between torts, equitable wrongs, marital wrongs and claims for salvage was also based upon the different kind of court that had jurisdiction.[19] As claims in contract and upon a tort were heard before the same common law courts, a tort could be defined negatively as 'an act or omission giving rise, in virtue of the common law jurisdiction of the Court, to a civil remedy which is not an action of contract'.[20]

Pollock's contract text was entitled *Principles of Contract at Law and in Equity*, showing that he thought that subject straddled the jurisdictional divide. Although at the outset Pollock states that the law of torts is dissimilar as a subject, he did include injunctions (an equitable remedy) within his text, and acknowledged that equity had concurrent jurisdiction in cases of deceit. It seems he wished to exclude wholly equitable wrongs, such as breach of confidence, including claims based upon them for compensation for consequential loss suffered, but not equitable remedies for common law wrongs. This bizarre half-historical division persists in most modern texts.

This is not a text concerned with civil wrongs properly understood at all. Pollock, astonishingly, states that '[t]he phrase *damnum sine iniuria*, which for the modern law is at best insignificant',[21] has been superseded.[22] Nobody who took the idea that torts are civil wrongs seriously could state such a thing.

Duxbury describes Pollock as 'Holmes's worker-bee wallflower sister'.[23] Within the law of torts this is fair, if mixed metaphor. Pollock's original

[16] Pollock, *The Law of Torts: A Treatise on the Principles of Obligations Arising from Civil Wrongs in the Common Law* (n 1) 2 (original emphasis).

[17] ibid.

[18] ibid 3.

[19] ibid 4. Of course we might then ask *why* the courts were divided in this way, but Pollock did not.

[20] ibid. 'Contract' here expressly includes 'supposed contracts', thereby including claims that we would now describe as being for restitution or based upon 'unjust enrichment'.

[21] ibid 22.

[22] See also ibid 23: 'the old-fashioned distinction between *mala prohibita* and *mala in se* is long since exploded'.

[23] Duxbury, *Frederick Pollock and the English Juristic Tradition* (n 2) 283.

contribution was that he sought to fit the law of torts as it was then understood within Holmes's new threefold scheme. To this end Pollock divided the categories of torts into three groups, as follows:

Group A.

Personal Wrongs.

1. Wrongs affecting safety and freedom of the person: Assault, battery, false imprisonment.
2. Wrongs affecting personal relations in the family: Seduction, enticing away of servants.
3. Wrongs affecting reputation: Slander and libel.
4. Wrongs affecting estate generally: Deceit, slander of title. Malicious prosecution, conspiracy.

Group B.

Wrongs to Property.

1. Trespass: (a) to land. (b) to goods. Conversion and unnamed wrongs *ejusdem generis*. Disturbance of easements, &c.
2. Interference with rights analogous to property, such as private franchises, patents, copyrights.

Group C.

Wrongs to Person, Estate, and Property generally.

1. Nuisance.
2. Negligence.
3. Breach of absolute duties specially attached to the occupation of fixed property, to the ownership and custody of dangerous things, and to the exercise of certain public callings. This kind of liability results, as will be seen hereafter, partly from ancient rules of the common law of which the origin is still doubtful, partly from the modern development of the law of negligence.[24]

Group A was Holmes's first class, where the defendant's conduct was 'wilful or wanton',[25] deserving of 'strong moral condemnation'.[26] Group B was Holmes's second class, the 'wrongs' of strict liability, where this 'moral element' was 'at first sight absent' and the law 'stricter, on the face of things, than morality'.[27] Group C was the intermediate class, where a 'man who fails to take order, in things within his control, against risk to others which he actually foresees, or which a man of common sense and competence would in his place foresee, will scarcely be held blameless by the moral judgment of his fellows'.[28]

[24] Pollock, *The Law of Torts: A Treatise on the Principles of Obligations Arising from Civil Wrongs in the Common Law* (n 1) 7.
[25] ibid 8.
[26] ibid 9.
[27] ibid 10.
[28] ibid 11.

V. MORALITY

Unlike Holmes, Pollock saw the law of torts as a form of enforced morality. It is usual to distinguish between true and conventional morality, but for Pollock, when it came to the conventional morality of Englishmen (which included Americans) as embodied in 'our lady the Common law', this was a distinction without a difference. The law of torts was based, he claimed, on the ethical precept of *alterum non laedere*, 'Thou shalt do no hurt to thy neighbour'. This he found similarly stated in Ulpian and the Church Catechism. Unsurprisingly, he was very sympathetic to Lord Atkin's subsequent invocation of the negative formulation of the Golden Rule in *Donoghue v Stevenson*[29] as the grounding principle behind liability for negligence. Despite the title of his book, Pollock saw the common law as moving towards a single unifying principle against inflicting harm in a morally blameworthy way: a law of tort, not a law of torts.[30]

Why the law should be in the business of enforcing morality, or *why* it should concern itself with the consequences of breaches of these duties of virtue after they have happened (why are they not so much spilled milk?) does not seem to have concerned him.

VI. 'ANOMALIES'

Pollock acknowledged that '[t]he real difficulty of ascribing any rational unity to our law of torts'[31] was created by Group B, where any element of want of virtuous behaviour was absent. As a person dealt with another's property 'at his peril', how could this be explained? If I honestly and reasonably build a house on your land believing that land to be mine, I commit the tort of trespass: why?

Pollock's explanation was one of historical accident. Claims for asserting title to land were initially done through the writ of right, whereas when compensation for loss was sought the claim was brought through the writ of trespass. The former was subject to archaic procedural hurdles, whilst the latter was not. As a result, the latter had come to swallow the former, with the result that, 'we may not actively approve, the inclusion of the morally innocent with the morally guilty trespasses in legal classification'.[32]

Three points should be noticed. First, Pollock's explanation shows how he believed the law of torts was disconnected from the (property) rights we had one against another. The proper province of the law of torts was not co-extensive with the violation of rights in his mind, but rather with holding the morally culpable responsible for the consequences of their actions.

[29] *Donoghue v Stevenson* [1932] AC 562 (HL).

[30] F Pollock, 'Review of JC Miles, A Digest of English Civil Law' (1910) 26 *LQR* 420, 421.

[31] Pollock, *The Law of Torts: A Treatise on the Principles of Obligations Arising from Civil Wrongs in the Common Law* (n 1) 12.

[32] ibid 16.

Second, he was wrong about the positive law, both in his day and now. Trespass to the person, including both false imprisonment and battery, and the torts of libel and slander do not differ from proprietary torts in the way he supposed. If I publish a statement about you that is defamatory, that I honestly and reasonably believe to be true, I commit a tort. If you detain me against my will, honestly and reasonably believing that you have statutory authorisation to do so, you commit a tort. If I kiss you, honestly and reasonably believing that you have given me permission to do so, when you have not, I commit a tort. Pollock seemed to believe that the elements for the torts of libel, false imprisonment or battery were the same as for their criminal law counterparts.[33] None of these is a wrong in private law that necessarily involves strong moral condemnation, indeed less so than for the 'intermediate' negligence-based category. This (basic) mistake undermined both his classificatory scheme and his view that the law of torts was closely tied to holding persons responsible for the losses caused by their moral failings.

Third, it is difficult to understand what role was left for the first category once the third had been admitted. If we accept that a defendant is *generally* liable for negligently leaving a defendant worse off than he otherwise would be, why would there be any need for the category where a higher degree of moral turpitude was shown? This distinction makes sense within the criminal law, where the more morally blameworthy may be subject to a more serious penalty, but if the universal remedy is one of compensation for loss, why would any litigant seek to rely on the category of intentional wrongdoing when mere negligence suffices?[34]

VII. INTENTIONAL HARM

Writing in the 1880s, Pollock, at the start of chapter II concerning 'Principles of Liability', stated that '[t]here is no express authority that I know of for stating as a general proposition of English law that it is a wrong to do wilful harm to one's neighbour without lawful justification or excuse'.[35] Given, however, that Pollock's starting point was that the blameworthy infliction of harm was the *central* case in the law of torts, this seems to pose a problem. He answers it by

[33] See, eg, his view that consent was no defence where a battery constituted a breach of the peace: ibid 141.

[34] For this end of the stick being firmly grasped, see D Howarth, 'Is There a Future for the Intentional Torts?' in P Birks (ed), *The Classification of Obligations* (Oxford, Clarendon Press, 1998).

[35] Pollock, *The Law of Torts: A Treatise on the Principles of Obligations Arising from Civil Wrongs in the Common Law* (n 1) 21. Because for Pollock the intentional infliction of harm was the central case of a tort, he had no room for any 'abuse of rights' doctrine. 'Abuse of rights' is more properly labelled 'abuse of liberties', and concerns the intentional infliction of harm in a way that the law confers no right on the claimant to stop. It is liability because there is no civil wrong, not because there is. See further Duxbury, *Frederick Pollock and the English Juristic Tradition* (n 2) 270–79.

stating that this is an accident of history. At one time there was no general law of contract, but only a list of certain kinds of agreement that could be enforced. Today, he argues, just as we have outgrown such pockets and are able to generalise a law of contract, so '[t]he three main heads of duty with which the law of torts is concerned – namely, to abstain from wilful injury, to respect the property of others, and to use due diligence to avoid causing harm to others – are all alike of a comprehensive nature'.[36]

Further, he claims that 'the commission of an act specifically forbidden by law, or the omission or failure to perform any duty specifically imposed by law, is generally equivalent to an act done with intent to cause wrongful injury'.[37] If, therefore, the legislature lays down that a particular action is unlawful, Pollock's view was that anybody harmed by the breach of this duty had an action. The statute might by implication *exclude* a private action, but there was no need to show that it created any particular right in the claimant – loss suffered as a result of the breach of a public duty sufficed.

This statement of general principle may have been plausible at the time of Pollock's first edition; it was not by the thirteenth in 1929. In the 1890s a trio of House of Lords decisions had firmly established that there was *no* principle in English law that the intentional infliction of harm is, alone, actionable: *Mogul Steamship Co Ltd v McGregor Gow & Co*,[38] *Bradford Corp v Pickles*[39] and *Allen v Flood*.[40]

Pollock maintained to the end his original formulation unchanged, and in later editions cited for the proposition an obiter dictum of Bowen LJ[41] from 1892, arguably before the contrary had been firmly established by higher authority, and a statement from Holmes J in the US Supreme Court decision in *Aikens v Wisconsin*,[42] at a point when the US and English authorities had clearly diverged from one another.

Pollock treated the high authority that was inconsistent with the central tenet of his account of the law of torts as either exceptional,[43] or best just ignored. Landon, the editor of the fourteenth and fifteenth editions of his text after Pollock's death, wrote that 'Pollock … refused to alter his exposition. There was a stubborn texture in him which made him unwilling to admit that his theories were erroneous, whatever the House of Lords might say'.[44] It is difficult to see

[36] ibid 22.

[37] ibid 23. Why?

[38] *Mogul Steamship Co Ltd v McGregor Gow & Co* [1892] AC 25 (HL).

[39] *Bradford Corp v Pickles* [1895] AC 587 (HL).

[40] *Allen v Flood* [1898] AC 1 (HL).

[41] *Skinner & Co v Shew & Co* [1893] 1 Ch 413 (CA) 422.

[42] *Aikens v Wisconsin* 195 US 194, 204 (1904).

[43] F Pollock, 'Allen v Flood' (1898) 14 *LQR* 129–32.

[44] PA Landon, *Pollock's The Law of Torts*, 14th edn (London, Stevens & Sons, 1939) 45. See also PA Landon comparing Pollock with Winfield (1954) 12 *CLJ* 80, 84: 'Winfield, on his part, always loyally accepted the decisions of the House of Lords'.

what choice Pollock had however. Either the apparent rule set down by these cases was wrong, or the entire account of the law of torts set out in his text was erroneous. It is a rare academic who is prepared to endanger his influence by explicitly calling back his earlier views for burning, and Pollock was not of that breed.

VIII. NEGLIGENT HARM

One might expect that if Pollock's view that there was a general principle against the intentional infliction of harm had proven erroneous, his equivalent claim in relation to causing it negligently would, *a fortiori*, suffer a similar fate. As we know, the opposite has proved true.

Pollock always included a chapter on negligence (although he did not refer to 'the tort of negligence'). His account is remarkably short on detail, however, with most of the chapter taken up with what needs to be proven to show that the defendant has been careless, and the defence of contributory negligence. He endorsed, as would be expected, the wide statement of principle of Brett MR in *Heaven v Pender*.[45] From the first we find

> the general rule that every one is bound to exercise due care towards his neighbours in his acts and conduct, or rather omits or falls short of it at his peril; the peril, namely, of being liable to make good whatever harm may be proved consequence of the default.[46]

He subsequently endorsed the wide statement of principle set down nearly 50 years later in that most trivial of famous cases, *Donoghue v Stevenson*,[47] although that case appeared three years after the last edition of his textbook to appear in his lifetime. Pollock had always, and rightly, been a critic of the privity fallacy,[48] the idea that to allow a claim for personal injuries where the defendant's conduct also constituted a breach of contract in relation to a third party, offended the doctrine of privity of contract. Lord Macmillan expressly relied on Pollock's textbook, unusual then during an author's lifetime, in rejecting this proposition (which is the important point that *Donoghue v Stevenson* actually decided), and adopted his explanation of the cases that had been thought to stand for it.

[45] *Heaven v Pender* (1883) 11 QBD 503 (CA) 507.

[46] Pollock, *The Law of Torts: A Treatise on the Principles of Obligations Arising from Civil Wrongs in the Common Law* (n 1) 353.

[47] *Donoghue v Stevenson* [1932] AC 562 (HL); F Pollock, 'The Snail in the Bottle and Thereafter' (1933) 49 *LQR* 22.

[48] Pollock, *The Law of Torts: A Treatise on the Principles of Obligations Arising from Civil Wrongs in the Common Law* (n 1) 448–49, explaining *Winterbottom v Wright* (1842) 10 M & W 1091, 152 ER 402.

Given Pollock's view that the law of torts was a form of codified personal morality, it is interesting to consider his views in relation to those features of the law of negligence that do not map on to this account, and that often bemuse student beginners.

So, what about duties of rescue? Good Englishmen no doubt pick up babies drowning in an inch of water, so why did the common law not hold them liable for not doing so? Pollock tells us that '[t]he law does not and cannot undertake to make men render active service to their neighbours at all times when a good or a brave man would do so',[49] but adds nothing to justify this assertion of impossibility.

What of the objective standard of care, that holds some people, through no moral fault of their own, to a higher standard than they can reach? Pollock considered the admission of evidence as to what the particular defendant foresaw as 'impracticable or useless',[50] and his justification for this rule centres upon its workability as a direction to juries.

IX. VICARIOUS LIABILITY

If we go back in time, the original justification for why a master could be held liable for the torts of his servant was that the acts of the latter were attributed to the former.[51] This entailed that both the master and the servant committed the same tort jointly. This 'master's tort' theory still has some defenders,[52] but the more 'modern' approach is to see vicarious liability as based upon a cocktail of the standard policy considerations for strict liability (deterrence, loss spreading and so on), although none of these appears to justify its central feature: that liability is dependent upon a tort having been committed by another.

Pollock claimed to have introduced the language of vicarious liability.[53] This fitted with his general view of torts as a set of liability rules, and he dismissed the traditional understanding based upon the attribution of action, *qui facit per alium facit per se*, as inapplicable outside of cases of expressly authorised action. However, he did not seek to explain the doctrine using the policy cocktail of more modern writers. Instead, he explained vicarious liability on the

[49] Pollock, *The Law of Torts: A Treatise on the Principles of Obligations Arising from Civil Wrongs in the Common Law* (n 1) 352.

[50] ibid 356.

[51] See the following decisions of Holt CJ: *Jones v Hart* (1698) 2 Salk 441, 91 ER 382; *Turberville v Stampe* (1697) 1 Ld Raym 264, 91 ER 1072; *Middleton v Fowler* (1698) 1 Salk 282, 91 ER 247; *Lane v Cotton* (1706) 12 Mod 472, 88 ER 1458; and *Hern v Nichols* (1708) 1 Salk 289, 91 ER 256.

[52] G Williams, 'Vicarious Liability and the Master's Indemnity' (1957) 20 *MLR* 220; EJ Weinrib, *The Idea of Private Law*, revised edn (Oxford, OUP, 2012) 186; R Stevens, *Torts and Rights* (Oxford, OUP, 2007) ch 11.

[53] Howe, *Holmes-Pollock Letters: The Correspondence of Mr Justice Holmes and Sir Frederick Pollock 1874–1932* (n 13) vol 1, 233.

basis that 'I am bound to see that my affairs are conducted with due regard to the safety of others'.[54] The idea (so far as discernible) seems to be that once the master has chosen that another will act on his behalf, he is responsible for the consequences of that choice.

X. LEGACY

As is well known, during Pollock's lifetime the main opponent of his generalised theory of liability based upon degrees of fault was Salmond. In the six editions of his (far more readable) textbook, Salmond never included 'negligence' as an independent tort or ground of liability. Salmond's formulation of the debate in 1910 was as follows:

> Does the law of torts consist of a fundamental general principle that it is wrongful to cause harm to other persons in the absence of some specific ground of justification or excuse, or does it consist of a number of specific rules prohibiting certain kinds of harmful activity, and leaving all the residue outside the sphere of legal responsibility?[55]

The most significant academic in Pollock's corner was Winfield,[56] whose textbook, unlike Salmond's, is still in use today.[57] With Salmond was Goodhart, the holder of the same chair in Jurisprudence at Oxford that Pollock had once held.[58]

Unfortunately, the way this debate was presented by Salmond and others makes it appear as if the matter is merely one of exposition: is there a general liability rule (with exceptions), or are there isolated islands of liability? Indeed, if our perspective is Holmes's one of *liability rules*, nothing of substance seems to turn on the question.[59] The rules can be presented and constructed in one way or the other with identical results in all cases, with neither one being any more 'right'. Further, Salmond, who was an excellent jurisprude whose work on rights pre-figured that of Hohfeld,[60] fails (as Pollock in his text consistently and maddeningly does) to distinguish between duties with correlative rights and *public* duties (such as that not to park on double yellow lines) over which

[54] Pollock, *The Law of Torts: A Treatise on the Principles of Obligations Arising from Civil Wrongs in the Common Law* (n 1) 68.

[55] JW Salmond, *The Law of Torts: A Treatise on the English Law of Liability for Civil Injuries*, 2nd edn (London, Stevens and Haynes, 1910) 8–9.

[56] PH Winfield, 'The Foundation of Liability in Tort' (1927) 27 *Columbia Law Review* 1; PH Winfield, *The Province of the Law of Tort* (Cambridge, CUP, 1931) 32–39.

[57] WE Peel and J Goudkamp, *Winfield and Jolowicz on Tort*, 19th edn (London, Sweet & Maxwell, 2014).

[58] A Goodhart, 'The Foundation of Tortious Liability' (1938) 2 *MLR* 1.

[59] See also P Mitchell, *A History of Tort Law 1900–1950* (Cambridge, CUP, 2015) 15, who accepts that 'for all of them the choice of definition was inextricably linked to fundamental questions about the law's nature, purpose and development', but does not explain why anybody should now care.

[60] JW Salmond, *Jurisprudence or The Theory of Law* (London, Stevens and Haynes, 1902).

nobody else has any control.[61] It is not and never has been the positive law, as Pollock consistently assumed, that anybody left worse off than they otherwise would be by another who breaks a (specific) legal duty has a claim against him.

Pollock's attempt to gather all of the law of torts under one general principle, that those responsible for harm through morally blameworthy behaviour should be held responsible, has, obviously, failed. Nearly one-and-a-half centuries since Pollock began work on a torts code for India, we have many separate torts, and the blameworthy causation of harm cannot explain them. However, the two ideas that he took from Holmes continue to fester.

First, scholars and – more importantly – courts continue to see torts in terms of liability formulae for compensation and not as civil wrongs. The most extreme form of this phenomenon is found in the area of the 'economic' torts, which I first studied 25 years ago. I had chosen to study 'Labour Law' as one of my options on the Oxford Jurisprudence BA. In order to understand the various statutory immunities for trade unions from civil action in trade disputes (and the withdrawal of those immunities where the union has failed to take various procedural steps such as ballots), it is first necessary to understand the economic torts. My regular tutor in 'Tort Law' (*sic*) did not teach the area, and so I was sent to a different tutor at another College who did. I was then presented with reading lists of staggering length, and expected to learn by rote the various formulae for relief that there were (and are).

These formulae seemed to have no rhyme nor reason to them. In this they resembled other areas of law I had been taught, such as equitable estoppel and constructive trusts, where the student was expected to take a leap of faith, accept that the rules existed, and then, through a feat of memory, remember the case names that stood for each element of each separate magic spell. Back then, being less world weary and with a better memory than now, I happily complied with the task expected of me. Around two weeks after the exams had taken place, however, most of what I had forced into my skull through an effort of will had disappeared.

On the 'torts as liability formulae' view, there is nothing wrong with a 'tort of conspiracy' (of which Pollock, alongside Winfield, was an early champion), as opposed to seeing conspiracy as only being a rule by which the actions of one party to an agreement may be attributed to another. As 'torts' are not required to relate to any particular right, just so long as they are consistent with one another, they can be constructed in almost any way we choose: a dash of illegality making up for a lower degree of blameworthiness, a drop of conspiracy lowering the threshold of what must be foreseen and so on.

[61] Pollock was, unsurprisingly, dismissive of Hohfeld. Howe, *Holmes-Pollock Letters: The Correspondence of Mr Justice Holmes and Sir Frederick Pollock 1874–1932* (n 13) vol 2, 63: 'it is strange how many rational beings believe the ultimate truths of the universe to be reducible to patterns on a blackboard'.

If we try to understand private law in general, and the law of torts in particular, as a series of liability spells, with formulae constructed on the basis of more or less arbitrary choices of here-today-gone-tomorrow judges, we have no basis for either understanding or assessing it. Worse, the law itself will have no stability, as any decision by any court, regardless of its priority in the legal pecking order, is always liable to be overturned. Without firm normative foundations, the law is just the contingent choices of mostly dead, nearly all white men.[62]

Second, although Pollock's Holmesian agenda of mapping all of the law of torts on to loss caused by different degrees of fault has few champions nowadays,[63] one element of it has triumphed: the 'tort' of negligence. This 'intermediate' category has come to dominate thinking and teaching of the law of torts. It is a mistake.

Legal categories are important, as we use them not just for exposition but to reason with. Once the law abandoned the forms of action, the 'causes of action' are grouped together as claims that arise for the same reason of justice. This enables us to start with the assumption that they will all show the same necessary features (eg, in contract: offer and acceptance, consideration, intention to create legal relations, certainty, etc). This is not true within the 'tort' of negligence, because the reasons for the different kind of rights that are covered are not the same.

Two examples illustrate the point. The law imposes a duty of care on all of us not negligently to injure the bodies of other people. This duty cannot be disclaimed, as it does not arise because voluntarily assumed. Prominent disclaimers of responsibility for the careful driving of a motor vehicle displayed on the roof will not avail the careless motorist. By contrast, some duties that care will be taken are not general but arise because they are voluntarily assumed (such as that of a bailee to a bailor). Such duties can be disclaimed by making it clear that the duty that would ordinarily be being undertaken is not.[64] The features of the two kinds of claim are not the same because they arise for different reasons, and so they should not be treated together. It may be objected that this difference is so obvious that nobody could make such a mistake, but this can be disproved by the positive law of England.[65]

Similarly, the *standard* of duty is not in fact the same. The duty the bailee assumes to the bailor is that *care will be taken* of the goods, not that the bailee

[62] The formula for intentionally inflicting physical or psychological harm in *Rhodes v OPO* [2015] UKSC 32, [2016] AC 219 similarly fails to identify the particular right in issue, omits to relate what must be intended or foreseen by the defendant to that right, and does not distinguish the issue of whether the defendant's conduct was potentially wrongful if it inflicted foreseeable psychological harm on the claimant from that of whether the appropriate remedy should be an injunction to stop such conduct before the wrong occurred. The result (no injunction) is correct.

[63] But see E Descheemaeker, *The Division of Wrongs* (Oxford, OUP, 2009).

[64] eg, *Hedley Byrne & Co Ltd v Heller & Partners Ltd* [1964] AC 465 (HL).

[65] *White v Blackmore* [1972] 2 QB 651 (CA) (Buckley and Roskill LJJ, Lord Denning MR in dissent): disclaimer effective to allow an occupier to negligently injure a bare licensee.

will be personally careful. This is the general position in relation to voluntarily assumed duties: they are non-delegable. If we lump the voluntarily assumed duties alongside those arising from our interest in our bodies and things, we shall lose sight of these distinctions. We shall also make many other mistakes (a common one being that because most of the duties in the 'tort of negligence' are not voluntarily assumed, none of them are).

It is common nowadays to divide thinkers into hedgehogs and foxes, lumpers and splitters, those preferring one big idea and those preferring many small ones. Within law there is no scope for this: each separate reason, whether big or small, has to occupy its correct space, neither too big nor too small. The 'tort of negligence' is too big.

It is probably too late to eradicate the 'tort of negligence' from our thinking altogether (although another child of Winfield, the 'quasi-contract', and my personal favourite the 'pseudo-quasi-contract', has almost disappeared), but we must at least refrain from thinking of it as a unified cause of action that enables us to use it for purposes of reasoning, as opposed to exposition.

Today, an even more sceptical approach to whether the law of torts is part of a law of civil wrongs than even Pollock would have countenanced has become prevalent. So Pollock, as we have seen, did not distinguish between duties owed *to* other individuals and public duties. More modern writers have gone further and have begun to treat the 'duty of care' in the law of negligence not as an actual duty at all but as a misnomer, much as the 'duty to mitigate' in the law of damages undoubtedly is.[66] The duty of care is portrayed as a 'control device',[67] into which are poured the various considerations for and against *liability* (eg, 'Will there be too many claims?'; 'Will defendants start behaving too defensively?') that are nothing to do with whether one party has a *duty* to another to take care not to injure him. This pushes Pollock and Holmes's line of thought further than they went, but they are the source.

XI. CONTRACT

In the field of contract, Pollock never adopted Holmes's approach. This may have been an accident of timing. They first met in 1874,[68] and Holmes's important publications were still to come.[69] Pollock completed his 600-page contract text in 1876, at the age of 32.

[66] If, following a wrong, my losses are increased by my own unreasonable behaviour, I cannot recover to that extent, but I breach no duty to anybody by so behaving.

[67] J Fleming, 'Remoteness and Duty: The Control Devices in Liability for Negligence' (1953) 31 *Canadian Bar Review* 471; *Dorset Yacht Co Ltd v Home Office* [1969] 2 QB 412 (CA) 426 (Lord Denning MR); *D v East Berkshire Community NHS Trust* [2005] UKHL 23, [2005] 2 AC 373 [94] (Lord Nicholls).

[68] Duxbury, *Frederick Pollock and the English Juristic Tradition* (n 2) 24.

[69] *The Common Law* was published in 1881.

The theoretical underpinnings of the work came instead from von Savigny[70] and the 'will theory' that he championed. On this approach, the obligation of performance is sourced in the subjective common intentions of the parties at the time of agreement. Under it, the contractual duties are of the same species as a vow or an oath. Good people are resolute and keep their vows, therefore where two parties form such a vow together they ought to keep it. This fitted with Pollock's more general view of seeing the law as a kind of codified personal morality.

Unfortunately, this Vulcan mind-meld view of the rights created by contracting not only has a poor fit with the positive law, it is normatively unappealing. It has continued, *faute de mieux*, to exercise considerable influence on English academic writing. Pollock, to his credit, although never freeing himself entirely from it, never ignored the features of English law that were inconsistent with it, and later editions downplayed its significance.[71] As a result, his influence on the law of contract has been less detrimental (and significant).

XII. HOW TO BE A JURIST

Contrary to the nineteenth-century view of Pollock and Holmes, law is not a science. Thankfully. Scientists are solely concerned with facts. Physicists are unconcerned with what gravity ought to be, but they want to know what it is. Biologists classify animals and plants according to facts in the world that have no moral significance. Some animals are carnivores, and there is no blame attached to that.

Judges have the authority to resolve for us the question of what the law, as a matter of posited fact, is. Jurists do not have this power. Once the United Kingdom (UK) Supreme Court has said, as it apparently has,[72] that those who pay bribes for honours can get back what they pay if the honour is not forthcoming, that is the end of the matter as a matter of the positive law. However unjustified that may be, or however inconsistent with the common law as it stood before they reached that decision. Everyone has no choice but to defer to them on this question of posited law as fact once they have acted.

Judges have no power authoritatively to determine the normative question of what the law ought to be. Nobody does, not judge or jurist. No deference to anybody by anybody is in order on this question, regardless of whether they have 'Professor' or 'Lady Justice' attached to their name.

[70] FC von Savigny, *System des heutigen romschen Rechts*, 9 vols (1840–51) vol iii, 258.

[71] See Duxbury, *Frederick Pollock and the English Juristic Tradition* (n 2) 194–95.

[72] *Patel v Mirza* [2016] UKSC 42, [2017] AC 467 [150] (Lord Neuberger), with express disapproval of *Parkinson v Royal College of Ambulance Ltd* [1925] 2 KB 1 (KBD).

On the law as science view, jurists are merely concerned with cataloguing the workings of the legal machine, and predicting what answer it will spit out. Within a common law system there is certainly a large (but diminishing) degree to which the role of description falls to the jurist. The judge-made law is found in the results of cases and, where they give them, the reasons for those results given by judges. These form precedents for future decisions. That is not, however, on its own a set of rules. What the posited rules are, as a matter of fact, must be inferred from the results and reasons. One central role of a textbook writer like Pollock was (and still is) to set out those rules, as deduced from the results and reasons in the cases. This inevitably involves generalising, and rationalising, the results in the specific instances and the sometimes inconsistent reasons given for them. Pollock, in performing this role, over-generalised in following Holmes in thinking the law could be understood in terms of harm caused by fault, and we still over-generalise today in thinking of a unitary 'tort' of negligence.

A jurist in this capacity faced with a decision of the High Court of Australia that is inconsistent with one of the UK Supreme Court has no basis for saying one is any more right or wrong than the other, unless one was given *per incuriam*. Those decisions now are the positive law facts in their respective jurisdictions. On this approach, the only way of assessing whether a decision is right (or wrong) is whether it is in conformity with the binding positive law as applicable at the time of judgment. In this (limited) role jurists have a strictly limited shelf life. Law moves on, the facts change. Further, compared with 1887, our law is increasingly found in legislation, not in the results of cases, and so this job of synthesising is not what is necessary. Ultimate appellate courts are also increasingly rendering this role redundant by refusing to confine themselves to giving reasons for the outcome of the instant case in front of them, instead setting out a more general rule that is to be applied in all cases (including the one they are hearing).

The (very valuable) job of the textbook writer of description is not 'theoretical' in any sense. Nor, once we have rejected Holmes's predictive theory of law, is it scientific. It is a job of reportage: the careful cataloguing of the positive law facts.

It is possible to engage in this endeavour without forming any view as to whether the body of law, as a matter of fact, you are cataloguing makes any normative sense whatsoever. It could be that what the jurist is describing is not only flawed, but also morally repugnant. Still, our jurist as reporter may be able to deduce from the judges' ordering the killing of members of a minority group on Mondays, Tuesdays and Wednesdays, and their repeated stated reason that they should be exterminated, that there is no rule against killing them on Thursdays either, whatever may be commonly supposed.

It may be that Holmes thought that the only proper province of the jurist was the scientific one of predicting what judges will do (the thought that led to legal realism and the exciting uncovering of all of the real facts outside of what the judges said in pursuit of this endeavour), but Pollock did not. His refusal to adjust his account in the light of *Bradford Corp v Pickles*[73] and *Allen v Flood*[74] was because his was a *theory* of law, not a description of it.

There is an uncrossable chasm between what the positive law is as a matter of *fact*, and what as a matter of justice the law *ought* to be. A proposition as to what the positive law *is* can only be refuted by proof of what, as a matter of fact, the posited rule *is*. A proposition as to what the law *ought* to be cannot be refuted by any number of facts, such as the result in cases, regardless of how many are assembled. This is the truth behind the proposition that 'it takes a theory to beat a theory'. Just as only proof of a fact can refute a proposition as to how the world is, only a better normative proposition can falsify another inconsistent normative proposition. The proper role of the jurist also includes determining whether the positive law measures up to what reasons of justice require.

However, jurists are not mere moral philosophers untethered by any results. Moral philosophers are forced to invent hypotheticals, often seemingly involving trollies. They then run online polls to test what the consensus is as to how they should be resolved ('20% say push the fat man into the trolley's path').

In law, by contrast, we have *millions* of actual real-world ethical problems that have been litigated, with a consensus tested and re-tested over time, often in different jurisdictions with different histories, as to how they should be answered. That does *not* entail that the answers given are presumptively correct. It does, however, enable us to go back and forth between our own suggested principles of justice and outcomes in real-world cases, challenging our own propositions as to what the law ought to be. Sometimes the outcomes will force us to adjust our suggested principle, sometimes we will conclude that the outcomes are wrong as the suggested principle cannot be improved upon. We can test ourselves against Bowen, Cardozo, Scrutton, Dixon, Denning and Hale. Often we conclude that they were right as to what the law ought to be, sometimes that they were wrong. They cannot answer that for us. Similarly, we can look to the arguments of Pollock, Posner, Atiyah, Birks and Stapleton, but nobody has any authority to resolve what justice requires.

Again, the case-law method can mislead us when it comes to separating the *is* from the *ought*. Counsel, in arguing their case, and judges, in giving judgment, rely both upon the *facts* of the positive law (the cases and statutes of the past) and the *reasons* of justice as to why one party or another ought to win. When we study law through judgments, we see, and are trained to employ together, both of these two streams. Those of us who write with a legal audience of judges or practitioners in mind may similarly seek to persuade by employing both the positive law facts and reasons of justice independent of the law. They are, however, quite separate.

[73] *Bradford Corp v Pickles* [1895] AC 587 (HL).
[74] *Allen v Flood* [1898] AC 1 (HL).

The entire point of a *theory* of what justice requires is to provide a benchmark against which the facts of the positive law may be assessed. Only a *theory* can enable us to say 'the positive law is wrong (or right)'. It can be no criticism of a *theory* of law that it indicates that certain cases were wrongly decided, or that particular statutes are unjustifiable. Indeed if your 'theory' is that all of the positive law everywhere is correct, even when the rules in different jurisdictions are exactly the opposite of one another,[75] that is not a 'theory' worth anything.

Some theories of law may conclude that large areas of it are without justification and should be abolished (eg, the later work of Patrick Atiyah), or less interestingly that the law is largely justifiable in terms of justice but that certain cases were wrongly decided or statutes unjustified (eg, me). It is no criticism of a *theory* of law that it is inconsistent with the positive law facts. A theory may be more or less interesting because of its divergence from the facts of the positive law, but it cannot be more or less correct.

Again, we see that the task of the jurist is not that of a scientist. Science is the art of prediction (hence the scientific method), legal theory is not. Jurists in their job of theorising about law have no lab. So I predict that the UK courts will follow the Supreme Court's decision in *Patel v Mirza*,[76] but my theory of justice tells me it is wrong. In my role as a barrister in giving advice to a client who wished to litigate the point, what would matter would be the prediction, not the theory. In my role as jurist the opposite is true.

XIII. POLLOCK AS JURIST

Pollock made three kinds of error, two analytical, the other normative. They are still common today.

The first analytical error was in what he thought constitutes law generally, and the law of torts in particular. Holmes's predictive theory of law has been discredited for over 70 years, most famously and powerfully demolished by HLA Hart in *The Concept of Law*.[77] No useful purpose would be served here by repeating Hart's devastating critique. Just as the absence of sanctions for breach in relation to large areas of public international law do not prove its non-existence, the abolition of civil recourse would not result in the law of torts in general, or of the obligation to pay damages, ceasing to be. Just as if we shut all the prisons and stopped the giving out of all sanctions there would still be a criminal law, the positive law rights of private law exist because they have been

[75] This seems to be the benchmark employed in J Goudkamp and J Murphy, 'Tort Statutes and Tort Theories' (2015) 131 *LQR* 133 and J Goudkamp and J Murphy, 'The Failure of Universal Theories of Tort Law' (2015) 21 *Legal Theory* 47.

[76] *Patel v Mirza* [2016] UKSC 42, [2017] AC 467.

[77] HLA Hart, *The Concept of Law*, 3rd edn (Oxford, OUP, 2012). The book started life as a series of lectures in 1952.

posited, not because of the existence of civil recourse. Confusion is perhaps more acute in the common law in this regard because the rules were and are (largely) posited through the process of civil recourse. Private law in its essence is the realm of *rights* and *duties*, not of *liabilities* to be sued and *powers* to sue.

That is not to deny that civil recourse is a good and important thing. Nor does it imply that the destruction in the UK of the ability of ordinary people to invoke civil recourse, through the elimination of civil legal aid and the introduction of court fees as a barrier to entry, is anything other than disgraceful. The ability to sue is not, however, a defining feature of the law of torts, and does not distinguish it in any useful way from, say, public law.

The second, and related, analytical error is the failure to understand, or perhaps to take seriously, that the common law of torts is concerned with civil wrongs. This led to several errors of exposition. This assertion leads us into Pollock's normative error, and a consideration of how we classify and compartmentalise law.

One of the roles of the jurist is to bring out and describe the formal distinctions that the law employs. So the distinction between public law duties (such as the duty not to commit insider trading) and private law duties (such as the duty not to trespass on my land) is a formal one. It is tempting (following Pollock) to think that this distinction turns upon how the duty will be enforced, and this thought was also encouraged by Hohfeld when he used the language of rights 'properly so-called' and 'claims' interchangeably. Once, however, we accept that the ability to *claim* (ie bring court proceedings) is not a necessary element of law at all, this cannot be correct. A more promising difference is that where the duty is one of right, the right holder has control, in the sense of the ability to waive the right (ie, give consent to the act that the obligor would otherwise be under a duty not to do). Where the duty is wholly public, and not dependent upon its private law counterpart, this is not true.[78]

Other formal distinctions may be made. All of the Hohfelidan distinctions between different classes of right (claim-rights, powers, privileges, immunities) are formal, telling us nothing at all about what if anything justifies them. The distinction between rights *in rem* and rights *in personam* is also wholly formal. Some more recently have argued that the law of trusts is given its unity by the *form* of rights that constitute a trust (rights that another not use his rights for his own benefit).[79]

The claim that 'the law of torts concerns the secondary obligations generated by the infringement of primary rights' is a formal claim of this kind. That does not make it empty or valueless if what we are trying to do is understand an area of the positive law. We might interpret the Holmes/Pollock view

[78] So if you kiss me with my consent you commit neither the tort nor the crime of battery. The crime is here parasitic upon the private wrong, but need not be so (eg, parking offences).

[79] eg, B Mcfarlane and R Stevens, 'The Nature of Equitable Property' (2009) 4 *Journal of Equity* 1.

that the law of torts concerns (the reversal of?) harm inflicted through fault in a similar way.

The law of contract, by contrast, is given its unity not by its form, but by a reason of justice: agreements ought to be kept. 'Unjust enrichment', if it exists as a single category within private law,[80] would also be united by a reason of justice. These reasons of justice are necessarily independent of the posited law itself.

Where the same reason of justice applies we can analogise across from one case to another. It is only through the appeal to a reason of justice that we can reason that one case is alike another, and so the same result ought to apply in both. So, the importance of the category of 'contract' is not just expository. It also enables us to reason by analogy: 'this is a claim in contract, such claims require feature X, therefore this claim should also require that feature (subject to any countervailing reason creating an exception)'.

Obligations to pay damages following a wrong take their unity from the persistence of the reason underlying the initial primary duty that has been breached. This now takes the form of a duty of next-best compliance: pay damages to ensure the claimant is placed in the position as near as money can do it to the wrong not having been committed.[81] Although this reason of justice has also been stated by different judges in giving judgment,[82] whether it is correct cannot be authoritatively determined by them. This reason of justice can be used to give civil wrongs a unity that is not just formal.

What of the primary rights themselves, upon which the justification for the secondary obligation depends? Pollock seemed to think of the common law as embodying the conventional morality of Englishmen. However, how is it legitimate to compel each of us by force of law to comply with this, even if we concluded that it perfectly reflected true morality?

In order to justify primary rights we require reasons that are of the same form. The question of what rights we have one against another that ought to be given the force of law is an entirely different question from that of how morally virtuous people ought to behave. By thinking that what the law as to our rights ought to be was answered by reference to the moral question of blameworthiness of conduct, Pollock was making a basic error.[83]

[80] Which I deny: see R Stevens, 'The Unjust Enrichment Disaster' (2018) 134 *LQR* 574.

[81] For several authors expressing the same idea in different terms, see N MacCormick, *Legal Right and Social Democracy* (Oxford, OUP, 1984) 212; E Weinrib, *The Idea of Private Law* (Cambridge, MA, Harvard University Press, 1995) 135; J Raz, 'Personal Practical Conflicts' in P Baumann and M Betzler (eds), *Practical Conflicts: New Philosophical Essays* (Cambridge, CUP, 2004); Stevens, *Torts and Rights* (n 52) 59; A Ripstein, 'As if it Never Happened' (2007) 48 *William and Mary Law Review* 1968. The best long treatment of the idea is J Gardner, 'What is Tort Law For? Part 1: The Place of Corrective Justice' (2011) 30 *Law and Philosophy* 1.

[82] *Livingstone v Rawyards Coal Co* (1880) 5 App Cas 25 (HL) 39 (Lord Blackburn), which is another case inexplicably omitted by Pollock from his torts textbook.

[83] For the same error, see Stevens, *Torts and Rights* (n 52) 332.

In a world of absolute liberties each of us would be free to stab one another in the neck, to steal a farmer's crops and to shout 'Fire'! in crowded theatres. Freedom for the pike is death for the minnow,[84] but we are all of us both pikes and minnows. In order for each of us to be able to choose how to live our own lives, it is necessary that we have rights against others that they refrain from interfering with this freedom. We have a right to be secure from interference by others in order that we may be free. The correlative general duties are ones to refrain from behaving in certain ways. This results in a system of equal freedom.

Some rights are not logically required by this reason of independence. It is possible to imagine a world of intelligent sharks, unable to possess material objects, who could make no use of things external to themselves. Human beings do not find themselves in such a world. The challenge is then how can we have rights to things external to ourselves, which are marvellously useful, in a way that is compatible with the freedom of each other?

Reasoning that we ought to have rights that enable each of us to be independent entails that I ought to have a right that you do not punch me on the nose, or negligently damage my lorry, or call me an axe murderer in print. It does not entail that I should have a right that you cure my illness, mend my broken bicycle, or speak well of me.

If we see rights as justified by seeking to ensure that each of us has equal freedom to live our lives, the absence of general rights that others take positive steps to confer benefits upon us follows as a matter of course. The point here is not that positive duties limit the freedom of the person subject to the duty, when a duty to refrain from acting in a certain way does not. All rights limit the freedom of others. Rather, your punching me interferes with my independence in a way that your failure to cure my illness does not. Similarly, this line of rights-based reasoning entails that the standard of duty imposed should be objective and uniform, personal blameworthiness or lack of virtue is not in issue.

The positive law, fortunately, generally reflects what it ought to be in this regard. The maxim of Jesus Christ that we should 'Do unto others as you would have them do unto you'[85] is, on this view, a maxim of personal morality not interpersonal moral right. The man who fails to pick up the baby drowning in an inch of water when he could, if he chose, easily rescue it is what is technically known as an 'arsehole'. He behaves in a way that is, as a matter of personal morality, deeply wrong and reprehensible. However, he does not, by his failure to rescue, wrong the child.

Again, the claim here is not that it is impossible to conceive, as a matter of analytic truth, of posited legal duties of easy rescue owed to other people.

[84] I Berlin, *Two Concepts of Liberty* (Oxford, Clarendon Press, 1958).

[85] Matthew 7:12; Luke 6:31.

We can imagine a system of positive law that imposed such duties, and we have a name for it: France.[86] Rather, the claims are that our common law is not such a system and that this conforms with our notions of interpersonal justice as a matter of morality.

Pollock's greater failure was not that his account of the law had a poor fit with the positive law of his time (although it did). Rather it was that he put forward an account with nothing normatively to be said for it, which has continued to have influence. The job of the jurist is not merely to set out the positive law facts that he got wrong, but to explain why a better account of what the law *ought* to be is available, that happily has a closer, but not perfect, fit with how it is.

XIV. ADDISON

It is tempting, but wrong, to forgive Pollock's introduction of errors as being the result of being a pioneer. After all, if you are first, you are bound to make mistakes that will later be corrected by others.

At the time of Pollock's text, the only English torts textbook in existence was *Addison on the Law of Torts*. This had been first published in 1860 by CG Addison, who had also produced a text on the law of contracts. This was a much more detailed practitioners' text of around twice the length of Pollock's work. It ran through eight editions, with the last in 1906.

Addison died in 1866, at the relatively young age of 54, and personally produced only the first two editions. The remaining six editions were produced by a variety of hands. The book suffered over time from having multiple successive authors, with no sole author for more than one edition. The title of the first two editions was *Wrongs and their Remedies*, with a sub-title of 'A Treatise on the Law of Torts'. After Addison's death it was styled '*Addison on the Law of Torts*'.

By far the most interesting edition is the fifth, by Lewis Cave QC (who also edited two editions of Addison's contract text) in 1879, the last before Pollock produced his work. Cave was appointed to the High Court bench shortly thereafter, which explains why he produced no further editions. He re-wrote the opening of the book concerning the nature of torts, and much else. He defined torts in terms of wrongs. He described these wrongs as the infringement of a right without lawful excuse. He emphasised from the outset the importance of the principle *ex damno sine injuria non oratorio actio*: 'it is essential to an action of tort that the act complained of should under the circumstances be legally wrongful as regards the person complaining; that is, it must prejudicially affect him in some legal right: merely that it will, however directly, do him harm in

[86] See J Kortmann, *Altruism in Private Law* (Oxford, OUP, 2005).

his interests, is not enough'.[87] He begins by listing the general rights we have one against another:

- Of Rights
  - Private Rights
    - Rights of personal security and liberty
    - Rights of reputation
    - Rights of property
      - Rights of trading
      - Rights of Contract
  - Public Rights
    - Actions for Public Nuisance
    - Public Officers
  - Statutory Rights and Duties

The error in that list is the inclusion of a 'right of trading', which is actually merely a liberty to trade, although that had not yet been authoritatively settled. Deceit, a difficult category for a rights theorist, has been omitted. Negligence as a separate 'tort' does not appear in the book, and neither do other 'wrongs' unrelated to any specific right, such as conspiracy. Overall, it is a sensible structure. The book is light on theory, as one would expect in a practitioners' text, but the implicit assumption of what a tort is, and how this determined the ordering of the subject, is sound.

Pollock makes no reference to Addison in his own textbook. In his review of Winfield's *The Province of the Law of Tort*,[88] he refers to 'Mr Addison for whose judgment nobody now cares a farthing (his book on Torts was only less bad than his book on Contracts)'.[89] He did so in criticising Addison's view (that Pollock and Winfield rejected) that the law of torts was incapable of reduction to a single principle against causing harm.

Looking back to Addison, therefore, we see that it was Pollock who introduced mistakes into English law that were not previously there, errors with which we are still living. It was his fault.

XV. LESSONS

Landon, the editor of the two editions of *Pollock on Torts* after Pollock's death, 'left the text and Pollock's footnotes exactly as they stood in the last edition

[87] L Cave (ed), *Wrongs and their Remedies: Being a Treatise on the Law of Torts*, 5th edn (London, Stevens & Sons, 1879) 1.
[88] Winfield, *The Province of the Law of Tort* (n 57).
[89] F Pollock, 'Book Review' (1931) 47 *LQR* 588, 589.

which he himself produced in 1929, save where the treatment is obviously out of date, when the new matter is indicated … by square brackets'.[90] As Landon himself stated in an obituary for Winfield, the book 'never quite shook off the fetters of the mid-Victorian era', which he contrasted with the 'lively and sometimes homely style' of Winfield's own book.[91] During Pollock's life, hardly anything changed from one edition to the next, so that the chapter on negligence, first written in 1886, 'remained in form, and to a large extent in substance, identical in all the editions from the first to the [last]'.[92] The American material in particular dated badly, as Pollock made no serious effort to keep it up to date. Winfield, in editing three editions of *Pollock on Contracts*, had taken the same approach as Landon, save for the addition of a chapter on damages that Pollock had not included. Treating law texts as Holy Writ that cannot be altered inevitably leads to their demise, and there were no further editions after these editors. (We may contrast *Dicey, Morris and Collins on the Conflict of Laws*, first published in 1896, now in its fifteenth edition,[93] still the leading work and showing no sign of faltering. In the eighth edition in 1967 Morris personally re-wrote the entire book. Without such occasional complete revision by a single hand, textbooks soon become tired and internally inconsistent. Little trace of Dicey's original work survives, despite the title.)

Great lawyers resemble great historians, not great philosophers. In philosophy, the towering figures of the past are all still read and reflected upon. Aristotle, Kant and Mill may be wrong, but they are not out of date. Great historians may sometimes live on through their prose (Gibbon) or because they are the only source for a factual account (Livy), but rarely from one generation to the next because of the brilliance of their analysis. If someone such as Pollock, a more important and prolific jurist than almost any of us can aspire to be, is now so much dust, what hope of immortality (or even some citations after retirement) is there for the rest of us?

Three answers may be given. The first is that we can all, at most, aspire to say one, or at most two, things of any significance. Wesley Newcomb Hohfeld was dead at 39, but his two articles on the nature of rights (which are really one and a half) outweigh the thousands of pages more that Pollock produced. Being prolific is not the point.

The second is that we can live on through the education of the young. The biggest influences on my legal life are those who have taught me (a process that did not end when I stopped being a student), not necessarily those whose work

[90] PA Landon (ed), *Pollock on Torts*, 15th edn (London, Stevens & Sons, 1951) v. Subject to an infamously vicious review by JG Fleming, 'Book Review' (1954) 1 *Sydney Law Review* 282.

[91] A McNair, 'Professor Sir Percy Winfield (1878–1953)' [1954] *CLJ* 80, 84.

[92] Landon, *Pollock on Torts* (n 91) 326.

[93] L Collins (ed), *Dicey, Morris and Collins on the Conflict of Laws*, 15th edn (London, Sweet & Maxwell, 2017).

I have read. Unfortunately for Pollock, he seems to have been a terrible teacher.[94] Lawson says of Pollock's time at Oxford:

> [I]t would have made little difference to the teaching of law in Oxford if Pollock had never been there. He was a bad lecturer who drew very poor audiences; so far as can be ascertained, he never taught any undergraduate in a private tutorial hour ... [and] 'his well-known difficulty of making oral communication with anyone with whom he was not naturally *en rapport* made him to all intents and purposes useless as a teacher.'[95]

Third, looking to the law to give us immortality is asking too much of it. The field of writers on the law is now much more crowded than it was in Pollock's day, and we have all been working busily away upon it. The law is stimulating and, despite cuts to academic pensions, provides most of us with enough to live on. That is enough.

[94] Duxbury, *Frederick Pollock and the English Juristic Tradition* (n 2) 53–54.

[95] FH Lawson, *The Oxford Law School 1860–1965* (Oxford, Clarendon Press, 1968) 72–73, taken from Duxbury, *Frederick Pollock and the English Juristic Tradition* (n 2) 53.

4

Professor Sir John Salmond (1862–1924): An Englishman Abroad

MARK LUNNEY*

NO SERIOUS TORT scholar in the Anglo-American world is unfamiliar with the notion that Sir John Salmond was an important tort scholar. Yet it is striking to reflect on the fact that Salmond's reputation as a tort scholar stems from only one piece of, albeit substantial, academic work: his treatise on the law of torts, first published in 1907.[1] In one sense, it is difficult to measure Salmond's influence, because while he did personally write and edit the first six editions of the text, it continued to be published for another 70 years after his death, with three editors of great distinction contributing to its longevity.[2] But whatever the efforts of its subsequent editors, they built on a platform of academic success and tribute that attached to Salmond's original text. This chapter reflects on some questions about Salmond's work: its relationship to his *Jurisprudence* text, why the book became so popular, and what influence, if any, the environment in which the book was written had on the final product.

I. A WINNER FROM THE START

Salmond published *Law of Torts* in 1907. According to RFV Heuston, a later editor of the book, the first edition was actually printed in New Zealand,

* Thanks are due to the participants in the Scholars of Tort Law workshop at Worcester College, Oxford, in April 2018 for helpful comments.

[1] For a full list of Salmond's published output, see A Frame, *Salmond: Southern Jurist* (Wellington, Victoria University Press, 1995) app A.

[2] WTS Stallybrass edited the 7th–10th editions, RFV Heuston the 11th–21st (and final) editions and RW Buckley the 19th–21st editions. The only other named editor was RS Chambers, who contributed with Heuston to the 18th edition. Not all of the later editions were well received: for critical reviews, see Review by J Spencer, '*Salmond on Torts*, 16th edn (1973)' (1975) 34 *CLJ* 334, and Review by A Hutchison, '*Salmond and Heuston on the Law of Torts*, 18th edn (1981)' (1982) 33 *Northern Ireland Legal Quarterly* 197. Much of this criticism derived from Heuston's editorial decision to maintain as far as possible the text he inherited (see Review by J Mesher, '*Salmond on the Law of Torts*, 17th edn (1977)' (1979) 30 *Northern Ireland Legal Quarterly* 82, 85).

though under the imprint of the London publishing firm Stevens & Haynes. The publishers rejected Salmond's offer to sell them the copyright and the book was effectively self-published, a decision apparently bemoaned many years later when through many editions it had been an outstanding commercial success.[3] At the time of its publication, Salmond had just ended his short tenure as founding Professor of Law at Victoria College in Wellington, New Zealand (now Victoria University of Wellington). Early in 1907, Salmond had been appointed as counsel to the Office of Law Drafting, and while he continued to teach at Victoria College after this appointment, he never again had a full-time academic role, becoming Solicitor-General of New Zealand in 1910 and a judge of the Supreme Court of New Zealand in 1920, a post he held until his death in 1924. While he discharged these offices with great distinction, they did not directly contribute to his standing as a tort scholar and will not be further discussed here.[4] Rather, the genesis of Salmond's 1907 treatise lies in his earlier career.[5] An Englishman born of Scottish parents, Salmond moved with his parents to Dunedin in New Zealand when he was 13. He obtained a BA and MA from the University of Otago in the early 1880s, before winning a scholarship to study law in England, which he did at University College London. Having successfully completed his degree, he returned to New Zealand, where after some delay he lectured in constitutional law at the University of Otago and began legal practice. His academic bent was clear, as during this time he published a number of articles and two collections of essays on constitutional law and jurisprudence.[6]

In 1897 Salmond moved to Adelaide in South Australia to take up a chair in the relatively new School of Law at the University of Adelaide.[7] During his time in Adelaide, in 1902 he published the first edition of his text on jurisprudence, a work that incorporated and built on many of the ideas in his *Principles of Jurisprudence* almost 10 years earlier.[8] While these works contained considerable discussions about the nature of civil liability, their focus was (broadly) analytical jurisprudence rather than practical civil law. This is not to say that the discussions were abstract – Salmond's aim was to explain the jurisprudence behind a working legal system – but the concern was not with legal rules in specific contexts. This narrower focus was the concern of the *Law of Torts*, and also of

[3] RFV Heuston, 'Sir John Salmond' (1963) 2 *Adelaide Law Review* 220, 222.

[4] For detail on this part of his career, see Frame, *Salmond: Southern Jurist* (n 1) chs 7–15.

[5] For greater detail, see ibid chs 1–6.

[6] JW Salmond, *Essays in Jurisprudence and Legal History* (London, Stevens & Haynes, 1891); JW Salmond, *The First Principles of Jurisprudence* (London, Stevens & Haynes, 1893). While published by a well-known London publisher, they were printed in Scotland and New Zealand respectively, a practice that, as noted, was followed for the *Law of Torts*.

[7] On Salmond's time in Adelaide, see V Edgeloe, 'The Adelaide Law School 1883–1983' (1983) 9 *Adelaide Law Review* 1, 12–15; Frame, *Salmond: Southern Jurist* (n 1) ch 5.

[8] AWB Simpson, 'The Salmond Lecture' (2007) 38 *Victoria University of Wellington Law Review* 669, 671.

his *Principles of the Law of Contracts*,[9] published posthumously after completion by Winfield. As Salmond wrote in the preface to the first edition of *Law of Torts*, his aim was to set forth 'the principles of the law of torts with as much precision, coherence and system as the subject admits of, and with as much detailed consideration as is necessary to make the work one of practical utility'.[10]

The reviews of the first edition were generally favourable, but varied depending on the nature of the publication. Practitioner and professional journals gave praise, but not necessarily because it was thought Salmond achieved his stated aim. The *Law Magazine and Review* noted Salmond was 'an academic lawyer rather than a practical one', and that the work's utility was 'to the student rather than a busy lawyer looking up points'.[11] A similar view was taken in the *South African Law Journal*: while the book was 'no compilation or stringing together of judgments, but a systematic and scientific exposition of the principles of the law of torts', it was thought it 'may contain too much historical matter for those who merely require a legal guide-book' but would be 'of the greatest assistance to the thoughtful lawyer'.[12] Reviews in the two major Anglo-American publications adopted a slightly different tone. In the *Harvard Law Review*, 'JS' (probably Jeremiah Smith) thought it 'worthy to be placed on the same shelf with Pollock or Clerk & Lindsell'.[13] While the book had the 'great merits of condensation and clearness – two qualities which are apt to go together', the author had done his own thinking and had expressed his thoughts in his own words. Although the book was conventional ('there is no striving after new or odd ways of "putting things", no love of novelty for its own sake'), no difficulties were avoided and the method of general statements and definitions followed by specific applications and illustrations clearly distinguished between what the law was and what the author thought it should be.[14] The discussions were 'always thoughtful and stimulating', even if they did not always convince.[15] The most detailed review was, perhaps, the least favourable. Thomas Beven, author of a contemporary text on negligence, thought the book presented the subject 'in a particularly concise and clear way' but did not shed much light on the moot problems of law.[16] As Beven noted, Salmond's book was one of 10 on torts published as new books or in new editions in the previous four years, and he judged it in light of this new plethora of material:

> The whole is well, carefully, accurately and thoroughly done. Indeed, had this book been published thirty years ago it would have marked a distinct advance on anything

[9] P Winfield, *Principles of the Law of Contracts* (London, Sweet & Maxwell, 1927).
[10] JW Salmond, *Law of Torts* (London, Stevens & Haynes, 1907) v.
[11] Review, '*Law of Torts* (1907)' (1907) 33 *Law Magazine and Review* 118.
[12] Review, '*Law of Torts* (1907)' (1907) 24 *South African Law Journal* 477. See also Review by J Adamson, '*Law of Torts* (1907)' (1908–9) 20 *Juridical Review* 84.
[13] Review by JS, '*Law of Torts* (1907)' (1908–09) 22 *Harvard Law Review* 69, 70.
[14] ibid.
[15] ibid 71.
[16] Review by T Beven, '*Law of Torts* (1907)' (1908) 24 *LQR* 84.

> previously written upon torts, but the last thirty years have witnessed a revolution in law-book writing, and the standard now required is so far in advance of what it once was that Mr Salmond must be content to take his place as one of a number of very capable writers.[17]

For Beven it was the student 'and also the practitioner who is a bit shaky in his groundwork' to whom the book would be of much service.[18]

The differing views of the academic and professional audiences reflect the transition that was taking place in legal writing at the end of the nineteenth century. Beven's reference to 'the last thirty years' in his review is a testament to the new kind of academic treatise that was being published in that period in an attempt at a scientific explanation of the common law.[19] Busy professionals had, then as now, much less time and interest in the philosophical grounding of the law with which they had to work. It was Salmond's didactic explanation of the law that they valued. Conversely, academic audiences were looking for something more, some kind of wider general theorising about the law of tort. Perhaps Salmond's *Law of Torts* was viewed slightly differently by academic reviewers because they knew Salmond had more to offer in this respect than he showed in his *Law of Torts*.

II. THE STRUCTURE OF THE *LAW OF TORTS*

Salmond makes no attempt in the treatise to explain the structure he adopted in *Law of Torts*. The book begins with a chapter on general principles of liability, moves to parties and remedies, and then describes, in a series of chapters, torts dealing with land (trespass, nuisance, interference with servitudes), goods, injuries to the person, liability for dangerous property, injuries to domestic relations, defamation and a miscellany of chapters at the end (deceit, intimidation), before finishing with the catch-all 'Residuary Forms of Injury'. He retained this structure throughout all six editions for which he was personally responsible. What is surprising about the structure of the book is not that it is in the form that it is. Rather, it is that Salmond made no attempt to explain the structure, because it reflects his fundamental views about civil liability. The structure of *Law of Torts* is derived from Salmond's analysis of legal relations contained in his earlier writings, in particular his earlier textbook on *Jurisprudence*. As Cook noted in 1919, 'one might read his *Torts* through and never realise that any such analysis as that found in the *Jurisprudence* [*sic*] had ever been made'.[20] Yet the

[17] ibid.
[18] ibid 85.
[19] See, generally, M Lobban, 'Mapping the Common Law: Some Lessons from History' (2014) 1 *New Zealand Law Review* 21, 58–60.
[20] WW Cook, 'Hohfeld's Contribution to the Science of Law' (1918–9) 28 *Yale Law Journal* 721, 729.

position is more complicated than Cook portrays. Certainly, there are parts of the book where the analytical jurisprudence propounded by Salmond could have been used to explain features of the law,[21] but Salmond's analysis is more than 'an academic exercise of theoretical interest only'.[22] Rather, his previous work was the reason the *Law of Torts* was structured the way it was.

In *Jurisprudence*, Salmond explained liability, including civil liability, through a series of correlative rights and duties of varying nature. The detail of this jurisprudence is not important for this chapter,[23] but it must be understood that Salmond's focus in his jurisprudential work was to explain the law as 'the rules recognised and acted on in courts of justice'.[24] Those rules were not simply commands issued by the state to its subjects as recognised under Austinian theory, but were also 'principles of right and wrong so far as recognised and enforced by the state in the essential function of administering justice'.[25] In maintaining this wider sense of right within a political community, the state applied the sanction of physical force in two different ways: enforcing rights, or punishing wrongs. The civil law was concerned with the former. In a civil claim, the claimant claimed a right that was secured by the court by the pressure of a remedy.[26]

A key question, then, was the content of the rights that would be enforced by the courts in this manner. Salmond first addressed this issue in his *First Principles of Jurisprudence* in 1893. At this stage of his thinking, Salmond had taken a different view about the primacy of rights in descriptions of the role of civil law:

> Now remembering the intimate relation shown in the last chapter to subsist between right, rights, wrongs and duties, it is clear that we may regard the administration of justice from the point of view of any of these. Instead of the definition already given, we may say that this function of the State consists in the protection of rights, the enforcement of duties, or the application of remedies to wrongs. The last of these is the most generally convenient, for the administration of justice has regard primarily to wrongs and only secondarily to rights and duties. The fact which puts the State in motion is not that a person has a right or is subject to a duty, but that he has suffered or inflicted a wrong.[27]

It is no surprise that when Salmond turned to examine each of these concepts in more detail, he began with liability, not rights. Moreover, when he did turn to

[21] ibid.

[22] A Dickey, 'Hohfeld's Debt to Salmond' (1971) 10 *University of Western Australia Law Review* 59, 64.

[23] On Salmond's analytical jurisprudence, see Simpson, 'The Salmond Lecture' (n 8); G Postema, *Legal Philosophy in the Twentieth Century: The Common Law World* (London, Springer, 2011) 18–25; G Postema, 'Legal Positivism: Early Foundations' in A Marmor (ed), *The Routledge Companion to Philosophy of Law* (Abingdon, Routledge, 2012) 44–45.

[24] JW Salmond, *Jurisprudence or The Theory of Law* (London, Stevens & Haynes, 1902) 11.

[25] ibid 55.

[26] ibid 68–69.

[27] Salmond, *The First Principles of Jurisprudence* (n 6) 48–49.

discuss the elements of rights, the content was abstract.[28] But more detail was provided in Salmond's discussion of property and obligations. In noting that wrongdoing resulted in a change to a person's interests, interests were defined as

> the aggregate of all the various elements or constituents of my well-being, the sum total of all those existing facts or circumstances which are advantageous to me; for example, my life, my health, my liberty, my reputation, my relations to other persons, and my power to make use of material objects.[29]

Salmond later divides interests into internal and external, the former encompassing life, health, freedom, and bodily and mental comfort, with the last of these including reputation, domestic relations, obligations, commercial or economic interests (eg goodwill), and real and corporeal property.[30]

When Salmond wrote his *Jurisprudence* text 10 years later his thinking had moved on. There was no ambivalence about the purpose of the administration of justice: it was the use of the physical force of the state in enforcing rights and punishing violations of them.[31] It was from this base that Salmond devised his famous series of correlatives and synonyms around rights, duties, wrongs, immunities, privileges and disabilities. Interests retained a place but as the foundation of rights, and rights needed to have an object.[32] The objects of the chief classes of legal rights were largely those that had been set out in 1893 as interests, albeit in a different order: rights over material things, rights in respect of one's own person (including a right not to be coerced or deceived contrary to one's desires or interests), the right of reputation, rights in respect of domestic relations, rights in respect of other rights (obligation in the 1893 version), rights over immaterial property (goodwill, trademarks, etc) and rights to services (including the *per quod servitium amisit* action and, rather curiously, a contract between physician and patient).[33]

It is unnecessary for present purposes to evaluate the rights' base that, by 1902, Salmond saw as the basis of civil law. Yet one striking question remains. Given the long journey that Salmond had made to reach this intellectual position, why was virtually none of it included in the *Law of Torts* five years later?[34] The most likely explanation is that Salmond saw the *Law of Torts*, as he asserted in the introduction, as a work having practical utility.

[28] ibid book II, ch 3, 202. Hence the very general statement that 'Every right is a right to the maintenance or advancement of some interest of him whose right it is'.

[29] ibid 175.

[30] ibid 180–85.

[31] Salmond, *Jurisprudence or The Theory of Law* (n 24) 217.

[32] ibid 227.

[33] ibid 227–30.

[34] There was no significant change, at least to this part of Salmond's thinking, in the second edition of *Jurisprudence*, also published in 1907 (JW Salmond, *Jurisprudence or The Theory of the Law*, 2nd edn (London, Stevens & Haynes, 1907). cf Pollock, who, in his initial classifications of wrongs, considered them as affecting various aspects of person and property without making it the basis of his preferred classification: F Pollock, *The Law of Torts: A Treatise on the Principles of Obligations Arising From Civil Wrongs in the Common Law* (London, Stevens & Sons, 1887) 5–9.

Traditional exposition of the common law in terms of rights protected did not always engage with the practical detail of how these rights were enforced in the courtroom.[35] If Salmond wanted his text to be practical, the kind of analytical jurisprudence that underlay his conclusions on rights would not necessarily fit that criterion, so he left it out. The book thus starts with a chapter on general principles of liability – the discussion of which had preceded rights in his *Principles of Jurisprudence* in 1893 but came several chapters after it in *Jurisprudence*. In 1893 Salmond the practitioner had recognised that the machinery of the state was usually invoked only when there was a wrong which had caused harm, and it no doubt seemed sensible to begin *Law of Torts* with a discussion of liability. None of this detracts from the notion that Salmond's structure in *Law of Torts* is based on the examples of rights he gave in 1902. Chapters V, VI, VII, VIII and IX (trespass to land, nuisance and interference with servitudes) and chapter X (conversion and injury to chattels) concern rights over material things; chapter XI (injuries to the person) covers rights in respect of one's own person; chapter XIII (injuries to domestic relations) deals with rights in respect of domestic relations and rights to services; and chapter XIV (defamation) covers the right of reputation. But the transfer of identified rights in *Jurisprudence* to *Law of Torts* is not complete. Deceit and injurious falsehood have their own chapter in *Law of Torts* and are not part of injuries to the person (as suggested in *Jurisprudence*). Moreover, injury to immaterial property is included in the final chapter on residuary forms of injury, where it sits, rather unhappily, with inducing breach of contract and breach of statutory duty, where any underlying links between the rights in issue is unexplored. But the most obvious outlier is chapter XII on liability for dangerous property. This kind of liability cut across several rights identified by Salmond in his earlier work, and is a recognition that, at least for practical purposes, some mention had to be made of some kind of generalised liability for negligence, an issue Salmond struggled with when writing the first two editions of *Law of Torts*.

III. SALMOND AND GENERAL THEORIES OF LIABILITY

Writing in the *Oxford History of the Laws of England*, Lobban notes that Salmond was the main rival text writer opposing Pollock's views as to the existence of universal duties requiring persons to avoid causing intentional or negligent harm without lawful justification or excuse.[36] For Salmond, such propositions did not accurately reflect the law as administered in the courts.

[35] Lobban, 'Mapping the Common Law: Some Lessons from History' (n 19) 21, 24.

[36] M Lobban, 'Tort' in Cornish et al (eds), *The Oxford History of the Laws of England*, Vol XII: *1820–1914* (Oxford, OUP, 2010) 893. See also G Williams, 'The Foundations of Tortious Liability' (1939) 7 *CLJ* 111; Lobban, 'Mapping the Common Law: Some Lessons from History' (n 19) 59–60.

Rather, the law of torts did not consist of these wide general principles subject to exceptions but was represented by a body of rules establishing specific injuries, and 'it was for my adversary to prove that the case falls within some specific and established rule of liability, and not for me to defend myself by proving that it is within some specific and established rule of justification or excuse'.[37] Mitchell makes the same point, something he explains as attributable in part to the different aims of Pollock and Salmond in writing their texts.[38] However, both Lobban and Mitchell cite from Salmond's second edition of 1910, because, as Mitchell notes in passing,[39] Salmond did not make this argument in the first edition. In fact, he took a diametrically opposite approach. In both editions Salmond discussed the notion of *damnum sine injuria*, but in the first edition he finishes with examples whereas in the second he raises the question about the nature of tortious liability. This is not the only fundamental change in this introductory section. When discussing the existence of a duty of care in negligence, in the first edition, after noting the variety of situations in which a duty may exist, he continued:

> In the present connection, however, there is one question as to this matter which may be appropriately considered: Is the duty of taking care one in which the law for special reasons establishes an exemption from it; or on the contrary is it the general rule that no duty of care exists, save when the law sees fit to establish it in special cases. On this question there is no adequate authority but on principle it is submitted that the first of these alternatives is correct, and that whenever any form of damage is of such a nature as to be actionable when done intentionally it is also actionable when done negligently save when an exemption from such liability is especially established by law. Such exemptions are no doubt numerous and important, but it would seem clear that they are exceptions and not the general rule.[40]

This section was omitted in the second and later editions.

Salmond did not acknowledge the changes he made to the introductory chapter in the preface to the second edition, but he did acknowledge that although Pollock held a contrary view that he would 'gladly accept as affording a comprehensive and logical basis for the law of torts', the actual contents of the legal system were contrary to this view.[41] The reference to Pollock is instructive, as there is good reason for thinking that Pollock's work influenced Salmond's thinking in the lead-up to the first edition of his own textbook. In his first edition of his textbook on torts Pollock explained tort law in terms of duties: 'And what

[37] JW Salmond, *The Law of Torts: A Treatise on the English Law of Liability for Civil Injuries*, 2nd edn (London, Stevens & Haynes, 1910) 9. For criticism that this approach made it impossible to escape from the 'mischiefs' of the forms of action and prevented a coherent articulation of protected rights, see J Gordley, 'The Common Law in the Twentieth Century: Some Unfinished Business' (2000) 88 *California Law Review* 1815, 1846–47.

[38] P Mitchell, *A History of Tort Law 1900–1950* (Cambridge, CUP, 2015) 17–18.

[39] ibid 18.

[40] Salmond, *Law of Torts* (n 10) 22.

[41] Salmond, *The Law of Torts: A Treatise on the English Law of Liability for Civil Injuries* (n 37) 9.

of *alterum non laedere*? "Thou shalt do no hurt to thy neighbor." Our law of torts, with all its irregularities, has for its main purpose nothing else than the development of this precept'.[42] Salmond produced something very similar in the first edition of his text:

> The law of torts exists for the purpose of preventing men from hurting one another, whether in respect of their property, their persons, their reputations, or anything else which is theirs. The fundamental principle of this branch of the law is: *Alterum non laedere* – to hurt nobody by word or deed. An action of tort, therefore, is usually a claim for pecuniary compensation in respect of the damage so suffered.[43]

The first edition then proceeded to a description of situations of *damnum sine injuria*, which cast immediate doubt on the generality of the principle just espoused as the foundation of the law of tort. Salmond recognised the difficulty but, whilst acknowledging the exceptions were various, proposed three general grounds of exemption, presumably to make it consistent with a general theory of liability for harm.[44] As noted, this was jettisoned in the second edition in favour of a law of torts of specific rules of liability, and the situations where no liability for harm arose were not only various but now 'not capable of exhaustive definition'. But the underlying general principle – *alterum non laedere* – was retained in all future editions for which Salmond was responsible.[45] In hindsight, Salmond could have arrived at a more consistent position by making more explicit the connection between property, persons, reputations – things which were theirs – and *damnum sine injuria*. In other words, his carefully considered jurisprudential position that rights, not duties, defined civil law could have explained why the law was the way it was.[46] Whatever the reason that Salmond never explicitly made the connection throughout the six editions he wrote, it is tempting to think that the initial difficulties of the first edition came from not wanting to deviate too much from the doyens of the scientific analysis of tort law, Pollock and Holmes.[47] Even when the second edition made something of a break, it did so on the basis of orthodoxy rather than through conviction in his own alternative structure.

[42] Pollock, *The Law of Torts: A Treatise on the Principles of Obligations Arising From Civil Wrongs in the Common Law* (n 34) 9.

[43] Salmond, *Law of Torts* (n 10) 7.

[44] ibid 8.

[45] The inconsistency was implicitly noted in the review in the *Juridical Review* of the third edition of *Law of Torts* (London, Stevens & Haynes, 1912), where the reviewer commented that to Scottish lawyers, 'who have been accustomed to regard the words "*alienum non laedere*" as an authoritative definition of principle underlying this branch of jurisprudence, the opinion of Sir Frederick Pollock will probably appear preferable': Review by GD Valentine, '*Law of Torts*, 3rd edn (1912)' (1912–13) 24 *Juridical Review* 334, 335.

[46] For analysis of this relationship, see JW Singer, 'The Legal Rights Debate in Analytical Jurisprudence from Bentham to Hohfeld' [1982] *Wisconsin Law Review* 975, 1042–49.

[47] On the influence of Pollock and Holmes on Salmond, see Lobban, 'Mapping the Common Law: Some Lessons from History' (n 19) 893; PS Atiyah, 'The Legacy of Holmes Through English Eyes' (1983) 63 *Boston University Law Review* 341, 352.

IV. SALMOND AND CULPABILITY

Apart from actionable damage – whatever the criteria that determined it – Salmond required one other general feature for the imposition of liability: *mens rea*.[48] Here he deviated from Pollock, who did not mention the term in his description of the conditions for liability. The use of a term with a familiar meaning in criminal law was no accident. For Salmond, 'pecuniary compensation is not in itself the ultimate object or a sufficient justification of legal liability'.[49] Rather, liability was imposed so that the creator of the harm could be punished.[50] In *Jurisprudence*, Salmond had made clear that the primary purpose of criminal punishment was deterrence,[51] and although the analysis is not explicitly extended in those works to civil justice, in *Law of Torts* Salmond emphatically restated the deterrent function of compensation.[52] From this perspective, a *mens rea* requirement was necessary, because no one 'can be deterred by a threat of punishment from doing harm and which he did his best to avoid'.[53] There were two forms of *mens rea* sufficient for civil liability – wrongful intent and negligence – and in most cases harm that was actionable if caused intentionally was also wrongful if caused negligently.[54]

While Salmond's views on negligence caused the greater controversy, it is also true that his discussion of intention was problematic. Again, this seems in part because of a reluctance to incorporate the fuller discussion in *Jurisprudence* into the *Law of Torts*. In *Jurisprudence*, Salmond explained that intention was the purpose or design with which an act was done.[55] The distinction between purpose and motive was clearly explained.[56] In *Law of Torts*, however, the only substantive discussion is about the relationship between wrongful intent and malice.[57] He distinguished between the different meanings of malice in determining wrongful intent and motive, noting that the latter was only exceptionally relevant in the law of torts. But his definition of the former required an element of knowledge by a defendant of the wrongfulness of the conduct, something he had explained in detail in *Jurisprudence*[58] but reduced to one sentence in *Law of Torts*. In the latter book, it was something of a sleight of hand to move, as he did,

[48] Salmond, *Law of Torts* (n 10) 9.
[49] ibid 10.
[50] ibid.
[51] Salmond, *Jurisprudence or The Theory of Law* (n 24) 71–82.
[52] Salmond, *Law of Torts* (n 10) 10.
[53] ibid. cf JB Ames, 'Law and Morals' (1908) 22 *Harvard Law Review* 97.
[54] Salmond, *Law of Torts* (n 10) 11.
[55] Salmond, *Jurisprudence or The Theory of Law* (n 24) 413.
[56] ibid 417–19.
[57] Salmond, *Law of Torts* (n 10) 15–18.
[58] Salmond, *Jurisprudence or The Theory of Law* (n 24) 414–15. Note, though, the inconsistency between stating that to trespass on A's land believing it to be one's own was not a wilful wrong (ibid 414) and that it is no defence to an action for trespass to land that the defendant believed the land to be his (ibid 461).

from a position that 'a malicious wrong in this sense is opposed to a negligent wrong and to one committed under an honest though mistaken claim of right' to malice as existing 'where any person wilfully does an act injurious to another without lawful excuse'.[59] This latter formulation – liability for which looks perilously close to a general principle of liability for intentionally caused harm – need not on its face require an act to be done with knowledge of its wrongfulness. To have accepted this, however, could have imposed liability in the absence of *mens rea*, something that was generally impermissible in Salmond's liability scheme. The result was, in effect, an extension of when malice could be implied from conduct – as discussed in the defamation case of *Bromage v Prosser*,[60] which he cited – to knowledge of wrongfulness of conduct.[61] It would have been analytically clearer, if question-begging, to have said that malice in law meant wrongful intention and 'includes any intent which the law deems wrongful and which therefore serves as a ground of liability'.[62]

The majority of Salmond's discussion of the two states of minds that satisfied the *mens rea* requirement is devoted to negligence. Intention and negligence were mutually exclusive, and absent an intention to cause a consequence the only basis to impose liability was negligence.[63] The careless man was 'he who does not care – who is not anxious or not sufficiently anxious that his activities shall not be the cause of loss to others'.[64] While inadvertence was often present, it was *not* the hallmark of negligence: even if consequences were foreseen, as long as they were not intended, liability had to be based on negligence. 'Recklessness' makes only a fleeting reference in the index when discussing liability for inaccurate statements under *Derry v Peek*.[65] The most conceptually difficult part of Salmond's analysis, however, is his view that the term 'negligence' could be used both subjectively (to connote a particular mental attitude) and objectively (to describe conduct produced by that mental attitude).[66] In his view, this dual usage, however, caused no difficulty, 'for negligence in the one sense is necessarily accompanied by negligence in the other also … Negligence in the subjective sense is opposed to wrongful intent; negligence in the objective sense is opposed to intentional wrongdoing'.[67] But lest it be thought this weakened negligence in the subjective sense as a ground of *mens rea*, Salmond emphatically denied that

[59] Salmond, *Law of Torts* (n 10) 15.

[60] *Bromage v Prosser* (1825) 4 B & C 247, 107 ER 1051.

[61] See also Salmond, *Law of Torts* (n 10) 18, where he refers to a person's intention as desiring the 'consequences' of his act (arguably neutral as to knowledge of wrongfulness) and also to the wilful wrongdoer 'who desires to do harm' (suggestive of knowledge of wrongfulness).

[62] Salmond, *Jurisprudence or The Theory of Law* (n 24) 419.

[63] Salmond, *Law of Torts* (n 10) 18–19.

[64] ibid 18.

[65] *Derry v Peek* (1889) 14 App Cas 337 (HL).

[66] Salmond, *Law of Torts* (n 10) 19–20.

[67] ibid 20.

negligence was 'a purely objective fact involving no characteristic or essential mental attitude at all'.[68]

Several questions arise from Salmond's position. First, the lack of concern about distinguishing between subjective and objective uses of negligence suggests Salmond saw no practical problem in the practice. The best evidence of subjective negligence was the failure to comply with an objective external standard of care. The subjective standard was effectively merged in the objective. Nowhere in *Law of Torts* does Salmond suggest that liability could be avoided by a defendant giving evidence that, subjectively, she did not have the necessary *mens rea* requirement for fault-based liability. In fact, in *Jurisprudence*, he accepted that there are times when such evidence is inadmissible. Dealing with the classic justification for an objective external standard of care – the defendant of below average capacity – he accepted that the person who was 'anxious to do the right, and yet may do the wrong, through sheer incapacity for adequate discrimination',[69] would be held liable for negligence. Why? Because the law 'finds it needful to act on general principles and to take no account of idiosyncracies'.[70] As was characteristic of Salmond, this was put down to evidentiary problems:

> In thus refusing to recognise and allow for individual differences of capacity, judgment or discretion, the law is moved by evidential difficulties which would attend the opposite course. It cannot inquire into the secrets of men's characters and capacities, and must therefore judge all men as if they reached the ordinary standard of human nature.[71]

But Salmond saw this as relevant only to the objective 'conduct' component of negligence. He could still maintain that negligence required culpable carelessness, and that 'he who is ignorant or forgetful, notwithstanding a genuine desire to attain knowledge or remembrance, is not negligent'.[72]

Salmond's attempts to maintain both subjective and objective components to negligence struggle to convince and, while he was not alone in holding this position,[73] the contemporary trend was against him.[74] His defence of the subjective standard was required to maintain a symmetry between intention and negligence, something required by systematisers of the law of tort, who saw the unifying theme for liability as based on a guilty mind.[75] Given this, objective

[68] ibid.

[69] Salmond, *Jurisprudence or The Theory of Law* (n 24) 437.

[70] ibid.

[71] ibid 438.

[72] ibid 449.

[73] See, eg, MM Bigelow, *The Law of Torts*, 8th edn (Boston, MA, Little Brown & Co, 1907) 19.

[74] Pollock, for example, noted the views of a 'learned and thoughtful writer Mr JW Salmond' on this point, but preferred his own objective theory as more convenient and more consistent with the authorities: F Pollock, *The Law of Torts: a treatise on the principles of obligations arising from wrongs in the common law*, 9th edn (London, Stevens & Sons, 1912) 450, fn (i).

[75] R Pound, *An Introduction to the Philosophy of Law* (New Haven, CT, Yale University Press, 1922) 157–58.

facts might not tell the whole truth, or at least the whole moral truth, because, to use one of his examples, an open trapdoor that caused injury might be the result of accident, negligence or intention.[76] His structure left no room for overlap: 'negligence was the opposite of intention, and since the latter is a subjective fact the former must also be so'.[77] Whatever the merits of that conclusion – which requires much greater justification than Salmond provides[78] – it could be maintained in practice only by an objective standard of negligent conduct that emasculated the subjective standard of any separate content. To the extent it did not, it was dangerous, as it would leave

> the general security unprotected against that vast amount of dangerous and harmful conduct that results not from inadvertence or indifference but from deficiencies in knowledge, memory, observation, imagination, foresight, intelligence, judgment, quickness of reaction, deliberation, coolness, self-control, determination, courage or the like.[79]

While Salmond was right to point out that context was important in determining negligence, this could comfortably be taken into account by the objective standard, and more abstract questions over the necessity to maintain a rigid division between culpable negligence and intention were left for academic dispute.

Given Salmond's views as previously described, it was inevitable that he would find strict liability problematic. He solved the problem of consistency with the general 'will' theory by saying such situations could be justified (as far as not historical anomalies) as based on a conclusive presumption of negligence. This was done because the difficulties of establishing 'the actual proof of the necessary *mens rea*' would place too great a burden on the claimant and limit the efficiency and certainty of the administration of justice.[80] However, Salmond's views on this subject changed between the writing of the first edition of his text on *Jurisprudence* in 1902 and the second in 1907 (the same year as *Law of Torts* was published). In the first edition, Salmond identified a general ground of absolute liability based on exceptionally dangerous activities (using *Rylands v Fletcher* and examples of non-delegable duties of care), and rejected the notion that these were in fact disguised negligence cases.[81]

By 1907 he abandoned this position, justifying any exceptions under the conclusive presumption of negligence rationale.[82] Perhaps wanting to minimise

[76] Salmond, *Jurisprudence or The Theory of Law* (n 24) 450–51.
[77] ibid 451.
[78] For an explanation of the will theory in this context, see Pound, *An Introduction to the Philosophy of Law* (n 75).
[79] HW Edgerton, 'Negligence, Inadvertence, and Indifference: The Relation of Mental States to Negligence' (1926) 39 *Harvard Law Review Rev* 849, 867.
[80] Salmond, *Law of Torts* (n 10) 11.
[81] Salmond, *Jurisprudence or The Theory of Law* (n 24) 456–57.
[82] Salmond, *Jurisprudence or The Theory of the Law* (n 34) 373.

this anomaly, and despite including *Rylands* as an example of inevitable accident, in *Law of Torts* he set out to show that *Rylands* was an example of fault-based liability. This he did by giving an extended meaning to the act of God defence recognised in *Rylands* itself. Defining the authorities as uncertain (without analysing or even identifying them) and saying there was good reason to interpret *Nichols v Marsland* broadly,[83] a House of Lords' decision applying the defence in a *Rylands* claim, without saying what it was, Salmond propounded the defence as applying to '*any event which could not have been prevented by reasonable care on the part of anyone*'.[84] Hence *Rylands* was only about imposing vicarious liability on the occupier for any negligence of persons lawfully on the premises with the permission of the occupier.

Even if *Rylands* could be explained away as consistent with *mens rea*, not all forms of strict liability could be. Salmond argued in *Law of Torts* that all cases of absolute liability (his term) could be divided into three classes: liability for inevitable accident, liability for inevitable mistake, and vicarious liability. The classification had its difficulties.[85] As inevitable accident was a ground of exoneration and inevitable mistake not so,[86] the symmetry intended by the use of 'inevitable' in both contexts seems to lie in the effect on liability of the claimant's reasonable conduct. As a reviewer of a later edition pointed out, however, 'inevitable' added nothing to the meaning of 'inevitable mistake', because the same rule applied irrespective of whether the mistake was reasonable or not.[87] Salmond adopted a slightly different classification in *Jurisprudence*, where he divided the instances into three different but related categories: mistake of law, mistake of fact, and accident. In both texts, 'accident' or 'inevitable accident' fitted well with the will theory of liability: only culpable conduct should attract liability as satisfying the *mens rea* requirement. But given that mistake, either as to fact or law, or whether inevitable or not, was not a general defence, it was much harder to square with a *mens rea* requirement. In both *Law of Torts*[88] and *Jurisprudence* evidentiary difficulties were again cited as the reason for the rule, but the detailed argument in the latter is unconvincing. Salmond thought the difficulties of making liability dependent on 'well nigh inscrutable conditions touching knowledge or means of knowledge of the law' insuperable: 'Who can say of any man whether he knew the law, or whether during the course of his

[83] *Nichols v Marsland* (1876) 2 Ex D 1 (HL).

[84] Salmond, *Law of Torts* (n 10) 200 (emphasis in original). Pollock's response was that he 'should be glad to think so if I could': Pollock, *The Law of Torts: a treatise on the principles of obligations arising from wrongs in the common law* (n 74) 503.

[85] J Smith, 'Tort and Absolute Liability: Some Changes in Classification II' (1916–17) 30 *Harvard Law Review* 319, 327.

[86] Salmond, *Law of Torts* (n 10) 11–12.

[87] Review by JCM, '*Law of Torts*, 6th edn (1923)' [1924] *Journal of The Society of Public Teachers of Law* 52, 53.

[88] Salmond, *Law of Torts* (n 10) 13.

past life he had an opportunity of acquiring a knowledge of it by the exercise of due diligence?'[89] The next justification was equally unconvincing:

> It is a public declaration by the state of its intention to maintain by force those principles of right and wrong which have already a secure place in the moral consciousness of men. The common law is in great part nothing more than the common honesty and common sense. Therefore although a man may be ignorant that he is breaking the law, he knows very well in most cases he is breaking the rule of right. If not to his knowledge lawless, he is at least dishonest and unjust.[90]

As a justification for a general rule that mistake of law was no defence, this was weak, and Salmond knew it, admitting in the end that there was no justification for the rule.[91] The same might for said for mistake of fact. To say that intentional interference with person, property, reputation or other rightful interest was done at a person's peril irrespective of a good faith and reasonable belief in the presence of a justification, did not explain how such a conception squared with a guilty mind.[92] In the end, Salmond had to admit simply that the success of the rule in civil law 'is due in part to its utility in obviating inconvenient or even impracticable enquiries, and in part to the influence of the conception of redress in minimising the importance of the formal conditions of penal liability'.[93]

Salmond's third example of absolute liability in *Law of Torts* was vicarious liability, one component of which was the liability of a master for his servant's torts. Such liability was justified either because the servant's tort was actually authorised by the master – the ground he had expounded for making a principal liable for the torts of an agent – or because there was negligence by the master in the selection of the employee or in supervising his work.[94] In *Law of Torts* there was no pretence that this reflected reality:

> Very often this presumption does not correspond with the facts; but the difficulty of actually proving some default on the part of the master would be so great, that it is better on the whole to create a legal presumption against the master, and even to make that presumption irrebuttable.[95]

The reason was explained in *Jurisprudence*: the employee could not pay, the employer probably could.[96] To hold the employer free from liability would

[89] Salmond, *Jurisprudence or The Theory of Law* (n 24) 458–59.
[90] ibid 459.
[91] ibid 459–60.
[92] ibid 461.
[93] ibid 462. cf J Smith, 'Tort and Absolute Liability: Suggested Changes in Classification' (1916–17) 30 *Harvard Law Review* 241; J Smith, 'Tort and Absolute Liability: Suggested Changes in Classification II' (1916–17) 30 *Harvard Law Review* 319; J Smith, 'Tort and Absolute Liability: Suggested Changes in Classification III' (1916–17) 30 *Harvard Law Review* 409, suggesting that absolute liability should be placed outside the law of tort.
[94] Salmond, *Law of Torts* (n 10) 78.
[95] ibid.
[96] Salmond, *Jurisprudence or The Theory of Law* (n 24) 468.

disturb a correspondence that was important to civil justice, but this was not the correspondence between *mens rea* and penal redress. It was between the capacity to do harm and the capacity to pay for it. This instrumental view was a long way from Salmond's core jurisprudential beliefs, but one should not be too critical; a convincing rationale for vicarious liability has proved elusive for many tort scholars. But what it does illustrate is that Salmond's tort text was not the place for a full reconciliation of the competing views. While there is considerable overlap, in *Law of Torts* Salmond was largely content to explain strict liability through evidentiary difficulties, something that was more easily comprehensible to the book's intended audience. But in time Salmond's frustration over the presence of liability without any, even vicarious, fault came to the fore in the *Law of Torts*. By the fourth edition in 1916, Salmond bemoaned the persistence of absolute liability, which, together with doubts over the scope of the duty of care, meant that, pending their authoritative settlement, 'any attempt to set forth the law of negligence in any systematic manner must necessarily be provisional'.[97]

Eventually, Salmond's somewhat dogmatic approach to legal developments outside his theory attracted adverse comment. While Salmond had been awarded the Ames Prize in 1910 for *Law of Torts*, American reviewers, by the third edition of 1912, began to note, among fulsome praise, shortcomings in the treatment of tort liability for mental suffering[98] and the absence of a broader treatment of negligence.[99] No doubt to Salmond's chagrin, it was said he had not followed Pollock's analysis of the subject but 'seems rather to have modelled his treatise on that of Addison',[100] a work that was very much less ambitious but also aimed at practitioners. For reasons that are not clear, Salmond also published a 'Summary' of the *Law of Torts*[101] along with the third edition, something that reviewers generally found unnecessary and counterproductive.[102] But if the practical side of *Law of Torts* was winning out, it was doing so at the expense of the wider theory. This is evident in comparing Winfield's review of the sixth edition – Salmond's last – to the seventh, the first edition prepared by Stallybrass. In the first review, Winfield politely notes that care had to be taken to ensure Salmond's text did not increase in size too much[103] and, more generally:

> Passing to other topics in the book, it may be suggested that the last word has yet to be said on the theoretical foundation of the law of torts; nor are we at all satisfied

[97] JW Salmond, *The Law of Torts: A Treatise on the English Law of Liability for Civil Injuries*, 4th edn (London, Stevens & Haynes, 1916) vi.

[98] Review by F Burdick, '*Law of Torts*, 3rd edn (1912)' (1912) 12 *Columbia Law Review* 658.

[99] Review by ERT, '*Law of Torts*, 3rd edn (1912)' (1912–13) 26 *Harvard Law Review* 282.

[100] Burdick, '*Law of Torts*, 3rd edn (1912)' (n 98).

[101] JW Salmond, *A Summary of the Law of Torts* (London, Stevens & Haynes, 1912).

[102] Burdick, '*Law of Torts*, 3rd edn (1912)' (n 98); ERT, '*Law of Torts*, 3rd edn (1912)' (n 99); Review, '*Law of Torts*, 3rd edn (1912)' (1912) 29 *South African Law Journal* 427; Review, '*Law of Torts*, 3rd edn (1912)' (1912) 28 *LQR* 430; cf Valentine, '*Law of Torts*, 3rd edn (1912)' (n 45).

[103] A reference to the section on remoteness of damage, which, as a result of *Re Polemis and Furniss, Withy & Co Ltd* [1921] 3 KB 560 (CA), increased from 10 to 40 pages.

> that the correct way of dealing with negligence in this branch of the law is not to discuss it under two distinct heads, first as one of the conditions grounding liability in various torts, and secondly as an independent tort.[104]

With Salmond dead and a new editor in place, Winfield was far more candid in his criticism of the original text in the seventh edition. Describing the difficulties Stallybrass had to encounter, he laid out the flaws of the text at the end of Salmond's stewardship:

> The first edition of Sir John Salmond's book was published nearly a generation ago. During that period many contributions of considerable value have been made here and in America not only to the general theory of the law of torts but also to its detailed doctrines. It must be confessed that the learned author, probably owing to the pressure of professional duties, took scarcely adequate account of these in his later editions. The last (in 1924) was distinctly disappointing. The section on 'Remoteness of Damage' was distended to forty-one pages of matter, much of which, however appropriate to the pages of a legal periodical, was out of place in a text-book. Theories as to the foundation of liability in tort and as to negligence stood where they were in the first edition, in spite of serious and increasing doubts as to their soundness. There was no improvement in a tendency to describe cases as irreconcilable which had often been rightly regarded by the Courts as distinguishable. And at times the impatience of a jurisprudent with the illogicalities of the Common Law led to broader generalisations than judicial decisions warranted. All this is not said in petty derogation of a great lawyer who has passed from us.[105]

On this reading, the longevity of Salmond's text lay as much in Stallybrass' surgery than in the quality of what Salmond left to him in the last edition he edited.[106] But it must be doubted if the weaknesses Winfield identified bothered the students, practitioners and judges who were now using Salmond. Its utility to them lay elsewhere.

V. THE SUCCESS OF SALMOND

However successful (or not) Salmond was in maintaining arguments over the whole of his general theory of civil liability, in practice Salmond's ability to capture the law in a series of relatively short paragraphs was masterly. Writing in 1960, RFV Heuston stated there were no fewer than 150 passages that had been the subject of express judicial approval in England or elsewhere in the common

[104] Review by P Winfield, '*Law of Torts*, 6th edn (1923)' (1924) 2 *CLJ* 128.

[105] Review by P Winfield, '*Law of Torts*, 7th edn (1928)' (1929) 45 *LQR* 128, 128–29. See also Review by PA Landon, '*Law of Torts*, 7th edn (1928)' (1928) 3 *Bell Yard* 42: 'The whole of Sir John Salmond's work was coloured by his desire to moralise the law of torts, and he fearlessly struggled for his principles against a succession of decisions during the last twenty years which were quite inconsistent with his views'.

[106] Winfield said as much: Winfield, '*Law of Torts*, 7th edn (1928)' (n 105) 129.

law world, and that the number of reported cases in which Salmond was cited by counsel 'is legion'.[107] The text was also credited with indirectly influencing decisions: even though it had been published only two years before, Spencer cited Salmond as representing the strain of academic opinion opposed to strict liability when discussing the decision of the Court of Appeal in *Wing v London General Omnibus Co*[108] rejecting the expansion of *Rylands v Fletcher* liability to the driving of motor vehicles.[109]

There is no doubt that *Law of Torts* was an influential text in the courts from soon after its publication. A search of reported cases in Australian jurisdictions reveals the first references to Salmond by counsel date from 1911[110] and by the judiciary from 1913.[111] While South Australia dominates the early references, by the end of the First World War and beyond Salmond is cited in cases by counsel and judges in all Australian jurisdictions. While most judicial references are supportive, examples can be found of judges expressly disagreeing with propositions expounded by Salmond, which is good evidence that Salmond went considerably further than providing a descriptive summary of the law.[112] In England and Wales, it took longer for Salmond to gain notoriety in the courts, and references seem initially to have been linked to individual judges. The first judicial reference in the authorised reports is by McCardie J in 1917,[113] who cited him five other times in the 1920s but was the only single judge to do so.[114] Scrutton LJ too seems to have been a fan and, from his first citing of *Law of Torts* in *The Koursk*[115] in 1924, was a member of every Court of Appeal bench where Salmond was cited until the mid-1930s.[116] Recognition in the House of Lords took longer – the first citation was not until 1945[117] – but well before then Salmond was regularly being cited by lower courts. Canadian courts were quicker off the mark: the first judicial citation was in 1914[118] and in the Supreme Court in 1919,[119] and Salmond has been regularly cited ever since. Perhaps surprisingly, American courts seem to have been the first of the non-New Zealand courts to

[107] Heuston, 'Sir John Salmond' (n 3) 223.

[108] *Wing v London General Omnibus Co* [1909] 2 KB 652 (CA).

[109] JR Spencer, 'Motor-Cars and the Rule in *Rylands v Fletcher*: A Chapter of Accidents in the History of Law and Motoring' (1983) 42 *CLJ* 65, 74.

[110] *McIntyre v Hams* [1911] SALR 16 (SC).

[111] *Young v Tilley* [1913] SALR 87 (SC).

[112] See, eg, *Young v Tilley* [1913] SALR 87 (SC); *Wardle v McInnes* [1930] SASR 450 (SC).

[113] *Maclenan v Segar* [1917] 2 KB 325 (KBD).

[114] *Baker v James Brothers & Sons Ltd* [1921] 2 KB 674 (KBD); *British Railway Traffic & Electric Co Ltd v The CRC Co Ltd* [1922] 2 KB 260 (KBD); *Transoceanica Societa Italiana di Navigazione v HS Shipton & Sons* [1923] 1 KB 31 (KBD); *Performing Right Society Ltd v Mitchell & Booker (Palais de Danse) Ltd* [1924] 1 KB 762 (KBD); *Gaylor & Pope Ltd v B Davies & Son Ltd* [1924] 2 KB 75 (KBD).

[115] *The Koursk* [1924] P 140 (CA).

[116] Scrutton had taught Salmond as a law student at University College London and was a referee for him for the Chair in Adelaide: Frame, *Salmond: Southern Jurist* (n 1) 24–25, 54.

[117] *Alexander v Tredegar Iron & Coal Co Ltd* [1945] AC 286 (HL) 294 (Viscount Maugham).

[118] *Skubiniuk v Hartman* (1914) 20 DLR 323 (Man QB).

[119] *Herdman v Maritime Coal Co* (1919) 49 DLR 90 (SCC).

incorporate Salmond into judgments, although this may also reflect different conventions as to citing living authors.[120] Whatever the reason, *Law of Torts* was first cited in the District of Columbia Court of Appeals in 1910,[121] and by 1939 had been cited in approximately 50 reported US cases, including a number of citations in the Court of Appeals of New York and one in the US Supreme Court.[122]

Perhaps the most interesting example of practitioner and judicial uptake is Salmond's home jurisdiction, New Zealand. While New Zealand citation of the tort text was the earliest among the major common law jurisdictions – the first references by counsel and judges is in May and July 1908[123] – it did not achieve any kind of supremacy, and other English tort texts were cited with at least the same degree of regularity by New Zealand courts during Salmond's life. This may reflect the sensitivities of citing an author who was playing an active role in the judicial system, both as Solicitor-General[124] and, from 1920, as a judge. In particular, during Salmond's judicial tenure (1920–24), while counsel continued to cite *Law of Torts* in argument (even to Salmond J[125]), there was a noticeable reluctance of the judges of the Supreme Court to cite one of their brethren in judgments.[126] Salmond too was understandably averse as a judge to explicitly citing his own work as an academic, but when the opportunity arose he did profess judicial opinions that coincided with his non-judicial writings. For example, in *Nash v Barnes*, one question was whether an innocent converter who had improved the goods was liable to the true owner for the improved value of the goods. Salmond had argued not in his text,[127] and his judgment adopted both the style and substance of the text in reaching the same conclusion:

> When A converts a chattel by delivering it to B, and B spends money on improving it, and then converts it by refusing to deliver it to the true owner, the owner, whether he

[120] A Braun, 'Burying the Living – The Citation of Legal Writings in English Courts' (2010) 58 *American Journal of Comparative Law* 27; N Duxbury, *Jurists and Judges: An Essay on Influence* (Oxford, Hart Publishing, 2001).

[121] *Sullivan v Capital Traction Co* (1910) 34 App DC 358.

[122] *McGuire v US* 47 S Ct 259, 260 (1927).

[123] *Byrne v Judd* (1908) 27 NZLR 1106 (CA) 1113 (counsel), 1116 (Denniston J), 1130 (Chapman J).

[124] From which position he sometimes argued tort cases on behalf of the Government: *Hill v The King* (1913) 33 NZLR 313 (CA); *Broad v The King* (1914) 33 NZLR 1275 (CA) (accidents at railway crossings).

[125] *Canning v The King* [1924] NZLR 118 (SC) 119.

[126] I have found only two references, one of which (*Connor v Howden* [1924] NZLR 181 (SC) 183 (Hosking J)) simply noted that counsel had accepted as correct the law cited in Salmond on Torts. The only substantive reference is in *Connor v Nelson, Moate & Co* [1925] NZLR 123 (Full Ct) 128, where *Law of Torts* was cited by the Full Court of the Supreme Court on the meaning of possession for occupiers' liability. Citation rates increased again after his death: there were two first-instance judicial citations in each of 1926 and 1927 (*Mazzola v Turnbull & Jones Ltd* [1926] NZLR 380 (SC) 382, 384 (Reed J); *Public Trustee v Waihi Gold-Mining Co Ltd* [1926] NZLR 449 (SC) 456, 458 (Stringer J); *Irwin v Hannah* [1927] NZLR 7 (SC) 10 (Alpers J); *Thomson v Hamilton* [1927] NZLR 11 (SC) 13 (Sim J)) and the Court of Appeal cited Salmond in 1928 (*Wackrow v Takapuna Jockey Club* [1928] NZLR 249 (CA) 255, 246).

[127] Salmond, *The Law of Torts: A Treatise on the English Law of Liability for Civil Injuries* (n 97) 366.

> sues A for the first conversion or B for the second, can recover only the value of the chattel as it stood at the time when it was first converted. Any other rule would work injustice. The true owner would make a profit out of the injury inflicted on him, and the innocent purchaser of a stolen article would incur a heavier liability than the thief himself.[128]

Exceptionally, Salmond's more general beliefs about the law of tort can be seen in his judgments. In *Holloway v Lamb* – on the liability of an employer for the acts of an independent contractor to whom the employer had delegated the obligation to ensure plant and premises were reasonably safe – it is hard to read his judgment without being reminded of Salmond's dislike of strict liability:

> Doubtless there are certain forms of absolute or vicarious liability which are ostensibly based on an alleged rule that a man cannot avoid liability for the non-performance of his duties by delegating the performance of them to other persons … This, however, is not a general principle …[129]

Yet the overwhelming impression from perusing Salmond J's tort judgments is that he understood his role as an appellate judge conventionally, applying established principles to resolve the case at hand and only rarely seeing the need for an incremental measure of judicial creativity. Increasingly, too, this was what was seen as valuable about his tort text. From a student perspective, *Law of Torts* by 1912 had become the accredited text for the LLB examination at Cambridge.[130] A reviewer of a later edition thought the book attractive to students from the point of view of examination purposes: 'The student gets what he wants, he is told what the law is, he is rarely left in doubt, which he detests'.[131] This may also have been its appeal to the judiciary.

The layout certainly helped the student and judge get what they wanted. Apart from chapters, the book is divided by paragraphs, which are numbered consecutively across the book rather than in each chapter. The paragraphs are further divided into subparagraphs and below, using numbers, letters and Roman numerals. The paragraph title sets out the general area to be discussed, with the following subparagraphs considering in more detail points raised in the introduction to the paragraph. As was common at the time, each subparagraph had its own heading and marginal note to aid in finding the relevant law. Even better for the student, in the first section of the book Salmond finished his discussion with a summary of the law he had just described,[132] although this is not done

[128] *Nash v Barnes* [1922] NZLR 303 (SC) 312 (Salmond J). For a similar approach, see *Knight v Bolton* [1924] NZLR 806 (SC) and Salmond, *The Law of Torts: A Treatise on the English Law of Liability for Civil Injuries* (n 97) 252 (liability in nuisance for acts of predecessor in title).

[129] *Holloway v Lamb* [1924] NZLR 913 (SC).

[130] ERT, '*Law of Torts*, 3rd edn (1912)' (n 99).

[131] JCM, '*Law of Torts*, 6th edn (1923)' (n 87) 53. For favourable student reviews of various editions, see Review, '*Law of Torts* (1907)' (1907) 29 *Law Students' Journal* 244; Review, '*Law of Torts*, 2nd edn (1910)' (1910) 32 *Law Students' Journal* 236.

[132] eg, in dealing with the *volenti* defence: Salmond, *Law of Torts* (n 10) 50–51.

consistently and it is not easy in hindsight to determine why particular topics were chosen for this treatment. In the section on conversion – a chapter that in early editions attracted mixed views[133] – he divides his discussion not only into main paragraphs but also into 23 numbered rules not necessarily corresponding to wider paragraphs. The book is laced with classification: the analysis of each chapter contains examples of subdivision for explanatory purposes to show an underlying system at play in tort law.[134]

Given the scale of Salmond's text, it is impossible to do more than identify some areas where innovation in the text is worthy of especial comment. Although not common, Salmond occasionally advocated reform of the law based on popular understanding. Hence he thought that 'assault' should cover the torts known conventionally as assault and battery, because in popular speech the term included both and 'there was no reason why legal terminology should not acknowledge the same use of it'.[135] This led to the oddity of describing a conventional assault as actionable as an attempt to commit an assault, something Jeremiah Smith of Harvard Law School thought resulted in a confusion of legal ideas.[136] It is hard not to see Salmond's experience as a practitioner being relevant to taking this view.

More cerebrally, Salmond spent considerable time on the tort of intimidation, teasing out potential consistencies between the two seminal cases of *Allen v Flood*[137] and *Quinn v Leathem*.[138] Here he did support a general principle of liability where an individual, irrespective of combination, conspiracy or agreement with others, intentionally and without lawful justification caused harm to a claimant by threatening other persons with harm unless they withdrew their service, custom or employment from him. While Salmond's text is largely apolitical, here he could not escape commenting on the Trade Disputes Act 1906 (UK), which immunised from liability certain acts and bodies in respect of action undertaken in furtherance of a trade dispute. He saw no principle of justice why 'these wealthy and powerful associations' had been raised above the law,[139] and similarly no reason why persons protected by the legislation should be exempted from his principle of liability, 'however oppressive, injurious and

[133] cf Beven's review of the first edition (Beven, '*Law of Torts* (1907)' (n 16) 85), stating that the rules 'only served to complicate and embarrass a doctrine of law fundamentally simple'. The rules were abandoned in the third edition. In contrast, Salmond's description of the history of the action attracted universal praise.

[134] Examples are too numerous to note in detail but for a flavour see in Salmond, *Law of Torts* (n 10), discussions of contributory negligence, 39 (three classes of defendant's knowledge), abatement of nuisance (notice requirements) 150–51, and liability for dangerous chattels, 359. This approach was popular with students: see Review by Studiosus Juris, *Law of Torts*, 3rd edn (1912)' (1913) 23 (June) *The Spike or Victoria College Review* 35.

[135] Salmond, *Law of Torts* (n 10) 338.

[136] JS, '*Law of Torts* (1907)' (n 13) 71.

[137] *Allen v Flood* [1898] AC 1 (HL).

[138] *Quinn v Leathem* [1901] AC 495 (HL).

[139] Salmond, *Law of Torts* (n 10) 58.

unjustifiable they may be'.[140] Whatever practical experience had motivated his advocacy of a change of terminology for battery, it did not extend to a subtle understanding of the class struggle.[141]

A couple of more detailed examples demonstrate the 'functional, clear and vigorous, if somewhat old fashioned' approach of the text.[142] Salmond's ability to produce meaning out of disorder is well illustrated by his discussion of the effect of intervening acts where the immediate cause of the harm was not the tortfeasor's conduct but a third party. Salmond discussed this under 'remoteness of damage', which he saw, correctly, as a remedial issue and placed in the chapter on judicial remedies.[143] Seeing remoteness as linked to his *mens rea* requirement for liability, damage was too remote if neither intended nor the natural or probable consequence of the tort. He recognised the similarity between the breach of duty enquiry in negligence and the test for remoteness, which resulted in ambiguity in the cases as to which issue was at play. A series of illustrative cases, largely without comment, are then included to highlight the principle. The structure is clear, as is the language. But when he turned to the vexed question of whether the same rules applied where the intervening act was wilful wrongdoing and not negligence, he gave unequivocal guidance: there seemed no reason in principle why they should not, because it could not be laid down as a matter of law that wilful wrongdoing could never be the natural and probable result of a defendant's wrong.[144] Compare that to the explanation provided in the eighth edition of *Addison on Torts*, published the previous year:

> Whoever does an illegal or wrongful act is answerable for all the consequences that ensue in the ordinary course of events, though those consequences be immediately and directly brought about by the intervening agency of others, provided the intervening agents were set in motion by the primary wrong-doer, or provided their acts causing the damage were the necessary or legal and natural consequence of the original wrongful act. If the wrong and the legal damage are not known by common experience to be usually in sequence and the damage does not, according to the ordinary course of events, follow from the wrong, the wrong and the damage are not sufficiently conjoined, as cause and effect, to support an action, unless it is shown that the wrong-doer knew, or had reasonable means of knowing, that consequences not usually resulting from his act were, by reason of some existing cause, likely to intervene so as to cause damage to another.[145]

[140] ibid 449.

[141] His view was well received in a number of reviews of the first edition: Review, '*Law of Torts* (1907)' (1907) 33 *Law Magazine and Review* 118; Review, '*Law of Torts* (1907)' (1907) 42 *Law Journal* 652.

[142] Heuston, 'Sir John Salmond' (n 3) 223.

[143] Salmond, *Law of Torts* (n 10) 103–13.

[144] ibid 112.

[145] W Gordon and W Griffith, *Addison's Law of Tort*, 8th edn (London, Stevens and Sons, 1906) 51. For an equally ambiguous explanation, see H Smith, *A Treatise on the Law of Negligence*, 2nd edn (London, Stevens and Sons, 1884) 19–20.

It is not surprising that Salmond's version was seen as a considerable advance on this menagerie of causal language.[146]

Another example of Salmond's ability to capture an essence from a morass of single examples is his well-known 'test' for scope of employment in vicarious liability. An act was within the course of employment if (apart from express authorisation) it was a wrongful and unauthorised *mode* of doing some act authorised by the master.[147] This is one of the most influential statements made in Salmond's text; it was stated together with the surrounding text as a correct statement of principle by the Privy Council in an appeal from Canada in 1942.[148] The use of the word 'mode' was an attempt by Salmond to capture the two ways in which an act could fall outside the course of employment: the nature of the act itself, or the intention with which it was done. Almost immediately, however, the role that Salmond had seen for intention was downplayed by the House of Lords' decision in *Lloyd v Grace, Smith & Co*,[149] holding that fraudulent conduct committed for an employee's own benefit could nonetheless fall within the course of employment. Salmond doubted the correctness of the decision and foresaw, correctly, that a decision such as that in *Morris v CW Martin & Sons Ltd*[150] nearly 50 years on would result from it, something he clearly thought was wrong.[151] The elegance of the linguistic formulation, Salmond's reluctance to change it and its practical usefulness in many cases of vicarious liability meant that it retained its judicial prominence, even though it was clearly problematic when liability was extended to cover deliberate, wrongful, self-serving acts of an employee.[152] It is a good example of how seductive Salmond's systematising could be, even if the law itself had taken a different turn.

A final example shows both the quality of Salmond's analysis and his ability to suggest changes based on that analysis, and, lastly, the need to respect the results reached in the cases. For some torts contributory negligence was a complete defence in English law in 1907. Salmond noted its effect but powerfully critiqued any attempt to rationalise it through some kind of remoteness argument. Arguing using analogies, he pointed out that this rationalisation could not explain why

[146] For fuller discussion of contemporary English texts on this point, see M Lunney, *A History of Tort Law in Australia 1901–1945: England's Obedient Servant?* (Cambridge, CUP, 2018) ch 5.

[147] Salmond, *Law of Torts* (n 10) 83.

[148] *Canadian Pacific Railway Co v Lockhart* [1942] AC 591 (PC (Can)) 599. See also *Deatons Pty Ltd v Flew* (1949) 79 CLR 370 (HCA).

[149] *Lloyd v Grace, Smith & Co* [1912] AC 716 (HL).

[150] *Morris v CW Martin & Sons Ltd* [1966] 1 QB 716 (CA).

[151] Salmond, *The Law of Torts: A Treatise on the English Law of Liability for Civil Injuries* (n 97) 99–100. Salmond was more perceptive than the *Law Quarterly Review* reviewer of the fourth edition ((1916) 32 *LQR* 330), who, while correctly noting that Salmond seemed to be surprised by *Lloyd v Grace, Smith & Co*, disagreed that it led to Salmond's view that the employer bailee would be liable for theft of bailed goods by the employee to whom the goods were entrusted – the result in *Morris v CW Martin & Sons Ltd*.

[152] eg, in cases involving sexual assault by employee carers, where it is sophistry to say that the employee's act was a mode, albeit a wrongful mode, of providing the caring service.

negligence that caused harm to two persons, only one of whom was guilty of contributory negligence, could be too remote as against one so as to deny liability but not against the other. Rather, the only explanation of the rule was as an example of the principle *in pari delicto potior est condition defendentis*.[153] Turning to the exception to the rule in *Davies v Mann*,[154] he saw it based in the 'last opportunity' rule, and justified the result in terms of direct and indirect cause.[155] This was not novel. But Salmond went on to integrate implicitly a *mens rea* component into the last opportunity rule. The rule only applied where the defendant knew of the danger and had the last opportunity to avoid it, or where he ought to have known of the danger in time to avoid it. If there was neither knowledge nor reason to know of the danger, Salmond submitted that the last opportunity rule did not apply: the parties here would be *in pari delicto*. There was no authority on this exception, but Salmond thought it sound in principle.[156] Even more ambitiously, Salmond tentatively proposed that the rule also should not apply where the defendant 'alone actually knows' of the danger created by the claimant's negligence. Here the rule in *Davies v Mann* would not apply, irrespective of whether the claimant had in fact the last opportunity to avoid the danger.[157]

No authorities were cited in support of the new rules Salmond was proposing; these were arguments from principle. They were succinct and practical yet, on a level not explained in his work of practical utility, consistent with his general theory of liability.[158] But here the need for an accurate exposition of the law came into conflict with Salmond's overall design for the law of tort. In the second edition, Salmond relegated his final proposition – that actual knowledge of a defendant might trump the plaintiff's later constructive knowledge – to a footnote of a summary of the three general propositions about when the last opportunity rule would apply.[159] The retreat was tactical rather than strategic, but the result was that this logical extension of Salmond's analysis went from the mainstream to the periphery. By the fourth edition of 1916, however, a very different tone was struck. The sections dealing with knowledge and means of knowledge and their relationship to the last opportunity rule, and the footnote dealing with a possible exception for actual knowledge, all disappeared, and the summary of the rule was a bland statement without any of the nuance in the earlier editions.

The footnote to this definition was decidedly defeatist:

> Although this principle may in general do substantial justice, it will probably produce in certain classes of cases results of an arbitrary and unreasonable nature. In former

[153] Salmond, *Law of Torts* (n 10) 31–33.
[154] *Davies v Mann* (1842) 10 M & W 546, 152 ER 588.
[155] Salmond, *Law of Torts* (n 10) 35–38.
[156] ibid 38–40.
[157] ibid 40–41.
[158] And attracted favourable comment in the review in the *Harvard Law Review*: JS, '*Law of Torts* (1907)' (n 13) 70.
[159] Salmond, *The Law of Torts: A Treatise on the English Law of Liability for Civil Injuries* (n 37) 41.

> editions of this book I endeavoured so to formulate the rule as to avoid such results. Further consideration, however, has led me to abandon any such attempt. At the best, the rule of contributory negligence is but a rough and ready method of doing justice as between persons both of whom are to blame, and it does not seem possible to establish any rule that is satisfactory in all its applications.[160]

Salmond was not averse to explaining compromises to principle on pragmatic grounds, but it is tempting to see this as part of the retreat from principled exposition that he highlighted in the preface to the fourth edition. His practical exposition remained unparalleled,[161] and when an academic reviewer wrote a joint review of Salmond's fifth edition and Pollock's eleventh edition, both of 1920, it was Pollock who was said to be freer in his criticism of decided cases than Salmond.[162] While both provided guidance in areas of uncertainty, '[the reader] will find the road indicated in more general terms [in Pollock] perhaps than in "Salmond on Torts"'.[163] Salmond's analysis of contributory negligence on the more concrete propositions appealed to judges no less because of his withdrawal from his logical conclusions; for example, the trial judge in *Joseph v Swallow & Ariell Pty Ltd*, a decision that went to the High Court of Australia,[164] cited Salmond's text as representing the law on the contributory negligence of a child. It is somewhat paradoxical that Salmond's increasing frustration at being unable to expound the law of torts as a coherent whole was mirrored by the increasing acceptance of this text as representing the law of torts as it was.

VI. SALMOND'S INFLUENCE: AN ENGLISHMAN ABROAD?

The most obvious difference between Salmond and his fellow tort text writers of the early twentieth century was not the philosophy behind, or the structure of, his text but the fact that he was not resident in England when he wrote it. What influence, if any, might this have had on the way Salmond chose to write about tort law and how the audience received it?

There is a striking dissonance between what Salmond thought he brought to writing a text from part of the empire and what those who enthusiastically received it thought he brought. Mitchell has argued that one of the factors

[160] Salmond, *The Law of Torts: A Treatise on the English Law of Liability for Civil Injuries* (n 97) 45, fn 11.

[161] Reviews of *Law of Torts* in practitioner journals were always favourable: for a flavour, see Review, '*Law of Torts* (1907)' (1907–08) 124 *Law Times* 218; Review, '*Law of Torts*, 2nd edn (1910)' (1911) 55 *Solicitors Journal* 252; Review, '*Law of Torts*, 5th edn (1920)' (1921) 41 *Canadian Law Times* 157.

[162] For a less forgiving practitioner view of the dissonance between Salmond's and Pollock's approaches (in Salmond's favour), see Review, '*Law of Torts*, 3rd edn (1912)' (1912) 56 *Solicitors Journal* 863.

[163] Review by AER, 'Pollock, *Law of Torts*, 11th edn (1920)' and 'Salmond, *Law of Torts*, 5th edn (1920)' (1921) 37 *LQR* 109.

[164] *Joseph v Swallow & Ariell Pty Ltd* (1933) 49 CLR 578 (HCA).

necessitating the search for general principles of (amongst others) tort law in the late nineteenth century was the fact that the common law had to be applied not just in England but in an increasingly diverse geographic and cultural empire.[165] With this in mind, Mitchell muses over a seeming paradox in Salmond's text. Despite the obvious differences between England and New Zealand, and an earlier article suggesting that inherent in applying the doctrine of precedent was some judicial lawmaking function,[166] Mitchell notes that Salmond's text was largely conventional.[167] It was the Englishman, Pollock, whose interest (for example) in an Indian Civil Code reflected a greater awareness of the place of the common law in the empire.[168]

What reasons might there have been for Salmond to adopt this approach? The first point to note is that any perceived limitation came from Salmond himself. It is striking how often reviewers of the book made positive mention of the fact that Salmond was writing from New Zealand. The *South African Law Journal*, for example, in its review of the first edition, thought that 'the colony of New Zealand has reason to be proud at having in its midst a jurist of such calibre'.[169] The *Law Magazine & Review* went further: the work under review 'is a striking instance, were such needed, of the growth of the Colonies, as demonstrating that the British Empire is a unit within which merit is recognised from whatever quarter it springs'.[170] Even Thomas Beven, in his review of the first edition, thought the book had particular interest, 'for it comes to us as an English law-book from the other side of the world'.[171] But Beven also noted a second peculiarity: that although well posted in the latest English cases, 'it did not refer to New Zealand decisions, some of which at least, might with advantage have been noticed'.[172] And by its review of the second edition of 1910, the initial enthusiasm for having an Antipodean author expressed by the *South African Law Journal* was decidedly more equivocal:

> We regret, however, that we have been unable to find a single reference to any New Zealand judgments. We believe that our learned author would have been well advised to insert some leading Australian or New Zealand decisions illustrating the uniformity of views in those countries with those of English judges cited in the text. The legal practitioner is ever on the lookout for cases in which certain principles have been applied to facts and sets of circumstances which happen to be closely related to, or even peradventure identical with, those submitted for advice, and an incalculable

[165] Mitchell, *A History of Tort Law 1900–1950* (n 38) 14–15.

[166] JW Salmond, 'The Theory of Judicial Precedents' (1900) 16 *LQR* 376.

[167] At least from the second edition; the change from the first to second edition has been discussed in section III.

[168] Mitchell, *A History of Tort Law 1900–1950* (n 38) 19.

[169] Review, '*Law of Torts* (1907)' (1907) 24 *South African Law Journal* 477, 478.

[170] Review, '*Law of Torts* (1907)' (1907) 33 *Law Magazine & Review* 118.

[171] Beven, '*Law of Torts* (1907)' (n 16) 84. See also the review of the first edition in the *Harvard Law Review* (n 13), noting Salmond's geographical provenance.

[172] Beven, '*Law of Torts* (1907)' (n 16) 86.

> service might possibly have been rendered in this direction by a reference to such a New Zealand or Australian case.[173]

The extract sets out perfectly the dilemma that someone in Salmond's position faced when deciding what to do with legal developments of the newly-emerging dominions. On the one hand, the common law, particularly in private law, was meant to be uniformly applied throughout the empire. If Australian or New Zealand case law was to be cited to add to the factual examples of the application of general principles, Salmond could well be forgiven for omitting them, as his book began life as something other than a compendium of authorities on discrete factual issues, however far it may have departed from this in later editions. But if Salmond discerned innovative developments in Antipodean case law, how was this to be reconciled both with the universality of common law principles throughout the empire and with the practical demands of precedent and comity, which required legal and cultural deference to decisions from the mother country?

The best way to understand Salmond's approach to the relationship between English and dominion law is through a version of cultural cringe. I have elsewhere argued that cultural cringe explanations lie at the heart of (misconceived) notions of the lack of judicial innovation in Australian tort cases in the first half of the twentieth century.[174] But while dominion judicial innovation could largely 'fly under the radar' while it stayed at home, Salmond was writing a book for the metropole. Paradoxically, as noted previously, this meant that he received no special preference from practitioners and judges in his home jurisdiction where he competed with other English tort texts. This was a price he had to pay if he wanted to be taken seriously, as to do that he needed to engage with English law as represented by English cases. His entreaty in *Essays in Jurisprudence and Legal History*[175] that any defects might be charitably attributed because the essays had been written 'at the ends of the earth', rendering historical research difficult, is testament to an anxious desire to be judged favourably where it mattered. Distance was still a tyranny, not a virtue, and it is interesting to note how Salmond described himself in the introduction to his books. In *Essays in Jurisprudence and Legal History*, he is simply a barrister of the Supreme Court of New Zealand; two years later he was LLB, MA, Barrister-at-Law and author of *Essays*. By the first edition of *Jurisprudence*, he was MA, LLB, Fellow of

[173] Review, '*Law of Torts*, 2nd edn (1910)' (1911) 28 *South African Law Journal* 132, 134; cf Review, '*Law of Torts*, 2nd edn (1910)' (1911) 55 *Solicitors Journal* 252, 253, where one New Zealand case was mentioned in the review of this edition (it was *Byrne v Judd* (1908) 27 NZLR 1106 (CA), the case where *Law of Torts* was first judicially cited in New Zealand). Salmond does not appear to have been much moved: by the fourth edition of 1916 there was only substantive discussion of two New Zealand cases. Australian jurisdictions did not move up from their zero in the first edition.

[174] Lunney, *A History of Tort Law in Australia 1901–1945: England's Obedient Servant?* (n 146) ch 2.

[175] Salmond, *Essays in Jurisprudence and Legal History* (n 6).

University College London and Professor of Law in the University of Adelaide. When *Law of Torts* came out he pulled out all the stops: MA, LLB, Fellow University College London, Barrister of the Supreme Court of New Zealand, Professor of Law in Victoria University College, Wellington, and Formerly Professor of Law at the University of Adelaide! His felt need to sell himself, including by reference to his status at University College London – which must have been honorific – is palpable, and it was only with later success that he described himself by his positions within the New Zealand Government and judiciary,[176] without reference to his earlier academic associations.

Yet it is too simplistic to see Salmond's need to be respected in the mainstream as simply obeisant cultural cringe. Mitchell notes that in an 1895 article in the *Law Quarterly Review*, Salmond refers to a fashion 'on this side of the Channel', a reference not to anything in New Zealand but to the English colloquial expression for the sea between England and France.[177] Mitchell finds this incongruous – which on one level it undoubtedly is – but it must be remembered that Salmond saw himself as part of a wider race of British peoples that inhabited various part of the globe. 'The Channel' was common language among that race, as it was in the metropole. Hence in reviewing the second edition of *Law of Torts*, the *Law Magazine and Review* could note that

> 'much water has flowed under London Bridge', and not only has the learned writer had more practical experience, but he has become the Solicitor-General in New Zealand. Whether consciously or unconsciously, this maturer experience is reflected in the tone of the revision of the present edition.[178]

The casual flitting between the waters of London Bridge and being Solicitor-General of New Zealand as contributing to the improvement in the new edition is characteristic of the community of common lawyers to which Salmond belonged. Finn notes that the progressive social changes taking place through legislation in New Zealand in the first decade of the twentieth century should not mask the fact that most New Zealand lawyers identified as 'Anglo-centric and prepared to relinquish any claims to intellectual independence in favour of deference to inherited English laws'.[179] But that they were 'less willing to challenge the dominant position of English legal practice and culture'[180] should not blind us to the intellectual endeavours made by those lawyers in applying 'their' common law in New Zealand. As that effort was almost completely ignored in the metropole, it is easy to forget that common lawyers in the dominions could

[176] As Solicitor-General and Justice of the Supreme Court. For detail on this stage of his career, see Frame, *Salmond: Southern Jurist* (n 1) chs 7–15.

[177] Mitchell, *A History of Tort Law 1900–1950* (n 38) 19. The article is JW Salmond, 'The Law of Nature' (1895) 11 *LQR* 121, 122.

[178] Review, '*Law of Torts*, 2nd edn (1910)' (1910) 36 *Law Magazine and Review* 365.

[179] J Finn, 'The Legal Environment of Salmond's Time' (2007) 38 *Victoria University of Wellington Law Review* 689, 717.

[180] ibid.

see the development of the shared common law as a corporate project.[181] That Salmond chose to contribute to the corporate project within narrower confines than later generations thought adequately reflected a New Zealand perspective, simply shows that the relationship between national identity and law is more nuanced and contextual than has traditionally been recognised.[182]

VII. CONCLUSION

Unlike the other tort scholars considered in this volume, Salmond's reputation was made through one piece of work: his treatise on tort. Its success was attributable, perhaps, to a mixture of Salmond's innate ability as an academic and to his experience as a practitioner. Salmond was interested in working legal systems. Even if we might wish for more of his theorising to appear in *Law of Torts*, it is there in the background. The structure of *Law of Torts* is discernible in his other great work, the *Jurisprudence* text. It is only by reading both together that one can understand the whole that formed the backdrop to the *Law of Torts*. Salmond thought deeply about the structure of torts and how best it should be explained. That he struggled at times to convince simply shows the enormity of the task on which he was engaged, a task made more difficult by the need to impose order within a structure still largely determined by more practical modes of thinking about the law of tort.

Yet it would be wrong to see any limitations on Salmond's attempts at systemisation as predetermined from the start. Salmond wanted to write a practical book, one that would be used by practitioners, courts and students. In doing so he hoped to shape the law as well as describe it. As time went by, and the law did not always in its developments conform to his preferred model for tort law, he was confronted with delicate questions as to the balance of prescription and description. While later editions of the book never went entirely in either of these directions, his problem was that his ability at exposition – the masterly phrase that captured the essence of a legal principle or rule – made the book so valuable to practitioners, judges and students that Salmond's more abstract ideas became less important.

The fact that Salmond's grand plan for the law of tort did not in its entirety make it to operational tort law should not mask the scale of Salmond's achievement. The greatest asset of the *Law of Torts* was that it was actually read and used by students, practitioners and judges in learning, arguing and

[181] On the academic connectedness of Britain and its colonies and dominions, see T Pietsch, *Empire of Scholars: Universities, networks and the British academic world 1850–1939* (Manchester, Manchester University Press, 2013).

[182] cf N Duxbury, 'English Jurisprudence Between Austin and Hart' (2005) 91 *Virginia Law Review* 1, 3, fn 9. Duxbury's interest was in jurisprudence written in England as opposed to English jurisprudence as possibly representative of national character (and excludes discussion of Salmond), and he also drew a distinction between English and British jurisprudence.

adjudicating on tort law. It provided a scholarly, internal perspective of tort law that the participants in the process absorbed and, through the recursive practices inherent in common law adjudication, reiterated as tort law.[183] If Salmond did not perhaps change general theories of tort law, few tort scholars of the twentieth century can claim Salmond's influence on the actual practice of tort law.

All of this suggests that Salmond well deserves a place in the pantheon of tort scholars. But, apart from the intrinsic merit of his content, perhaps his greatest achievement was to be a New Zealander who wrote a book that English and other common lawyers thought valuable. Noting, inaccurately, his death in 1917, the *Solicitors Journal* observed he was a busy practitioner, a successful advocate and a great jurist, 'although the forum in which he achieved fame was that of a somewhat remote colony'.[184] This revealing statement shows the hurdles that colonial lawyers had to overcome to contribute to their common law. No other colonial legal figure came close to Salmond's influence in England, the dominions and in other parts of the common law world through his works on jurisprudence and torts. At least for us ex-colonials of the dominions, perhaps Salmond's greatest legacy is as a genuine Imperial citizen.

[183] For an example of its ubiquity, see Colin Watson, Letter to the Editor, 'How News of the World Fell to Mr Murdoch' *Guardian* (31 January 1981) 8: '[the] public is about as interested in the fate of *The Times* and its distinguished supplements as would the readers of Agatha Christie be in the possibility of the going out of print of Salmond on Torts'.

[184] (1917) 61 *Solicitors Journal* 361. The error was corrected the following week.

5

Professor Francis Hermann Bohlen (1868–1942)

MICHAEL D GREEN*

I. INTRODUCTION

As one of the Reporters for the *Restatement (Third) of Torts*,[1] I have developed a fascination with those who went before me in restating torts for the American Law Institute (ALI). Of course, there was William Prosser, the Chief Reporter for the *Restatement (Second) of Torts*,[2] who dominated the academic torts scene in the middle of the twentieth century by leveraging his restating with treatise writing and academic work. Chris Robinette has already done important work uncovering aspects of Prosser's career, including for this volume.

Much less well known is Francis H Bohlen, the Reporter for the first *Restatement of Torts*.[3] But what did Bohlen really do? And how much of it is of lasting importance? I am grateful to the sponsors of the workshop that led to the present collection for providing me an opportunity to further explore this somewhat obscure character and the role he played in the development of tort law. Unfortunately, in pursuing this topic, I was unable to locate any of Bohlen's private papers. The Biddle Law Library at the University of Pennsylvania has none of Bohlen's personal papers, the compendium of library private papers has

* I am indebted to Melissa McKinley for her superb research assistance in the preparation of this chapter.

[1] *Restatement (Third) of Torts: Liability for Physical & Emotional Harm* (Philadelphia, PA, American Law Institute, 2010 & 2012).

[2] *Restatement (Second) of Torts* (Philadelphia, PA, American Law Institute, 1965).

[3] *Restatement of Torts* (Philadelphia, PA, American Law Institute, 1934). I find Bohlen more interesting than Prosser, both because he is largely unknown today and because so much of his work was carried forward by Prosser and influences courts to this day. See text accompanying n 28.

no listing for Francis Bohlen and my casual efforts to locate any of his descendants were unproductive.[4]

Because of space constraints, I was forced to make a choice between depth and breadth in my assessment of Bohlen. Because I have had a long interest in two issues that Bohlen addressed, I have chosen depth rather than breadth, although I hedge my bet just a bit. Thus, I focus in this chapter on the adoption in the first *Restatement* of the three elements that make up the famous *Carroll Towing* test formulated by Learned Hand. Notwithstanding the contrary claim of William Landes and Richard Posner,[5] a balancing test of the sort Hand made famous was not well-established in the cases of Bohlen's era, nor, unsurprisingly, in the treatises that catalogued the common law of torts.[6] The path that led him to adopt that principle and his role in furthering it is one of my primary foci. The second aspect I investigate is the treatment of factual cause and proximate cause by Bohlen in the first *Restatement*. It is no secret that those topics were among the weaker aspects of the first *Restatement* (and, unfortunately, largely carried forward by Prosser in the *Restatement (Second)*), such that the *Restatement (Third)* started almost from ground zero in its treatment of these subjects.

II. ORGANISING TORT LAW

The single matter of breadth I indulge in is Bohlen's role in providing structure and organisation to this topic. With the assistance of a research assistant, I surveyed every torts treatise, English[7] or American, published in the period 1895–1930, a time when they might have had an impact on Bohlen's restatement work, that I could locate.[8] While the torts treatises of Bohlen's day had

[4] I was able to locate and review minutes of many of the Advisory Committee meetings held by the ALI to discuss drafts of the *Restatement* prepared by Francis Bohlen. Professor Andrew Kaufman, who reviewed them while writing his biography of Benjamin Cardozo, put me on to them. These minutes were apparently the personal copies of a Harvard Law School faculty member, either Warren Seavey or Edward Thurston, both of whom served as Advisors for the first *Restatement*. See AL Kaufman, *Cardozo* (Cambridge, MA, Harvard University Press, 1998) 652, fn 7. I did find in one of the minutes of a later meeting the handwritten name 'Edward Thurston', although Kaufman reports that these and other materials from the first *Restatement* were donated by Warren Seavey.

[5] See n 33.

[6] See the discussion in the text accompanying nn 41–53.

[7] I included English treatises because Bohlen's work frequently engaged with English cases and treatises. See, eg, FH Bohlen, 'The Basis of Affirmative Obligations in the Law of Tort' (1905) 53 *University of Pennsylvania Law Review* 337 (critiquing Thomas Beven's treatment of superseding cause in his treatise); FH Bohlen, 'The Rule in Rylands v Fletcher' (1911) 59 *University of Pennsylvania Law Review* 423, 425, 427 (citing the Clerk and Lindsell treatise).

[8] Unless there was a substantial change across editions, I focused on editions closest to when Bohlen was working on the first *Restatement*, beginning in 1923. See EA Jaggard, *Handbook on the Law of Torts* (St Paul, MN, West Publishing Co, 1895); WB Hale, *Handbook on the Law of Torts* (St Paul, MN, West Publishing Co, 1896); H Smith, *A Treatise on the Law of Negligence* (St Louis, MO, FH Thomas Law Book Co, 1896); TW Saunders and EB Wright, *The Law of Negligence*,

not reached a uniform understanding of the way to organise the subject, many authors began with an initial overview of the general principles of tort law.[9] From there, authors diverged into chapters on causes of action, such as defamation, or Lord Campbell's Act, or affected persons or parties to actions, such as married women, railroads or lunatics, and then generally concluded with defences or remedies, though these organisational schema lack consistency past the initial overview chapters.[10] Both American and British versions of these treatises maintained the same organisation systems across successive editions.[11] Additionally, although the treatises mostly covered the same topics, the depth and detail on each subject varied considerably.[12] Virtually none had a chapter or even a section on causation; what coverage they offered was often buried in treatment of remoteness of damage. Factual causation was largely ignored.

Despite the variation, none of the systems of organisation resembled the organisational system adopted in the *Restatement* by Bohlen, which relied predominantly on a combination of legally protected interests and specific types of wrongful conduct and conduct, for example ultrahazardous activity, subjecting one to strict liability. Bohlen's organisation does not appear to

2nd edn (London, Butterworth & Co, 1898); TG Shearman and AA Redfield, *A Treatise on the Law of Negligence*, 5th edn (New York, Baker, Voorhis & Co, 1898); SD Thompson, *Commentaries on the Law of Negligence in All Relations* (Indianapolis, IN, Bowen–Merrill Co, 1901); EB Kinkead, *Commentaries on the Law of Torts* (San Francisco, CA, Bancroft–Whitney Co, 1903); JF Clerk and WHB Lindsell, *The Law of Torts*, 3rd edn (London, Sweet & Maxwell, 1904); FA Erwin, *A Summary of Torts*, 2nd edn (New York, LJ Tompkins, 1906); WE Gordon and WH Griffith (eds), *A Treatise on the Law of Torts*, 8th edn (London, Stevens, 1906); MM Bigelow, *The Law of Torts*, 8th edn (Boston, MA, Little Brown & Co, 1907); J Lewis (ed), *A Treatise on the Law of Torts*, students' edn (Chicago, IL, Callaghan, 1907); T Beven, *Negligence in Law*, 3rd edn (London, Steven and Haynes, 1908); A Underhill, *A Summary of Torts*, 10th edn (London, Butterworth & Co, 1922); JW Salmond, *The Law of Torts: A Treatise on the English Law of Liability for Civil Injuries*, 6th edn (London, Stevens and Haynes, 1924); FM Burdick, *The Law of Torts*, 4th edn (Albany, NY, Banks & Co, 1926). Although a year earlier than the period I selected, I nevertheless included F Pollock, *A Treatise on the Law of Torts*, 3rd edn (St Louis, MO, FH Thomas Law Book Co, 1894), because of its influential status and because it is more supportive of Landes and Posner than the other treatises.

[9] See, eg, Pollock, *A Treatise on the Law of Torts* (n 8) xi–xxvi. See also JCP Goldberg and B Zipursky, 'Thomas Cooley (1824–98) and Oliver Wendell Holmes Jr (1841–1935): The Arc of American Tort Theory' (describing organisation of Thomas Cooley's treatise) and M Lunney, 'Professor Sir John Salmond (1862–1924): An Englishman Abroad' (describing organisation of John Salmond's treatise) (chs 2 and 4 of the present volume respectively). But see Saunders and Wright, *The Law of Negligence* (n 8) ix.

[10] See, eg, Beven, *Negligence in Law* (n 8) ix (transitioning from negligence principles to authoritative parties); Bigelow, *The Law of Torts* (n 8) ix (addressing specific torts after an overview chapter).

[11] See, eg, Bigelow, *The Law of Torts* (n 8) ix–xii (American version); MM Bigelow, *The Law of Torts*, 2nd edn (Cambridge, CUP, 1903) ix–xii (British version); Pollock, *A Treatise on the Law of Torts* (n 8) vii–xxvi (American version); F Pollock, *The Law of Torts*, 9th edn (London, Stevens and Sons, 1912) ix–xxiv (British version).

[12] See, eg, Shearman and Redfield, *A Treatise on the Law of Negligence* (n 8) 26–44 (discussing proximate cause principles for an entire chapter); Thompson, *Commentaries on the Law of Negligence in All Relations* (n 8) 43–162. But see Saunders and Wright, *The Law of Negligence* (n 8) 14 (omitting discussion of proximate cause except for a brief mention as an element of contributory negligence).

spring from the treatises of his day, but rather to have been borrowed from the organisation followed in his text on torts and, to a lesser extent, the Ames and Smith casebook.[13] Learned Hand put this point eloquently in a memorial to Bohlen:

> [Torts] lacked structure; and Bohlen's work has consisted principally in trying to impose some pattern upon the amorphous material. It was a task of great difficulty and demanded much acuteness, and an endurance of unending verbal refinements which would have prostrated a less determined man.[14]

[13] FH Bohlen, *Cases on the Law of Torts*, 2nd edn (Indianapolis, IN, Bobbs–Merrill Co, 1925) (starting with all of the intentional torts, subdivided by the interest protected, consent and privilege, then proceeding to the negligence cause of action, beginning with whether the right to vote is legally protected, concluding with defences, and then covering deceit, defamation, malicious prosecution and abuse of process); JB Ames and J Smith, *A Selection of Cases on the Law of Torts* (Cambridge, MA, Harvard University Press, 1919) (beginning with torts interfering with bodily and tangible property integrity, proceeding then to some intentional torts, negligence and defences thereto, strict liability, and concluding with dignitary torts, deceit and interference with contract and prospective economic advantage). To hedge my bet just a bit more, Bohlen's scholarly career, aside from his restating, reminds me of Gary Schwartz's. Bohlen took on a wide variety of torts topics, ranging from consent to the liability of children and insane persons, to affirmative duties to riparian rights, and did not return to any subject on which he had previously written and double dip (see FH Bohlen, *Studies in the Law of Torts* (Indianapolis, IN, Bobbs–Merrill Co, 1926) 291, 378, 543 and 577). Early in his career, he addressed the emerging field of workers' compensation and developed a theory to justify the emerging statutes that required employers to compensate injured workers (see GL Priest, 'The Invention of Enterprise Liability: A Critical History of The Intellectual Foundations of Modern Tort Law' (1985) 14 *Journal of Legal Studies* 461, 466). I believe that Priest misreads Bohlen to have employed his benefit theory to justify a negligence regime. Rather, Bohlen accepted negligence for risk creation by the defendant. His benefit theory was designed to justify affirmative duties to protect, not as a basis for imposing liability on those whose risk-creating conduct caused harm, such as product manufacturers. Bohlen was a progressive on privity. He wrote an early article advocating its demise, on which Cardozo, with whom Bohlen had a close and mutually admiring relationship, relied in *MacPherson v Buick Motor Co* 111 NE 1050 (NY 1916) (see LH Eldredge, 'Francis Hermann Bohlen' (1943) 91 *University of Pennsylvania Law Review and American Law Register* 387, 389; GE White, *Tort Law in America: An Intellectual History* (New York, OUP, 1980) 264, fn 128). These are notable contributions for a legal scholar in their own right, yet ones that are left behind in this chapter. Patrick Kelly covers a number of these contributions in more detail and with lavish praise in P Kelly, 'The First Restatement of Torts: Reform by Descriptive Theory' (2007) 32 *Southern Illinois University Law Journal* 93.

[14] L Hand, 'Francis Hermann Bohlen' (1943) 91 *University of Pennsylvania Law Review* 386, 386. See also B Cardozo, *Selected Writings of Benjamin Nathan Cardozo*, ed ME Hall (New York, Fallon Law Book Co, 1947) (ALI lecture at which Cardozo described positively Bohlen's new arrangement, a departure from a system that 'did much, I think, to choke and stunt the law of torts'); WL Prosser, 'Book Review, The Law of Torts' (1959) 47 *California Law Review* 418, 418. Notwithstanding Hand, Prosser and Cardozo's views, Leon Green was harshly critical of the *Restatement's* organisation, as he was for virtually every aspect of the *Restatement* (L Green, 'The Torts Restatement' (1935) 29 *Illinois Law Review* 582, 585–86). There is a level of animosity between Bohlen and Green for which I have been unable to find a credible explanation: see FH Bohlen, 'Should Negligent Misrepresentations Be Treated as Negligence or Fraud?' (1932) 18 *Virginia Law Review* 703 (nastily criticising Green's commentary on an earlier article by Bohlen). I do not find Edward White's explanation that this stemmed from Green's disappointment about Bohlen's failure adequately to join the realists persuasive: White, *Tort Law in America: An Intellectual History* (n 13) 81–83. The extent of vituperation in Green's criticism suggests something more personal than Bohlen's stance toward the realist movement.

It should not go without saying that the ALI's *Restatements* have had a tremendous impact on the common law.[15] When the *Swift v Tyson*[16] model of federal law, providing greater consistency and clarity to the common law, went by the board in 1938 with *Erie Railroad v Tompkins*,[17] that function was left primarily to the ALI and its *Restatements*, which had begun emerging. And torts is the subject where the ALI's work has most influenced the courts.[18] Bohlen, and the other Reporters of the initial round of *Restatements*, all leaders in their respective fields, deserve considerable credit for that influence.

III. BOHLEN'S BACKGROUND

I omit most of the biographical details about Bohlen, save for a few salient ones that situate him in the legal landscape in which he operated.[19] Bohlen completed his legal education at the University of Pennsylvania in 1892 and began teaching at Penn immediately thereafter as a fellow and later, after a term in practice and travel, as an assistant professor in 1901.[20] Bohlen's legal career spans the formalist or legal science period and the realist era.[21] It also spans the era when tort law left behind the shackles of the writ system and began working out a regime based on protected interests and different categories of culpable conduct.[22] He began work on the first *Restatement of Torts* in 1923, shortly after the formation of the ALI, when his former Dean at Penn and the

[15] See, eg, A Elson, 'The Case for an In-Depth Study of the American Law Institute' (1998) 23 *Law and Social Inquiry* 625, 625 ('For almost 75 years the [ALI] has made a substantial contribution to the development of the law. It has successfully enlisted leading law scholars, lawyers, and members of the judiciary of exceptional distinction and prestige in this effort. Its standing and reputation are unique'); RA Warshak, 'Parenting by the Clock: The Best-Interest-of-the-Child Standard, Judicial Discretion, and the American Law Institute's "Approximation Rule"' (2011) 41 *University of Baltimore Law Review* 83, 86 ('ALI's Restatements of the Law – formulated by influential jurists, bar leaders, and law professors – profoundly influence American law').

[16] *Swift v Tyson* 41 US 1 (1841).

[17] *Erie Railroad Co v Tompkins* 304 US 64 (1938).

[18] See MD Green and O Moréteau, 'Restating Tort Law: The American and European Styles' (2012) 3 *Journal of European Tort Law* 281, 285 (as of date of article, over 200,000 court citations to *Restatements*; 70,000 to torts *Restatements*).

[19] A reasonable and affectionate treatment of Bohlen's life, including his education and youth, can be found in WD Lewis, 'Francis Hermann Bohlen' (1943) 91 *University of Pennsylvania Law Review and American Law Register* 377.

[20] ibid 379.

[21] Several different terms have been employed to characterise the dominant mode of legal thought in the late 19th and early 20th centuries. I use the terms 'formalist' or 'conceptualist', which are among those frequently employed. See, generally, TC Grey, 'Langdell's Orthodoxy' (1983) 45 *University of Pittsburgh Law Review* 1, 2 (employing the phrase 'classical orthodoxy'); White, *Tort Law in America: An Intellectual History* (n 13) 31–37 (employing the phrase 'legal science').

[22] In only the second preliminary draft of the *Restatement* prepared by Bohlen, he explained that the writs of trespass *vi et armis* and trespass on the case had only pleading significance, and then only in jurisdictions that retained common law pleading. See *Restatement of Torts*, Preliminary Draft No 2 (Philadelphia, PA, American Law Institute, 10 December 1923). Bohlen found the need, repeatedly, in his scholarly work to return to an explanation of the writ system in order to analyse

first Director of the ALI, William Draper Lewis, appointed him as the Reporter. Bohlen was then 55.[23]

In 1925, Bohlen moved to Harvard Law School where he taught for three years; he returned to Penn in 1928. Bohlen worked on the *Restatement* for a total of 14 years,[24] until his health deteriorated so significantly that he was unable to continue. Others completed the later chapters of that work, but Bohlen is responsible for what we would consider the core of tort law. Thus, although Bohlen was working at a time when the realist movement was taking hold,[25] his training and a substantial portion of his career were during the formalist reign. And the first *Restatement of Torts*, like the others of its generation, certainly reflects Bohlen's formalist roots.[26] One more aspect of Bohlen worthy of mention is his scepticism about juries. Bohlen repeatedly wrote of his belief that juries were biased toward compensating victims, and remarked on this matter even in his last article, which reflected on the prior 50 years in tort law.[27]

My interest in Bohlen has been enhanced over the years as I have come to appreciate how much of his work was carried forward in the *Restatement (Second)*. William Prosser is largely credited (or blamed) for everything in the *Restatement (Second)*. However, as I wrote in an earlier article that investigated that widely held assumption by looking at a sample (approximately 10 per cent) of sections in the two *Restatements*:

> We found that almost two-thirds of the Second Restatement's sections were the same as the first Restatement. Ten percent of the first Restatement sections were omitted because the areas of unfair competition and trade regulation had been taken over by statutory provisions rather than being governed by common law. Of the approximately 25% percent that did change, almost three quarters changed only moderately

whichever subject he was addressing. See, eg, FH Bohlen, 'Liability in Tort of Infants and Insane Persons' (1924) 23 *Michigan Law Review* 9, 13.

[23] See Lewis, 'Francis Hermann Bohlen' (n 19) 377.

[24] Lewis writes (ibid 381–82) that 'the work on the Restatement of Torts absorbed a large part of his time'. All in all, Bohlen was remarkably prolific, producing preliminary drafts often on a monthly basis and meeting with the advisors to the project just as frequently, yet publishing 10 major articles during the period from 1923 to 1934 when he was actively restating and preparing two new editions of his casebook.

[25] See G Gilmore, *The Ages of American Law* (New Haven, CT, Yale University Press, 1977) 12. Edward White explained how Bohlen's career spanned two eras in legal thinking, which required Bohlen to rethink his conceptualist training. See White, *Tort Law in America: An Intellectual History* (n 13) 75–83.

[26] See Green and Moréteau, 'Restating Tort Law: The American and European Styles' (n 18) 289 (characterising the first torts *Restatement* as having 'little if any explanation, no discussion of policy or the tensions that exist in the law, and no citations to relevant cases or other legal materials'). The last of those three assessments of the first *Restatement of Torts* is incorrect. Cases supporting the black letter were contained in a separate document entitled 'Explanatory Notes', rather than the current practice of including them in 'Reporters' Notes' contained in the main volume. See, eg, *Restatement of Torts*, Explanatory Notes to Tentative Draft No 4 (Philadelphia, PA, American Law Institute, 6 April 1929).

[27] FH Bohlen, 'Fifty Years of Torts' (1937) 50 *Harvard Law Review* 725, 728.

while the remainder were substantially different from their predecessors. The Second Restatement did have a significant number of new sections (135) that both filled in gaps in the coverage of the first Restatement and others that addressed newly developed issues. Among the most notable new provisions were § 402A, adopting a strict products liability standard, § 433B, which shifted the burden of proof to apportion causation when multiple tortfeasors caused only a part of the plaintiff's harm and addressed liability in the alternative causation circumstance popularly known as the 'two hunters' case, and §§ 652A–652I, which covered protection of the interest in privacy.[28]

IV. INCORPORATING RISK–BENEFIT ANALYSIS

Let me proceed to Bohlen's and the first *Restatement*'s role in employing a risk–benefit standard for negligence. *Carroll Towing*[29] is, of course, the most famous legal articulation of this idea, as evidenced by its presence in every contemporary torts casebook, at least at the turn of the twenty-first century,[30] and in each of the three editions of the *Restatement of Torts*.[31] Its fame has spread beyond US borders and is well known not only in other common law countries but in civil law systems as well.[32]

Several years ago, I explored the claim of William Landes and Richard Posner that tort law reflects rules that further economic efficiency.[33] In that account,

[28] Green and Moréteau, 'Restating Tort Law: The American and European Styles' (n 18) 290 (footnote omitted). Prosser's laissez-faire approach to the first *Restatement* may have been influenced by the deep respect Prosser had for Bohlen.

[29] *United States v Carroll Towing Co* 159 F 2d 169 (2d Cir 1947).

[30] PJ Kelley, 'The Carroll Towing Company Case and the Teaching of Tort Law' (2001) 45 *St Louis University Law Journal* 731, 732–33 (footnotes omitted).

[31] *Restatement of Torts* (n 3) §§ 291–93; *Restatement (Second) of Torts* (n 2) §§ 291–93; *Restatement (Third) of Torts: Liability for Physical & Emotional Harm* (n 1) § 3.

[32] In my experience, European tort academics are familiar with and use *Carroll Towing* (n 29) or the Hand formula as a shorthand term to invoke balancing risk and benefit. The *Principles of European Tort Law*'s coverage of negligence, while not cast in *Carroll Towing* terms, includes the 'dangerousness of the activity' and the 'costs of precautionary or alternative methods': European Group on Tort Law, *Principles of European Tort Law* (Vienna, Springer, 2005) art 4-104. The leading Canadian torts treatise cites and discusses *Carroll Towing*: see A Linden and B Feldthusen, *Canadian Tort Law*, 10th edn (Toronto, LexisNexis, 2015) § 5.3. For work from other countries employing *Carroll Towing* or Hand, see L Leysser, 'El Análisis Económico del Derecho Civil en Italia un Inventario Histórico-Bibliográfico Mínimo' (2001) 42 *Themis* 317, 334 (noting the Hand formula's reputation in Peru); J Noll, 'Das Prinzip des "Cheapest Cost Avoider" in der Rechtsprechung des OGH – Beispiele aus jüngerer Zeit' (2003) 9 *Manz* 471 (arguing that two Austrian Supreme Court rulings were based upon the Hand formula). One notable exception is Spain, where a prominent torts academic there reports that neither the courts nor traditional commentators mention the *Carroll Towing* formula with the exception of a few law and economics scholars whose work has not had any appreciable impact outside that school: email from Professor Miquel Martin Casals to Michael D Green (23 July 2018).

[33] MD Green, 'Negligence = Economic Efficiency: Doubts >' (1997) 75 *Texas Law Review* 1605, 1606 and fn 7. The Landes and Posner claim is contained in WM Landes and RA Posner, *The Economic Structure of Tort Law* (Cambridge, MA, Harvard University Press, 1987) 85–86

Carroll Towing,[34] and its algebraic risk–benefit formula, plays a central role. Let me put aside the debate over whether *Carroll Towing* reflects a conscious (or subconscious) effort to further economic efficiency[35] or merely reflects a reasonableness balancing test,[36] as that matter is not pertinent to the question at hand.[37] What I found is that far from being seminal, *Carroll Towing*'s risk–benefit balancing had been preceded, as Landes and Posner claimed, but that there was very little such precedent, contrary to their claims,[38] until the first *Restatement*.[39]

Indeed, Bohlen, influenced by Henry Terry, deserves considerable credit for planting the seeds that have flourished into an explicit risk–benefit standard for negligence and providing the law and economics movement fertile fodder for its work.[40] It is quite plausible that Bohlen played a critical role in Learned Hand's

('[Judge] Hand was purporting only to make explicit what had long been the implicit meaning of negligence; ... something like the Hand Formula has long been used to decide negligence cases').

[34] *Carroll Towing* (n 29). Judge Hand had provided a non-algebraic, descriptive version of this risk–benefit test in three earlier cases (see *The Charles H Sells* 89 F 2d 631, 633 (2d Cir 1937); *Gunnarson v Robert Jacob, Inc* 94 F 2d 170, 172 (2d Cir 1938); *Conway v O'Brien* 111 F 2d 611, 612 (2d Cir 1940), all asserting that the degree of care required is found by balancing three factors: likelihood of injury, seriousness of injury, and cost of avoiding the risk).

[35] As William Landes and Richard Posner have famously claimed (see Landes and Posner, *The Economic Structure of Tort Law* (n 33)).

[36] But the Learned Hand formula can also be understood non-instrumentally to reflect the Golden Rule: 'And as ye would that men should do to you, do ye also to them likewise': Luke 6:31 (King James). In other words, treat others – with regard to risks resulting from your activities – as if they were of equal value and respect as yourself. Thus, non-instrumentalists can also embrace a *Carroll Towing* standard for negligence. See, eg, GT Schwartz, 'Contributory and Comparative Negligence: A Reappraisal' (1977) 87 *Yale Law Journal* 697, 702–03; EJ Weinrib, 'Toward a Moral Theory of Negligence Law' (1983) 2 *Law & Philosophy* 37, 54; R Dworkin, *Law's Empire* (Cambridge, MA, Belknap Press, 1986) 295–309; JJ Thomson, *The Realm of Rights* (Cambridge, MA, Harvard University Press, 1990) 243–46; DG Owen, 'The Moral Foundations of Products Liability Law: Toward First Principles' (1993) 68 *Notre Dame Law Review* 427; GT Schwartz, 'Contributory and Comparative Negligence: A Reappraisal' (179) 87 *Yale Law Journal* 697, 702–03; EJ Weinrib, 'Toward a Moral Theory of Negligence Law' (1983) 2 *Law and Philosophy* 37, 54; GC Keating, 'Must the Hand Formula Not Be Named?' (2015) 163 *University of Pennsylvania Law Review Online* 367, 370 ('Inquiring in this way is a kind of ordinary moral and legal reasoning, not a foray into economics or philosophy.'); JJ Thomson, *The Realm Of Rights* (Cambridge, MA, Harvard University Press, 1990) 243–46; BC Zipursky, 'Sleight of Hand' (2007) 48 *William and Mary Law Review* 1999, 2001 ('Although the Hand Formula analysis of negligence certainly has seen its share of detractors, it is an analytical doctrine that has tended to cut across political and ideological lines').

[37] On the different normative interpretations of the *Carroll Towing* formula, see SG Gilles, 'On Determining Negligence: Hand Formula Balancing, the Reasonable Person Standard, and the Jury' (2001) 54 *Vanderbilt Law Review* 813.

[38] 'The Hand formula appears to be an accurate description of the negligence standard ... in diverse periods and jurisdictions' (Landes and Posner, *The Economic Structure of Tort Law* (n 33) 102).

[39] See first *Restatement of Torts*, Explanatory Notes to Tentative Draft No 4 (n 26) 5 ('The comparison between the social utility of the act and the magnitude of the risk involved in it is occasionally, but only occasionally, stated as the basis of decision in negligence cases').

[40] I draw on my earlier work, Green, 'Negligence = Economic Efficiency: Doubts >' (n 33), in this discussion of Bohlen and the first *Restatement*'s contribution to a risk–benefit standard for negligence.

first articulation of a risk–benefit standard in 1938 descriptively rather than algebraically, and finally in 1947 in *Carroll Towing*, as I explain below.

Let me back up a bit and consider what explicit risk–benefit existed in negligence law prior to its adoption in the first *Restatement*. Very little, it turns out. Frequently cited as exemplary of the turn-of-the-century approach to negligence is *Chicago, B & QR Co v Krayenbuhl*.[41] *Krayenbuhl* is one of two early cases cited by Landes, Posner[42] and others[43] as reflecting a risk–benefit approach to negligence.[44] In *Krayenbuhl*, a four-year-old child was injured when playing on the defendant railroad company's unguarded and unlocked turntable. After the court concluded that the attractive nuisance doctrine applied and thus imposed a duty of reasonable care on the railroad, the court adumbrated a clear risk–benefit test to flesh out the reasonableness standard, and began with reassurance that a negligence regime would not shut down the commerce of the Industrial Revolution:

> It is true … 'the business of life must go forward'; the means by which it is carried forward cannot be rendered absolutely safe. Ordinarily, it can be best carried forward by the unrestricted use of private property by the owner; therefore the law favors such use to the fullest extent consistent with the main purpose for which, from a social standpoint, such business is carried forward, namely, the public good. Hence, in order to determine the extent to which such use may be enjoyed, its bearing on such main purpose must be taken into account, and a balance struck between its advantages and disadvantages. If, on the whole, such use defeats, rather than promotes, the main purpose, it should not be permitted; on the other hand, if the restrictions proposed would so operate, they should not be imposed. The business of life is better carried forward by the use of dangerous machinery; hence the public good demands its use, although occasionally such use results in the loss of life or limb. It does so because the danger is insignificant, when weighed against the benefits resulting from the use of such machinery, and for the same reason demands its reasonable, most effective, and unrestricted use, up to the point where the benefits resulting from such use no longer outweigh the danger to be anticipated from it. At that point the public good demands restrictions. For example, a turntable is a dangerous contrivance, which facilitates railroading; the general benefits resulting from its use outweigh the occasional injuries inflicted by it; hence the public good demands its use. We may conceive of means by which it might be rendered absolutely safe, but such means would so interfere with its beneficial use that the danger to be anticipated would not justify their adoption;

[41] *Chicago, B & QR Co v Krayenbuhl* 91 NW 880 (Neb 1902).

[42] The other case referred to by Landes and Posner was from Scotland. See Landes and Posner, *The Economic Structure of Tort Law* (n 33) 86–87 (discussing *Mackintosh v Mackintosh* 2 M 1357, 1362–63 (2d Div 1864)).

[43] MA Kotler, 'Competing Conceptions of Autonomy: A Reappraisal of the Basis of Tort Law' (1992) 67 *Tulane Law Review* 347, 381; EC Lyons, 'Balancing Acts: Intending Good and Foreseeing Harm – The Principle of Double Effect in the Law' (2005) 3 *Georgetown Journal of Law and Public Policy* 453, 491–93. But see Zipursky, 'Sleight of Hand' (n 36).

[44] Landes and Posner cite other cases but they are of later vintage, after Bohlen was engaged in drafting the first *Restatement* (Green, 'Negligence = Economic Efficiency: Doubts >' (n 33) 1616).

> therefore the public good demands its use without them. But the danger incident to its use may be lessened by the use of a lock which would prevent children, attracted to it, from moving it; the interference with the proper use of the turntable occasioned by the use of such lock is so slight that it is outweighed by the danger to be anticipated from an omission to use it; therefore the public good, we think, demands the use of the lock. The public good would not require the owner of a vacant lot on which there is a pond to fill up the pond or inclose the lot with an impassable wall to insure the safety of children resorting to it, because the burden of doing so is out of proportion to the danger to be anticipated from leaving it undone … But where there is an open well on a vacant lot, which is frequented by children, of which the owner of the lot has knowledge, he is liable for injuries sustained by children falling into the well, because the danger to be anticipated from the open well, under the circumstances, outweighs the slight expense or inconvenience that would be entailed in making it safe …[45]

This is plainly a court that recognised that a marginal improvement in safety, a lock for the turntable, was such a slight burden as to be 'outweighed by the danger to be anticipated from an omission to use it'.[46] We are here comparing the costs of injury prevention with the expected costs of accidents to determine the standard of care imposed on the railroad.

Notwithstanding *Krayenbuhl*, there is very little evidence of courts' using a risk–benefit standard in the run-up to Bohlen's work on the *Restatement*. Oliver Wendell Holmes's assessment of negligence focused on the foreseeability of harm to further his deterrence concerns and paid no attention to the social utility of the act.[47] Holmes was not alone. As mentioned in section II, I conducted a survey of every torts treatise, English or American, published in the period between 1895 and 1930 that I could locate.[48] What emerges is that the risk–benefit standard articulated by the Nebraska Supreme Court in *Krayenbuhl* appears quite rarely. The treatises almost exclusively define negligence in general terms of ordinary or reasonable care in the circumstances, and infrequently make reference to differing degree of danger, probability of harm or burden of precaution as variables to be considered in the assessment of negligence or reasonable care.[49] Although one does find an occasional reference to

[45] *Krayenbuhl* (n 41) 882–83.

[46] ibid 883.

[47] OW Holmes Jr, *The Common Law* (New York, Dover Publications, 1991) 93–96.

[48] I also included two treatises on railroad law that contain substantial discussions of negligence and negligence standards. See SE Baldwin, *American Railroad Law* (Boston, MA, Little Brown & Co, 1904); BK Elliott and WK Elliott, *A Treatise on the Law of Railroads*, 2nd edn (Indianapolis, IN, Bobbs–Merrill Co, 1907).

[49] By the time of his fourth edition in 1916, John Salmond was an exception. In explaining factors that would inform reasonableness, Salmond identified the magnitude of the risk created by defendant's conduct and the benefit to be gained by the conduct (JW Salmond, *The Law of Torts: A Treatise on the English Law of Liability for Civil Injuries*, 4th edn (London, Steven and Haynes, 1916) 28). Frederick Pollock also identified the 'magnitude and the apparent imminence of the risk' as informing the 'caution that is required' (Pollock, *A Treatise on the Law of Torts* (n 8) 533).

Krayenbuhl within these treatises, rarely is the case cited for its risk–benefit standard.[50] Most of the prominent negligence cases of the day could be read as consistent with a risk–benefit test, but they are far more vague in their characterisation of the relevant negligence standard and certainly susceptible of alternative interpretations.[51] The dominant explanation of negligence in judicial opinions, as in the treatises, is that it entails exercising 'reasonable care' or that which a 'reasonable or prudent man' would employ. Indeed, in *Krayenbuhl*, for all of the court's risk–benefit proselytising, we find out later in the opinion that the jury was instructed with the standard reasonable-care instruction that included nothing about comparing costs of precaution with the risks that could be eliminated by employing a lock on the railroad's turntable.[52] And if citation by other courts makes a leading case, *Krayenbuhl* is no *Palsgraf*.[53]

[50] See, eg, Lewis, *A Treatise on the Law of Torts* (n 8) 737 (mentioning *Krayenbuhl* (n 41) in the discussion on liability for children); Elliot and Elliot, *A Treatise on the Law of Railroads* (n 48) 730 (citing *Krayenbuhl* for a proposition on effective pleading).

[51] See, eg, *Sioux City & P R Co v Stout* 84 US (17 Wall) 657, 659 (1873) (suggesting that the critical inquiry with regard to the defendant's negligence was whether there was a probability or likelihood of the railroad turntable's causing harm to children); *Alabama Great S Ry v Moody* 9 So 238, 240 (Ala 1890) ('[A] company fulfils its duty, when it adopts those [safety devices] in ordinary use by prudently conducted and well-regulated [rail]roads engaged in like business, under like circumstances'); *Koelsch v Philadelphia Co* 25 A 522, 524 (Pa 1893) ('A higher degree of care and vigilance is required in dealing with a dangerous agency than in the ordinary affairs of life or business, which involve little or no risk of injury to persons or property … [and] every reasonable precaution suggested by experience and the known dangers of the subject ought to be taken'); *Mather v Rillston* 156 US 391, 399 (1895) (imposing a super-negligence standard – that one 'must [use] all appliances readily attainable [and] known to science for the prevention of accidents' – on a mine operator for operations entailing 'great and unusual danger'); *Last Chance Mining & Milling Co v Ames* 47 P 382, 384 (Colo 1896) (holding the golden rule instruction erroneous because it imposed a higher standard of care than that required by law); *Galveston, H and SA Ry v Gormley* 93 Tex 393, 399 (1898) (stating that the precautions required by the defendant depend on the extent of the danger involved).

[52] *Krayenbuhl* (n 41) 883: '[T]he company was required to exercise reasonable care in the placing and fastening of the turntable and having the same fitted with such appliances as would make it reasonably safe in the situation where it was placed, under the circumstances as disclosed in this case'.

[53] *Palsgraf v Long Island Railroad Co* 162 NE 99 (1928). *Krayenbuhl* (n 41) was not cited by the Nebraska Supreme Court with regard to the meaning of negligence for 70 years (see *Gubalke v Estate of Anthes* 202 NW 2d 836, 839 (Neb 1972)). Four other courts have cited it for its statements that include a balancing of risks and benefits; those cases were all decided at least 50 years after *Krayenbuhl* (see *Niegos v Indiana Harbor Belt Ry* 116 NE 2d 550, 552–53 (Ind App 1954); *Graci v United States*, 301 F Supp 947, 956 (ED La 1969), aff'd, 456 F 2d 20 (5th Cir 1971); *Hall v El DuPont de Nemours & Co* 345 F Supp 353, 366 (EDNY 1972); *Clayton v Penn Cent Transp Co* 376 NE 2d 524, 526 (Ind Ct App 1978)). *Krayenbuhl* was cited earlier by two courts, but the references were for the proposition that negligence requires reasonable precautions (see *Heller v New York, NH & HR Co* 265 F 192, 198 (2d Cir 1920); *Oldon v Ottertail Power Co* 65 F 2d 893, 894 (8th Cir 1933)). Another case, decided 40 years after *Krayenbuhl*, cited it for the proposition that balancing certain factors, including the probability of injury and precautions necessary to prevent injury, is 'just another way of saying that the standard of care is that which would be exercised by an ordinary prudent person under the same or similar circumstances' (*Indiana Harbor Belt Ry Co v Jones* 41 NE 2d 361, 364 (Ind 1942)).

Indeed, Bohlen's writing at the time of *Krayenbuhl* did not reflect anything resembling a risk–benefit standard for negligence. Bohlen wrote his first article on the subject of torts in 1901.[54] His second torts article was published the following year.[55] Both of these articles, in keeping with the dominant mode of scholarship of the day, consist almost exclusively of a discussion of appellate cases and the rules of law to be derived from them.[56] While neither of the articles has as its central concern the standard for negligence, they provide considerable signals about Bohlen's early views on this question. Bohlen repeatedly suggested that the essential condition for negligence is that a foreseeable risk of a 'probable' injury exists.[57] Nowhere did Bohlen discuss or acknowledge that the magnitude of the danger that results from the 'probable' risk of injury might be a relevant variable, or that the difficulty of preventing the risk is of concern.[58] Indeed, there are indications that he contemplated that once a probable injury is identified, the actor must take whatever precautions are necessary to prevent the harm, regardless of the costs in doing so (or benefit of not doing so).[59] On occasion, Bohlen equated this standard to that of the 'average reasonable man – not the ideal citizen, but the normal one'.[60] Bohlen's first edition of his casebook, published in 1915, had the chapter addressing negligence entitled 'Acts Wrongful Because Probably Injurious to Others'.[61]

[54] See FH Bohlen, 'The Probable or the Natural Consequence as the Test of Liability in Negligence' (1901) 49 *The American Law Register* 79; FH Bohlen, 'Right to Recover for Injury Resulting from Negligence Without Impact' (1902) 50 *The American Law Register* 141, 149.

[55] See Bohlen, 'Right to Recover for Injury Resulting from Negligence Without Impact' (n 54) 141.

[56] See ibid; Bohlen, 'The Probable or the Natural Consequence as the Test of Liability in Negligence' (n 54).

[57] See Bohlen, 'The Probable or the Natural Consequence as the Test of Liability in Negligence' (n 54) 82, 83–85, 151; Bohlen, 'Right to Recover for Injury Resulting from Negligence Without Impact' (n 54). Bohlen's first edition of his casebook, published in 1915, took the same approach. The chapter addressing negligence was entitled 'Acts Wrongful Because Probably Injurious to Others' (FH Bohlen, *Cases on the Law of Torts*, 1st edn (Indianapolis, IN, Bobbs–Merrill Co, 1915). Bohlen cites no sources in support of his statements that 'probable' injury is the key to negligence.

[58] In discussing the duty owed by a railroad to a prospective passenger waiting on the platform for the arrival of a train, Bohlen stated that the railroad should 'take such precautions as are reasonably sufficient to protect the passenger from any danger which he or she may probably be subjected to by his position as such' (Bohlen, 'Right to Recover for Injury Resulting from Negligence Without Impact' (n 54) 152). He also suggested local governments responsible for roadways owed a duty to make and maintain 'a road in such condition as to render all ordinary travel safe' (ibid 153).

[59] In this respect, Bohlen's view resembles *Bolton v Stone* [1951] AC 850 (HL) 867, where Lord Reid, acknowledging that the magnitude of risk was relevant in determining negligence, stated 'I do not think it would be right to take into account the difficulty of remedial measures'. The UK approach to the question of the role of precaution cost in determining negligence is ambivalent (see K Oliphant (ed), *The Law of Tort*, 3rd edn (London, LexisNexis, 2015) §§ 13.22–13.23). *Winfield & Jolowicz* is less ambivalent than Oliphant, stating that the magnitude of the risk has to be balanced against the burden of precaution, although the authors do recognise that if the risk is remote, no precautions may be required: E Peel and J Goudkamp, *Winfield & Jolowicz on Tort*, 19th edn (London, Sweet & Maxwell, 2014) §§ 6-020, 6-023.

[60] Bohlen, 'The Probable or the Natural Consequence as the Test of Liability in Negligence' (n 54) 83.

[61] Bohlen, *Cases on the Law of Torts* (n 57) 188. The second edition, published 10 years later, had a similar title for its negligence chapter: 'Acts Involving an Undue Probability of Material Harm to

In the same year that Bohlen's casebook appeared, Henry Terry wrote a now famous[62] article[63] about negligence. He set forth, somewhat clumsily,[64] a risk–benefit test. Several examples that accompanied his test plainly recognise a trade-off between avoiding risk and the costs of doing so.[65] Terry also observed that his analysis was likely inapplicable to non-enterprise activity (although that is not the terminology he used). Terry identified behaviour that had no apparent purpose or benefit; here, I believe he was referring to non-purposive behaviour by individuals that is careless or inadvertent, and he asserted that liability did not necessarily follow from the absence of any purpose or benefit. Rather, he invoked a different test: one of reasonable conduct.[66]

Early drafts of the *Restatement*, prepared in 1923, reflected Bohlen's earlier probable injury view and did not recognise Terry's different perspective. The first

the Legally Protected Interests of Others' (Bohlen, *Cases on the Law of Torts* (n 13) 168). But this edition, unlike the first, contained a cryptic footnote citing Henry Terry's article on negligence, with a pinpoint cite to Terry's discussion of negligence involving a balancing of the magnitude of risk with the benefits to be gained by undertaking the risk.

[62] The article was largely ignored until the second half of the 20th century, after *Carroll Towing* (n 29) (and the first *Restatement of Torts*) when the law and economics school and other scholars turned their attention to risk–benefit balancing and what it meant for tort law. I can find only two cases that cited the article prior to its adoption in the first *Restatement of Torts*, neither of which evidenced any interest in the risk–benefit test contained therein (see *Charbonneau v MacRury* 153 A 457 (NH 1931); *Patton v City of Grafton* 180 SE 267, 270 (W Va 1935)). Typical early academic citation to Terry's article was in a case note as support for some aspect of negligence law, only on one or two occasions for its risk utility discussion (see, eg, [n. d.], 'Recent Decisions' (1932–33) 10 *New York University Quarterly Law Review* 527, 545 fn 11).

[63] HT Terry, 'Negligence' (1915) 29 *Harvard Law Review* 40. Terry hinted at his balancing theory of negligence in a treatise he wrote 20 years earlier (see HT Terry, *Some Leading Principles of Anglo-American Law* (Philadelphia, PA, T & JW Johnson & Co, 1884) § 206: 'If I borrow a friend's diamond ring, I may not, for the purpose of saving myself trouble, omit to take precautions for its safety which no one would think of requiring from me about a borrowed newspaper … The amount of risk that can be reasonably run is necessarily different according to the value of things at risk').

[64] eg, Terry needed three factors, including such concepts as the 'collateral object' the injurer seeks to obtain with her conduct, to express the notion of the burden of precaution (Terry, 'Negligence' (1915) (n 63) 43). He also got caught up in distinguishing between legally cognisable interests and those that are not in articulating his factors (ibid 44).

[65] I do not know where Terry found the inspiration for his work, but there is not much evidence to support Greg Keating's claim that it was the result of careful reading and synthesis of the case law (Keating, 'Must the Hand Formula Not Be Named?' (n 36) 369). Terry's article reads as if the principles expressed were handed down from Mt Sinai as adjuncts to the 10 commandments. He does not explicitly or implicitly claim that his principles came from careful case reading and analysis. In 15 pages of text explaining negligence, Terry cites but 24 cases in 20 footnotes (Terry, 'Negligence' (n 63)). And, as explained in the text to nn 47–61 above and in n 66 below, there was very little cost benefit in the cases of Terry's era.

[66] (Terry, 'Negligence' (n 63) 46–47. This observation was not lost on Bohlen who, later in the same *Restatement of Torts* commentary about courts basing their decisions on a comparison of the risks and utility of an act, continued (*Restatement of Torts*, Tentative Draft No 4 (Pennsylvania, American Law Institute, 6 Apr 1929) § 172 commentary at 8): '[S]uch cases are comparatively rare. In the vast majority of cases the acts which do harm to others and the negligent character of which is under investigation, consist of inadvertence, carelessness, unskillfulness, inadequate preparation or the failure to give a warning. In such cases the problem is rarely presented. There is usually no social utility in such conduct. There may, however, be cases in which inadvertence may be justifiable. No man can under all circumstances be attentive to everything at once.'

Preliminary Draft of the *Restatement* prepared by Bohlen describes negligence as conduct that 'a reasonable man would recognise as posing *an undue probability of harm*'.[67] The Draft contains no further explanation of the undue probability concept.[68] While Bohlen adhered to his undue probability characterisation, the seeds for his later transformation are revealed in another passage where he referred to an act 'containing a probability of injury to the interests of others out of proportion to the utility of the act'.[69]

By the time the first *Restatement* was published in 1934, Bohlen had changed his mind and accepted Terry's conception of negligence. Sections 291–93 of the *Restatement* articulate, albeit also clumsily, a risk–benefit standard for negligence that invokes the benefit to be gained by the defendant's conduct and the probability and magnitude of any harm that may result.[70] Bohlen plainly had changed his mind prior to that, in a Preliminary Draft circulated in 1927 to Advisors,[71] and indeed suggested a balancing approach in a 1924 article he wrote.[72]

[67] *Restatement of Torts*, Preliminary Draft No 1 (Philadelphia, PA, American Law Institute, 10 December 1923) 7, 9 (emphasis added).

[68] Preliminary Draft No 2 contained a black-letter section reflecting the same view (first *Restatement of Torts*, Preliminary Draft No 2 (n 22) § 1(b)): 'Section 1. A substantial impairment of the physical condition of another's body or physical pain thereto, unless privileged, subjects the person causing it to a liability to the person the physical condition of whose body is impaired: … (b) if it results from conduct which a reasonable man would recognize as creating an undue probability of a substantial impairment of the physical condition of the other's body or physical pain thereto …'

[69] First *Restatement of Torts*, Preliminary Draft No 1 (n 67); Bohlen provided no explanation for the two different standards for negligence contained in this Draft.

[70] First *Restatement of Torts* (n 3) §§ 291–93.

[71] 'If the act is one which a reasonable man would recognize as creating a risk of bodily harm to another, the risk is unreasonable if the risk involved in the act is of such magnitude as to outweigh its social utility': *Restatement of Torts*, Preliminary Draft No 18 (Philadelphia, PA, American Law Institute, 4 October 1927) § 6. Quite similar language was contained in § 172 of a Tentative Draft that was circulated to the ALI membership and discussed at the annual meeting in 1929. There were no comments about this aspect of the draft at the annual meeting.

[72] FH Bohlen, 'Mixed Questions of Law and Fact' (1924) 72 *University of Pennsylvania Law Review* 111, 111 (standard of care is whether a reasonable person would 'have realized that his conduct contains a probability of harm … out of proportion to its social value and utility'). In the same article, Bohlen expressed scepticism about the jury's ability adequately to value the social utility of the defendant's conduct (ibid 119). At the end of his career, in his last article, Bohlen included a paean to Terry's article (Bohlen, 'Fifty Years of Torts' (n 27) 1226 (footnote omitted)): 'In the twenty-ninth volume of the Harvard Law Review there appeared an analysis of unreasonable and, therefore, negligent conduct which still serves as a starting point for modern research and speculation. In it Henry T Terry first brought into the open the now accepted view that in determining the negligence of the defendant's conduct the utility of the end served by it both to the actor and through him to society was to be weighed against the magnitude of the risk to which it subjected others. His analysis went deeper than this. It stated the factors which were to be considered in determining the utility of the conduct and in determining the magnitude of the risk. In the latter he included the extent of the likelihood that some harm would be done, the value of the interest endangered by the conduct, and the gravity of the harm which might result to such interest. This analysis, sloganized by Dean Pound's striking phrase "the balancing of interests", has been universally accepted in the law school world and has been followed in practice, though not always in words, by many courts.'

Patrick Kelley has unearthed an explanation for how Terry's views found their way into the *Restatement*, based on a slim volume written by Donald King after Warren Seavey's death (but which credits Seavey as a co-author).[73] Kelley identifies Seavey as having influenced Bohlen to adopt the Terry balancing view of negligence:

> The puzzling appearance of Terry and Seavey's general theory of negligence liability in Bohlen's Restatement may be explained by a reference in Warren Seavey's posthumously-published memoirs. In the summer of 1927 Seavey was teaching in the summer school at Yale, rooming with his friend, Edward S Thurston, the assistant reporter for the negligence restatement. Seavey wrote,
>
>> Most of my time was spent in preparing a draft of a chapter for the Torts Restatement, since Bohlen had gone to Europe, leaving us to do the spade work. Finding that Thurston had the same ideas that I did, I would write out a few pages and Thurston would check what I had written to check for inaccuracies ... When Bohlen returned he was disgruntled, since we had not followed his directions, but he let most of it stand. It became the basis for that which was finally incorporated into the Restatement.
>
> In the fall of 1927 and the Spring of 1928, Bohlen and his Advisers were working on the first part of the Negligence materials (Chapter I: General Principles), which wound up embodying Terry and Seavey's theories of negligence. That chapter, therefore, must have been what Seavey and Thurston were working on in the summer of 1927.[74]

Kelley adds his assessment that 'Seavey worked hard to convince Bohlen' and that Seavey 'clearly succeeded in persuading Bohlen of the accuracy of his theory'.[75]

I find the Seavey explanation unlikely. First, the Seavey article that Kelley cites does not focus on the content of negligence.[76] Rather, it is concerned with which acts and states of mind are based on subjective as opposed to objective criteria, as its title makes plain. That issue was a burning one for commentators at the end of the nineteenth century and early into the twentieth century. While Seavey's article does articulate a balancing test for negligence, that was in service to Seavey's efforts to characterise all of the matters that required assessment as to whether they should be determined based on objective or subjective criteria.

[73] WA Seavey and DB King, *A Harvard Law School Professor: Warren A. Seavey's Life and the World of Legal Education* (Buffalo, NY, William S Hein, 2004). The book is primarily written in the first person of Seavey and explains that it contains the 'recollections of Professor Warren Seavey, written when he was alive and then preserved by his family' (ibid viii). It was published 39 years after Seavey's death.

[74] See Kelly, 'The First Restatement of Torts: Reform by Descriptive Theory' (n 13) 109–10 (footnotes omitted).

[75] ibid 110.

[76] Indeed, Seavey explicitly denied that the article was about determining when a risk was sufficiently undue that liability should be imposed: 'What constitutes the "undueness" [of a risk] is not within the limits of this paper' (WA Seavey, 'Negligence – Subjective or Objective?' (1927) 41 *Harvard Law Review* 1, 7.

Seavey made no effort to argue that the balancing factors he identified should be (or were) the ones used by courts.[77]

Second, as Kelley appreciated, the King/Seavey passage does not identify the subject of the chapter that Seavey and Thurston worked on during the summer of 1927. While work was in progress on negligence, there were several other topics about negligence that were being developed other than the three sections that covered risk–benefit in the final published *Restatement*.[78] Most importantly, it appears that Bohlen's transformation preceded the summer of 1927 when Eldredge and Seavey were at work. In a 1926 book, *Studies in the Law of Torts*, a collection of the articles he had written over the past 25 years, he reflected in a 'Note' about his first article,[79] which suggested that negligence depended alone on a 'probability' of injury.[80] 'The article is immature', Bohlen wrote, and then itemised several difficulties with it.[81] Among them, notably, was his recognition that the likelihood of injury was not the sole determinant of negligence, citing the 'very valuable' article by Henry Terry that elaborated on the factors, along with the probability of harm, that determine whether an act is negligent.[82] And, as mentioned previously, Bohlen recognised balancing factors in an article published in January 1924,[83] even as early as December 1923 in his first Preliminary Draft for the *Restatement*.[84] Bohlen's recanting of his prior views, again occurring before Seavey and Eldredge's summer, contains none of the reluctance suggested by the Seavey and King claim.[85] Indeed, Bohlen had presented his reformed view of negligence to the *Restatement* Advisors just before the summer of 1927, where the three factors are referred to along with the explanation that they were systemised by Henry Terry in his 1915 article.[86]

[77] See ibid 7, 8, fn 7.

[78] *Restatement of Torts* (n 3) §§ 291–93. The first *Restatement of Torts* contained over 200 black-letter sections applicable to negligence. It seems more likely that Seavey and Eldredge's efforts were focused on working out the role of subjectivity and objectivity in determining negligence, which was the subject of Seavey's 1927 article. Indeed, that is what the Seavey and King book says, referencing the 1927 article, 'when Thurston and I wrote the first chapter on negligence we used it as a basis' (Seavey and King, *A Harvard Law School Professor: Warren A Seavey's Life and the World of Legal Education* (n 73) 98).

[79] See Bohlen, 'The Probable or the Natural Consequence as the Test of Liability in Negligence' (n 54).

[80] Bohlen, *Cases on the Law of Torts* (n 13). The following year, Bohlen circulated Preliminary Draft No 18, which contained his first effort at a risk–benefit test. See n 71.

[81] Bohlen, *Cases on the Law of Torts* (n 13).

[82] ibid 31–32. Indeed, a year earlier, Bohlen cited, albeit obscurely, the Terry article in the second edition of Bohlen's torts casebook (see n 61).

[83] See n 72.

[84] See text accompanying n 69.

[85] Bohlen went on to fully embrace risk–benefit balancing. The third edition of Bohlen's casebook, published in 1930, contained *Krayenbuhl* for the first time. Bohlen footnoted the court's statement of risk–benefit as negligence with a reference to, among other sources, section 172 [the section in Tentative Draft No 4 containing a risk–benefit standard] of the *Restatement of Torts*.

[86] American Law Institute, *Torts Conference Minutes* 3–4 (Pennsylvania, PA, 14 June 1927). Curiously, I cannot identify the Preliminary Draft containing discussion of this matter. Preliminary Draft No 17 (Philadelphia, PA, American Law Institute, 14 February 1927) was about intentional

Finally, there are several inaccuracies about *Restatements* and Seavey's involvement in them that gives one pause about accepting all of the claims in the King book.[87]

So, in the end, how much credit does Bohlen deserve for recognising that negligence often entails a trade-off between risk and precaution? My best judgement is, along with Henry Terry and Learned Hand, a considerable amount. Terry needed Bohlen and the *Restatement* to get his views out to a wider legal audience. And, as I explain below, there is reasonably good evidence that Judge Hand was influenced by the *Restatement* when he wrote the several opinions leading to *Carroll Towing*.

Hand's first articulation of a risk–benefit test occurred 10 years before *Carroll Towing*, in *The Charles H Sells*,[88] although he stated it linguistically and without mathematical symbology but more crisply than the prior versions by Terry and Bohlen.[89] The genealogic connection to *Carroll Towing*, is, however, unmistakable: 'As in all such situations [determining the appropriate standard of care] the legal standard is the function of three variables: the actuarial possibility that the event will occur; the gravity of the damage, if it does; the expense and effort necessary to fend against it'.[90] *Sells* was decided three years after the negligence volume of the *Restatement* was published and 10 years after Bohlen first set forth a balancing of the risk (which consists of the magnitude of harm discounted by the probability it will occur) created by conduct against its social utility in a Preliminary Draft.[91] Hand was a co-founder of the ALI and a member of the ALI Council from its inception in 1923. Hand was also quite active in reviewing *Restatement* drafts during the period when Bohlen was preparing drafts of the *Restatement of Torts*. Hand was present at the October 1927 Advisory Committee meeting at which there was considerable discussion

torts and the next draft, denominated '18-R' was dated 4 October 1927. Perhaps that draft is a revision of an earlier draft distributed before the June meeting that has not been preserved by HeinOnline, my source for preliminary drafts of the *Restatement*.

[87] Among the ones I was able to identify, King states (Seavey and King, *A Harvard Law School Professor: Warren A Seavey's Life and the World of Legal Education* (n 73) 68) that Seavey, after Bohlen died, was commissioned by the ALI to change prior work that he believed erroneous. That would have been impossible, as the first two volumes of the *Restatement*, covering intentional and negligent torts, had been published in 1934, eight years before Bohlen's death in 1942. The book (ibid 72) states that Seavey was a 'chief Reporter' of the *Restatement*. While he did contribute as Reporter for several later portions of the *Restatement*, he was not the chief Reporter. At another point, the book incorrectly dates the submission of an article to the *Harvard Law Review* as 1928 – the article was published in 1927 (ibid 98).

[88] *The Charles H Sells* (n 34).

[89] On the differences between Terry, Bohlen and the first *Restatement*, on the one hand, and *Carroll Towing* (n 29), on the other, see Gilles, 'On Determining Negligence: Hand Formula Balancing, the Reasonable Person Standard, and the Jury' (n 37) 827–31.

[90] *The Charles H Sells* (n 34) 633.

[91] Although Hand did not cite §§ 291–93 of the *Restatement of Torts* in any of the cases mentioned in n 34, that was consistent with his practice of refraining from citing restatements (see G Gunther, *Learned Hand: The Man and The Judge* (New York, Knopf, 1994) 413). It was a practice he occasionally violated (see, eg, *Siegmann v Meyer* 100 F 2d 367, 368 (2d Cir 1938)).

of Bohlen's proposal to use the Terry framework for negligence in the *Restatement*, although apparently not on the day (the meeting went for four days) that Bohlen presented Terry's idea in the meeting.[92] Patrick Kelley, independently, reached the same conclusion about the provenance of *Carroll Towing*, citing Hand's commitment to and involvement in the ALI along with his interest in developing legal thought.[93]

What would have happened if Bohlen had not picked up on Terry and incorporated his negligence balancing in the first *Restatement*? That is a hard question to answer. As previously explained, notwithstanding the law and economics claims,[94] the *Carroll Towing* test was not embedded in tort law and could be found in only a few scattered cases.[95] Indeed, *Carroll Towing* was not welcomed with open arms by the torts community. The first time that it was cited by a court for its risk–benefit standard was in 1963.[96] The casebooks of the 1950s were only mildly more attentive.[97] Regular reliance on *Carroll Towing's* risk–benefit test in court opinions and legal scholarship had to wait until the 1970s and the rise of the law and economics movement.[98] Cost–benefit analysis, a central concept in economics, surely would have embraced whatever hints or strands of it existed in legal sources, at least for those doing descriptive work. Surely, *Carroll Towing* and the *Restatements* gave greater succour to those doing law and economics, but there were other strands that existed independent of those pillars.

[92] *Restatement of Torts Minutes of Conferences* (Philadelphia, PA, American Law Institute, 20–23 October 1927 (copy in Harvard Law School Law Library)). Of course, the possibility exists that Hand was informed of Bohlen's decision to use Terry's factors at another time during the meeting. Cardozo was also present. Although not relevant to my subject, I cannot resist reporting that one year before *Palsgraf* (n 53), Cardozo and Hand rehearsed the Cardozo–Andrews debate in *Palsgraf* about duty to the plaintiff–duty to the world that played out in the majority and dissenting opinions in *Palsgraf*.

[93] Kelley, 'The Carroll Towing Company Case and the Teaching of Tort Law' (n 30) 732.

[94] See Landes and Posner, *The Economic Structure of Tort Law* (n 33).

[95] See *Restatement of Torts*, Explanatory Notes to Tentative Draft No 4 (n 26).

[96] See *Wildwood Mink Ranch v United States* 218 F Supp 67, 75 (D Minn 1963). Robert Strassfeld pointed out to me that in the pre-computer legal research era, how a case was categorised for West headnote purposes played a significant role in who and how many researchers found it. All four headnotes and key numbers of *Carroll Towing* (n 29) were placed in the 'Shipping' category.

[97] I located seven books published during the 1950s, excluding prior editions of the same text. *Carroll Towing* (n 29) was a principal case in only the text co-authored by Prosser and a 1959 book by Gregory and Kalven; it was cited in one other (see WA Seavey et al, *Cases and Materials on the Law of Torts* (St Paul, MN, West Publishing Co, 1957); YB Smith and WL Prosser, *Cases and Materials on Torts*, 2nd edn (Brooklyn, NY, Foundation Press, 1957); CO Gregory and H Kalven Jr, *Cases and Materials on Torts* (Boston, MA, Little Brown & Co, 1959)). *Carroll Towing* was ignored in four other casebooks of the decade (see H Shulman and F James Jr, *Cases and Materials on the Law of Torts*, 2nd edn (Brooklyn, NY, Foundation Press, 1952); FH Bohlen, *Cases on the Law of Torts*, 5th edn (Indianapolis, IN, Bobbs–Merrill Co, 1953); CM Hepburn, *Cases on the Law of Torts*, 3rd edn (St Paul, MN, West Publishing Co, 1954); L Green et al, *Cases on the Law of Torts* (St Paul, MN, West Publishing Co, 1957)).

[98] Westlaw searches found that 80% of court citations to *Carroll Towing* (n 29) or the Hand formula occurred after 1969, while over 99% of citations in secondary sources occurred in that same time frame.

V. THE FIRST RESTATEMENT AND CAUSATION

The second aspect of Bohlen's work I would like to address is his *Restatement* work on causation.[99] For reasons explained below, this is not celebratory: rather it is descriptive, first; critical, second. For purposes of this discussion, I shall use 'factual cause' to address the matter of whether the defendant's act was a necessary condition (*sine qua non* or 'but for') for the plaintiff's harm and 'scope of liability', to determine whether, despite the existence of tortious conduct and factual cause, the defendant will not be held liable. Those are the clearest terms to describe those two different concepts, even if the latter is not widely adopted at this time.[100]

By way of introduction, as with negligence, Bohlen's early writings expressed some primitive ideas on the subject of scope of liability.[101] Like his earlier writings on negligence, he repudiated some of that work, writing in 1926 in the midst of his restating work, about the state of flux in tort law and the extent to which time and societal evolution had changed terminology and substance.[102]

To proceed, it might be well to explain the framework adopted by Bohlen in the *Restatement*. Bohlen began with an umbrella term for causation, 'Legal Cause',[103] although he recognised that 'Proximate Cause' was in much wider use.[104] Thus, Bohlen, in one of the initial *Restatement* efforts, sought to use the *Restatement* as a platform for changing legal terminology. That is, as subsequent

[99] Aside from two early articles on scope of liability, all of Bohlen's work in this area was confined to the *Restatement of Torts*.

[100] Although it is employed by the leading US torts treatise and by at least a couple of leading US torts casebook (see DB Dobbs et al, *The Law of Torts*, 2nd edn (St Paul, MN, West Publishing Co, 2011) ch 18; DB Dobbs et al, *Torts and Compensation: Personal Accountability and Social Responsibility for Injury*, 7th edn (St Paul, MN, West Publishing Co, 2013); MA Franklin et al, *Tort Law and Alternatives: Cases and Materials*, 10th edn (Washington, DC, Foundation, 2016).

[101] Specifically, Bohlen expressed the view that liability should extend to all consequences that were the result of the 'natural laws of cause and effect', but that intervening causes could break the chain of causation (Bohlen, 'The Probable or the Natural Consequence as the Test of Liability in Negligence' (n 54) 80). The idea that liability was limited to the natural and probable consequences of tortious conduct was prevalent at the time (see, eg, F Pollock, *The Law of Torts*, 10th edn (London, Stevens and Sons, 1916) 40). Bohlen ignored factual cause in his discussion of the requisites for causation to be satisfied in a negligence case (FH Bohlen, 'Probable or the Natural Consequence as the Test of Liability in Negligence (part 2)' (1901) 49 *American Law Register* 148). Nowhere in these articles does he mention 'substantial factor' as a test or element for causation, confirming that it was Jeremiah Smith's work on this subject that influenced Bohlen to adopt it in the *Restatement of Torts*. See text accompanying nn 108–152.

[102] Bohlen, *Studies in the Law of Torts* (n 13) v–vi.

[103] *Restatement of Torts* (n 3) § 431.

[104] Bohlen explained the reason for this was that the modifier 'proximate' suggested that only those acts or conduct that were nearest to the harm or latest in the chain of events leading to the harm were the ones to which liability attached (see *Restatement of Torts*, Explanatory Notes to Preliminary Draft No 46 (Philadelphia, PA, American Law Institute, 3 December 1931) 3). Apparently the first (entirely unself-conscious) use of 'legal cause' to mean the appropriate causal relationship for liability to be imposed was in a Queen's Bench case involving a gratuitous bailment, *Coggs v Bernard* (1703) 2 Ld Raym 909, 92 ER 107.

events reveal, risky business.[105] *Restatements*, notwithstanding the persuasive effect they have had on courts for decades, are often inadequate to the task of revising long-established and well-entrenched legal language. Bohlen's move was especially daring given that the *Restatements* had no track record at the time to provide an informed assessment of how much they might influence the courts for which they were intended. Replacing proximate cause with legal cause does not extirpate any uses of the former in the court opinions that had already been published and which were contained in the casebooks from which law students learn the law.

Bohlen initially adopted 'legal cause' in the *Restatement* chapters on intentional torts, which he prepared before the negligence materials.[106] In doing so, he distinguished 'actual cause', by which he meant factual cause (*causa sine qua non*), from legal cause, which encompassed both actual cause and scope of liability.[107] Those provisions were expanded in the negligence materials.

The structure that Bohlen chose for legal cause in the negligence materials was borrowed from a series of articles on cause and scope of liability by Professor (previously Judge) Jeremiah Smith.[108] In the first of those articles, Smith laid out the two issues posed by legal cause, a term that he unabashedly and without explanation employed, despite the greater popularity of proximate cause:[109]

1. Was defendant's tort in fact the cause of plaintiff's damage?
2. If so, is there any arbitrary rule of law absolving defendant from liability for all, or any part of, the damage of which his tortious conduct was in fact the cause?[110]

[105] Fully cognisant of Bohlen's failure to move legal terminology from proximate cause to legal cause, Bill Powers and I faced two different efforts to do the same. One, during 'Apportionment of Liability', was to adopt a more accurate term than joint and several liability, which concededly is poor at describing what it is about. My recollection is that Bob Keeton was the leader of those advocating this change. We successfully resisted that effort, although there was significant sentiment in support, on grounds similar to those expressed in the text along with the fact that few were misled by the inaccurate terminology. The second was with regard to the name of the principle that limits liability notwithstanding a breach that factually caused plaintiff's harm in the 'Liability for Physical and Emotional Harm Restatement'. We began with proximate cause but acceded, though not without reluctance, to a proposal to replace it with 'scope of liability'. We ultimately accepted the latter because of the continuing confusion that proximate cause has produced, both because it is frequently used to mean three different things and because it is so inaccurate in describing what it is about – neither proximity nor cause (at least in a factual cause sense). Only time will tell whether our judgement was correct.

[106] See *Restatement of Torts*, Tentative Draft No 1 (Philadelphia, PA, American Law Institute, 5 April 1925) § 6. Six months earlier, in a Preliminary Draft, Bohlen had black-letter language employing legal cause that was quite similar to the one in Tentative Draft No 1, save that there was no explanatory commentary in the Preliminary Draft (see *Restatement of Torts*, Preliminary Draft No 10 (Philadelphia, PA, American Law Institute, 25 November 1924) § 6).

[107] ibid § 6 cmt. In that cleavage, Bohlen was ahead of a number of contemporary treatises, which treated causation (or more commonly 'remoteness of damage') as a unitary concept that would negate liability if it did not exist (see, eg, Hale, *Handbook on the Law of Torts* (n 8) 43–44).

[108] J Smith, 'Legal Cause in Actions of Tort' (1911–12) 25 *Harvard Law Review* 103 ('Smith I'); J Smith, 'Legal Cause in Actions of Tort' (1911–12) 25 *Harvard Law Review* 223 ('Smith II'); J Smith, 'Legal Cause in Actions of Tort' (1911–12) 25 *Harvard Law Review* 303 ('Smith III').

[109] See Smith I (n 108) 106: 'Indeed the expression "proximate cause" is generally used instead of "legal cause", and it is often under the former head that one must look in digests for authorities on causation.'

[110] ibid 123.

In the overview section on legal cause, § 431, Bohlen echoed Smith's structure:

> LEGAL CAUSE; WHAT CONSTITUTES
>
> The actor's negligent conduct is a legal cause of harm to another if
>
> (a) his conduct is a substantial factor in bringing about the harm, and
> (b) there is no rule of law relieving the actor from liability because of the manner in which his negligence has resulted in the harm.[111]

Beyond the black letter, comment *a* explained why a philosophic conception of causation (Mill's view that all antecedent necessary conditions are causes) is different from the legal conception; that was also drawn from Smith's article.[112] To combat the overbroad philosophic definition of cause,[113] Bohlen employed the limiting concept of 'substantial factor'. Embedded in the substantial factor requirement was a *sine qua non* element.[114] However, *sine qua non* was not sufficient to constitute a substantial factor; something more was required. Bohlen explained that something more:

> The negligence must also be a substantial factor as well as an actual factor in bringing about the plaintiff's harm. The word substantial is used to denote the fact that the defendant's conduct has such an effect in producing the harm as to lead reasonable men to regard it as a cause using that word in the popular sense in which there always lurks the idea of responsibility, rather than in the so-called 'philosophic sense', which includes every one of the great number of events without which any happening would not have occurred. Each of these events is a cause in the so-called 'philosophic sense' yet the effect of many of them is so insignificant that no ordinary mind would think of them as causes.[115]

My view is that the causation and scope of liability provisions in the first *Restatement* missed a significant opportunity to provide a coherent and sensible structure for these elements, and instead adopted and perpetuated an unfortunate structure and substance for causation and scope of liability. The substance, architecture and terminology of causation in the first *Restatement* is confused and confusing, and in some instances has cast a dark and perplexing pall over the subject to this day. By the time Bohlen was restating causation, the tools

[111] *Restatement of Torts* (n 3) § 431; see also § 9 cmt *b*.
[112] cf ibid § 431 cmt *a*.
[113] What Bohlen failed to appreciate in accepting the concern that the philosophic concept of causation (all necessary antecedents) is too broad, is that tort law has other means to screen those necessary antecedents from being subject to liability. Those means include negligence by a juridical person, scope of liability, duty and legally cognisable harm. Nicholas St John Green, 50 years earlier, and cited in the Smith articles from which Bohlen borrowed so extensively, explained this point (see NJ Green, 'Proximate and Remote Cause' (1870) 4 *American Law Register* 201, 211–12). Bingham, in 1909, provided a straightforward definition of cause, 'a condition, force, or omission was a cause of a status if that identical status would not have occurred but for the contribution of the condition, force or omission' (JW Bingham, 'Some Suggestions Concerning "Legal Cause" at Common Law' (1909) 9 *Columbia Law Review* 16, 23).
[114] See *Restatement of Torts* (n 3) § 431(a).
[115] ibid § 431 cmt *a*.

were available, if not well accepted, to take a path that articulated a more coherent and logical framework and substance for causation and scope of liability. Unfortunately, Bohlen chose another path. The *Restatement (Second)* adopted his architecture, terminology, and the vast majority of the substance of the core provisions on cause and scope of liability identified above,[116] so Prosser deserves some share of comparative responsibility, although his is for nonfeasance as contrasted with Bohlen's misfeasance.[117] Some, although thankfully not all, of the terminology in the first *Restatement* has been adopted by courts and therefore embedded in legal usage.

Those are provocative claims, I recognise, and perhaps outside the theme of this volume in celebrating our famous predecessors. What I wish to critique is Bohlen's (i) causation architecture; (ii) terminology, specifically the confusing use of 'substantial factor'; (iii) substance, in demanding the 'more than' but-for required for factual cause; and (iv) failure to clarify the jumble of scope of liability law and provide coherent treatment of that subject, adopting, among others, a hindsight test like that advocated by Judge Andrews dissenting in *Palsgraf*.[118] In the course of this critique, I point out treatments of these matters contemporaneous with Bohlen's work that, had he attended to them, would have provided a huge improvement to the first *Restatement*'s coverage of causation. Tempering this critique, I must acknowledge that the state of the case law and treatises on these matters at the time left a great deal to be desired in terms of clarity and consistency but that was precisely the reason for the formation of the ALI and its preparation of *Restatements*.

Consider the architecture of causation coverage in the first *Restatement*. There appears to be a chapter devoted to the topic, chapter 16, comprising 33 black-letter sections.[119] Yet the very first section reveals that one needs to look elsewhere (§ 281(b)) to find additional requirements about causation. Section 281, which provides the elements for a negligence cause of action,

[116] Including down to individual comments contained in the *Restatement of Torts*. One significant change in the *Restatement (Second) of Torts* (n 2) occurred in § 281 cmt *j*. That comment made an actor who threatened harm to a legally cognisable interest of another liable for all harm to the other, regardless of whether the harm was different from the harms whose risk made the actor's conduct tortious. That comment in the *Restatement (Second) of Torts* reversed the position of the first *Restatement of Torts* (n 3) § 281 cmt g, which distinguished between interests in bodily integrity and interests in property and provided that an actor whose negligence threatened harm only to one such interest would not subject the actor to liability if harm to the other interest occurred.

[117] Curiously, Prosser was critical of the use of causal terminology to deal with scope of liability issues (WL Prosser, *Handbook of Torts*, 4th edn (St Paul, MN, West Publishing Co, 1971) 311: 'The tendency of courts to state these considerations in terms of causation often obscure the real issues involved').

[118] Although Judge Andrews is often credited with the hindsight test for determining scope of liability, it had gained some limited traction well before *Palsgraf* (n 53). See Smith II (n 108) 246.

[119] See *Restatement of Torts* (n 3) §§ 430–62.

includes an unnamed requirement that adopts both *Palsgraf*[120] and a harm within the risk standard,[121] independent of the legal cause element.[122] Yet in the factual causation title, Bohlen, in dealing with substantial factor,[123] adopted a hindsight test – whether, looking back after the harm, it appears extraordinary that the tortious act caused the harm.[124] Thus, without acknowledging it, the *Restatement* contained two different tests for scope of liability, neither of which is contained within the title concerning scope of liability. Indeed, the placement of a hindsight test in the factual causation title was so obviously a misplacement that the ALI attempted in 1948, in an unfortunately obscure volume, to seek to correct that mistake.[125]

In the title covering scope of liability, the *Restatement* begins with five black-letter sections that identify what is not outside the scope of liability,[126] and then proceeds over the remaining 22 sections to consider the effect of a variety of different intervening acts and forces that do or do not constitute superseding causes that prevent the tortious actor from being held liable.[127] Nowhere in that title is there a general test describing when harm resulting from tortious conduct is within the actor's scope of liability.[128] This focus on superseding

[120] *Palsgraf* (n 53) was decided in 1928 during the drafting of the first *Restatement*. For a thorough account of the cross-influence of the *Restatement* and *Palsgraf*, see Kaufman, *Cardozo* (n 4) 286–302.

[121] Actually § 281(b) expressly contains only a harm with the risk standard, 'the conduct of the actor is negligent with respect to [a protected interest] or any other similar interest of the other'. However, commentary to that section also imports the rule of *Palsgraf*, albeit without telling the reader whether this is duty, scope of liability or some other unidentified matter (§ 281 cmt *c*). And the first *Restatement* nowhere identifies duty as an element of a negligence claim (§ 281), which contains four elements: (i) negligence; (ii) *Palsgraf* and harm within the risk; (iii) legal cause; and (iv) lack of contributory negligence.

[122] Bohlen might better have just quit after § 281(b) and one section on factual cause, which is just about what the *Restatement (Third)* did.

[123] By placing a test for scope of liability in a section about factual case and the role of substantial factor, Bohlen cemented the confusion over whether substantial factor is an element of factual cause or scope of liability. See text accompanying nn 139–141.

[124] *Restatement of Torts* (n 3) § 433(b). This is consistent with Bohlen's article on scope of liability, in which he advocated both a hindsight test and a test invoking intercession of other causes that interfered with 'the ordinary natural laws of cause and effect' (Bohlen, 'The Probable or the Natural Consequence as the Test of Liability in Negligence' (n 54) 80).

[125] *Restatement of Torts* (Philadelphia, PA, American Law Institute, 1948 Supp) § 433.

[126] eg, *Restatement of Torts* (n 3) § 435 (neither unforeseeability of extent nor manner of harm prevents an actor from being liable).

[127] Warren Seavey, four years after the first *Restatement* was published, identified two different tests for scope of liability contained within it, the risk standard in § 281 and the series of sections on superseding causes (WA Seavey, 'Mr Justice Cardozo and the Law of Torts' (1939) 39 *Columbia Law Review* 20, 38; (1939) 52 *Harvard Law Review* 372, 290; (1939) 48 *Yale Law Journal* 390, 408 (parallel publication of the same Symposium articles)).

[128] What tests are provided are contained in passages outside the scope of liability title. See text accompanying nn 119–122.

causes reflected the formalist efforts to pursue law-as-science.[129] As Bill Powers put it:

> The style of argument was pseudoscientific and deductive, focusing on causal 'links' in the chain between the defendant's conduct and the plaintiff's injury. For example, an intervening human cause or an act of God might break a direct 'chain' of causation …[130]

We should recognise that this occurred at a time when the scope of liability determination took on much greater importance because contribution between jointly and severally liable tortfeasors was not available.

An even more serious problem with the first *Restatement*'s architecture is its use of an umbrella term to encompass two very different concepts: factual causation and limitations on the liability of a tortious actor who has caused legally cognisable harm. Proximate cause was the popular umbrella term,[131] but Bohlen, as explained, replaced it with legal cause. While there was good reason for leaving proximate cause behind,[132] there were even better reasons for eliminating any umbrella term at all and treating causation and scope of liability as the two distinct elements that they are.[133]

[129] And indeed these efforts were contained in an early article by Bohlen on scope of liability (see Bohlen, 'The Probable or the Natural Consequence as the Test of Liability in Negligence' (n 54) 80: 'Where such a rule of conduct established by public policy for the good of all is violated, the wrongdoer should answer for all the consequences brought about by the working out of the injurious tendency of this wrongful act until the ordinary natural laws of cause and effect are diverted by some outside agency.' A year before the first *Restatement* was published, Fowler Harper took issue with the formalist approach to superseding causes, contending that the foreseeability of the intervening act was the critical matter in determining whether it was a superseding cause that negated liability for the earlier negligent actor (see FV Harper, *A Treatise on the Law of Torts* (Indianapolis, IN, Bobbs–Merrill Co, 1933)). Harper's position on this is reflected, almost 80 years later, in the *Restatement (Third) of Torts* (n 1) § 34.

[130] WC Powers Jr, 'Reputology' (1991) 12 *Cardozo Law Review* 1941, 1951. See also White, *Tort Law in America: An Intellectual History* (n 13) 101–02.

[131] CE Carpenter, 'Workable Rules for Determining Proximate Cause – Part I' (1932) 20 *California Law Review* 229, 232 (proximate cause is 'used almost universally by the courts').

[132] See *Restatement (Third) of Torts* (n 1) § 29 cmt *b*. Bohlen articulated these reasons in Bohlen (n 27) 1228.

[133] The conflation of factual cause and proximate cause in the first *Restatement* has been criticised since shortly after it was published (see Green, 'The Torts Restatement' (n 14) 606–07). For other scholars favouring the separation of factual cause and proximate cause, see HLA Hart and AM Honoré, *Causation in the Law*, 2nd edn (Oxford, OUP, 1985) 110; J Stapleton, 'Legal Cause: Cause-in-Fact and the Scope of Liability for Consequences' (2001) 54 *Vanderbilt Law Review* 941; RW Wright, 'Once More into the Bramble Bush: Duty, Causal Contribution, and the Extent of Legal Responsibility' (2001) 54 *Vanderbilt Law Review* 1071, 1073; DA Logan and WA Logan, *North Carolina Torts*, 2nd edn (Durham, NC, Carolina Academic Press, 2004) § 7.10. There is a general consensus in contemporary work that the two should be kept separate. Both leading US torts treatises and the leading Canadian treatise agree, as do a number of contemporary casebooks (see FV Harper et al, *Harper, James & Gray on Torts*, 3rd edn (New York, Aspen Publishers, 2006) § 20.2, fn 1; Linden and Feldthusen, *Canadian Tort Law* (n 32) (containing separate chapters on factual causation and scope of liability); VS Schwartz et al, *Prosser, Wade and Schwartz's Torts: Cases and Materials*, 13th edn (Washington, DC, Foundation Press, 2015) (containing separate chapters on factual causation and legal or proximate cause); DB Dobbs et al, *Hornbook on Torts*, 2nd edn (St Paul, MN, West Publishing Co, 2016) § 15.3; Franklin et al, *Tort Law and Alternatives: Cases and Materials* (n 100) (containing separate chapters devoted to factual cause and scope of liability).

There are four reasons for decoupling factual cause and scope of liability. First, this permits courts and factfinders to focus on the issue that is truly in dispute. Second, even when the two matters are each at issue, having distinct treatment for each clarifies analysis and avoids confusion – confusion that continues to this day when umbrella terms, whether proximate cause or legal cause, are used. Third, separation enables courts and juries to address scope of liability matters without confusing and inapt causal language.[134] Lastly, eliminating use of an umbrella term quells usage of it to mean three different things: factual cause, scope of liability, and both.[135]

Scholarship at the time, although surely not all of it, had clearly distinguished between factual cause and recognised that scope of liability was not about factual cause.[136] Jeremiah Smith reported that in some cases 'it is difficult to tell upon which of these three questions [negligence, factual cause and scope of liability] the decision really turned. The issues were not kept separate and distinct as they should have been.'[137] Bohlen, himself, had made the distinction between actual cause and legal cause in an early draft of the *Restatement* (although the section overall was quite confusing), but that provision disappeared in the final version.[138]

Terminologically, adoption of a substantial factor test for factual causation was an unfortunate mistake.[139] Substantial factor involves an evaluative assessment that is contrary to the counterfactual dichotomous analysis demanded by

See also Peel and Goudkamp, *Winfield & Jolowicz on Tort* (n 59) ch 7 at 161–206 (containing separate subchapters on causation in fact and remoteness of damage). The case law, unfortunately, to this day, remains muddled.

[134] See *Restatement (Third) of Torts* (n 1) § 29, Rptr's note to cmt g.

[135] See DW Robertson, 'The Common Sense of Cause in Fact' (1997) 75 *Texas Law Review* 1765, 1776 and fn 43 (identifying three distinct ways in which 'substantial factor' is employed in the *Restatement*).

[136] See Bingham, 'Some Suggestions Concerning "Legal Cause" at Common Law' (n 113) 23 and 35 (distinguishing between but-for causes and 'legally blameable' causes, the latter of which is 'not a causal question at all'; denominating it a causal matter 'is misleading'); Smith II (n 108) 242; JA McLaughlin, 'Proximate Cause' (1925) 39 *Harvard Law Review* 149, 153; Carpenter, 'Workable Rules for Determining Proximate Cause – Part I' (n 131) 229 (footnote omitted) ('[c]ause in fact is essential to liability, but liability must be further delimited').

[137] See Smith II (n 108) 242. Similarly, Henry Terry also reported on courts that failed to correctly identify the issue as one of factual cause or scope of liability (HT Terry, 'Proximate Consequences in the Law of Torts' (1914–1915) 28 *Harvard Law Review* 10, 16). See also L Green, *Rationale of Proximate Cause* (Kansas City, KS, Vernon Law Book Co, 1927) 155: 'The only regret is that the two problems [factual cause and scope of liability] were confused and the impression left that the court thought that "expectation or probability" had a part in determining the causal relation between the collision and the losses claimed'; Green, 'The Torts Restatement' (n 14) 604–05 (criticising the *Restatement of Torts* for using legal cause – 'here are two essential phases of liability expressed in the term *cause*, and they can never be kept separate if the same word is used to express both ideas') (original emphasis).

[138] See *Restatement of Torts*, Tentative Draft No 1 (Philadelphia, PA, American Law Institute, 5 May 1925) § 6 cmt ('An act or omission may be the actual cause of an invasion of which it is not the legal cause.').

[139] Bohlen adopted the phrase from an article by Jeremiah Smith (Smith III (n 108) 309–10). There was very little use of the term in either court opinions or the torts treatises at the time Bohlen was preparing the causation materials for the *Restatement*.

the *sine qua non* test for causation.[140] Given the inconsistent architecture of the first *Restatement* and the evaluative nature of the phrase, it is no surprise that many courts and commentators understand it to be about scope of liability rather than factual cause.[141]

Structurally, there is considerable confusion about whether the 'more than' but-for is about factual cause, limitations on liability or, as modern minds have difficulty wrapping their heads around, a unitary causation concept that encompasses both factual cause and limitations on liability in a single element.[142] Indeed, there is even more confusion about whether 'substantial factor' is limited to factual causation or also encompasses at least some aspects of scope of liability, or even contains the scope of liability limits. Recall that § 431 required both a substantial factor and the absence of a 'rule of law relieving the actor of liability because of the manner in which his negligence has resulted in the harm'.[143] That might mean that 'substantial factor' encompasses factual cause, while rules of law negating liability are about scope of liability.[144] Section 432 suggests that substantial factor is about factual cause as it requires that the tortious conduct be a *sine qua non* to constitute a substantial factor. In the 1948 revisions to the initial set of *Restatements*, Lawrence Eldredge, a former student of Bohlen who later assisted Bohlen in the latter stages of his *Restatement* work and then continued work on the *Restatement* after

[140] AC Becht and FW Miller, *The Test of Factual Causation in Negligence and Strict Liability Cases* (St Louis, MO, Washington University Studies, 1961) 131–34.

[141] Ironically, during an Advisor's meeting, 'substantial effect' was recommended for use as the test for scope of liability (*Restatement of Torts Minutes of Conferences* (Philadelphia, PA, American Law Institute, 20–21 February 1931) 10–13). Prosser, while preparing the *Restatement (Second) of Torts*, wrote 'the "substantial factor" element deals with causation in fact' (*Restatement (Second) of Torts* (n 2) § 433 Rptr's note). By the fifth edition of his treatise (after he had died) the view had changed: 'The "substantial factor" formulation is one concerning legal significance rather than factual quantum' (WP Keeton et al, *Prosser and Keeton on the Law of Torts*, 5th edn (St Paul, MN, West Publishing Co, 1984) § 41. Harper, James and Gray's treatise understands Bohlen's use of substantial factor in the first *Restatement of Torts* as addressing scope of liability (Harper et al, *Harper, James & Gray on Torts* (n 133) § 20.6), but then waffles and acknowledges that maybe it was about factual cause (ibid 224–25, fn 46). See also Carpenter, 'Workable Rules for Determining Proximate Cause – Part I' (n 131) 234–35. For courts that have used substantial factor for scope of liability, rather than factual-causation purposes, see, eg, *Tetro v Town of Stratford* 458 A 2d 5 (Conn 1983); *Haynes v Hamilton County* 883 SW 2d 606, 612 (Tenn 1994).

[142] I did find indications of this conceptualisation in the torts literature of the era before Bohlen began restating (see T Beven, *Negligence in Law*, 2nd edn (London, Steven and Haynes, 1895) 95; Thompson, *Commentaries on the Law of Negligence in All Relations* (n 8) 59). Yet this account for the *Restatement* seems unlikely given Bohlen's recognition of actual cause and its distinction from a causal relationship sufficient to impose liability during his earliest work on causation in the *Restatement* (see *Restatement of Torts* (n 3) § 6).

[143] *Restatement of Torts* (n 3) § 431.

[144] For those who believe 'substantial factor' contains at least some elements of scope of liability, see, eg, Green, 'The Torts Restatement' (n 14) 605; R Wright, 'The Grounds and Extent of Legal Responsibility' (2003) 40 *San Diego Law Review* 1425, 1447.

Bohlen's passing, wrote that 'the "substantial factor" element deals with causation in fact while the other element deals with a legal policy relieving the actor of liability for harm he has, as a matter of fact, caused'.[145] Prosser, both when he was working on the *Restatement (Second)* and in his treatises, maintained that 'substantial factor' was about factual causation.[146]

Yet Bohlen identified a clearly evaluative component to 'substantial factor', requiring that the more-than but-for cause element would 'lead reasonable men to regard it as a cause'.[147] Factual cause, being about who did what to whom, is not a judgmental matter but an inquiry into historical facts.[148] Pointing even more directly at scope of liability is § 433, which identifies four factors 'important in determining whether negligent conduct is a substantial factor in producing harm'.[149] None of those factors is about factual cause.[150]

The origin of the substantial factor test was the same as the source for the legal cause terminology and structure – Jeremiah Smith. In his work on scope of liability, Smith coined, out of whole cloth,[151] the term and test for scope of liability. His work is very clearly about scope of liability and not about factual cause, nor about a combination of the two.[152]

Substantively, adoption of substantial factor was an even graver mistake. The more-than but-for it required for factual cause is unjustified.[153] A straw that breaks a camel's back is a cause of the camel's back being broken just as

[145] First *Restatement of Torts* (Philadelphia, PA, American Law Institute Supp, 1949) § 433 reason for changes.

[146] *Restatement (Second) of Torts*, Council Draft No 10 (Philadelphia, PA, American Law Institute, 16 October 1961) § 433 cmt *e* ('the "substantial factor" element deals with causation in fact'). See also § 433B (alternatively referring to cause in fact as 'cause' and 'substantial factor'); § 546 (in section titled 'causation in fact', using 'substantial factor' in the black letter and explaining in comment, 'this section deals only with the question of causation in fact'); Prosser, *Handbook of Torts* (n 117) 287.

[147] *Restatement of Torts* (n 3) § 431, cmt *a*. Only after his death did the successor authors of his treatise decide that substantial factor was about scope of liability. See WL Prosser, *Handbook of Torts*, 5th edn (St Paul, MN, West Publishing Co, 1980) § 52.

[148] To be sure, factual cause determinations require inference, as all causation matters are proved through circumstantial evidence rather than direct evidence. Whether the circumstantial evidence is sufficient to permit an inference is, indeed, a judgmental matter.

[149] *Restatement of Torts* (n 3) § 433.

[150] For example, one factor is an aspect identified by Judge Andrews, dissenting in *Palsgraf* (n 53), about whether, from an ex post perspective, it is highly extraordinary that the negligence brought about harm (First *Restatement of Torts* (n 3) § 433(b)). That is purely a scope of liability matter that has nothing to do with factual cause.

[151] I have been unable to find the 'substantial factor' usage in any case, article or treatise prior to when Smith first published his series of articles about scope of liability in 1911. See n 108.

[152] Smith II (n 108) 227.

[153] I can find no effort by Bohlen to justify a 'more than' requirement for factual cause. Prosser, while revising the first *Restatement of Torts*, attempted such a justification in Reporter's notes and in his treatise. Prosser cited three cases that he characterised as eliminating liability, 'where the defendant's conduct has played a clear, but insignificant, part in producing the result' (*Restatement (Second) of Torts* (n 2) App § 432, Rptr's note). See also WL Prosser, *Handbook on the Law of Torts*, 3rd edn (St Paul, MN, West Publishing Co, 1964) 240.

surely as is the large load of hay also loaded on the camel.[154] Yes, we may want to eliminate a small contribution to an outcome when there are other, greater contributions that are themselves sufficient to cause the outcome, but that is better done through the element of scope of liability as opposed to factual causation.[155] At the same time, some courts have ignored the but-for test embedded in the *Restatement*'s adoption of it and used it to mean something less than but-for causation.[156] Yes, there may be situations in which we want to permit a plaintiff to recover without proof of factual cause,[157] but we should be transparent about that instead of employing 'substantial factor' to obscure what is going on.[158]

As a stand alone test for factual cause, as it remains in some jurisdictions, 'substantial factor' provides no analytical framework or guidance for the jury in deciding whether factual causation exists. It results in defaulting to a jury's unbridled intuition about factual cause. Unless one believes that the jury should not only decide facts but should also be free to provide law, 'substantial factor' is an unfortunate substitute for an appropriate test for causation.[159]

'Substantial factor' does serve one useful purpose: § 432(2) addresses over-determined outcomes, permitting each of the independently sufficient acts to be a substantial factor and therefore a cause, even though neither is a but-for cause. Indeed, the first court that adopted the 'substantial factor' test in 1920 employed it for just that purpose.[160] Providing a mechanism for making acts that over-determine the outcome to be factual causes does not, however, require use of 'substantial factor' along with its negative baggage. The *Restatement (Third)* accomplishes this in just such a way: 'If multiple acts occur, each of which … alone would have been a factual cause of the physical harm at the same time in the absence of the other act(s), each act is regarded as a factual cause of the harm.'[161]

[154] For courts that have used the 'substantial factor' requirement to impose a more onerous burden on the plaintiff with regard to factual cause than merely establishing but-for causation, see *Challis Irr Co v State* 689 P 2d 230, 235 (Idaho Ct App 1984); *Shyface v Sec'y of HHS* 165 F 3d 1344, 1352–53 (Fed Cir 1999). See also *Culver v Bennett* 588 A2d 1094 (Del 1991); *Ten Hagen v DeNooy* 563 NW 2d 4 (Iowa 1997).

[155] And in any case not an issue Bohlen faced in the pre-toxic era when varying doses of a toxic agent were provided by different defendants.

[156] See, eg, *Roberson v Counselman* 686 P 2d 149 (Kan 1984); *Hake v Manchester Twp* 486 A 2d 836 (NJ 1985); *Mayhue v Sparkman* 653 NE 2d 1384 (Ind 1995).

[157] See generally, S Steel, *Proof of Causation* (Cambridge, CUP, 2015).

[158] An example is asbestos exposure to multiple defendants' products, such that plaintiff cannot know which defendant(s)' products caused the harm. See *Rutherford v Owens-Ill, Inc* 941 P 2d 1203 (Cal 1997).

[159] Dobbs et al, *The Law of Torts* (n 100) § 14.6. 'Substantial factor' was also used in early lost-chance cases and in enhanced injury cases to facilitate doing justice, but at the cost of obscuring what should have been a better explanation of why a but-for test was inappropriate. See *Restatement (Third) of Torts* (n 1) § 26, cmt *j* and Rptr's note.

[160] *Anderson v Minneapolis, St Paul & Sault Ste Marie Ry Co* 179 NW 45 (Minn 1920). That same court later criticised the test as an ordinary standard for causation. See *Seward v Minneapolis St Ry Co* 25 NW 2d 221, 224 (Minn 1946) (using 'substantial factor' for factual cause 'leave[s] the jury afloat without a rudder … and to decide the case according to whim rather than law').

[161] *Restatement (Third) of Torts* (n 1) § 29.

In short, there never was a need for 'substantial factor' with regard to causation; it introduced an evaluative component that has no rightful place at the factual causation table. It is unnecessary to deal with over-determined outcomes, has obscured the central aspect of factual cause and has created unnecessary confusion, as virtually all contemporary commentators agree.[162] The *Restatement (Third)* turned its back on substantial factor for all purposes, yet it continues to play its unfortunate role in tort law today.[163] Given that there was no basis in case law for use of 'substantial factor' during the first *Restatement* drafting, and the primary advocate for it coined it for purposes of scope of liability, Bohlen's adoption of it must count as an unfortunate and substantial error of judgement.

Bohlen's substantive efforts on scope of liability leave a great deal to be desired as well: the first *Restatement* contains three different options, a harm within the risk standard, a hindsight test,[164] and a series of black-letter sections

[162] See Green, 'The Torts Restatement' (n 14) 606; CO Gregory, 'Proximate Cause in Negligence – A Retreat From Rationalization' (1938) 6 *University of Chicago Law Review* 36, 59–61; Becht and Miller, *The Test of Factual Causation in Negligence and Strict Liability Cases* (n 140) 130–34; R Strassfeld, 'If ...: Counterfactuals in the Law' (1992) 60 *George Washington Law Review* 339, 355; B Black and DH Hollander Jr, 'Unravelling Causation: Back to Basics' (1993) 3 *University of Baltimore Journal of Environmental Law* 1; Robertson, 'The Common Sense of Cause in Fact' (n 135) 1776 ('By using the term [substantial factor] in three different senses, the *Restatement (Second) of Torts* has contributed to a nationwide confusion on the matter'); DB Dobbs, *The Law of Torts* (St Paul, MN, West Publishing Co, 2000) § 171; WV Dorsaneo III, 'Judges, Juries, and Reviewing Courts' (2000) 53 *Southern Methodist University Law Review* 1497, 1528–30 (substantial factor 'render[s] the causation standard considerably less intelligible'); Stapleton, 'Legal Cause: Cause-in-Fact and the Scope of Liability for Consequences' (n 133) 945, 978 ('The obfuscating terminology of legal cause, proximate cause and substantial factor should be replaced'); Wright, 'Once More into the Bramble Bush: Duty, Causal Contribution, and the Extent of Legal Responsibility' (n 133) 1080; DA Fischer, 'Insufficient Causes' (2005) 94 *Kentucky Law Journal* 277, 277 ('Over the years, courts also used the substantial factor test to do an increasing variety of things it was never intended to do and for which it is not appropriate. ... [T]he test now creates unnecessary confusion in the law and has outlived its usefulness'). Professors Hart and Honoré are critical of it even when over-determined harm exists, when the but-for test is inadequate: Hart and Honoré, *Causation in the Law* (n 133) 124 ('Little, however, seems to be gained by describing, even to a jury, such cases in terms of the admittedly indefinable idea of a "substantial factor"'). Even the venerable Prosser treatise, in its final publication, turned its back on 'substantial factor' as a useful concept for causation: see WP Keeton et al, *Prosser and Keeton on the Law of Torts*, 5th edn Supp (St Paul, MN, West Publishing Co, 1988) § 41 ('Even if "substantial factor" seemed sufficiently intelligible as a guide in time past, however, the development of several quite distinct and conflicting meanings for the term "substantial factor" has created a risk of confusion and misunderstanding, especially when a court, or an advocate or scholar, uses the phrase without indication of which of its conflicting meanings is intended.').

[163] *Restatement (Third) of Torts* (n 1) § 26, Rprtr's note to cmt *j*.

[164] Charles Carpenter wrote of the hindsight test, 'it seems extraordinary that anyone should seriously propose it as a test. It is pure fantasy ... it is misleading and would frequently impose liability where there is no warrant for it in the cases. There is nothing in the cases to suggest it' (Carpenter, 'Workable Rules for Determining Proximate Cause – Part I' (n 131) 245–46). Yet, interestingly, that is exactly what Cardozo proposed at an Advisors meeting at which scope of liability was the subject (*Restatement of Torts Minutes of Conferences* (Philadelphia, PA, American Law Institute, 12 November 1930) 1): 'liability is imposed even though [the consequence] was not foreseen if, looking back, it appears that it is not so extraordinary that it seems unjust or inexpedient').

on what constitutes and does not constitute a superseding cause that prevents liability. The risk test is misplaced completely outside the treatment of legal cause and contained in an overview section listing the prima facie elements of a negligence claim.[165] Commentators during that period had identified both the risk standard and its close relative, foreseeability, as tests for limitations on scope of liability.[166] Courts and treatises used a variety of plausible-sounding verbal articulations that turned out to be mostly nonsense.[167] How much confusion and incoherence might have been avoided if Bohlen had adopted one of those tests and labelled it as the basis for limiting liability despite duty, negligence and factual cause?[168]

I may be unfair to Bohlen on this latter matter of clarity with regard to scope of liability. There was little agreement among scholars addressing the matter at the time Bohlen was working, with many making the case for their own preferred theory for an appropriate test and claiming that test best explained the

[165] Courts at the time were treating these issues as a matter of proximate cause rather than as bearing on negligence or some other element of a negligence cases (see Carpenter, 'Workable Rules for Determining Proximate Cause – Part I' (n 131) 231, fnn 4–5).

[166] For scholars proposing a foreseeability test, see F Pollock, 'Liability for Consequences' (1922) 38 *LQR* 165, 167 (arguing that a foreseeability test avoided inappropriate terms such as 'natural' and 'probable' and provided an 'intelligible' standard); A Goodhart, 'The Unforeseeable Consequences of a Negligent Act' (1930) 39 *Yale Law Journal* 449, 458–61; PH Winfield, 'The Restatement of Torts – Negligence' (1935) 13 *New York University Quarterly Law Review* 1, 3. But see Beven, *Negligence in Law* (n 8) 89, fn 2 (foreseeability 'is utterly immaterial to limit liability once negligence has been established'). Surely Beven failed to appreciate that the foreseeable risks that made the defendant negligent may not have been the same risks that produced the plaintiff's harm. Indeed, Bohlen, himself, employed a risk standard in the first *Restatement of Torts*, but unaccountably situated it outside coverage of legal causation. See nn 119–121.

[167] eg, in requiring that the harm be a 'natural' consequence, which presumably excluded 'unnatural' consequences. But what are unnatural consequences? Bohlen, in an early article, spoke of 'consequences which flow in an unbroken natural sequence from … [the defendant's] act, not merely those he could have foreseen' (Bohlen, 'Right to Recover for Injury Resulting from Negligence Without Impact' (n 54) 148). Similar is requiring the tortious conduct to be the 'efficient' cause (Kinkead, *Commentaries on the Law of Torts* (n 8) 538). What, pray tell, is an 'inefficient' cause? Nor is a 'natural and continuous sequence' any more useful in determining the scope of liability. As Jeremiah Smith, on whom Bohlen relied in his treatment of causation, wrote, quoting Nicholas St John Green: 'Now all these expressions are vague: they mean little; and in the majority of instances in which they are employed they probably mean nothing. No person who uses one of them, if asked what he means by it, can give a well-defined explanation. Such sentences are not a solution of a difficulty; they are stereotyped forms for gliding over a difficulty without explaining it. When a court say [*sic*] this damage is remote, it does not flow naturally, it is not proximate; all they mean, and all they can mean, is that under all the circumstances they think the plaintiff should not recover. They did not arrive at the conclusion of themselves by reasoning with those phrases, and by making use of them in their decision they do not render that decision clearer to others. The employment of such phrases has never solved one single difficulty' (Smith I (n 108) 108, fn 19); cf *Shadday v Omni Hotels Management Corp* 477 F 3d 511, 513 (7th Cir 2007) (Posner J) (characterising 'intervening and supervening cause that severs the causal chain' language as 'legal mumbo-jumbo').

[168] Yes, it is true that *Polemis* had been decided in England and adopted a direct/remote test for proximate cause in 1921 (*Polemis and Furness Withy & Co Ltd Re* [1921] 3 KB 560 (CA)).

case law or was preferable to other tests.[169] The notion of distinguishing among foreseeability of the type of harm, extent of harm and manner in which the harm occurred (even if those distinctions are sometimes not quite so distinct) had yet to be clearly made and accepted. Moreover, courts used proximate cause to address a variety of problems, many of which had to do with duty, breach, legally protected interests and factual cause.[170] I have the benefit of hindsight, which Bohlen did not.

Bohlen's effort to transform causation terminology from proximate cause to legal cause has largely failed. Despite commitment to that language for some 75 years by both the first and second *Restatements*,[171] courts continue to use proximate cause in preference to legal cause.[172]

In short, the treatment of causation and scope of liability in the first *Restatement* is quite weak. Virtually all of its flaws were carried over in the *Restatement (Second)*, and its influence has been substantial. Courts are confused or misled into thinking that factual causation requires more or less than a *sine qua non* for factual causation. Juries are instructed with an evaluative term for factual causation. Umbrella terms of proximate cause or legal cause are used incorrectly and confusingly to mean factual cause, scope of liability or both. Clarity, consistency and coherence, the goals of the founders of the ALI, remain largely absent from this area of law, facilitated by the missed opportunity in the first *Restatement*.

VI. CONCLUSION

There is much to admire in Francis Bohlen's career and torts work. He was a prolific scholar throughout his career, preparing and updating a popular casebook, publishing 34 law review articles in the top journals (although there were far fewer non-elite journals in his day), all while organising and drafting the *Restatement of Torts*, a monumental effort that provided a coherent structure and clarity to the law of torts after its publication. It must be mentioned that the ALI's torts *Restatements* have been the most cited of all of the different subject-matter *Restatements* the ALI has published. Bohlen successfully negotiated the

[169] For a critical canvassing of many of those efforts, see Carpenter, 'Workable Rules for Determining Proximate Cause – Part I' (n 131) 235–46.

[170] See ibid 246–57. Although claiming that some scholars had exaggerated the extent, Carpenter observed '[t]he confusion and contradiction as to proximate cause in judicial opinion are great' (ibid 257).

[171] The *Restatement (Third) of Torts* avoided both of these terms, instead employing factual cause and scope of liability (*Restatement (Third) of Torts* (n 1) §§ 26, 29).

[172] See *Marshall v Nugent* 222 F 2d 604, 610 (1st Cir 1955) ('perhaps, the phrase "legal cause", as used in [*Restatement of Torts* § 431], is preferable to "proximate cause"; but the courts continue generally to use "proximate cause"'); Dobbs, *The Law of Torts* (n 100) § 15.2 n 4. A Westlaw search of usage in state courts during the decade between 1950 and 1960 reveals that 'proximate cause' was used 20 times more often than 'legal cause'.

transition away from legal formalism, frequently questioning formalist renditions of tort law, arguing against opacity in doctrinal provisions and exploring public policy consideration with regularity in his work.[173] Much of his legal scholarship, combined with his restating, resolved and clarified murky tort issues of the day, such as how reckless and negligent misrepresentations should be dealt with given the existing body of law on deceit.[174]

This chapter has not been able to catalogue or discuss all of those contributions to tort law. Instead, it follows the adoption of cost–benefit factors into the standard for negligence by Bohlen in the first *Restatement*. That story reveals a scholar who, with maturity, changed his mind on the subject and gave a significant boost to an idea that had largely been out of the sight of courts, commentators and treatises of the day. His work probably was the genesis of Learned Hand's adoption and algebraification of the idea that culminated in *Carroll Towing*. Yet, at the same time, we must acknowledge that if cost–benefit had not been adopted in the *Restatement* and Hand never championed the idea, the law and economics movement of the latter half of the twentieth century would have pursued and developed it.

It seems ungracious in a chapter of a monograph celebrating the heroic historical figures of tort law to be critical of one of them, even if limited in scope. Yet causation and scope of liability are of central concern in tort law. And I am firmly of the conviction that Bohlen's work in this area was subpar terminologically, structurally, conceptually, and substantively and terribly consequential because of the influence of the *Restatement*. The legacy of his efforts continues to this day in contemporary tort law and, despite the efforts of numerous commentators and the *Restatement (Third)*, is likely to continue for many more decades.

[173] See, eg, Bohlen, 'Should Negligent Misrepresentations Be Treated as Negligence or Fraud?' (n 14) 704.

[174] ibid. The core of Bohlen's resolution of the limits on liability for negligent representation are widely accepted and are contained in the recently approved Liability for Economic Harm piece of the *Restatement (Third) of Torts* (see *Restatement (Third) of Torts: Liability for Economic Harm*, Tentative Draft No 1 (Philadelphia, PA, American Law Institute, 4 April 2012) § 5).

6

Professor Sir Percy Winfield (1878–1953)

DONAL NOLAN*

I. INTRODUCTION

SIR PERCY WINFIELD is arguably the most influential scholar of the English law of tort in the relatively short history of the subject. Measuring scholarly influence is not easy, particularly in law, where at least three different audiences are discernible: legal practitioners (including judges), students and fellow scholars. Nevertheless, in Winfield's case the claim to scholarly influence is a strong one. Some seven decades after his death, his work is still cited regularly by the courts,[1] the textbook that bears his name has achieved canonical status,[2] and his ideas continue to influence the thinking of tort scholars across the common law world.[3] It is difficult to think of another scholar whose impact on the subject is truly comparable to Winfield's. Although Sir Frederick Pollock was the pioneer of the serious scholarly study of tort law in England,[4] his writings on tort are now much less frequently cited than Winfield's, and

* An earlier version of this chapter was presented at the Edinburgh/Oxford obligations workshop in Edinburgh in October 2018, and I am grateful to the participants for their comments. I am also indebted to Eleni Katsampouka for her excellent research assistance, and to Paul Mitchell and Mark Lunney for their helpful comments on an earlier draft.

[1] For a recent example, see *Network Rail Infrastructure Ltd v Williams* [2018] EWCA Civ 1514, [2018] 3 WLR 1105 [38] (Sir Terence Etherton MR).

[2] For the latest edition, see WE Peel and J Goudkamp, *Winfield & Jolowicz on Tort*, 19th edn (London, Sweet & Maxwell, 2014).

[3] For a recent example, see C Essert, 'Nuisance and the Normative Boundaries of Ownership' (2016) 52 *Tulsa Law Review* 85, 105. A crude measure of Winfield's scholarly influence is the number of times that his articles are cited by the writers of other articles, as indicated by a citation search on HeinOnline. This measure unquestionably significantly understates the overall number of citations of Winfield's work in the periodical literature, particularly outside the United States. Nevertheless, the total number of citations to Winfield's principal tort articles in January 2018, excluding self-citations, was an impressive 650.

[4] As Winfield himself pointed out: PH Winfield, 'The Law of Tort, 1885–1935' (1935) 51 *LQR* 249, 262.

his textbook survived him by only a couple of decades. The New Zealander Sir John Salmond was by any account a scholar of English tort law of great standing, but while his textbook ran to 21 editions, the last edition was published over 20 years ago, and his other writings on tort are few and far between. In the modern era, John Fleming and Patrick Atiyah were figures of monumental importance, but Winfield appears a more central figure in the history of English tort law than either. In Fleming's case, this is because Fleming spread his wings more widely in jurisdictional terms, targeting his work as much at American and Australian audiences as at English ones. And in Atiyah's case, this is because the extraordinary range of his scholarly interests meant that his work on tort law, though of lasting significance, was not sufficiently extensive for it to achieve as pervasive an influence as that of Winfield.

Comparisons of this kind can of course be criticised on a number of grounds, and my purpose in making them is simply to highlight what I see as being, by any measure, the extraordinary and enduring influence of Winfield as a scholar of English tort law. For in writing this chapter, I have two goals in mind. One is simply to pay tribute to the work of a scholar whom in the course of my researches I have come to admire greatly. And the other is to seek to explain Winfield's undoubted scholarly success. Needless to say, the twin tasks I have set myself will require that I sometimes pass judgement on particular writings that Winfield published or particular arguments that he put forward. However, I am mindful of Neil Duxbury's warning that 'intellectual histories that come replete with ticks and crosses tend to arouse suspicion',[5] and have certainly not sought to conduct a comprehensive evaluation of the strengths and weaknesses of Winfield's tort scholarship.

The chapter is divided into three main sections. Section II ('The Life') consists of a short biography of Winfield. In section III ('The Work') can be found a discussion of his principal writings on tort law, their reception and their influence. And in section IV ('The Scholar'), I seek to identify Winfield's key characteristics as a scholar. A brief conclusion follows.

II. THE LIFE

Percy Henry Winfield was born on 16 September 1878 in Stoke Ferry, Norfolk. After grammar school in King's Lynn, Winfield went up to St John's College, Cambridge to read law, which he did with great distinction, heading the first class in both parts of the Law Tripos. Winfield was called to the Bar by the Inner Temple in 1903, but after only a year or two of practice on the south-eastern circuit, he returned to Cambridge to teach, first solely as a private coach, and later also giving lectures and classes for the Law Faculty. During the

[5] N Duxbury, *Frederick Pollock and the English Juristic Tradition* (Oxford, OUP, 2004) 327.

First World War, Winfield served in the Cambridgeshire Regiment, and was seriously wounded in action near Morlancourt in August 1918. He returned to Cambridge the following year, where he was appointed to lectureships at St John's and Trinity Colleges and completed the work he had begun before the war on abuse of legal procedure. Following the publication of his two monographs on that subject – one on the history, and one on the present law[6] – Winfield was elected to a fellowship of St John's in 1921. A university lectureship followed five years later, and in 1928 Winfield was elected to the newly established Rouse Ball Professorship of English Law, which he held until his retirement in 1943. He was knighted in 1949, four years before he died at his home in Cambridge at the age of 74. A career academic, he had spent virtually all of his professional life in Cambridge, apart from forays to Harvard in 1923 to lecture on English legal history, and to Calcutta in 1930 to deliver the Tagore law lectures.

One explanation of Winfield's success was unquestionably his work ethic. Despite a truly punishing coaching and lecturing load, it appears that he began working in earnest on the history of abuse of legal procedure in 1911, and (allowing for the interruption of the war) he was from that point onwards an 'energetic and determined scholar'[7] whose commitment to research and writing seems never to have wavered. According to McNair:

> However busy he became in his busy life, there was always in the background a piece of private work – a book, an article, or a piece of research – to which he could turn and in which he could find a change. He was a prodigious worker and I am confident that there is no man, alive or dead, who has lived so much as Winfield in the Squire Law Library, old and new.[8]

Nor were Winfield's exertions confined to teaching and research. A leading figure in the creation of the modern Cambridge law faculty, he also edited the *Cambridge Law Journal* for two decades (1927–47), and even took over the *Law Quarterly Review* for a period in 1929 when the editor was abroad. In addition, Winfield served as a member of the Council of the Senate of Cambridge University for eight years, as a magistrate for a quarter of a century (1925–49), as a deputy county court judge, as a member of the Lord Chancellor's committees on law revision and law reporting, as Reader in Common Law to the Council of Legal Education, as Vice-President of the Selden Society and as President of the Society of Public Teachers of Law (1929–30).

[6] PH Winfield, *The History of Conspiracy and Abuse of Legal Procedure* (Cambridge, CUP, 1921); PH Winfield, *The Present Law of Abuse of Legal Procedure* (Cambridge, CUP, 1921). Winfield's original intention had been to publish a single volume on the subject, but the historical aspects were separated out in order to create a work suitable for inclusion in a new series of *Cambridge Studies in Legal History*: see Winfield, *The History of Conspiracy and Abuse of Legal Procedure*, xv.

[7] SJ Bailey, 'Percy Henry Winfield, 1878–1953' (1955) 41 *Proceedings of the British Academy* 329, 330.

[8] A McNair, 'Professor Sir Percy Winfield (1878–1953)' [1954] *CLJ* 80, 80.

At the conferral of an honorary doctorate by the University of London in 1949, Winfield was described as 'the most distinguished academic lawyer of our time'.[9] According to the Public Orator, there was no 'teacher of law in recent times whose writings are cited by practitioners and listened to by judges with greater respect'.[10] Similar accolades were bestowed on him after his death, both in terms of his general scholarly reputation and the high esteem in which he was held by bench and Bar. An obituary in the *Manchester Guardian* said, for example, that '[i]t would be hard to overestimate Sir Percy's contribution to the development of the common law in our time – particularly in the province of tort'.[11] And Winfield's former antagonist,[12] PA Landon, said of him in a *Cambridge Law Journal* appreciation that:

> It would be a mistake to think that Winfield's influence on different branches of the law was confined to the academic sphere. Many members of the judiciary, including more than one of the Law Lords, would readily have acknowledged the great assistance which they received, in personal contact with Winfield, in deciding upon the facts of a particular case.[13]

A year later, Harry Street described Winfield as 'one of the great academic English common-lawyers of this century'.[14]

III. THE WORK

Although my subject-matter is Winfield's writings on tort, it may assist in understanding that work to appreciate his scholarly range and to have some sense of his endeavours in other fields of law. McNair observes that '[t]here were few branches of law in which he had never worked',[15] a claim borne out by perusal of Winfield's many book reviews for the *Cambridge Law Journal*, which demonstrate his familiarity with a remarkably wide variety of legal subjects, including administrative law, intellectual property law, commercial law, conflict of laws and evidence.[16] Winfield's range was particularly evident early on in his career,

[9] *The Eagle* (St John's College, Cambridge, 1950) 54(236) 64.

[10] ibid.

[11] Obituary, 'Sir Percy Winfield' *Manchester Guardian* (8 July 1953) 12.

[12] See pp 177–79.

[13] PA Landon, 'Professor Sir Percy Winfield (1878–1953)' [1954] *CLJ* 83, 85.

[14] H Street, '*Winfield on Torts: Sixth Edition*' (1955) 3 *Journal of the Society of Public Teachers of Law (New Series)* 51, 51 (review).

[15] McNair, 'Professor Sir Percy Winfield (1878–1953)' (n 8) 81.

[16] According to CJ Hamson, 'Winfield, of all Cambridge lecturers I have heard, had the most extensive and most accurate knowledge of the relevant case law over the most extended common law fields' (CJ Hamson, 'Law Teaching Methods at Cambridge' (1956) 3 *Journal of the Society of Public Teachers of Law (New Series)* 161, 168).

when he wrote extensively on legal history[17] and international law.[18] After his election to the Rouse Ball chair, Winfield's scholarly focus narrowed somewhat, and he devoted an increasing amount of his time to the law of tort, though he also found the time to write on contract and (particularly towards the end of his life) on 'quasi-contract', or restitution. Following the death of Salmond – whom he never met[19] – Winfield had taken over his unfinished book on contract, which was published as a co-authored work in 1927.[20] This seems to have stoked his interest in the subject, and thereafter he published seven articles in the *Law Quarterly Review* on contract and quasi-contract/restitution,[21] and a short book on the latter subject,[22] as well as editing three editions of Pollock's contract treatise between 1942 and 1950.[23]

Unquestionably, however, Winfield's greatest contribution to legal scholarship came through his extensive writings on the law of tort. Winfield's tort scholarship can be divided into three parts: his articles on tort and its history; his monograph on *The Province of the Law of Tort* ('*Province*');[24] and his famous *Text-Book of the Law of Tort* ('*Text-Book*'), which ran to five editions under his pen.[25] These will be the focus of the discussion that follows, but before that mention should also be made of his twin monographs on the abuse of legal procedure,[26] and of the four editions of his *Cases on the Law of Tort*.[27] The case book (compiled as a companion to the textbook) consists almost entirely of case extracts, and is of little scholarly significance. The early volumes on abuse

[17] See especially PH Winfield, *The Chief Sources of English Legal History* (Cambridge, MA, Harvard University Press, 1925). Like many of Winfield's books, this work was based on lectures he had given, in this instance at Harvard in 1923.

[18] TJ Lawrence and PH Winfield, *The Principles of International Law*, 7th edn (London, Macmillan, 1925); and TJ Lawrence and PH Winfield, *A Handbook of Public International Law*, 10th edn (London, Macmillan, 1930). See also his short later work on the subject, based on lectures given to army officers during the war: PH Winfield, *The Foundations and the Future of International Law* (London, CUP, 1941).

[19] J Salmond and PH Winfield, *Principles of the Law of Contract* (London, Sweet & Maxwell, 1927) iii.

[20] ibid.

[21] PH Winfield, 'The American Restatement of the Law of Restitution' (1938) 54 *LQR* 529; PH Winfield, 'Some Aspects of Offer and Acceptance' (1939) 55 *LQR* 499; PH Winfield, 'Necessaries under the Sale of Goods Act, 1893' (1942) 58 *LQR* 82; PH Winfield, 'Mistake of Law' (1943) 59 *LQR* 327; PH Winfield, 'Quasi-Contract Arising from Compulsion' (1947) 63 *LQR* 35; PH Winfield, 'Quasi-Contract for Work Done' (1947) 63 *LQR* 35; PH Winfield, 'Equity and Quasi-Contract' (1948) 64 *LQR* 46.

[22] PH Winfield, *The Law of Quasi-Contracts* (London, Sweet & Maxwell, 1952).

[23] PH Winfield, *Pollock's Principles of Contract*, 11th edn (London, Stevens & Sons, 1942); 12th edn (London, Stevens & Sons, 1946); 13th edn (London, Stevens & Sons, 1950).

[24] PH Winfield, *The Province of the Law of Tort* (Cambridge, CUP, 1931).

[25] PH Winfield, *Text-Book of the Law of Tort* (London, Sweet & Maxwell, 1937). The subsequent editions written by Winfield were published in 1943, 1946, 1948 and 1950.

[26] See n 6.

[27] PH Winfield, *Cases on the Law of Tort* (London, Sweet & Maxwell, 1938). The subsequent editions were published in 1941, 1945 and 1948.

of legal procedure are of much greater importance, and established Winfield's reputation as a legal scholar of real weight. However, they are likely to be of limited interest to the modern tort lawyer. And while they do demonstrate some of Winfield's qualities as a scholar – in particular his depth of knowledge, seriousness of purpose and historical expertise – both books are rather dry, and lack the lightness of touch, style and wit of his later work. While WS Holdsworth wrote enthusiastic reviews of both books in the *Law Quarterly Review*,[28] in the *Cambridge Law Journal* Roscoe Pound was less effusive, commenting critically on the conservatism of the works, and observing that:

> Dr Winfield shows capacity for a high order of juristic criticism and his reluctance to engage in constructive juristic thinking, perhaps imposed by a conservative regard for the conventions of English law-writing in the past generation, is to be regretted.[29]

A. Articles

Winfield wrote 17 significant articles on tort law and its history, many of which are regularly cited to this day. Among the most famous of these works are the seven that were included in a collection of 15 of Winfield's articles published the year before he died as *Select Legal Essays*.[30] The essays in the collection were chosen not by Winfield himself, but by his former colleagues at Cambridge,[31] and the selection doubtless reflects their perceived significance. Largely the choices made have survived the test of time, though to a modern eye it is perhaps surprising that Winfield's overview of 'The Law of Tort, 1885–1935'[32] was preferred to his articles on privacy[33] and wrongful death.[34]

A general observation that can be made about these works is that it is impossible, when considering the contribution Winfield made to the study of tort through his periodical writings, to separate the historical aspects of his work from his discussions of the contemporary law. The inseparability of these two aspects of his writings can be seen in the articles themselves, where historical analysis is intertwined with discussion of contemporary case law and consideration of possible future developments. However, it is also observable in the reputation that Winfield built on the back of these publications, which is part legal historian, part 'modern' tort lawyer. In retrospect, therefore, the fact that Winfield's early reputation was built on twin volumes on the same topic

[28] WS Holdsworth, 'Conspiracy and Abuse of Legal Process' (1921) 37 *LQR* 462; WS Holdsworth, '*The Present Law of Abuse of Legal Procedure*' (1922) 38 *LQR* 102 (review).
[29] R Pound, 'The History of Conspiracy and Abuse of Legal Procedure' (1922) 1 *CLJ* 156, 162.
[30] PH Winfield, *Select Legal Essays* (London, Sweet & Maxwell, 1952).
[31] SJ Bailey, 'Editorial Preface', ibid, iii.
[32] Winfield, 'The Law of Tort, 1885–1935' (n 4).
[33] PH Winfield, 'Privacy' (1931) 47 *LQR* 23.
[34] PH Winfield, 'Death as Affecting Liability in Tort' (1929) 29 *Columbia Law Review* 239.

published in the same year, one of which dealt with the subject's history and the other with the 'present law', is highly prescient. The intermingling of historical and (contemporary) doctrinal analysis is a leitmotif of Winfield's tort scholarship, most obviously apparent in his articles on the subject.

Another general point that can be made about Winfield's articles on tort is that it is largely through this work that a modern tort lawyer will probably come into direct contact with Winfield's scholarship. Though *Province* seems to have made a strong impression on Winfield's contemporaries, it is not widely read today. And although (as we shall see) there are many traces of the original work in the modern editions of the textbook that bears Winfield's name, these are only echoes or fragments of his authorial voice, mediated through the prism of the 15 editions of the work published since his death and of the six other scholars responsible for them. By contrast, Winfield's articles continue to be read and relied upon – at least by judges and scholars anyway – and so it is through these works that the contemporary reader is most likely to encounter his scholarship in its pure form.

As befits Winfield's broader scholarly trajectory, many of the earlier articles are largely historical. The first, on 'The History of Maintenance and Champerty',[35] was later subsumed into Winfield's history of abuse of legal procedure, but 'The Myth of Absolute Liability'[36] and the trilogy of articles on negligence – 'The History of Negligence in the Law of Torts',[37] 'Trespass and Negligence'[38] (co-authored with Arthur Goodhart) and 'Duty in Tortious Negligence'[39] – are classic works, and served as benchmarks for the historical scholarship that succeeded them.[40] Nor was the influence of these works confined to historical debates. Winfield's preference for the language of 'strict liability' over 'absolute liability'[41] is reflected in modern usage, for example, while his claim in the first article on the history of negligence (published in 1926) that '[n]egligence in the law of torts has a double meaning', in that it might signify both 'a definite tort' and 'a possible mental element in the commission of some other … torts',[42] provided the intellectual underpinning for the judicial recognition, six years later, of an independent cause of action for negligence.[43]

[35] PH Winfield, 'The History of Maintenance and Champerty' (1919) 35 *LQR* 50.

[36] PH Winfield, 'The Myth of Absolute Liability' (1926) 42 *LQR* 37.

[37] PH Winfield, 'The History of Negligence in the Law of Torts' (1926) 42 *LQR* 184.

[38] PH Winfield and A Goodhart, 'Trespass and Negligence' (1933) 49 *LQR* 359.

[39] PH Winfield, 'Duty in Tortious Negligence' (1934) 34 *Columbia Law Review* 41.

[40] See, eg, MJ Prichard, 'Trespass, Case and the Rule in *Williams v Holland*' [1964] *CLJ* 234, 234, describing the latter articles as providing – with CHS Fifoot, *History and Sources of the Common Law: Tort and Contract* (London, Stevens & Sons, 1949) – 'the standard accounts of the development of the tort of negligence'.

[41] Winfield, 'The Myth of Absolute Liability' (n 36) 51. See also PH Winfield, 'Nuisance as a Tort' (1931) 4 *CLJ* 189, 193–94.

[42] Winfield, 'The History of Negligence in the Law of Torts' (n 37) 196.

[43] *Donoghue v Stevenson* [1932] AC 562 (HL). After Winfield's death, he was credited in an obituary with playing a 'great part' in bringing about the recognition of negligence as a separate head of liability: see Obituary (n 11) 12.

In a similar fashion, Winfield's influential excavation of the origins of the duty of care concept provided the basis for his conclusion that the 'duty idea' might well in theory 'be eliminated from the tort of negligence, for it got there only by a historical accident and it seems to be superfluous',[44] which appears to be the earliest example of the duty-of-care scepticism that has been a persistent theme of scholarship on the subject to this day.[45]

Particularly impressive examples of Winfield's periodical writings, in my view, are his articles on privacy and nuisance, both published in the same year as *Province* (1931).[46] By comparison with the works on strict liability and negligence, the balance here is more towards analysis of the law as it currently stands and (particularly in the piece on privacy) its future direction. In these two articles, Winfield demonstrates those qualities as a scholar of contemporary tort law that would later make his *Text-Book* such a resounding success. The subjects are well chosen, and fill gaps in the existing literature, and the discussion is lively and engaging, yet founded on a solid base of knowledge and understanding. It is no surprise that more than 80 years after their publication both articles continue to be recommended by the authors of a textbook as further reading on the topics in question.[47]

In an echo of the taxonomical approach that underpinned *Province*, Winfield's article on nuisance considered the relationship between nuisance and 'three other branches of the law of tort',[48] namely the rule in *Rylands v Fletcher*, negligence and trespass to land. The treatment of these relationships is largely persuasive, and remains of great value.[49] Unlike some judges,[50] Winfield considered that the *Rylands* rule was not 'merely a species of nuisance', and that the two doctrines 'were related to one another as intersecting circles, not as the segment of a circle to the circle itself'.[51] His examination of the relationship between nuisance and negligence is also illuminating, highlighting as he does the very different meaning that attaches to the central notion of 'reasonableness' in the two causes of action.[52] Finally, Winfield brings his

[44] Winfield, 'Duty in Tortious Negligence' (n 39) 66.

[45] For my own contribution to this stream of scholarship, see D Nolan, 'Deconstructing the Duty of Care' (2013) 129 *LQR* 559, where I survey earlier examples.

[46] Winfield, 'Privacy' (n 33); Winfield, 'Nuisance as a Tort' (n 41).

[47] See S Deakin, A Johnston and B Markesinis, *Markesinis and Deakin's Tort Law*, 7th edn (Oxford, OUP, 2012) 465 ('Nuisance as a Tort'), 746 ('Privacy').

[48] Winfield, 'Nuisance as a Tort' (n 41) 189.

[49] Winfield's article was implicitly criticised by Wolfgang Friedmann for being a 'strictly historical and analytical survey', which failed to 'investigate the sociological scope and function of the various actions' (see W Friedmann, 'Modern Trends in the Law of Torts' (1937) 1 *MLR* 39, 42–45). However, the criticism seems unfair, since Winfield's aim was quite simply different from Friedmann's, and both articles were valuable – and remain so – for different reasons. Furthermore, the passage of time reveals weaknesses not only in aspects of Winfield's approach, but also in key tenets of Friedmann's own 'functional' analysis.

[50] See, in particular, *Cambridge Water Co Ltd v Eastern Counties Leather plc* [1994] 2 AC 264 (HL); and *Transco plc v Stockport MBC* [2003] UKHL 61, [2004] 2 AC 1.

[51] Winfield, 'Nuisance as a Tort' (n 41) 195.

[52] ibid 199–200.

historical learning to bear in his brief (but convincing) discussions of the difficult boundary between nuisance and trespass, and of what he called 'the confusing medley of remedies'[53] for damage caused by fire.

While Winfield's article on nuisance is unquestionably a classic, his piece on privacy was even more ground-breaking, the first significant attempt by an English scholar to argue for the recognition of a general tort of invasion of privacy.[54] As Paul Mitchell has pointed out, Winfield's intention in publishing this article seems to have been to influence the outcome of the appeal to the House of Lords in *Tolley v JS Fry & Sons Ltd*,[55] since he considered that the decision of the Court of Appeal in that case 'highlighted an important gap in the scope of protection offered by English tort law'.[56] Winfield drew upon a range of other jurisdictions in putting forward his argument that 'our law probably lags behind the needs of a community in which intrusion on privacy is apt to take offensive forms' in the light of recent societal and technological developments, such as the rise of photography and modern advertising techniques.[57] But although his article made 'a compelling argument for judicial recognition of a right to privacy',[58] the House of Lords decided *Tolley* on different grounds, and it was not until the passage of the Human Rights Act 1998, nearly three-quarters of a century later, that the courts developed a cause of action along the lines that Winfield had suggested.[59] The episode demonstrates Winfield's characteristic prescience, but also his practical engagement with the task of developing the law in the light of what he called 'social exigencies'.[60] Furthermore, in this instance Winfield's attempt to bring about legal change was not limited to his own writings,[61] for it seems that he also encouraged the publication in the same year – and, presumably, again with the appeal in *Tolley* in mind – of two more avowedly comparative articles on the same subject, which focused on the protection of privacy in German and Swiss law,[62] and in French law,[63] respectively. Nor did he give up the fight after *Tolley v Fry*; he continued to argue for a tort of invasion of privacy in his academic writings,[64] and some eight years later,

[53] ibid 203.

[54] As he himself said, at the time English law was 'pretty nearly destitute of literature on the topic' (Winfield, 'Privacy' (n 33) 23).

[55] *Tolley v JS Fry & Sons Ltd* [1931] AC 333 (HL). See Winfield, 'Privacy' (n 33) 34, where Winfield points out that the House of Lords has a 'free hand' in the matter, and ibid 39, where he identifies two ways in which they might play it.

[56] P Mitchell, *A History of Tort Law 1900–1950* (Cambridge, CUP, 2015) 177.

[57] Winfield, 'Privacy' (n 33) 30.

[58] Mitchell, *A History of Tort Law 1900–1950* (n 56) 177.

[59] See p 201.

[60] Winfield, 'Privacy' (n 33) 34.

[61] See Mitchell, *A History of Tort Law 1900–1950* (n 56) 177–78.

[62] HC Gutteridge, 'The Comparative Law of the Right to Privacy: Law of Germany and Switzerland' (1931) 47 *LQR* 203.

[63] F Walton, 'The Comparative Law of the Right to Privacy: Law of France' (1931) 47 *LQR* 219.

[64] See, eg, *Text-Book* (n 25) 669; PH Winfield, 'Restatement of the Law of Torts: Volume IV' (1940) 18 *New York University Law Quarterly Review* 66, 82.

amidst moves to reform the law of defamation, he wrote to *The Times* drawing attention to the lack of legal protection against statements that were offensive but true.[65]

The most theoretical of the articles on tort in *Select Legal Essays* is 'The Foundation of Liability in Tort', which was published in 1927.[66] Although frequently cited, this is perhaps the least satisfying of the articles to a modern reader, reflecting as it does a contemporary debate aspects of which now appear somewhat arcane and even misguided. That debate has been extensively discussed elsewhere,[67] and little is to be gained by reprising it here. Winfield summarised the question in issue in the debate as follows:

> Is the English law of torts based on the principle that (1) all injuries done to another person are torts, unless there is some justification recognized by the law; or on the principle that (2) there is a definite number of torts outside which tort liability does not exist?[68]

However, he immediately mixed that question up with what looks to be a very different one, namely whether the courts 'have full power to create new torts'.[69] Having gone on to demonstrate (straightforwardly enough) that the answer to the second question was affirmative, he then concluded that the correct answer to his original question must be the first one. This was, however, a non-sequitur, as Glanville Williams pointed out in an article that effectively brought the debate to a close by showing that the protagonists had largely been at cross-purposes.[70]

Winfield was a major player in what has come to be known as the 'tort or torts' debate, and restated his position a number of times,[71] although in the aftermath of Williams' article – and another by Arthur Goodhart trenchantly criticising Winfield's position[72] – he did eventually concede ground to the alternative view.[73] For present purposes, my interest lies in what, if anything, his participation in the debate tells us about Winfield as a scholar. For a start,

[65] PH Winfield, 'Law of Libel' (Letter) *The Times* (6 February 1939) 13.

[66] PH Winfield, 'The Foundation of Liability in Tort' (1927) 27 *Columbia Law Review* 1.

[67] For an excellent overview, see Mitchell, *A History of Tort Law 1900–1950* (n 56) ch 2.

[68] Winfield, 'The Foundation of Liability in Tort' (n 66) 1.

[69] ibid.

[70] GL Williams, 'The Foundation of Tortious Liability' (1939) 7 *CLJ* 111. As Williams said (with considerable understatement), '[t]he question whether existing rules of liability are or are not elastic is not quite the same as the question of whether there *is now* a general principle of liability in tort': ibid 113(original emphasis). The non-sequitur had previously been pointed out by Edward Jenks in a review of *Province*: E Jenks, 'The Province of Tort in English Law' (1932) 14 *Journal of Comparative Legislation and International Law* 207, 210.

[71] In addition to the 'Foundations' article, see also *Province* (n 24) 32–39; Winfield, 'The Law of Tort, 1885–1935' (n 4) 249–50; and *Text-Book* (n 25) 15–21.

[72] AL Goodhart, 'The Foundation of Tortious Liability' (1938) 2 *MLR* 1.

[73] See PH Winfield, '*Pollock's Law of Torts*' (1939) 55 *LQR* 450, 450–51 (review) (also crediting PA Landon for his partial change of heart); PH Winfield, *A Text-Book of the Law of Tort*, 2nd edn (London, Sweet & Maxwell, 1943) 20–21.

it shows his intellectual debt to Pollock. As Winfield himself acknowledged,[74] Pollock and Salmond were the heavyweights among his predecessors as scholars of English tort law, and as a disciple of Pollock it was no surprise that Winfield should take his side in a dispute that went to the heart of the intellectual fissure between the two. It also perhaps demonstrates Winfield's limitations as a scholar. Whereas the more doctrinal articles on privacy and nuisance show him at his best, when he ventures into more abstract, theoretical territory, his touch seems less sure. Finally, the debate evidences Winfield's progressive attitude towards the law and legal development. What really seems to have animated Winfield's writing on the topic is the same underlying conviction that drove his intervention on privacy, namely the belief that the law of tort must adapt to the changing needs of society, and the recognition that new causes of action might sometimes be needed in response to new social problems. Winfield's role in the debate therefore casts him in a positive light,[75] even if the arguments that he marshalled in support of his view that the law of tort 'is based upon a general principle that all harm to another person is presumptively unlawful'[76] were less than persuasive.[77]

B. *The Province of the Law of Tort*

Province was published in 1931, and was based on the Tagore law lectures that Winfield had delivered in the University of Calcutta the year before. As Mitchell says, in this work Winfield 'advanced a distinctive thesis about the foundations and scope of tortious liability'.[78] To the modern reader, the book seems innocuous enough, but at the time of its publication, *Province* appears to have been little short of scholarly dynamite, and in some quarters it provoked a very strong reaction indeed. To some extent, this may have been attributable to the nature of the work, for it seems to be the first English monograph on tort, which was still then a very young subject, and had hitherto been the subject only of treatises and articles. But to some extent, it was also attributable to Winfield's scientific and taxonomic approach to his chosen subject-matter, which seems to have ruffled the feathers of the notoriously conservative entity that was English inter-war legal academia.[79]

Although my main interest lies in the reception of *Province*, a brief consideration of the work itself is needed, both for context and because it sheds

[74] Winfield, 'The Law of Tort, 1885–1935' (n 4) 262.

[75] For a sympathetic assessment of Winfield's involvement in the debate, which is less critical of his arguments than I am inclined to be, see Mitchell, *A History of Tort Law 1900–1950* (n 56) 29–36.

[76] *Province* (n 24) 36.

[77] His argument perhaps reaches its lowest point in his attempt to explain away *Mayor of Bradford v Pickles* [1895] AC 587 (HL): Winfield, 'The Foundation of Liability in Tort' (n 66) 11.

[78] Mitchell, *A History of Tort Law 1900–1950* (n 56) 8.

[79] See pp 187–88.

some light on Winfield's merits as a scholar. The book is somewhat imbalanced by the disproportionately long chapter on tort and quasi-contract, which accounts for almost a third of the text, and amounts to a mini-monograph on the latter subject. That chapter is of limited significance for our purposes, though it is important to note that Winfield's temerity in calling attention to that neglected area of law – which he memorably described as a 'no man's land, not in the sense that there are constant battles for it, but that nobody wants it'[80] – accounts for a good deal of the critical reaction to *Province*'s publication. Setting that chapter aside, the book consists of an introductory chapter, followed (predictably) by a historical outline of the development of tort as a legal category, a short general chapter in which Winfield puts forward a rather uninspiring – though subsequently influential[81] – definition of what he calls 'tortious liability' and reprises his position on the general liability principle, and then a series of chapters exploring the relationship between that head of liability and other fields of law, such as contract, quasi-contract, crime, property and so on. The book closes with chapters on limitation and on alternative definitions of tort put forward by other writers. The chapters exploring what Winfield is careful to describe as the '*liaisons*'[82] (rather than the boundaries) between tort and other legal categories are the heart of the text, and in them we again find the Winfield leitmotif of historical investigation blending into more conceptual analysis. And at times – for example in his discussion of the relationship between tort and property – we also see just how sophisticated a legal thinker Winfield was. As with his many of his articles, the book largely passes the test of time, and modern scholars have been commendatory of Winfield's taxonomical endeavours.[83]

Of more interest to me, however, is the force of the critical response that *Province* generated. The rather defensive opening chapter, in which Winfield went out of his way to justify the project – tellingly, in both theoretical and practical terms – suggests that he himself realised that the book might provoke a negative reaction. A flavour of the lack of enthusiasm in some quarters for Winfield's attempt to place the law of tort on a more scientific footing is apparent from the underwhelming review of *Province* by Winfield's mentor, Pollock,

[80] *Province* (n 24) 118.

[81] '[P]robably the most cited definition (or rather, characterization) of tort': E Descheemaeker, *The Division of Wrongs* (Oxford, OUP, 2009) 205. See also JA Jolowicz and TE Lewis, *Winfield on Tort*, 8th edn (London, Sweet & Maxwell, 1967) viii ('Winfield's famous definition').

[82] *Province* (n 24) v.

[83] See, eg, P Birks, 'Equity in the Modern Law: An Exercise in Taxonomy' (1996) 26 *University of Western Australia Law Review* 1, 26 ('[Winfield] was committed to accurate classification and, within the common law in the narrower sense, did more than anyone to promote a vigorous taxonomic debate'); Descheemaeker, *The Division of Wrongs* (n 81) 280 (Winfield 'thought through these issues probably harder than anyone else'); Mitchell, *A History of Tort Law 1900–1950* (n 56) 23 ('[*Province*] was a distinctive and important contribution' to contemporary debates about the nature and foundations of tort law).

in the *Law Quarterly Review*, who said that 'it made rather hard reading' – surely an instance of the pot calling the kettle black[84] – and that there was 'to the present writer's taste, rather too much talk about definitions'.[85] While the approach of the book might be suitable for legal academics, he wrote, 'the profession at large … may be allowed a little grumble'.[86] A review in the *Times Literary Supplement* (*TLS*) was more critical still.[87] After taking a swipe at the 'long and ponderous' chapter on tort and quasi-contract, and at Winfield's definition of 'tortious liability', the reviewer observed:

> Lest it be supposed that any theorizing is to be deprecated it will be found that judgments in cases of tort frequently contribute something towards a general theory of tort. But the general theory of tort thus built up is essentially inductive, and it is thereby the better adapted to subserve functions of the Law, which are and should be organic.[88]

Winfield was not inclined to take criticism lying down, and a squabble between Winfield and the reviewer in the letters pages of the *TLS* followed.[89] This was not the only spat inspired by the publication of *Province*. Another, more famous, *contretemps* – this time between Winfield and the arch-conservative Oxford law don PA Landon – played out in the pages of *Bell Yard*.[90] In retrospect, parts of the review of *Province* by Landon that lit the fuse seem almost comical, but the very fact that a tort scholar of Landon's standing could react to the book in such a manner tells us a great deal about the intellectual environment in which Winfield was operating. Although much of the substance of Landon's review consists of perfectly reasonable criticisms of particular aspects of Winfield's thinking on tort, it is the more general critique of the very nature of Winfield's enterprise that is most revealing. Early in the review, Landon merely emphasises the novelty of that enterprise:

> The book is primarily of an academic character … English students are not so familiar as are American readers with books of this type, and it is as well to make it quite clear that the book is concerned, not so much with stating the law as it is, as with making suggestions for its rearrangement on a more logical basis.[91]

However, this seemingly detached and neutral tone does not last, and Landon soon makes it abundantly clear that he has no sympathy for this kind of

[84] On Pollock's own style, see ch 3 by Robert Stevens in this volume.

[85] FP, '*The Province of the Law of Tort*' (1931) 47 *LQR* 588, 588 (review).

[86] ibid.

[87] RE Negus, 'The Law of Tort' *The Times Literary Supplement* (25 June 1931) 509.

[88] ibid.

[89] See PH Winfield, 'The Law of Tort' (Letter) *The Times Literary Supplement* (2 July 1931) 528; RE Negus, 'The Law of Tort' (Letter) *The Times Literary Supplement* (9 July 1931) 547; PH Winfield, 'The Law of Tort' (Letter) *The Times Literary Supplement* (16 July 1931) 564.

[90] For a more detailed account of this episode, see Mitchell, *A History of Tort Law 1900–1950* (n 56) 26–29. And for a brief but revealing sketch of Landon, see FH Lawson, *The Oxford Law School, 1850–1965* (Oxford, OUP, 1968) 130–31.

[91] PA Landon, 'The Province of the Law of Tort by Percy H Winfield' (1931) 8 *Bell Yard* 19, 19.

scholarship at all. A flavour of his critique can be gleaned from the following passage, in which he piles into Winfield's identification of categories of liability (such as 'quasi-contract') separate from tort and contract:

> [Winfield's analysis] is speculation. It is not English law. Our categories were fixed by the Commissioners … who drafted the Common Law Procedure Act, 1852. Professor Winfield tilts in vain against a dichotomy which has received the approval of generations of lawyers and, in the second schedule to that Act, the sanction of the Legislature.[92]

More generally, Landon argued that it was folly 'to try to force our grossly unscientific system into a Procrustean bed of juristic categories', as evidenced by the fact that that was 'what they are doing in America'.[93] Winfield hit back in the next issue of the journal, demonstrating his rhetorical powers in a merciless assault on Landon's reactionary attitudes, while also defending himself vigorously against Landon's criticisms of his positions on specific questions.[94]

In a sign of the way the wind was blowing, two of Landon's colleagues at Oxford – WTS Stallybrass, the editor of *Salmond on Torts*, and the legal historian WS Holdsworth – moved to defend Winfield. According to Holdsworth, in a review of *Province* in which he did not mention the *Bell Yard* controversy but seemed to have it in mind:

> [The qualities of *Province*] may no doubt draw upon it the denunciation of those lawyers who prefer to follow faithfully the conservative traditions of the profession. But this is inevitable. We should not be surprised to find that leading practitioners in the King's courts in Edward I's reign made similar criticisms upon those more Romanesque and, to their eyes, unpractical parts of Bracton's book, which, in the succeeding centuries, proved to be of considerable practical importance in shaping modern English law.[95]

In a more direct intervention in *Bell Yard* itself, Stallybrass was unable to resist the temptation to ridicule Landon,[96] but he also made the telling observation that the gist of what he called 'a most entertaining and instructive controversy'[97] lay in the different views that the protagonists held 'as to what is the proper subject of study in a university and as to the true function of the academic lawyer'.[98] Like the *TLS* reviewer, Landon clearly conceived of the role of the law teacher and legal scholar very narrowly, as limited to the exposition of the

[92] ibid 20.
[93] ibid 21.
[94] PH Winfield, 'The Province of the Law of Tort: A Reply' (1932) 9 *Bell Yard* 32.
[95] WS Holdsworth '*The Province of the Law of Tort*' [1932] *Journal of the Society of Public Teachers of Law (Old Series)* 40, 43 (review).
[96] '[N]o one quite knows exactly under what letters patent he holds his mandate to speak for the whole London Bar': WTS Stallybrass, 'Landon v Winfield: An Intervention' (1932) 10 *Bell Yard* 18, 23.
[97] ibid 27.
[98] ibid 19. A similar point is made by Mitchell, *A History of Tort Law 1900–1950* (n 56) 35–36.

current law, by way of teaching and writing. Trying to rationalise the common law was both pointless and dangerous, and suggesting ways in which it could be improved an impertinence. By contrast, Winfield's more expansive view of the legal academic's function extended beyond mere exposition to encompass scientific analysis of legal doctrine and (as his intervention on privacy demonstrated) pointing the judiciary and the legislature in the direction of beneficial reforms. Of course, that vision is now entirely orthodox, but it should not be forgotten that it was works like *Province* that showed the way.

C. *A Text-Book of the Law of Tort*

By contrast with *Province*, Winfield's famous tort textbook was (in Mitchell words) 'at first glance, a more conventional work'.[99] And yet by the standards of its day, the *Text-Book* was also innovative, though this time more in terms of its style than its substance. The *Text-Book*, which was intended primarily for students,[100] apparently developed out of the detailed syllabus that Winfield gave those who attended his lectures,[101] and the origins of the text in undergraduate tuition may explain the light and arresting tone. Undoubtedly the modern feel of the work[102] goes a long way to explaining its success, particularly when one recalls that the existing tort treatises of note were *Pollock*, with its long paragraphs and overblown Victorian prose, and *Salmond*, with its numbered lists of propositions and paucity of case discussion. For a law student in the late 1930s, *Winfield* would have been a welcome breath of fresh air.

Another important point to note about the *Text-Book* is that it was published in 1937, when Winfield was in his late fifties, had probably been teaching tort for upwards of 30 years[103] and had already published a raft of articles on diverse aspects of the subject. The *Text Book* is therefore the product of a mature, established scholar, steeped in its subject-matter and very well used to expounding it to students. This of course gave the *Text-Book* authority and gravitas, and helped to ensure its accuracy: quite simply, Winfield knew what he was talking about. However, it may also partly explain the book's stylistic attractions.

[99] Mitchell, *A History of Tort Law 1900–1950* (n 56) 8.

[100] See *Text-Book* (n 25) v.

[101] 'The story is told that year by year Sir Percy's lecture notes issued to his pupils grew larger and larger until there was nothing for it but to write a book to replace them' (Obituary (n 11) 12). See also Landon, 'Professor Sir Percy Winfield (1878–1953)' (n 13) 83; and Hamson, 'Law Teaching Methods at Cambridge' (n 16) 167.

[102] 'It was the first sort of really modern [tort] book': L Dingle and D Bates, 'Conversations with Professor Tony Jolowicz: Third Interview (Published Works)' (Barrington, 17 April 2009) at www.squire.law.cam.ac.uk/eminent-scholars-archiveprofessor-ja-jolowicz/conversations-professor-ja-jolowicz-third-interview, 220.

[103] It is difficult to know what subjects Winfield taught in his early private coaching, but it seems likely that he covered the foundational common law subjects, such as contract and tort. He lectured in tort from 1919 until his retirement in 1943.

Whereas a younger, less famous scholar might have felt the need to demonstrate his learning with detailed expositions and extensive footnotes that would have weighed down the text, Winfield had the confidence to say only what he thought the student needed to hear, and not to include 'more references than were strictly necessary',[104] safe in the knowledge that his earlier writings showed the depth of the scholarly foundations on which the *Text-Book* was built.[105]

The organisation of the *Text-Book* demonstrates Winfield's pragmatism, faced as he and other textbook writers are with the impossibility of reducing the common law of torts to a systematic and logical structure.[106] Sensibly, the material was largely organised around specific torts, despite the author's adherence to the general liability principle. More generally, he avoided an overly scientific approach, which he said 'would merely mean an attempt to wrench intractable material into neat shapes that would have little real connection with either the history or the present substance of the topic'.[107] Although it has been claimed that Winfield adopted an interest-based classification,[108] this is true only in the loosest of senses – wrongs to the person, wrongs to property, wrongs to the person or property, etc. (Aspects of this very basic classification jar a little today, so that for example 'nuisance' sits alongside negligence as a wrong 'to person or to property' rather than alongside trespass to land as a real property tort.) And near the end Winfield abandons this approach and slips into the conduct-based approach adopted in the US *Restatement of the Law of Torts*, so that, for example, we find side-by-side two chapters entitled 'Strict Liability: *Rylands v Fletcher*' and 'Strict Liability: Animals'. The structure may have been influenced by the similar approach taken by Courtney Kenny in his casebook on tort,[109] and this in turn may have reflected the structure of Kenny's lectures on tort at Cambridge, which Winfield would presumably have attended as a student.[110] One does not in any case get the impression that Winfield worried

[104] AL Goodhart, '*A Text-Book of the Law of Tort*' (1938) 54 *LQR* 126, 131 (review).

[105] For example, while he mentions in the chapter on negligence his argument (in Winfield, 'Duty in Tortious Negligence' (n 39)) that the duty of care is superfluous, he then says that 'repetition of the reasons which have led me to this conclusion would be out of place here' (*Text-Book* (n 25) 429).

[106] The chapters in the *Text-Book* are as follows: 1. Meaning of the Law of Tort; 2. General Conditions of Liability in Tort; 3. Capacity; 4. Remedies; 5. Joint Tortfeasors; 6. Locality of Tort; 7. Death in Relation to Tort; 8. Classification of Particular Torts; 9. Trespass to the Person; 10. Injuries Affecting Family Relationships; 11. Defamation; 12. Trespass to Land; 13. Trespass to Goods; 14. Conversion and Other Injuries to Goods; 15. Deceit; 16. Negligence; 17. Conspiracy; 18. Nuisance; 19. Strict Liability: *Rylands v Fletcher*; 20. Strict Liability: Animals; 21. Dangerous Chattels; 22. Dangerous Land and Structures; 23. Dangerous Operations; 24. Interference with Contract or Business; 25. Abuse of Legal Procedure; 26. Miscellaneous and Doubtful Torts; 27. Extinction of Liability in Tort; 28. Tort and Contract.

[107] *Text-Book* (n 25) 218.

[108] Descheemaeker, *The Division of Wrongs* (n 81) 243. For a thorough exploration of the various approaches that have been adopted to the structuring of English tort law, see ibid ch 7.

[109] CS Kenny, *Cases on the Law of Tort*, 5th edn (Cambridge, CUP, 1928).

[110] According to Kenny, writing in 1904, he had lectured on the subject 'for upwards of ten years past' (ibid v). Winfield's undergraduate years were 1896–99.

much about the organisation of the work going forward: the sequence and the titles of the 28 chapters in the fifth edition (his last) exactly replicate those in the first.

Whereas the reception of *Province* had been mixed, the *Text-Book* seems to have met with almost universal acclaim.[111] In the *Law Quarterly Review*, Arthur Goodhart was fulsome in his praise: the book was not only accurate, clear and comprehensive, but also characterised by 'an unusual charm of style and a brilliant analysis of the more difficult problems'.[112] Goodhart also drew attention to the manner in which Winfield had brought his historical learning to bear, commenting that '[a]gain and again the author's profound knowledge of legal history enables him to explain some doubtful point'.[113] According to a review by Holdsworth, the book 'combine[d] great learning with a clear and attractive style' and would 'be of equal value to the student and to the practitioner',[114] while T Ellis Lewis, who later took over the work, could scarcely contain his enthusiasm in the *Cambridge Law Journal*, describing the book as 'an outstanding production' and predicting – accurately – that 'its rare charm of style, its enlivening, amusing and interesting references, its accuracy and clarity, and its method of approach will make it the most popular book on tort'.[115] Nor did the positive view of the *Text-Book* wane over time. The then Mr Justice Denning remarked in a review of the third edition that '[t]he place which was first occupied by *Pollock*, and to which *Salmond* succeeded, is now filled by *Winfield*'.[116] By the sixth edition, the same reviewer said simply that 'Winfield on *Tort* is one of the great textbooks of the law'.[117] Denning's emphasis in his reviews on the book's standing among legal practitioners was echoed by other commentators, such as SJ Bailey, Winfield's successor as Rouse Ball chair, who said in his memoir of him in the *Proceedings of the British Academy* that 'The *Textbook* spread Winfield's reputation outside the academic world into solicitors' offices, barristers' chambers, into the courts of law, and among lawyers and law students wherever the Common Law is known.'[118]

The survival of Winfield's *Text-book* into the twenty-first century is in part attributable to the quality and success of the original product, but it also owes a great deal, of course, to the efforts of subsequent editors of the text.[119] Particular mention should be made in this respect of Tony Jolowicz, who undertook

[111] An exception is a critical review by Cecil Wright: see p 185.
[112] Goodhart, '*A Text-Book of the Law of Tort*' (n 104) 127.
[113] ibid 128.
[114] WS Holdsworth, '*A Text-Book of the Law of Tort; Cases on the Law of Tort*' [1938] *Journal of the Society of Public Teachers of Law (Old Series)* 38, 38 (review).
[115] TEL, '*A Text-Book of the Law of Tort*' (1938) 6 *CLJ* 457, 457 (review).
[116] AT Denning, '*A Text-Book of the Law of Tort*' (1947) 63 *LQR* 516, 516 (review).
[117] AT Denning, '*Winfield on Tort*' [1955] *CLJ* 113, 113 (review).
[118] Bailey, 'Percy Henry Winfield, 1878–1953' (n 7) 334.
[119] Despite Winfield's own scepticism on the subject: 'As a general rule, an edition of a standard book by any one except its author is a scientific failure' (PHW, '*[Salmond's] The Law of Torts*' (1929) 45 *LQR* 128, 128 (review)).

a major overhaul of the work in the 1960s that probably ensured its survival, and of Horton Rogers, whose careful stewardship of the text over no fewer than nine editions (four more than the author himself) meant that it retained its reputation for clarity and accuracy throughout English tort law's most turbulent years. The contrast with *Pollock* and *Salmond* is instructive. After Pollock's death, his treatise was edited by PA Landon, who took the conservative approach – also adopted by Winfield in his editions of Pollock's work on contract – of preserving Pollock's text in its entirety and marking out his own additions with square brackets. Needless to say, with a subject as dynamic as tort law, this was not a recipe for success, and the second edition that Landon edited was also the last.[120] The after-life of *Salmond* was of course much longer and more distinguished, and the text ran to 21 editions – two more than *Winfield & Jolowicz*'s current tally – before petering out in the 1990s, some 70 years after Salmond's death. Nevertheless, it is plausible to suppose that the eventual demise of *Salmond* is traceable in part to the less appealing features of the original text, particularly in its later editions under Salmond's pen,[121] as well as to the cautious approach of its subsequent editors, who never gave the work the drastic makeover that it needed to remain a serious contender in a textbook market peppered with works written for a contemporary audience.[122] As John Spencer observed in a review of a new edition of what had then become *Salmond & Heuston* in the 1970s, 'the book is now beginning to show evident signs of being the sixteenth edition of a book which first appeared in 1907'.[123]

The impact and influence of the subsequent editors of Winfield's *Text-Book* raise the question of the extent to which his scholarship continues to animate the work that bears his name. A systematic investigation of that question would be a colossal task, but some general observations can none the less be made. Winfield himself entrusted the book to his colleague T Ellis Lewis, who bore sole responsibility for one edition and then helped Jolowicz with a further three. In the sixth edition,[124] Ellis Lewis filled out the text by about a hundred pages, added more references to decisions and literature from other jurisdictions, and also made some other, relatively minor changes, such as dropping the short chapter on dangerous operations. These changes, though conservative, were well received.[125] There was then a gap of nine years until the next, seventh, edition,

[120] PA Landon, *Pollock's Law of Torts*, 15th edn (London, Stevens & Sons, 1951). Duxbury also makes the point that the fact that Pollock approached tort via its underlying principles meant, paradoxically, that his text dated quickly: Duxbury, *Frederick Pollock and the English Juristic Tradition* (n 5) 249.

[121] For critical comments by Winfield in this respect, see Winfield, '*[Salmond's] The Law of Torts*' (n 119) 128–29.

[122] Lawson, *The Oxford Law School, 1850–1965* (n 90) 130, comments that WTS Stallybrass, who edited the first four editions after Salmond's death, 'edited that famous work with great piety, keeping the original author's text whenever possible'.

[123] JR Spencer, '*Salmond on Torts*' (1975) 34 *CLJ* 334, 334 (review).

[124] TE Lewis, *Winfield on Tort*, 6th edn (London, Sweet & Maxwell, 1954).

[125] According to Cecil Wright, the result of Ellis Lewis's endeavours was 'a much better book': CA Wright, 'The English Law of Torts: A Criticism' (1955) 11 *University of Toronto Law Journal* 84, 87.

for which Jolowicz took control.[126] Over the course of the seventh and eighth editions the book was transformed, with the material completely reorganised (albeit for practical rather than 'scientific' reasons[127]), new chapters added on topics such as breach of statutory duty, employers' liability, vicarious liability and damages, and the treatment of negligence significantly expanded. Although naturally further reorganisation took place in later editions, it was the overhaul in the seventh and eighth editions that really produced the core structure of the modern work known as *Winfield & Jolowicz*.

How much of Winfield's scholarly voice remained in the work after that overhaul? In an interview in 2009, Jolowicz said that he asked for his name to be added to the book's title because he 'didn't really leave an awful lot [of the original] in it', and that 'the order and method' was 'to a substantial extent, different in my editions from the original'.[128] But although Jolowicz's impact on the work was undoubtedly profound – it might well not have survived, one suspects, but for his endeavours – he may be guilty of a little exaggeration here, and his intimation that he completely rewrote the book is not borne out by contemporary reviews of the editions for which he was responsible. In a review of the seventh edition, for example, Street praised Jolowicz for his 'excellent judgment in deciding when to re-write and when to leave alone',[129] while a reviewer of the ninth edition congratulated him and his co-editors on 'performing the difficult task of writing a modern treatise while still incorporating part of Winfield's text', but suggested that it might have been better to have written a completely new work.[130] And indeed, reading the editions written by Winfield alongside the latest *Winfield & Jolowicz*, one regularly comes across remnants or vestiges of the original author's text. A good example is the continued use in the current work of his definitions of core concepts, some of which have survived more or less unscathed. His definition of nuisance as an 'unlawful interference with a person's use and enjoyment of land, or of some right over, or in connection with it'[131] is almost precisely replicated in the current edition

See also the positive reviews of the sixth edition by Street, '*Winfield on Torts: Sixth Edition*' (n 14) and Denning, '*Winfield on Tort*' (n 117).

[126] Jolowicz says in the preface to that edition that Ellis Lewis – who was returning to health after a period of illness – was responsible for only three chapters: JA Jolowicz and TE Lewis, *Winfield on Tort*, 7th edn (London, Sweet & Maxwell, 1963) v. The same was true of the eighth edition: Jolowicz and Lewis, *Winfield on Tort*, 8th edn (n 81) viii. In the ninth edition, Donald Harris took over two of the three chapters for which Ellis Lewis had previously been responsible, leaving him with only the chapter on animals: JA Jolowicz, TE Lewis and DM Harris, *Winfield & Jolowicz on Tort*, 9th edn (London, Sweet & Maxwell, 1971) v.

[127] Jolowicz and Lewis, *Winfield on Tort*, 7th edn (n 126) v.

[128] Dingle and Bates, 'Conversations with Professor Tony Jolowicz: Third Interview (Published Works)' (n 102) 220. See also ibid 223 ('we rewrote a great deal').

[129] H Street, '*Winfield on Tort: Seventh Edition*' (1964) 8 *Journal of the Society of Public Teachers of Law (New Series)* 36, 36 (review).

[130] DM Kloss, '*Winfield and Jolowicz on Tort*' (1972) 12 *Journal of the Society of Public Teachers of Law (New Series)* 191, 191 (review).

[131] *Text-Book* (n 25) 462.

of *Winfield & Jolowicz*, for instance,[132] and the same is true of his definition of trespass to land as 'unjustifiable interference with possession of it'.[133] Winfield's identification of what he considered to be the three ingredients of the tort of negligence has also survived into the modern text,[134] and indeed has influenced English thinking on negligence more generally,[135] despite its obvious flaw in conflating into the third 'ingredient' (after duty and breach) three quite distinct concepts, namely damage, causation and remoteness.

Winfield's influence on the modern work that bears his name is also discernible at a more fundamental level. As with a house built centuries ago, with some parts added later, and some parts long since demolished, it is still possible to observe the imprint and the consequences of the original design. To give an example, as a teacher of tort, I have always found the chapters on negligence in *Winfield & Jolowicz* less useful than those on the nominate torts. And looking back at the early editions, one can discern the likely origins of this disparity in the strengths and weaknesses of Winfield's own treatment of these topics. The discussion in the *Text-Book* of trespass to the person, deceit, nuisance, animals and so forth is a *tour de force*, with clear, straightforward definitions and explanations of complex concepts and questions,[136] enriched as always by Winfield's historical expertise. By contrast, the discussion of negligence is disappointing, even if full account is taken of the relative youth of that cause of action at the time.[137] In a book of some 700 pages, only 27 are devoted to what was even then by far the most important tort in practice.[138] And the discussion, which is divided into the three 'ingredients' of duty, breach and causation, is unsatisfying. The treatment of duty is largely historical, with no real effort made to explain its modern significance. The section on breach tells the reader little about what actually constitutes negligence, a concept that Winfield mischaracterises as a

[132] Peel and Goudkamp, *Winfield & Jolowicz on Tort*, 19th edn (n 2) para 15-008. The only differences are that an 'or' has replaced the 'and', and the second 'of' has been removed. It is now also made clear that this is a definition of *private* nuisance.

[133] cp *Text-Book* (n 25) 324 with Peel and Goudkamp, *Winfield & Jolowicz on Tort*, 19th edn (n 2) para 14-001.

[134] cp *Text-Book* (n 25) 427 with Peel and Goudkamp, *Winfield & Jolowicz on Tort*, 19th edn (n 2) para 5-002.

[135] See, eg, C Witting, *Street on Torts*, 15th edn (Oxford, OUP, 2018) 26.

[136] For a flavour of the clarity and precision of Winfield's exposition, see, for example, the treatment of (a) the unloaded gun issue in assault (*Text-Book* (n 25) 227–28); (b) the relevance of means of escape in false imprisonment (ibid 233–34); (c) *Derry v Peek* (1889) 14 App Cas 337 (HL) in deceit (ibid 410–15); (d) 'reasonableness' (ibid 468–69) and 'who can be sued' (ibid 483–92) in nuisance; and (e) the distinction between nuisance and *Rylands v Fletcher* (ibid 521).

[137] See also Wright, 'The English Law of Torts: A Criticism' (n 125) 87: 'This reviewer never considered Winfield's treatment of negligence as satisfactory'. Winfield's limitations as a negligence scholar are also apparent from his article on the volume of the *Restatement of the Law of Torts* devoted to the topic: see PH Winfield, 'The Restatement of the Law of Torts: Negligence' (1935) 13 *New York University Law Quarterly Review* 1.

[138] As Denning said in his review of the third edition, '[a]ctions for personal injuries now take up most of the time of the Courts, and more space might be devoted to the problems to which they give rise' (Denning, '*A Text-Book of the Law of Tort*' (n 116) 517).

state of mind, despite the fact that earlier writers, such as Pollock and Holmes,[139] had argued persuasively that in its legal sense it meant the failure to meet an objective standard of reasonable conduct.[140] (As Cecil Wright later observed, this was bound to lead to nothing 'but confusion and misunderstanding, particularly to a student'.[141]) A discussion of contributory negligence dominates the section on causation. Remoteness and what Winfield called 'dangerous operations' are dealt with elsewhere.[142] More generally, one gets the impression once again that Winfield is less secure when dealing with more abstract or general topics. The second chapter, on 'General Conditions of Liability in Tort', is also disappointing, mixing up defences with liability questions, and failing to differentiate sufficiently between propositions relating to tort as a whole and those relevant only to negligence.

The weaknesses that undoubtedly exist in the *Text-Book* were highlighted in an article about the sixth edition by the Canadian tort scholar Cecil Wright, published in the *University of Toronto Law Journal* in 1955.[143] In a review of the first edition, Wright had expressed 'a slight feeling of disappointment, – not with what the author has done but with what ... he might have done and which the reviewer believes ought to be done'.[144] The general treatment of the subject was little different from that in other English books – such as *Pollock* and *Salmond* – that 'failed to address the basic problem in the law of torts', namely the 'adjustment of conflicting claims or interests'.[145] Wright reiterated and extended his critique of the *Text-Book* in the 1955 article, which serves as an interesting contrast to Landon's attack on *Province*, for whereas Landon lambasted Winfield for his radicalism, 24 years later Wright was taking him to task for his conservatism. As was the case with Landon, the bulk of Wright's article is made up of entirely reasonable criticisms of particular aspects of Winfield's analysis – his devotion of a chapter to 'dangerous chattels', for example, and his failure to deal properly with breach of statutory duty[146] – and

[139] See Duxbury, *Frederick Pollock and the English Juristic Tradition* (n 5) 242.

[140] It might be thought in Winfield's defence that this was a common view at the time, but David Ibbetson argues that 'by the beginning of the twentieth century the objective standpoint was becoming dominant': D Ibbetson, 'The Tort of Negligence in England' in N Jansen (ed), *The Development and Making of Legal Doctrine* (Cambridge, CUP, 2010) 51. And although Salmond had been guilty of the same error as Winfield, by the time the *Text-Book* was written Stallybrass had put matters straight in *The Law of Torts* (see ibid).

[141] Wright, 'The English Law of Torts: A Criticism' (n 125) 87.

[142] For remoteness, see *Text-Book* (n 25) 71–88 (in the chapter on 'General Conditions of Liability in Tort'). 'Dangerous operations' had their own chapter (ch 23), which was removed by Ellis Lewis in the sixth edition.

[143] Wright, 'The English Law of Torts: A Criticism' (n 125). For an insightful examination of Wright's own tort scholarship, see RB Brown, 'Cecil A Wright and the Foundations of Canadian Tort Law Scholarship' (2001) 64 *Saskatchewan Law Review* 169.

[144] CA Wright, '*A Text-Book of the Law of Tort*' (1938) 16 *Canadian Bar Review* 237, 238 (review).

[145] ibid.

[146] Wright, 'The English Law of Torts: A Criticism' (n 125) 96 and 94 respectively.

yet for me it is again the general premises that underlie the critique that are of particular interest.

It should be borne in mind here that Wright's target was the 'English treatment' of '[a] number of situations in the law of torts, and particularly the law concerning liability for negligence', and that the new edition of the *Text-Book* was merely a 'focal point' for his analysis.[147] According to a later commentator, the gist of Wright's critique of the English literature was that 'it simply attempted to summarize the decisions of English appellate courts, failed to adequately conceptualize the law of torts, and gave little attention to the need for tort law to fulfil social needs'.[148] There is some truth in this, but in fact Wright's critique of the *Text-Book* was more complex. At times it smacks of legal realism, as when he writes that the book does not 'get to the fundamental problems of *fact*' but instead over-emphasises 'the language of legal concepts'.[149] And yet Wright was no realist,[150] and the bulk of his article consists of criticisms of Winfield's treatment of particular topics, tied together by the general theme that the book is not sufficiently ambitious in its conceptual analysis, particularly when it comes to the law of negligence. Tellingly, Wright was much more favourably disposed towards the American treatment of the subject,[151] and his criticisms of the *Text-Book* can be contrasted with his adulatory review of William Prosser's treatise on American tort law,[152] published four years after Winfield's first edition, which he termed 'excellent in every respect'.[153]

To put Wright's attack on the *Text-Book* in context, we need to remember that the later years of Winfield's life coincided with the first stirrings of what would eventually amount to a complete transformation of Commonwealth tort scholarship in the 1950s and 1960s, culminating in the 1970s in a widespread belief that large swathes of tort law would be replaced with social insurance along the lines of the New Zealand accident compensation scheme.[154] This post-war *Zeitgeist* was exemplified by Jolowicz's decision in the eighth edition of the *Text-Book* (published in 1967) to replace Winfield's conceptual definition of tortious liability with the statement that 'the law of tort may be said to be concerned with the allocation or redistribution of those losses which are bound to occur in our society'.[155] Winfield cannot have been oblivious to the storm

[147] ibid 84.

[148] Brown, 'Cecil A Wright and the Foundations of Canadian Tort Law Scholarship' (n 143) 209.

[149] Wright, 'The English Law of Torts: A Criticism' (n 125) 85.

[150] According to Brown, Wright was 'deeply concerned about the threat realism posed to legal doctrine' (Brown, 'Cecil A Wright and the Foundations of Canadian Tort Law Scholarship' (n 143) 188).

[151] See, eg, Wright, '*A Text-Book of the Law of Tort*' (n 144) 238.

[152] WL Prosser, *Handbook of the Law of Torts* (St Paul, MN, West Publishing, 1941).

[153] CAW, '*Handbook of the Law of Torts*' (1941) 19 *Canadian Bar Review* 551, 552 (review).

[154] For a discussion of the early thinking along these lines in the English context, see M Lobban, 'English Jurisprudence and Tort Theory' in M Lobban and J Moses (eds), *The Impact of Ideas on Legal Development* (Cambridge, CUP, 2012) 134–38.

[155] Jolowicz and Lewis, *Winfield on Tort*, 8th edn (n 81) 1.

clouds that were gathering on the horizon. After all, Wright had published an article in the *Cambridge Law Journal* in the early 1940s where he described tort law as a loss adjustment mechanism,[156] to which Winfield as editor had added a note commending it as 'of general interest'.[157] And he would of course also have been familiar with the burgeoning literature in the American law reviews along these lines,[158] and to the way in which American works such as Prosser's incorporated this perspective into their treatment of the subject. And yet there is absolutely no sign whatsoever of this new thinking even in the last edition of the *Text-Book* that Winfield wrote, published in 1950. In a review of the seventh edition, Harry Street – the author of the first new tort textbook to appear in England after Winfield's, which took full cognisance of the new thinking[159] – commented that '[o]ne would wish that almost the only statement in this long book about the increasingly important topic of insurance should not be wrong'![160] The result was that by the mid-1950s, a book which had been commended for its modernity in the 1930s already looked rather dated.

Nevertheless, when evaluating Winfield's work on tort as a whole, one cannot help feeling that, if it was attacked both by conservatives for being too progressive and also by progressives for being too conservative, he was probably striking a reasonable balance for his time. (That Winfield saw himself as walking something of an intellectual tightrope is suggested by the fact that Wright received a letter from him after the former's critical review of the first edition of the *Text-Book* in which Winfield had indicated that a book of the kind that Wright wanted to see 'would so shock the traditional attitude of the profession as to be commercially impossible'.[161]) And it must also be said that when the social and political conditions in which tort law operates are constantly changing, a historical and doctrinal perspective of the kind that Winfield adopted can prove to be of more enduring relevance than scholarly writing that more obviously tacks to the prevailing winds.

IV. THE SCHOLAR

When considering Winfield as a scholar, it scarcely needs to be said that full account must be taken of the broader intellectual context. Posterity has not been kind to English academic law in the period during which he was working.

156 CA Wright, 'Introduction to the Law of Torts' (1942–44) 8 *CLJ* 238.

157 ibid 238 fn.

158 See, eg, WG Friedmann, 'Social Insurance and the Principles of Tort Liability' (1949) 63 *Harvard Law Review* 241.

159 H Street, *The Law of Torts* (London, Butterworths, 1955). Although Street's book could have toppled *Winfield* off its perch, it had its own shortcomings, as Glanville Williams pointed out in a penetrating review: see G Williams, '*The Law of Torts*' [1956] *CLJ* 251 (review).

160 Street, '*Winfield on Tort: Seventh Edition*' (n 129) 36.

161 Wright, 'The English Law of Torts: A Criticism' (n 125) 85.

It was a small and insular world, and the bulk of its 130 or so inhabitants[162] were uninspired and uninspiring.[163] Many law teachers did no research at all, and the work that was done tended to be practitioner-oriented and pedestrian. Later commentators have said that in England '[a]cademic law remained a fairly moribund, amateurish profession throughout the first half of the twentieth century',[164] and that it reached its nadir between the wars.[165] Seen in this light, Winfield's achievement is particularly impressive.

As for Winfield's own scholarly mindset, we can gain some insight into this from his inaugural lecture on 'Law Reform'.[166] Steeped in the English common law tradition, he is favourably disposed towards it, and operates on the working assumption that the law-makers have broadly speaking got things right:

> [W]hat I urge is that the bulk of English law is rational and well adapted to current needs. This is a mere truism to most of you, but great men like Bentham often forgot it, and lesser men who assume that whatever is, is wrong, have never remembered it.[167]

Winfield's positive disposition towards the common law is also revealed by his review of Leon Green's *Judge and Jury*, where he defends the law of tort against Green's 'thunderstorm of criticism', much of which strikes him as 'destructive rather than constructive'.[168] On the whole, he believes, the English courts 'have dealt with troublesome problems in a tolerably sensible fashion', and his impression is that the same is true of the American courts.[169] The qualifiers are important. Winfield was certainly not uncritical in his attitude towards the law, and was at pains to make clear in his lecture that he 'was not denying for a moment that there are many bad things in English law – sheer bad rules that stick in it from our early history, like rubbish carried down by a glacier'.[170] Unlike realists such as Green, however, Winfield's starting point was that the common law was broadly 'sensible'. It did not follow that it could not be improved, though such improvement was best effected organically, through judicial development and piecemeal codifications, rather than through some grand rationalising scheme.[171]

[162] See W Twining, *Blackstone's Tower: The English Law School* (London, Sweet & Maxwell, 1994) 25–26.

[163] See, eg, the devastating assessment of LCB Gower, 'English Legal Training' (1950) 13 *MLR* 137.

[164] N Duxbury, *Jurists and Judges: An Essay on Influence* (Oxford, Hart Publishing, 2001) 71.

[165] JW Bridge, 'The Academic Lawyer: Mere Working Mason or Architect?' (1975) 91 *LQR* 488, 491.

[166] PH Winfield, 'Law Reform' (1928) 44 *LQR* 289.

[167] ibid 290.

[168] PHW, '*Judge and Jury*' (1931) 47 *LQR* 594, 595 (review).

[169] ibid 595.

[170] Winfield, 'Law Reform' (n 166) 289–90.

[171] 'Any scheme ... of codifying here and now the whole of English law is both useless and mischievous' (ibid 293). See also *Text-Book* (n 25) 5 ('a great deal of harm would be done to our law of tort by its reduction to a statutory code').

Consistently with his essential conservatism – a quality he described as 'a valuable asset for stability in law'[172] – Winfield was impatient of grand theories not grounded in the lived reality of the law over the course of its history, and the present needs of the community. In his essay on 'Ethics in English Case Law', he wrote:

> [T]here is not the faintest trace in current English case law of any attempt on the part of the judges to make the law conform to any ideal ethical standard. Where there is any scope for the application of morals to the law, what they do apply is the practical morality which is prevalent for the time being in the community. They have no general formula, whether utilitarian or otherwise, as to what morality *ought* to be. It is enough for them if they can keep abreast of what it *is* now.[173]

Note that Winfield is not arguing here that there is no relationship between ethics and the law. On the contrary, while recognising that the two are distinct, he believed that it was impossible to 'escape from the moral element in law',[174] or 'to make or to administer a civilised system of law without taking account of current ethical ideas'.[175] His point is rather that the common law reflects the ethics and the morality of the community it serves, and not some overarching philosophical theory. This in turn echoed his broader belief, expressed in his inaugural lecture, that '[l]aw, in the main, has discharged its function, if it corresponds with reasonable accuracy to the existing needs of the community'.[176]

After Winfield's death, his scholarly success was ascribed, in part, to 'his intolerance of legal theories, however elegant, which would be unworkable in practical law',[177] or in other words (as Bailey put it) to the fact that 'he kept his feet on the ground':

> One of his great qualities ... was that he did not invent or criticize for the sake of cleverness: he took the law as it stood, remembering its background and its purpose, its courts, its practitioners, and the lives of men.[178]

Though conservative, Winfield was also a progressive. In *Province*, he said that some 'of the boldest plans for reconstructing the framework of the law of tort have originated in the United States', and that while in certain instances it would be 'perilous' to teach these in English law schools, they did 'at least mark progressive thought', which was 'preferable to the view which deprecates definition because exactness in it is impossible'.[179] Winfield's progressive attitudes are also evident from his writings on restitution – he expresses his approval, for example, of the effective 'obliteration' of the distinction between common law

[172] Winfield, 'The Province of the Law of Tort: A Reply' (n 94) 32.
[173] PH Winfield, 'Ethics in English Case Law' (1931) 45 *Harvard Law Review* 112, 132–33.
[174] ibid 118.
[175] *Text-Book* (n 25) 26.
[176] Winfield, 'Law Reform' (n 166) 290.
[177] 'Sir Percy Winfield' *The Times* (8 July 1953) 8.
[178] Bailey, 'Percy Henry Winfield, 1878–1953' (n 7) 335.
[179] *Province* (n 24) 5–6.

and equity in the *Restatement of the Law of Restitution*[180] – and in his opinions on legal education, as set out in his Presidential Address to the Society of Public Teachers of Law in 1930. The 'highest aim of legal education', he argues, 'ought to be the inculcation of broad principles and of sound methods of thinking',[181] and he goes on to express forward-thinking views on matters such as the teaching of civil procedure, which he says could profitably be studied by means of lectures and books (and not only by practice), 'provided the reasons … for seemingly arbitrary rules' were identified.[182]

As for the scholar's role within the common law system, the first pages of *Province* suggest that Winfield saw this as both theoretical and practical. The scholar must advance the subject in scientific terms, by making it more rational and comprehensible (not least to students), and yet at the same time scholarship could also point the way towards the resolution of problems that came before the courts, and improve the advice lawyers gave to their clients. Winfield saw the textbook – which might be read, as his was, not only by students, but also by practitioners – as a particularly powerful weapon in the academic's armoury, as he made clear in this passage from his inaugural lecture:

> I now pass to the last source of English law – text books. They are the humblest in authority but, to my mind, the most important agencies for improving the form of the law and, to some extent, its substance … The ideal pattern for them would be a statement of what the law has been, what it is now, and what it ought to be. It is quite impossible to achieve the second of these aims without taking account of the first: and the third follows as a natural consequence.[183]

When reading Winfield's writings, one comes across certain themes or traits again and again, and in the remainder of this section, I would like to bring out what I see as being the most persistent and recurrent of these. We have already seen that Winfield could be described as a conservative, and also as a progressive. But he was also many other things, including a pragmatist, a scientist, a historian, a comparativist and a stylist. Again, when looking at these characteristics we need to put them in context. Some – such as his practical outlook, and his desire to put the law on a more rational footing – were observable in most tort scholarship of the period.[184] Others – his openness to other legal systems, for instance, and his engaging style – were less common, and so more distinctive. All went to make up a multi-faceted, but remarkably consistent, scholarly persona.

[180] Winfield, 'Equity and Quasi-Contract' (n 21).

[181] PH Winfield, 'Reforms in the Teaching of Law' [1930] *Journal of the Society of Public Teachers of Law (Old Series)* 1, 3.

[182] ibid 7.

[183] Winfield, 'Law Reform' (n 166) 295–96.

[184] See Mitchell, *A History of Tort Law 1900–1950* (n 56) 33 (scientific aspirations), 35 (pragmatism). The same is true, at least to some extent, of Winfield's historical approach: see Lobban, 'English Jurisprudence and Tort Theory' (n 154) 130.

A. The Pragmatist

Winfield's pragmatism has already been adverted to, for example in the discussion of the organisation of his *Text-Book*.[185] It was connected to his conservatism, and yet also distinct from it. It undoubtedly played a significant part in his scholarly successes. And it is a theme that recurs throughout his work. Numerous examples could be given, particularly from *Province*, perhaps because he felt it necessary to emphasise his practical outlook in what was his most theoretical work. Hence, he stresses in that book that he is keen not to alienate two of his potential audiences, namely practitioners and students. His view on a particular question, he notes, 'has the great advantage of coinciding with the opinion of practitioners, and that ought to be the aim of every writer on jurisprudence if by any reasonable intendment it can be reconciled with scientific analysis'.[186] Later on, he observes that the 'advisability of adopting [a particular classification] is somewhat doubtful from the teaching point of view'.[187] And in his *Text-Book*, he again kept his intended audiences firmly in mind.[188] Winfield was also accepting of the essential illogicality of the law, which he saw as an inevitable consequence of the process of its development. The separation of the law of trusts from the rest of private law, for example, was 'unfortunate' as a matter of logic, 'but it is inevitable that a completely logical scheme of the law is impossible. What jurists have to construct is the physiology of a living body, not the anatomy of a skeleton.'[189]

Winfield's pragmatism is perhaps most explicit in his comments on law reform. In a review of a recent report proposing reforms to the law of evidence, for example, he said that '[m]ost reformers spoil their chance of success by attempting too much', and that others pinned their faith 'on theoretical improvements, without much regard to the material that must be sifted before a sound practical amendment of the law is possible'.[190] Indeed, he went so far as to say in his lecture on law reform that 'no author who is not a practitioner ought to recommend a reform without consulting some practical expert in that part of the law which he is expounding'.[191]

As those observations demonstrate, Winfield was acutely conscious of the practicalities of the law's operation. In a book review he says, for example (with reference to the law of contributory negligence), that 'what is wanted in this

[185] See pp 180–81.

[186] *Province* (n 24) 104. Note also his concern not to put off practitioners suspicious of 'unfamiliar terms' when framing his definition of tortious liability (ibid 32).

[187] ibid 243.

[188] See, eg, *Text-Book* (n 25) 191 ('too technical for reproduction in a students' book').

[189] *Province* (n 24) 114. cp P Birks, *An Introduction to the Law of Restitution* (Oxford, Clarendon Press, 1985) 1.

[190] PH Winfield, '*The Law of Evidence: Some Proposals for its Reform*' (1928) 3 *CLJ* 323, 323 (review).

[191] Winfield, 'Law Reform' (n 166) 296.

branch of the law, as in others, is a rule that will work, not one that will satisfy a metaphysician or a logician'.[192] Similarly, in a discussion of interference with marital relations he comments that while a particular attitude that he ascribes to 'average people' may be 'deplored by the moralist', 'its existence is a fact and the law has to deal with average people'.[193] And in a letter to *The Times* urging reform of the law of libel he comments that, 'however confident they may be of a favourable result, what authors would prefer is freedom from the fear of litigation rather than success (and probably expensive success) in it'.[194]

B. The Scientist

Winfield's conservatism and pragmatism went hand-in-hand with a rationalising tendency that he characterised as 'scientific'.[195] Examples of Winfield's 'scientific' mindset abound. When welcoming the American *Restatement of Restitution*, for example, he said that it was particularly important 'to all of us on this side of the Atlantic who are anxious to find a scientific basis for our system as distinct from the purely practical application of isolated rules'.[196] And in his defence of *Province* against Landon's critique in *Bell Yard*, Winfield says that he had 'tried to put the existing common law into a more scientific form':

> Of course my critic will retort, 'You can't treat it in scientific fashion.' To that I have no rejoinder, except that if this had been the attitude of the writers of text-books on any branches of our law, we should still be studying nothing more shapely than alphabetical abridgments and books of entries.[197]

Winfield's scientific tendencies (and capabilities) are indeed particularly apparent in *Province*, especially in the short but brilliant chapter on tort and property, where he argues that:

> In theory, one might expound the law solely by reference to legal rights, leaving all legal duties to be inferred from the statement of rights … On this hypothesis the law of tort could be eliminated as a separate division of the system. All the duties comprised in it could be deduced from statements of the various rights *in rem* comprised under the rights to property, to personal security and to reputation. But, for historical reasons, English law has never reached this abstraction. To begin with,

[192] PH Winfield, '*The Law of Torts*' (1935) 51 *LQR* 388, 389 (review).
[193] PH Winfield, 'Restatement of the Law of Torts: Volume III' (1939) 17 *New York University Law Quarterly Review* 1, 17.
[194] PH Winfield, 'Authors and the Law of Libel' (Letter) *The Times* (17 March 1936) 12.
[195] On the influence of 'scientific' thinking on common law scholarship at this time, see Lobban, 'English Jurisprudence and Tort Theory' (n 154) 130–31, who conceives of it as an aspiration that the common law should develop towards being 'a coherent and well-ordered system of norms'.
[196] Winfield, 'The American Restatement of the Law of Restitution' (n 21) 529.
[197] Winfield, 'The Province of the Law of Tort: A Reply' (n 94) 34.

> like any other legal system, it has been compelled to plod along from the simple idea of a 'wrong' to the complicated idea of a 'right'.[198]

We can also see those tendencies in Winfield's dislike of what he called 'hair-splitting' attributable to accidents of history – examples are the direct/indirect distinction in trespass to the person,[199] much of the law of defamation,[200] and the law's differing treatment of dangerous chattels and ruinous houses[201] – and in his contempt for 'rhythmical inanities' like 'respondeat superior',[202] and for the maxims (such as *sic utere tuo ut alienum non laedas*) he dismisses as 'unfortunate scraps of Latin'.[203]

However, while the desirability of putting the law on a more rational footing was a consistent theme of Winfield's scholarship, it was also explicitly tempered by his belief that the common law was incapable of a wholly logical analysis, and his anxiety not to alienate his intended audiences. The resultant tension is clearly apparent, for example, in his article on the duty of care. As a legal scientist (and as a historian and comparativist), he perceives that the duty concept is unnecessary, and that it makes the law 'overweighted and unscientific'.[204] But at the same time, as a pragmatist, he accepts that the concept is too firmly embedded in the law to be removed, and in any case considers that for all its faults its removal would 'inflict much too great a shock on ingrained habits of legal thought' to be desirable.[205]

C. The Historian

It is impossible to over-emphasise the extent to which Winfield's tort scholarship was imbued with his historical learning. To give just one example from the many that could be given, the distinctive view that he put forward in *Province* about the nature of tort was grounded in historical analysis of the development of tort liability.[206] There is an irony in the fact that Winfield was forced to divide his early work on abuse of procedure into separate volumes dealing with 'history' and 'the present law', since in much of his later work the two are so closely

[198] *Province* (n 24) 204–05. Eight decades later, the plodding continues: see R Stevens, *Torts and Rights* (Oxford, OUP, 2007); and D Nolan and A Robertson (eds), *Rights and Private Law* (Oxford, Hart Publishing, 2012).

[199] See PH Winfield, 'The Restatement of the Law of Torts: Intentional Harms' (1935) 12 *New York University Law Quarterly Review* 557, 561.

[200] *Text-Book* (n 25) 258. See also Winfield, 'Law of Libel' (n 65) 13 ('a branch of the law which carries too much dead timber from the past and which has not grown sufficiently for present needs').

[201] *Text-Book* (n 25) 589.

[202] ibid 125.

[203] ibid 339 (and see also at 468). Elsewhere, he dismisses the '*sic utere*' maxim as 'that blessed refuge of mental inertia' (Winfield, 'Duty in Tortious Negligence' (n 39) 47).

[204] Winfield, 'Duty in Tortious Negligence' (n 39) 64.

[205] ibid 58.

[206] See Mitchell, *A History of Tort Law 1900–1950* (n 56) 21–23.

intertwined that separating them would be impossible. Nor would Winfield have accepted the validity of the distinction in any case. For him, the law and its history were inseparable.[207]

Winfield's historical outlook was both a reflection of, and reflected in, his essential conservatism, and admiration for the common law. As Mitchell says:

> Winfield was very much writing within the common law tradition – he had a deep respect for, and intellectual interest in, the historical development of common law concepts, and tended to argue for legal changes that would reflect, or at least be consistent with, that development.[208]

And yet at the same time, Winfield's background as a legal historian also ties in to some of his other scholarly traits, such as his progressive tendencies, his quest for rationality and his pragmatism. Far from making him reactionary in his attitudes, Winfield's understanding of the law's history enabled him to take up iconoclastic positions, where appropriate. Hence, he was able to make a persuasive argument that the duty of care was superfluous, because he could show that it was the result of a historical accident, and a fairly recent one at that. Similarly, he could demonstrate that an irrationality in the present law was merely a hangover from some past period of the law's development, which now served no purpose, or the result of some wrong turning taken centuries earlier. Either way it could safely be reformed. For example, the legislative reversal of the common law rule against a plaintiff's suing joint tortfeasors separately could be welcomed, because the rule was the result of a 'procedural shibboleth', and in any case a decision from 1412 suggested that the law had once been otherwise.[209]

Winfield's pragmatism is illustrated by the fact that his interest in legal history was an avowedly practical one. He valued legal history not as an intellectual pursuit in its own right but as a tool, the use of which could help explain the present state of the law and inform its future development.[210] So the references to history in his *Text-Book* were justified because sometimes they were necessary to explain the reason for a rule (which would in turn help to arouse the student's interest in the topic),[211] and for the most part law reform was 'likely to be a half-witted affair' unless legal history was '*applied to it*'.[212]

[207] See ibid 20.

[208] ibid 9.

[209] PH Winfield, 'Recent Legislation on the English Law of Tort' (1936) 14 *Canadian Bar Review* 639, 656–57. The legislation in question was the Law Reform (Married Women and Tortfeasors) Act 1935.

[210] See, eg, PH Winfield, '*Law and Other Things*' (1938) 6 *CLJ* 461, 462 (review) (commending Lord Macmillan's view of '[t]he real practical value of history to the lawyer').

[211] *Text-Book* (n 25) v. See also, eg, *Province* (n 24) 44 ('[i]t is almost impossible to give an intelligible account of the relation of contract to tort at the present day without frequent reference to the history specially affecting them').

[212] Winfield, 'Law Reform' (n 166) 296 (emphasis added). See also PH Winfield, '*A History of English Law*' (1926) 42 *LQR* 394, 395 (review) ('To show the reason for a particular rule is the best way of guaranteeing sane reform of it'). It seems that Winfield practised what he preached in this respect: Mitchell points out that – unlike the Law Revision Committee's earlier reports – its report

In Winfield's view, the value of history to a lawyer lay in the fact that it was 'often difficult to state what the law is without knowing something of its history and always dangerous to attempt reform of the law without it'.[213]

D. The Comparativist

Although Winfield was not a comparative lawyer, he demonstrates a ready familiarity with other legal systems, both within and beyond the common law world, and he frequently brings this knowledge to bear on the problems of English law. This trait is particularly apparent in his periodical writings. An exemplar is his article on privacy, discussed earlier,[214] but his comparative mindset can also be seen clearly in, for instance, his late paper on tort in the conflict of laws, where he refers to the law in France, Italy, Germany, Austria, Switzerland, Latin America, Scandinavia and South Africa.[215] By contrast, Winfield seems to have deliberately toned down his comparative inclinations in his *Text-Book*, perhaps for fear of turning off students and practitioners.[216]

Winfield was keen to emphasise the benefits of comparative analysis to other English scholars, many of whom were doubtless possessed of a more insular outlook. He concluded his inaugural lecture with a plea to his audience to devote more study to comparative law, which he said was 'intimately allied'[217] with legal history: '[I]n some topics its study seems to me highly advisable and perhaps essential. Whether we consider the past, present or future of English law, there is much to be gained from it.'[218]

Winfield suggested that such work 'might begin with a comparative study of Scots law', books on which were more accessible than those on foreign systems. In an observation that continues to resonate to this day, he expressed surprise 'that while the vision of our comparative lawyers sweeps across oceans to America and Europe, it is apt to glance lightly at Scotland'.[219] This was a theme he returned to a year later, in a review of a book on the Scots law of contract in the *Law Quarterly Review*:

> English lawyers in general know as much about Scots law as they do about French or German law … considering the extent to which Roman law is taught in many English

on contributory negligence 'sought to give a historical explanation for the current position', and speculates that 'this might well have been prompted' by Winfield's involvement in its drafting (Mitchell, *A History of Tort Law 1900–1950* (n 56) 316).

[213] Winfield, '*Law and Other Things*' (n 210) 462.

[214] See p 173.

[215] PH Winfield, 'The Law of Tort: Conflict of Laws' (1949) 35 *Transactions for the Year* 133.

[216] Not completely however. For comparative references in the *Text-Book* (n 25) see, eg, 64 (necessity), 69 (abuse of rights) and 116–17 (insanity). Then again, in the preface to the sixth edition, Ellis Lewis specifically draws attention to the fact that he has increased the references to decisions and commentary in other common law countries: Lewis, *Winfield on Tort*, 6th edn (n 124) v.

[217] Winfield, 'Law Reform' (n 166) 301.

[218] ibid 300.

[219] ibid 304.

> universities, it does seem a pity that Scots law, in so far as it is a derivative from the older system, is not used more by way of instructional illustration.[220]

Winfield's intellectual open-mindedness is most obvious, though, in his interest in, and frequent references to, American developments and American scholarship.[221] This is a constant refrain throughout his work, and may date back to his time in Harvard in 1923. He saw particular value in the *Restatement of the Law of Torts*,[222] and devoted no fewer than four articles to a close examination of it, one for each volume.[223] In the third of those articles, Winfield warned English lawyers that they must regard themselves as incompletely equipped for their profession unless the *Restatements* formed part of their library,[224] and in the final article he said:

> For the English writer, teacher and student, the value of the Restatements is very great ... the [dawning interest in them among English practitioners] will quicken when it is realised that some regions of the common law that are as yet *terra incognita* in the English system have been explored and charted by the American courts.[225]

It is also striking that so many of Winfield's major periodical writings on tort were published in American and Canadian journals – no fewer than nine of the 17 publications that I have categorised as such.[226] This again demonstrates the extent of Winfield's engagement with other common law systems, while also suggesting that he was keen to reach audiences beyond these shores. And it is noteworthy that in the year in which the first two of Winfield's *Restatement* articles were published, Cecil Wright claimed that he had found nowhere in England 'any discussion of the utility to be derived from the study of American, or even "colonial", decisions or doctrine'.[227] This is at least an indication that Winfield's curiosity about developments across the Atlantic was unusual, even

[220] PH Winfield, '*The Law of Contract*' (1929) 45 *LQR* 535, 535 (review).

[221] This did not pass unnoticed in the US: see WA Seavey, '*The Province of the Law of Tort*' (1931) 45 *Harvard Law Review* 209, 209 (review) ('To these questions the author brings a more complete knowledge of current American discussions and a more sympathetic treatment of them than, at least until recently, has been usual in English writers').

[222] Winfield, 'The Law of Tort, 1885–1935' (n 4) 112.

[223] Winfield, 'The Restatement of the Law of Torts: Intentional Harms' (n 199); Winfield, 'The Restatement of the Law of Torts: Negligence' (n 137); Winfield, 'Restatement of the Law of Torts: Volume III' (n 193); Winfield, 'Restatement of the Law of Torts: Volume IV' (n 64).

[224] Winfield, 'Restatement of the Law of Torts: Volume III' (n 193) 22.

[225] Winfield, 'Restatement of the Law of Torts: Volume IV' (n 64) 67. For other examples of Winfield's interest in American law, see, eg, Winfield, '*[Salmond's] The Law of Torts*' (n 119) 129; Winfield, '*Negligence in Law*' (1929) 3 *CLJ* 480, 481 (review); Winfield, 'The American Restatement of the Law of Restitution' (n 21); Winfield, *Pollock's Principles of Contract*, 11th edn (n 23) iii; and PH Winfield, 'Annual Survey of American Law' (1947) 9 *CLJ* 366. It is scarcely surprising that when the Porter Committee on the Law of Defamation wanted a report on the American law in that area, it was Winfield to whom they turned (see Mitchell, *A History of Tort Law 1900–1950* (n 56) 330).

[226] I am grateful to Paul Mitchell for pointing this out to me.

[227] CA Wright, 'The American Law Institute's Restatement of Contracts and Agency' (1935–1936) 1 *University of Toronto Law Journal* 17, 23.

if Wright's failure to exempt the Rouse Ball Professor from his criticism also suggests that his search for such discussions was not a very thorough one.

Finally, it is important to emphasise that, as with legal history, Winfield's appreciation of the potential benefits of comparative analysis was an essentially pragmatic one. The American legal system was particularly useful for English lawyers, he argued, because 'it was naturally more fertile in reported decisions' than English law, and hence 'many a point *primae impressionis* before an English court has already been decided in one or more of the United States'.[228] And more generally:

> [The] true practical value [of comparative law] lies in the information which it would place in the hands of the legislator in one country when he seeks to make or to reform a branch of the law, which has been adequately covered by the law in another country. That information may be of positive assistance; but even if it be a mere danger signal, it will save the law maker from being trapped into a false analogy.[229]

E. The Stylist

Winfield's engaging style is a consistent theme of reviews of his *Text-Book*. According to a reviewer of the second edition, for example:

> The whole book is written with a clarity which is deceptive. It all seems so straightforward, until one tries one's hands at a little re-phrasing. Then it becomes clear that there has been that careful polishing and reshaping … which alone can produce the finished article.[230]

As the reviewer points out, Winfield is adept at producing 'the telling phrase which drives home the point',[231] as when he is explaining that while a corporation is an artificial person, that does not mean it is fictitious: 'A wooden leg may be artificial; it is not a fiction.'[232]

A number of other features of Winfield's style can be highlighted. One is that he does not waste words. He says what needs to be said, and no more. He defines trespass to land, for example, simply as 'unjustifiable interference with possession of it',[233] and his summaries of the facts of cases are concise and to the point – in one instance a single short sentence.[234] Second, he uses examples in a systematic way to aid understanding, particularly in his *Text-Book* (the opening chapter is a good illustration of this). Third, his writing has a homely

[228] Winfield, 'Annual Survey of American Law' (n 225) 367.
[229] Winfield, 'Law Reform' (n 166) 303.
[230] DWL '*A Text-Book of the Law of Tort*' (1942–44) 8 *CLJ* 338, 338 (review).
[231] ibid.
[232] Winfield, *A Text-Book of the Law of Tort*, 2nd edn (n 73) 120, fn.
[233] *Text-Book* (n 25) 324.
[234] 'The defendant's monkey bit the plaintiff' (Winfield, *Cases on the Law of Tort* (n 27) 229). The case was *May v Burdett* (1846) 9 QB 101.

quality to it, which pulls the reader in, rather than pushing them away. Hence in his account of dangerous chattels, he starts with the observation that 'the law expects of a man a great deal more care when carrying a pound of dynamite than a pound of butter',[235] and in his discussion of nuisance he expresses a preference for the 'homely phrases' 'Give and Take', 'Live and Let Live', over the '*sic utere*' maxim.[236] Finally, he has a dry wit, which pops up unexpectedly to enliven potentially dull raw material.

Winfield's clear and precise exposition of the law was also a feature of his lectures at Cambridge,[237] and seems to have been the result of a conscious effort on his part. This is suggested by a comparison of his descriptions of the law on abuse of procedure in his 1921 monograph on the topic and in his 1937 *Text-Book*. Whereas many scholars would simply have repeated more or less word-for-word the original phrasing, Winfield seems to have gone out of his way to tighten it up, with the result that precisely the same point is made more concisely and transparently in the later work. Winfield's concern with matters of style is also apparent from his discussions of the writings of others. He says, for example, of William Blackstone's *Commentaries*, that '[t]he general learning of the book is admitted, but even that is outstripped by its style',[238] while commenting disparagingly on the 'rather arid style' of *Salmond on Torts*.[239] When assessing Winfield's own scholarship, it would be a grave mistake to dismiss the attractive style of his writing as a triviality. On the contrary, a contemporary commentator attributed much of the success of the *Text-Book* to Winfield's use of 'pungent phrase[s] and homely illustration[s]',[240] while MJ Prichard later suggested that the tendency of scholars to follow Winfield in dating the tort of negligence to the period from 1825 onwards was 'a tribute to the effectiveness of his celebrated aphorism about the homicidal tendencies of railway trains towards Ministers of State and wandering cows'.[241]

Needless to say, a proper appreciation of Winfield's style and wit can be gained only by the reading of his works, but a flavour of it can be conveyed by some examples:

- '[T]ill [the nineteenth century] the history of negligence is a skein of threads, most of which are fairly distinct, and no matter where we cut the skein we shall get little more than a bundle of frayed ends.'[242]

[235] *Text-Book* (n 25) 566.
[236] ibid 468.
[237] See McNair, 'Professor Sir Percy Winfield (1878–1953)' (n 8) 82.
[238] Winfield, *The Chief Sources of English Legal History* (n 17) 338.
[239] Winfield, 'The Law of Tort, 1885–1935' (n 4) 262.
[240] Bailey, 'Percy Henry Winfield, 1878–1953' (n 7) 335.
[241] Prichard, 'Trespass, Case and the Rule in *Williams v Holland*' (n 40) 234–35. For the aphorism in question, see Winfield, 'The History of Negligence in the Law of Torts' (n 37) 195.
[242] Winfield, 'The History of Negligence in the Law of Torts' (n 37) 185.

- 'In *Langridge v Levy* [the duty idea in negligence] was no more than a cloud upon the horizon. In *Winterbottom v Wright* it was beginning to cast shadows.'[243]
- 'Common employment, that galling pack upon the back of our law.'[244]
- 'It is the ill fate of public policy that, like a football, everybody kicks it although it is essential to the game.'[245]
- 'Instead of sprawling in vaporous fashion across the legal atmosphere like a genie of the *Arabian Nights*, [public policy] is shrinking [in the seventeenth and eighteenth centuries] to certain departments of the law; but no one had yet thought of imprisoning it in a jar, and indeed no one has ever been able to do that.'[246]
- 'A full apology [requires] a complete withdrawal of the imputation ... To say that a man has manners that are not fit for a pig and then to retract that by saying that his manners are fit for a pig would merely aggravate damages.'[247]
- 'The facts were as follows. Mr Grant ... bought from M's shop a pair of "Golden Fleece" pants which M had purchased in a consignment from the manufacturers ... The Golden Fleece unfortunately proved to be the robe of Nessus.'[248]
- '[W]e may doubt whether even a man of no more than average balance would throw a squib into a crowd to save his gingerbread from ruin.'[249]
- 'If [the married woman] was the spoiled child of Equity, she was also the Cinderella of the Common Law.'[250]
- 'It was pregnant with a good deal more mischief than was ever born of it.'[251]
- 'One feels inclined to reverse a cliché and to say that bad law makes hard cases.'[252]
- '[T]he savage animal is peculiar to neither time nor clime.'[253]

[243] Winfield, 'Duty in Tortious Negligence' (n 39) 54.
[244] PH Winfield, '*Negligence in Delict*' (1939–41) 7 *CLJ* 302, 303 (review).
[245] PH Winfield, '*Fender v St John-Mildmay*' (1938) 54 *LQR* 155, 155 (note).
[246] PH Winfield, 'Public Policy in the English Common Law' (1928) 42 *Harvard Law Review* 76, 84.
[247] *Text-Book* (n 25) 323.
[248] PH Winfield, '*Grant v Australian Knitting Mills Ltd*' (1936) 52 *LQR* 12, 12–13 (note). The case in question was *Grant v Australian Knitting Mills Ltd* [1936] AC 85 (PC).
[249] *Text-Book* (n 25) 60.
[250] ibid 106.
[251] ibid 195 (of the maxim *actio personalis moritur cum persona*). Winfield first used this metaphor in his earlier article on wrongful death (Winfield, 'Death as Affecting Liability in Tort' (n 34) 248–49), but that version was less elegant ('It was pregnant with mischief to which it never gave birth'), which is again indicative of Winfield's having consciously worked on polishing his prose. The inspiration for the metaphor may have been Psalm 7.14.
[252] Winfield, 'Recent Legislation on the English Law of Tort' (n 209) 654.
[253] *Text-Book* (n 25) 550.

V. CONCLUSION

An advantage of considering a scholar's work with the benefit of hindsight is that it enables us to assess how prescient he or she was. In Winfield's case, this is yet another respect in which he and his writings impress the modern reader. Some of Winfield's suggestions as to how the law should be improved were adopted in his lifetime, and in these cases one can only speculate as to his influence on the development in question, while also bearing in mind that its timing may indicate that Winfield's view was also by then the dominant one. A good example is his proposal that the complete defence of contributory negligence be replaced with an apportionment regime akin to that of the Maritime Conventions Act 1911, which he first made in two 1935 articles[254] and then again in his *Text-Book*.[255] In 1939, the Law Revision Committee (LRC) published a report recommending this reform, which Winfield helped to draft;[256] the change itself was effected by the passage of the Law Reform (Contributory Negligence) Act 1945.[257] And another example is his attack on the privity of contract fallacy,[258] the year before the House of Lords abandoned it in *Donoghue v Stevenson*.[259]

Perhaps more impressive, however, are the examples of reforms advocated by Winfield that did not come to pass until decades after his death. Four examples can be given. First, some 30 years before *Hedley Byrne & Co Ltd v Heller & Partners Ltd*[260] Winfield questioned why a claim could not be brought for negligent, as opposed to fraudulent, misrepresentation.[261] Second, he argued consistently for the extension of the tort of malicious prosecution to civil proceedings,[262] a reform enacted only recently by decisions of the Privy Council[263] (where Winfield's writings were called in aid[264]) and the Supreme Court.[265] Third, he drew attention to the complex legal issues raised by the

[254] Winfield, 'The Law of Tort, 1885–1935' (n 4) 255; Winfield, 'Restatement of the Law of Torts: Negligence' (n 137) 17.

[255] *Text-Book* (n 25) 451.

[256] Law Revision Committee, *Eighth Report (Contributory Negligence)* (Cmd 6032, 1939).

[257] See further on the work of the LRC on contributory negligence and the passage of the legislation, Mitchell (n 56) ch 13; and J Steele, 'Law Reform (Contributory Negligence) Act 1945: Collisions of a Different Sort' in TT Arvind and J Steele (eds), *Tort Law and the Legislature: Common Law, Statute and the Dynamics of Legal Change* (Oxford, Hart Publishing, 2013).

[258] *Province* (n 24) 73–76.

[259] *Donoghue* (n 43).

[260] *Hedley Byrne & Co Ltd v Heller & Partners Ltd* [1964] AC 465 (HL).

[261] Winfield, 'The Law of Tort, 1885–1935' (n 4) 258; Winfield, 'Restatement of the Law of Torts: Volume III' (n 193) 8–9. For the possibility that Winfield's Cambridge lectures may have influenced Lord Devlin's analysis in *Hedley Byrne* (n 260), see P Mitchell, '*Hedley Byrne & Co Ltd v Heller & Partners Ltd* (1963)' in C Mitchell and P Mitchell (eds), *Landmark Cases in the Law of Tort* (Oxford, Hart Publishing, 2010) 195–96.

[262] Winfield, 'The Law of Tort, 1885–1935' (n 4) 261; Winfield, 'Restatement of the Law of Torts: Volume III' (n 193) 16; *Text-Book* (n 25) 653.

[263] *Crawford Adjusters (Cayman) Ltd v Sagicor General Insurance (Cayman) Ltd* [2013] UKPC 17, [2014] AC 366.

[264] ibid [42], [50] (Lord Wilson).

[265] *Willers v Joyce* [2016] UKSC 43, [2018] AC 779.

unborn child, arguing in particular that an action should be maintainable by a child with a disability caused by a pre-natal injury[266] – legislation to this effect was passed only in 1976.[267] And finally, and perhaps most famously, we have seen that Winfield argued forcefully for the recognition of a civil cause of action for invasion of privacy.[268] Although this has not yet occurred, the extension of the action for breach of confidence to provide a remedy for the unauthorised disclosure of private information in the wake of the Human Rights Act 1998 at least went some way towards filling the gap in English law that Winfield had identified some 70 years earlier.[269]

One of my aims in this chapter was to search for explanations for Winfield's extraordinary success as a tort scholar. Pulling the strings together, a number of reasons for the impact and endurance of his writings can be identified: his technical brilliance; his intellectual openness; his clear and attractive style; his prescience and forward-thinking approach; his thoroughgoing pragmatism; and a measure of good fortune (most obviously in the form of those who took his *Text-Book* forward after his death). Underlying all of this, however, lay an even more basic foundation for his scholarly achievements, namely a profound and very broad knowledge of the common law and its history. Those countless long days in the Squire Law Library had their pay off.

In *Foundations of Legal Liability*, published just after Winfield's return to academic life following his brief career in practice, Thomas Atkins Street issued the following warning to scholars of the common law:

> The mass of the common law is so formidable, and its complexity so pronounced, that even the stoutest investigator may well quail upon undertaking the task of philosophic inquiry. Too often he proceeds with insufficient knowledge of details, and with little or no insight into the processes which have made the law what it now is. One who makes this fatal blunder is naturally appalled at the outset by the vast pile of matter presented for his consideration, and he is naturally tempted to lay his foundation upon *a priori* speculations instead of searching it out from the body of the law. The scholar who yields to this temptation turns his eyes from the true source of light and is irresistibly carried into barren fields of research.[270]

Though we can be confident that he would have read that passage, we cannot know whether it made an impression on Winfield as a young scholar. But what we can be certain of is that Winfield's own eyes remained resolutely on 'the true source of light', and that as a result his writings continue to illuminate the subject to which he devoted so much of his life.

[266] Winfield, 'Restatement of the Law of Torts: Volume IV' (n 64) 83; PH Winfield, 'The Unborn Child' (1942) 8 *CLJ* 76 (also published in (1942) 4 *University of Toronto Law Journal* 278).

[267] Congenital Disabilities (Civil Liability) Act 1976.

[268] See pp 173–74.

[269] *Campbell v MGN Ltd* [2004] UKHL 22, [2004] 2 AC 457.

[270] TA Street, *Foundations of Legal Liability*, Volume 1: *Tort* (Northport, NY, Edward Thompson, 1906) xxiv.

7

Professor Leon Green (1888–1979): Word Magic and the Regenerative Power of Law

JENNY STEELE

I. INTRODUCTION

'NOTHING FADES SO fast as history', as Leon Green reflected:[1] '[I]t is impossible after a few years to recreate the environment out of which a decision came'.[2] We should do our best to sketch that environment so far as we can, but only the peaks of the faded environment remain accessible to us, and the thoughts that motivated the court can only be conveyed by the merest, unreliable words.[3] Judicial pronouncements are of

[1] L Green, 'Tort Law Public Law in Disguise' (1959–60) 38 *Texas Law Review* 1, 3.

[2] The important thing is to understand that this is the case, that we can appreciate only the 'peaks' of this environment, and that the environment makes a difference to the understanding of a decision. It strikes me that there has been increasing appreciation of the value of particular historical study in private law, and that this encourages an appreciation of openness to environment, as well as an attempt to understand the environment in which cases arose and were decided. The work of AWB Simpson has been particularly influential here (eg, AWB Simpson, *Leading Cases in the Common Law* (Oxford, Clarendon Press, 1995)). Notice also the series of *Landmark Cases* volumes, including C Mitchell and P Mitchell (eds), *Landmark Cases in the Law of Tort* (Oxford, Hart Publishing, 2010); and the co-edited collection, TT Arvind and J Steele (eds), *Tort Law and the Legislature: Common Law, Statute, and the Dynamics of Legal Change* (Oxford, Hart Publishing, 2013).

[3] The 'doctrinal word' is known to be 'the least reliable, though the most indelible phase of the judicial process' (Green, 'Tort Law Public Law in Disguise' (n 1) 3–4). Elsewhere, arguing that the search for a 'language technic' has been 'the falsest hope of legal scholarship', Green quoted Ehrlich: 'words are extremely imperfect tools ... nobody has ever succeeded in mastering real things by means of mere words' (L Green, 'The Duty Problem in Negligence Cases' (1928) 28 *Columbia Law Review* 1014, 1018, citing E Ehrlich, 'Judicial Freedom of Decision: Its Principles and Objects' in E Bruncken and LB Register (trs), *The Science of Legal Method* (Boston, MA, Boston Book Co, 1917) 47, 69). Freedom of decision is one of the key themes of Green's work, as it was of the collection of essays, by a number of European scholars, containing Ehrlich's contribution. See the review by WH Page, '*Science of Legal Method: Select Essays by Various Authors*' (1918) 12 *The American Political Science Review* 312 (review).

a part with their times: we 'can no more make use of the power that flowed through the words of Coke and Blackstone and Marshall than we can of the life contemporary with that power'.[4] Important themes of the vitality of law, the nature of 'power' as a sort of life force,[5] and the necessity and inadequacy of words are illustrated by these brief observations.

The same problem is likely to be true of academic writings, posing a challenge for those of us contributing to this volume. As the only trans-Atlantic interpreter, the issue may be all the greater. The environment of Leon Green's early work is very different from my own. A long-faded struggle against formalism, both in the courts and in the law schools, preoccupied the legal realists of the 1920s and 1930s and gave their analysis of law its significance as a living and evolving force.[6] As usual, Green captured his own part of this in evocative terms: as he put it, through his collection of essays, *The Litigation Process in Tort Law*,

> runs a clear and binding theme – the creative and regenerative power of law. This flow of life in a subject matter thought by so many to be as dead and motionless as the stones of the earth is the most exciting and important discovery a law student can make.[7]

Equally, the relationship between functions of judge and jury in civil claims, including the division between legal and factual questions, dominated much of Leon Green's early work,[8] and was never far from the forefront of his analysis of duty and proximate cause.

Today, formalism in this particular sense is rather remote from the issues that preoccupy tort scholarship; and it strikes me that Green's deep concern with process and the division between judge and jury decisions, though shared by many in his time and place and of great significance in debates about the division between duty and cause, for example, is easy to overlook, particularly in a jurisdiction where juries rarely play any role in the law of tort.[9] Add to all

[4] Green, 'The Duty Problem in Negligence Cases' (n 3) 1019.

[5] The complexity of Green's use of 'power', and potential for misreading, are explored in section IV of this chapter.

[6] On the struggle generally, see N Duxbury, *Patterns of American Jurisprudence* (Oxford, OUP, 1997); and W Twining, *Karl Llewellyn and the Realist Movement*, 2nd edn (Cambridge, CUP, 2014).

[7] L Green, *The Litigation Process in Tort Law: No Place to Stop in the Development of Tort Law*, 2nd edn (Indianapolis, IN, Bobbs-Merrill Co, Inc, 1977) ix.

[8] L Green, *Judge and Jury* (Kansas City, KS, Vernon Law Book Co, 1930).

[9] According to GE White, *Tort Law in America: An Intellectual History*, expanded edn (Oxford, OUP, 2003) 77, 'Other torts scholars, such as Holmes, had seen the importance of judge-jury relations in negligence, but none before Green had shown so powerfully the capacity of generalized tort principles to fragment in their application.' The significance of judge and jury is particularly easy to overlook in the writer's jurisdiction, where jury trial is relevant only to a small and shrinking range of tort cases. In English libel cases now, where juries until recently retained the most significance, the presumption lies against jury trial: Defamation Act 2013, s 11. Peter Cane has pointed out that Green's *Judge and Jury* was a significant influence on the work of John Fleming, and was much cited in the first edition of Fleming's *The Law of Torts*: P Cane, 'Fleming on Torts: A Short Intellectual History' (1998) 6 *Torts Law Journal* 216.

of this Grant Gilmore's remark, in a different context, that '[i]t is, no doubt, as difficult for the English to understand Americans (or vice versa) as it is for men to understand women',[10] and I would appear to be facing a formidable set of hurdles. And yet Green's work in some instances is still sympathetic, perhaps for its heartfelt quality and iconoclasm, and at points still revelatory or at least thought-provoking. Indeed, I suggest that his work retains its resonance for contemporary debates, despite the fading of his own environment, and despite the adverse reviews his work tends sometimes now to command. It is worth engaging with this work, both in its own right and because of its influence on those who followed – some of whom had a much more direct connection with practical legal change.[11] But in addition, since one of Green's themes was dynamic adaptation, we may also learn more about elements of our contemporary debates as products of their own environment.

After this introduction, the chapter will turn first to Green's extraordinary use of language and metaphor, an unusual beginning but in my view a significant factor in his contribution and legacy (though bringing the danger, contrary to what Green hoped, of more heat than light). I then turn briefly to Green's biography and timeline, and sketch the key points of substance his work on tort offered. I then attempt some appraisal of Green's work, including a measure of his contribution against some of the more unsympathetic criticisms of it.

II. LANGUAGE

It is unusual to place style of communication at the top of an analysis of legal scholarship, but it strikes me as essential to remark on Green's unique use of language and metaphor, which burns with frustration and impatience for the law to get on. As if to emphasise that Green's work marked a transition to a new

[10] G Gilmore, '*Karl Llewellyn and the Realist Movement* by W Twining' (1974) 22 *American Journal of Comparative Law* 812, 813 (review). Luckily for any woman seeking an academic career in law, he added that such attempts to communicate are not without interest.

[11] I am grateful to participants in the workshop at which the chapters that constitute this volume were presented for pointing out the influence of Green on two American Law Institute Reporters, William Prosser and Gary Schwartz, as well as on Fleming James, Robert Keeton and John Fleming, the last of these having considerable impact in the UK and Australia. Green had no blueprint for the development of the law, consistent with his belief that legal decisions respond to their environmental facts. Invited to comment on Jeffrey O'Connell's proposal for broadening no-fault liability beyond automobile cases (J O'Connell, 'Expanding No-Fault Beyond Auto Insurance: Some Proposals' (1973) 59 *Virginia Law Review* 749), Green described it as 'a worthy inspiration of an able daydreamer'. Somewhat colourfully, he added that '[i]f our people continue to maintain a free society, my perspective is that No-Fault will be woven into the texture of tort law in a manner that will not conflict with our goals of peace, happiness, health, justice, economic welfare, law and order here on earth and in heaven hereafter' (L Green, 'No-Fault: A Perspective' [1975] *Brigham Young University Law Journal* 79, 80). In other words, no-fault was already with us, to an extent, and would continue to be developed so far as it was useful, all things considered: typically, this is not the narrative of blueprints or grand plans, and it denies any one overriding value.

and 'modern' era, Francis Bohlen (in a long and not especially positive review of *Judge and Jury*) complained that the style was 'eager and rhetorical', and drew a parallel to similar events in the world of art:

> Words are often used [by Green] not so much to define thoughts as to evoke emotional reactions. Like much modern art the book releases the author's personality but it often fails to give anything approaching a definite outline of the ideas which he intends to express.[12]

Perhaps Green would not have minded this any more than the modern artists.[13] His severe criticisms of 'word magic' were directed to attempts to wring some sort of definitive meaning out of mere language – or more seriously perhaps, to create such meaning through it, contriving verbal formulae that would bind future courts to definitive outcomes (an affliction he thought to affect the *Restatement* project, just as much as the practice of the courts). Within a few sentences of his essay on 'The Duty Problem in Negligence Cases'[14] (and before any reference to the duty problem, or indeed the law of negligence), Green refers to 'holy words', 'sacred words', 'word ritual' and 'word worship' – it could be argued that his primary, at times obsessive, target was not doctrine as such but the confusion of doctrine with verbal formulae, and of these verbal formulae with the law itself. Where this leaves the role of substance, as opposed to process, in the law is a question returned to in section IV of this chapter.

Green's key theme, underlying his distaste for 'word magic', was change, both the fact of social change and law's need to respond to it, and the irritation of legal baggage that obstructed its rational progress. Perhaps Bohlen was right that the vivid language performed a role not unlike the role of new techniques in modern art. As Hughes expressed it, artists in the late nineteenth and early twentieth centuries were confident that 'art, in the most disinterested and noble way, could find the necessary metaphors by which a radically changing culture could be explained to its inhabitants'.[15] It seems quite possible that 'affect' is as important as detailed analysis in Green's legacy.[16] Bohlen also complained of Green's 'modernistic tendency', 'to believe that what has been thought in the past is necessarily wrong', seeking to argue that the most valuable insights

[12] FH Bohlen, '*Judge and Jury*' (1931–32) 80 *University of Pennsylvania Law Review* 781, 781 (review).

[13] R Hughes, *The Shock of the New: Art and the Century of Change*, 2nd edn (New York, McGraw-Hill, 1991).

[14] Green, 'The Duty Problem in Negligence Cases' (n 3).

[15] Hughes, *The Shock of the New: Art and the Century of Change* (n 13) 9. Hughes begins his work with the words of Péguy in 1913, that 'the world has changed less since the time of Jesus Christ than it has in the last thirty years'. What matters is not whether this assertion was correct, but the perception that this was the case.

[16] See F James, 'To Leon Green' (1977–78) 56 *Texas Law Review* 535, 535–36: 'Leon's writings together with memories of his class became beacon lights in the transition from a railroad attorney's point of view to that which Fowler Harper and I tried to express in our textbook'. Notice the emphasis, which I think is not trivial, on a 'point of view'; but also the acknowledged influence of Green on a succeeding generation of influential scholars.

of the essays under review were in reality extensions of what had been said or appreciated before.[17] For Green, the necessity of change was as applicable to legal scholarship as it was to the rationality of the law of tort.[18]

On reading Green's work, nobody who sympathises with any part of it (and there are some who do not) could struggle to find an evocative quote. His facility with words, and his ability to strike ruthlessly (even if expressively) at a point through a colourful aphorism, may be unparalleled in tort scholarship – to the extent that David W Robertson, on the occasion of a symposium to mark Green's retirement from active research and teaching in 1977 (at the age of 89),[19] was able to make up the final half of his appreciation entirely in the words of Leon Green, grouped according to his key concerns.[20] Somewhat ironically for a scholar whose most visceral criticism as we have seen was directed at 'word magic' and the dominance of verbal formulae in the law,[21] the vibrant words of Leon Green are the aspect of his work most capable of commanding attention into a new century. But these are not words of the same character as those through which, as Green thought, futile attempts were made to freeze the law in place. They are simple, direct and colourful, using numerous analogies and permutations as Green sought new ways to skewer obfuscatory notions such as 'proximate cause', which in his view needed to be cleared away, or at least to lose their mystique in order to allow rational growth in the law.[22] My impression is that these words were not chosen primarily to dazzle or impress, and were not a repeat of the 'intentional mystification'[23] Green attacked, but reflected a constant desire to elucidate and to strip away verbal mystique.

At its most powerful, the vision was close to apocalyptic. Lawyers must work with doctrine, and this is unavoidable, but it is also dangerous (apparently for them, as well as for the law):

> They may become obsessed and imprisoned; they may seek to scale the heaven of certainty and universal justice through their doctrinal perfection. But, like any other tower of Babel, the confusion of doctrine will inevitably craze the workers and wreck the structure ... Doctrine will ultimately destroy every code, written or unwritten, substantive and procedural ... With change of environment accumulations of

[17] Bohlen, '*Judge and Jury*' (n 12) 781.

[18] Notice his retrospective comment about the first attempt at a *Restatement of Torts*: 'It so happened ... that most of the restaters came out of the 19th century, taught by 19th century law teachers and taught by 19th century cases. That accounts in part for the fact that the first Torts Restatement is so musty with 19th century terminology and ideas': L Green, 'Fifty Years of Tort Law Teaching' (1966–67) 61 *Northwestern University Law Review* 499, 505.

[19] Green contributed a new article to the collection: L Green, 'Political Freedom of the Press and the Libel Problem' (1977–78) 56 *Texas Law Review* 341.

[20] DW Robertson, 'The Legal Philosophy of Leon Green' (1977–78) 56 *Texas Law Review* 393.

[21] The 'first requisite' for intellectual freedom is a 'wholesome fear of words' (Green, 'The Duty Problem in Negligence Cases' (n 3) 1017).

[22] A very similar project inspired the law reformers of the first half of the 20th century in England, but without the same rhetorical or theoretical investment.

[23] Robertson, 'The Legal Philosophy of Leon Green' (n 20) 405.

> doctrine must sometimes be left as ruins while new doctrine is built on a new foundation site. This is the story of common law for six hundred years.[24]

The imagery is born of genuine and, it would seem, enduring[25] frustration at artificial factors that would prevent law's evolution to new environments. But underlying all this was a faith in the wisdom, intelligence and social power of the law and its power of regeneration, which from some contemporary perspectives could be thought complacent, and even to verge on the naive. Green might well have seen it as reflecting the virtues and the challenges of public service, as well as the capacity of expertise free from the clutter and mystification of restrictive doctrine. Importantly, it also reflects the nature of 'power' that Green attributed to the law. Here there is some complexity in Green's language over time; but I suggest that this was not naked instrumental power nor purely government or administrative power, but a 'social power' derived from law's openness to the very aspects of society from whose needs it springs, consistent with the sense that 'power' is akin to a life force. That is, it seems to me, identifiably consistent with a private law vision,[26] responsive to the disputes from which tort springs, despite the language of public interest and administration that Green brings to bear upon it.[27]

III. BIOGRAPHY, KEY CONTRIBUTIONS AND TIMELINE

I do not set out to produce a new biography of Leon Green, and so deal with biographical details only briefly and derivatively.[28] I shall, however, spend a little time in contemplation of this timeline in terms of Green's intellectual 'environment', as he himself might have put it. Born in 1888 and raised in Louisiana, Green moved to Texas in 1908 after a serious bout of malaria. He was a practising lawyer before he was an educator or academic, and a successful businessman before he was a lawyer at all. Leaving his business interests, he passed the state Bar examination in 1912 after a single year of legal study, resuming law school studies part time from 1912 to 1915 whilst he also worked in practice. His perspective on the law was, initially at least, that of the practical lawyer, and as Robertson put it, as a young practitioner 'his powers of

[24] L Green, 'Tort Law Public Law in Disguise: II' (1959–60) 38 *Texas Law Review* 257, 268. Green offered examples of the 'rubble' that had been cleared away as wreckage in the past: 'the forms of action, common law pleading' and 'negligence law in the industrial employer-employee cases' (ibid).

[25] The article just quoted was published some decades into Green's scholarly career.

[26] It is unlikely, however, to accept a clear demarcation between public and private law.

[27] Evident, for example, in Green, 'The Duty Problem in Negligence Cases' Green (n 3).

[28] I draw here on Robertson's account: Robertson, 'The Legal Philosophy of Leon Green' (n 20). That account was based partly in conversations with Leon Green, and partly in an unpublished note written by Green and included (at least at that time) in the Faculty Writing Collection in the University of Texas Library. Robertson also edited Green's correspondence with Charles McCormick: DW Robertson and R Meyer (eds), *Correspondence between Leon Green and Charles McCormick 1927–1962* (Littleton, CO, Fred B Rothman and Co, 1988).

observation and curiosity were not dimmed or diminished by much in the way of formal education'.[29] The contrast with today's professionalised academic route is plain (though by no means unique to Green). Unlike Holmes, he did not reach law via a literary or philosophical education. Throughout his career, Green's writings continued to smack of first-hand observation, rather than ideological or even scholarly allegiance. His concern with process as more important in the development of the law than abstract principle, and of law as a process of administration, could be attributed to these practical origins, for all that it also fitted the realist movement as a whole.[30] Robertson reports that although both Jerome Frank and Karl Llewellyn identified Green as among the first group of legal realists,[31] for his part '[he] could never see himself as part of a school or movement', writing that he had not to his knowledge made use of the term 'realism', and claiming not to understand what it meant.[32]

After graduation in 1915, Green joined the Faculty at Texas, where he remained until 1918,[33] and which he joined again in 1920, still practising law on the side. He joined the Faculty at Yale on a temporary basis in 1926, then on a permanent basis in 1927.[34] His stay at Yale (the hotbed, of course, of the realist movement) was relatively short: he accepted the Deanship at Northwestern University in 1929, and remained there for 18 years, before returning to Texas as Distinguished Professor in 1947. He did not retire from active teaching and writing for another 30 years, and passed away in 1979.

A. Substantive Contributions

Green was of course no 'system builder'.[35] He did not seek to impose a pattern for the law of tort, which might in any case have been an attempt to constrain

[29] Robertson, 'The Legal Philosophy of Leon Green' (n 20) 397.

[30] Robertson reports that Green recalls being involved in the trial of a damages claim on the day of his first graduation from Law School: ibid 394.

[31] ibid 399; J Frank, *Law and the Modern Mind* (New York, Tudor Publishing Co, 1930); KN Llewellyn, 'Some Realism About Realism – Responding to Dean Pound' (1930–31) 44 *Harvard Law Review* 1222. Underscoring the independence of Green's thought, Llewellyn identified Green as preceding him in his identification of judicial decisions as often being after-the-fact rationalisations of the result, rather than accounts of the reasons that led to the decision (KN Llewellyn, 'Law and the Modern Mind: A Symposium' (1931) 31 *Columbia Law Review* 82, 84 (review); Robertson, 'The Legal Philosophy of Leon Green' (n 20) 399, fn 26).

[32] L Green, 'Innocent Misrepresentation' (1932–33) 19 *Virginia Law Review* 242, 247; Robertson, 'The Legal Philosophy of Leon Green' (n 20) 399. This should in no way obstruct us in recognising Green as a realist: see, eg, the discussion of Hagan's identification of key realist themes, all of them exemplified by Green, in final section IV of this chapter: text to n 78. But he may have been a 'natural' realist, rather than primarily attaching himself to, and learning from, a 'movement'.

[33] Robertson, 'The Legal Philosophy of Leon Green' (n 20) 395, recounts that Green was found unfit for active service on account of a knee injury.

[34] He had meantime accepted the Deanship at North Carolina, but was released from this commitment when the depression hit the state, depleting the resources of the Faculty.

[35] I Englard, 'The System Builders: A Critical Appraisal of Modern American Tort Theory' (1980) 9 *Journal of Legal Studies* 27, discussing a later brand of tort theory he dubbed 'remarkable' in its determination to found a general theory, given the realist heritage of American law.

its constant regeneration. But he also recognised the stability that common law could attain, and reflected on the sources of both stability and change. Green would not have championed a single or small range of 'instrumental' concerns for the law of tort to advance, any more than he would have countenanced its organisation around a key few concepts, and never sought any type of 'covert' operation via the law: all decision-making factors and processes, in his view, should be made plain, so far as this could be achieved.[36] Aside from liberation from the mindset that held tort back from rational and useful development, he had no set blueprint for its future. This would be dependent on its environment, and the intelligence of future decisions. His most constant attempt at substantive influence was in removal of 'proximate cause' from the lexicon of lawyers, in return for a much greater focus on issues of duty (or legal rules) and risk, and simplification of the notion of causation. This was only ever unfinished business, at best. Whilst in the UK, 'proximate cause' is a rather rare category (used extensively in insurance law, with its own implications,[37] but largely displaced by notions of foreseeability or scope of duty in the law of tort), in the United States (US) it continues in common use.

Green did not leave a textbook on torts in the traditional sense that might encourage a revised mapping of the law of torts. Presumably, any idea that he might have developed a legal test to be named after him (like 'the Salmond test' in the English law of vicarious liability) would have been an incongruous insult. He was not an American Law Institute Reporter like Prosser, suffering significant misgivings about the 'restatement' process, and more so about its results. Green did, however, create a number of casebooks, illustrating his seriousness about legal education. It has been said that legal realism was partly responsible for the longevity of the case method: 'While … no legal realist would have wished to use the case method as Langdell and his successors had used it, they saw nevertheless that it provided a superb means of encouraging a broadly sceptical approach to the study of law.'[38] For Green, this was no compromise, and certainly no failure, and the development of casebooks was an essential contribution to the understanding of the law of tort: exposure to the cases in all their detail was an empowering mode of education, making the student a 'critic' and equipping him (or sometimes her[39])

[36] Always, however, he recognised that doctrinal expression was necessary: doctrine was, essentially, 'the language of lawyers', or one of the instruments with which they worked: 'Doctrines, theories, formulas, *etc.*, serve somewhat the same purposes for the judge that microscopes, powerful lights, chemical reagents serve for the medical man': L Green, 'The Torts Restatement' (1934–35) 29 *Illinois Law Review* 582, 588.

[37] See the discussion by R Merkin and J Steele, 'Causation and Proportional Recovery' in K Barker and R Grantham (eds), *Apportionment in Private Law* (Oxford, Hart Publishing, 2018).

[38] Duxbury, *Patterns of American Jurisprudence* (n 6) 142.

[39] The experience of war-time teaching seems to have had an impact. From expressing anxiety in a letter of 30 September 1940, that Faculties might soon be teaching 'girls and cripples', as they had in 1917, by 22 October 1943, Green was reporting to his fellow Dean that of the current first year at Northwestern, '[a]lmost one-third are women, and some very smart ones in both senses'.

to judge afresh.[40] Facts, rather than concepts, were paramount in understanding the law. For Green, it was the problem to which law responded, not the concept it used in doing so, that was of most significance. His casebook on torts, fittingly, was organised according to the context in which problems arose, rather than around legal categories.[41] Equally, it was the *decisions* of courts, not their presentation of the rationale, that needed to be studied to understand the wisdom of the law and the intelligence of the judges – and he was a believer in both. The resulting particularism in his work is not its most appealing feature, but it indicates the way he thought that legal scholarship, and legal education, should operate.

What, then, was the breadth of Green's substantive concerns around the law of tort? He was a prolific contributor.[12] His first contributions, of which he remained enduringly proud, provided a critique of the law's inconsistent

An editorial footnote to MacCormick's letter to Green of 7 October 1940 (in which there is a reference to 'first year men') suggests the extent of change: in 1940, in Texas, the first year comprised 24 women and around 700 men, far short of the third reported by Green in 1943: Robertson and Meyer, *Correspondence between Leon Green and Charles McCormick 1927–1962* (n 28). In relation to the 'girls' attending during the First World War, the biography of Alice Sheffield on the pages of the Texas Law Faculty provides some information. Alice Sheffield was enrolled in 1914 and graduated in 1918: 'In her small class with only thirty-five students, female students, Alice Sheffield, Helen Lord Leary, Bertha Lewis, Mildred Marshall, Annie Maxwell, and Nellie Gray Robertson, constituted 17% of the class.' Doubtless the proportion increased considerably as the war continued. Alice Sheffield, it is recorded, had a highly successful legal career with the Gulf Oil Corporation, and became a major benefactor of the University of Texas: 'Alice Sheffield' *Tarlton Law Library* (Austin) at tarlton.law.utexas.edu/first-year-societies/alice-sheffield. Nellie Gray Robertson was the first female county attorney of Texas, and was nominated to be Chief Justice in the all-female Texas Supreme Court of 1925, but was disbarred for falling short of the required years' service. She was replaced by another woman, and for a few months the all-woman Texas Supreme Court was a reality: LJ Kaspar, 'Meet Nellie Gray Robertson, The First Female County Attorney in Texas' *The Prosecutor* (March–April 2014) at http://www.tdcaa.com/journal/meet-nellie-gray-robertson-first-female-county-attorney-texas. It appears the Court was convened to hear the case of an influential Society that did not accept female members (and in which most male attorneys had a personal interest): MG Ramos, *Texas Almanac* (1998–99) at texasalmanac.com/topics/history/texas-all-woman-supreme-court.

[40] Green, 'Fifty Years of Tort Law Teaching' (n 18) 503: in one of many references to doctrine as akin to theology, Green compares the critical impact on students with 'the undermining of sectarian theology by the Sunday schools'. Duxbury, *Patterns of American Jurisprudence* (n 6) outlines the general explosion of casebooks associated with the realist movement.

[41] CO Gregory, 'Leon Green's Contributions to a Better Understanding of the Law of Torts' (1948–49) 43 *Illinois Law Review* 15. Gregory's observations extend to the reasons why the casebook was not more widely used: 'Looking back to the early thirties, I now wonder why more of us did not hail Mr Green as our prophet and adopt his casebook. Beyond any doubt, most of the younger torts professors of that time were very much aware of him, read everything he wrote, including large parts of his casebook, and were much influenced by him. But I can state the reasons why I did not adopt his casebook. It was much too long and heavy, for one thing, although his second edition, published in 1939, is much more compact; and, because he included materials in almost every conceivable social situation which arose in torts litigation, it was repetitious' (ibid 19). In terms of brevity, an approach organised around simple principles rather than the response to social contexts will always have an advantage.

[42] J Jackson, 'Bibliography of Leon Green' (1977–78) 56 *Texas Law Review* 381. The bibliography appears at the end of Green's own contribution (Green, 'Political Freedom of the Press and the Libel Problem' (n 19)) and is not listed separately in the 'Contents'.

treatment of trespassers, and particularly child trespassers, who were injured by dangers on premises – a particular illustration, for Green, of the way in which nineteenth-century doctrines and defences had lingered in the law to deny protection. Green was influential in gaining alteration to the 'turntable' cases, expanding the remedies for such trespassers in recognition of the very different capacity to manage and bear the risk applying to each party, and was recognised as such.[43] The obfuscation of accumulated doctrine appeared to Green to be preventing a sound treatment of these cases, and was part of his concern that the law was not successfully adapting in ways that would leave the concerns and environment of the nineteenth century behind. That these complex edifices clearly operated to protect one powerful set of interests at the expense of more defenceless claimants will have helped to colour his belief that the substance of the law, and its responsiveness to environment, was more significant than the words and 'reasons' on which so much attention was generally lavished.

Another early but eventually lifelong target was the doctrine of 'proximate cause' in negligence cases, which in Green's estimation was beyond repair and threatening to wreck damages trials. The term 'proximate cause' attracted Green's most visceral criticism, being written off as (amongst other things) a farcical piece of hocus-pocus.[44] In its place, Green assigned to judges the key parts of the legal enquiry required in negligence cases, leaving juries to deal with a single 'factual' enquiry as to causation, as well as the questions of negligence and damage. Green proposed introducing a 'new step' in which the judge should determine the 'limits of protection' afforded by the rule invoked by a litigant. This was, in effect, 'scope of duty' analysis, though Green in its first incarnation used the word 'rule' rather than duty.[45] Analysis using the terminology of duty would follow.[46] This would place in the hands of judges, rather than laymen, resolution of the crucial question in play, namely who should bear which risks. As the key issue in question, this should not be hidden from sight but made

[43] L Green, 'Landowner v. Intruder; Intruder v. Landowner – Basis of Responsibility in Tort' (1922–23) 21 *Michigan Law Review* 495. There was some controversy over the role played by another, more established author: MO Hudson, 'The Turntable Cases in the Federal Courts' (1922–23) 36 *Harvard Law Review* 826, who was also cited by Prosser as influential in the changing law. Green believed that his insights had been taken up and used: Robertson, 'The Legal Philosophy of Leon Green' (n 20) 398, fn 22.

[44] L Green, *Rationale of Proximate Cause* (Kansas City, KS, Vernon Law Book Co, 1927) 199 (hocus-pocus), 200 (farcical).

[45] He noted, however, earlier work by Nicholas St John Green, which had similarly analysed the cases in terms of 'duty', and thought this an appropriate alternative terminology: N Green, 'Proximate and Remote Cause' (1869–70) 4 *American Law Review* 201. As Robertson explains (Robertson, 'The Legal Philosophy of Leon Green' (n 20) 404, fn 55), this article was originally published unsigned, and reprinted in N Green, *Essays on the Law of Tort and Crime* (Menasha, WI, George Banta Publishing Co, 1933).

[46] Green, *Rationale of Proximate Cause* (n 44); cp L Green, 'Duties, Risks, Causation Doctrines' (1962–63) 41 *Texas Law Review* 42, on the same themes, updated (now, the focus is on competition between causation and duty language to analyse the extent of tort liability).

apparent for all involved. Democracy, Green was confident, was mature enough to accept this role for the judge; there was no longer a need to pronounce judgment from behind a veil, allowing 'word magic' to prevail.

In determining whether the damage fell within the protection of the legal rule (duty), all of the factors involved would be consciously weighed, rather than any one factor acting as a 'trump' in which law had often become a game of chance.[47] Part of the objective was clarity: it would be much clearer at which stage an unsuccessful claim had failed; was the hazard outside the protection of the rule, for example, or was there an absence of right on the part of the claimant, or a lack of evidence of wrongdoing? It is in this sense true that Green proposed a *process* – a series of questions allocated to judge or jury – rather than substantive rules for the resolution of negligence cases. The purpose of his focus on the rule or duty was to ensure that the process was appropriate, clear and rational. Notably, his assault on words was not nihilistic. Rather, the rational process for resolving the real issues lay in other routes. And while Green identified vested interests as being served by the verbal formulae deployed by the courts, he plainly thought that rational answers fitting underlying social needs could be sensed by the courts, provided they could slough off the distraction of verbal formulae. He was, in many respects, a deep believer in the common law.

Green's thoughts on both duty and proximate cause seem to have been at least consulted in the *Restatement* process,[48] but Green was enormously dismissive of the result, both in terms of what it sought to do and in terms of the substance of the attempt.[49] This partly reveals the divergence in general theories of law between those of Green and those of those most closely involved in drafting the first *Restatement*. Green's relationship to 'realism' was never clearer than in his comment on the *Restatement of Torts*. His scathing assessment of the *reduction* of 'law' to 'black letter'[50] content reaches a peak in his complaint that in offering authoritative answers to hypothetical questions, the law professor, whether in the classroom or in the *Restatement*, claims for himself the role of judge, jury and appellate court rolled into one. The law should be free to develop in

[47] Green did not share any discomfort with the weighing of incommensurables: it was better that this be done openly. The notion of a 'game of chance' in which one factor is the trump is well illustrated by the traditional rule of contributory negligence (as opposed to its proportional variant).

[48] RE Keeton, 'A *Palsgraf* Anecdote' (1977–78) 56 *Texas Law Review* 513, indicates that the judgments of both Cardozo and Andrews in *Palsgraf* might have been influenced by Green. Green's views were closer to those of Cardozo, since Andrews paid too much attention to notions of cause; but he was also critical of Cardozo in some respects. In discussion, he declined to state prescriptive solutions to the questions posed, preferring to point to the ways in which the issues should be structured by the court, and thought both judges had ducked the real issues: see White, *Tort Law in America: An Intellectual History* (n 9), ch 3, 'The Impact of Realism on Tort Law: 1910–1945'.

[49] Green 'The Torts Restatement' (n 36).

[50] The expression is used by Green to refer to the bold sections of the *Restatement* that sought to crystallise the law of tort.

response to the issues raised by new cases. This is partly because torts cases had so far defied prediction, so that the attempt at prescription of outcomes was a vain one. But it was not only that. Quite simply, such propositions were not 'law'; for law was the result of the process mandated by 'our form of government' for producing judgment. Part of the problem was that such propositions and formulae, designed to guarantee a particular result, second-guessed the decisions of laymen in the jury – they belittled that part of the process. But more profoundly, they were merely propositions. Law was not to be found in this content but in the judgment of those assigned the task of judging – both judge and jury: 'No formulation of propositions designed to give automatic answers to cases as they come to court is of very much value, nor are such propositions "law" in the general usage of the term'.[51]

I have said that Green also had more substantive concerns about the first *Restatement*. We can learn much about Green's general approach to the law of tort from these concerns. Among them, Green objected to the structure that had been adopted for the *Restatement*; he also had particular criticism for the sections dealing with negligence and the 'ridiculous' section on causation, which were close to the heart of his main contributions to tort law.

As to the first, Green objected that the *Restatement* had accepted and adopted Professor Bohlen's classification of the law of torts. This he found cumbersome, contradictory, incomplete and generally unhelpful. He had objections to the way in which protected interests were listed, which, he argued, was not a list of protected interests at all but incorporated the means by which those interests might be invaded, contributing to the messy and hybrid nature of the project. More fundamentally, though, Green's view was that there could not be a successful restatement of tort law, 'except as it may be based on specific groups of cases closely related factually'.[52] This could include road traffic and transportation, for example; or problems of land occupiers in relation to hazards of fire, water and animals; or physician cases, and so on. In Green's view, '[t]he restatement of the law as to them is not by any means so difficult of generalization as are the attempts to generalize rules, which apply to many divergent groups of cases'.[53] His point was that such cases would raise all the applicable doctrines, which were apt to cross categories, and might resolve them in distinctive ways related to their 'environmental facts'. That battle, to organise our presentation of tort around groups of cases in specific contexts, has generally been lost, at least where textbooks and restatements are concerned. A case could still be made, however, that Green's approach is the reality of most scholarly treatment, as well as legal advice and decision-making, in relation to professional negligence, road traffic cases, medical cases, employer–employee cases and so on.

[51] Green, 'The Torts Restatement' (n 36) 598.
[52] ibid 588.
[53] ibid.

The summit of Green's disapproval of the first *Restatement* lay, however, with its treatment of negligence and of causation. The section on the 'General Negligence Formula' was castigated for failing to mention the duty problem, and for 'loading' all the associated problems onto a new 'illusory' concept,[54] namely 'legal cause'. 'Legal cause' was further elaborated in the section on 'Causation', which Green described as the most remarkable section of the *Restatement*. Here, the *Restatement* directed attention to whether the manner in which the invasion has occurred 'is such that the law regards it as just to hold the actor responsible for such harm'. As Green saw it, this dragged in all the difficulties of the duty problem, which he had worked so hard to reorient away from 'proximate cause'. In an analysis that maps well with the recent history of 'duty of care' in English law at least, Green underlines the great importance of the 'judge's function in the determination of duty'.[55] If we concede that the claimant had suffered damage, caused by the defendant's conduct, and the defendant was found to be negligent, should liability be imposed? The judge could make his judgment final on this point (ie, make the judgment one of law):

> He may say there is no duty, or that the duty was not owed to the plaintiff, or to the particular interest of the plaintiff which has been hurt, or finally was not designed to afford protection against such hazard as actually befell the plaintiff.[56]

Thus for Green the duty problem delineated the reach of negligence liability – and it had been entirely omitted from the general statement of what negligence was. For Green, a range of factors would determine what judgment was reached as to duty. At the time of the *Restatement*, he named these 'administrative policy, moral policy, economic policy, preventive policy, and the all-comprehensive "justice" policy'.[57] The mention of 'policy' is a red flag to many contemporary tort scholars. In other versions of Green's account of the duty problem, the listed areas of 'policy' are referred to instead as 'factors',[58] and the word 'policy' did not have the heavy significance attributed to it in contemporary legal scholarship, where it is contrasted with issues of 'principle'.[59] Notably, the factors listed include morality and ethics, prevention (an actual impact on behaviour and protection) and justice, though these would have to compete against more pragmatic questions of administration and economics. These had nothing to do with 'causal relation', and the *Restatement* therefore confused cause with duty.

This was the major opportunity, which Green thought, in terms that still ring clear, had been lost: the opportunity to state the considerations that go to

[54] ibid 602.
[55] ibid 606.
[56] ibid 605.
[57] ibid 606.
[58] Green, 'The Duty Problem in Negligence Cases' (n 3).
[59] Influential here is the work of Ronald Dworkin: see, especially, R Dworkin, *A Matter of Principle* (Cambridge, MA, Harvard University Press, 1985).

the determination of duties and their limitations in *particular* cases. In fact that opportunity had been 'worse than lost', as all the difficulties had been dumped onto 'legal cause'. Memorably, Green complained of the drafters of the *Restatement* that '[i]f they had been inspired by all the imps that can bring confusion into the administration of law, they could not have succeeded in their attempt in that respect more overwhelmingly'.[60] Prescient in one sense was the prediction that if courts were to be gullible enough to absorb the 'synthetic pretender', legal cause, into the law, 'it will take a century to get rid of it'.[61] The century is approaching, and legal cause is still with us.

Certain elements of Green's body of work could be seen as extensions of his work on proximate cause, for example his engagement with the emergence of comparative negligence reforms,[62] rolling back one of the extreme defences, in Green's view, created by and for the nineteenth century. Later, he objected to the apparent simplicity of reliance on foreseeability as attempted by English and Commonwealth law through the *Wagon Mound*,[63] despite its apparent fit with his general preference for emphasis on duty over proximate cause and with the 'risk principle'. The idea of a single notion that could be used at all stages of the negligence enquiry contradicted Green's belief in the multiple factors that necessarily inform sound decision-making.[64] Over a long period of time, Green championed the significance of protection for 'relational' interests in the law, such as the relationship between employer and employee, or between family members, although it is recounted that he later dropped these from his torts casebook in favour of their inclusion as part of other topics.[65] He interpreted defamation and communication in terms of 'relational' interests.[66] His work on the legal issues involved in the 'sit down strike' extended his exploration of relational interests as recognised aspects of the law.[67] In one of his later books, he proposed an insurance solution for the exceptional area of road traffic, to be

[60] Green, 'The Torts Restatement' (n 36) 607.

[61] Green included a conciliatory footnote at the end of the article, which acknowledged the work of the American Law Institute and opined that a restatement could be useful but that we did not yet know how to do it: ibid 607, fn 33. Perhaps he had been asked to tone down the criticism, but the footnote does very little to dampen the overall nature of the article to which it is attached.

[62] In fact, the relationship may be the other way around, as proximate cause emerged from the contributory negligence case: proximate cause, in Green's view, was 'the most extravagant development of that ruthless defense' (L Green, 'The Duty Problem in Negligence Cases: II' (1929) 29 *Columbia Law Review* 255, 266).

[63] *Overseas Tankship (UK) Ltd v Morts Dock and Engineering Co (The Wagon Mound)* [1961] AC 388 (PC).

[64] L Green, 'Foreseeability in Negligence Law' (1961) 61 *Columbia Law Review* 1401.

[65] L Green, 'Basic Concepts: Persons, Property, Relations' (1938) 24 *American Bar Association Journal* 65; Gregory, 'Leon Green's Contributions to a Better Understanding of the Law of Torts' (n 41) 21.

[66] L Green, 'The Right to Communicate' (1960) 35 *New York University Law Review* 903.

[67] TW Arnold, 'Leon Green: An Appreciation' (1948–49) 43 *Illinois Law Review* 1; L Green, 'Case for the Sit-Down Strike' (24 March 1937) 90 *The New Republic* 199.

administered by the courts and to replace the law of negligence,[68] a few years ahead of the well-known (and more practically detailed) no-fault proposals of Keeton and O'Connell.[69] He wrote about the communication torts, including misstatement, libel and privacy, but in this area as in others, he did not have the coordinated impact of William Prosser. He recognised, but did not elaborate on, the insight – a 'completed revolution' – in the Supreme Court's extension of constitutional protection with respect to personal, political and economic rights.[70] While the status of such rights might have had the capacity to create tensions with his overall realism, the point is that Green's account of the social power of law is exemplified by this unexpected revolution – accomplished, as he puts it, by 'gaining power and support with each decision'.[71] These rights, furthermore, he describes as relational – as concerning 'the citizen's relations to our democratic society'.[72]

B. Timeline

Green's career began at the time that legal realism was in the ascendant, and when the restrictive doctrines of the nineteenth century still exerted an influence upon the law of tort. Theorising law's regenerative power was important. His retirement came at the end of another important era in private law. The start of the 1980s is generally identified as the key time at which 'new contractualism' and new styles of regulation were born. The year of Green's death marked the election of Margaret Thatcher's Conservative Party to government in the UK, followed closely by Ronald Reagan's 1980 victory in the US presidential elections, marking the beginning of a trans-Atlantic growth in new uses for freedom of contract. In the era that followed, the law of tort perhaps adjusted with greater restrictiveness, and less willingness to spread risks away from the individual – or at least has begun to find some 'stopping places'.[73] Part of this occurred through pressure from without, via powerful 'tort reform' movements in both the US and Australia. For defenders of tort law, these movements may appear to offer extra reasons for adherence to doctrine and principle, as democracy appears to have moved beyond an acceptance, as Green confidently perceived, in the wisdom and intelligence of judging.

[68] L Green, *Traffic Victims: Tort Law and Insurance* (Evanston, IL, Northwestern University Press, 1958).
[69] RE Keeton and J O'Connell, *Basic Protection for the Traffic Victim: A Blueprint for Reforming Automobile Insurance* (Boston, MA, Little, Brown & Co, 1965).
[70] Green, 'Fifty Years of Tort Law Teaching' (n 18) 503.
[71] ibid.
[72] ibid.
[73] The subtitle of Green's essay collection, *The Litigation Process in Tort Law*, is '*No Place to Stop in the Development of Tort Law*'. See Green, *The Litigation Process in Tort Law* (n 7).

Perhaps, however, Green would simply observe that the environment was no longer that in which expanding tort liability could flourish. Priority to the individual now had a different meaning: not individual protection, but individual responsibility for self-protection. Undoubtedly, to pursue this in realist fashion would involve charting not just new reactions to the pragmatic aspects of the law, but also potentially a new moral and ethical stance. The grand sweep of tort law, according to Green, had already moved from an ethic of trespass and strict liability in feudal societies, to an ethic of negligence and collectivist interest in the nineteenth century. In the twentieth century, negligence had finally developed to protect the individual, given a new recognition that this could be achieved without undue damage to collective interests. I myself have used different terminology, referring to the shift into the twentieth century as revolving around a 'security' revolution and collective means of providing security to individuals, in which tort law was one aspect.[74] I have suggested that in our new century, a concern with the costs of this security – including the costs of insurance, and who is to bear it – is underpinned by new dimensions of responsibility. We do not know how Green would have responded to these new challenges to the law of tort, but it seems unlikely he would have sought the answer in countervailing substantive legal concepts and principles, as some contemporary tort scholarship does. It strikes me that Green's ideas about the factors that allowed tort's regeneration are just as pertinent to understanding the restriction of tort law and its current application in a more particular and environmentally cautious fashion.

On the other hand, Green's confidence about the political acceptability of legal judgment without the obfuscation of doctrinal veils may be objected to as a product of its own environment, from very different perspectives. There are those who wish to define legal decision-making as somehow surpassing its environment – as promising the protection of the individual against collective decision-makers, or of private law's legitimacy against politics. On the other hand, there are those who absorb the contingency and indeterminacy of doctrine revealed by Green and others, and who seek to show the possibility of alternative accounts built around other discourses, such as feminism.[75] Striking, to me, is that current exercises in judgment rewriting, initiated by the feminist judgments project,[76] build themselves upon a deep engagement with the facts of

[74] J Steele, 'Risk Revolutions in Private Law' in S Worthington, A Robertson and G Virgo (eds), *Revolution and Evolution in Private Law* (Oxford, Hart Publishing, 2018).

[75] E Rackley, C McGlynn and R Hunter (eds), *Feminist Judgments: From Theory to Practice* (Oxford, Hart Publishing, 2010).

[76] ibid; similar exercises have been completed or initiated in a range of jurisdictions including Canada, Ireland, Australia, New Zealand, USA, India and Africa. For published collections, see H Douglas, F Bartlett, T Luker and R Hunter (eds), *Australian Feminist Judgments: Righting and Rewriting Law* (Oxford, Hart Publishing, 2014); KM Stanchi, LL Berger and BJ Crawford (eds), *Feminist Judgments: Rewritten Opinions of the United States Supreme Court* (Cambridge, CUP, 2016); M Enright, J McCandless and A O'Donoghue (eds), *Northern/Irish Feminist Judgments: Judges'*

a case and an appreciation that how these are presented is fundamental to the reaching of decisions, a move long advocated by Green (though, as we have seen, he showed no particular signs of feminism). Diversity may be one aspect of the current era's 'rebuilding of conscience', never anticipated by Green.

What Green propounded was not critical of law, as opposed to the narrow reading of doctrine in general, and in particular instances. His vision of law was bound up with principles of good administration in the broadest sense of the term, and judging had a special place marked by the quality of its participants, its reliable 'good sense' and its closeness to the environment in issue. This view was undoubtedly of its time, and is certainly that of a legal insider. It does not pay much attention to the factors that motivate and restrain particular actors, whether these are judges, insurers, legislators or litigators. But it also does not make the judge a manipulator of instrumental factors so much as a faithful servant of the public, in the contexts that law facilitates. Its trustfulness is apparent, as it tends to assume that constraints are barriers to the proper responsiveness of courts to their environment. As a true realist, Green's perception was that law was a practical and useful discipline, which he saw as safest in the hands of those engaged in its practice, and without the distraction of conceptualism.[77]

IV. APPRAISAL

Here I try to consider aspects of Green's tort scholarship more deeply by measuring his contribution against some critical dismissals from contemporary tort theorists.

Overall, I think it is fair to say that in recent years, Leon Green's scholarship has had a critical press among tort scholars – though at the same time it is attributed with significant influence. An important criticism, given the focus of his substantive contribution, is that Green was, in common with other influential US thinkers (and some English ones), a duty-sceptic, a position that has influenced successive *Restatements on Torts*.[78] This position is regarded as having been inherited from Oliver Wendell Holmes. I am not convinced that

Troubles and the Gendered Politics of Identity (Oxford, Hart Publishing, 2017); E McDonald, RL Powell, M Stephens and RC Hunter (eds), *Feminist Judgments of Aotearoa New Zealand – Te Rino: A Two-Stranded Rope* (Oxford, Hart Publishing, 2017).

[77] Notice Green's presentation of his *Traffic Victims: Tort Law and Insurance* as 'an experiment based on the most reliable social invention of modern times – insurance – and under the control of the most reliable and respected institutions of government – the courts' (Green, *Traffic Victims: Tort Law and Insurance* (n 68) 103). More recent work has explored the role of insurance and insurers more critically, while building on the perception that its influence is enormous. As just one (outstanding) example, see KS Abraham, *The Liability Century: Insurance and Tort Law from the Progressive Era To 9/11* (Cambridge, MA, Harvard University Press, 2008). We can place Green's writings within the 'progressive era' of Abraham's title.

[78] JCP Goldberg and BC Zipursky, 'The *Restatement (Third)* and the Place of Duty in Negligence Law' (2001) 54 *Vanderbilt Law Review* 657.

it is pertinent to describe Green as a duty-sceptic. Indeed, despite Green's relentless attack on the use of legal language and concepts, he accepted that these were inevitable and useful, so long as their role was properly understood. Doctrines were the laboratory equipment of the lawyer, not the outcome of their enquiries: they focused the attention, acted as shorthand and provided a structure to decision-making. They were means, not outputs. What, then, were Green's thoughts about 'duty' in the law of torts?

In *Rationale of Proximate Cause*, as we have seen,[79] Green advocated that the issues dealt with under the heading of 'proximate cause' were more appropriately thought of in terms of the legal rule that was being applied to the defendant's conduct. This was then a matter for judge, rather than jury. In a footnote, he accepted that for 'legal rule', we could instead substitute the notion of 'duty'. He also castigated the drafters of the *Restatement of Torts* for neglecting the notion of duty. Into duty, and not into the notion of legal cause, should be inserted all the factors that would determine the proper limits of liability. To some, this will be duty-scepticism in a disguised form (and certainly in a different form from the one that caused duty to disappear from the *Restatement*): it would appear to propose duty merely as an amalgamation of policy factors, designed to limit liability rather than to establish it. This approach is not, however, explained by a view that there was no legal rule. Rather, it is based on a view that the rules were neither particularly determinate, nor infinite in their scope. The *scope* of the applicable rule, or of the duty, was what the judge needed to determine in Green's additional step. There is more to say on the apparent treatment of duties as merely limiting devices, and it is returned to below.

Goldberg and Zipursky suggest that Green's view of duty, like that of Prosser, was that it collapsed into breach, citing a (relatively impenetrable) section of his essay on 'The Duty Problem in Negligence Cases'.[80] Here, while accepting the difficulty, I do not think that Green argued that duty collapsed into breach: this would undo all his work in treating duty questions as questions of law for the judge, and as distinct from the question of negligence, which was for the jury. Indeed, ambiguity between duty and breach was his primary complaint about Cardozo's judgment in *Palsgraf*.[81] On the contrary, in the passage referred to, he was particularly criticising the 'danger' or 'foreseeability' theory of duty of care in negligence, derived from *Heaven v Pender*.[82] Here, as in other work, he doubted the feasibility of having the same test for duty of care as for breach. His point was that in adopting this test, many courts had behaved *as though*

[79] See n 44 and accompanying text.

[80] Goldberg and Zipursky, 'The *Restatement (Third)* and the Place of Duty in Negligence Law' (n 78) 715–16, referring to Green, 'The Duty Problem in Negligence Cases' (n 3) 1028–30.

[81] Green, 'Duties, Risks, Causation Doctrines' (n 46) 62: 'Even today it is not unusual for a court to confuse the function of the court to determine the scope of the duty with its function to determine the sufficiency of the evidence to raise the issue of negligence, as is so graphically illustrated in Cardozo's opinion in the *Palsgraf* case.'

[82] *Heaven v Pender* (1883) 11 QBD 503 (CA).

they were passing the test for duty to the jury, under cover of the fact that it had the same nature as the test for breach. In reality, Green argued, they were not doing any such thing, but by implication admitting that the duty existed and that there was a question of breach to be tried. The collapse of duty into breach was, in fact, precisely what Green was arguing against. As a determinant of duty, danger or foreseeability was at fault for its ambiguity, as resembling a jury question, but it was in any case too simple. Citing Cardozo, and at the same time questioning its compatibility with Cardozo's embrace of 'danger' in *Palsgraf*, Green noted that negligence is 'the law of the dangerous machine':[83] logically, danger could not be the determinant of duty in relation to the dangerous machine. By making danger the hallmark of duty, surely all our activities would swiftly be curtailed. Pragmatically, and realistically, there must be limits to the notion of duty in negligence, suitable to its environment. These could not be supplied by the element of foreseeability or anticipated danger, for negligence otherwise would cease to be appropriate to the environment that had created it.

Much more plausible is the alternative criticism that Green simply saw duty in terms of a matrix of policy factors for the determination of the court: that he saw its usefulness in terms of process (placing the decision with the judge, not the jury), but not in terms of substance. Green did indeed believe that multiple factors were used, and should be used, by the courts in determining the question of duty of care. In his two essays on 'The Duty Problem in Negligence Cases',[84] he grouped these as the administrative factor; the ethical or moral factor; the economic factor; the prophylactic factor; and the justice factor. He spent most space on the first of these, the administrative factor, arguing that the courts would never move forward in the recognition of duties in new circumstances unless they were content that the law could deal with this in terms of its own administration. He may not have been right that this is always the first concern of the courts, but it seems plain to me that it is such a consideration. Having spent considerable time on the administrative factor, the other factors, more than a little hastily, he bundled together. He argued that no case that created serious tension at any of these stages would have any longevity. Does this mean that Green believed in the notion that duties exist only in the form of an ex post policy decision by the courts?

Not necessarily. The factors set out were used in determining the limits of legal rules and duties. It may well be that in doing this, they presuppose the recognition, as a matter of law, of those rules and duties. The factors are notions about the institutional limits to duty recognised by the law, but most particularly the law of negligence. Green saw negligence as creating particular

[83] Green, 'The Duty Problem in Negligence Cases' (n 3) 1033.

[84] Green, 'The Duty Problem in Negligence Cases' (n 3); Green, 'The Duty Problem in Negligence Cases: II' (n 62).

problems unknown elsewhere in the law of torts. These problems were related to the potential breadth of liability for inadvertent harms in a society where such harms are endemic. As it happens, Green made plain, many years after his essays on 'The Duty Problem in Negligence Cases', that he considered duties to be a common feature of all tort law. At the base of every tort case, he argued, must be a duty: liability 'must rest upon some rule or principle of law'.[85] The court must rule on the duty question, because 'it is the court's function to say whether there is any law to cover the risk of injury'.[86] Green's initial analysis of the duty 'problem' primarily in terms of placing the limits of liability owed its origins to the way in which duty questions had emerged in the common law. These, he argued, were initially used as limiting doctrines. Occupiers of land, for example, owed 'no duty' to injured trespassers. By contrast, '[d]uty as a creative concept for extending the protection of the law to the rapidly increasing toll of deaths and personal injuries resulting from the risks imposed by machine and other enterprise activities of the 1800's was slow in emerging'.[87] Gradually, the law had come to use duty as a *positive* notion in a series of different contexts, ultimately covering most of the risks of enterprise.

It seems fair to say that Green thought that duties were the foundation of tort law, and that their existence was a question of law. In negligence cases in particular, defining the limits of these duties was a challenging exercise requiring the judgment of the court. But to act as a limiting device was not the sole function of the duty. This is plainly illustrated by Green's criticism of the *Restatement*'s assertions that no duty could be involved in liability for ultra-hazardous activities, nor in intentional torts: 'At the base of *every* tort case in which liability is imposed on a defendant, there *must* be a duty.'[88] Green proposed that the duty not to cause intentional harm could be interpreted as a duty to respect the personality of others: everyone 'owes a duty to respect the personality of his fellow man'.[89] The factors that were spelt out by Green as relevant to defining the presence of a duty of care in negligence were associated with the exercise of reason in relation to protection from the 'everyday hurts' of society. Those factors would vary with time and context – there is no alternative but to apply judgment, and they are not unitary. But I do not think that Green was a sceptic about the existence of obligations between people, nor about law's role in defining these, nor about the social significance of offering protection against harm. Among the broad set of factors listed by Green, only the 'economic' factor appears to point outside the law itself or the relationship of the parties,[90] and it may be thought a necessary prescription for the survival of a body of law that

[85] Green, 'Duties, Risks, Causation Doctrines' (n 46) 45.
[86] ibid 59.
[87] ibid.
[88] ibid 45.
[89] ibid 47–48.
[90] There may be much argument about the 'administrative' factor. This appears to be a factor concerned with what law itself can manage at any particular time.

it should not cause significant economic disruption. Tort duties should not be destabilising, but they should also be moral, just and convenient, and this was essential for the stability of the law.

Green was well aware that this contradicted Holmes's approach. Green argued that it was the notion of duty that Holmes was really seeking when he looked for a way to express the limits of liability for inadvertent harm. In his view, Holmes was hampered by the nature of liability for negligence in the nineteenth century – the notion of duty had not yet coalesced. Perhaps this simply reflects the fact that Green was no philosopher and did not fully appreciate Holmes's stance against duty. One cannot ignore, however, that much of Green's contribution to tort was devoted to advancing duty analysis as the missing factor in the *Restatement*, and in any approach to the limits of protection based on legal or proximate cause – the duty 'problem' was specifically encountered in relation to negligence; but duties were found throughout the law of tort.

Green's supposed duty-scepticism is merely regarded as symptomatic by his contemporary doubters. How does his work measure up against other charges levelled at it? John Goldberg has lamented that Green, like William Prosser, loved tort law only for the power it holds.[91] He portrays Green as a cynical instrumentalist, interested in a form of naked power that tort law conferred. I suggest that Green's admiration for the law of tort was not dependent on its ability to pursue ends of his own devising, though like all of us he thought the law 'wise' when its answers corresponded with his own. Rather, he thought tort law had emerged as a socially useful means of protecting interests of individuals against the hurts created by everyday society. Where inadvertent harm was concerned, it could not protect against all such hurts, because this would be inconsistent with today's environment. There lay the essential element of judgment: in determining which such hurts fell to be protected. It is true that Green talked in terms of the 'power to judge', a power that was conferred on courts, but he was adamant that this should not be anticipated by professors or others engaged in determining which outcomes should be *predetermined* in what circumstances. It is true that he also spoke of tort in terms of 'government power' to determine particular disputes. That did not mean that the power was to be exercised without reason, and without reference to legal rules and duties (as we have already seen). Law was functional, and in the legal process power was conferred, and exercised. But the function of law was not to be powerful, nor to serve some hidden external goal or goals. Rather, the role of law was to serve the needs of the community. The 'power' of private law is to a large extent social power.

[91] JCP Goldberg, 'Unloved: Tort in the Modern Legal Academy' (2002) 55 *Vanderbilt Law Review* 1501, 1510: 'Prosser, Green, and their intellectual heirs never loved tort law for what it is. They loved it only for the power it creates: not only power in judges and juries, but also power in the armchair policymakers (law professors) who would advise them.' The latter is of course the mirror image of Green's complaints about the authors of the *Restatement*, who took upon themselves (in his view) the role of judge and jury in an attempt to determine outcomes for future cases.

In a rather uncharacteristically abstract essay, 'My Philosophy of Law',[92] Green stated that three elements were involved in the composition of law: (i) wisdom; (ii) power; and (iii) process. For Green, there need be no choice between these in terms of which was the dominant element. Power was discussed by Green in terms of both governmental power (the conferred power to decide) and social power. Social power, Green argued, 'has its sources in the activities in which human beings engage – in thought, in labor, in trade, in industry, in play, in music, in prayer, in war, in charity, in all the multitudinous activities to which people devote their energies'.[93] Social power is harnessed by government to protect the more urgent interests of human beings – both by law and by other processes.[94] In its social power, law was part of life at large. The institutions of government, for Green, 'are responses to the needs of the day as required by the interests of people active in society'. What lawyers did was primarily to devise means of supporting social activities:

> [L]awyers take a little paper and a little ink into which they breathe the spirit of the law. These creations ... result in finished products designed to enable people to carry on their activities with a speed and safety which most of us are not prepared to appreciate. These are the creations which control and protect people in a free society.[95]

It could be argued that for Green, law's power is built upon social power; and the admiration that Green held for the law was not for its ability to confer power per se, but for its ability, as he perceived, to achieve protection for a free and active society.

It has also been suggested that Green saw it as vital that tort law have minimal content.[96] This I think is true in important respects. Green thought the *process* of decision-making and the power to judge were essential elements of study, and that these had been underestimated. As we have seen, he also considered that there was no replacement for the jurisdiction of the court to decide. A range of potential answers would be socially acceptable: there was no basis on which to say that a particular outcome was certain. Indeed, doctrine for Green, in an anti-Dworkinian twist, 'has little integrity' and generates instability – the stability of law must be sought elsewhere:

> The dangers of doctrine are difficult to escape. It has little integrity. It lends itself to usage far beyond the boundaries of its origin. It can be stretched or contracted to meet the needs of the moment and is always colored by the desires of the

[92] L Green, 'My Philosophy of Law', in a collection bringing together a number of theorists: Julius Rosenthal Foundation for General Law, Northwestern University, *My Philosophy of Law – Credos of Sixteen American Scholars* (Boston, MA, Boston Law Book Co, 1941).

[93] Green, 'My Philosophy of Law' (n 92) 135.

[94] These other processes are effective where social needs are 'too subtle' for formal government, and include thousands of social conventions.

[95] Green, 'My Philosophy of Law' (n 92) 139–40.

[96] Goldberg, 'Unloved: Tort in the Modern Legal Academy' (n 91).

> user … It feeds on itself; hardens into clichés and blocks the arteries of thought … The more passionately embraced the deadlier its kiss.[97]

Even so, this did not amount to a thesis that tort was or should be empty of content. Green accepted that a decision reached by a judge as a matter of law would retain significance for future courts, while a jury's determination was good for one time only. Notions of duty in particular classes of case were to be found in and derived from law. And legal doctrine, while unreliable and indeterminate in itself, was a handy shorthand means of summarising decisions and guiding future courts. Green thought the majority of the law of torts to be reduced to quite specific legal rules and duties, protecting clear interests: it was the amorphous law of negligence that posed most problems. Certainly, Green thought that many of the defences that had been introduced to limit liability for negligence, and other doctrinal creations such as proximate cause, should be removed in order to permit the law's development. Thus, he believed in minimal obstacles in the realisation of the law, so far as society is ready for its growth. But this is not to say that doctrine as a whole – the content of the law in this sense – could or should be swept away. There were forces for stability, as well as for change, in the law, but these could as well be found in consistency of pragmatic judgment as in doctrine. With more open attribution of reasons to different stages in the decision-making process, these forces would become clearer.

This answer partly also provides our response to the next accusation, that Green treats tort suits essentially as an occasion for regulation or legislation. The power to judge is not, on Green's account, the basis for a power grab; and generally speaking, it does not treat the dispute itself as merely the occasion for something else. True it is that in 'Tort Law Public Law in Disguise', Green set out the belief that 'we the people' are a party to every law suit, and that the interests of the community are the most important interest in play.[98] In some senses, I think this is an unfortunate gloss on his earlier explanation in terms of administration, morality, economics, prevention and justice.[99] Was Green suggesting that tort suits should be used to advance extrinsic goals, or did he simply mean that there is a public interest in the promotion of these factors – just as there is a public interest in the protection of privacy, for example, or reputation? In a tamer moment, Green expressed the interests served by tort law and its functions quite conventionally: 'The functions of tort law are to compensate, indemnify, prevent, mitigate or penalize harms to which persons are subjected by the activities of other persons.'[100] If there is a public interest in achieving these goals to an extent that is compatible with society's activities and purposes, this is not surprising.

[97] Green, 'Tort Law Public Law in Disguise: II' (n 24) 266.
[98] Green, 'Tort Law Public Law in Disguise' (n 1) 1.
[99] Green, 'The Duty Problem in Negligence Cases' (n 3).
[100] L Green, 'The Study and Teaching of Tort Law' (1955–56) 34 *Texas Law Review* 1, 4.

Overall, in Green's vision, tort law responds to the dangers of human activity, and this is why it expands, though it does so only where all the factors mentioned are broadly in alignment. The solution of disputes must respond to the facts of the case with reference to the law, to good sense and to the needs of 'we the people'. Judges must engage in 'delicate and ... profound probing',[101] to determine the soundest answer. The exercise is shamelessly multi-factorial, and courts are still the right people to be engaging in this process: they have the power to judge. To say that this is a branch of government is to draw attention to the fact that law fulfils social purposes – including a process for compensation and determination of protection – and to the fact that it is a specific, and rightly prized, instance of government.

A. Modern Resonance

As has already been suggested, Green did not predict the major challenge to tort law represented by the insurance crisis and 'tort law reform', nor the diversity movement that would seek to alter the make-up of the branch of government, as he would put it, engaged with judging. His optimism about tort, the courts, insurance and free judgment belongs to an extended progressive era. Insurance crisis, tort reform and diversity are elements of the more recent scene that he did not anticipate. The last of these, however, builds upon the notion that we have gone wrong by focusing upon the machinery (doctrine) and not the engineers (the judges)[102] – though Green's variation of this expressly refers to 'trust': that the sense of the judge matters more than the existing doctrinal content of the law. It is a more critical, less complacent but still optimistic reading of the same phenomenon.

Staying closer to the operation of negligence law, it is not only American tort law that shows signs of concept-scepticism and adherence to a more pragmatic approach, even as available (and now imprecise) verbal formulae continue to multiply. The English approach to negligence law from *Caparo*[103] onwards could even be said to be predicated on the hopelessness of clear and binding doctrine, even as it multiplies new verbal formulae and new uses of existing ones. It distances itself from these as 'tests' and describes them as guides to reasoning, which are used even in defiance of any definition. This is of course open to criticism but, as Green once put it, once underlying concerns are 'reduced to pattern',[104] decision-making does indeed become more predictable, within certain specific areas, and in these circumstances, 'doctrine' is rendered

[101] Green, 'Tort Law Public Law in Disguise: II' (n 24) 269.
[102] Green, 'The Duty Problem in Negligence Cases' (n 3) 1019.
[103] *Caparo Industries Plc v Dickman* [1990] 2 AC 605 (HL).
[104] Green, 'Tort Law Public Law in Disguise' (n 1) 2.

less dangerous: it is the understanding of what lies beneath the words, rather than the words themselves, that provides the law's stability.

At the same time, there are strands of contemporary legal scholarship that are impatient of this sort of pragmatism and particularism, and which reject all elements of Green's approach and his presumed legacy. These tend to be presented as relating to a more traditional approach to legal scholarship. But that may be misleading. Utilising Green's perception of the significance of environment, these strands might simply reflect elements of today's legal environment: the struggle for protection of civil or human rights perhaps, or a more generally increased need to rationalise the distinctiveness and independence of the legal branch, by drawing more attention to reason than to wisdom; or, perhaps, a sense that private law will be protected from interest politics, or from suspicion of meddling in areas that are primarily for legislation, if its special nature as private – a matter between parties – can be validated.

For all that I have tried to avoid a caricature of some of Green's key positions, there is no doubt that his campaign to liberate the development of tort from the grip of prescriptive doctrinal understanding and to assess it as an exercise of wisdom, power and process, does not commend itself to those who seek to define tort in terms of a conceptual framework. Green did not deny that tort had content; but definition of that content did not appear to him to be the most useful or important element in its study. The point of tort was to protect, avoid, compensate and so on. But the best blueprint for allowing the law of tort to achieve these functions effectively was to empower the courts.

Hanoch Dagan has recently proposed that realism should be understood in terms of its analysis of law as a set of institutions that must accommodate three irresolvable tensions: between power and reason; science and craft; and tradition and progress.[105] Hagan's main concern is with the jurisprudential heritage of realism, and his discussion does not refer to Leon Green. Nevertheless, Green's work could be said to illustrate all of these tensions. Jurisprudential realists, according to Dagan, are *interested in* the presence of these tensions. Green, perhaps, exemplified them.

Green was very far from mistrustful of the common law, and did not think he was suggesting a break from its traditions. For him, trust could more readily be placed in the judges than in their words. He perceived himself to be correcting relatively new misunderstandings, for example about the restraining power of *stare decisis*, over and above the liberating qualities he perceived it to contain;[106] or about the naturalness of fault liability. Fault liability was natural,

[105] H Dagan, 'The Real Legacy of American Legal Realism' (2018) 38 *OJLS* 123; H Dagan, *Reconstructing American Legal Realism and Rethinking Private Law Theory* (New York, OUP, 2013).

[106] Green saw the doctrine as containing elements of custom and practice, adherence to form and appeal to principle. The last of these, he proposed, 'opens the storehouses of wisdom and experience outside the law': L Green, 'The Development of the Doctrine of Stare Decisis and the Extent to Which it Should Be Applied' (1945–46) 40 *Illinois Law Review* 303, 321.

Green argued, but to a *particular* environment: nineteenth-century courts had 'developed the defensive doctrines of tort law as naturally as the weeds and flowers come to the landscape in response to spring',[107] and in this natural (not manipulative) way the liberation of defendants from liability had been accomplished 'under cover of fault'. By the time he began his scholarship, it was time to recognise this, and to allow a break from this protectionism to take root just as naturally.

Oddly, despite his challenging and critical language, Green's approach was (deeply) optimistic about the common law. He was a debunker, but still a believer: there was simply no need for mystification. In Green's own words, 'There is no warrant for the fear that a fluid language and adjustable rules are undependable. We have never had any other sort, although we have lost much by not recognizing that fact.'[108] Exploring both the stability of judgment and the capacity of law to remain at the same time constantly unfinished,[109] was at the core of Green's almost romantic attachment to the common law.

[107] L Green, 'The Thrust of Tort Law Part I: The Influence of Environment' (1961–62) 64 *West Virginia Law Review* 1, 9.

[108] Green, 'The Duty Problem in Negligence Cases' (n 3) 1019.

[109] Its unfinished quality was, for Green, the 'most beautiful' aspect of the law: Green, 'Basic Concepts: Persons, Property, Relations' (n 65) 69.

8

Professor William Lloyd Prosser (1898–1972)

CHRISTOPHER J ROBINETTE*

I. INTRODUCTION

IN A 1952 letter to his mother, William Lloyd Prosser wrote, 'I shall probably be the last of a generation that really made the law of Torts over and did quite a job of it'.[1] Prosser sounds boastful, but he was not exaggerating. In terms of shaping doctrine, John CP Goldberg calls him 'the most important American tort scholar of the twentieth century'.[2]

His reputation and influence stem from multiple sources.[3] First, and most significantly, there is his treatise, known as 'Prosser on Torts'.[4] The treatise has been celebrated far beyond the dreams of typical academic authors: 'Prosser on Torts! It has a completed sound, a belonging sound, a natural sound, a sound to be remembered for years to come.'[5] Ken Abraham and Ted White recently stated the treatise was not only the most influential torts treatise, but for nearly

* For reviewing and improving earlier drafts, I thank Ken Abraham, Martha Chamallas, Mary Davis, Don Gifford, Sheila Scheuerman, Brian Tamanaha and Ted White. For helpful comments, I thank the participants in the Scholars of Tort Law workshop at Oxford: Guido Calabresi, Peter Cane, Paula Giliker, John Goldberg, James Goudkamp, Mike Green, Mark Lunney, Paul Mitchell, Donal Nolan, Jenny Steele, Rob Stevens and Ben Zipursky. For excellent research, I thank Ed Sonnenberg and Alexander Beale.

[1] Letter from William L Prosser to Zerelda Ann Huckeby Prosser (22 September 1952) (on file with author).

[2] JCP Goldberg, 'Prosser, William L' in RK Newman (ed), *The Yale Biographical Dictionary of American Law* (New Haven, CT, Yale University Press, 2009) 439–40.

[3] The next two paragraphs, with minor changes, are taken from CJ Robinette, 'The Prosser Letters: 1917–1948' (2016) 101 *Iowa Law Review* 1143, 1144–45.

[4] WL Prosser, *Handbook of the Law of Torts* (St Paul, MN, West Publishing Co, 1941). Subsequent editions were published in 1955, 1964, and 1971. A fifth edition was published after Prosser's 1972 death: WP Keeton (ed), *Prosser and Keeton on the Law of Torts*, 5th edn (St Paul, MN, West Publishing Co, 1984).

[5] J Wade, 'William L. Prosser: Some Impressions and Reflections' (1972) 60 *California Law Review* 1255, 1255.

50 years, it was 'arguably the leading single-volume treatise in American legal scholarship'.[6] Second, Prosser served as the Reporter for the *Restatement (Second) of Torts*, which has been described as 'the most influential of the American Law Institute's volumes restating and reshaping American law'.[7] Third, he authored a casebook that has gone through 13 editions and, 46 years after his death, remains the leader in a competitive market.[8]

Through these works and dozens of law review articles, Prosser exerted considerable influence on the development of several specific tort doctrines, notably strict products liability, privacy and intentional infliction of emotional distress. Regarding products liability, Prosser's 1941 treatise called for strict liability for injuries caused by products[9] three years prior to Justice Roger Traynor's concurrence in *Escola v Coca Cola Bottling Co*.[10] His 1960 article 'The Assault Upon the Citadel'[11] has been described as 'a model of how legal scholarship can serve to further doctrinal change in a common law subject'.[12] Moreover, in drafting the products liability sections of the *Restatement (Second) of Torts*, especially §402A, Prosser legitimised strict products liability.[13] Regarding privacy law, Prosser's scholarship established the division of the vague tort right of privacy into four separate causes of action.[14] Prosser's 1960 article 'Privacy',[15] followed by the privacy provisions in the *Restatement (Second) of Torts*, 'came to supplant Warren and Brandeis's work as the touchstone of privacy jurisprudence'.[16] Finally, Prosser's 1939 article on the intentional infliction of emotional distress[17] legitimised that cause of action as an independent tort. In the article, Prosser announced that courts had created a 'new tort';[18] one scholar noted, 'Prosser's statement had an element of accuracy. But it was also

[6] KS Abraham and GE White, 'Prosser and His Influence' (2013) 6 *Journal of Tort Law* 27, 28.

[7] HA Johnson, 'So What Is a Rumination, Anyway: Tales of Professor Wex S Malone' (1996) 56 *Louisiana Law Review* 493, 493.

[8] Email from Christopher Hart, Director of Sales and Account Management, Found. Press, to author (7 February 2018) (on file with author). The first edition was published in 1952: YB Smith and WL Prosser, *Cases and Materials on Torts* (Brooklyn, NY, Foundation, 1952). The most recent edition was published in 2015: VE Schwartz et al, *Prosser, Wade and Schwartz's Torts: Cases and Materials*, 13th edn (St Paul, MN, Foundation, 2015).

[9] Prosser, *Handbook of the Law of Torts* (n 4) 688–89.

[10] *Escola v Coca Cola Bottling Co* 150 P 2d 436, 440 (Cal 1944).

[11] WL Prosser, 'The Assault Upon the Citadel (Strict Liability to the Consumer)' (1960) 69 *Yale Law Journal* 1099.

[12] GE White, *Tort Law in America: An Intellectual History* (Oxford, OUP, 2003) 169.

[13] *Restatement (Second) of Torts* (Philadelphia, PA, American Law Institute, 1965) §§ 402A–402B.

[14] The four privacy torts are: (1) intrusion upon plaintiff's seclusion or solitude; (2) public disclosure of embarrassing private facts; (3) publicity that places the plaintiff in a false light in the public eye; and (4) appropriation for the defendant's advantage of the plaintiff's name and likeness. *Restatement (Second) of Torts* (Philadelphia, PA, American Law Institute, 1977) §§ 652B–652E.

[15] WL Prosser, 'Privacy' (1960) 48 *California Law Review* 383.

[16] J Kahn, 'Bringing Dignity Back to Light: Publicity Rights and the Eclipse of the Tort of Appropriation of Identity' (1999) 17 *Cardozo Arts and Entertainment Law Journal* 213, 223.

[17] WL Prosser, 'Intentional Infliction of Mental Suffering: A New Tort' (1939) 37 *Michigan Law Review* 874.

[18] ibid 874.

unnecessarily modest. A major contribution to the "creation" of the "new tort" had been made by Prosser himself.'[19]

Instead of his well-known influence on these discrete torts, this chapter will focus more broadly on Prosser's overall effects, particularly regarding the paramount tort of negligence. Prosser attempted to adjust negligence to two Realist challenges: Realists' belief in the public nature of seemingly private disputes and the undermining of certainty caused by emphasising the facts of each case. To the first challenge, Prosser reconceptualised the elements of negligence as involving public policy choices. To the second, Prosser attempted to present a negligence formula that was both flexible and predictable. Prosser succeeded on the first issue but failed on the second, with far-reaching consequences for tort law as a compensatory mechanism.

Thus, in section II, I describe a significant shift that Prosser helped bring to tort law: an increased emphasis on social policy and factors. Section III discusses Prosser's motivations therefor. Prosser wanted to make the law more transparent and practical, and he believed that these changes would lead to increased compensation for the injured. At the same time, Prosser tried to cabin the unpredictability in negligence. In section IV, I describe some of the effects of Prosser's work. Although, initially, tort law became more compensatory, the trend has reversed. Moreover, Prosser failed to cabin the uncertainty of negligence. Uncertainty creates unpredictability, delays and transaction costs, hurting both plaintiffs and defendants. One response by institutional defendants has been to seek relief from tort law in the form of liability-limiting tort reforms. Prosser's infusion of policy provided a basis for overturning prior compensatory gains. Thus, increased obstacles await plaintiffs seeking compensation. Section V briefly describes a potential response to the problem to which Prosser contributed. Prosser's considerable efforts to make tort law more just, intelligible and compensatory have somewhat backfired. A part of William Prosser's legacy in the law of torts is unintended consequences.

II. TORTS MADE OVER

A. General Approach

William Prosser's influence on tort law did not result from his creativity. Regarding his role in legitimising strict products liability, Ted White stated, 'Only his bold stroke of stripping strict liability from its "illusory contract mask" and declaring its status as a tort doctrine ranked as a genuinely creative effort.'[20] George Priest even suggested that Prosser's 'extraordinary influence over the direction

[19] White, *Tort Law in America: An Intellectual History* (n 12) 102.
[20] ibid 173.

of the law' was '[p]erhaps because Prosser never threatened originality'.[21] Instead, White has argued Prosser was successful because of his 'consensus' approach to tort law. In an ongoing dispute between doctrinalists, who saw tort as bound by doctrine, and Realists, who believed in the primacy of the facts of each case and social policy, Prosser managed to make everyone happy.

Prosser combined 'the insights of Realism and the countervailing demands of doctrinally oriented theories of tort law'.[22] He did this in two ways. First, he tried to impose some order on the Realists' functional view of torts as a chaotic mass of cases, while retaining necessary flexibility. Prosser 'treated tort law as a collection of doctrines, each of which was capable of being reduced to a general formula that articulated its salient features'.[23] At the same time, these formulae 'represented only simplified aggregates of countless cases, no one of which precisely embodied all the elements of the formula'.[24] The goal of this method, as Prosser said in his treatise, was 'to make the rule sufficiently flexible to allow for the particular circumstances, and yet so rigid that lawyers may predict what the decision may be, and men may guide their conduct by that prediction'.[25] Second, working within this doctrinal framework, Prosser introduced Realist innovations. Prosser explicitly infused doctrine with social policy and factors. Social policy corresponded to the Realists' focus on the public nature of seemingly private disputes. The result of Prosser's efforts, particularly in the treatise, was that he 'had made Realist-inspired innovations in tort law part of the received orthodoxy of the field'.[26]

The formats of Prosser's most influential projects, a treatise and a Restatement, emphasise his acceptance of the importance of doctrine and predictability. But he did not see tort law as static. In the opening sections of his treatise,[27] first published in 1941, Prosser presented his conception of tort law. The third section, entitled 'Social Engineering',[28] includes Prosser's idea that policy is important in deciding tort cases. After announcing that tort law is a 'battleground of social theory',[29] Prosser stated society has 'some concern even with

[21] GL Priest, 'The Invention of Enterprise Liability: A Critical History of the Intellectual Foundations of Modern Tort Law' (1985) 14 *Journal of Legal Studies* 461, 465.

[22] White, *Tort Law in America: An Intellectual History* (n 12) 157.

[23] ibid.

[24] ibid.

[25] Prosser, *Handbook of the Law of Torts* (n 4) 18.

[26] White, *Tort Law in America: An Intellectual History* (n 12) 163.

[27] In defending their focus on Prosser's treatise in discussing his work, John Goldberg and Ben Zipursky cited three reasons. First, 'it is important simply because of its huge influence on lawyerly and judicial understandings of duty and other basic feature of negligence law'. Second, it embodies the received wisdom about duty, in particular, passed down from Oliver Wendell Holmes, Jr and Leon Green. This point also emphasises that Prosser's influence did not stem from his originality. Third, 'it is a prolonged and highly effective brief on behalf of an instrumentalist understanding of negligence': JCP Goldberg and BC Zipursky, 'The Moral of Macpherson' (1998) 146 *University of Pennsylvania Law Review* 1733, 1754, fn 76.

[28] Prosser, *Handbook of the Law of Torts* (n 4) 15.

[29] ibid.

the single dispute involved in a particular case'.[30] When the effects of precedent are considered, 'others now living and even those yet unborn may be affected by a decision made today'.[31] Thus, there is good reason 'to make a conscious effort to direct the law along lines which will achieve a desirable social result, both for the present and for the future'.[32]

The primary purpose of tort law is still to make a 'fair adjustment of the conflicting claims of the litigating parties'.[33] But 'public policy' is also involved in private cases.[34] Prosser noted, 'When the interest of the public is thrown into the scale and allowed to swing the balance for or against the plaintiff, the result is a form of "social engineering".'[35] Prosser's form of social engineering was explicitly utilitarian; it 'deliberately seeks to use the law as an instrument to promote "the greatest happiness of the greatest number", which by common consent is the object of society'.[36]

The next section Prosser dedicated to 'Factors Affecting Tort Liability'.[37] Courts must 'balanc[e] the individual and social interests involved in tort cases'.[38] In so doing, courts are influenced not only by the 'weight attached to the particular interest',[39] but also by other considerations.

> Among these are:
>
> a. The moral aspects of the defendant's conduct.
> b. The historical development of the law.
> c. The difficulty or convenience of administration of a proposed rule.
> d. The capacity of the respective parties to bear the loss.
> e. The possible prevention of future torts.[40]

The first thing to notice about the factors list is that it is not exclusive. It begins with 'Among these are'. There may be others. The second thing to notice is the variety of the factors: morality, history, administrative convenience, loss-spreading and deterrence. Then Prosser warned that 'no one of them is of such supervening importance that it will control the decision of every case in which it appears'.[41]

Stepping back from Prosser's description of what is required of courts in tort cases, one is struck by the difficulty of the endeavour. The court must balance the particular interests of the plaintiff and defendant. Then the court must take

[30] ibid 16.
[31] ibid.
[32] ibid.
[33] ibid 15.
[34] ibid.
[35] ibid 17.
[36] ibid.
[37] ibid 18.
[38] ibid.
[39] ibid.
[40] ibid.
[41] ibid.

societal interests into consideration and weigh them as well. All the while, the court must, at a minimum, give consideration to morality, history, administrative convenience, loss-spreading and deterrence.

B. Negligence

Consistent with his general approach, Prosser infused policy and factors into the elements of negligence.

i. Duty

Like other abstract concepts, Prosser was not fond of 'duty': 'Its artificial character is readily apparent.'[42] To Prosser, duty was empty: 'It is a shorthand statement of a conclusion, rather than an aid to analysis in itself.'[43] Prosser's attitude toward duty did not change; over a decade later, he stated, 'There is a duty if the court says there is a duty; the law, like the Constitution is what we make [of] it.'[44]

Because he saw duty as vacuous, Prosser presented the element as one of policy, '"duty" is not sacrosanct in itself, but only an expression of the sum total of those considerations of policy which lead the law to say that the particular plaintiff is entitled to protection'.[45] He reiterated the point in a later passage, '[t]he real problem, and the one to which attention should be directed, would seem to be one of social policy'.[46] John Goldberg and Ben Zipursky summarise Prosser's conception of duty as follows: 'Thus, whenever they had rendered "no-duty" decisions, the courts had actually determined that there was some policy reason not to apply the default rule of compensation for harm caused by unreasonable acts'.[47]

Factors also play a role in Prosser's duty. Many of the factors to be considered involve policy. Thus, he wrote that 'Various factors undoubtedly have been given weight, including convenience of administration, capacity of the parties to bear the loss, a policy of preventing future injuries, the moral blame attached to the wrongdoer, and perhaps many others.'[48] Prosser later added that 'There is room for argument that the foreseeability of harm to the plaintiff should be but one factor in determining the existence of a duty, and not always conclusive.'[49]

[42] ibid 180.

[43] ibid.

[44] WL Prosser, 'Palsgraf Revisited' (1953) 52 *Michigan Law Review* 1, 15, reprinted in WL Prosser, *Selected Topics on the Law of Torts* (Ann Arbor, MI, University of Michigan Press, 1953) 213.

[45] Prosser, *Handbook of the Law of Torts* (n 4) 180.

[46] ibid 185.

[47] Goldberg and Zipursky, 'The Moral of Macpherson' (n 27) 1763.

[48] Prosser, *Handbook of the Law of Torts* (n 4) 181.

[49] ibid 185.

The Prosser-inspired duty analysis is the clear majority rule in the United States. In a 1997 article, Peter Lake reviewed the duty jurisprudence of all fifty states in the United States. Referring to the 'Prosser (Green)' approach, as an acknowledgement that Prosser relied heavily on and cited Leon Green in the treatise, Lake defined the approach as 'policy-based, multi-factor balancing tests'.[50] Lake declared 'an overwhelming majority of American jurisdictions treat questions of duty in negligence law substantially' according to the Prosser (Green) approach.[51] Lake produced an appendix describing the duty cases in each state.[52] Prosser's influence is absent in only a handful of states. As an example of Prosser's effect, Lake singled out California for discussion. The effects of California's duty decisions 'cannot be (and have not been) underestimated'.[53] And the California Supreme Court 'specifically created [its] list of factors with Prosser (Green) in mind'.[54]

ii. Breach

To a lesser extent, Prosser influenced the importance of policy and factors in the element of breach. Prosser's factors are familiar. He contended that 'Against this probability, and gravity, of the risk, must be balanced in every case the utility of the type of conduct in question.'[55] Policy is important on both sides of the equation. When weighing the factors, the social value of the interests is a prime consideration. Prosser said that 'Chief among the factors which must be considered is the social value of the interest which the actor [defendant] is seeking to advance.'[56] For example, he wrote that '[t]he public interest will justify the use of dangerous machinery, so long as the benefits outweigh the risks'.[57] Social value is not limited to use in considering the defendant's behaviour. Breach 'is determined by balancing the risk, in light of the social value of the interest threatened, and the probability and extent of the harm, against the value of the interest which the actor is seeking to protect, and the expedience of the course pursued'.[58] Not surprisingly, determining when a party has breached can

[50] PF Lake, 'Common Law Duty in Negligence Law: The Recent Consolidation of a Consensus on the Expansion of the Analysis of Duty and the New Conservative Liability Limiting Use of Policy Considerations' (1997) 34 *San Diego Law Review* 1503, 1505.

[51] ibid.

[52] ibid 1529–70.

[53] ibid 1515–16.

[54] ibid 1534. For this proposition, Lake cited *Biakanja v Irving* 320 P 2d 16, 19 (Cal 1958), in which the court listed factors and immediately cited multiple pages from the 2nd volume of Prosser's treatise.

[55] Prosser, *Handbook of the Law of Torts* (n 4) 222.

[56] ibid.

[57] ibid.

[58] ibid 223. Compare the formula Prosser provided to his Torts students three years earlier. When describing 'what the reasonable man will do', Prosser instructed that one weighs the balance between two things. On one side was the seriousness of risk and certainty of risk and on the other was the cost of obviating the risk, which included the importance of doing what the defendant wanted to do

be uncertain: 'it is seldom possible to reduce negligence to any definite rules … conduct which would be proper under some circumstances becomes negligent under others'.[59]

As on duty, Prosser was not an originator on breach. He did, however, endorse and disseminate a viewpoint that had only recently received widespread attention. Mike Green, reviewing authorities from around the turn of the twentieth century, concluded that, at that time, Prosser's type of balancing test 'was not the dominant force providing content to the negligence standard for liability'.[60] Green further reviewed the scholarship of Francis Bohlen, the Reporter for the first *Restatement of Torts* and the dominant torts figure in the United States in the first several decades of the twentieth century. He noted Bohlen's early view on breach reflected a conception of torts as a closed system for doing justice between the parties: 'the essential condition for negligence is that a risk of "probable" injury exists'.[61] By 1924, two years after Bohlen had been named Reporter, his views 'had changed dramatically'.[62] Bohlen included 'utility of the act' by the defendant into the calculus.[63] He did so out of concern for the value of defendant's conduct to society,[64] essentially a matter of policy.

Bohlen, as Reporter, adopted a factors-balancing test for breach in the *Restatement*. He considered that 'the risk is unreasonable and the act is negligent if the risk is of such magnitude as to outweigh what the law regards as the utility of the act or of the particular manner in which it is done'.[65] The *Restatement* provided that 'what the law regards as the utility of the actor's conduct' is 'determined in light of the social value the law attaches to the interest in question'.[66] Social value focused on benefits to 'the whole community'.[67] Thus, factors and policy were present in the version of breach adopted by the

and the social utility advantages to the defendant. CJ Robinette, 'The Prosser Notebook: Classroom as Biography and Intellectual History' (2010) 2010 *University of Illinois Law Review* 577, 617–18 (describing notes taken by a student in Prosser's 1938–39 Torts course at the University of Minnesota Law School).

[59] Prosser, *Handbook of the Law of Torts* (n 4) 223.

[60] MD Green, 'Negligence = Economic Efficiency: Doubts' (1997) 75 *Texas Law Review* 1605, 1617.

[61] ibid 1623, citing FH Bohlen, 'Right to Recover for Injury Resulting from Negligence Without Impact' (1902) 50 *American Law Register* 141, 147, 150.

[62] Green, 'Negligence = Economic Efficiency: Doubts' (n 60) 1623.

[63] ibid 1624, citing FH Bohlen, 'Mixed Questions of Law and Fact' (1924) 72 *University of Pennsylvania Law Review* 111, 114.

[64] Green, 'Negligence = Economic Efficiency: Doubts' (n 60) 1624.

[65] SG Gilles, 'On Determining Negligence: Hand Formula Balancing, the Reasonable Person Standard, and the Jury' (2001) 54 *Vanderbilt Law Review* 813, 823–24, citing *Restatement of Torts* (Philadelphia, PA, American Law Institute, 1939) § 291.

[66] Gilles, 'On Determining Negligence: Hand Formula Balancing, the Reasonable Person Standard, and the Jury' (n 65) 828, citing *Restatement of Torts* (Philadelphia, PA, American Law Institute, 1939) §1.

[67] ibid 829, citing *Restatement of Torts* (Philadelphia, PA, American Law Institute, 1939) §292, cmt *a*.

Restatement two years prior to the publication of Prosser's treatise. Bohlen, however, acknowledged that the *Restatement* standard was 'a shift in the formal doctrinal test for negligence'.[68] Thus, Prosser endorsed an understanding of breach that had only recently gained widespread attention and, through the influence of the treatise, helped establish it.

One more point may be instructive. Stephen Gilles has argued the *Restatement*'s balancing test was anchored in morality, specifically the concept of equal respect for others. This was because it required that

> the reasonable person's *judgments* about risks 'give to the respective interests concerned the value which the law attaches to them', and 'give an impartial consideration to the harm likely to be done the interests of the other as compared with the advantages likely to accrue to his own interests'.[69]

Prosser's conception of breach, involving factors and policy, does not emphasise the moral notion of equal respect for others.

iii. Proximate Causation

For Prosser, proximate causation, used to limit liability, was a matter of policy. He argued that 'This limitation is sometimes, but rarely, one of the fact of causation. More often it is purely one of policy, not connected with questions of causation at all.'[70] He delivered the same message to his students. In describing proximate cause, he stated '[T]he question is should [defendant] be legally responsible?'[71] The question 'has nothing to do with causation. It is a matter of policy'.[72]

Although the tie to factors is not as strong in Prosser's understanding of proximate causation as it is in duty and breach, it is nonetheless there. In one sense, as with duty, the policies to be considered are themselves factors. Prosser spoke of 'various considerations of policy',[73] meaning a court might have to consider multiple items in the name of policy. In another sense, Prosser believed proximate cause involves 'a number of distinct problems',[74] such that the facts and circumstances of each case must be taken into consideration to determine which problem is involved. In the treatise, Prosser noted these problems

[68] ibid 838, citing *Restatement of Torts*, Commentary on Section 172, Tentative Draft No. 4 ('The comparison between the social utility of the act and the magnitude of the risk is occasionally, but only occasionally, stated as the basis of decision in negligence cases').

[69] Gilles, 'On Determining Negligence: Hand Formula Balancing, the Reasonable Person Standard, and the Jury' (n 65) 832, citing *Restatement of Torts* (Philadelphia, PA, American Law Institute, 1939) §283, cmt *d* (explaining that the reasonable person is 'reasonably "considerate" of the safety of others and does not look primarily to his own advantage').

[70] Prosser, *Handbook of the Law of Torts* (n 4) 312.

[71] Robinette, 'The Prosser Notebook: Classroom as Biography and Intellectual History' (n 58) 612.

[72] ibid 612–13.

[73] Prosser, *Handbook of the Law of Torts* (n 4) 311.

[74] ibid.

included, but were not necessarily limited to, causation-in-fact, apportionment of damages, liability for unforeseen consequences and intervening causes.[75] An earlier list included six problems, with the caveat that the list was 'by no means exclusive'.[76]

When Prosser's conception of each element is analysed separately, it is striking that each involves policy. This raises the question of why multiple elements involving policy are needed. After providing his 1938–39 torts class with the five elements of negligence – duty, standard of conduct, breach of duty, causation and damage – Prosser is recorded as stating, 'The five elements are really all the same thing. You can only define one in terms of the other four.'[77] Indeed, Prosser's approach has been described as flattening negligence to focus on whether the act was unreasonable; essentially reducing negligence to breach, and that being partially a policy question.[78]

III. GOOD INTENTIONS

In effectuating these shifts in tort law, Prosser was motivated to make the law more intelligible, fair and, ultimately, more compensatory.

A. Demystifying the Law

To understand Prosser's approach to law, it is instructive to understand his attitude towards theory, professors generally and himself. William Prosser hated 'academic theory'. After his 1952 meeting with Adlai Stevenson, the Democratic candidate for President of the United States in 1952 and 1956, Prosser compared him favourably to Woodrow Wilson, the 28th President of the United States, when he wrote that Stevenson 'does not have Wilson's colossal conceit and academic theory approach to everything'.[79] Similarly, when a professor with whom his father had worked died, Prosser stated he had liked the man, 'although I never saw anyone who better typified the wool-gathering theorist'.[80]

In Prosser's view, many professors were faulty; instead of being useful, they lived lives of abstraction. As a young man, Prosser discussed an article in which

[75] ibid 320.

[76] WL Prosser, 'The Minnesota Court on Proximate Cause' (1936) 21 *Minnesota Law Review* 19, 21.

[77] Robinette, 'The Prosser Notebook: Classroom as Biography and Intellectual History' (n 58) 613.

[78] Goldberg and Zipursky, 'The Moral of Macpherson' (n 27) 1741–42, 1762–63.

[79] CJ Robinette and K Graham, 'The Prosser Letters: Scholar as Dean' (2017) 10 *Journal of Tort Law* 99, 142.

[80] ibid 143, fn 350.

the author argued the reason that professors made less money than janitors is that they were less valuable. Paraphrasing the argument, Prosser stated 'that everybody could get along quite comfortably if all the professors alive were killed off with an ax, but that in this era of steam heat janitors are a necessity'.[81] Prosser agreed: 'When I write a textbook on education, I am going to make that my opening sentence.'[82] When he became a professor, his initial impressions were mixed, but he found the 'fairly complete detachment from the world'[83] and the 'general abstraction'[84] to be negative.

Prosser saw himself as worldlier and more grounded. Unlike others who 'take the veil',[85] Prosser knew that the law was about 'a lot of low-browed individuals … shaking their fists under each other's noses down at the District Court'.[86] Prosser presented himself in this practical manner, humorously and emphatically, in his 1942 book review entitled 'My Philosophy of Law'.[87] Prosser started by recalling his philosophy course at Harvard as an undergraduate as follows: 'The philosophy people all used a lot of words like theological and categorical imperative, and they all disagreed with one another most hideously. I can see from this book that they still do.'[88] He recalled the definition of a philosopher as 'a blind man in a dark cellar at midnight looking for a black cat that isn't there'.[89] By extra-curricular research, Prosser had found a philosopher who appealed to him, 'He was a Persian named Omar, who made tents for a living, and took up philosophy as a sideline, probably because there wasn't enough money in it as a regular job.'[90] Omar's 'theory was that you couldn't possibly figure it out anyway and it was a waste of time to try, and that the thing to do was to forget it and go out and get drunk'.[91] When Prosser reviewed the volume he found that the 15 different authors had found 15 different cats.[92] When it came time for Prosser to write about his own philosophy of law, he found 'that I haven't any'.[93] Prosser 'had always supposed that law was the product of a

[81] Robinette, 'The Prosser Letters: 1917–1948' (n 3) 1156, citing a letter from William L Prosser to Zerelda Ann Huckeby Prosser (22 March 1920).

[82] ibid.

[83] ibid 1179, citing a letter from William L Prosser to Zerelda Ann Huckeby Prosser (28 October 1930).

[84] ibid. It is likely Prosser's attitudes were shaped by his father, Charles Allen Prosser. Known as the 'Father of Vocational Education', Charles believed in the separation of vocational from general education and that general education should be made more 'practical': ibid 1184, citing John Gadell, 'Charles Allen Prosser: His Work in Vocational and General Education' (August 1972) (unpublished PhD dissertation, Washington University in St Louis, MO).

[85] Robinette, 'The Prosser Letters: 1917–1948' (n 3) 1175, citing a letter from William L Prosser to Zerelda Ann Huckeby Prosser (2 May 1929).

[86] ibid 1179, citing a letter from William L Prosser to Zerelda Ann Huckeby Prosser (28 October 1930).

[87] WL Prosser, 'My Philosophy of Law' (1942) 27 *Cornell Law Quarterly* 292.

[88] ibid 293.

[89] ibid 294.

[90] ibid 293.

[91] ibid.

[92] ibid 294.

[93] ibid 295.

lot of pulling and hauling in society, a set of rather inadequate compromises brought about by very headstrong mules all going in different directions, and that the reason it is in a mess is that society is in the same kind of mess'.[94]

William Prosser thus wanted to make the law more practical and to simplify it. In his mind, that meant two things. First, either eliminating or making more intelligible abstract, theoretical concepts. Duty and proximate cause are prime examples. The concepts were woven into tort law, so eliminating them was unlikely. He could, instead, make them more concrete. Thus, they were not really what they purported to be, but instead were practical policy decisions to be made by courts. If duty is meaningless, at least courts could compensate people or make them safer. It was tangible and intelligible. For example, in discussing proximate cause in terms of policy considerations, Prosser stated that 'The tendency of courts to state these considerations in terms of causation often obscures the real issues involved.'[95] If the real issues were discussed openly, better decisions would be made. Moreover, it was more honest than hiding behind empty terms and deceptive reasoning.

The second way to simplify the law was to favour general principles over detailed rules. Prosser stated this forcefully in a 1953 letter to his mother. Describing a deans' meeting in which the group discussed 'Lecturer' in terms of tenure, salary and duties, Prosser's frustration was palpable:

> Everyone on the university has the typical layman's desires to reduce everything to a set of detailed rules covering every possible contingency and complication, which of course drives a lawyer frantic because he knows that it can't be done, that something unanticipated will always come up and mess the whole thing up, and simple general principles with some kind of tribunal to decide how they apply to the particular case are always best. The whole university lives in a state of almost abject terror of ever having to make a decision on individual responsibility in a case not covered by a definite rule laid down in advance. The result is that the rules are so complicated that no one can fine [*sic*] out what they are, and are almost unintelligible.[96]

Again in the name of transparency and intelligibility, Prosser preferred 'simple general principles' with specific applications to be decided by a tribunal under the facts and circumstances of each case, and not a complex system put in place

[94] ibid 294.

[95] Prosser, *Handbook of the Law of Torts* (n 4) 311. Compare his attitude about the intentional infliction of emotional distress, in which he argued that courts were finding liability for that tort but calling it something else. He stated that '[t]he tendency remains, however, to find some other foundation for the action, however strained, and to disguise the real basis of recovery under some other name': Prosser, 'Intentional Infliction of Mental Suffering: A New Tort' (n 17) 880. Many 'problems could be dealt with in far more intelligent fashion if we were to jettison the entire cargo of technical torts with which the real cause of action has been burdened, and recognize it as standing on its own feet': ibid 892.

[96] Robinette and Graham, 'The Prosser Letters: Scholar as Dean' (n 79) 123, citing a letter from William L Prosser to Zerelda Ann Huckeby Prosser (11 April 1953). Note there is an error in the article; the last word of the quotation printed in the article is 'intelligible' when the word in the letter is actually 'unintelligible'.

ex ante. This idea is consistent with Prosser's hatred of abstract, theoretical principles. They are vague and less easily applied by a tribunal.

The idea is also consistent with Prosser's repeated invocation of the need for 'common sense' with regard to doctrine after doctrine. Proximate cause 'is, in the last analysis, nothing more than a question of common sense'.[97] In drawing lines for purposes of the intentional infliction of emotional distress, '[s]o far as the elimination of trivialities is concerned, it calls for nothing more than ... common sense'.[98] *Res ipsa loquitur* requires the jury to use 'common sense', that is, if the jury bothered 'to give it a name at all'.[99] In fact, Prosser considered the entire doctrine as calling for nothing other than common sense, and he thought it should be abolished.[100] Prosser's idea was to provide a simple general principle to a tribunal, provide the facts and circumstances, and let the tribunal use its common sense.

B. Compensating the Injured

In addition to making the law more intelligible, Prosser believed the inclusion of policy and factors would make it fairer and more compensatory. Besides explaining an abstract, theoretical concept such as duty, reconstructing it with the more concrete idea of policy had another advantage. Prosser believed duty was being illegitimately used to limit liability. As Goldberg and Zipursky phrased it, Prosser thought duty was 'a child of anti-regulatory, laissez-faire ideology'.[101] He believed duty had been introduced into tort law, 'perhaps more or less unconsciously, to limit the responsibilities of growing industry within reasonable bounds'.[102] Thus, Prosser was hostile to 'no duty' limitations throughout his career.

As seen, Prosser reconstructed duty as an issue of 'social policy: whether the defendants in such cases should bear the heavy negligence losses of a complex civilization, rather than the individual plaintiff'.[103] What Prosser considered as policy is telling:

> Because these defendants are in large measure public utilities, governmental bodies, industries, automobile drivers, and others who by rates, prices, taxes, or insurance are better able to distribute the loss to the general public, many courts may reasonably consider that the burden should rest upon them, and experience no great difficulty in finding a 'duty' of protection.[104]

[97] Prosser, 'The Minnesota Court on Proximate Cause' (n 76) 69.

[98] Prosser, 'Intentional Infliction of Mental Suffering: A New Tort' (n 17) 878.

[99] WL Prosser, 'Res Ipsa Loquitur in California' (1949) 37 *California Law Review* 183, 193.

[100] ibid 220, 232. This dovetails with his hatred of abstract concepts. He thought *res ipsa loquitur* was nothing other than circumstantial evidence and the Latin title added nothing but confusion.

[101] Goldberg and Zipursky, 'The Moral of Macpherson' (n 27) 1761.

[102] ibid, citing Prosser, *Handbook of the Law of Torts* (n 4) 179.

[103] Prosser, *Handbook of the Law of Torts* (n 4) 185.

[104] ibid.

Prosser thus thought of policy as generally favouring compensation of the injured.

Prosser often invoked policy as the explanation for compensating injuries. Several examples he provided to his students are illustrative. In the area of premises liability, 'social policy' was invoked as the reason for liability. While discussing *Palmer v Gordon*,[105] Prosser is recorded as stating that 'it is comparatively slight burden on D to require him to use reasonable care not to injure a known trespasser by D's affirmative act … Social policy makes D liable'.[106] While covering a case on landlord–tenant injuries, Prosser discussed the rationales for holding the landlord liable. One of the rationales was the pure policy rationale of loss-spreading. He said that 'the landlord is probably more able to pay – and in better position to distribute the loss'.[107]

Prosser thus saw policy and factors as having the beneficial effect of compensating the injured. As Walter Olson critically described it, 'Prosserism came to stand in short-hand for the proposition that society could and should make tort law into a sort of surrogate social insurance to help accident victims'.[108] Indeed, in evaluating Prosser's motivation, it is important to recall that at the time his views developed, injured victims not recovering in tort would bear the cost of injury themselves. In 1940, only 9 per cent of the population had private health insurance,[109] and Medicare and Medicaid were not adopted until 1965.[110] The worse the injuries, the more devastating the financial loss.

C. Salvaging Predictability

At the same time Prosser incorporated policy and factors into negligence, he consciously attempted to manage a separate Realist challenge to negligence. Realists' emphasis on the facts of each particular case undermined the importance of doctrine and predictability. Extreme Realists, such as Leon Green, adopted a functional approach to tort law. Pursuant to functionalism, cases were organised by type, such as automobile accidents, instead of by doctrine, such as negligence.[111] In Realist literature, torts was seen as 'a shapeless mass; its leading principle, negligence, as inherently variegated and fluid; its rules in a constant state of change; its boundaries uncertain'.[112]

[105] *Palmer v Gordon* 53 NE 909 (Mass 1899).

[106] Robinette, 'The Prosser Notebook: Classroom as Biography and Intellectual History' (n 58) 613.

[107] ibid 615.

[108] W Olson, *Schools for Misrule* (New York, Encounter Books, 2011) 58.

[109] R Bovbjerg et al, 'US Health Care Coverage Costs: Historical Development and Choices for the 1990s' (1993) 21 *Journal of Law, Medicine & Ethics* 141, 144.

[110] KS Abraham, *The Liability Century: Insurance and Tort Law from the Progressive Era to 9/11* (Cambridge, MA, Harvard University Press, 2008) 86.

[111] White, *Tort Law in America: An Intellectual History* (n 12) 87.

[112] ibid 145–46.

Prosser recognised the value in flexibility, but he knew it had to be bounded for torts to be a cohesive subject. Thus his goal 'to make the rule sufficiently flexible to allow for the particular circumstances, and yet so rigid that lawyers may predict what the decision may be, and men may guide their conduct by that prediction'.[113] As an example of Prosser's methodology, White examined his treatment of last clear chance. Prosser began his discussion by dismissing several 'doctrinal' explanations for the concept, and then conceded each state treated it differently.[114] Prosser then tried to bring order to the chaos. Despite the forgoing, there are 'situations' that 'may be classified'.[115] Prosser presented three types of last clear chance cases: 'helpless plaintiff' cases, 'inattentive plaintiff' cases, and cases where the defendant's 'antecedent negligence' prevented him from avoiding injury to the plaintiff even though he had exercised the last clear chance to prevent the injury.[116] Prosser is then able to announce that 'nearly all courts' allow a plaintiff to recover in the first category; in the second category 'most courts' allow a plaintiff to recover if the plaintiff was actually discovered but 'nearly all' courts deny recovery if defendant only should have discovered the plaintiff; in the last category there is no recovery.[117] One could thus make sense of last clear chance by focusing on the state of the plaintiff or, failing that, on the character of the defendant's original negligence.[118] Prosser's categorisation is appealing; it depends on the facts of the case, but it provides predictable resolutions.

IV. ACHIEVING COMPENSATION

Just as Prosser was a consensus figure or moderate in the dispute between Realists and doctrinalists, he played a similar role regarding compensation. He, like most academics of the time, favoured increased compensation, but he wanted to make the existing tort system more compensatory. In a sense, the idea was to incorporate a more compensatory function into a system whose primary function had been focused on punishing blameworthy conduct.[119] More radical supporters of compensation would have replaced tort law with compensation programmes.

The problem with incorporating compensation into negligence is that the fit between the two, including the fit of aspects for which Prosser himself was responsible, is uneasy. The policy factors Prosser fused into negligence are not static. Although Prosser saw policy as generally pro-compensation, modern

[113] Prosser, *Handbook of the Law of Torts* (n 4) 18.
[114] White, *Tort Law in America: An Intellectual History* (n 12) 158–59.
[115] ibid 159.
[116] ibid.
[117] ibid.
[118] ibid.
[119] ibid 62.

courts invoke policy factors generally to the contrary. Taken to the extreme, Prosser's infusion of policy can be used to justify the limitations of liability imposed by modern tort reforms. Moreover, the negligence standard itself, with its unpredictability, delay and transaction costs, is inconsistent with compensating injured victims. Prosser recognised the importance of predictable rules for negligence, but was unsuccessful in drawing proper boundaries.

A. Policy

Prosser's conception of policy as generally pro-compensation was formed in an era where Realist influences were strong. Realists emphasised a sense of interconnectedness and favoured loss-spreading, which meant expanding tort liability. But policy is not static. Policy arguments favouring the limitation of liability can and have been made on the part of institutional defendants. In the course of analysing the general contraction of tort liability in the 1980s, Gary Schwartz noted the change in public policy analysis. In the 1960s, the energy was with the liberal left, with Schwartz observing that 'By the 1980s, however, much of the intellectual vitality in public-policy analysis had switched to the neo-conservatives or to rejuvenated traditional conservatives.'[120] Liability should be limited, for example, in order to reduce liability insurance rates and, in turn, retain needed services and products; keep costs manageable for consumers; provide jobs. In other words, policy is a two-way street.[121]

Lake recognised this over two decades ago. He noted that 'Prosser (Green) notions, and even California-influenced variants, have been used to *limit* liability and/or *curtail* the growth of liability law. Duty has thus been used in conservative ways.'[122] Consider *Strauss v Belle Realty Co*,[123] in which a tenant in an apartment building in New York City was injured in the common area of the building during a blackout. The court denied recovery on the basis of a lack of duty. It explained that policy played an important role in duty analysis, and one of the policies it followed was to protect against crushing liability.[124] The court stated that 'The courts' definition of an orbit of duty based on public policy may at times result in the exclusion of some who might otherwise have recovered for losses or injuries if traditional tort principles had been applied.'[125]

[120] GT Schwartz, 'The Beginning and Possible End of the Rise of Modern American Tort Law' (1992) 26 *Georgia Law Review* 601, 694.

[121] Goldberg and Zipursky have been making this point for a long time. JCP Goldberg and BC Zipursky, 'The Restatement (Third) and the Place of Duty in Negligence Law' (2001) 54 *Vanderbilt Law Review* 657, 734–35.

[122] Lake, 'Common Law Duty in Negligence Law: The Recent Consolidation of a Consensus on the Expansion of the Analysis of Duty and the New Conservative Liability Limiting Use of Policy Considerations' (n 50) 1527.

[123] *Strauss v Belle Realty Co* 482 NE 2d 34 (NY 1985).

[124] ibid 36.

[125] ibid.

The dissentient, citing a later edition of the Prosser treatise, did not dispute policy was a relevant factor in a duty analysis. Instead, he argued the majority ignored the countervailing policy argument that the defendant, a public entity, could more easily spread the loss.[126]

The example Lake provided in his article introduces another concern about emphasising the role of policy in tort law. In *Hawks v State Department of Public Safety*,[127] a mother sued the state for a five-year delay in finding the remains of her murdered daughter. The court, citing Prosser's treatise, held the state had no duty to the mother. Consistent with Prosserian duty analysis, the court listed the factors of policy to be considered.[128] In finding no duty existed, the court concluded that '"the consequences to the community" of imposing liability for a negligently-conducted investigation or identification are considerable'.[129] The court added that 'A decision by this court that imposed a duty of care on the police would open [up] the judicial floodgates to allow review of all identifications and permit liability in those determined with twenty-twenty hindsight to have been negligently conducted.'[130] Thus far, the court's language was restricted to using policy in a conservative way to limit liability. But it then stated that 'Such a decision would invariably lead to the diversion of resources from other projects and investigations. Decisions regarding the allocation of limited resources are better left to the executive branch.'[131] Most significantly, the court cited an earlier case, with approval, that stated that '[C]ourts are ill-equipped to investigate and balance the numerous factors that go into an executive or legislative decision'.[132]

This raises a concern about institutional competence. If decisions in tort law are to be made by weighing policy factors, should those be made by judges or legislatures? As Goldberg and Zipursky stated, if tort law is about policy decisions, 'it makes perfect sense to think such policy choices would be more effectively made by legislatures and administrators'.[133] After all, legislators are more directly accountable to the people. Moreover, legislatures have the resources to study issues comprehensively and extensively, but courts are restricted to deciding individual disputes as they arise.

Beginning in the 1970s, legislatures have increasingly passed liability-limiting tort reforms that are detrimental to a compensatory tort system. At first, the reforms came in waves. The first, in the mid-1970s, focused on medical malpractice. Practically every state legislature passed some restrictions. Common responses included caps on pain and suffering; regulating fees of plaintiffs'

126 ibid 38, 40.
127 *Hawks v State Department of Public Safety* 908 P 2d 1013 (Alaska 1995).
128 ibid 1016.
129 ibid 1017.
130 ibid.
131 ibid.
132 ibid.
133 Goldberg and Zipursky, 'The Restatement (Third) and the Place of Duty in Negligence Law' (n 121) 735.

attorneys; shortening statutes of limitations; requiring periodic payments as to future awards; and altering or eliminating the collateral source rule.[134] The second wave, in the mid-1980s, focused on protecting tort defendants. Reforms focused on damage caps, joint and several liability, and the collateral source rule.[135] A third wave arose in the early 1990s with legislation similar to the second wave.[136]

Tort reforms have become perpetual. As the editor of TortsProf Blog, I monitor these reform proposals, and they are constant. Kentucky is a good example. As I was writing this section, the Kentucky Senate passed a bill to reform medical malpractice law. The bill would: (i) impose a certificate of merit requirement, forcing plaintiffs to file a certificate by an expert stating the case had merit before suit could be filed; (ii) impose caps on contingency fees for plaintiffs' attorneys; (iii) allow healthcare providers to express condolences without the statement being introduced into evidence; and (iv) regulate fees for copying medical records.[137] Only a year ago, Kentucky imposed a requirement of going through medical malpractice panels before suit could be filed.[138] That bill failed multiple times before it finally passed, which is another hallmark of tort reform. If a bill does not pass, it is often introduced again the following year until it does.

Significantly, the language used by advocates of tort reform is Prosserian, though he would have invoked it to contrary purposes. The American Tort Reform Association is the only national organisation in the United States dedicated exclusively to reforming tort law. The mission statement on its website includes the following:

> These lawsuits are bad for business; they are also bad for society. They compromise access to affordable health care, punish consumers by raising the cost of goods and services, chill innovation, and undermine the notion of personal responsibility. The personal injury lawyers who benefit from the status quo use their fees to perpetuate the cycle of lawsuit abuse. They have reinvested millions of dollars into the political process and in more litigation that acts as a drag on our economy. Some have compared the political and judicial influence of the personal injury bar to a fourth branch of government.
>
> ATRA works to counter that influence by challenging this status quo and continually leading the fight for common-sense reforms in the states, the Congress, and the court of public opinion.[139]

[134] Franklin et al, *Tort Law and Alternatives: Cases and Materials*, 10th edn, (Westbury, NY, Foundation, 2016) 824.

[135] ibid.

[136] ibid 827.

[137] Staff, 'Medical tort-reform bill moves to House' *The Ohio County Monitor* (2 March 2018).

[138] MC Ksiazek, 'Bill Creating Medical Malpractice Panels Passes in Kentucky' *The National Law Review* (6 March 2017) at https://www.natlawreview.com/article/bill-creating-medical-malpractice-panels-passes-kentucky (accessed 30 October 2018).

[139] American Tort Reform Association, 'Mission', *ATRA*, at http://www.atra.org/about/mission/ (accessed 3 November 2018).

Note the concern that lawsuits are bad for 'society' and that ATRA wants to re-establish 'common sense'. Note the existence of policy arguments, 'They compromise access to affordable health care, punish consumers by raising the cost of goods and services, chill innovation, and undermine the notion of personal responsibility.' And note that this all leads to the legislature. Plaintiffs' lawyers are investing money into 'the political process'. Thus, ATRA must respond by fighting back in the political process in 'the states, the Congress, and the court of public opinion'.

B. Unpredictability

Realists valued allowing courts the flexibility to achieve justice on the basis of the particularised facts of the case. But factors and case-by-case analysis make the law unpredictable. Prosser recognised the tension. Recall his comment in the treatise that his goal was to make the rule sufficiently flexible to allow for the particular circumstances, but sufficiently rigid to be predictable.[140] White was not impressed with the results. Reviewing Prosser's treatment of last clear chance, he described Prosser's attempt to classify the doctrine. The classifications 'left a sense of tidiness',[141] but 'they were nearly useless as predictive rules'.[142] White continued:

> Prosser's approach was rather to create pseudo-rules, classifications that purported to summarize the 'state of the law' in a given area of Torts, but in fact were simply devices that aided in summary and synthesis of a disparate mass of material.[143]

White opined that 'Prosser's efforts were only to wrest some surface intelligibility from the chaos of the cases before him.'[144]

In essence, Prosser's attempt in the treatise to make rules rigid enough to be predictable was often inadequate. In a recent email, White commented on Prosser's efforts to cabin negligence within predictable boundaries:

> Prosser didn't want tort law to just end up being a mass of policy decisions. On the other hand he recognized the contingency and, at some level, the illusory quality of doctrines associated with negligence. So what I think he tried to do was to present the clearest summary of tort doctrine he could find, so that the doctrinal elements he identified with tort actions would be enduring. The problem was that although his summaries made for very good synthetic overviews for casebooks and treatises, they didn't work very well as rules to be applied across a range of cases. Too much indeterminacy. That's why I think of them as 'pseudo-rules'.[145]

[140] See n 25.
[141] White, *Tort Law in America: An Intellectual History* (n 12) 160.
[142] ibid.
[143] ibid 161.
[144] ibid.
[145] Email from G Edward White, David and Mary Harrison Distinguished Professor of Law, University of Virginia School of Law, to author (19 March 2018) (on file with author).

Prosser's failure to balance flexibility and predictability, although not surprising, leaves in place a significant problem with negligence, particularly as a compensation mechanism. The lack of predictability, the uncertainty, in the negligence standard is immense.[146] The basic standard of 'reasonableness under the circumstances' is vague and invites arguments over what, exactly, the relevant circumstances were at the time of the incident and how those circumstances should be interpreted. Even garden variety cases can get bogged down into dueling sets of facts and interpretations thereof.

Ken Abraham focused on the basic uncertainty of the negligence standard by describing the job given to a finder of fact. The finder of fact must (i) find the empirical facts, such as what the defendant did; (ii) determine what kind of care and how much of it was reasonable in those circumstances; and (iii) decide whether the defendant behaved with the amount of care identified in step (ii).[147] He further distinguished between 'bounded' and 'unbounded' cases. Unbounded cases exist when the finder of fact uses its 'own general normative sense of the situation, informed by individual experience and by the evidence submitted by the parties'.[148] By contrast, in bounded cases, 'the source of this content is a pre-existing, concrete norm that exists independently of the finder of fact's individual sense of the situation'.[149] Examples of bounded cases include cases involving custom, professional standards or statutes.[150]

Abraham argued the negligence decision is typically an act of unbounded norm creation.[151] The example he offered, 'the simplest of negligence cases',[152] is of a slip and fall, allegedly caused by inadequate snow removal from a sidewalk. In such a case, among other things, the finder of fact would have to decide 'whether the homeowner exercised reasonable care to make her property safe for the plaintiff'.[153] On this question, the relevant factors include a long list: how much snow the defendant removed initially, whether she performed an inspection of the condition of the steps on subsequent occasions, the visibility of the ice, the number and steepness of the steps, whether there was a railing, the amount of time the steps were exposed to direct sunlight during the day, and the snow removal practices of others in the neighbourhood.[154] Abraham commented on all of the 'decision points' facing the finder of fact:

> [E]ach of these items of evidence is a potential predicate for the application of a norm to the facts of the case – for example, that a homeowner should remove all but

[146] The next several paragraphs are adapted from CJ Robinette, 'Party Autonomy in Tort Theory and Reform' (2013) 6 *Journal of Tort Law* 173, 183–86.

[147] KS Abraham, 'The Trouble with Negligence' (2001) 54 *Vanderbilt Law Review* 1187, 1190–91.

[148] ibid 1190.

[149] ibid.

[150] ibid 1199–1202.

[151] ibid 1191.

[152] ibid 1193.

[153] ibid.

[154] ibid.

> the tiniest bits of snow from steps, that subsequent inspection is (or is not) necessary, or that greater care should be exercised if the steps are not in strong sunlight for several hours each day. But unless one or more of these precautions is mandated by statute or ordinance ..., the failure of the defendant to employ the precaution is simply an optional basis for the negligence decision by the finder of fact [who] ... is simply directed to weigh all the evidence in deciding whether the defendant was or was not negligent.[155]

Uncertainty is even worse in more complicated cases, such as medical malpractice. First, there is a laundry list of potentially negligent defendants, including, but not limited to, physicians, hospitals, equipment and pharmaceutical manufacturers – all or none of whom could be responsible for the plaintiff's injuries. Moreover, a landmark study by the prestigious Institute of Medicine found that adverse results from healthcare are often caused by complex, multicausal, systemic interactions, and not from the fault of a single individual.[156] This is contrary to typical medical malpractice litigation in which, according to an extensive study by the American Psychological Association, plaintiffs' lawyers generally focus on proof of the supposed monocausal mistakes of individuals.[157]

Second, fault in the medical context, whether multi- or monocausal, is often difficult to prove because of the intricate nature of the human body. The body is composed of elaborate, interlocking parts that take years of study to properly understand. It is not surprising that jurors and even judges, as triers of fact, find it difficult to separate adverse consequences due to medical negligence from pre-existing conditions that further developed during treatment. The difficulty is exacerbated by the time limits a trial places on the ability to educate jurors on the complex variables in malpractice cases. Third, jurors are often presented with conflicting, and confusing, expert testimony regarding a defendant's negligence or lack thereof.

It does not follow that determinations of fault in medical malpractice are arbitrary. The best available data demonstrate there is a correlation between fault and payment to claimants.[158] A study by the Harvard School of Public Health, however, found that the assessment of liability pursuant to tort law was correct less than three-quarters of the time.[159] Thus, given on average five years to reach the correct conclusion,[160] the tort system is still incorrect over one-quarter of the time. There is even more reason for claimants to be apprehensive.

[155] ibid.

[156] LT Kohn et al, *To Err is Human: Building a Safer Health Care System* (Washington, DC, National Academy Press, 1999).

[157] N Feigenson, *Legal Blame* (Washington, DC, American Psychological Association, 2000) 151–69.

[158] PG Peters Jr, 'What We Know about Malpractice Settlements' (2007) 92 *Iowa Law Review* 1783, 1785.

[159] DM Studdert et al, 'Claims, Errors, and Compensation Payments in Medical Malpractice Litigation' (2006) 354 *New England Journal of Medicine* 2024, 2028.

[160] ibid 2031.

In a separate meta-study, an error rate for and against each party was derived. The studies demonstrate that plaintiffs win about 10 to 20 per cent of the cases with weak evidence of negligence and 50 per cent of the cases with strong evidence thereof.[161] In other words, plaintiffs win between 10 and 20 per cent of cases they should likely lose, but lose a staggering one-half of cases they should likely win.

Medical malpractice is not alone in increasing the uncertainty of the vague negligence standard. Products liability, traceable to Prosser, exhibits similar shortcomings. Consider David Owen's discussion of the standard of liability in products cases:

> [T]he design and warnings 'defect' notions … are surrounded by shrouds of mist. The mist exists, of course, only in the middle of the spectrum, and cases do arise at either extreme, where the product is clearly defective or not. Yet for the great number of cases in the middle, the legal 'tests' of liability for such defects are by their nature so vague that they are often effectively meaningless as guides for design engineers attempting to comply with the law … One indeed may ask whether 'law' itself exists in such terrain, or whether 'lawless' is the better word to describe the prevailing 'rule' of random guilt. The very notion of how much design safety is enough, and to a lesser extent how much safety information is enough, involves a morass of conceptual, political, and practical issues on which juries, courts, commentators, and legislatures strongly disagree.[162]

Such unpredictability by itself is problematic. Plaintiffs, and plaintiffs' lawyers, are uncertain whether and how cases should be pursued. Defendants and their lawyers are uncertain whether liability is likely once a claim is made. In addition, unpredictability increases delay and transaction costs as parties attempt to answer those questions.

There is a significant amount of evidence substantiating the problem of delay in tort law.[163] Consider again the study conducted by the Harvard School of Public Health on a random sample of 1,452 closed medical malpractice claims from five liability insurers.[164] Of the claims examined, as noted, the average time between injury and resolution was five years.[165] Moreover, one in three claims took six years or more to resolve.[166] Consider also a 1999 study conducted by Jeffrey O'Connell and Craig Stanton.[167] The authors examined four torts

[161] PG Peters, Jr, 'Doctors & Juries' (2007) 105 *Michigan Law Review* 1453, 1464.

[162] DG Owen, 'Problems in Assessing Punitive Damages against Manufacturers of Defective Products' (1982) 49 *University of Chicago Law Review* 1, 37.

[163] This paragraph is adapted from J O'Connell and CJ Robinette, *A Recipe for Balanced Tort Reform* (Durham, NC, Carolina Academic Press, 2008) 41–43.

[164] Studdert et al, 'Claims, Errors, and Compensation Payments in Medical Malpractice Litigation' (n 159).

[165] ibid 2031.

[166] ibid. Compare the three to four-year time period based on 1984 data from the United States Congress's General Accounting Office: D DeWees et al, *Exploring the Domain of Accident Law* (Oxford, OUP, 1996) 121.

[167] J O'Connell and CA Stanton, 'Justice Delayed is … Delay Ignored: The Indifference of Judges and Law Professors to Legal Lassitude' (1999) 49 *DePaul Law Review* 489.

casebooks widely used in the United States to determine the length of time between incident and appellate decision. In order to enhance the quality of the results, cases were limited to those decided after 1950 (to eliminate the effect of major changes such as the adoption of the Federal Rules of Civil Procedure). Furthermore, areas where the law varies significantly from state to state and the law is exceptionally vague (such as injuries involving solely emotional harm, and cases in which the incident could not be traced back to a specific date) were excluded. The authors compiled a list of 51 cases. The average length of time between the incident and appellate opinion was 6.94 years,[168] with appellate judges then ordering remands or new trials in almost half the cases. Many cases lasted between six and 10 years, and in certain instances between 10 and 13 years.[169]

Delay can be detrimental for tort defendants, and even worse for plaintiffs. Defendants such as manufacturers and healthcare providers are distracted from their primary work. Prolonged litigation reduces the amount of time that can be devoted to more productive endeavours. Injured plaintiffs, who may have mounting medical bills and lost wages, are forced to endure extended uncertainty and find ways to make ends meet while awaiting resolution. As the Harvard School of Public Health authors stated of the medical context, 'These are long periods for plaintiffs to await decisions about compensation and for defendants to endure the uncertainty, acrimony, and time away from patient care that litigation entails.'[170]

The unpredictability and delay also increase transaction costs.[171] During the period of delay, as lawyers and experts grapple with all of the factors, facts and circumstances, they are billing busily. Plaintiffs' lawyers typically work on contingency fees of 33 per cent to as high as 50 per cent of gross recovery. By contrast, defendants (or, often, their insurers) pay lawyers an hourly fee or, more recently, a flat fee per case, with payment being made win or lose. In addition to

[168] ibid 494.

[169] ibid 490.

[170] Studdert et al, 'Claims, Errors, and Compensation Payments in Medical Malpractice Litigation' (n 159) 2031. Delay, of course, is not restricted to tort law. A number of factors contribute to delay: particular case types, locale, the number of litigants and whether alternative dispute resolution was involved are among them. M Heise, 'Empirical Analysis of Civil Litigation: Torts Trials in State Courts' in J Arlen (ed), *Research Handbook on the Economics of Torts* (Cheltenham, Edward Elgar Publishing, 2013) 21. Additionally, commentators often warn about the limitations of available data and analyses thereof. ibid 22. One significant weakness is the lack of sufficient longitudinal data. Nevertheless, what data there are indicate that the average time from filing to disposition of tort cases is several months longer than in contract cases. TH Cohen, 'Expeditiousness and Delay in State Courts: An Exploration of Case Processing Time in Civil Trials' (1 July 2010) at https://papers.ssrn.com/sol3/papers.cfm?abstract_id=1633501 at 11. Moreover, the gap would be much greater had automobile accidents, comprising over half of all tort claims, not been routinised. Those claims were routinised because the level of uncertainty was inefficient, there was a sufficient volume of claims and repeat players were on both sides of the claims. See CJ Robinette, 'Two Roads Diverge for Civil Recourse Theory' (2013) 88 *Indiana Law Journal* 543.

[171] The next two paragraphs are adapted from Robinette, 'Party Autonomy in Tort Theory and Reform' (n 146) 182–83.

lawyers, at least in medical malpractice and products liability cases, both parties are paying expert witnesses. In the medical malpractice context, Gary Schwartz (writing in 2002) estimated that a plaintiff's malpractice expenses were approximately $50,000, *not including attorneys' fees*.[172] In the early 1990s, a litigation guide for products liability included several examples of a plaintiff's advanced expenses totalling several hundreds of thousands of dollars.[173]

Transaction costs substantially impact the amount of money eventually reaching the injured plaintiff. According to data from the 1980s, tort law's administrative costs were 53 per cent of net plaintiff benefits,[174] meaning more money was spent on transaction costs than plaintiffs received. There was a disparity among torts; 'plaintiffs' net compensation as a percentage of the total expenditures was 52 percent for auto torts and 43 percent for all other torts'.[175] More recent data are consistent with the earlier findings. The Harvard School of Public Health study found that 54 per cent of the money expended on the medical malpractice claims in its sample was spent on transaction costs, leaving plaintiffs with 46 per cent.[176]

Thus, even as the tort system expanded to compensate more plaintiffs, its willingness to consider factors and facts and circumstances made it unpredictable. Considering all of the facts and circumstances consumes both time and money. Protracted, bitter, costly disputes are less appealing to plaintiffs and, more importantly, plaintiffs' lawyers, who will not be paid if they estimate the possibility of recovery incorrectly. Nor is such a system appealing to defendants who are spending more time and money involved in litigation.

C. Effects

If one were to predict an outcome based on the unpredictability, delay and transaction costs of tort lawsuits combined with the prevalence of pro-defendant policies, particularly enacted as tort reforms, it would have to be that plaintiffs receive compensation less often. One would expect fewer plaintiffs to want to pursue tort claims, and, even more importantly, fewer plaintiffs' attorneys willing to risk pursuing tort claims. The data bear this out.

It has been known for some time that the number of tort trials has been decreasing. The Bureau of Justice Statistics announced in 2005 that the number

[172] GT Schwartz, 'Empiricism and Tort Law' (2002) 2002 *University of Illinois Law Review* 1067, 1071.

[173] J Vargo, *Products Liability Practice Guide* (Newark, Lexis, 1992) 42.065a.

[174] J Kakalik and N Pace, *Costs and Compensation Paid in Tort Litigation* (Santa Monica, CA, RAND, 1986) 70.

[175] ibid.

[176] Studdert et al, 'Claims, Errors, and Compensation Payments in Medical Malpractice Litigation' (n 159) 2031.

of tort trials in federal district courts fell almost 80 per cent from 1985 through 2003.[177] The Bureau listed as contributing factors, '[t]he growing use of alternative dispute resolution as well as the increased complexity and costs inherent in taking a case to trial'.[178]

Even more significant is that the number of *claims* has dropped precipitously. Last summer, Joe Palazzolo published an article in the *Wall Street Journal* in which he announced:

> Fewer than two in 1,000 people – the alleged victims of inattentive motorists, medical malpractice, faulty products, and other civil wrongs – filed tort lawsuits in 2015, an analysis of the latest available data collected by the National Center for State Courts shows. That is down sharply from 1993, when about 10 in 1,000 Americans filed such suits.[179]

Tort cases declined from 16 per cent of civil filings in state courts in 1993 to about 4 per cent in 2015, a difference of more than 1.7 million cases nationwide.[180]

A study conducted by researchers at Northwestern University and the University of Illinois found a 57 per cent nationwide decline in malpractice claims paid by doctors or their insurers between 1992 and 2012, and a similar drop in the number of malpractice lawsuits. The highest drop was in claims of less than $50,000, likely because the increasing litigation costs made them too expensive to pursue.[181] Claims in Texas, where comprehensive reforms were passed in 2003, fell 27 per cent between 1995 and 2014, according to a separate study. Non-automobile accident claims in Texas fell 60 per cent over the same period.[182] Moreover, these reductions are absolute and not as a percentage of the population, which has continued to grow.

One possibility, of course, is that claims are being settled not only prior to trial, but prior to filing of suit as well. Data from the insurance industry, however, show that the percentage of bodily-injury claims has been declining since the 1990s.[183]

Why have such suits declined? Because of a host of factors, 'including state restrictions on litigation, the increasing cost of bringing suits, improved auto safety and a long campaign by businesses to turn public opinion against plaintiffs and their lawyers'.[184] In other words, the only factor not related to the

[177] Bureau of Justice Statistics, 'Number of Federal Tort Trials Fell by Almost 80 Percent from 1985 through 2003' (17 August 2005) at http://www.dcinjuryfacts.com/files/numberofclaims.pdf (accessed 3 November 2018).

[178] ibid.

[179] J Palazzolo, 'We Won't See You in Court: The Era of Tort Lawsuits is Waning' *Wall Street Journal* (24 July 2017).

[180] ibid.

[181] ibid.

[182] ibid.

[183] ibid.

[184] ibid.

factors and policy is the technological improvement in automobiles. The article quoted Senior Judge Gregory Mize of the District of Columbia Superior Court, 'People are just not filing cases like they used to. They are not seeking trials like they used to. It's so expensive and time-consuming.'[185]

Thus, the number of injured persons claiming for compensation is down dramatically. In the absence of data suggesting that the number of injuries is also down dramatically, one has to conclude that the compensation function of tort has been seriously curtailed.[186]

V. NEXT STEPS

Though the focus of this piece is the contributions of William Prosser to tort law, I would be remiss if I did not briefly address the problem to which he contributed. White described tort law as a field uncertain whether its primary function is admonitory, one based in conduct that is wrongful, or compensatory, providing the injured with resources to allay their injuries.[187] This division tracks the debate in tort theory about whether tort does and should achieve individualised justice between the parties, or whether it is and should be an instrument to achieve regulatory goals such as compensation and deterrence. I consider that debate something of a distraction. Claims of both types currently inhabit the system.[188]

Wrongs cases have always existed in tort law. As a clear example, consider a battery suit brought by the victim against the rapist. Schwartz invoked such a case in the late 1970s,[189] and noted it was not based on instrumentalism. Such a suit 'does not really depend on the general assessment of the overall wealth distribution between men and women'.[190] Instead, it 'rests on corrective justice' because 'rape is an act that is morally wrong'.[191] Moreover, its wrongness is not based on an efficiency comparison of the victim's pain and the rapist's satisfaction; 'from a moral perspective, the latter is illegitimate'.[192]

Cases better suited for compensatory treatment, however, exist in the tort system, too. But tort law, as seen, is not currently compensating well or efficiently.

[185] ibid.

[186] Another possibility is that the system is eliminating 'frivolous' cases. The data, however, suggest that frivolous cases, though they exist, are not a substantial problem. Studdert et al, 'Claims, Errors, and Compensation Payments in Medical Malpractice Litigation' (n 159) 2031–32 write that 'portraits of a malpractice system that is stricken with frivolous litigation are overblown … The vast majority of resources go toward resolving and paying claims that involve errors'. See also DA Hyman and C Silver, 'Medical Malpractice Litigation and Tort Reform: It's the Incentives, Stupid' (2006) 59 *Vanderbilt Law Review* 1085, 1101–03.

[187] White, *Tort Law in America: An Intellectual History* (n 12) 291.

[188] Robinette, 'Two Roads Diverge for Civil Recourse Theory' (n 170).

[189] GT Schwartz, 'Economics, Wealth Distribution, and Justice' (1979) 1979 *Wisconsin Law Review* 799.

[190] ibid 1809, fn 64.

[191] ibid 1809.

[192] ibid.

Many individualised justice scholars will, undoubtedly, feel vindicated and feel no need to do anything. There are two reasons that is a bad idea. First, as White chronicled, as an historical matter tort law tends to shift back and forth between private law and public law impulses, meaning another shift towards compensation is predictable. As a specific application of this idea, consider the compensatory effects that particular types of injuries have had on tort law over time. In the early 1900s, workplace accidents were taken out of tort law and workers' compensation was created. One of the major motivating factors in the movement was the work of Crystal Eastman in her book *Work Accidents and the Law*.[193] She chronicled the plight of the families of workers injured primarily in Pittsburgh steel mills. John Witt credits Eastman with 'organiz[ing] work-accident debates around the image of the wounded family'.[194] Similarly, the push to reform tort law for automobile accidents was caused by the 'hellish carnage'[195] that automobiles created. Tort law was again reformed, this time to adopt no-fault automobile laws in some states; unlike workers' compensation, no-fault was integrated into the tort system.[196] Products injuries were the impulse to move to products liability, partially based on a compensatory rationale, and wholly within tort law itself.[197] Finally, even in a period where compensatory impulses are muted within tort law, Bob Rabin noted they surface often in response to mass disasters, with the most significant example being the September 11th Victim Compensation Fund.[198]

The second reason is more significant, yet more difficult for me objectively to demonstrate.[199] I believe the motivation for the majority of people filing tort claims in the modern tort system is to be compensated. By which I mean they pursue claims primarily because they need money to cover their medical bills and/or lost wages. I practised law for seven years, with a substantial portion of my clients as plaintiffs in tort cases. I had some clients I felt wanted vindication; they pursued claims because they believed their rights were violated and they wanted justice. This, however, was a small portion of my clients, and they tended to be suing in the types of cases not comprising the majority of tort actions (for example, false imprisonment and defamation cases). By contrast,

[193] PU Kellogg (ed), *Work Accidents and the Law* (New York, Charities Publication, 1910).

[194] JF Witt, *The Accidental Republic: Crippled Workingmen, Destitute Widows, and the Remaking of American Law* (Cambridge, MA, Harvard University Press, 2004) 130.

[195] J Simon, 'Driving Governmentality: Automobile Accidents, Insurance, and the Challenge to Social Order in the Inter-War Years, 1919–1941' (1998) 4 *Connecticut Insurance Law Journal* 521, 540.

[196] CJ Robinette, 'Why Civil Recourse Theory Is Incomplete' (2011) 78 *Tennessee Law Review* 431, 468–70.

[197] ibid 471–75.

[198] RL Rabin, 'Jeffrey O'Connell and the Compensation Principle in Accident Law: Institutional and Intellectual Perspectives' (2013) 6 *Journal of Tort Law* 3, 24–26.

[199] Obtaining data on why plaintiffs file tort suits would be valuable. I have tried, and failed, to design a survey that would receive sufficient, objective responses. I hope to try again soon.

the overwhelming majority of my clients seemed to me to have a compensatory motivation. Contrary to the view of aggressive plaintiffs, they were generally very reluctant to sue at all, but doing so was often the only way to obtain needed funds.

Thus, both wrongs-based and compensatory cases are currently in the tort system. The crucial issue that should be engaged by tort scholars is how to divide claims worthy of individualised justice treatment from those better suited to treatment as routinised compensatory cases. For individualised justice cases, perhaps the factors and the close attention to facts and circumstances make sense. They may even be worth the associated delay and transaction costs. After all, determining whether one has been wronged is a serious inquiry. But, as seen, these features are often counterproductive to compensating the injured. A tort reform that successfully separated claims that should be treated as wrongs from those better suited to compensatory treatment, likely involving a simpler, cheaper procedure and perhaps decreased amounts of pain and suffering, would be fairer than current tort reform efforts, yet potentially generate the savings desired by business groups.[200]

VI. CONCLUSION

William Prosser was the most influential American tort scholar of the twentieth century. Because of his consensus approach to law and his writing skills, including an unusually vivid style, he was able to shift the law in his preferred direction. Though most of his ideas were not original – he called himself a 'packrat'[201] – he was able to express those ideas in a way that others found persuasive. His intentions were good. He wanted to simplify the law and make it more practical. Moreover, in an era where losses often truly stayed where they fell because of a lack of health insurance, Prosser wanted to compensate the injured. The results, however, have been disappointing.

It is unfair to give Prosser too much credit for moving tort law in a compensatory direction. Again, many of the ideas he espoused were not his own. The advent of liability insurance was a major factor, though Prosser did not overly rely on it as a rationale to expand liability.[202] But he did make the Realist ideas of policy and factors a part of accepted orthodoxy within tort law. Both those

[200] Robinette, 'Party Autonomy in Tort Theory and Reform' (n 146) contains my preliminary thoughts on the matter.

[201] White, *Tort Law in America: An Intellectual History* (n 12) 176, citing WL Prosser, *Law of Torts*, 3rd edn (St Paul, MN, West Publishing Co, 1964) xi.

[202] Prosser, 'The Assault Upon the Citadel (Strict Liability to the Consumer)' (n 11) 1122 ('insurance is obviously not to be ignored; but it is a makeweight').

who laud him[203] and those who do not[204] attach his name to the tort law that came after him.

Similarly, it is unfair to put too much of the share of blame on Prosser for the unintended consequences of the retrenchment of tort law that followed its expansion. Gary Schwartz mentioned changes in the composition of the judiciary.[205] Advances in technology have made tort cases more complex, thus more unpredictable, slow and expensive. But Prosser pointed the law in a particular direction, and the retrenchment follows logically from the direction in which he pushed. In addition to Schwartz's suggestion about judicial composition, he also focused on costs and changes in public policy,[206] reasons consistent with Prosser's influence.

It is painful to emphasise the failings of a figure of such obvious work ethic and talent. If the next generation of tort scholars is able to learn from his mistakes, and find a way to vindicate those who should be vindicated and compensate those who should be compensated, it will provide Prosser's work in torts with a worthy coda.

[203] Lake, 'Common Law Duty in Negligence Law: The Recent Consolidation of a Consensus on the Expansion of the Analysis of Duty and the New Conservative Liability Limiting Use of Policy Considerations' (n 50) 1528.

[204] Goldberg and Zipursky, 'The Moral of Macpherson' (n 27); Olson, *Schools for Misrule* (n 108).

[205] Schwartz, 'The Beginning and Possible End of the Rise of Modern American Tort Law' (n 120) 685.

[206] ibid 689–94.

9

Professor Fleming James Jr (1904–1981)

GUIDO CALABRESI

I. A SURPRISING BACKGROUND

'JIMMY' JAMES, AS he was universally called, was my teacher both in torts and in civil procedure in my first term at the Yale Law School in the fall of 1955. He became my mentor and friend, helping to bring me back to Yale, as a faculty member, in 1959. My first article, which with his help led to my receiving a Full Professorship at the Law School two years later, was an almost unchanged revision of a paper I had written in the fall of 1956. It was, in many ways, a somewhat critical reaction to his view of tort law as he had expressed it in class and in our out-of-class conversations. It also represented an answer to many questions that the casebook he used in torts seemed to ask. The questions were undoubtedly there, but neither he nor his co-author, Harry Shulman, seemed to know precisely why. I have used that casebook – now in its sixth edition[1] and put out by others, some of whom were also Jimmy's students – in each of the nearly 60 years that I have taught torts. I used it just last term! Why the questions are there, what they had to do with Jimmy's scholarship and his view of torts, what that view of torts was and how it came to be are all parts of the story I shall try to tell today.

In writing this chapter, I have re-read most of Jimmy's articles. And I still refer, from time to time, to his massive encyclopedia of torts[2] (written with his colleague, Fowler Harper) when, as a Federal Court of Appeals Judge, I have a difficult torts case. (Harper's own copy with an inscription to me by Jimmy sits behind my desk in my Judicial Chambers.) But in truth, I could have written this piece entirely from memories of the conversations that I had with Jimmy.

[1] H Shulman et al, *Law of Torts: Cases and Materials*, 6th edn (New York, Foundation Press, 2014).

[2] FV Harper and F James Jr, *The Law of Torts* (Boston, MA, Little, Brown and Co, 1956).

In these conversations, he stated forthrightly what his view of torts was, and what he thought his role as a Law Professor, who had been a torts lawyer (and the latter is not unimportant), should be in furthering that view.

Re-reading his articles has been useful because, in fact, Jimmy's view is stated quite explicitly in some of them. Still I cannot hide from you the fact that my knowledge of Jimmy and his vision of torts remains first and foremost a personal one. And so, while I shall give citations as I deem appropriate, I also from time to time in this chapter rely on recollections alone. Nor is this bad, I think. I am 86 years old and those recollections will not long be available, while Jimmy's writings will continue to be there for all to read long after I and my memories of Jimmy are gone.

Who was Fleming James, Jr, what was his family, professional and academic background? And how did this background shape his vision of law and of legal scholarship? A few words on this are, I believe, useful. Jimmy's father, also named Fleming James, was a minister and a missionary in China. While going to Divinity School, he also got a PhD in classics. Jimmy was born in China and was brought up in a deeply white, Anglo-Saxon Protestant religious family, which believed that knowledge of the Classics and of the Bible were a fundamental part of a youngster's education. His father became a Professor at the Berkeley Divinity School in New Haven. At the time this was an independent Episcopal (Church of England) seminary. (It remains the latter but now is part of the Yale Divinity School.) As a result, like me, James went to Yale College and Yale Law School as a faculty brat. But, very unlike me, he studied classics in Yale College, won the Samuel Henry Galpin Latin Prize and, as far as I know, ignored economics.

He was also brought up to believe that a mission in life was essential to being a decent person, and that furthering that mission was what life was all about. Jimmy, himself, was profoundly secular. And he had early come to view most puritanical restrictions as absurd. (He was not quite as 'wild' as many of his law school faculty contemporaries, but he certainly loved a good time.) Still a sense of mission was a profound part of Jimmy's being.

It became in him the mission of the Social Democrat, of the 'Labourite' reformer I suppose one would say in England, rather than a churchly one. But it was definitely still there. The abuses of the poor and needy by past and present powers that be – these were the moneylenders that Jimmy sought to drive from the Temple that he considered the Law to be. And he meant to do it mainly through his teaching and scholarship, but also by working directly with various state agencies, especially after his mandatory retirement as a teacher when he became the head of Connecticut's Labor Board.

And yet there was also another side of Jimmy's ancestry that I believe is not generally known. He never mentioned it to me and, as far as I know, never wrote about it. I only learned of it doing research for this chapter. This side made him fear abuses by the government, and made him something of a Libertarian among Social Democrats. His opposition to government actions against 'subversives' did not come simply from a revulsion at the McCarthyism of his time or as a reaction to the 'Red Scares' of his youth. It had deeper and quite unusual roots.

Jimmy's grandfather, also named Fleming James, was born in Virginia in 1835. He went to the University of Virginia and then an Episcopal Seminary in the South. In 1869 he was an Episcopal Minister working in St Luke's Hospital in New York. During a trip to Baltimore, while he was with a friend (who later became the Anglican Bishop of Kentucky), his friend was asked by some not very active parishioners to preside at a family funeral. The friend declined, saying he was otherwise engaged. Fleming James did not say no. And so it happened that Jimmy's grandfather presided at the reinternment of John Wilkes Booth, Lincoln's assassin![3]

He was severely hounded and quickly fired from his Hospital job. He may, thereafter, have had difficulties. I found him employed in 1879, and then just as an Assistant Minister, in Ohio – a state with parts that had distinctly Southern leanings. Finally, in 1892, when attitudes towards the Confederacy had changed and its position, all-too-often, had come to be romanticised as the Lost Cause, he became a professor in a seminary in Pennsylvania.

The grandfather may well have had Confederate sympathies. It is said that he was at Pickett's charge at Gettysburg.[4] But he firmly decried Lincoln's assassination. And, in presiding at the funeral, he was just doing a priest's job. Still, the Government, in the best of causes – the punishment of conspirators in Lincoln's assassination – was not about to make distinctions. And neither were many private individuals who feared government disfavour.

Now Jimmy was even further removed from those who may have defended opponents of Lincoln than he was from his churchly upbringing. He was a committed integrationist, and a fierce supporter of the Warren Court. And his grandfather, as I said, seems never to have been mentioned by him. Indeed, Jimmy's father called himself Fleming James not Fleming James, Jr, and Jimmy was Fleming James, Jr, not 'the third'. Moreover, Jimmy's father's obituary, after noting his defence of labourers and the underdog, goes out of its way to emphasise his work on inter-racial relations. Still, I rather think that governmental extremism – even in a good cause – remained an underlying fear that Jimmy had. And I believe this not only influenced his determination to protect civil liberties generally, but also led to some scepticism of the role of government in tort law.

His view of torts, as we shall see, should have made him fight for a totally centralised social insurance – like social security. He often recognised this fact.

[3] After his death in 1865, Booth had been unceremoniously buried in a storage room. Near the end of his administration, the Southern-leaning President Andrew Johnson, having survived impeachment by one vote, authorised the Booth family to re-inter him. Soon after, however, Ulysses S Grant, the commander of the Union Armies who had been elected President at the end of 1868, took office.

[4] T Alford, *Fortune's Fool: The Life of John Wilkes Booth* (Oxford, OUP, 2015) 331.

But he also hesitated and frequently suggested the benefits of 'half-way measures', like the tort law that he advocated or like limited government programmes such as Worker's Compensation. I always wondered about this. I now believe that somewhere, in the back of Jimmy's very Yankee consciousness, the treatment of his Southern grandfather had left its mark.

After Yale College, Jimmy went to Yale Law School, which was already a centre of interest in Law and the Social Sciences. The great Arthur Corbin had, with the help of Harvard's Roscoe Pound, managed to get Yale to hire Wesley Hohfeld. Hohfeld died very young in the Influenza Pandemic of 1918. But in the four or so years that he was at Yale, he had a profound effect on the place. As a result, when Jimmy talked 'pure theory', which was rarely, he would revert, rather uncomfortably I thought, to Hohfeldian categories.

Jimmy talked some about his time in college and law school. And some of his quirks are easily traceable to these times: 'Alternatives', the Latin prize winner insisted, refers to two possibilities only, not more. 'You can call it Thucydides or you can call it Mustard Plaster', the classically trained legal realist would thunder, 'but it's all proximate cause just the same'. But he spoke more often and enthusiastically about his work, after law school, as a defence lawyer for the New Haven Railroad. It was there that Jimmy saw tort law, as it actually played out in practice, and it was there that he learned how important procedural rules and burdens of proof can be in a tort case. He was not a practitioner that long. But it was long enough for Jimmy to see how often a tort recovery was the only thing between a decent survival and total destruction for injured victims in an America without any real 'safety net', how often an injured victim's basic needs could only be met through torts. And it was also long enough both to make him want to teach procedure as well as torts, and to make him appreciate how important a good *lawyerly* argument can be to winning one's case. This will be seen again and again in his articles, which, in the most lawyerly of ways, marshalled the cases and materials in favour of the doctrinal definitions that furthered Jimmy's policy goals.

II. SPREADING: A REALIST'S VIEW OF TORTS

When Jimmy joined the Yale Law School faculty, Yale was well on its way to becoming the leading school devoted to legal realism. And, in a way, Jimmy fit right in. To the realists the immediate object of legal scholarship was not only the relatively trivial task of showing how much law depended on the whims of the law makers (including judges). It was also to show – either through empirical work or by using the Social Sciences – how ineffective, wrong-headed, unintelligible or simply obsolete (in terms of any possible sound policies) the dominant doctrinal rules in one's field were. Many of the most influential legal realists, like Wesley Sturges, were in spirit and action nihilists. They were magnificent destroyers of the 'wrongheaded' dogmas of their fields, and were happy to leave it at that.

But the greatest realists were not satisfied with destroying the old and absurd. They sought somehow – however difficult it was, and however limited in time the results of their efforts might prove to be – to construct new rules, new doctrines that might more adequately respond to the needs of their times. They wanted to rebuild their fields of law, after destroying the old rules, so that the law in these fields might better serve what the 'constructive realist' deemed to be proper, modern policy goals.

Jimmy was fully at home with this approach. He could urge us to '*Ecrasez l'infame*' (wipe out the unworthy) with the best of them. But his missionary spirit led him always to reconstruct, to rebuild, to make better the rules of his chosen field, torts. The object was to make the law of torts, as much as reasonably possible, serve the proper needs of those most in need of it, as he had come to see them as a defence lawyer for the railroad. It never was to make the law logically or philosophically pure.

In an interesting side reference that recalled his religious background, but which spoke of his view of the proper role of law in a society, Jimmy wrote 'The Sabbath must serve persons, not persons the Sabbath.' And again more directly, playing off language by Oliver Wendell Holmes and speaking scornfully of those who would adhere to obsolete rules for their logical elegance and regardless of their practical effect on people, James wrote that these are 'men who propose to sacrifice good sense to a syllogism – and an outworn syllogism at that. Was Don Quixote ever more quixotic?'[5]

To Jimmy, the coming of liability insurance had made most of the rules and structures of traditional tort law obsolete. This was not only with respect to certain specific doctrines – such as intrafamily immunities, governmental immunities, charitable immunities and the like.[6] It was, much more importantly, with respect to the object of tort law generally. His 1948 article, 'Accident Liability Reconsidered: The Impact of Liability Insurance', says it directly and concisely.[7] After a bow to the supposed philosophical fairness and deterrent effects of traditional tort rules, he says 'these matters of fairness and deterrence were all considered on the assumptions that plaintiff and defendant were alone involved and that what happened between them was the real issue – that tort liability was paid for out of the defendant's own pocketbook'.[8] But with the coming of insurance this was no longer the case, and most of the old rules no longer made sense.

The existence of insurance led him to be sceptical of the deterrent effect of tort law, even apart from insurance. Accident avoidance, he thought 'can best be

[5] F James Jr, 'Contribution Among Joint Tortfeasors: Replication' (1941) 54 *Harvard Law Review* 1178, 1183.

[6] F James Jrand JV Thornton, 'The Impact of Insurance on the Law of Torts' (1950) 15 *Law and Contemporary Problems* 431.

[7] F James Jr, 'Accident Liability Reconsidered: The Impact of Liability Insurance' (1948) 57 *Yale Law Journal* 549.

[8] ibid 549.

[achieved] through the pressure of safety regulations with penal and licensing sanctions, and of self-interest in avoiding the host of non-legal disadvantages that flow from accidents'.[9] But given liability insurance, whatever the safety effects of making defendants liable might conceivably once have been, they were no longer significant now. Tort liability was no longer 'paid for out of the defendant's pocketbook', and deterrence of undesirable behaviour by accident causers had become a mighty weak reed upon which to rest a field of law.

Had Jimmy been a nihilistic legal realist he would have stopped there, and have amused himself and his students by describing the fatuousness of torts rules, given the practical absence of the personal liability on which they were based. And we would not then be discussing him today. But Jimmy was a builder and a missionary; he could not leave it at that. In the same article I just cited he says, 'There is however an altogether different approach to tort law … As a class the victims of … accidents can ill afford the loss they entail … [and] wherever there is widely held insurance, tort liability no longer merely *shifts* a loss from one individual to another but it tends to *distribute* the loss'.[10] Moreover, 'while no social good may come from the mere shifting of a loss, society does benefit from the wide and regular distribution of losses, taken alone'.[11] Furthering this 'principle of (decentralized) social insurance' became for Jimmy 'the principal job of tort law today'.[12]

All this meant to him 'that when courts talk and reason about a rule of law as though the judgment were to come out of the defendant's pocket, they are often thinking in terms of complete unreality'.[13] (Here the destructive part of Jimmy's legal realism.) But 'this fact of insurance *does* mean that some of the benefits and values of social insurance are actually attained under our present system'.[14] And this 'invites an appraisal of existing or proposed rules of law in terms of how they serve the possible objectives of social insurance'.[15] It was expanding this distributional, spreading role of torts that became the object of Jimmy's missionary zeal and lawyerly acumen.

A couple of things deserve specific note. Jimmy is talking about the socially beneficent effects of broad distribution of losses. He is not focused on the possibly good effects deriving from placing losses on the wealthy rather than on the poor. I am sure that he believed in wealth distribution of that sort as desirable as well. But that – deep pocket – approach was not for him the object of tort law. It was the best spreader, not the wealthiest, that torts should seek out and hold liable. And spreading to Jimmy meant meeting the, broadly defined, *needs* of

[9] ibid 549–50.
[10] ibid 549–51 (original emphasis).
[11] ibid 550.
[12] ibid.
[13] ibid 552.
[14] ibid (original emphasis).
[15] ibid.

victims. It did not mean making them whole, and returning them to a, perhaps very wealthy, *status quo ante* the accident.[16]

The second thing to note is that while Jimmy seeks to rely on non-civil liability ways of deterring bad conduct, and hence of avoiding undesirable accident costs, and while he does not think such deterrence is the primary job of torts once insurance is available, he does feel the need to consider whether the 'spreading of losses' through insurance will lead to more accidents. He asks '[D]oes [insurance] dilute the deterrent effect of liability upon the individual? Does this dilution tend to foster irresponsibility, or are there countervailing forces brought into play which promote accident prevention – perhaps even more than the fear of individual liability would do?'[17] One might expect from this that Jimmy was on the brink of moving to the kind of structural deterrence analysis that characterised my work. It looks as if, back in 1948, Jimmy was about to begin what rather simplistically has come to be viewed as the Law and Economics approach to torts.

That, however, is not the case. Jimmy relies on purely empirical data that, he says, have shown that insurance and insurance companies have fostered safety. There is really no theory or convincing explanation behind the assertion. He attributes it to insurance companies' wealth and their capacity to teach. 'This has put insurance companies in a strategic position effectively to carry out programs to promote safety',[18] and they 'have contributed materially to the education of the general public along this line'.[19] But why insurance companies might spend their moneys on this is not examined. And the effect of insurance rates on safety is treated only in passing, mainly to say that it is unlikely that the risk of higher individual rates as a result of accident involvement affords more than 'some slight motive to be careful':[20] 'the effect of any individual's conduct on the general rate structure is so little, that the motive can hardly be strong'.[21] And, he then asserts that 'safe driver reward plan[s] for individual automobile owners … have been pretty generally abandoned … because of the administrative difficulties they entailed'.[22]

He does say, at the end of this very brief discussion, '[insurance] companies do exert an influence for safety by rejecting risks which have had bad experience or accepting them only at higher premiums'.[23] But that is essentially the sum and substance of his discussion.

[16] This aspect of James's theory is discussed at length and particularly well in an early article by JCP Goldberg, 'Misconduct, Misfortune and Just Compensation: Weinstein on Torts' (1997) 97 *Columbia Law Review* 2034.

[17] James, 'Accident Liability Reconsidered: The Impact of Liability Insurance' (n 7) 557.

[18] ibid 559.

[19] ibid 560.

[20] ibid.

[21] ibid.

[22] ibid 561.

[23] ibid.

Jimmy was simply not interested in these possible economic incentives. He was not an Economist and did not much care about Economics. Was it the classicist's traditional scorn for the dismal science? Or was it the minister's son's discomfort with its narrow-minded materialism? I do not know. As we shall see, he pays due respect to the concept of 'Enterprise Liability', which he attributes primarily (and not incorrectly) to Albert Ehrenzweig.[24] But one feels (and I can confirm this from conversations) that these citations are there because they help him marshal forces in favour of rules of tort law that will put losses on the best spreaders. Not until late in life does he come to think that enterprise liability can have a significant beneficent deterrent effect.

The most important thing to note in understanding Jimmy's view of torts is that he believed that tort law was only a half-way house on the way to a system of social insurance that would bring about full spreading. As he said specifically in his debate with Charles O Gregory about the merits of the common law rule barring contribution among joint tortfeasors (about which more later), 'Both of us [ie, Gregory and I] believe that a comprehensive scheme of social insurance for accidents is a better ultimate solution of the problem of civil liability … We divide only on the question of what to do in the meanwhile.'[25] Whether that system of social insurance would resemble Workers Compensation, something like what has come to be known as the New Zealand plan, or direct government insurance of a social security type, is something on which Jimmy displayed considerable uncertainty. (Was it memories of his grandfather?) But that it would come, he did not doubt. It was his view of what to do in the meantime that makes Fleming James's contributions to tort law so interesting: redefine tort rules so that, wherever possible, losses are placed on the best spreader, and do this both by *adhering* to anachronistic old rules that lead to this and by *supporting* any changes in rules that further spreading.

A more precise description of this strategy as applied to various doctrinal issues will follow. For now it is enough to end this section with Jimmy's own words describing the problem as he saw it and what should be done about it. In 'Accident Liability Reconsidered', Jimmy concluded:

> The accident problem of our mechanical age calls for two things: accident prevention and the compensation of the victims of accidents that *do* happen. As for that branch of the law which is concerned with civil damages or their equivalent, it is doubtful whether it contributes very much to accident prevention. But if it does, that contribution will not be diminished by further steps towards assurance of compensation and widespread distribution of the loss; indeed such changes – or at least some of them – may well further the cause of safety. The main job of accident law is, therefore, to promote the well-being of accident victims if this can be done without

[24] AA Ehrenzweig, *Negligence Without Fault: Trends Toward an Enterprise for Insurable Loss* (Berkeley, CA, University of California Press, 1951) (reprinted at (1966) 54 *California Law Review* 1422).

[25] James, 'Contribution Among Joint Tortfeasors: Replication' (n 5) 1178.

> imposing too great a social cost in other directions. It is the writer's conclusion that a system of social insurance can do this. The expressed doctrines of tort law are not well adapted to such an end. They are horse and buggy rules in an age of machinery; and they might well have gone to the scrap heap some time ago had not the tremendous growth of liability insurance and the progressive ingenuity of the companies made it possible to get some of the benefits of social insurance under – or perhaps in spite of – the legal rules. What we have as a result is only a partially satisfactory solution. Many who cause accidents are still financially irresponsible and not covered by insurance. Even where this is not the case, many needy victims are still barred because of the fault principle, and many others fail to get what they are legally entitled to under existing law, because of the weakness of their bargaining position. Even if the present system improves, it is not likely to be permanent, but rather to yield to a system of full social insurance with the government playing a role at least as important as that which it plays in workmen's compensation. The question of how long the present system will endure is likely to depend on how progressive and far-sighted the insurance companies are, and on the success of such legislative half-way measures as compulsory insurance, financial responsibility laws, and the like. While it does endure, no analysis or appraisal of tort problems or tort law in the accident field can be really helpful unless it takes full account of the fact and operation of liability insurance. The present article is simply intended to suggest ways in which this may be done.[26]

How Jimmy applied this vision to various areas of tort law and how he argued for his vision are what I must turn to next.

III. SPREADING APPLIED

Jimmy's devotion to the notion that modern tort law should view spreading of losses as its primary function can be seen, dramatically sometimes, in the positions he took both in furthering and in resisting changes in some, then current, tort doctrines, depending on whether they aided or hindered loss spreading. I shall discuss a few areas, with direct reference to his writings.

The first is Jimmy's seemingly bizarre and ultimately losing position on contribution among joint tortfeasors. The classic rule, logically akin to the rule of contributory negligence, was that whichever joint tortfeasor happened to be burdened by the plaintiff with a loss, that is where it stayed. There were, of course, some 'indemnity' exceptions to this rule, just as there were exceptions to placing the whole loss on a negligent plaintiff. But the principle was the same: if your negligence was in part responsible for your bearing a loss, you could not diminish your burden by shifting part of the loss to another negligent party who had also been a cause of the loss. Thus a contributorily negligent victim could not get 'contribution' from the negligent defendant who had harmed him, and

[26] James, 'Accident Liability Reconsidered: The Impact of Liability Insurance' (n 7) 569–70 (emphasis added) (footnote omitted).

a negligent joint tortfeasor could not get contribution – from the negligent, other tortfeasor – simply based on the fact that the other tortfeasor's actions were also a cause of the loss.

Both contributory negligence and the rule of no contribution came under significant attack and were pretty much abolished in the twentieth century. During the debates that presaged the changes, many treated the rules as logically similar and used the same arguments against both. A few argued for the abolition of the rule of no contribution among joint tortfeasors but for the retention of contributory negligence. Jimmy was one of very few pushing strongly for comparative negligence but, nonetheless, for retaining the rule of no contribution. Why?

Those who pushed for the abolition of the rule of no contribution while retaining contributory negligence based their argument on the notion that both rules had philosophical merit, but that the rule of no contribution gave rise to dangers of bribery and bad behaviour. Unlike the loss (in contributory negligence situations) that fell on the particular plaintiff by chance, the bearer of the undivided loss in the no-contribution situation was the result of a human decision. The plaintiff chose the defendant from whom to collect his joint judgment. This, the opponents of that rule argued, could lead to one defendant paying the plaintiff (under the table, so to speak) to get him to collect the damages from the other defendant. And this evil could readily be avoided by allowing contribution among defendants.

Jimmy based his argument for retention of the no-contribution rule while abolishing contributory negligence on the same factual difference between the two. But for him it cut the other way. He was always sceptical of 'fraud' arguments in torts. (He believed that there were many effective criminal sanctions that could control these. He also thought, as a result of his experience in practice, that juries were very good at discerning fraud.) What then, in practice, motivated a plaintiff to collect fully, or much more, from one defendant rather than from the other? It was because one defendant was insured, or large enough to self-insure, and collection from that defendant was much easier.

If that was so – and of course it was – what would be the effect of *allowing* contribution? It would be virtually none when both defendant parties were, in fact, insured. Repeat players, like insurance companies, could readily and cheaply deal with that situation by contracts providing for contribution if they wished. In such situations, the 'contribution' suit would only add administrative costs. Allowing contribution through a law suit would matter, though, if one defendant was insured (or large enough to be self-insured) and the other was not. But then the effect of contribution would be to place a significant part of the loss on a party who could not spread it, to re-concentrate a well-spread loss. And this, of course, was anathema to Jimmy. Contributory negligence ran exactly the other way. Quite apart from the fact that dividing is itself a form of spreading (this would apply to contribution among joint tortfeasors as well), it was the fact that liability insurance is far more frequent than accident insurance.

Unlike what would happen if the rule of no contribution were abolished, abolishing contributory negligence would, for this reason, have important pro-spreading consequences.

The logic of fault and symmetry among legal rules all favoured abolition of both.[27] And Jimmy's great friend, Gregory (who was the brother-in-law of Jimmy's former dean and friend, Judge Charles E Clark) thought that such logic should govern. He too believed that tort law should ultimately be replaced by some form of social insurance. But until it was, the logic of fault-based liability should govern.[28] To Jimmy, moving toward greater spreading came first, and no amount of symmetry or 'obsolete' fault logic should stand in the way. The elegant debate, an article by James,[29] a reply by Gregory,[30] a replication by James[31] and a rejoinder by Gregory[32] in the 1941 *Harvard Law Review*, is as good a start for understanding what Jimmy was about as there is.

Equally demonstrative of Jimmy's approach, and perhaps even more dramatic, was his position on the question of collateral damages. Here James attacked what plaintiffs defended. Today the so-called tort reformers (who in reality most often are simply representatives of injurer categories – just as the defenders of the 'justice' of the American tort system of the late twentieth century are most often simply plaintiffs' lawyers) also vehemently attack the collateral damage rule because of the possibility of double recovery that it affords plaintiffs. What led Jimmy, so often on the plaintiff's side, to oppose the rule and to look sceptically even on subrogation? The reason is obvious. Jimmy usually favoured plaintiffs because in most instances that would lead to greater spreading. The collateral damage rule, in his view, did not, and neither would subrogation.

Jimmy's discussion in 'Social Insurance and Tort Liability: The Problems of Alternative Remedies' details his position.[33] He begins by presenting the use of social insurance and its benefits: 'Such legislation is based on a faith that the general welfare is best served by protecting individuals from the consequences of pecuniary loss [from] … accident, old age, sickness, and unemployment'[34] through spreading of losses. He then notes the very different ways this can be done:

> The broadest possible scheme would largely disregard the source of loss and distribute its cost … by general taxation … The philosophy of workmen's compensation,

[27] CO Gregory, 'Contribution Among Joint Tortfeasors: A Defense' (1941) 54 *Harvard Law Review* 1170.

[28] CO Gregory, 'Rejoinder' (1941) 54 *Harvard Law Review* 1184.

[29] F James Jr, 'Contribution Among Joint Tortfeasors: A Pragmatic Criticism' (1941) 54 *Harvard Law Review* 1156.

[30] Gregory, 'Contribution Among Joint Tortfeasors: A Defense' (n 27).

[31] James, 'Contribution Among Joint Tortfeasors: Replication' (n 5).

[32] Gregory, 'Rejoinder' (n 28).

[33] F James Jr, 'Social Insurance and Tort Liability: The Problem of Alternative Remedies' (1952) 27 *New York University Law Review* 537.

[34] ibid (footnote omitted).

> on the other hand, is that losses should be allocated to the enterprise that … causes the losses, and ultimately distributed among those who consume its products. Under such a system there is room for private insurance [by the enterprise] … Still a third type of scheme seeks to distribute its costs [through] … voluntary accident or health insurance …[35]

Significantly, Jimmy does not suggest any preference among these. He then notes that tort law has gone from a system in which 'there was no machinery for, nor any thought of, widely distributing losses'[36] to one in which 'something of the philosophy of social insurance has crept'[37] in. What should happen, he asks, when these different approaches 'overlap and so present problems of cumulative or alternative remedies'?[38] In other words, he puts the problem of collateral damages in its broadest possible context, that of overlapping forms of social insurance, that is, of overlapping ways to spread losses.

James says the possibilities are four: (1) 'abolishing one (or more) of the remedies'; (2) 'compelling claimant to elect one'; (3) 'allowing the claimant to have the cumulative benefits of two (or more) remedies'; and (4) 'allowing the claimant to pursue both (or all) remedies but limiting his total recovery to the maximum amount he could recover from a single source'.[39] After suggesting that abolition of all but one might well be desirable, he notes that 'general abolition of the tort remedy, as an across-the-board solution of our present problem, is most unlikely'.[40] He points to the fact that neither England under Atlee, nor Communist Russia nor Saskatchewan have done without torts despite broad social insurance. And he adds that it is 'probably just as well … not so much because it is needed as a deterrent to carelessness, for … that … has been greatly overemphasized', but, and this is typical James, 'because we may find we don't want to rip any more of the threads of individualism out of our social and economic fabric than we must in order to take adequate care of the basic human needs of all our people'.[41]

In other words, the conservative in Jimmy comes out. Do not make radical change. Head in the direction of widespread spreading, of social insurance. But, because full social insurance will not happen, since abolition of torts is most unlikely and because such rapid change may well do other, not clearly defined harms, work within the system. Bend its rules so that it achieves the goal, without hastily destroying any parts of it! And the goal – always the goal – is to achieve wide distribution of losses, or, as he puts it, taking 'adequate care of … basic human needs'.[42] Once the problem is stated that way, it is easy to see

[35] ibid 537–39 (footnote omitted).
[36] ibid 540.
[37] ibid.
[38] ibid (footnote omitted).
[39] ibid 541.
[40] ibid 542.
[41] ibid.
[42] ibid.

why Jimmy's solution is to limit the claimant's total recovery to the maximum amount that any one of the alternative systems would give him.

If the object is spreading the loss, allowing double recovery does nothing to further such spreading. It puts the excess loss on the defendant, who may be a better spreader than the plaintiff in general, but who is not a better spreader than a plaintiff in this situation. Such a plaintiff, whether through private or public insurance or tort recovery, has had his basic loss borne by an excellent spreader. And however good a spreader the defendant may be, placing that loss on him either does nothing (if he is also insured) or leaves some concentrated loss on him (if he is not). He may be able to spread that loss pretty well, but not as well as if it had not been so allocated.

This not only applies to a plaintiff's 'double recovery', but also counsels against subrogation. In subrogation cases, the plaintiff has been compensated in a way that has spread the loss. The plaintiff's insurance company or the government – both superb – have borne part of the loss; the defendant has borne whatever the plaintiff's insurer or the government has not. What is to be gained (in terms of *spreading*) by having the insurer or the government shift this burden to the defendant? Nothing. If the defendant is insured, no harm occurs but no spreading benefit occurs either, and unnecessary administrative costs are borne. If the defendant is not insured then a widely spread loss is to some extent re-concentrated by being placed on the defendant, who may be a better spreader than the plaintiff but not than the plaintiff's insurer or the government.

Notice that Jimmy's conclusion would not hold were Jimmy concerned with wealth distribution, with shifting burdens from the poor to the rich. The defendant might well be wealthier than those who bore the cost of the plaintiff's insurance or who, through general or other taxes, paid for the governmental pay outs. But, as I suggested earlier, while Jimmy politically certainly favoured wealth redistribution, it was not *deep pocket* but *spreading capacity* that motivated his rebuilding mission in torts.

Notice also, and this is most important, that other possible reasons for wanting to put the burden of this accident on the defendant category are of no real concern to James. The notion that this defendant should bear the loss because he had done wrong, and should not benefit merely because the plaintiff he injured had chosen to pay for private insurance or to work for a company that paid him less but helped cover his injuries, is of no real significance to Jimmy. (In other words, he is not interested in making the plaintiff, who paid for private insurance, 'whole'.) And he is equally uninterested in the notion that such a faulty party should not bear less loss merely because the government has chosen to alleviate the suffering of its injured citizens.

This is not surprising in view of Jimmy's aforementioned discounting of fault as a moral basis of liability (given the generality of insurance), or (for the same reason and more) of fault-based liability as a significant deterrent of accidents. What needs underscoring, though, is that Jimmy's position here also means a rejection of the importance of placing a loss on the defendant *category*, where it was placed, perhaps, because that category was the best avoider of accidents or the best 'chooser' between safety and accident costs. If the decision to hold defendants liable was made because the defendant category was 'the cheapest cost avoider' (whatever that means), then the abolition of the collateral rule and of subrogation means that some of the pressure to decide what safety is worth having has been removed from the party society had decided was best suited to bear that pressure. In Jimmy's 'Social Insurance and Tort Liability' – in the context of subrogation – there is just a hint of this possible concern. But it is quickly discarded.

In 1952, then, Jimmy might cite Ehrenzweig and use his term 'Enterprise Liability'. He might even, in passing, mention that worker's compensation had been supported by some who had argued that the cost of accidents, like the cost of the materials used in production, should be on the producer. But one cannot avoid the conclusion that he neither knew nor much cared about what those terms and arguments meant. If they led to the assignment of costs to those who were better spreaders of basic needs, he would happily cite the arguments. But if they led in the opposite direction, the goal of spreading always dominated.

I do not have time, nor is it necessary, to go into as much detail with respect to other positions that Jimmy had that were distinctly pro-spreading. Unlike the previous two, the reason for these positions are obvious and can be discerned even from a brief mention. After an important article in the *Tulane Law Review* in 1954 in which Jimmy describes, defines and discretely urges the expansion of vicarious liability, because of its spreading benefits,[43] Jimmy wrote a brief piece in the *University of Florida Law Review* excoriating 'imputed negligence' and arguing against the seductive, but to him wrong-headed, symmetry of the 'both ways test'.[44] That test would make assignment of liability based on the negligence of another depend on the existence of the same relationship between the negligent party and the innocent party, whether the other's negligence is imputed or made the basis of vicarious liability. The beneficent spreading effects of making innocent insured car owners vicariously liable for injuries caused even by non-agent drivers are obvious. Imputing the contributory negligence of such drivers to the innocent car owners serves no similar purpose. Nuff said!

Any number of articles supporting moves toward strict defendant liability in various areas of torts could also be cited.[45] As could articles urging the abolition

[43] F James Jr, 'Vicarious Liability' (1954) 28 *Tulane Law Review* 161.

[44] F James Jr, 'Imputed Negligence and Vicarious Liability: The Study of a Paradox' (1957) 10 *University of Florida Law Review* 48.

[45] The failure of the Columbia (and to some extent Yale) attempt of 1929 to bring about third-party non-fault liability for automobile accidents is decried by James, as is the lack of spreading the cost of auto accident injuries that persisted as a result. F James Jrand SC Law, 'Compensation for Auto Accident Victims: A Story of Too Little Too Late' (1952) 26 *Connecticut Business Journal* 70. One wonders whether this had an effect on the development, by Jimmy's friend, Bob Keeton, of the Keeton-O'Connell first-party, non-fault plan, not long after: RE Keeton and J O'Connell, *Basic Protection for the Traffic Victim* (Boston, MA, Little, Brown and Co, 1965).

of defendant immunities or of other rules that kept juries from deciding whether to impose liability. In all these situations, procedural rules and burdens of proof are examined; always with the goal of furthering greater likelihood that defendants would be held liable, because defendants were (Jimmy believed) by and large better spreaders.

This belief, and hence his advocacy of standards and rules that gave rise to greater likelihood of defendant liability, is open and explicit, as is his advocacy of greater access to juries, with repeated citations to a student piece by the then still unknown Richard M Nixon, who discussed in legal realistic terms the choice between judge and jury decisions regarding breach of duty, emphasising the relative biases of the different decision makers. Nixon, for that reason, argued for more judge-made decisions; Jimmy, on the same basis, urged more jury ones. (The article was an excellent one in its time; it remains in the Shulman and James casebook at my insistence and gives rise – after the students are surprised to learn that the author named Nixon is the former President – to a short sermon on the difference between brains and character.) In his discussion of all of these issues, Jimmy's mastery of procedure, and of the practical effect of different procedural rules, is manifest. And it is always employed to further spreading, to make tort law more into a form of social insurance while retaining its basic structure. The goal is the same, and is never hidden as various procedural and burden assignment devices are marshalled in its favour.

More interesting to me, though, is James's article written later, but in the same vein, on additurs and remittiturs.[46] For here, Jimmy, the frequent plaintiff's advocate, is anything but 'simply' that. He argues that courts should have and should use the power to grant additurs, in effect to be able to put pressure to increase damage verdicts, in cases where juries, for whatever reason, gave inadequate recoveries. But he also strongly supports the use of judicially ordered remittiturs to bring excessive verdicts into line. Once again, it can be seen that Jimmy is not for plaintiffs per se or because they often are poorer than defendants. He favours their recoveries when this leads to a greater spreading of basic losses. Excess damages, given because juries took a 'scunner' to some hapless or nasty defendant, do not do this. And to Jimmy that is reason enough for judicial intervention.[47] Additurs are harder to accomplish, but Jimmy tries to make them easier. When juries, for whatever reason, have failed to bring about the desired spreading (social insurance) result, courts should do what they can to make it happen.

[46] F James Jr, 'Remedies for Excessiveness or Inadequacy of Verdicts: New Trial on Some or All Issues, Remittitur and Additur' (1963) 1 *Duquesne University Law Review* 143.

[47] As John Goldberg points out, in his excellent article, discussing James's influence on Judge Jack B Weinstein, the same desire to avoid recoveries that go beyond the spreading of basic needs, broadly defined, explains James's support (picked up by Judge Weinstein) of relatively low recovery settlements in mass tort cases: see Goldberg, 'Misconduct, Misfortune and Just Compensation: Weinstein on Torts' (n 16).

IV. SELLING SPREADING

But how and why did this single-minded vision of what tort law was about make James so important an American twentieth-century legal scholar? It was due to the effectiveness and scholarliness of his advocacy. The openness and honesty of what he was trying to achieve, combined with his capacity for marshalling and analysing cases and materials, and his respect for opponents made him formidable. He was, in other words, a terrific *lawyer* and used his lawyerly skills to great advantage. There is not time to demonstrate all this in detail. A short description and citation of a few articles will suffice. For those who want more, I suggest a close examination of the Harper and James 'encyclopedia' of torts.[48]

But let me begin. Fleming James's skill at translating his view of what he thought torts law should become into what torts law, to a fair extent, actually came to be is best seen by reading a series of articles he wrote in the early 1950s. There were many: I shall only talk about some of them.

In one of the first of these, 'Proof of the Breach in Negligence Cases (including Res Ipsa Loquitur)',[49] James seeks to demonstrate, and further, the trend of sending more cases to the jury. There were various reasons for the trend. To him, however, this was desirable primarily because he thought the jury both saw through fraudulent claims and, in cases of serious injury, was sympathetic to placing the burden on parties who were insured or could otherwise spread well.

He is quite open about this. Thus, in discussing *res ipsa* he says 'the persistence and expansion of the "doctrine" – in spite of trenchant and penetrating logical criticism – may well be attributable to the strong general trend towards strict liability and social insurance – a trend which is corroding a system of liability nominally based on fault'.[50] In an accompanying footnote[51] he takes that view back to Smith's famous 1914 article on the significance of Workers Compensation,[52] and then cites his own works for the desirability of this, and Nixon(!) on why juries would foster it.

His technique seems remarkably neutral, while in fact being powerfully advocative. Thus, in a preceding footnote, after listing case after case that expands the doctrine because of 'the trend toward stricter liability',[53] he makes the following, seemingly obvious empirical remark:

> Within the confines of common law negligence courts may infer negligence and impose liability more frequently because, as complicated manufactured articles

[48] Harper and James, *The Law of Torts* (n 2).

[49] F James Jr, 'Proof of the Breach in Negligence Cases (Including Res Ipsa Loquitur)' (1951) 37 *Virginia Law Review* 179.

[50] ibid 198–99 (footnotes omitted).

[51] ibid 199.

[52] J Smith, 'Sequel to Workmen's Compensation Acts' (1914) 27 *Harvard Law Review* 235.

[53] James, 'Proof of the Breach in Negligence Cases (Including Res Ipsa Loquitur)' (n 49) 199 n 59.

> achieve greater perfection, it becomes increasingly probable that an otherwise unexplained mishap is attributable to negligence on the part of the manufacturer or the person in control at the time.[54]

That statement, a mild enough reflection of 'facts', together with the previous one about the growth of strict liability amount to a strong argument as to why, in the world of the 1950s, courts should, in almost all cases, either find against the party who is, in fact, the best spreader, or let the jury do so. And, even more effective, the combination of the two constitutes a statement that that *is* the way the law is, the way recent past cases *should be read* to be.

The article, as a whole, does the same with respect to burdens of proof generally. It begins with a lucid and neutral discussion of the different meanings of the term 'burden of proof', and with the statement that 'The plaintiff has the burden of proving each of the essential elements of a cause of action for negligence.'[55] But then case after case and circumstance after circumstance is given a *plausible* (and that is crucial) reading in the direction that lessens the practical impact of that burden. In doing this he regularly marshals his knowledge of procedure and how it works to further his preferred reading.

The second article, on 'Assumption of Risk', begins by separating out the doctrine's 'secondary sense' as nothing more than 'a form of contributory negligence' and excluding it from a serious discussion of the term.[56] The article then gives the classic, unexceptional definition of assumption of risk in its 'primary sense', of '*volenti non fit injuria*'. But the bulk of the piece is, in fact, a very effective analysis designed to convince the reader that many, many cases in which the doctrine was applied in the past simply do not make sense 'now', if one takes the doctrine's alleged requirements of knowledge and voluntariness of choice seriously. The object, clearly, is to try to get rid of an awful lot of very unpleasant nineteenth- and early twentieth-century precedents, and thereby limit a doctrine that frequently put losses on a very poor spreader indeed.

This works to some extent, but nowhere near well enough for James. And this may explain his later, losing fight to have the *Restatement (Second) of the Law of Torts* get rid of assumption of risk as a separate defence. This attempt is well described in a 1968 article (one of his last substantive torts articles), 'Assumption of Risk: Unhappy Reincarnation'.[57] It is not that Jimmy did not recognise some sense to the doctrine. Even in spreading terms there surely are situations in which the plaintiff, because he understands the risks that he is truly choosing to take, may be the one who has most likely covered those risks by insurance. But most of the old cases, as Jimmy demonstrated, do not really describe those 'plaintiff–best bearer' situations. How, then, to get rid of these precedents? Jimmy's solution was to eliminate the doctrine as a separate defence and make

[54] ibid.
[55] ibid 179.
[56] F James Jr, 'Assumption of Risk' (1952) 61 *Yale Law Journal* 141.
[57] F James Jr, 'Assumption of Risk: Unhappy Reincarnation' (1968) 78 *Yale Law Journal* 185.

the concepts behind it part of what defines a defendant's duty. In urging this[58] he relies on his reading of a 1910 article by Francis H Bohlen, 'Voluntary Assumption of Risk'.[59] But I think his object is simpler: assumption of risk carries with it a truck full of bad precedents; there is something to the notion of assumption of risk, but we should start with as clean a slate as possible.

His attempt failed (even his friend Robert Keeton was on the other side). And the *Restatement (Second)* retained assumption of risk as a separate defence.[60] I, myself, believe it was good that it failed, because whether one is concerned with assigning liability to the best decision maker for the reasons associated with my category deterrence analysis, or for reasons grounded in burdening the best spreader, the *language* of assumption of risk, which focuses on the plaintiff and his knowledge and capacity to choose, is better suited to the task than James's proposed 'no duty' rules. Duty questions linguistically focus more on defendants, and hence get somewhat in the way of examining what the plaintiff is capable of doing. But if one is as determined as Jimmy was to put losses on the best spreader, then the elimination of the traditional defence with all its unfortunate luggage may well have seemed more important to him than those 'linguistic' (are they really just that?) niceties.

Other articles, discussing different areas of tort law and reading the cases to move their meanings in the direction James wanted, followed in quick succession in the 1950s. In 1953, 'Scope of Duty in Negligence Cases' analyses duty.[61] It begins as always with a straight traditional definition and then goes on to read the definition and the cases, plausibly, as James would have them read, to further greater defendant liability, and hence greater spreading. 'Vicarious Liability',[62] in 1954, and 'Products Liability', in 1955,[63] together with 'General Products: Should Manufacturers be Liable without Negligence?',[64] do the same for those two fundamental areas of tort law. Characteristically, they always do it in the same way: honesty in what the object is; a traditional start and definitions; and a lawyerly reading of the definitions and cases to demonstrate a strong trend toward results that further spreading, and hence bring about James's desideratum of tort law as a – middle way – form of social insurance.

Much of this, of course, becomes effective through his successful role in the American Law Institute (ALI) and the making of the *Restatement (Second)*. Though I am a longtime member of the ALI, I have never been active and know little of its politics now, let alone then. So I cannot say how Jimmy used his lawyerly skills, made allies with those who, perhaps for other reasons, wanted

[58] ibid.

[59] FH Bohlen, 'Voluntary Assumption of Risk' (1906) 20 *Harvard Law Review* 14.

[60] James, 'Assumption of Risk: Unhappy Reincarnation' (n 57) 188.

[61] F James Jr, 'Scope of Duty in Negligence Cases' (1953) 47 *Northwestern University Law Review* 778.

[62] James, 'Vicarious Liability' (n 43).

[63] F James Jr, 'Products Liability' (1955) 34 *Texas Law Review* 44.

[64] F James Jr, 'General Products – Should Manufacturers Be Liable Without Negligence?' (1957) 24 *Tennessee Law Review* 923.

the law to move the same way and brought about a *Restatement* that certainly furthered his goals. That *Restatement* – unlike the most recent one on products liability, which, at least for the moment, has been properly rejected by several important states[65] – became a self-fulfilling prophecy. James's reading of the cases often became how the *Restatement* described the law to be or to be trending towards, and in time it became what the law actually was.

Torts never came fully to be the social insurance system, achieved indirectly and locally, that James wished it to be. But it certainly got much closer to that goal by the time James died, in 1981, than it had been when he started writing.

V. ECONOMICS, TORTS AND SPREADING

Fleming James did not write many substantive tort law articles after the 1950s. He wrote wonderful appreciations of his torts friends – Chief Justice Traynor,[66] Dean Leon Green,[67] Fowler Harper[68] – as well as of his non-torts mentors – the great Arthur Corbin,[69] JW Moore[70] and Wesley Sturges.[71] He wrote about particular problems associated with the coming of comparative negligence.[72] He also wrote about legal education issues, law school history[73] and the role of torts in the curriculum.[74] And he, of course, kept his great tort encyclopedia up to date. But his creative work in the field was by and large done.

This did not mean, however, that he stopped thinking deeply and well about it. Here the story becomes somewhat personal, and a slight detour is needed to put matters in context. The Shulman and James textbook from which Jimmy taught torts and from which I first learned the subject, asks any number of questions that can best be described as 'law and economic' ones.[75] How could that be, given that James, the classicist, did not give a hoot about economics and Shulman, his co-author, though perhaps more sympathetic to the field, was no more knowledgeable? The answer lies in the casebook's origins. The ancestor

[65] See, eg, *Bifolck v Philip Morris, Inc* 152 A3d 1183, 1201 (Conn 2016) (declining to adopt the *Restatement (Third)* and describing how California, Hawaii, Kansas, New Mexico, Pennsylvania and Florida have taken similar positions). New York has also declined to follow the *Restatement*.

[66] F James Jr, 'A Tribute to the Imaginative Creativity of Roger Traynor' (1974) 2 *Hofstra Law Review* 445.

[67] F James Jr, 'To Leon Green' (1978) 56 *Texas Law Review* 535.

[68] F James Jr, 'Fowler Vincent Harper' (1965) 74 *Yale Law Journal* 604.

[69] F James Jr, 'Arthur L Corbin' (1967) 76 *Yale Law Journal* 884.

[70] F James Jr, 'In Honor of James William Moore: Forward' (1974) 83 *Yale Law Journal* 880.

[71] F James Jr, 'In Memoriam' (1963) 72 *Yale Law Journal* 642.

[72] F James Jr, 'Connecticut's Comparative Negligence Statute: An Analysis of Some Problems' (1974) 6 *Connecticut Law Review* 207.

[73] F James Jr, 'The Law School: From Hutchins to Rostow' (1960) 6 *Yale Law Report* 1; F James Jr et al, 'Current Issues in Legal Education (A Survey)' (1960) 9 *Cleveland-Marshall Law Review* 582.

[74] F James Jr, 'The Torts Curriculum: An Overview' (1973) 42 *University of Cincinnati Law Review* 435.

[75] H Shulman and F James Jr, *Law of Torts: Cases and Materials*, 1st edn (New York, Foundation Press, 1942).

of the book was a set of materials put together by Walton Hamilton and Harry Shulman. Hamilton was an institutional economist, much like the young Ronald Coase had been. And like the then Coase, he was ideologically of the left, and out of favour with classical economists. The Yale Law School, devoted to legal realism and the social sciences, made him a professor. And one of the early things Hamilton did at Yale was to put together, with Shulman, materials for a 'modern' torts course. He then turned away (from torts to anti-trust law) and left the torts materials to be refined and used by Shulman and his young colleague James. By the time I came to the Law School in 1955, Hamilton was long gone and his role in the creation of the materials essentially forgotten. But it remained in the book's structure and in the questions it posed.

Having been very well trained in economics in Yale College and at Oxford, I responded to all those hidden cues. And that was, I am sure, the source of my role in the beginning of the law and economics movement, which people date from the start of 1961, when Ronald Coase's great article[76] and my first piece appeared independently and contemporaneously.[77] But what was all that to James, who still had the classicist's disdain for economics?

I believe that what struck him immediately about what I said in his class and in the paper I wrote in 1956 (which derived from his class, and which soon after I joined the faculty in 1959 became my 1961 article) was my emphasis on general or category deterrence. It was not any claims of economic efficiency, whatever that might be, that really interested him. But the notion that tort law might, after all, have an important deterrent effect, often *precisely because* of the existence of insurance, was one that he understood and liked. It explained, in a way that had been too vague for him earlier, the 'enterprise liability' positions that he had cited when they seemed to support spreading. It gave him a theoretical basis for the safety improvements that he had said insurance companies seemed to bring about. And, most important, it often was consistent with losses being put on really good spreaders. It might, in other words, lead to a torts-based social insurance system that was consistent with 'free enterprise' and in which government played a role, but only a limited one.

He refers to all this in two of three, short but significant articles from the middle of the 1960s. Thus, in his 1966 *California Law Review* article, he says that coverage of such risks 'by the victim's own accident or health insurance, or by the state',[78] though plausible, is unrealistic. He cites Ehrenzweig for the proposition that self-insurance is unlikely.[79] And, he adds, 'As for state insurance against such risks, a good case can indeed be made for it, yet it has its disadvantages.'[80]

[76] RH Coase, 'The Problem of Social Cost' (1960) 3 *Journal of Law and Economics* 1.

[77] G Calabresi, 'Some Thoughts on Risk Distributions and the Law of Torts' (1961) 70 *Yale Law Journal* 499.

[78] F James Jr, 'The Untoward Effects of Cigarettes and Drugs: Some Reflections on Enterprise Liability' (1966) 54 *California Law Review* 1550, 1556.

[79] ibid.

[80] ibid (footnote omitted).

Then, in the accompanying footnote he writes '[f]or example, the approach of enterprise liability, in contrast to that of state insurance, would preserve more of the values of the free enterprise system', and cites a 1965 article by me.[81]

But this did not mean that he bought this because it served some high theoretical economic goal. Thus, in an earlier note in the same piece, after citing Ehrenzweig and his enterprise liability arguments for placing pharmaceutical and cigarette costs on the producers, he says '[i]mplicit in this line of reasoning may be another which suggests a similar result'.[82] He then cites my 1961 article, 'Some Thoughts on Risk Distribution and the Law of Torts', as well as the more recently published 1965 article I mentioned above.

He says those articles suggest that the 'optimum allocation of resources in a free enterprise system requires each enterprise to pay its own accident costs'.[83] But he then goes on to express his scepticism of economic theory's giving a truly helpful answer. Relying on Blum and Kalven's first article in what at the time became a celebrated debate with me,[84] he suggests that 'the economist [may] indeed contribute little or nothing useful to the solution'[85] of the question of whether the cost is one of the producer or of the consumer. Nevertheless, he goes on to conclude for very practical, empirical reasons that losses left on consumers are much less likely to bring about the desired *category deterrent effect* than if the losses were put on the producer. And he asserts that 'surely little quarrel can be had with a political or judicial judgment which attributes to the maker's enterprise the cost of unreasonable dangers which inhere in his product'.[86]

All this is stated more fully and centrally in his remarkable 1965 *Tennessee Law Review* article, 'An Evaluation of the Fault Concept'.[87] This article can truly be said to reflect James's views at the end of his scholarship, and I would urge those who would like to understand him to read it if no other.

He begins by acknowledging that recent 'economic analysis … has caused [him] to do a good deal of thinking about the [the fault concept] and … justifies a review of it here'.[88] He then characteristically gives an elegant description, and in a way defence, of fault-based liability as it was when it first developed. Next, he points out its undermining over time, and concludes by emphasising the fundamental change brought about by insurance:

> The real defendants today – the persons who actually foot the bill for liability – are rarely the active participants in an accident who were guilty of whatever fault

[81] ibid, fn 27.

[82] ibid 1551, fn 6.

[83] ibid.

[84] WJ Blum and H Kalven Jr, 'Public Law Perspectives on a Private Law Problem – Auto Compensation Plans' (1964) 31 *University of Chicago Law Review* 641, 723.

[85] James, 'The Untoward Effects of Cigarettes and Drugs: Some Reflections on Enterprise Liability' (n 78) 1151, fn 6.

[86] ibid.

[87] F James Jr, 'An Evaluation of the Fault Concept' (1965) 32 *Tennessee Law Review* 394.

[88] ibid.

> there was. Rather, the brunt of liability today is borne, in the first instance, by innocent absentees – employers and liability insurance companies. And if distribution of losses occurs after that, the aliquot parts of this burden, like the gentle rain from heaven and the quality of mercy, fall indifferently on the just and the unjust.
>
> … No longer is the law limited to the stark and simple alternatives of either letting a loss lie where it fell, or shifting it entirely to the one who caused it. Liability insurance and large scale production provide means for the wide distribution of losses, thereby minimizing their disutility according to insurance principles.[89]

Thus far Jimmy James of the 1950s. But he goes on and cites a new reason why 'the fault system can no longer be justified':

> This point of view, which may be called enterprise liability, is most simply stated by the proposition that an activity like motoring should pay for the accident loss it causes because, as a general proposition, each enterprise in our society should pay its own way.[90]

He notes Keeton and O'Connell's adoption of this viewpoint[91] and then goes into an extended discussion of my early writings, saying that he believes they 'may go to the root of the matter … and it is worth anyone's while to read what (Calabresi) has written on the matter'.[92]

But after this description of my position in economic terms, he focuses ultimately on category deterrence:

> If a system which compelled motoring to pay its own way should increase the cost of motoring, this might well result in fewer cars and fewer miles driven. And this, in turn, would tend to reduce the number of motor accidents. This is what Calabresi calls 'general deterrence' as distinguished from the specific deterrence of faulty driving behavior.[93]

Significantly, his scepticism of economics as *the* answer remains. He makes a bow to what is now called the symmetry of causation – '[i]f you remove the pedestrian you will just as surely prevent [a car–pedestrian] accident as if you remove the motorist'[94] – but then says '[w]hatever the economist may think of the matter, I suggest that it is equitable to consider'[95] the risk as one-sided and one that should be on driving. And, characteristically, he finds the answers to

[89] ibid 398–99.

[90] ibid 399–400.

[91] The third 1960s article, F James Jr, 'The Future of Negligence in Accident Law' (1967) 53 *Virginia Law Review* 911, focuses on the Keeton and O'Connell proposals, in RE Keeton and J O'Connell, *Basic Protection for the Traffic Victim* (Boston, MA, Little, Brown and Co, 1965), and concludes, desirable though they may be, they, like general social insurance, will not fully replace ordinary tort law.

[92] James, 'An Evaluation of the Fault Concept' (n 87) 400.

[93] ibid 400–01.

[94] ibid 402.

[95] ibid.

the question of whether the pedestrian–auto accident is a cost of driving or of walking by returning to insurance and how in practice it works:

> Pedestrians as well as motorists could of course insure against losses from auto-pedestrian accidents. In this case the protection would take the form of accident insurance rather than liability insurance. If now such insurance were compulsory or widely held and if it covered only the type of risk here involved then the premiums would roughly reflect the accident cost which is allocated by the present system to the activity of walking, and pedestrians would have brought home to them the extent of this cost. If it should be found excessive this would presumably be reflected in a reduction in the amount of walking and consequently in the number of auto-pedestrian accidents. But no such thing is likely in fact to occur.[96]

Allocating the cost of auto–pedestrian accidents to pedestrians will not, therefore, be likely to reduce such accidents by the kind of general deterrence that would result from allocating these costs to motoring. Pedestrians do not constitute an 'actuarial class' for which we can 'evaluate the risk of such costs in the future'; and the allocation of these accidents costs to them rather than to motorists has additional disadvantages. Since pedestrians are far less likely to be insured than motorists, there would be much less chance that victims of such accidents would receive compensation, or that these accident losses would be put into the channels for widely distributing them.

For these varied reasons, allocation of the cost of motor vehicle accidents to motorists seems to give promise of being the most feasible and just solution of one of our major unsolved problems.[97]

In other words, when one takes spreading, as well as my category deterrence, into account, the symmetry of causation problem is solved and the solution leads to no-fault allocation of motor vehicle costs to motorists!

Jimmy and I talked about all this at the time he was writing his mid-1960 articles. And I know that it was not the desire to achieve some undefined and probably impossible economic optimum that moved him. It was the realisation that costs put on the enterprise, on the driver or on their insurance companies were much more likely to lead to a reduction of undesired harms than costs left on consumers or pedestrians: '[W]here "the loss is left with the consumers" a very few individuals among them bear the whole loss, each of his own injury. And it seems doubtful indeed that users as a class … will be as likely to evaluate the risk (or cost) as accurately as if each were charged his aliquot share',[98] as would happen if the cost was placed on producers or insurance companies.

[96] ibid 403.

[97] ibid.

[98] James, 'The Untoward Effects of Cigarettes and Drugs: Some Reflections on Enterprise Liability' (n 78) 1551, fn 6.

This is, of course, straight category deterrence analysis. And the fact that it so often coincided with placing the costs on a very good spreader – perhaps not the *best* spreader (the state) but still a very good one – brought Jimmy great joy. The role of torts as a middle ground 'social insurance' system, which involved the state but only to a limited extent, was vindicated. And James, the social democrat who had some deep-seated worries about possible state abuse, could not be more pleased.

He showed his pleasure with me in many ways, some of which are relevant to this chapter. In 1965, when he was writing these articles and in them adding category deterrence to his spreading rationale, he gave me, on Fowler Harper's death, Harper's original first edition copy of their joint tort encyclopedia. Harper had left it to James and James passed it on to me. He inscribed it as follows: 'With that special affection a teacher has for a student who has pushed the quest further'. In other words, 'thanks youngster for adding category deterrence as a reason why together with the achieving of spreading, torts, with liability properly placed on the insured or self-insured party, turns out to be a pretty good social insurance system in a predominantly free enterprise society'.

He also made sure that I got to know and became close to Jan Hellner, his good friend and the dominant Swedish private law professor. Hellner was a great scholar and a lovely person. But the point of getting us together was not merely the joining of friends. Hellner was working out Scandinavian approaches to accident liability. He was concerned with the same social insurance – spreading – issues that were at the core of James's thought. But he also worried about how to achieve deterrence in countries that – though socialist – were not totally command oriented. James thought I might be of help to Hellner. But, even more important, he believed Hellner might be useful to me in applying my ideas to societies (perhaps Jimmy thought of a future, less free-enterprise America) where 'liberal' social democracy was taking hold.

VI. CRITICISM AND INFLUENCE

Before concluding, a few words of criticism are, I think, appropriate, as are some words to recognise explicitly Jimmy's profound influence on members of the next generation who themselves became central to the development of modern tort Law.

A. Criticism

First the criticism. What always puzzled me about Jimmy's early but persistent view that spreading of losses was the basic goal of tort law, and that deterrence of accidents could be comfortably left to criminal law, was his seeming failure to recognise how many horribly unspread burdens criminal law imposes on those subjected to its penalties. Jimmy the railroad lawyer had seen the dire effect of catastrophic accidents on accident victims. Jimmy the labour and consumer advocate could sympathise with unions and the poor worker. But in his reliance on criminal law to deter accidents, Jimmy seems almost oblivious to the dangers of police stereotyping, and to the catastrophic effects that criminal prohibitions can have, and will have, if penal sanctions are treated as the principal means of accident prevention. Perhaps some recognition of these effects underlay Jimmy's happy acceptance of my category deterrence analysis. Category deterrence, after all, permits the combining of non-penal financial incentives permitting safety with the broad spreading of the economic costs of accidents. But if that explained in part his favourable response to my work, he never said so.

No, I fear that the dangers of penal sanctions were simply something James did not focus on. And that lack remains a problem with his basic approach. Deterrence of needless accidents is an important aim of torts law. And finding a way of deterring that does not crush individuals – that spreads the burden – is a crucial component of the field. As such, Jimmy's too ready reliance on penal sanctions for the deterrence side is properly criticised.

B. Influence, Generally

As to Jimmy's influence on individuals who have played a significant role in the development of torts in the generation after his, I shall briefly mention two, and then discuss at greater length his influence on me. Those I first mention are meant just to be representative.

John Goldberg, some 20 years ago, wrote a splendid article describing in elegant detail James's influence on Judge Jack Weinstein, who was then and remains today – in his high nineties – perhaps the pre-eminent Federal District Judge in America.[99] To anyone acquainted with the American judiciary to show, as Goldberg does, that 'Judge Weinstein's work on mass torts is best understood as part of [the] approach to torts, developed by James'[100] is to demonstrate, beyond peradventure, James's significance.

If James's influence on Judge Weinstein is representative of his importance to the judiciary, James's influence on Jeff O'Connell is symbolic of his significance to the American academic world. I cannot overstate the number of times that Jeff told me how important to his thought and work James was. The essence

[99] Goldberg, 'Misconduct, Misfortune and Just Compensation: Weinstein on Torts' (n 16).
[100] ibid 2044, fn 39.

of O'Connell's many reform proposals was always: speedy and administratively efficient payments that covered the basic needs of accident victims and in that way spread accident losses.[101] All this is straight James.[102]

C. Influence, Calabresi

Jimmy's influence on me, and through me on those whose thinking about torts I may have affected, is manifest. Most obvious is the importance in my writings of what I called 'secondary cost avoidance' (reducing the costs that inhere in unspread losses). This is, of course, the part of my work that is most difficult for those attached to classical economic theory to accept. (Here one may usefully contrast Patrick Atiyah's review of my book, *The Cost of Accidents*,[103] praising that part,[104] with Richard Posner's review, totally puzzled by it.[105])

The same point is made expressly by George Priest in his article, 'The Rise of Law and Economics',[106] and even more in his forthcoming book on the same topic. In his article he writes:

> Having at Guido's urging, read Fleming James, I appreciate his point entirely that it is impossible otherwise to understand Guido's contribution to Legal Scholarship … Guido's, *The Costs of Accidents* … represents an acceptance of James's conclusions, with the most persuasive economic analysis justifying them.[107]

Priest then goes on to suggest that he believes this emphasis on secondary cost avoidance is understandable but wrongheaded. (I believe that classical economists are wrong and that economic theory can and should take secondary costs into account, but that is neither here nor there.) In any event, my emphasis on secondary costs is surely straight Fleming James. To him, they were the be-all and end-all of Accident Law; to me they are only one crucial part, but Jimmy's influence cannot be doubted.

[101] See, eg, J O'Connell and C Robinette, *A Recipe for Balanced Tort Reform: Early Offers with Swift Settlements* (Durham, NC, Carolina Academic Press, 2008); J O'Connell, *Ending Insult to Injury: No Fault Insurance for Products and Services* (Chicago, IL, University of Illinois Press, 1975); RE Keeton and J O'Connell, *Basic Protection for the Traffic Victim; A Blueprint for Reforming Automobile Insurance* (Boston, MA, Little, Brown and Co, 1965).

[102] Others could readily be mentioned. For instance, Paul Mitchell's fine chapter in this volume (ch 10), demonstrates Fleming James's influence on John Fleming.

[103] G Calabresi, *The Costs of Accidents* (New Haven, CT, Yale University Press, 1970).

[104] PS Atiyah, 'Book Review: The Costs of Accidents by Guido Calabresi' (1970) 44 *Australian Law Journal* 297.

[105] RA Posner, 'Book Review (reviewing Guido Calabresi, The Cost of Accidents: A Legal and Economic Analysis (1970))' (1970) 37 *University Chicago Law Review* 636.

[106] G Priest, 'The Rise of Law and Economics: A Memoir of the Early Years' in F Parisi and CK Rowley (eds), *The Origins of Law and Economics: Essays by the Founding Fathers* (Cheltenham, Edward Elgar, 2005).

[107] ibid 379, fn 29.

The second and more important influence of James on me is equally obvious. To James, torts was exclusively a public law subject. The significance of the individual injurer/victim relationship was to James so trivial (given the presence of insurance) that it could essentially be ignored in thinking about a proper system of tort law. Now I do not go anywhere near that far. Indeed, as I grow older, I become more and more conscious of how complex and multifaceted any field of law is. And this is especially true of a common law field, like torts. As a result, I have come to appreciate that there are many significant private law desiderata that attach to this field. There are relationships that, though attenuated by the presence of liability insurance, cannot be ignored, and which must somehow be 'substituted' for, if one moved totally to a 'party independent' system like that of New Zealand.

That said, however, Jimmy's influence remains on me. And I often find myself wondering at the obtuseness of those who do not recognise the fundamental centrality, also, of the public side of torts. However much one might wish to ignore it, tort law does to a significant extent determine which accidents, how many accidents, how much safety and what kinds of safety costs a society will have. And it also determines what categories of people and activities will bear the costs of safety and of accidents. Moreover, it does this in many ways, regardless of the relational – private law – significance of its rules.

James, until his last years, was not particularly conscious of some of the public sides of torts (the deterrent sides). But from the very beginning he was focused on 'What categories of people and activities will bear the costs of accidents and of safety'. And he considered that question as a public law, political and judicial question. The recognition that torts today is at least as much a public law subject as it is a private one, is fundamental to my view of the subject. It is, moreover, one that was instilled in me from my first day in Law School in 1955 by Fleming James.

The third influence is perhaps more subtle, but it is every bit as important. Many people view my contributions to tort law as centrally located in the law and economics movement. Indeed, they attribute the founding of that movement to me, and to (the much greater theorist) Ronald Coase, and its spread to that outdoer of Huxley and Melanchthon in propagation, Richard Posner. And I guess that is fair enough. But my relationship to economics, and hence to law and economics, has always been a peculiar one. Unlike Jimmy, I was *very* well trained in the field both at Yale and at Oxford, with three Nobel Prize winners as tutors. But, like Jimmy, and in part I think because of him, I have never thought that the goal, the object, of tort law could be the accomplishment of some kind of perfect or near perfect economic efficiency. I am, like him, and perhaps because of him, sceptical of the existence of any such thing, and even more so of the capacity of any legal system to achieve it, if it exists.

What for me is useful about economic thinking is that it tells us that *incentives* are crucial and helps us to understand how they work. The essence of this is found in my article with Melamed, generally called 'The Cathedral'.[108] There are three ways in which a society orders relationships: agreement, incentives and command. They meld into each other far more than people think. Still they are, by and large, emphasised in different fields of law: contracts, torts, and regulation/criminal law. Fleming James was sceptical that incentives remained important in torts with the advent of insurance. So for much of his life he looked to command and contract to deal with the questions of how many and which accident costs a society wished to tolerate. And he set about, through spreading, to try to lessen the harm of the accidents that did occur.

The way he did it, with the help of the ghost of Walton Hamilton, however, showed me that a massive amount of room for the use of incentives remained in the field, mainly, if not entirely, at a category/public level rather than at an individual/private level. At the end of his life as a scholar, James came to see this, but surely not because the use of 'incentives' in torts fostered some theoretical economic heaven. I believe his way of thinking is particularly important today, when those who would like to make torts an entirely private law field act as if they have won the war (though they have not even gained a foothold) when they demonstrate the fatuousness of that economic heaven.

It is no more a successful criticism of cost allocations as a way of creating economically wise incentives to say that they do not approach, let alone achieve, economic efficiency, than it is a successful criticism of compensation, as a goal of tort law, to demonstrate – the obvious – that full compensation is impossible. Moreover, one can show the same to be true of all the possible goals of tort law. And this includes what to James was his mission – the reduction of secondary costs of accidents by making tort law rules favour the spreading of losses wherever possible. Perfection, in spreading, might seem to be achievable through fully centralised governmental social insurance. But Fleming James – the grandson of an unfortunate priest – had his doubts. And rightly so, for with full governmental social insurance, the role of deterrence would fall to the criminal law, which, as I noted earlier, can, and often does, impose terribly *unspread* penalties to achieve its aims.

This scepticism of perfectibility – even in what was his chosen goal, his secular mission – may well have been his most important gift to me. I certainly have taken it to heart when I talk and write about law and economics in general and, most especially, in torts.

VII. CONCLUSION

How then should one conclude? Fleming James believed wide spreading of losses was *the* goal of torts in the American society of his time. He argued for

[108] G Calabresi and AD Melamed, 'Property Rules, Liability Rules, and Inalienability: One View of the Cathedral' (1972) 85 *Harvard Law Review* 1089.

it with remarkable success (and occasional failures – contribution among joint tortfeasors, collateral damages and, to a lesser extent, assumption of risk). And he moved tort law so that it became more congruent with this end. He did this by using his lawyerly skills and his procedural know how, both in his analysis of the cases and in the convincing of his fellow torts professors engaged in the writing of the *Restatement (Second) of Torts*. He also did it by his influence on many 'students' who became judges and law professors. Toward the end of his scholarly life he came to see that cost allocations to create category incentives might also have a place in torts law. But he always viewed such deterrence as secondary to, and primarily significant for, the backing it gave to his spreading goal. In all this, he clearly viewed torts as a public law subject, and felt that philosophical musings on the relationships between individual victims and individual injurers were a profound waste of time. Some of his views have been surpassed, some have been made more nuanced and incorporated into other scholarly conceptions of tort Law. But a remarkable amount of his thinking remains central to understanding tort law today.

10

Professor John G Fleming (1919–1997): 'A Sense of Fluidity'

PAUL MITCHELL*

I FIRST CAME across Fleming in a preliminary meeting with my tort tutor. We were being told which textbook to purchase. 'Well, I suppose you should get Winfield and Jolowicz', he said, mournfully. A pause. We waited. 'The best book is Fleming.' Another pause. 'But that's Australian … sort of.' We all bought Winfield. But the sense that Fleming was both uncategorisable and not for children was enticing enough to make some of us seek him out later.

I think the tutor's advice was right. Fleming is not a beginner's book – the analysis is too compressed, too dense to be immediately accessible – and the book's multi-jurisdictional approach (spanning across the common law world) is problematic for students destined to be examined in only the law of one jurisdiction. In truth first-year undergraduates were not the target readership.[1] But there is also a deeper, structural sense in which Fleming should not be the first writer one reads. That is because his work as a whole (not just the torts treatise) is essentially agonistic. To understand Fleming, it is necessary to understand what he is struggling against, what he is reacting to. Of course, finding oneself at odds with accepted thinking is hardly unusual for a scholar of any significance, but with Fleming the agonism was both structural and defining; it went much further, and ran far deeper, than a mere departure from orthodoxy. In his iconoclastic vision, venerable legal institutions ranging from the doctrine of precedent to the law faculties of certain universities, were unceremoniously toppled from their plinths, and the attitudes of complacency and deference to authority which sustained them were held up to mockery. Sometimes the antagonist is large and self-evident; sometimes it is more elusive, and has to be pieced together from close readings and silences in the texts. On occasion the struggle even seems to have been to come to terms with Fleming's own past and education. As will be

* I very gratefully acknowledge the comments of Anthony Julius, Mark Lunney and participants at the Scholars of Tort Law workshop on an earlier version.

[1] P Cane, 'Fleming on Torts: A Short Intellectual History' (1998) 6 *Torts Law Journal* 216, 222.

seen, the essentially confrontational nature of many of Fleming's book reviews and case notes makes these shorter pieces (which are often overshadowed by his torts treatise) particularly illuminating of his animating concerns.

I. LIFE AND WORK

'Born in Berlin, John Gunther Fleming went to school at Brentwood in Essex before going up to read jurisprudence at Brasenose College, Oxford.' This was how *The Times* summarised Fleming's early life.[2] It was both strictly accurate and, to the extent that it encouraged readers to infer a British childhood, entirely misleading: Fleming was born Alfred Gunther Kochmann, the son of Wilhelm Kochmann, a successful banker. He grew up in Berlin until, in 1935 at the age of 15, he was sent to school in England. Within a year he had obtained the qualifications needed for admission to Oxford. By the age of 19, he had gained a first-class honours degree in jurisprudence.[3] He stayed on at Oxford, despite a short period of internment as an enemy alien, to read for the Bachelor of Civil Law, but left before taking his degree in order to join up. Distinguished military service took him to Italy, North Africa and Austria. In 1943 he changed his name to John Gunther Fleming. Following demobilisation he was called to the Bar and appointed to a lectureship at King's College London; at the same time he began work on his doctoral thesis under the supervision of Professor GC Cheshire in Oxford.[4]

The thesis was on matrimonial causes in private international law, and this, along with issues in succession and equity, formed the subject-matter of his earliest publications.[5] He became a British citizen in 1947, received his doctorate in 1948 and, the following year, emigrated to Australia, taking up a lectureship at Canberra University College.[6] His arrival in Australia coincided with a change in his academic interests: he began to write about obligations, initially the law of contract, but then, beginning in 1952 with an arresting article on 'The Action Per Quod Servitium Amisit', on tort.[7] Fleming's earlier publications had been

[2] 'John Fleming' *The Times* (4 October 1997) 25.

[3] 'University News' *The Times* (13 July 1939) 18; he took his degree a couple of days later: 'University News' *The Times* (17 July 1939) 8.

[4] M Lunney, 'Legal Émigrés and the Development of Australian Tort Law' (2012) 36 *Melbourne University Law Review* 494, 507–08.

[5] 'John Gunther Fleming: A Bibliography of his Publications 1947–1998' in P Cane and J Stapleton (eds), *The Law of Obligations: Essays in Celebration of John Fleming* (Oxford, Clarendon Press, 1999) 411.

[6] A copy of the naturalisation certificate, dated 15 May 1947, is held at the National Archives HO 334/179/26583. A definitive account and analysis of Fleming's Australian period is offered by M Lunney, 'Fleming's *Law of Tort*: Australian-Made or Foreign Import? Australia's Role in Making the "King" of Torts' (2013) 36 *Australian Bar Review* 39.

[7] JG Fleming, 'The Action Per Quod Servitium Amisit: A Challenge to Judicial Technique' (1952) 26 *Australian Law Journal* 122.

heavily analytical in a rather conventional way; the work on tort, by contrast, was radical, original and probed at the very basis of tort liability. After 1956, when Fleming delivered his inaugural lecture as the Robert Garran Professor of Law at Canberra, tort was his exclusive academic focus.

His academic interests might have been settled, but his professional life was not – not quite. From at least the early 1950s he had been an admirer of American legal theorists – particularly the realists and Roscoe Pound.[8] A visiting professorship at Berkeley in 1958 proved that the admiration was mutual. Both Fleming and Berkeley would have liked him to move immediately, but the US government policy on such recruitments imposed a two-year hiatus. Eventually, in 1961, Fleming took up the post at Berkeley, which he held until his retirement. The torts treatise, first published in 1957 when he was still at Canberra, went through a further eight editions under his sole authorship, and he was a prolific contributor to legal journals. In 1972 his involvement with journals took on a different dimension when he became editor-in-chief of the *American Journal of Comparative Law*. He would hold this post until 1985. By the end of his career he had been hailed as 'the doyen of living tort writers'.[9] His successor as editor-in-chief at the *American Journal of Comparative Law* concluded a short tribute to Fleming, written to mark his death in 1997, as follows:

> We have lost a courageous, feisty, plain-spoken, and deeply learned man, one whom the tragedies and cataclysms of this century marked but did not press down, a scholar and a bon vivant, an excellent critic and an equally excellent colleague and friend.[10]

II. LEGAL FORMALISM: BIPOLARITY

Much of the force and originality of Fleming's work flowed from emphasising his opposition to legal formalism. At the time Fleming was developing his intellectual position on tort, legal formalism was perhaps not so much a distinctive philosophical position (although it had roots in the work of John Austin) as an all-pervasive assumption that the form and, in particular, the formal limits of tort law were both essential and unchangeable attributes. Fleming's work engaged vigorously with two manifestations of legal formalism: the bipolar nature of decision-making in tort cases; and the boundary between tort and other legal categories.

Fleming's response to the inherently binary, bipolar nature of judicial decision-making in tort was to problematise it. He was fascinated by situations

[8] JG Fleming, 'Book Review' (1953) 69 *LQR* 271.

[9] *Hunter v Canary Wharf Ltd* [1997] AC 655 (HL) 717 (Lord Cooke).

[10] R Buxbaum, 'John G Fleming 1919–1997' (1997) 45 *American Journal of Comparative Law* 645.

where the inevitable basic form of litigation – claimant versus defendant – obscured or concealed the underlying issue. He had an abiding interest in the 'collateral source' rule, that is to say, the rule that determined whether benefits received by a claimant from a source other than the defendant's payment of damages should reduce the defendant's liability, writing two major articles on the topic.[11] One of his earliest pieces on tort explored a similar theme, using an Australian High Court decision that had refused to confine actions for loss of services to domestic contexts as the point of departure in a search for the rationale for allowing such claims generally.[12] Fleming found that rationale in the importance of having a legal mechanism for the recovery of costs incurred by an employer in providing benefits (such as medical care) to an employee injured by the defendant. As Fleming was quick to point out, the problem was tripartite: a rule permitting the employer to recover from the tortfeasor needed to be complemented by a rule preventing the tortfeasor from also being liable for the value of those benefits to the victim/employee.

In the loss of services situation an exclusive focus on the accident victim and tortfeasor thus risked overlooking the position as between different parties in another case arising from the same event. The problem of bipolarity here was essentially a problem of coordination of legal rules. But the critique of bipolarity also applied and was, in some ways, more powerful, when the third party was nebulous or its interests were not backed by a legal right. For example, in his searching analysis of remedies for defamation, Fleming drew attention to how badly the conventional remedy of damages served the public interest in the correction of falsehoods.[13] He advocated the 'widest possible deployment' of the remedies of right to reply and retraction in order to 'help to break the traditional deadlock faced by the law of defamation between the individual's interest in his reputation and the general concern in the free flow of accurate information'.[14] No single individual stood for this 'general concern', but there was a powerful argument for law to be tailored to its needs.

Perhaps Fleming's most eloquent articulation of this critique of bipolarity came in his acerbic article on the availability of damages for lost years in personal injury claims.[15] The basic legal question was simple: could a claimant whose life expectancy had been reduced by a tortiously suffered injury recover damages to reflect the earnings that he would have received had he lived for his pre-accident lifespan? The English Court of Appeal had recently held that

[11] JG Fleming, 'The Collateral Source Rule and Loss Allocation in Tort Law' (1966) 54 *California Law Review* 1478; JG Fleming, 'The Collateral Source Rule and Contract Damages' (1983) 71 *California Law Review* 56.

[12] JG Fleming, 'Action for Loss of Services' (1959) 22 *MLR* 682.

[13] JG Fleming, 'Retraction and Reply: Alternative Remedies for Defamation' (1978) 12 *University of British Columbia Law Review* 15, 16.

[14] ibid 30.

[15] JG Fleming, 'The Lost Years: A Problem in the Computation and Distribution of Damages' (1962) 50 *California Law Review* 598.

such claims were not available. Fleming took issue with the Court of Appeal's reasoning on its own terms (see section IV), but was even more exercised by what he saw as a general failure to engage with the fundamental underlying question, which he identified as 'the distribution of compensation among the various interests, including those of dependants, who are liable to suffer prejudice presently and in the future as the result of an accident'.[16] The point was that if a claimant received compensation for the earnings that he would have received in the years he had now lost, the claimant's dependants' claims for loss of dependency would be correspondingly reduced, and often extinguished altogether. The dependants' position would turn on what testamentary provision the tort victim had made for them and the size of his estate, rather than being based on a fatal accident claim. As Fleming put it, the key question in the 'lost years' cases was whether the fatal accidents legislation should be seen as providing protection to dependants before the tort victim's death; in other words:

> is the statute content to let [the dependants] remain dependent upon [the tort victim's] unfettered discretion regarding their future welfare or does it purport to intervene after his injury and abridge his management for the sake of safeguarding their interests against the risk of his wasting their patrimony?[17]

Focusing on the position as between the tortfeasor and tort victim almost guaranteed that the position of dependants, for whom so much was at stake, would be overlooked. In the article's conclusion Fleming drew a general lesson: 'this complex situation, like so many others involving multiple party interests is singularly taxing to a system of law which is primarily geared to the adversary process'.[18]

Fleming's analyses of the collateral source rule, the continued availability of the action for loss of services, remedies for defamation and damages for lost years demonstrated how focusing on the two parties before the court could distort and inhibit the development of appropriate tort doctrines. But the emphasis on the parties and the individual decision could also be unfortunate for a broader reason, in that it tended to distract attention from the fact that the individual decision was part of a system. Innovations that were ostensibly unobjectionable in an individual case could have alarming systemic implications, to which Fleming was alert. Perhaps the most egregious example – certainly, I suspect that Fleming would have thought it was the most egregious – was the campaign by Melvin Belli, a high-profile personal injury plaintiffs' attorney, to increase the quantum of personal injury awards. His *Ready for the Plaintiff*[19] inspired one of Fleming's most devastating reviews, the tone of which can be gathered from

[16] ibid 598.
[17] ibid 607.
[18] ibid 618.
[19] MM Belli, *Ready for the Plaintiff* (New York, Henry Holt & Co, 1956).

its final short paragraph: 'Mr Belli is a dangerous man, and this is a dangerous book, particularly in the hands of the less discriminating reader. I hope it will not be read by many.'[20]

Fleming identified many shortcomings, in content, in style and in taste, but his most telling point was to highlight Belli's failure even to *recognise* the inevitable systemic consequences of his proposals. 'Perhaps the most serious weakness in the author's thesis', Fleming wrote,

> is his failure to address himself to the fundamental question whether our society can afford at the same time to compensate all (or all deserving) casualties of motor traffic and other high-accident producing activities, and still maintain or even increase the level of awards for which he is so ardently pressing. This problem is not solved by asking the silly rhetoric question whether the particular accident victim would have been prepared to sacrifice his leg for $200,000 or any other sum.[21]

Here, vividly, was a demonstration of how focusing on the individual parties to litigation missed the point.

III. LEGAL FORMALISM: CATEGORIES

A second manifestation of legal formalism against which Fleming positioned himself was the deference to legal categories, in particular the distinctions between different torts and the distinction between tort and other legal areas (such as contract). A readiness to think across the boundaries between different torts can already be seen in his earliest publication on tort, 'The Action Per Quod Servitium Amisit'.[22] Here an argument about the way that changing social conditions can lend new significance to old legal forms moves from a close analysis of the action for seduction to a reflection on the developing law of duty of care in negligence. The article saw itself as addressing the modern structure of tort liability, not just one specific tort.

When it came to the relationship between tort and other legal categories, Fleming was positively enthusiastic about transgressing boundaries. He praised the infusion of 'public values' which Canadian tort law had experienced as the result of the indirect effect of the Charter of Rights and Freedoms,[23] and argued for a more fluid border between contract and tort. On this latter point, his deep knowledge of German law allowed him to make an eloquent and paradoxical contribution. The demarcation between contract and tort in English law was particularly problematic when tort was invoked to provide

[20] JG Fleming, 'Book Review' (1958) 46 *California Law Review* 137, 138.
[21] ibid.
[22] Fleming, 'The Action Per Quod Servitium Amisit: A Challenge to Judicial Technique' (n 7).
[23] JG Fleming, 'Libel and Constitutional Free Speech' in P Cane and J Stapleton (eds), *Essays for Patrick Atiyah* (Oxford, Clarendon Press, 1991) 335.

a remedy which the law of contract seemed to have deliberately withheld. Thus, in *Hedley Byrne & Co Ltd v Heller & Partners Ltd*,[24] for instance, no consideration had been given for a promise to supply a banker's reference; in *Ross v Caunters*[25] and *White v Jones*,[26] a solicitor had breached his contract with his client but all the loss had fallen on the client's legatees, who had no relationship of privity with the solicitor. In all three cases, tort remedies had been recognised (although the detailed facts of *Hedley Byrne* prevented the claim from succeeding). Fleming pointed out the contrast with German law, where similar problems had been solved by modifying the application of the relevant contractual doctrines.[27] Ironically, as Fleming also pointed out, German law had been driven to use contractual solutions for difficulties created within delict[28] – there is a sense in his writings that he regarded these kinds of ad hoc borrowings as unavoidable.

However, that was not to endorse the indiscriminate use of whatever legal materials lay to hand in order to create a claim. One of the cases that gained Fleming's highest praise was the Supreme Court of Canada's decision in *London Drugs Ltd v Kuene & Nagel*.[29] There the claimant had contracted for storage of a valuable transformer on terms that limited the warehouse company's liability to C$40. The transformer was damaged by the company's employees' carelessness. The claimant sued the employees personally, in negligence, hoping thereby to circumvent the limitation clause. The Supreme Court denied the claim for a variety of reasons. The majority allowed the employees to avail themselves of the limitation clause – an essentially contractual solution. Fleming was not entirely convinced by this line of reasoning; he was more taken with the analysis of McLachlin J, which held that the duty of care owed by the employees was modified by the contractual matrix. But it was his overall characterisation of the case that really catches the reader's eye. The Supreme Court, he observed,

> has thus once again … demonstrated its independence and inventiveness of thought in the field of civil liability, untrammelled by the orthodoxies of yesteryear, in order to reach a decision congruent with its, and our, sense of today's realities.[30]

'The orthodoxies of yesteryear' here are the doctrine of privity of contract and the idea of contract and tort as separate domains. What was so important to Fleming was that these legal platitudes were not mistaken for absolute truths. As he had put it in 1957, 'It cannot be too often reiterated that legal

[24] *Hedley Byrne & Co Ltd v Heller & Partners Ltd* [1964] AC 465 (HL).
[25] *Ross v Caunters* [1980] Ch 297 (Ch D).
[26] *White v Jones* [1995] 2 AC 207 (HL).
[27] JG Fleming, 'Comparative Law of Torts' (1984) 4 *OJLS* 235; JG Fleming, 'The Solicitor and the Disappointed Beneficiary' (1993) 109 *LQR* 344.
[28] J Fleming, 'Tort in a Contractual Matrix' (1993) 5 *Canterbury Law Review* 269, 279.
[29] *London Drugs Ltd v Kuene & Nagel* [1992] 3 SCR 299 (SCC).
[30] JG Fleming, 'Employee's Tort in a Contractual Matrix: New Approaches in Canada' (1993) 13 *OJLS* 430, 435.

concepts ... are means, not ends';[31] the ends the categories served were decisions 'congruent with ... our sense of today's realities'. If the legal propositions conflicted with the appropriate decision, it was the legal propositions that should yield.

In taking this approach to legal categories, and making them subservient to other ends, Fleming was departing from the more traditional view, which accorded the categories greater priority. As I mentioned earlier, legal formalism of this kind was not particularly associated with one individual writer – it was an all-pervasive general attitude. However, some writers committed themselves to more extreme forms of it than others; at the end furthest from Fleming one could find the views of those like PA Landon, whose definition of tort was 'a breach of duty which would have been remediable before 1852 by one of the writs of trespass, case, and detinue'.[32] 1852 was crucial, because that was the date of the Common Law Procedure Act, which had abolished the requirement to plead cases using the forms of action. It was a vision of tort law that unashamedly delighted in 'the orthodoxies of yesteryear'.

Landon would have taught Fleming in Oxford. He had put forward his definition of tort in an article published in 1931, and there is no reason to think that he would not have used it in his lectures.[33] It is tempting to wonder whether Landon's ultra-conservative approach is not at least partly responsible for the fact that Fleming did not turn his attention to torts until over a decade after having attended Landon's lectures. Certainly it is easy to imagine the young Fleming emerging from the lecture theatre feeling that other subjects had more to offer him. But even when he came to write his torts treatise, Fleming had not forgotten his old lecturer. Footnote 1 on page 1 of chapter 1 set out three definitions of tort: Winfield's, Salmond's and Landon's.[34] Winfield's was introduced as '[t]he best-known definition'. Salmond's was offered without comment. Here is what Fleming said about Landon's:

> There is some subtle humour, for those with a bent for antiquarian curiosities, in the proposal by Mr Landon ... to define tort as 'a breach of duty which would have been remediable before 1852 by one of the writs of trespass, case and detinue.'[35]

One of the hallmarks of agonistic writers is their propensity to engage in what Harold Bloom calls 'misreading' of their predecessors, in order to assert and create their own place in the tradition.[36] To recharacterise Landon's definition as

[31] JG Fleming, 'Vicarious Liability for Breach of Statutory Duty' (1957) 20 *MLR* 655, 656.

[32] PA Landon, 'The Province of the Law of Tort' (1931) 8 *Bell Yard* 19, 20. For the context, and a sense of the debate to which Landon was contributing, see P Mitchell, *A History of Tort Law 1900–1950* (Cambridge, CUP, 2015) ch 2, esp 26–29.

[33] FH Lawson, *The Oxford Law School 1850–1965* (Oxford, Clarendon Press, 1968) 131 describes Landon as 'an excellent lecturer, especially on the law of torts, exciting the opposition of his best hearers by his attachment to past orthodoxies'.

[34] JG Fleming, *The Law of Torts* (Sydney, Law Book Co of Australasia, 1957) 1.

[35] ibid.

[36] H Bloom, *The Anxiety of Influence: A Theory of Poetry*, 2nd edn (Oxford, OUP, 1997) 5.

comedy – as, quite literally, a joke – is a perfect example of such a misreading. It was not the only aspect of his Oxford experience that Fleming would come to define himself against.

IV. PRECEDENT

There is a close link between legal formalism and precedent: a commitment to traditional legal categories tends to go hand-in-hand with a deferential attitude towards earlier judicial pronouncements. So it is not entirely surprising to discover that Fleming, with his sceptical attitude to legal formalism, had a corresponding wariness about precedent. As with Fleming's approach to legal formalism, it is illuminating first to identify his antagonists, and then to trace the emergence of his own position.

Some of Fleming's wittiest and most cutting commentary was inspired by excessive deference to precedent. He observed of the Court of Appeal's reasoning in *Oliver v Ashman*,[37] for example, that it manifested

> the typically English concern with inconclusive dicta in earlier cases ... [which] was strongly reminiscent of such necromantic rites as the viewing of chicken gizzards by the ancient Roman augurs and the still extant English practice of foretelling the future from random patterns of tea leaves.[38]

There is a kind of subdued pun here, playing on *ratio decidendi/obiter dictum* and rational/irrational, which enables Fleming to (mis)characterise the Court of Appeal's judgment as irrational. The truth was that the Court of Appeal's decision manifested a commitment to a kind of rationality that Fleming thought both misguided and inferior to his own analytical approach. But, rather than presenting his analysis as a rival, alternative rationality, his bracketing of the Court of Appeal's reasoning with augury and tasseography allows him to claim that his is the first valid analysis of the problem. The urge to claim priority is another hallmark of agonistic writing.[39]

Fleming's move to Australia also made him alive to a different dimension of excessive deference – the habit of Australian courts to follow English decisions. His 1953 review of GW Paton's *The Commonwealth of Australia*[40] regretted that work's lack of 'a sensitive discussion of the present-day Australian tragedy of choosing the easy path to imitation, often a generation behind the English prototype, rather than consistently adopting an attitude of independent valuation'.[41] Conversely, six years later, he would salute – in an English

[37] *Oliver v Ashman* [1962] 2 QB 210 (CA).

[38] Fleming, 'The Lost Years: A Problem in the Computation and Distribution of Damages' (n 15) 601, fn 11.

[39] Bloom, *The Anxiety of Influence: A Theory of Poetry* (n 36).

[40] GW Paton, *The Commonwealth of Australia: The Development of Its Laws and Constitution* (London, Stevens, 1952).

[41] Fleming, 'Book Review' (1953) 69 *LQR* 123, 124.

journal – a decision of the High Court of Australia as 'providing further evidence of the High Court's growing spirit of independence towards the English judiciary, born of increasing confidence and perhaps even a consciousness of superiority'.[42]

Fleming's attitude could partly be explained by his conviction that English courts' decisions were often not worth deferring to: he would allude, for instance, to English courts' 'intrepidity for sacrificing common sense to the inexorable demands of a spurious logic which has contributed so much to forfeiture of their erstwhile leadership of the common law'.[43] But his position also had deeper roots. The review of Paton complained of the absence of 'an appraisal of judicial quality and achievement along lines familiar in American writing'.[44] The sentence from his note on the Australian High Court case quoted above continued by saying that the decision 'opens a window upon the extent to which the judicial attitude to *stare decisis* is influenced by the individual judge's strength of conviction regarding the substantive issue in the case before him'.[45] This was precisely the kind of issue on which American legal writers were eloquent.

Fleming was well-versed in the American legal writing of the period. His warm review of Roscoe Pound's *Justice According to Law*[46] hailed Pound as 'the outstanding jurist of our time',[47] and was only tempered by two reservations. First, he identified that Pound had nothing new to say in the work under review: 'all that is found in this little book has been stated before by him, particularly in his *Social Control Through Law*'.[48] Only a reviewer with extensive knowledge of Pound's oeuvre could have made that point. Second, Fleming felt that Pound judged the realists too harshly: 'though the so-called realists are prone to spoil their case by exaggeration and over-emphasis, they have undoubtedly contributed insights into the administration of the law which deserve a fairer appraisal than their denigration as a "cult of the ugly"'.[49]

Quite how much Fleming felt that the American realist school could bring to the understanding of precedent could be seen in a review he wrote of two tort casebooks – one by WL Morison,[50] the second by Cecil A Wright.[51] The point of the review was to confront Morison's traditional, orthodox work with Wright's radically different approach as a way of highlighting 'the divergence of teaching techniques between the North American casebook method

[42] Fleming, 'Action for Loss of Services' (n 12) 683. The case was *Commissioner for Railways (NSW) v Scott* (1959) 102 CLR 392 (HCA).

[43] Fleming, 'The Lost Years: A Problem in the Computation and Distribution of Damages' (n 15) 612.

[44] Fleming, 'Book Review' (n 41) 124.

[45] Fleming, 'Action for Loss of Services' (n 12) 683–84.

[46] R Pound, *Justice According to Law* (New Haven, CT, Yale University Press, 1951).

[47] Fleming, 'Book Review' (n 8).

[48] ibid 273.

[49] ibid.

[50] WL Morison, *Cases on Torts* (Sydney, Law Book Co of Australasia, 1955).

[51] CA Wright, *Cases on the Law of Torts* (Toronto, Butterworth & Co, 1954).

[exemplified by Wright] and the traditional pattern of instruction followed in most British and Australian law schools [typified by Morison]'.[52] It was a contest between Morison's 'conservatism' and Wright's 'spirit of adventure';[53] readers will perhaps not need to be told whom Fleming declared the winner.

Morison's book followed the familiar format of extracting passages from judgments, a strategy which Fleming immediately objected to:

> [T]he material is pre-digested and in that process loses most of its nourishing quality, because the student is spared that essential, if arduous, task of analysing legal problems and evaluating the judicial reaction to them for himself. It hardly needs a reminder that, since much of the life-blood of the legal process is already drained away through the filter of law reporting (see Llewellyn, *The Bramble Bush*, and Frank, *Courts on Trial*), this further process of distillation produces a degree of abstraction which cannot fail to distort seriously a realistic perception of law in operation.[54]

As Fleming explained, the underlying problem here was the kind of legal education for which such casebooks were created, which was founded on assertions of general principle in lectures and textbooks:

> A casebook suited to this pattern of education inevitably reflects its preoccupation with so-called *leading* cases, singling out for attention the *ipse dixit* of the highest appellate courts whilst underplaying the uncertainties of the legal process, and thereby perpetuating the make-believe of jural generalizations.[55]

Wright's book came from a very different place: 'Refusing to regard law as an aggregate of static solutions clothed in oracular pronouncement, the stress is on the experimental nature of court reactions to the manifold social conflicts of our time'.[56] Divergent rulings and dissents were included, 'with a view to stimulate questioning rather than submission'.[57] This radically different approach was underpinned by a vision of legal education that was a very long way from Morison's.

> Rather than cramming the student's mind with detailed information of an abstract nature, the object of education is to make him detect legal problems embedded in a hard crust of facts, to develop a critical faculty in the evaluation of fact situations and the judicial reaction to them, to approach case-reading not with a view to extracting theoretical information so much as to observe the court's method of tackling a concrete problem, to familiarize himself with the course of trial and appellate practice and appreciate the significance of proof on the outcome of litigation. For short, the emphasis is on case-study rather than study of abstract judicial opinions, on the Concrete rather than Generalization.[58]

[52] JG Fleming, 'Book Review' (1956) 2 *Sydney Law Review* 212, 212.
[53] ibid 214.
[54] ibid 213.
[55] ibid.
[56] ibid 214.
[57] ibid.
[58] ibid.

Fleming fully appreciated, and embraced, the fact that this emphasis on the concrete could be unsettling and even subversive. In a passage where metaphors of struggle could hardly have been more prominent, he commented that

> the more meticulous the attention given to a court's wrestling with a concrete problem, the more sceptical we grow of the mechanistic theory of judicial adjudication. It becomes more obvious that there are influential factors other than the mere application of verbal formulae which shape conclusions, that precedents are only guide-posts or 'starting points' of legal reasoning, that the 'agony of decision' is constantly present.[59]

Fleming published this hugely important double review in the *Sydney Law Review* volume covering 1956 to 1958, and the date is surely significant. He was still the Robert Garran Professor of Law at Canberra University College (that is how he signed the review), but would be taking up a visiting professorship at Berkeley in 1957–58 and then, ultimately, moving there permanently.[60] The review seems to capture him on that threshold, both looking back at the constraining conservatism of Australian law schools and forwards to the more adventurous possibilities of the United States. Whatever the delays with his visa, he was already in California in spirit.

But while the review gives a powerful sense of a particular moment in Fleming's life, it also articulated beliefs to which he had been, and would continue to be, committed for his entire career. At the heart of these beliefs was a fundamental scepticism about judicial language. He shared the realists' conviction that judicial reasoning never provided a complete account of the true motivations for a decision. It followed, therefore, that the lavish attention given to judicial language in traditional casebooks was misplaced – nearly 40 years after the double review, he would praise the Supreme Court of Canada for an analysis of precedents 'paying more attention to the actual decision than what the court said in explanation'.[61]

He practised what he preached. The foreword to the torts treatise drew attention to the relative sparsity of quotations from judges, and the commitment to an American-inspired approach to precedent was prominent enough to provoke the one notably negative review that the work received.[62] Perhaps the most interesting example of Fleming's commitment to legal realism in his own practice was his famous essay, 'Remoteness and Duty: The Control Devices in Liability for Negligence'.[63] This piece, published about five years before the

[59] ibid.

[60] For a vivid account of the protracted nature of the move, drawing on Fleming's correspondence, see Lunney, 'Fleming's *Law of Tort*: Australian-Made or Foreign Import? Australia's Role in Making the "King" of Torts' (n 6) 224–27.

[61] JG Fleming, 'Employee's Tort in a Contractual Matrix: New Approaches in Canada' (1993) 13 *OJLS* 430, 439.

[62] EG Coppel, 'Book Review' (1957) 1 *Melbourne University Law Review* 272.

[63] JG Fleming, 'Remoteness and Duty: The Control Devices in Liability for Negligence' (1953) 31 *Canadian Bar Review* 471.

double review, took as its point of departure an envious glance at the United States, where,

> during the last generation at any rate, realistic comprehension of the functional operation of the devices employed in negligence litigation has become almost a commonplace ... By comparison, all too often our approach to the problems surrounding negligence liability cannot be regarded as other than immature.[64]

Although Fleming was writing in a Canadian journal, while holding a position in Australia, 'our' here essentially meant English law. The central thrust of Fleming's critique was that there had been a general failure to articulate the central problem in negligence. That problem was how to limit liability; and the array of legal doctrines associated with negligence should be judged by their contribution to resolving it. Seen in this light, the current doctrines' greatest shortcoming was their failure to capture the underlying policy interests in play. Crucially, Fleming was not arguing that doctrinal flaws were leading to frequent unjust outcomes – on the contrary, 'in the largest number of negligence cases the decisions as such can meet the standards of an exacting critic'.[65] The problem, rather, was that the judicial opinions accompanying those decisions 'are all too often couched in phraseology which suppresses the vital "inarticulate major premise" beneath a manipulation of verbal formulas'.[66]

The middle sections of the article supported this thesis with compelling analyses of the use of remoteness of damage and duty of care as control devices. As he moved towards his conclusion Fleming indicated that only a modified duty of care test – one that took account, for instance, of the different policy factors relevant to recovery for psychiatric injury and purely economic loss – had the potential to be an adequate and coherent control device.[67] But the conclusion itself struck a rather more ambivalent note:

> The conclusion I seek to commend is the relative unimportance of formalizing the structural analysis of negligence cases. The particular method adopted by the court is of as little consequence to the actual decision reached as the verbal formula through which it finds expression. Neither could be of substantial significance unless we were employing 'self-determining words with fixed content, yielding their meaning to a process of inexorable reasoning'. But, as we need hardly remind ourselves, the reality behind law-making through the judicial process lies elsewhere.[68]

This sounds dismayingly like an admission of defeat, an acceptance that we can never truly access 'the reality behind law-making through the judicial process'. In a sense it is the realist scepticism about judicial language taken to its logical

[64] ibid 472.
[65] ibid 473.
[66] ibid.
[67] ibid 495.
[68] ibid 502. The quotation was from F Frankfurter, 'Twenty Years of Mr Justice Holmes' Constitutional Opinions' (1923) 36 *Harvard Law Review* 909, 912.

(and extreme) conclusion. But, as a conclusion, it is hardly very satisfying: if we are to discard judges' own explanations for their decisions as mere surplusage, we desperately need some kind of alternative explanatory framework to make sense of things. What could that framework look like? Fleming's later writings would attempt to set it out.

V. TEMPORALITY

One of the most distinctive features of Fleming's tort scholarship was its readiness to invoke a grand historical narrative about the law of negligence. As he explained in the preface to a special issue on contemporary roles of the law of tort in the *American Journal of Comparative Law* for 1970, there were three phases:

> It was the task of the nineteenth century to create a law of compensation compatible with the requirements of the awakened giant of free enterprise. The age of negligence was born, and with it the vestiges of an older, stabler society, linked to notions of strict liability, were cast off. The last fifty years have been occupied with adjusting the law of torts to the phenomenon of liability insurance which destroyed the assumption of individual responsibility and familiarized us with the reality of spreading or pooling losses among large sections of the community. But ere yet this revolution has run its full course, the next stage is already in the offing; the message, unmistakable for those who care to read, spells nothing short of the displacement of tortious liability by systems of direct compensation, private and public.[69]

The sense of an inevitable acceleration towards accident compensation schemes as replacements for tort was amplified and elaborated in his 1973 article, 'The Decline and Fall of the Law of Delict',[70] where the imminent enactment of New Zealand's Accident Compensation Scheme was seen as bringing the future into the present day. Significantly, in that later paper, Fleming emphasised the continuities between the second and third phases of tort's history: both were grounded in collectivism. The difference between them was that, while the collectivism of the New Zealand scheme was overt, the collectivism in asking who was best placed to bear the loss was implicit – a doctrine like vicarious liability, for example, was an instance of 'creeping collectivism' because it departed, subtly, from the tenet of individual responsibility.[71] Fleming's use of vicarious liability in this context also highlighted a rather different, and less attractive, aspect of his grand historical narrative: it was not historically accurate – vicarious liability in its recognisably modern form dated from

[69] JG Fleming, 'Contemporary Roles of the Law of Torts' (1970) 18 *American Journal of Comparative Law* 1, 1.

[70] JG Fleming, 'The Decline and Fall of the Law of Delict' (1973) 6 *Comparative and International Law Journal of Southern Africa* 259.

[71] ibid 261.

the 1840s, arguably earlier. This was a clue to the fact that Fleming was not interested in the past for its own sake.

The historical narrative was so important to Fleming because it gave tort a purpose, one might even say a destiny, which intertwined tort's fate with wider social changes. For, in essence, Fleming was portraying negligence as first a symptom then an attempt to mitigate the effects of the Industrial Revolution. The social, economic, political and cultural significance of industrialisation was – and would continue to be – a central theme of scholarship in the humanities. Fleming only very rarely referred to specific works dealing with this theme – for example, when invoking Karl Renner's thesis that legal institutions could survive radical alterations in social conditions by making use of fictions[72] – but he was clearly aware of it. In particular, his historical narrative can be seen as implicitly engaging with, and responding to, Marx's analysis of the connection between the relations of production and their corresponding legal superstructure.

One of the central insights of Marxist analysis was to highlight that there was an inevitable interconnection between the material conditions of economic production and the social institutions (such as law) adopted by a community.[73] In some writers' analyses the connection proposed was a crudely direct one. Fleming, in the passage quoted above from his 1970 preface, seemed to be positing such a direct causal link between industrialisation and the legal test for negligence. However, in earlier work, particularly his 'The Role of Negligence in Modern Tort Law', he had been more careful.[74] Here he criticised (unspecified) 'economic determinists' for claiming that the negligence standard had been produced by the Industrial Revolution; the truth, Fleming pointed out, was that it had been created by the Romans.[75] But that was not to say that the Industrial Revolution was irrelevant: the fault doctrine thrived because it 'responded adequately to the fundamental needs of a developing economy'.[76] There was, in other words, a deep and mutually sustaining relationship between the conditions of production and the legal doctrine.

Fleming's analysis of tort's second stage of development seems to have undergone its own period of change. In 1967 he argued that the pendulum had begun to swing against fault because of doubts about 'its adequacy to cope with the problems posed by the highly technological society of our time'.[77] Legal doctrine was, again, being explained by direct reference to societal conditions. However, as Fleming continued his analysis, it became clear that he identified

[72] Fleming, 'The Action Per Quod Servitium Amisit: A Challenge to Judicial Technique' (n 7) 122–23; Fleming, 'Action for Loss of Services' (n 12).

[73] The canonical text is K Marx, 'Preface to *A Contribution to the Critique of Political Economy*', available in RC Tucker (ed), *The Marx-Engels Reader*, 2nd edn (New York, Norton, 1978). For an excellent explanation of the issues, see H Collins, *Marxism and Law* (Oxford, OUP, 1982) ch 2.

[74] JG Fleming, 'The Role of Negligence in Modern Tort Law' (1967) 53 *Virginia Law Review* 815.

[75] ibid 817. Fleming saw little point in the independent study of Roman law: Fleming, 'Comparative Law of Torts' (n 27).

[76] Fleming, 'The Role of Negligence in Modern Tort Law' (n 74) 818.

[77] ibid 819.

a crucial intermediary factor, without which changes in negligence would not have been possible:

> By far the most pervasive catalyst of loss spreading has proved to be liability insurance; for it has made it possible to gear conventional rules of law, without any radical reform of those rules themselves, to the changing needs of a technological society.[78]

In Fleming's 1970 summary, quoted above, liability insurance has been promoted from intermediary to underlying cause. His more extended account, from 1973, showed that this was a deliberate move away from economic determinism:

> Clearly the decision of the law to give its nod of approval to liability insurance was a critical turning-point in the annals of delictual liability. Implicit was the choice that abandoning the principle of individual responsibility was a price worth paying for the double benefit of at once safeguarding the defendant from the potentially ruinous consequences of an adverse judgment and assuring his victim of actual compensation instead merely of an empty verdict against a defendant who was more likely than not financially irresponsible.[79]

Fleming's sense of tort's historical trajectory was not merely ornamental: it was a critical, evaluative tool to be deployed in his analyses of contemporary controversies. He used it in at least two distinctive ways. The first was to marginalise unhelpful precedents: these could often be seen as contingent on the (now altered) social conditions in which they had been decided. They should, in Fleming's phrase, be seen as 'no more than tentative experiments in technique'.[80] The second informed Fleming's sense of the role of legal writers, and could be seen particularly vividly in his appreciative review of *Prosser on Torts*.[81] One of the many aspects of the work that he admired was Prosser's 'conscious[ness] of his ability … to help along judicial change-in-the-making'.[82] The example Fleming particularly had in mind was Prosser's contribution to recent changes in the law of product liability, which had been inspired by an emphasis on 'maximum pressure for accident prevention, capacity to absorb and distribute losses, and the relative inability of the consumer to protect himself'.[83] 'In short', Fleming continued,

> a new reasoning has emerged which is quite alien to the classical or conventional theories of civil responsibility on which most of us were nurtured in an earlier day, and one which possibly represents a drift towards collectivism which those less attuned to the temper of our times have reason to deplore as an aberration from the ancient verities of individualism, puritanism, and maximum freedom from social responsibility. Yet this breakthrough in the area of products liability is but a symptom

[78] ibid 837.
[79] Fleming, 'The Decline and Fall of the Law of Delict' (n 70) 260.
[80] Fleming, 'Remoteness and Duty: The Control Devices in Liability for Negligence' (n 63) 476.
[81] JG Fleming, 'Book Note' (1964) 52 *California Law Review* 1068 (reviewing WL Prosser, *Prosser on Torts*, 3rd edn (St Paul, MN, West Publishing Co, 1964)).
[82] ibid 1068.
[83] ibid.

> of a more general restlessness and change in orientation that osmotically, as it were, is insinuating itself throughout the whole of tort law, communicating a sense of fluidity in which precedents must justify themselves anew on their own, independent merit.[84]

The best kind of legal writer, who was attuned to the temper of his times, would respond to this restlessness and help to take the law where it needed to go – the writer had become a key agent of legal change.

This deep commitment to approaching the law with an eye to its future was not always straightforward. To the extent that the future was understood to mean the inevitable dominance of compensation systems, Fleming admitted that he found it difficult to commit wholeheartedly: '[my] preference for comprehensive accident compensation has not weaned [me] from a life-long addiction to the intellectual allures of traditional tort law', he once confessed.[85] It might also be difficult to extricate oneself from the opposing gravitational force-fields of past, present and future, as Fleming found when writing about *Pigney v Pointers Transport Services Ltd*.[86] In this case, an English court of first instance had allowed full recovery in a claim for negligence where the accident victim had committed suicide as a result of depression brought on by the accident. Fleming was troubled. The claimant's deliberate act of self-harm seemed to break the chain of causation; furthermore, cases decided under the workmen's compensation scheme had denied recovery for the consequences of suicide:

> [T]he policy underlying social welfare legislation would, if anything, tend to favour rather more comprehensive protection than a system of loss allocation, like the common law, which is still largely geared to individualistic notions of fault and, despite the widespread incidence of indemnity insurance, continues to pretend that the defendant's own purse is the sole source of all compensation.[87]

A footnote to this sentence added that, 'perhaps, it should not be overlooked' that the defendants in the case were 'almost certainly covered by liability insurance'.[88]

The case, and Fleming's uncharacteristically conflicted analysis of it, highlighted the difficulty of writing to judicial change-in-the-making. He could not resist the temptation of pointing out how, viewed in its own orthodox legal terms, the judgment was unconvincing. But that criticism immediately deconstructed itself, because the notion of individual responsibility for tort damages was a pretence, not only in general but also – almost certainly – in this particular case as well. The presence of insurance made the decision look a lot less objectionable; it also raised doubts about whether it had been right to deny recovery under

[84] ibid 1068–69.
[85] Fleming, 'Comparative Law of Torts' (n 27) 236.
[86] *Pigney v Pointers Transport Services Ltd* [1957] 1 WLR 1121 (Norwich and Norfolk Summer Assizes).
[87] John G Fleming, 'Liability for Suicide' (1957) 31 *Australian Law Journal* 587, 589.
[88] ibid.

the 'social insurance' of workmen's compensation. One might have expected Fleming here to invoke a legal realist explanation – to stress what the court had done, not what it had said. But, on this occasion at least, he seemed reluctant to make that move, concluding his note with the rather conventional observation that 'of all the progeny spawned by *Re Polemis*, Pilcher J's decision is certainly the oddest'.[89]

VI. SELF-IDENTIFICATION

Fleming's view of history profoundly shaped his work; the same is true of his personal history. On some aspects of it he could be outspoken. There are several contenders for the accolade of Fleming's most devastating book review, but his savaging of PA Landon's edition of *Pollock's Law of Torts*[90] has a compelling claim.[91] Landon had retained the text of the final edition written by Pollock (in 1929), and that decision, Fleming wrote, 'lends the book an antiquarian flavour which in the Olympian atmosphere of Oxford might be regarded as a commendation but elsewhere could be diagnosed as a symptom of sterility'.[92] Where Landon had added new material it tended to reflect his 'predilection' for jargon, his 'enthusiasm for the propagation of diehard points of view' and – perhaps most damningly – 'prejudices' rooted in 'an unwillingness to recognise the social changes of our time'.[93] The portrayal of Oxford – where Fleming had been a student – and of Landon – who had taught him – bore eloquent witness to their influence on him.

Fleming's personal history also seems to have shaped his work in more subtle ways. His successor as editor-in-chief of the *American Journal of Comparative Law* described him (in a passage already quoted) as a man 'whom the tragedies and cataclysms of this century marked but did not press down'.[94] One such marking related to Fleming's own sense of identity. After leaving Germany he had, quite literally, to reinvent himself when Gunther Kochmann became John Fleming. There was, possibly, a pragmatic reason for this linked to his military service.[95] But it was not, of course, merely a matter of changing his name – he changed his nationality, and assimilated in other ways. For example, in a review of Giorgio del Vecchio's *Justice*[96] in the *Law Quarterly Review*, he observed that

[89] ibid.

[90] PA Landon, *Pollock's Law of Torts*, 15th edn (London, Stevens & Sons, 1951).

[91] JG Fleming, 'Book Review' (1954) 1 *Sydney Law Review* 282.

[92] ibid 282.

[93] ibid 283.

[94] Buxbaum, 'John G Fleming 1919–1997' (n 10) 646.

[95] Lunney, 'Fleming's *Law of Tort*: Australian-Made or Foreign Import? Australia's Role in Making the "King" of Torts' (n 6) 214; Lunney, 'Legal Émigrés and the Development of Australian Tort Law' (n 4) 508, fn 65.

[96] G del Vecchio, *Justice: An Historical and Philosophical Essay* (Edinburgh, Edinburgh University Press, 1952).

the book was 'in many respects representative of critical idealist philosophical thought of the twentieth century'.[97] Which was not a good thing:

> It might as well be frankly admitted that the idea of inter-subjective correlation as an a priori concept of justice derived from trans-subjective consciousness may prove not a little unpalatable for those of us in the Anglo-Saxon world who have not been sufficiently 'conditioned' by a century or more of this type of obscurantist German epistemology.[98]

This is the authentically weary tone of a pragmatic Englishman confronted with the excesses of Continental philosophy. Why was Fleming writing like this? Who did he want readers to think he was?

One answer is 'not German, obviously', and it is quite remarkable how little he gave away about his origins in his early work. On the rare occasions when a German source is alluded to – as with his citation of Renner in 'The Action Per Quod Servitium Amisit' – there is almost a feel of pantomime in his referring only to his compatriot Kahn-Freund's *translation*.[99] He did not review a German book until 1967,[100] and seems only ever to have published one article in German (he published two in Italian). It is probably not a coincidence that the review was for the *American Journal of Comparative Law*, where an interest in German law was not out of place; but, even here, Fleming's self-identification was striking. The book's author, he observed, 'takes his place besides the ever increasing phalanx of modern European writers who have fallen under the spell of our own common law methods'.[101] There is no sense that Fleming identified himself with those 'European writers': the demonstrative affectionate possessiveness of 'our own' speaks volumes for where he felt he belonged. Conversely, when reviewing another, less impressive, German work in the same journal, Fleming was unsparing:

> True to the conventional German academic tradition the author, a professorial aspirant understandably concerned with his own professional survival, deploys more ingenuity in pursuing the will o' the wisp of theoretical subtleties (*Dogmatik*) … than in developing functionally valuable insights … [One of the book's] flaw[s] is the pervasively naive assumption … that the contemporary German institutional model yields criteria of universal *validity* (*vide* the constant appeal to 'sachgerecht', ie proper).[102]

[97] Fleming, 'Book Review' (n 8) 271.

[98] ibid.

[99] Fleming, 'The Action Per Quod Servitium Amisit: A Challenge to Judicial Technique' (n 7) 122–23.

[100] JG Fleming, 'Book Review' (1967) 15 *American Journal of Comparative Law* 579 (reviewing W Marschall von Bieberstein, *Reflexschäden und Regressrechte* (Stuttgart, Kohlhammer Verlag, 1967)).

[101] ibid 580.

[102] JG Fleming, 'Book Review' (1971) 19 *American Journal of Comparative Law* 805, 805–06 (reviewing W Gitter, *Schadensausgleich im Arbeitsunfallrecht* (Tübingen, JC Mohr, 1969)).

We have already seen that Fleming could be a devastating reviewer, but there seems to be a further factor in play here – perhaps it was the memory of a German system that had threatened more than merely his professional survival – and the tone is starting to veer towards contempt, both for the system and its products. At the same time we should note the implicit claims to linguistic and institutional expertise that create the platform for the criticisms – Fleming was, perhaps, starting to feel happier about acknowledging a Germanic element in his professional identity. In any event, from the early 1970s onwards, his work overtly engages far more with German sources than it had done previously.

VII. CONCLUSION

Twenty years after his death, some aspects of Fleming's work remain extraordinarily vivid, while others seem very remote. His analysis of duty of care may be over 60 years old but it retains an astonishing urgency and value; the importance of legal categories being means not ends has never been more compellingly articulated and illustrated. On the other hand, tort's inevitable replacement by compensation systems seems unlikely to happen anytime soon, and legal change inevitably makes commentaries on some aspects of earlier law feel rather stale. The torts treatise lives on, but I would suggest that it is not so much Fleming's specific analyses of particular points that we should value today as the priorities and attitudes that they exemplify. His work is a constant reminder of the importance – and rewards – of the kind of restlessness that had excited him when he glimpsed it in the background of Prosser's book on torts. Existing structures were there to be challenged and interrogated, not meekly accepted or deferred to; history could be a critical and potentially subversive tool, not just a daunting heap of constraining precedents. At his best, Fleming makes readers feel exactly what he had felt when he looked over Prosser's shoulder: an exhilarating sense of the possibilities and fluidity of tort.

11

Professor Patrick Atiyah (1931–2018)

JAMES GOUDKAMP*

I. INTRODUCTION

IT WAS MORE common in the past than it is today for legal scholars' interests to span multiple fields. This situation is no doubt due in large part to there being much less law in earlier times than there is at the present day. However, Patrick Atiyah's repertoire was nevertheless unusually diverse. He was a legal polymath whose expertise extended to tort law, contract law, legal history, general jurisprudence and legal institutions. Throughout his career, Atiyah drew profitably upon his great learning in various fields in aid of analyses that he advanced in other areas. Atiyah's writings were published between the mid-1950s and the late 1990s, although they were primarily produced prior to 1988, at which time Atiyah retired as Professor of English Law at the University of Oxford. Within the law of torts, his publications mainly concerned the personal injury context.

Atiyah's three principal publications regarding tort law are the books *Vicarious Liability in the Law of Torts*,[1] *Accidents, Compensation and the Law*,[2] and *The Damages Lottery*.[3] This chapter examines the contribution of each of these works to scholarly thinking about tort law generally. However, it is convenient to say a few brief words about these texts by way of introduction. *Vicarious Liability in the Law of Torts*, which was published in 1967, was largely aimed at laying out the law regarding vicarious liability. Although it was thus mainly a work of doctrinal scholarship, one of its distinguishing features was the frequent recourse made in it to legal policy. Another distinctive characteristic

* William Twining provided me with several valuable insights regarding Atiyah's tort scholarship for which I am most grateful. I am also grateful to Václav Janeček and Harold Luntz for providing me with helpful reactions on drafts of this chapter. I am also indebted to Mengfei Ying for her careful research assistance.

[1] PS Atiyah, *Vicarious Liability in the Law of Torts* (London, Butterworths, 1967).

[2] PS Atiyah, *Accidents, Compensation and the Law* (London, Weidenfeld & Nicolson, 1970).

[3] PS Atiyah, *The Damages Lottery* (Oxford, Hart Publishing, 1997).

is the extensive reference made to the law of other jurisdictions, especially that in the United States.

In 1970, Atiyah's path-breaking *Accidents, Compensation and the Law* was released. It offered a comprehensive survey of the many systems by which compensation could be recovered for personal injury and death resulting from accidents. In some ways, *Accidents, Compensation and the Law* was an extension of *Vicarious Liability in the Law of Torts*. It powerfully developed a host of ideas that were embryonic in its forerunner, in particular the idea that tort law was fundamentally and hopelessly deficient as an accident compensation system. However, on the whole, *Accidents, Compensation and the Law* struck out in a wholly new direction. It did not draw upon tort law as an organising device. And it also differed greatly from *Vicarious Liability in the Law of Torts* in that doctrinal analysis of the law was very much of secondary concern to the objective of understanding mechanisms of compensating for personal injury and death caused by accidents in their social context. Atiyah authored a further two editions of *Accidents, Compensation and the Law*[4] before he handed responsibility for the book to Peter Cane.

In 1997, upon his being coaxed briefly out of retirement, Atiyah published *The Damages Lottery*. That work – Atiyah's final contribution to legal scholarship – comprises a withering attack on the tort system as a mechanism for compensating for personal injury and death. In some respects, *The Damages Lottery* merely distils ideas that Atiyah advanced almost 30 years earlier in *Accidents, Compensation and the Law*: he considered the tort system to be just as defective and irrational as he had found it in 1970 (if not more so). However, in other ways, *The Damages Lottery* stands apart from *Accidents, Compensation and the Law*, not least because Atiyah changed his position on certain key issues, because he developed new criticisms, especially the idea that the tort system stimulates a damaging 'culture of blame', and because he gave the agenda for reform heightened prominence.

Before proceeding, it is important for the discussion that follows to emphasise just how far Atiyah's interests extended beyond the law of torts. Atiyah's unusually wide range is noteworthy because it is obvious that his learning in other fields impacted significantly upon his thinking about tort law, with the result that Atiyah's writings on tort cannot be properly understood in isolation. Relatedly, it is also important to appreciate that Atiyah pursued his interests across multiple fields more or less simultaneously throughout essentially the full length of his career. He can usefully be compared in this regard with Glanville Williams, who serves as an interesting contrast (because both their interests and their careers overlapped, because their styles were similar in various ways, and because they were both leading lights in their chosen fields). Williams began

[4] PS Atiyah, *Accidents, Compensation and the Law*, 2nd edn (London, Weidenfeld & Nicolson, 1975); PS Atiyah, *Accidents, Compensation and the Law*, 3rd edn (London, Weidenfeld & Nicolson, 1980).

his career working in tort[5] and contract[6] before abandoning those fields,[7] at a relatively early stage, for the criminal law. He became increasingly fixated by the minutiae of the criminal law as the years passed by. Conversely, Atiyah maintained his mastery of multiple areas over essentially the entirety of his professional life. This undoubtedly increased the effectiveness with which he was able to cross-fertilise.

Atiyah was at least as well known as a contract law scholar as for his contributions to tort law. In 1957, Atiyah released his classic *The Sale of Goods*.[8] He authored eight editions of that work in total. In 1961, Atiyah's *An Introduction to the Law of Contract*[9] appeared on bookshelves. Atiyah published five editions of that text before responsibility for it passed into the capable hands of Stephen Smith. In 1979, Atiyah published *The Rise and Fall of Freedom of Contract*,[10] which is a *tour de force* that explores the development of, and influences on, the English law of contract, and which advances the claim that 'far from being the typical case of obligation', promise-based liability 'may be a projection of liabilities based on benefit or reliance'.[11] In 1982, *Promises, Morals, and the Law*[12] arrived in bookstores. In that text, Atiyah offered a radical account of the nature of promissory obligations, which account was influenced by his study of how tort law operated in practice.[13] In 1986, Atiyah republished a selection of his essays on contract in a single volume.[14] Again, the extent to which Atiyah brought to bear his learning in tort law in his quest to understand contract is a highly conspicuous feature of that book.[15]

[5] See, eg, G Williams, *Liability for Animals: An Account of the Development and Present Law of Tortious Liability for Animals, Distress Damage Feasant and the Duty to Fence in Great Britain, Northern Ireland and the Common-Law Dominions* (Cambridge, CUP, 1939); G Williams, *Joint Torts and Contributory Negligence: A Study of Comparative Fault in Great Britain, Ireland and the Common-Law Dominions* (London, Stevens, 1951).

[6] See, eg, R McElroy and G Williams, *Impossibility of Performance: A Treatise on the Law of Supervening Impossibility of Performance of Contract, Failure of Consideration, and Frustration* (Cambridge, CUP, 1941); G Williams, *The Law Reform (Frustrated Contracts) Act, 1943: The Text of the Act with An Introduction and Detailed Commentary* (London, Stevens & Sons Ltd, 1944); G Williams, *Joint Obligations: A Treatise on Joint and Joint and Several Liability in Contract, Quasi-Contract and Trusts in England, Ireland and the Common-Law Dominions* (London, Butterworths, 1949).

[7] Save for brief returns to tort law in G Williams and B Hepple, *Foundations of the Law of Tort* (London, Butterworth, 1976) and G Williams and B Hepple, *Foundations of the Law of Tort*, 2nd edn (London, Butterworth, 1984).

[8] PS Atiyah, *The Sale of Goods* (London, Pitman, 1957).

[9] PS Atiyah, *An Introduction to the Law of Contract* (Oxford, Clarendon Press, 1961).

[10] PS Atiyah, *The Rise and Fall of Freedom of Contract* (Oxford, OUP, 1979).

[11] ibid 4.

[12] PS Atiyah, *Promises, Morals, and the Law* (Oxford, Clarendon Press, 1982).

[13] ibid 185–88 (arguing that promises can be understood as admissions of prior obligations, and developing this analysis with reference to examples drawn from personal injury litigation).

[14] PS Atiyah, *Essays on Contract* (Oxford, OUP, 1986).

[15] See, eg, ibid 8–9, 64 (arguing that contract and tort 'are merging' and that the idea 'that contract law is "based" on agreements or voluntarily incurred obligations, while tort law is "based" on legally imposed obligations … is misconceived'); ch 10 (considering the fact that misrepresentation 'occupies a hazy and undefined area generally thought to lie along the boundaries of tort and contract' (at 275)); and 379–85 (considering the impact of the expansion of liability in tort on how the law of contract should be understood).

Beyond the English law of torts and contract, Atiyah was also profoundly interested in comparative law. In particular, he studied from a distance tort law in the United States, and wrote several major articles in which he ruminated on the differences between tort law in the United States and in England.[16] He considered that tort law in the United States was particularly ripe for comparative investigation '[b]ecause American litigiousness affects the whole world'.[17] Atiyah also thought that American tort law should be studied in so far as it stood as a warning. He wrote that the American tort experience had 'produced a crisis, an explosion of litigation, and a correspondingly disastrous effect on insurance premiums in various fields of activity, not to mention other unsatisfactory by-products'.[18] Atiyah's study of American tort law culminated with the publication in 1987 of his *Form and Substance in Anglo-American Law*,[19] which he co-authored with the American law professor Robert Summers.[20] Although tort law featured prominently in that text, it travels well beyond that field, and is ultimately concerned with the differences and similarities between the two countries in terms of their legal institutions and the style of legal reasoning generally employed. Atiyah also published several other important works that were concerned primarily with the nature of the English legal system.[21]

Finally, although Atiyah had all of the qualities of a world-class doctrinal scholar, a significant proportion of his work was highly philosophical in nature, especially certain of his writings regarding the theory of contract law and the nature of promises. Joseph Raz, no less, in a well-known review of Atiyah's *Promises, Morals, and the Law*, wrote:

> [T]he book fulfils its promise in being a genuinely interdisciplinary study. Atiyah is not a philosopher using a few legal cases as illustration, nor is he a lawyer who uses the occasional philosophical argument. He is a great legal scholar who has studied the philosophical issues in detail and who speaks with equal confidence in both fields.[22]

[16] See, eg, PS Atiyah, 'No Fault Compensation: A Question That Will Not Go Away' (1980) 54 *Tulane Law Review* 271; PS Atiyah, 'American Tort Law in Crisis' (1987) 7 *OJLS* 279; PS Atiyah, 'Tort Law and the Alternatives: Some Anglo-American Comparisons' (1987) 6 *Duke Law Journal* 1002.

[17] Atiyah, 'Tort Law and the Alternatives' (n 16) 1004.

[18] Atiyah, 'American Tort Law in Crisis' (n 16) 293.

[19] PS Atiyah and RS Summers, *Form and Substance in Anglo-American Law: A Comparative Study of Legal Reasoning, Legal Theory, and Legal Institutions* (Oxford, Clarendon Press, 1987).

[20] *Form and Substance in Anglo-American Law* provided the inspiration for the conference *Obligations IX: Form and Substance in the Law of Obligations* (2018) held at Melbourne Law School and the associated edited collection: A Robertson and J Goudkamp (eds), *Form and Substance in the Law of Obligations* (Oxford, Hart Publishing, 2019).

[21] See, eg, PS Atiyah, *Pragmatism and Theory in English Law* (London, Stevens & Sons, 1987); PS Atiyah, 'Common Law and Statute' (1985) 48 *MLR* 1; PS Atiyah 'Justice and Predictability in the Common Law' (1992) 15 *University of New South Wales Law Journal* 448.

[22] J Raz, 'Book Review: Promises, Morals, and the Law by Patrick Atiyah' (1982) 95 *Harvard Law Review* 916, 917.

Rather unexpectedly, given his willingness to grapple with philosophy in the field of contract, Atiyah adopted, on the whole, a very different approach in his tort scholarship. By and large, he shunned and, indeed, was derisory of, efforts to theorise tort law, whether in economic or moral terms. For example, in one article, Atiyah wrote:

> There is something paradoxical, almost comical, about the fact that, in the last decade or so, the main thrust of the literature on this question [ie, whether tort law can be justified on the grounds of efficiency] has concerned the highly abstract and theoretical economic arguments about efficiency in the resource allocation sense. Once it had been thoroughly and convincingly demonstrated that the tort system was, by any comparable standard, highly inefficient in practice, new legal and economic theorists appeared on the scene to assure us that it was, nevertheless, extremely efficient in theory.[23]

This chapter unfolds in the following way. Each of Atiyah's three principal books regarding tort law is discussed *seriatim*. The concern is not, for the most part, to engage with their substance but, rather, to understand their impact upon subsequent scholarly thinking regarding tort law. Thereafter, additional insight as to the influence of Atiyah's work is offered by way of a citation analysis. This analysis compares the significance of Atiyah's three books in Australia, the United Kingdom and the United States, and also considers Atiyah alongside several other leading twentieth-century Commonwealth torts scholars. Some more impressionistic and qualitative thoughts are also ventured as to Atiyah's past and continuing impact as regards tort law.

II. *VICARIOUS LIABILITY IN THE LAW OF TORTS* (1967)

Atiyah's earliest contributions to tort law comprised short articles[24] and case notes.[25] *Vicarious Liability in the Law of Torts* was his first major work in the field, and in it Atiyah developed certain ideas that he would advance with increasing urgency throughout his career. *Vicarious Liability in the Law of Torts*, which Robert Stevens described in 2007 as 'still the leading text on vicarious liability',[26] was presented by Atiyah as having been 'written mainly for practitioners'.[27] Although it is true that much of the book is expository in nature, it is nonetheless clear that Atiyah's principal audience is not, in fact, practising lawyers but legal scholars, and that his real interest lay in legal policy. Thus, the book commenced with an exploration of the master's tort theory

[23] Atiyah, 'No Fault Compensation' (n 16) 279. Consider, also, the passage set out in the text accompanying n 86, below.

[24] PS Atiyah, 'Causation, Contributory Negligence and Volenti Non Fit Injuria' (1965) 48 *Canadian Bar Review* 609; PS Atiyah, 'Negligence and Economic Loss' (1967) 83 *LQR* 248.

[25] See, eg, PS Atiyah, 'A Re-examination of the *Jus Tertii* in Conversion' (1955) 18 *MLR* 97.

[26] R Stevens, *Torts and Rights* (Oxford, OUP, 2007) 259.

[27] Atiyah, *Vicarious Liability in the Law of Torts* (n 1) v.

and the servant's tort theory[28] followed by an excursus of what Atiyah called 'The Social Justification for Vicarious Liability'.[29] Further, large tranches of the text are highly critical of the law of vicarious lability, which is something that one tends not to see in arid practitioner-oriented books. Atiyah laid siege to several key aspects of the law of vicarious liability, including the control test, which he argued was a deficient way of identifying the existence of a contract of service,[30] and tests for determining liability in the case of borrowed servants.[31] This willingness to question basic principles of tort law would grow throughout Atiyah's career.

One feature of *Vicarious Liability in the Law of Torts* that distinguished it from most other legal writing of the same era was Atiyah's concern with the social impact of the relevant law. In developing his arguments, Atiyah placed significant weight on 'the widespread practice of insuring against legal liabilities', and on the resulting reality that 'the person who pays the damages is rarely the person who was at fault'.[32] He also drew attention to the fact that 'some proportion of the cost of accidents – at least those involving death and personal injury – will be borne by the taxpayer if it is not borne by anyone else'.[33] Although these observations, and Atiyah's approach in general, may appear trite and unremarkable today, they were anything but when *Vicarious Liability in the Law of Torts* was written. The simple fact is that Atiyah's analysis constituted a radical break from the then conventional mode of legal scholarship. In the decades preceding Atiyah's arrival onto the scene, English torts scholars, and indeed legal academics more generally, eschewed policy-based analysis.[34] Instead, they tended to mimic the approach taken by judges, who had firmly embraced the Austinian positivist tradition, and confined themselves to the role of synthesising principles from the case law.[35] Atiyah's nakedly policy-based reasoning, and willingness to explore the practical impact of the law of vicarious liability, amounted to a root-and-branch rejection of the prevailing academic style.

In *Vicarious Liability in the Law of Torts* Atiyah sowed the seeds for his later, sustained assaults on the fault principle. He wrote:

> If a person is injured in an accident and is unable to work, the loss is never thrown entirely onto him. Where there is legal liability the loss is thrown on the person at fault, and, in general, through him onto some insurance fund. Where on the other hand there is no legal liability the loss is thrown partly on the man himself and

[28] ibid ch 1.
[29] ibid ch 2.
[30] ibid 45–49.
[31] ibid ch 18.
[32] ibid 14.
[33] ibid.
[34] A good example of this style is J Salmond, *The Law of Torts: A Treatise on the English Law of Liability for Civil Injuries* (London, Stevens & Hayes, 1907).
[35] For further discussion of this theme, see B Hepple, 'Negligence: The Search for Coherence' (1997) 50 *Current Legal Problems* 69, 76.

> partly on the state. The state in turn meets the cost partly by a charge on industry through national insurance, and partly by general taxation. When this broad picture is considered the whole element of fault in the law of torts comes to look a good deal less relevant to modern conditions. In the last analysis the law (including in this, law of a public nature) must allocate the losses caused by accidents, only part of which will fall within the scope of the law of torts anyhow. The question which has to be decided is generally not, what individuals should bear this burden?, but, what class of society should bear the burden? Take road accidents. Here the burden is principally cast on motorists who pay for the cost of road accidents caused by negligence through their insurance premiums. But those accidents not caused by, or not capable of being proved to have been caused by, negligence, will be paid for partly by those injured themselves, and partly by the state. Questions of fault are really irrelevant here. The policy issue which will have to be faced sooner or later is whether the cost of all road accidents (and not only those proved to have been caused by negligence) should not be borne by the motoring community.[36]

Again, it is easy, with the benefit of modern spectacles, to underestimate the great significance of this passage. However, it is important to remember that this constituted a profound rejection of the then dominant style of tort scholarship, and indeed of the prevailing understanding regarding tort law more generally. Atiyah was writing at a time when the fault principle was in the ascendency and when essentially the whole tort system was thought properly to be premised on the understanding that it was the fault of the defendant that justified the imposition of liability.[37]

III. *ACCIDENTS, COMPENSATION AND THE LAW* (1970)

Accidents, Compensation and the Law, which was written while Atiyah was based in Canberra, launched the *Law in Context* series. William Twining, the series co-editor, who had been a colleague of Atiyah when they were both teaching in Khartoum, reveals that he had invited Atiyah to write a book for the series about regulation or commercial law in practice.[38] Although it was an entirely

[36] Atiyah, *Vicarious Liability in the Law of Torts* (n 1) 14–15.

[37] The dominant view is encapsulated by Ames's well-known remark that 'The early law asked simply, "Did the defendant do the physical act which damaged the plaintiff?" The law of today, except in certain cases based upon public policy, asks the further question, "Was the act blameworthy?" The ethical standard of reasonable conduct has replaced the unmoral standard of acting at one's peril': JB Ames, 'Law and Morals' (1908) 22 *Harvard Law Review* 97, 99. Another prominent statement in support of the dominant understanding is Lord Macmillian's comment in *Read v J Lyons & Co Ltd* [1947] AC 156, 171 that 'the process of evolution has been from the principle that every man acts at his peril and is liable for all the consequences of his acts to the principle that a man's freedom of action is subject only to the obligation not to infringe any duty of care which he owes to others … the emphasis now is on the conduct of the person whose act has occasioned the injury'.

[38] W Twining, 'Reflections on Law in Context' in P Cane and J Stapleton (eds), *Essays for Patrick Atiyah* (Oxford, OUP, 1991) 2.

sensible proposal (contextual analyses in those areas were badly needed),[39] had it been accepted, understanding regarding the law's treatment of accidents would have been profoundly impoverished. Twining records that Atiyah said that he was 'bored with contract and commerce'[40] and wanted to produce 'a book on torts',[41] and that he proceeded to assemble *Accidents, Compensation and the Law* in short order. My sense is that Atiyah had almost certainly done much of the thinking that underpinned *Accidents, Compensation and the Law* when he wrote *Vicarious Liability in the Law of Torts*.

Atiyah described the agenda of *Accidents, Compensation and the Law* as being to offer 'a comprehensive survey of all aspects of the problem of compensation for accidents'.[42] Thus, the text was organised around a single factual paradigm – accidents causing personal injury and death – rather than a traditional legal category.[43] This meant that the book was not confined to causes of action in tort but encompassed the myriad mechanisms by which redress can be obtained for personal injury and death, such as private insurance and criminal compensation schemes. This approach enabled Atiyah to examine, for example, the cause of action in negligence *qua* compensation system alongside the plethora of other compensation arrangements. Looking at tort law in this way led Atiyah to conclude that it was a dismal and wasteful failure: it afforded highly preferential treatment to a tiny minority of accident victims who, by chance, were able to prove that they had been injured by someone else's fault. His ultimate assessment was that '[w]hat is surely needed is a single comprehensive system based on the existing social security system, but with benefits as adequate as society can afford'.[44] *Accidents, Compensation and the Law* has (rightly) been described as a 'path-breaking and devastating critique of the tort system'.[45]

Three features of *Accidents, Compensation and the Law* merit particular mention for present purposes. First, the book represented a concerted effort to cut free from traditional classifications to which torts scholars were generally wedded (or, as Atiyah may have thought, by which they were imprisoned) and to look at a particular *problem* of significant social importance – accidents resulting in personal injury and death – from a legal perspective. The traditional way in which torts scholars proceed is to bring together for consideration under one roof all civil wrongs other than breaches of contract and equitable wrongs. The difficulty that Atiyah perceived in this methodology was that it resulted in torts

[39] It would not be until 2007 that a book on regulation appeared in the *Law in Context* series: B Morgan and K Yeung, *An Introduction to Law and Regulation: Text and Materials* (Cambridge, CUP, 2007). The series still lacks a book on commercial law.

[40] Twining, 'Reflections on Law in Context' (n 38) 2.

[41] ibid.

[42] Atiyah, *Accidents, Compensation and the Law* (n 2) xiv.

[43] Atiyah may well have looked askance at the present edited collection due to its focus on tort law.

[44] Atiyah, *Accidents, Compensation and the Law* (n 2) 572.

[45] J Conaghan and W Mansell, 'Review Article: From the Permissive to the Dismissive Society: Patrick Atiyah's Accidents, Compensation, and the Market' (1998) 25 *Journal of Law & Society* 284, 284.

that were largely addressed to one particular issue being treated alongside torts that were really aimed at a very different problem. Although not the first work to reject the strictures of existing legal classifications,[46] *Accidents, Compensation and the Law* was nonetheless pioneering in its approach. Atiyah's hope was that the book

> may provide some encouragement towards the break up of existing courses and syllabuses on the law of torts. I have for long felt that the law of torts as at present delineated is not a coherent or satisfactory subject for study by university students. It includes too many diverse groups of law. For example, economic torts are today almost entirely concerned with industrial relations and with fair trade compensation. To teach these subjects properly requires far more attention to other aspects of the law and practice than can possibly be accommodated in a torts course. On the other hand, to teach them at all means that less time and room is available in a torts course for teaching the law of negligence as in my view it should be taught, namely as one part of a complex system of compensation for accidents.[47]

The extent to which this hope was realised is debatable. However, Richard Lewis claims that '[t]he pedagogical revolution eventually precipitated by *Atiyah's Accidents, Compensation and the Law* has influenced all but the most ostrich-like of undergraduate tort courses'.[48] Harold Luntz reports that he structured his *Torts: Cases and Commentary*[49] in view of Atiyah's approach.[50]

Second, *Accidents, Compensation and the Law* constituted a categorical rejection of approaches that concentrated on doctrine at the expense of legal policy and the practical operation of the law. The book was fundamentally concerned with the social reality of personal injury litigation and the institution of liability insurance in particular. Accordingly, Atiyah described the relevant

[46] It was preceded by T Ison, *The Forensic Lottery: A Critique on Tort Liability as a System for Personal Injury Compensation* (London, Staples, 1967); JG Fleming, *An Introduction to the Law of Torts* (Oxford, Clarendon Press, 1967); and DW Elliott and H Street, *Road Accidents* (Harmondsworth, Penguin, 1968).

[47] Atiyah, *Accidents, Compensation and the Law* (n 2) xv.

[48] R Lewis, 'Criticisms of the Traditional Contract Course' (1982) 16 *Law Teacher* 111, 111.

[49] H Luntz and D Hambly, *Torts: Cases and Commentary* (Sydney, Butterworths, 1980).

[50] Luntz wrote (H Luntz, 'A Personal Journal Through the Law of Torts' (2005) 27 *Sydney Law Review* 393, 401): 'I attended the annual conference of the Australasian Law Schools Association (as ALTA was then called) in Adelaide. At the conference, Atiyah put forward his model for teaching an accident compensation course instead of the traditional torts course. At first I was sceptical as to the feasibility of this, given the requirements for admission to the profession, but of its merits I had no doubt. It was one of the inspirations for the case book that I produced with David Hambly and Robert Hayes, Torts: Cases and Commentary (1980). The other model for the case book was the one produced by Bob Hepple and Martin Matthews, Tort: Cases and Materials (1974). Bob Hepple had taught me at Wits, though not torts. He had escaped to England, where he went on to an eminent career (he is now Sir Bob). There was no doubt that his approach to the law of torts accorded with my own. We did not abandon the traditional intentional torts completely, though I left the writing of those chapters largely to my co-authors. Negligence, however, was in the forefront and dominant throughout. I wrote a long introductory chapter, seeking to place the law of torts in its social context and emphasising its actual operation. It also drew attention to the alternatives to the law of torts for compensating victims of accidents.'

law simply as a means to an end rather than (as is the case with conventional textbooks) the end in itself. Consequently, while certain areas of tort law were treated fairly fully in *Accidents, Compensation and the Law*, such as the tort of negligence, other parts of tort law that are often treated extensively in torts textbooks, such as the law of nuisance and the action in *Rylands v Fletcher*, were barely mentioned at all.[51]

Third, although *Accidents, Compensation and the Law* is fundamentally a book about accident compensation in the United Kingdom, it offered significant engagement with the tort system and enormous associated literature in the United States.[52] In *Accidents, Compensation and the Law*, Atiyah said that he proceeded in this way partly because the tort system in that jurisdiction had been the subject of far more intense investigation,[53] and he clearly drew much of his inspiration for his critiques of the English tort system from earlier denunciations of tort law that had been made by American scholars, especially Fleming James.[54] Atiyah's engagement with the United States literature extended to his crossing swords with several American scholars, especially Guido Calabresi,[55] whose work he realised was of great significance.

The two subsequent editions of *Accidents, Compensation and the Law* that Atiyah authored maintained much the same message as the first, although my impression of those subsequent editions is that Atiyah adopted an increasingly hostile view of the tort system as a mechanism for compensating for personal injury and death. The second edition was largely prompted by the implementation of the New Zealand Woodhouse Scheme.[56] The third edition was provoked by the publication of the Pearson Commission's Report.[57] The Pearson Report

[51] The first edition of *Accidents, Compensation and the Law* contains just over two pages of text on 'Rylands v Fletcher, Nuisance and Animals': Atiyah, *Accidents, Compensation and the Law* (n 2) 168–70. The relevant text was left largely unchanged in the second and third editions: Atiyah *Accidents, Compensation and the Law*, 2nd edn (n 4) 152–54; Atiyah, *Accidents, Compensation and the Law*, 3rd edn (n 4) 163–66.

[52] Atiyah's most sustained treatment of United States torts scholarship is his review article of OS Gray (ed), *Harper, James and Gray The Law of Torts* (Boston, MA, Little, Brown & Co, 1986) in Atiyah, 'American Tort Law in Crisis' (n 16).

[53] Atiyah complained that 'the information available with regard to the tort system [in England] is seriously deficient and I have often had to fall back on the fruits of American research' (Atiyah, *Accidents, Compensation and the Law* (n 2) xv). He added '[t]o those familiar with American work it will be obvious how much I owe to the masters of American tort law of the past decade, and to the protagonists of the present day' (ibid xviii).

[54] One suspects, in particular, by F James, 'Accident Liability Reconsidered: The Impact of Liability Insurance' (1948) 57 *Yale Law Journal* 549. Atiyah considered that 'James was one of the first lawyers to systematically downgrade the importance of the deterrence aspect of tort law': see Atiyah 'American Tort Law in Crisis' (n 16) 288.

[55] See, eg, Atiyah, *Accidents, Compensation and the Law* (n 2) ch 4, on 'general deterrence'; and PS Atiyah, 'Book Review: The Costs of Accidents by Guido Calabresi' (1970) 44 *Australian Law Journal* 297.

[56] In the form of the Accidents Compensation Act 1972 (NZ). See Atiyah's remarks in the preface to the second edition: Atiyah, *Accidents, Compensation and the Law*, 2nd edn (n 4) xii.

[57] *The Report of the Royal Commission on Civil Liability and Compensation for Personal Injury* (Command 7054, 1978). See Atiyah's remarks in the Preface to the third edition: Atiyah, *Accidents, Compensation and the Law*, 3rd edn (n 4).

yielded a prodigious amount of statistical information regarding the tort and liability insurance systems that was vitally relevant to *Accidents, Compensation and the Law* given its agenda. The Report also acted as a punching bag for Atiyah, and on the whole he (rightly) treated its proposals with contempt and incredulity.[58]

IV. *THE DAMAGES LOTTERY* (1997)

The Damages Lottery warrants extended discussion because it provoked much more debate than either *Vicarious Liability and the Law of Torts* or *Accidents, Compensation and the Law*.

A. A Prelude

It is necessary to preface the analysis of *The Damages Lottery* by mentioning Atiyah's important essay 'Personal Injuries in the Twenty-First Century: Thinking the Unthinkable'.[59] That contribution, which appeared in 1996 in a collection of essays edited by Peter Birks, was a prelude to *The Damages Lottery*. In it, Atiyah made two overarching claims, which he described as follows:

> It is one of the functions of the academic lawyer from time to time to think the unthinkable, and to challenge some of the most fundamental assumptions of our legal system. Few assumptions are more basic than the idea that if someone wrongfully does you an injury you should be entitled to sue him, and to think of abolishing this right without providing any real replacement is to go about as far as one can in thinking the unthinkable. Yet I want in all seriousness to float the suggestion that the action for damages for personal injuries should largely be abolished, and its replacement left to the free market.[60]

Atiyah developed the first of these claims – the retrenchment claim – by contending that tort compensation is, in effect, a type of welfare benefit, and by asserting that it is bizarre that 'welfare' benefits available through tort law are continuing

[58] eg, in relation to the Pearson Commission's proposal to extend strict liability for dangerous things and activities, Atiyah wrote in the third edition that 'the Commission appears to have paid inadequate attention to the implications of these proposals, nor do they really attempt any serious justification of them in principle. … The truth is that these proposals of the Commission were ill-thought out and are unlikely to be implemented. We need waste no further space on them' (Atiyah, *Accidents, Compensation and the Law*, 3rd edn (n 4) 165–66). His overall assessment was that 'the Pearson Commission's Report has proved a great disappointment. Although there are a great many detailed recommendations, there is a marked lack of over-all principle, of underlying strategy. And on the crucial question of abolition, in whole or in part, of the right of action in tort, the Commission have provided no leadership' (ibid 623 (footnote omitted)).

[59] PS Atiyah, 'Personal Injuries in The Twenty-First Century: Thinking the Unthinkable' in P Birks (ed), *Wrongs and Remedies in the Twenty-First Century* (Oxford, Clarendon Press 1996).

[60] ibid 1.

to be increased at a time when the tendency is to curtail the welfare state, especially in circumstances where those benefits are being increased by judges and, hence, without any oversight or authorisation by Parliament. Atiyah suggested that this raised 'a serious constitutional question'.[61] He also cast doubt on attempts to justify the tort system on the basis that, for example, it tended to ensure that accidents occurred at an efficient rate.

The retrenchment claim had been fully developed by Atiyah, although with differences in emphasis, in *Accidents, Compensation and the Law*. However, the second claim – that tort law, once largely abolished, should not be replaced by anything – was entirely novel. It was animated by an understanding on the part of Atiyah that the tort system effectively

> forces us all to have insurance coverage which is not the coverage many of us would choose to have in the open market, if insurance against personal injury was the kind of insurance people bought for themselves, as they buy household insurance, or holiday insurance, or motor comprehensive insurance.'[62]

Absent the tort system, people would, he argued, instead tend to buy loss insurance, which would permit them to choose the level of cover that suited them.

B. Atiyah's Theses

Just a year later, in 1997, *The Damages Lottery* burst onto the scene. Its title, an obvious allusion to Terrence Ison's *The Forensic Lottery*,[63] showed the influence of that work on Atiyah's thinking. In *The Damages Lottery*, Atiyah built upon the foundations that he had laid down in his essay. He made the same two overarching claims, although he developed his case in support of each of them in rather different ways than he had previously. As to the retrenchment claim, Atiyah complained that the tort system 'is as unjust and inefficient as it could be'[64] and 'built on … rotten foundations'.[65] He endeavoured to make good this argument by way of a loose federation of propositions between which he regularly glided. Five ideas seem to have been particularly important to him, and it is worth setting them out in some detail.

First, Atiyah drew attention to the fact that the tort system determines both the entitlement to compensation and the quantum of compensation based on luck rather than on (for example) need.[66] He observed that accident victims

[61] ibid 26.

[62] ibid 33 (footnote omitted).

[63] T Ison, *The Forensic Lottery: A Critique on Tort Liability as a System of Personal Injury Compensation* (London, Staples, 1968).

[64] Atiyah, *The Damages Lottery* (n 3) 2.

[65] ibid 93.

[66] I engaged with the idea of compensation awarded on the basis of need in J Goudkamp, 'Reforming English Tort Law: Lessons from Australia' in E Quill and R Friel (eds), *Damages and Compensation Culture: Comparative Perspectives* (Oxford, Hart Publishing 2016).

often have little or, more often, no control over whether or not they are injured in compensable circumstances, which usually means being injured by the fault of someone who holds third-party insurance or who is employed by a government department. In Atiyah's words, 'it is almost pure chance whether an injured person ends up with damages'.[67]

Second, Atiyah observed that only a tiny fraction of the very many people in society who suffer disability are eligible to receive tort compensation.[68] Most people who suffer disability are not entitled to tort compensation and instead need to look to other sources of support, such as the social security system. Those alternative compensation systems offer assistance at much less generous levels than the tort system which, uniquely among compensation systems, is committed to the principle that the compensation awarded should place the claimant into the position that he or she would have occupied but for the defendant's tort. Thus, the tort system creates, in Atiyah's words, 'a highly privileged class of accident victims'.[69]

Third, Atiyah emphasised the fact that defendants hardly ever pay tort compensation personally. In fact, he observed, it is the premium-paying population or taxpayers who pay.[70] The upshot of this situation, Atiyah pointed out, is that the relatively small number of people who are 'fortunate' enough to be injured in circumstances that attract tort compensation are compensated by substantially the same group of people who fund the various other, much less generous compensation systems.

Fourth, Atiyah argued that the tort system had been 'stretched' in many ways over the course of the twentieth century in favour of claimants. The consequence of this 'stretching' had been to increase the number of disabled persons who were eligible for tort compensation. Although it is understandable that judges (who are principally but not exclusively responsible for the 'stretching') might want to treat accident victims sympathetically, Atiyah argued that this 'stretching' simply made the tort system even more absurd. He developed the following vivid analogy in support of this contention:

> The basic problem is that those who are compensated with damages are in a tiny minority of all victims of accidents and disabilities, and the more we squeeze into this category, the less money is likely to be available for the great majority of those victims. It is rather as though, faced with a hundred homeless people living on the street, we picked out one or two and lodged them in the Ritz at our expense. If we then stretch things a little more here and a little more there, perhaps we could afford to help one or two more of the homeless and put them in the Ritz too. But we shall then find that the bill from the Ritz is so large that we shall have little or nothing to

[67] Atiyah, *The Damages Lottery* (n 3) 2149.

[68] '[O]f all the disabled or handicapped people in society, … only a tiny minority obtain damages at all': ibid 99.

[69] ibid 103.

[70] '[T]he whole public pays': ibid 111.

> spend on the remaining still sleeping on the street. So stretching things will actually have made things worse.[71]

Fifth, Atiyah argued that the tort system is unjust, highly inefficient, has a host of highly undesirable side-effects and is largely devoid of redeeming features. He referred, for example, to the fact that the tort system is delay-stricken and enormously expensive to administer relative to other systems of delivering compensation. Atiyah also contended that the tort system was liable to encourage an unhealthy 'blame culture'. And he poured scorn on suggestions that tort law can be justified on the grounds that it punishes where punishment is deserved, deters unwanted behaviour and serves a useful role as a public accountability mechanism.

As to the other overarching claim made in *The Damages Lottery* – that after tort law has been largely eliminated nothing need be put in its place – Atiyah contended that many of his attacks on the tort system applied equally to the social security system, such as his view that the tort system encourages malingering,[72] is prone to exploitation by claimants who falsely assert that they have suffered mental injuries[73] and lends credence to the unattractive idea that individuals are entitled to have governments care for their every need.[74] However, it appears that Atiyah's most fundamental reason for not suggesting that a social security system should fill the gap left by the retrenchment of tort law is the fact that welfare state ideals had fallen out of favour.

Atiyah did not actually go quite as far as saying that the state should not put anything in the void left by the retrenchment of the tort system. In the case of road accidents, Atiyah favoured total removal of the tort system and a compulsory loss insurance regime being installed in its place. Atiyah argued for this limited state involvement on the basis that if buying insurance were optional, few would purchase it and many would be left without cover. However, in the case of other accidents, Atiyah preferred to leave it up to individual citizens to decide whether to purchase loss insurance. He accepted that a society security safety net would be required for people who could not, even after the savings that would be made by dispensing with the requirement of purchasing liability insurance, afford cover.

C. The Intended Audience

Atiyah directed *The Damages Lottery* at the layperson.[75] He wrote in the Preface that '[t]his book is designed for the ordinary reader who may, perhaps, have

[71] ibid 32.
[72] ibid 12–13.
[73] ibid 61–62.
[74] ibid 184.
[75] *The Damages Lottery* was not the only popular text that Atiyah wrote. See also PS Atiyah, *Law and Modern Society* (Oxford, OUP, 1995).

read accounts of strange cases in which huge damages have been awarded for bizarre events, and wonders whether the law has gone mad'.[76] Atiyah positioned *The Damages Lottery* in this way because he thought that it might be the only hope of achieving the change that he desired. Efforts (his own included, through *Accidents, Compensation and the Law*) to effect change by influencing academic opinion had (predictably) been in vain, and Atiyah considered that institutions that might be capable of prompting the legislature to enact the required root-and-branch reforms had been 'captured' by the tort system. He thus sought to sway public opinion in the hope that doing so would elicit a groundswell of support for change. Atiyah wrote:

> The one body which might have been able to [achieve the reforms required] – the Law Commission – is far too closely wedded to the system and its underlying value structure, to be able to bring to bear the independent scrutiny the system needs. In the long run the only solution to the difficulty must lie in educating the public to understand more fully the nature of the system we live under, and who pays its costs.[77]

Consistently with that objective, *The Damages Lottery* is almost devoid of footnotes and citations, brief (it runs to just under 200 pages) and written in a highly accessible style. Moreover, and in a radical break from the way in which legal academics in Commonwealth jurisdictions tend to write, *The Damages Lottery* is a highly partisan project that heaps invective on the tort system. On account of these features, *The Damages Lottery* is the antithesis of a dreary academic text. Arthur Ripstein writes that '*The Damages Lottery* is written with great passion and urgency. Readers unfamiliar with Atiyah's earlier work are likely to experience the thrill of reading an exposé.'[78] In a recent lecture, Lord Sumption observed that *The Damages Lottery* is 'one of the most eloquent polemics ever to be directed against a firmly entrenched principle of law'.[79]

Despite Atiyah's approach, *The Damages Lottery*, not unexpectedly, apparently made little or no impression on society's attitude towards tort law. In a country in which tort law occupies a very fringe role in the lives of most people,[80] an apathetic public was seemingly essentially unmoved by the problems Atiyah identified. However, *The Damages Lottery* quickly garnered attention for its significant scholarly value. Two critics refer to it as

> a sustained, relentless (and highly accessible) examination of the problems which beset personal injury litigation, exposing the system as indefensible (both rhetorically

[76] Atiyah, *The Damages Lottery* (n 3) vii.
[77] ibid 173.
[78] A Ripstein, 'Some Recent Obituaries of Tort Law' (1998) 48 *University of Toronto Law Journal* 561, 567.
[79] J Sumption, 'Abolishing Personal Injuries Law: A Project', Personal Injuries Bar Association Annual Lecture (2017) 1.
[80] 'Nobody in England would regard tort law as playing more than a very peripheral role in the life of the society': Atiyah, 'Tort Law and the Alternatives' (n 16) 1044.

and legally), unjustifiably expensive, and producing a fundamentally unfair distribution of the 'compensation cake'.[81]

D. The Retrenchment Claim

The retrenchment claim, although deeply controversial, was certainly not new. Atiyah himself had, of course, argued in *Accidents, Compensation and the Law*[82] for the substantial abolition of tort law in the personal injury context. And impassioned calls for the abolition of tort law, for essentially the same reasons that Atiyah gave, had been made previously elsewhere.[83] How did scholars react to Atiyah's articulation of the retrenchment argument? Those who reject the retrenchment argument generally contend that it overlooks the fact that tort law is ultimately a system of interpersonal justice. In his well-known response to *The Damages Lottery*, Andrew Burrows contends:

> My central defence of the tort system rests on it being a system of individual responsibility. It pins responsibility for compensating another on an individual because of what the individual has done, or has not done. … A central flaw in the argument put by critics of tort is to assume that because individual defendants rarely pay the damages themselves, tort cannot stand up as a system of individual responsibility. … But whether the defendant pays the damages himself or herself is not of central importance. What is important is that the defendant is made legally responsible for ensuring that the plaintiff is paid compensation. It is the pinning of that legal responsibility on the defendant that is at the heart of the tort system.[84]

In a similar vein, Ripstein contends:

> Atiyah's rhetoric obscures the role of responsibility in tort law. Atiyah … put[s] forward a litany of examples in which the law has been 'stretched' by plaintiffs seeking compensation from defendants whose responsibility is dubious. As he describes the cases, the defendants typically appear blameless. In some of them, we are left with the impression that if anyone ought to have been more careful, it was the plaintiff. Reflection on these examples is supposed to lead us to conclude that people should insure against their own carelessness, and perhaps also against their own bad luck. They should bear the costs of their choices, rather than trying to displace those costs onto others. Because they are examples in which we are not inclined to think that the defendant is not [sic] responsible for the plaintiff's injury, though, they distract us from the cases that are of central concern of the tort system, namely, those in which the defendant *is* responsible.[85]

[81] Conaghan and Mansell, 'Review Article: From the Permissive to the Dismissive Society' (n 45) 286.

[82] See the text accompanying n 44, above.

[83] Especially in Ison, *The Forensic Lottery* (n 63).

[84] A Burrows, *Understanding the Law of Obligations: Essays on Contract, Tort and Restitution* (Oxford, OUP, 2000) 122–23.

[85] Ripstein, 'Some Recent Obituaries of Tort Law' (n 78) 565–66 (original emphasis). Consider also Stevens, *Torts and Rights* (n 26) 325.

Atiyah pre-empted these criticisms and wrote in his essay that foreshadowed *The Damages Lottery*:

> I am aware that many lawyers and philosophers who have discussed the moral foundations of tort liability take the view that insurance is irrelevant to the moral basis of the wrongdoer's liability. Either he pays the damages, we are told, or he pays an insurance premium which is actuarially sound and this amounts to the same thing. Yet in most cases outside the road accident sphere the guilty party does not even pay the insurance premium. Except for some (though not, of course, all) road accidents, most tort liability for personal injuries is these days imposed on corporations or public authorities of some kind, and it is the employer or the authority which pays the premium or acts as a self-insurer. So (with the same exception) not only is it the case that the damages are hardly ever paid by the guilty party, but the insurance premiums are hardly ever paid by him either ... The employer or insurer, who is not to blame, pays the damages; the wrongdoer, who is to blame, does not pay. How then can it possibly be argued that the tort system is one of corrective justice?[86]

However, this retort does not really meet Burrows' and Ripstein's point. Their argument is not that the ubiquity of liability insurance prevents tort law from being understood in terms of personal responsibility because tortfeasors must pay damages or must pay premia. Instead, it is that arrangements in relation to insurance say nothing about tort law *qua* personal responsibility system, because insurance merely enables wrongdoers to discharge liabilities that descend upon them. A sounder way by which Atiyah might have sought to defuse the criticisms concerned is to contend that even if the tort system, despite the fact that the actual wrongdoers normally do not pay, is a system of personal responsibility, it does not follow that retaining it, with all its prolificacy, waste, delay and the like, is justified. Atiyah did not see things in quite this way, however, being unwilling to accept that the tort regime can be understood as a system of personal responsibility in the first place.

Another and quite different rebuttal of the retrenchment claim is that it is imprecise. The objection is that Atiyah failed to make it sufficiently clear which parts of tort law should be done away with and which aspects preserved. Burrows writes:

> A major problem with the arguments advanced by the critics of tort is that the precise subject-matter under attack is never made entirely clear.
>
> If we first of all confine ourselves to tort, is it the whole of tort or only parts of it that are under attack? While the main focus is clearly on negligently caused personal injury and death, what about intentionally caused personal injury (through the tort of trespass to the person)? What about strict liability causing personal injury (through, for example, the tort of breach of statutory duty or the Consumer Protection Act 1987)? And is the attack also intended to knock out negligently, or intentionally, caused property damage or pure economic loss? What about the torts of defamation and nuisance?

[86] Atiyah, 'Personal Injuries in The Twenty-First Century' (n 59) 13 (footnote omitted).

> It is not obvious that the critics of tort have properly considered this issue. …
>
> [A] lack of clarity [in this regard] is to be found in *The Damages Lottery*. Atiyah writes, 'In general this book is not concerned with … intentional torts, and certainly no proposal will be found here to abolish or reduce the liability of a person who commits an intentional tort. But there are some cases which do raise issues with intentional torts which are really identical to issues which arise with negligence. These cases concern the liability of employers or others for the actions of a wrongdoer. When, for instance, a policeman uses excessive force in arresting someone (and thereby commits a tort) the police authority will be liable for the damages, just as much as the policeman himself. This kind of liability – which is actually the liability of the public in the last resort – is very much the concern of this book, and raises problems in no way different from the liability of police officers for negligence. But apart from that this book is not concerned with intentional torts which do not give rise to anything like the volume of claims and litigation which negligence does.'
>
> But what is it that links the police or employer intentional torts with negligence, yet does not link other intentional torts with negligence?[87]

To a degree, the complaint is a valid one. The scope of the retrenchment claim is not specified with the precision that one would hope to see in, for example, a statute that was carving out one area of law from a larger field. However, it must be remembered that Atiyah was concerned in *The Damages Lottery* to write an accessible polemic about tort law as a compensation system.[88] It would have been incompatible with that objective to condescend to a fine-grained analysis of the specific causes of action that should be expelled from the law of torts in so far as they afford redress for personal injury and death.

Connected with the imprecision objection is the suggestion that, regardless of which parts of tort law Atiyah thought should survive, Atiyah offered no rational basis, and could offer no rational basis, for stopping at any particular point. Atiyah placed great weight on the fact that defendants do not personally pay damages awards that are made against them.[89] However, if it is that fact that contributes to tort law's problematic state, several other parts of the law of obligations should be abolished too. Burrows makes the point forcefully:

> If one is criticising the tort system on the basis that defendants do not themselves pay the damages … why is the whole system of civil wrongs (and indeed aspects of the law on unjust enrichment) not subjected to the same attack?[90]

One possible answer to Burrows is that tort law is different from other departments of private law in that it is one of a plethora of compensation systems that are all funded by substantially the same people (ie the premium-paying population and taxpayers), and that it makes no sense to have different regimes that afford widely disparate levels of support to different groups of

[87] Burrows, *Understanding the Law of Obligations* (n 84) 126–127 (footnote omitted).
[88] See the text accompanying n 75, above.
[89] See the text accompanying n 70, above.
[90] Burrows, *Understanding the Law of Obligations* (n 84) 128.

people based on luck. Contract law and the law of unjust enrichment do not resemble tort law in this regard.

A final but important point in evaluating the retrenchment argument, as presented by Atiyah, concerns Atiyah's jaundiced opinion of claimants and claimants' lawyers generally. Atiyah implies that accident victims as a class are prone to exaggerate their symptoms and refrain from rehabilitating themselves with a view to maximising their monetary recovery. Thus, he writes that an accident victim who has entitlements in tort 'may simply assume that he can never lead a normal life again, never work again, and make no effort to rehabilitate himself'.[91] Atiyah also expressed scepticism as to whether many recognised psychiatric illnesses actually exist. He said that '[g]iving ... perfectly natural conditions fancy names like "post-traumatic stress" does not actually demonstrate that they have a real, objective existence, though judges striving not to appear old-fashioned fuddy duddies, are naturally persuaded by the doctors that they have'.[92] Atiyah also criticised claimants for partaking in the tort system instead of accepting responsibility for their own problems,[93] and lawyers for their facilitative role. He argues that the tort system may encourage 'behaviour ... which ... help[s] to foment claims or litigation – lawyers may ... start advertising'.[94] There are formidable difficulties with this collection of claims. Atiyah cites no evidence – let alone any credible evidence – in support of his apparent suggestion that claimants generally are prone to malinger, and his view that one should respond sceptically when invited to conclude on the basis of medical evidence that a given condition is a psychiatric illness is downright surprising. Further, it is difficult to fault accident victims for choosing to exercise rights that the law confers upon them, or lawyers for assisting claimants to invoke those rights. Atiyah seems not to have considered the possibility that lawyers who advertise, far from engaging in discreditable behaviour, are, in fact, performing a public service.[95]

E. Atiyah's Volte-face

A striking feature of *The Damages Lottery* is that it involves a significant change of position by Atiyah. Although Atiyah continued to favour retrenchment of the

[91] Atiyah, *The Damages Lottery* (n 3) 12.

[92] ibid 61.

[93] ibid 138–143. Cf Atiyah's remark that 'we should not blame ... (in general) the people who take advantage of [the tort system] to claim what they are entitled to' (ibid 155).

[94] ibid 28.

[95] An immense literature exists regarding the desirability of permitting lawyers to advertise. Contributions include Note, 'Advertising, Solicitation and the Profession's Duty to Make Legal Counsel Available' (1972) 81 *Yale Law Journal* 1181; M Walker, 'Advertising by Lawyers: Some Pros and Cons' (1979) 55 *Chicago-Kent Law Review* 407; G Hazard, R Pearce and J Stempel, 'Why Lawyers Should be Allowed to Advertise: A Market Analysis of Legal Services' (1983) 58 *New York University Law Review* 1084.

tort system as a mechanism for dispensing compensation for personal injury and death, instead of arguing for the installation of a comprehensive society security system he contended that nothing should replace tort law (except in the context of road accidents and subject to a safety net for people who cannot afford to buy insurance). Burrows chides Atiyah for this volte-face. He writes:

> One must have concerns, about Atiyah's willingness to argue so vehemently for such radically different conclusions in such a relatively short space of time. Critics would say that, had policy-makers applied his arguments in the 1970s, we would have abolished the tort system and instead had in place a wide-ranging social welfare scheme for the benefit of the injured. Yet only fifteen years later those policy-makers would have been condemned by Atiyah for creating a misconceived new system which should be abolished. Those concerned with legislative reform may be forgiven for thinking that such a willingness to 'switch horses' means that one must not take Atiyah's views too seriously. Fascinating, beautifully expressed and brilliantly argued as they are, they may be the stuff of classrooms and academic conferences and not for the real world.[96]

With respect, this criticism is unjustified. In the first place, the political currents in the United Kingdom ebbed rather differently in 1970 when *Accidents, Compensation and the Law* was published from the way in which they flowed in 1997, when *The Damages Lottery* appeared. Atiyah, as he made clear, changed tack precisely because the prevailing political ideology had shifted.[97] He realised that his earlier proposals, not having been acted upon in the 1970s, would not now be implemented.[98] More fundamentally, the mere fact that Atiyah changed his mind does nothing to undermine the case that he presented in favour either

[96] Burrows, *Understanding the Law of Obligations* (n 84) 122.

[97] 'I now see no likelihood whatever of large, bureaucratic, welfare schemes of the Woodhouse type, coming back into fashion in the near future, or even the next half century, either in the UK or elsewhere. It is not simply a matter of left-wing or socialist parties winning elections. As everyone knows, there has been a massive, world-wide reaction against bureaucratic welfare schemes in the past decade' (Atiyah, 'Personal Injuries in The Twenty-First Century' (n 59) 34).

[98] This point has been convincingly made by Edwin Peel. Peel wrote (E Peel, 'Book Review of Understanding the Law of Obligations: Essays on Contract, Tort and Restitution by Andrew Burrows' (1997) 115 *LQR* 335, 340–41) that 'one particular attack on [Atiyah] does seem a little unfair. Atiyah has, indeed, performed a volte-face in *The Damages Lottery* (1997) in which he now argues that the tort system should be abolished and replaced with nothing at all, save the hope that individuals with more money in their pockets will be encouraged to take out personal accident insurance. This contrasts starkly with the stance he took in *Accidents, Compensation and the Law* (now in the hands of Peter Cane) where he advocated the abolition of the tort system and its replacement with some form of enhanced publicly-funded no fault compensation scheme. The unfairness lies in suggesting that Atiyah would now condemn any policy-makers who might have acted on his earlier proposals. The fact of the matter is that they did not, and a fairer interpretation of this change of approach might be to congratulate Atiyah on his political astuteness. Still faced with the obvious failings of the existing tort system, but all too well aware that no political party is looking to extend the social welfare system, Atiyah has adopted the pragmatic approach so prevalent in much of Burrows' writing by seeking a solution which would be politically acceptable and therefore represent an attainable goal.'

of the social security solution or of the loss insurance solution. Atiyah may well have been wrong to abandon the former as the type of reform for which society should strive. Equally, prior acceptance of another view does nothing to show that a newly held position is wrong. The fact of the matter is that Atiyah's exceptional intellectual honesty and preparedness to revisit his earlier views and shift his position where he felt that doing so was appropriate is a desirable quality in a scholar rather than a shortcoming.

F. The Loss Insurance 'Solution'

The second major claim made by Atiyah in *The Damages Lottery* (ie, that loss insurance should be allowed to fill the gap left by tort law), which claim I suspect was heavily influenced by his experience in the law of contract, has apparently persuaded few, if any, scholars. Ripstein writes:

> In the end, the main benefit Atiyah's alternative offers to the needy is reduced prices for goods and services, and perhaps reduced taxes, because manufacturers will not need to buy liability insurance. No numbers are offered, but even this promised side benefit sits uneasily with his other arguments. He is attuned to the ability of companies to pass the costs of liability insurance on to their customers. In contrast, he does not consider the ability of those with market power to pass the costs of their own first-party coverage on to their customers. Nor does he mention that under his proposed system, people would need to pay for their own first-party insurance, including insurance against the carelessness of others.[99]

Joanne Conaghan and Wade Mansell argue:

> Atiyah has not solved the problem of the damages lottery, but has simply substituted one system of arbitrary and fortuitous distribution for another. In what sense is it more justifiable for protection from injury or illness to depend on ability to pay premiums rather than on what causes the injury or illness in question? It is only if one accepts that the distribution of wealth is itself just (rather than the random product of a socio-economic system where there is, too often, little correspondence between individual merit and financial reward) that its outcomes appear defensible.[100]

Bob Hepple says:

> [W]hen I hear the words 'free market' I reach for my begging bowl. Would low income earners be able to afford first-party insurance? How would unemployed people or unwaged women at home be protected? How would the private insurance market react to the abolition of tort law?[101]

[99] Ripstein, 'Some Recent Obituaries of Tort Law' (n 78) 564 (footnote omitted).
[100] Conaghan and Mansell, 'Review Article' (n 45) 291–92.
[101] B Hepple, 'Negligence: The Search for Coherence' (1997) 50 *Current Legal Problems* 85.

Other commentators have been similarly unkind to Atiyah's proposal, for substantially the same reason. Pat O'Malley wrote, in relation to Atiyah's first-party insurance solution to the damages lottery:

> It has to be said that this is the kind of vague utopianism for which socialists and supporters of welfare state policies have been vilified for decades. Worse, this Faith in Markets is coupled with an almost complete wishing away of the very troubling complexities.[102]

O'Malley proceeds to criticise Atiyah for not having thought through in any detail how his proposed safety net would function. In a similar vein, John Keeler doubts that loss insurance is a promising alternative to the tort system given its apparently limited popularity at the present.[103] Jeffrey O'Connell and Christopher Robinette write that 'Atiyah is merciless and effective in flaying tort law for its hopeless inadequacies'.[104] However, they, too, dissent from his loss insurance proposals on the basis that he goes too far in saying that 'efficiency and corrective justice in tort law … do not matter at all'.[105]

One additional objection to Atiyah's argument in favour of allowing loss insurance to fill the gap left by the removal of the tort system concerns his suggestion that loss insurance should be compulsory in relation to road accidents. The first difficulty here is that it is not at all clear why road accidents should be singled out for separate treatment, or why Atiyah thought, as he apparently did, people would be less likely to purchase loss insurance voluntarily in this setting. Another problem is that the idea of making loss insurance compulsory rather cuts against his idea that the *Zeitgeist* requires individuals to look after themselves.

V. INFLUENCE

How is Atiyah's influence on scholarly thinking regarding tort law to be determined? And to what extent does his thinking continue to affect the writing of today's torts scholars? One way of answering those questions is by analysing citations of Atiyah's work. The burden of this section is to provide that analysis. Before proceeding, it is worth observing that Atiyah's scholarship has been included in one previous citation analysis.[106] Although that study, which

[102] P O'Malley, 'Book Review: The Damages Lottery by Patrick Atiyah' (1999) 16 *Law in Context* 123, 127.

[103] J Keeler, 'Thinking Through the Unthinkable: Collective Responsibilities in Personal Injury Law' (2001) 30 *Common Law World Review* 349, 350.

[104] J O'Connell and CJ Robinette, 'The Role of Compensation in Personal Injury Tort Law' (1999) 32 *Connecticut Law Review* 137, 147.

[105] ibid 148.

[106] BS Markesinis and J Fedtke, *Engaging with Foreign Law* (Oxford, Hart Publishing, 2009) 111–12.

was conducted by Basil Markesinis and Jörg Fedtke, is not limited to Atiyah's writings in tort law, it is nonetheless of interest. The investigators report citation rates for Andrew Ashworth, Patrick Atiyah, Peter Birks, Roy Goode and Guenter Treitel for the period 1980 to 2000 in the periodical literature in (among other countries) the United States and England. Markesinis and Fedtke explain that those scholars were included within their study on the basis that 'no English colleague would, we believe, argue that [they] are not among the leaders of our profession' and because '[a]ll also taught (or teach) core subjects'.[107]

Eight hundred and ninety-four citations of Atiyah's work were identified in scholarly literature in the United States. That rate was by far the highest, with the next highest figure being 164 citations of Andrew Ashworth's writings. Two hundred and seven citations of Atiyah's work were recorded in the English academic literature. The next highest figure related to Peter Birks, whose work had been referred to 144 times. These figures are particularly striking given that Atiyah had retired in 1988, whereas all of the other writers were at the height of their powers throughout the study period. All things being equal, one would reasonably expect to observe greater academic interest in contemporaneous publications than in older writings, not least because the more dated a contribution, the less relevant it is likely to be to scholars who are interested in the law as it presently stands. Markesinis and Fedtke also examined citations of the same scholars' writings for the period 2001 to 2005. By this time, the picture had changed significantly: Atiyah's writings were still the most frequently cited in the United States at 259 citations, but Andrew Ashworth, in second place, had closed much of the gap, his work having been cited 182 times. As regards citations in the English academic literature, Atiyah had tumbled to third place with 51 citations, behind Peter Birks, who had 193 citations, and Andrew Ashworth, whose work was cited 77 times.

The following methodology was used for the citation analysis that follows. All citations of Atiyah's three principal contributions to tort law – *Vicarious Liability in the Law of Torts*; *Accidents, Compensation and the Law*; and *The Damages Lottery* – in articles, case notes and book reviews published prior to 31 December 2017 in Australia, the United Kingdom and the United States were identified. The citations were located by way of database searches on Westlaw UK, Lexis and HeinOnline. In the case of *Accidents, Compensation and the Law*, which saw three editions authored by Atiyah and a further five editions under the authorship of Peter Cane, only citations to editions for which Atiyah was responsible were counted. Self-citations by Atiyah were disregarded as were, in order to avoid double counting, republications of works that cited one of the three books in issue. No attempt was made to examine citations in books (there being no straightforward way to perform any such examination). If any given source referred to one of Atiyah's three works in question, a single citation was

[107] ibid 111.

recorded in respect of that source, irrespective of the number of times the book in issue was cited in it. Accordingly, no significance was attached to the weight that a given writer attached to Atiyah's scholarship: a single reference to one of Atiyah's books in issue was accorded the same significance as a substantial review article of one of Atiyah's three texts. Endeavouring to ascribe the weight given to Atiyah's books would have greatly complicated the exercise and, in a sense, rendered the tally of citations more imprecise, because, for example, it would have been debatable how to treat a publication that referred explicitly (say) once to one of Atiyah's three books by name but then discussed it indirectly thereafter. Similarly, no attempt was made to discriminate between the various purposes for which Atiyah's work concerned were cited (for example, to indicate approval or disagreement, for a description of the positive law, and so on). The results of the analysis are shown in Table 11.1.

Table 11.1 Citations of Atiyah's principal contributions to tort law scholarship

	Australia	United Kingdom	United States	**Total**
Vicarious Liability in the Law of Torts	37	82	50	169
Accidents, Compensation and the Law	52	134	125	311
The Damages Lottery	31	73	36	140
Total	120	289	211	620

Pausing here, it is clear from these results that, of the three texts under investigation, *Accidents, Compensation and the Law* made by far the largest mark in terms of citations. That is, perhaps, unsurprising in circumstances where that book ran to more than one edition, unlike the other two works concerned, and given that it is the most substantial by far of the three publications. Also of interest is the fact that Atiyah's work gained more traction (in terms of citations) in the United Kingdom than elsewhere, although interest in *Accidents, Compensation and the Law* was fairly similar on both sides of the Atlantic. That result may be thought to be somewhat surprising given, first, the fact that the market for legal scholarship in the United States dwarfs that in the United Kingdom, second, Atiyah's extensive engagement with United States scholarship in *Accidents, Compensation and the Law*,[108] third, the fact that Atiyah's policy-driven style of analysis is much more familiar in the United States than in the United Kingdom and, fourth, the findings of Markesinis and Fedtke's study.[109]

[108] See the text accompanying nn 52–55, above.
[109] See the text accompanying n 107, above.

How did Atiyah's impact, understood in terms of citations, fare relative to that of other leading twentieth-century Commonwealth torts scholars? Table 11.2 records the number of times (as of 31 December 2017) the tort-related periodical writings of several other great Commonwealth torts scholars (or scholars whose interests included tort law) were cited in periodical publications according to searches performed on HeinOnline.[110] Perhaps unsurprisingly, given that John Fleming spent a large proportion of his career at Berkeley[111] and published much of his work in United States journals and reviews, Fleming's work had the greatest impact by far (in terms of the number of citations).

Table 11.2 Citations of leading 20th-century Commonwealth torts scholars

PS Atiyah	284
JG Fleming	891
Harold Luntz	18
Harry Street	32
Tony Weir	11
Glanville Williams	199

Although these results are of interest, they should not be taken too seriously in circumstances where they have not been informed by citations of the scholars' books or by those of their periodical contributions that do not appear on HeinOnline. Furthermore, publications in United States journals and reviews are overrepresented on HeinOnline, and a prominent publication in the United States thus has the potential to distort the results. Indeed, in some ways, the results contained in Table 11.2 are principally a measure of the degree to which the scholars in issue penetrated the United States market in tort scholarship than anything else.

Putting the numerical picture to one side, from a more qualitative perspective, what impact has Atiyah's writings on tort law had on the thinking of prominent torts scholars? It is obvious that Atiyah's work has made a major mark on several leading thinkers, even if they have not necessarily followed Atiyah down all of the principal avenues he travelled. It seems likely that John Fleming was significantly influenced by Atiyah's work in a sceptical assessment that he wrote regarding the future of tort law,[112] despite only fleeting references to

[110] The vast majority of the publications concerned were authored by the scholar of interest writing alone. However, a few contributions were co-authored, and these were included in the results.

[111] Fleming spent two years as a visiting professor at Berkeley in 1958 and 1959, before relocating permanently to Berkeley in 1961, where he remained for the rest of his career: RM Bauxman, 'John G Fleming – 1919-1997' (1997) 45 *American Journal of Comparative Law* 645, 645.

[112] JG Fleming, 'Is There a Future for Tort?' (1984) 58 *Australian Law Journal* 131.

Atiyah's writings in the article in question. Harold Luntz's understanding of tort law was profoundly shaped by Atiyah's vision. Luntz was persuaded by Atiyah's critiques of the tort system and attempts to justify it,[113] and considered those criticisms to show conclusively that the tort system should be jettisoned and a comprehensive no-fault system installed in its place.[114] As with Luntz, Atiyah's assaults on the tort system persuaded Peter Cane that *qua* mechanism for providing compensation to victims of accidents, it had few redeeming features. However, Cane was unconvinced by Atiyah's proposal that tort law should be largely abolished and nothing installed in its place. Instead, he prefers a 'two-tier system in which cover for losses and expenses above a certain minimum would be voluntary', but contends that 'up to that minimum level, people should not be left to the vagaries of the "free market"'.[115]

My sense is that Atiyah's writings in tort are, regrettably, no longer featuring in the works of tort theorists as prominently today as they once did. This is particularly so in the case of scholars who are concerned to advance moral accounts of tort law, which accounts are now in vogue. Ernest Weinrib did not refer once to Atiyah in his landmark *The Idea of Private Law*.[116] John Gardner similarly fails to engage with Atiyah's work in any of his major writings on tort law.[117] John Goldberg and Ben Zipursky in their important work have made reference to Atiyah's scholarship only in passing.[118] No doubt, the reason why these writers have apparently side-lined Atiyah is that his view that tort law is a clumsily and grossly inadequate compensation system does not fit their respective understandings of tort law. Another reason for the lack of engagement with Atiyah's writings may be to do with the fact that Atiyah was deeply sceptical of efforts to justify tort law in theoretical terms. It appears that Atiyah's intensely functionalist reasoning has become unfashionable.

[113] In a personal reflection written in the twilight of his career, Luntz describes in detail the impact that Atiyah's writings had made on him: Luntz, 'A Personal Journal Through the Law of Torts' (n 50) 401, 404, 411, 415.

[114] See, eg, H Luntz, 'Compensation for Injuries Due to Sport' (1980) 54 *Australian Law Journal* 588; H Luntz, 'Proposals for a National Compensation Scheme' (1981) 55 *Law Institute Journal* 745; H Luntz, 'National Compensation Scheme: A Further Contribution' (1982) 56 *Law Institute Journal* 35; H Luntz, 'The Case for No-Fault Accident Compensation' (1985) 15 *Queensland Law Society Journal* 161; H Luntz, 'Reform of the Law of Negligence: Wrong Questions – Wrong Answers (2002) 25 *University of New South Wales Law Journal* 836; H Luntz, 'Guest Editorial: Medical Indemnity and Tort Law Reform' (2003) 10 *Journal of Law and Medicine* 385; H Luntz, 'Looking Back at Accident Compensation: An Australian Perspective' (2003) 34 *Victoria University of Wellington Law Review* 279; H Luntz, 'The Australian Picture' (2004) 35 *Victoria University of Wellington Law Review* 879; H Luntz, 'A View from Abroad' (2008) *New Zealand Law Review* 97.

[115] P Cane, *Atiyah's Accidents, Compensation and the Law*, 8th edn (Cambridge, CUP, 2013) 493.

[116] E Weinrib, *The Idea of Private Law* (Cambridge, MA, Harvard University Press, 1995).

[117] J Gardner, 'What is Tort Law For? Part 1. The Place of Corrective Justice' (2011) 30 *Law & Philosophy* 1; J Gardner, 'What is Tort Law For? Part 2. The Place of Distributive Justice' in J Oberdiek (ed), *Philosophical Foundations of Tort Law* (Oxford, OUP, 2014).

[118] See, eg, JCP Goldberg and BC Zipursky, 'Tort Law and Moral Luck' (2007) 92 *Cornell Law Review* 1123, 1146–67, fn 84; JCP Goldberg and BC Zipursky, 'Torts as Wrongs' (2010) 88 *Texas Law Review* 917, 924.

VI. LEGACY

Tony Weir was not a person who dispensed praise lightly or withheld criticism where he felt that criticism was deserved.[119] In a book review published in 1992 of *Essays for Patrick Atiyah*,[120] he (rightly) wrote that Atiyah 'is unrivalled in the number, scope and quality of his contributions to English scholarship in the last 40 years'.[121] Atiyah, perhaps uniquely among the great legal scholars of the twentieth century, rose to the apex of more than one major field simultaneously. He was a masterful expositor of the law, but first and foremost he was an inquisitor, who was able, with unparalleled ability, to synthesise and marshal a vast array of sources convincingly to bear out his arguments.

[119] Consider T Weir, 'Book Review: The Law of Contract by Hugh Collins' (1986) 45 *CLJ* 503.
[120] P Cane and J Stapleton (eds), *Essays for Patrick Atiyah* (Oxford, Clarendon Press, 1991).
[121] T Weir, 'Book Review: Essays for Patrick Atiyah edited by Peter Cane and Jane Stapleton' (1992) 51 *CLJ* 374, 374.

12

Mr Tony Weir (1936–2011)

PAULA GILIKER

I. INTRODUCTION

THE VALUE OF the contribution of John Anthony (or Tony) Weir to tort law scholarship and notably comparative tort law scholarship cannot be doubted. His obituary in *The Times* newspaper described him as possessing 'extraordinary learning and intelligence, idiosyncratic ideas and tastes, and a great generosity of character', and as being 'all that a cloistered don should be'.[1] Eminent French comparative law scholar Xavier Blanc-Jouvan described him as 'in the world of legal scholars, one of the brightest minds of his generation'.[2] Brought up and schooled in Scotland (at Fettes College in Edinburgh), Weir won a scholarship to study Classics at Trinity College, Cambridge at the age of 16, but deferred for two years to undertake national service with the Cameronians, rising to second lieutenant. While at Trinity, he changed to law, gaining a first in his Part II examinations. Having spent 1960–62 as a graduate student at Tulane University Law School in New Orleans (which would result in four substantial pieces, written in collaboration with Pierre Catala, on French and English tort law), he was elected a Fellow of Trinity College, Cambridge, from 1962,[3] and, in the Faculty of Law, was a lecturer

[1] 'Tony Weir' *The Times* (9 February 2012). The Cambridge University website also noted, 'A Fellow of Trinity College, Tony had been a teaching member of the Faculty since 1963. He will be remembered for his lively lectures, delivered with sharp wit and full of insights, and for his scholarship in Comparative law and the Law of Torts': 'Death of Mr Tony Weir' (13 December 2011) at www.law.cam.ac.uk/press/news/2011/12/death-mr-tony-weir/1715. Although Weir made clear that he did not want a *Festschrift* in his honour, tributes to his work include a collection of essays in a special volume of the *Tulane Law Review* in 2013 (see, in particular, Shael Herman's introduction, 'Friendship's Bounty' (2013) 87 *Tulane Law Review* 717) and a seminar organised by the British Association of Comparative Law in September 2012.

[2] X Blanc-Jouvan, 'In Memoriam: John Antony [*sic*] Weir (1936–2011)' (2012) 64 *Revue internationale de droit comparé* 327, 329 (translation by Giliker).

[3] Weir remained committed to his college, Trinity College, Cambridge, all his life. The College, after consulting with alumni, has now set up a fund to assist students in his honour, the Donoghue and Stevenson Law Fund (see at www.trin.cam.ac.uk/alumni/giving-to-trinity/the-donoghue-and-stevenson-law-fund), named, naturally, after Weir's two cats: Donoghue and Stevenson.

from 1963–79 and Reader from 1979–2003. At the time of his death in 2011, Weir was an Emeritus Reader in Law at the University of Cambridge. Despite his strong affiliation to Trinity, Weir was a frequent visitor to universities in the United States (US) (notably Tulane and Cornell), France, Italy, Germany and Switzerland, where he made many strong friendships that lasted to his death.

His was an extraordinary career, which included the publication of two leading tort textbooks (his *Casebook on Tort* reaching 10 editions), 18 contributions to edited collections, 23 articles, 35 case notes and 50 book reviews, published in English, French and German, together with translations of nine books from French, German and Latin, most famously Zweigert and Kötz's *Introduction to Comparative Law*.[4] His Clarendon Law lectures on economic torts, published in 1997,[5] give us an insight into Weir as a tort scholar. The back cover to the book describes the lectures as 'exciting and provocative … contain[ing] a number of controversial propositions, defended with vigour by [their] author.' We gain an impression, therefore, of a critical and intellectually vigorous mind, ready to pierce the conventions of the common law. Indeed, Ken Oliphant in his review described the lectures as 'lively, entertaining and stimulating … No staid academic treatment this! Weir writes in the genre that he has made his own – the legal polemic – splendidly disdainful of conventional proprieties'.[6]

In this chapter, I consider Weir in several roles he made his own (tort lawyer, comparative lawyer and translator), and the specific nature of his contribution as a textbook writer and prolific author of case commentaries. The chapter will also examine how a leading comparative lawyer, fluent in many languages, can be, in parallel, a Eurosceptic. During the 2016 UK referendum on European Union (EU) membership, a number of colleagues commented to me that Weir would have been a Brexiteer, fighting against the 'evils' of Europe. As will be seen, Weir's contribution as a scholar of tort law is important, both in his distinctive style and because of its impact on fellow academics, generations of students and judges.

II. WEIR AND THE LAW OF TORT: TEXTBOOK WRITER AND CASE NOTE COMMENTATOR

A. The Textbook Writer

The contribution of Tony Weir to the law of tort is profound. Anyone who has studied law at an English or Welsh university (or even beyond) in the last 50 years will be familiar with his *A Casebook on Tort* (first edition appearing

[4] K Zweigert and H Kötz, *Introduction to Comparative Law*, 3rd edn, tr Tony Weir (Oxford, OUP, 1998). Weir had also translated the two previous versions (1977 and 1992).

[5] T Weir, *Economic Torts* (Oxford, Clarendon Press, 1997).

[6] K Oliphant, 'Book Review' (1999) 62 *MLR* 320.

in 1967) and his Clarendon textbook, *An Introduction to Tort Law*, which first appeared in 2002 with its second, and final, edition in 2006. The judiciary is equally conversant with his work. In *Henderson v Merrett Syndicates Ltd*,[7] Lord Goff sought to resist 'the temptation of elegance' offered by Weir's reference to the French doctrine of *non cumul*, under which the concurrence of claims in contract and tort is outlawed.[8] On Weir's death, Carnwath LJ paid tribute to his work in *Barr v Biffa Waste Services Ltd*,[9] remarking that '[t]he matter is stated simply and accurately by Tony Weir (whose death last December was a sad loss to all who knew him or learnt from him)'.[10] Lord Rodger commented extra-judicially that he found inspiration in every edition of the *Casebook*: 'it was surely not least because his pointed remarks were fun to read and, even more importantly, stuck in the mind long after a more pedestrian explanation would have been forgotten'.[11]

Weir's appeal to the reader, then, can perhaps be summed up with his stated goal in writing *A Casebook on Tort*: to comment and discuss the law in a manner 'occasionally extreme, in the hope of stimulating a response and of dispelling the aura of inevitability which the judgments themselves properly exhale'.[12] The provocative nature of his statements render them, at the very least, memorable, and provide the student with a succinct insight into the operation of the law of tort and the often difficult decisions of principle the courts are forced to address.

In this section I shall consider one example taken from chapter 14 of Weir's *Casebook*, which illustrates his distinctive style as a textbook writer. The chapter concerns defamation. While setting out the relevant law with typical clarity, this is a topic on which Weir is not afraid to state his views. He describes defamation as the 'most difficult of all torts. It is certainly the oddest.'[13] He then lists its oddities: liability is extinguished by the death of either party; trial by jury is available at the instance of either party (this is pre-Defamation Act 2013); there is a one-year time bar; in contrast with negligent misstatement, there is a presumption of falsity; damages extend to emotional and financial harm (neither of which, in Weir's view, should be readily redressible in the law of tort). 'Are we still in the law of tort?' he asks. 'Liability in defamation is extremely easy to incur,

[7] *Henderson v Merrett Syndicates Ltd* [1995] 2 AC 145 (HL) 186.

[8] T Weir, 'Complex Liabilities' in A Tunc (ed), *International Encyclopaedia of Comparative Law*, vol XI (Tübingen, JCB Mohr, 1976) para 52.

[9] *Barr v Biffa Waste Services Ltd* [2012] EWCA Civ 312, [2013] QB 455 [72]. See also *JGE v Portsmouth Roman Catholic Diocesan Trust* [2012] EWCA Civ 938, [2013] QB 722 [45] (Ward LJ).

[10] The work cited by Carnwath LJ is Weir's *An Introduction to Tort* Law, 2nd edn (Oxford, Clarendon Press, 2006) 160, which explains in very lucid terms the concept of 'reasonable user' in private nuisance.

[11] Lord Rodger of Earlsferry, 'Humour and Law' [2012] *Scots Law Times* 202, 203.

[12] T Weir, *A Casebook on Tort*, 1st edn (London, Sweet & Maxwell, 1967) (Preface).

[13] T Weir, *A Casebook on Tort*, 10th edn (London, Sweet & Maxwell, 2004) 519.

especially if you say anything interesting.'[14] Certain targets are easy for him. The jury escalation of damages awards and judicial intervention to control them in cases such as *John v Mirror Group Newspapers*[15] provoke the comment that the courts need to do more to prevent the law's 'becoming as absurd, complex and unfair as it is'.[16] His attack on the tort of defamation is devastating:

> The defects of the present law arise because it uses a single remedy, the action for damages, in order to perform three distinct purposes: (a) to permit people to clear their reputation from unfounded allegations; (b) to allow people to claim compensation for the harm they suffer because others have abused their freedom of speech; and (c) to repress gratuitous vituperation, scurrilous disparagement and malignant calumny. Only for (b) is damages the appropriate remedy. For (a) we need a procedure for retraction or correction, and for (c) we need the public stocks.[17]

Weir's argument in a nutshell is that freedom of expression is often at its most useful when it is critical and puncturing the reputations of the great and (not so) good.[18]

Weir's views on defamation reveal much about him as a scholar and lawyer. He is well versed in the law (that goes without saying) but also ready to set out his ideological stall and criticise principles of tort law developed over centuries.[19] His criticism is unsparing – of the courts, the legislator, the claimants who take 'advantage' of these rules, and law reform bodies of which he is dismissive in the extreme.[20] His skills as a comparative lawyer also give him further food for thought, notably in relation to the US and Australia, but also with the European Court of Human Rights (ECtHR) receiving a rare nod of approval due to its intervention in *Tolstoy Miloslavsky v UK*.[21] Such analysis is, however, fleeting, Weir typically keeping his interests in tort law development and comparative law separate. For Weir, the common law should evolve organically, and this would not be assisted by furtive glances overseas. Johnston notes Weir's conviction that the right answer could be reached through reasoning in a principled manner from case law.[22] Reasoning, then, from principle,

[14] ibid 520. This view was no doubt shared by controversial columnists such as Julie Burchill: see *Berkoff v Burchill* [1996] 4 All ER 1008 (CA), on which Weir comments, 'how can a jury possibly know whether the claimant's reputation has actually been damaged [by words imputing ugliness]': Weir, *A Casebook on Tort* (n 13) 529.

[15] *John v Mirror Group Newspapers* [1997] QB 586 (CA) (characterised by Weir as the result of a 'doubtless musical jury' responding to 'some trivial aspersion which can have done him no harm whatsoever': Weir, *A Casebook on Tort* (n 13) 522).

[16] Weir, *A Casebook on Tort* (n 13) 522.

[17] ibid 523.

[18] Weir, *An Introduction to Tort Law* (n 10) 176.

[19] See P Mitchell, *The Making of the Modern Law of Defamation* (Oxford, Hart Publishing, 2015).

[20] 'The emanations of the Law Commission are omitted because so many of their proposals in this area of law are daft': Weir, *A Casebook on Tort* (n 13) vii.

[21] *Tolstoy Miloslavsky v UK* (1995) 20 EHRR 442.

[22] D Johnston, 'A Case, a Statute, and Some Thoughts on the Proper Role of Policy' (2013) 87 *Tulane Law Review* 887, 891.

Weir comes to a clear conclusion: 'Defamation taints all those who come into contact with it.'[23]

Defamation remains a 'distinct' tort. While it more often than not slips off the tort law university syllabus, due to lack of space, in favour of its more energetic fellow torts, negligence and nuisance, it provides an insight into how tort law is capable of protecting a variety of interests beyond that of personal injury and damage to property, and of adapting to different forms of wrongful behaviour. (Weir would not, of course, agree, regarding it as a blot on the landscape of the law of torts.) Lunney, Nolan and Oliphant in their textbook comment:

> No areas of the law excite more interest, or controversy, than the law of defamation … and privacy … [T]hey raise issues of real importance, relating to the appropriate balance to be struck between freedom of expression (guaranteed by Article 10 ECHR) and individual interests to reputation and private information.[24]

As these authors indicate, the modern discussion of defamation has progressed beyond Weir's critique – to a new statute (the Defamation Act 2013) and a focus on the tension between European Convention rights (Articles 10 and 8 ECHR). This does not mean, however, that his voice of criticism has nothing to add. It is important to test the status quo, to challenge the validity of accepted views, although it is perhaps fortunate that individuals such as Bill Roache ('[t]he surprisingly numerous viewers of Coronation Street may know that for over thirty years he played the role of Ken Barlow'[25]) did not also choose to avail themselves of Weir's work, as some of his comments in the *Casebook* and *An Introduction to Tort Law* might well have brought him into closer contact with defamation law than he would have liked.

B. The Case Note Commentator: Working as a Miniaturist

For many academics, however, Weir is perhaps better known as a prolific common law *arrêtiste* – a master of the succinct summation of legal cases, whilst wielding his intellectual scalpel. Hector MacQueen has commented that 'Tony was the acknowledged master of the case note in academic journals (above all, the *Cambridge Law Journal*): terse offerings of sharp legal insight along with the ever-present dry humour which in combination none could rival.'[26] Joe Thomson, another fellow Scot, is equally effusive:

> The case note has I think gone out of fashion. The research big brothers do not think that it is REF worthy. Young clever academics feel that it will distract them from

[23] Weir, *A Casebook on Tort* (n 13) 568.

[24] M Lunney, D Nolan and K Oliphant, *Tort Law: Text and Materials*, 6th edn (Oxford, OUP, 2017) 716.

[25] Weir, *A Casebook on Tort* (n 13) 568.

[26] 'Tony Weir', *Scots Law News* (15 December 2011) at www.sln.law.ed.ac.uk/2011/12/15/tony-weir.

> bigger more important projects. Then, as some of us know only too well, there is the real prospect of upsetting more sensitive members of the judiciary. The point is, of course, that it is difficult to write a good case note. It necessitates the ability to précis accurately, an art which has almost died out in the age of information overkill on the internet. The author must have deep knowledge of the relevant legal rules if he is to provide a more principled solution to that of senior judges who have had the advantage of argument from learned counsel. Yet when everything comes together a case note can give the reader immense delight as well as legal insight. So on my desert island I would have to have the collected case notes of Tony Weir, that Scot who lived in voluntary exile in Cambridge. Compared to his clever, witty and stimulating comments, much longer articles on the same subject betray themselves to be … of little, if any, intellectual sustenance.[27]

Thomson captures in this quotation many of the attributes that continue to draw academics to Weir's notes today – a genuine insight into a legally significant case with a degree of brevity that, in the world of the Research Excellence Framework, few are encouraged to exercise. But also the confidence to say the 'unthinkable' – that judges are incorrect, that victims can be unmeritorious, that the courts should say no to compensation. One can only imagine how Weir would comment on recent cases on vicarious liability such as *Mohamud v Wm Morrison Supermarkets plc*[28] and *Armes v Nottinghamshire CC*,[29] where the Supreme Court Justices were willing to extend liability without fault on the basis of vague principles of social justice. Weir noted in 1973 that

> [d]efendants' insurance … does affect the incidence and extent of tort liability, by increasing it … [I]t is much easier to award damages to the victim if one assumes that the defendant is not going to have to pay them out of his own pocket.[30]

In 2017, the Supreme Court in *Armes* freely acknowledged that

> vicarious liability is only of practical relevance in situations where (1) the principal tortfeasor cannot be found or is not worth suing, and (2) the person sought to be made vicariously liable is able to compensate the victim of the tort.[31]

Weir's soundbites, often provocative, always thoughtful, have stimulated generations of lawyers to consider how tort law works, and its role in the legal system and in society in general.

In this section, I examine two of Weir's most celebrated case notes, both published in the *Cambridge Law Journal*.[32] The first was published in 1963 at

[27] J Thomson, 'Northern Lights: Some Personal Reflections on Scottish Legal Scholarship' [2014] *Juridical Review* 83, 87–88.

[28] *Mohamud v Wm Morrison Supermarkets plc* [2016] UKSC 11, [2016] AC 677.

[29] *Armes v Nottinghamshire CC* [2017] UKSC 60, [2018] AC 355.

[30] Published posthumously as 'Subrogation and Indemnity' (2012) 71 *CLJ* 1, 2.

[31] *Armes* (n 29) [63].

[32] Weir's case notes for the *Cambridge Law Journal* may be found in a collection published after his death: *Tony Weir on the Case* (Oxford, Hart Publishing, 2012), reviewed by E Descheemaeker (2013) 112 *Revue trimestrielle de droit civil* 722.

the start of Weir's Cambridge career, before, in the words of Lord Rodger, John Anthony Weir 'had found both his scholarly persona, "Tony Weir", and what was to be his trademark learnedly witty voice';[33] the second in Weir's sixties, towards the end of his career.

i. JA Weir, 'Liability for Syntax' – Case Note on Hedley Byrne v Heller *[1964] AC 465*

The facts and significance of this case are well known. Breaking from previous law, the House of Lords accepted in *Hedley Byrne & Co Ltd v Heller & Partners Ltd*[34] that a claimant could bring an action for pure economic loss caused by a negligent misstatement. On this basis, the bank that had wrongly advised Hedley Byrne (a firm of advertising agents) that they could safely extend credit to a company, Easipower, on whose behalf they had entered into various advertising contracts, would have been liable but for the fact that the reference had been given 'without responsibility'. Thus was opened a door for recovery for pure economic loss in negligence, subsequently extended by the House of Lords in *Henderson v Merrett Syndicates Ltd*[35] and *White v Jones*.[36]

Weir's view was that such a step ignored the context in which the loss was suffered. The case for change, he argued, was hardly compelling:

> They [the claimants] made bad business deals, having taken only a free opinion before hazarding their wealth in the hope of profit, no part of which, had it eventuated, would they have transferred to the honest person whom they now seek to saddle with their loss. The defectiveness of a system which refuses in such a case to sever the risk of loss from the chance of profit is not obvious ... A free tip is relevantly distinguishable from a remunerated opinion, as social practice shows; the guest thanks the hostess, but the hostess chides the cook.[37]

He also expressed disgust that such sympathy was wasted on *advertising agents* who had the temerity to sue for misrepresentation![38]

For Weir, then, the whole idea of voluntary assumption of responsibility or a special relationship rang strangely in the law of tort:

> [T]he plaintiffs here could have found a credit investigation agency; had they done so, the system would have afforded them a remedy, through the appropriately commercial institution of contract, against such of their advisers as were careless; the risk on the adviser would be justified by the fee.[39]

[33] Rodger, 'Humour and Law' (n 11) 203.
[34] *Hedley Byrne & Co Ltd v Heller & Partners Ltd* [1964] AC 645 (HL).
[35] *Henderson v Merrett Syndicates Ltd* (n 7).
[36] *White v Jones* [1995] 2 AC 207 (HL). For Weir's case note on *White v Jones*, see 'A Damnosa Hereditas?' (1995) 111 *LQR* 357.
[37] JA Weir, 'Liability for Syntax' (1963) 21 *CLJ* 216, 218–19. See, more generally, T Weir, 'Recovery in Tort for Economic Loss' (1997) 94 *British Insurance Law Association Journal* 14.
[38] See also Weir, *A Casebook on Tort* (n 13) 61.
[39] Weir, 'Liability for Syntax' (n 37) 218.

The main thrust of his argument lay, as Basil Markesinis identified in the *Law Quarterly Review* in 1987,[40] in the fact that this decision blurred the line between contract law (where recovery for pure economic loss is not a problem and indeed the main source of claims) and tort law (traditionally focusing on non-consensual obligations protecting the health and property of claimants). In other words, creating a form of liability 'akin to contract' not only disturbed the clarity of the contract/tort division, but also distorted the distribution of risk within society. Was this so deserving a claim as to justify the uncertainty as to the scope of recovery that followed? Weir later dismissed Jane Stapleton's arguments[41] of the need to find a principled approach to pure economic loss as providing consolation after the event, rather than recognising the need for clear guidance: 'what is wrong with just line-drawing, or even slightly unjust line-drawing, when a line has to be drawn somewhere is quite beyond me'.[42]

Such views exemplify Weir's understandable unease in turning a careless adviser into an unpaid and involuntary guarantor of a contractual debt. The success of *Hedley Byrne* did not dissuade Weir of the validity of his criticism, but rather seemed to make his disapproval more forthright with age. Fundamentally, Weir asserted, the difference between the various interests – between a man's pocket and his person, his good name and his personal property – is quite great enough to justify different rules, particularly if they result in a coherent legal framework. Commenting 21 years after his original case note, Weir's view of *Hedley Byrne* remained unchanged and, certainly, less inhibited:

> Never has there been such a judicial jamboree as *Hedley Byrne* [1964] AC 465, where one almost has the feeling that their Lordships had been on a trip to Mount Olympus and perhaps smoked a joint on the bus. *Something* certainly went to their heads, presumably not the merits of the claim, which they dismissed.[43]

It is hard to imagine a law professor willing to express such comments in print today!

ii. T Weir, 'Swag for the Injured Burglar' – Case Note on Revill v Newbery *[1996] QB 567*

A *bête noire* of Weir, notably as he grew older, was what we might now call 'the compensation culture'. In several case notes, Weir took issue with the

[40] BS Markesinis, 'An Expanding Tort Law – The Price of a Rigid Contract Law' (1987) 103 *LQR* 354.

[41] See J Stapleton, 'Duty of Care and Economic Loss: A Wider Agenda' (1991) 107 *LQR* 49; and J Stapleton, 'Duty of Care Factors: A Selection from the Judicial Menus' in P Cane and J Stapleton (eds), *The Law of Obligations: Essays in Celebration of John Fleming* (Oxford, Clarendon Press, 1998).

[42] T Weir, 'Errare Humanum Est' in P Birks (ed), *The Frontiers of Liability*, vol 2 (Oxford, OUP, 1994) 107.

[43] ibid 105.

policy choices of the courts in failing to respect the personal autonomy of claimants. Why should the courts interfere with the personal choices of individuals simply on the basis that they led to personal injury? Unsurprisingly, one target for his wrath was the decision in *Revill*, which dealt with the plight of 76-year-old pensioner, William Newbery, who had taken to sleeping in his allotment shed to protect it from vandals and thieves. He had been rudely awakened at about two o'clock in the morning of Saturday, 12 March 1988, by the 21-year-old claimant and his older friend, Grainger, who were attempting to break into his shed, at the end of an active night's work that included breaking into two car showroom portacabins, setting alight one of them and stealing two motor cars. Newbery reacted by loading his shotgun and shooting Revill through a small hole in the door of his shed. Revill brought a claim against Newbery for negligence. For the Court of Appeal, the mere fact that the claimant had been engaged in criminal activities at the time he suffered injury was not sufficient of itself to debar him from claiming damages for those injuries. By introducing the Occupiers' Liability Act 1984, which imposed a duty of care on occupiers towards trespassers, Parliament could be taken to have decided that burglars should not be treated as outlaws and that *some* duty of care was owed towards them.[44] On this basis, the judge had been entitled to find that the defendant was negligent by reference to the standard of care to be expected from the reasonable man placed in the situation in which he found himself, but damages would be reduced by two-thirds for contributory negligence.

Contrast Weir's view:

> [T]he Court of Appeal explicitly disregarded the fact that the plaintiff was a criminal, as well as the fact that the defendant was the occupier of the premises being burgled. This deliberate refusal to take manifestly material considerations into account can only confirm the layman's view that 'the law is an ass – an idiot'.[45]

Legally Weir is correct to identify that this decision did require the courts to take what he regarded as a radical step. The case concerned an activity on land and, despite the loose wording of section 1(1)(a) of the Occupiers' Liability Act 1984,[46] which refers to dangers arising due to the state of the premises or things done or omitted to be done on them, the general understanding is that occupiers'

[44] 'It seems to me to be clear that, by enacting section 1 of the Act of 1984, Parliament has decided that an occupier cannot treat a burglar as an outlaw and has defined the scope of the duty owed to him. As I have already indicated, a person other than an occupier owes a similar duty to an intruder such as the plaintiff': *Revill v Newbery* [1996] QB 567 (CA) 577 (Neill LJ).

[45] T Weir, 'Swag for the Injured Burglar' (1996) 55 *CLJ* 182, 182.

[46] Section 1(1) reads: 'The rules enacted by this section shall have effect, in place of the rules of the common law, to determine – (a) whether any duty is owed by a person as occupier of premises to persons other than his visitors in respect of any risk of their suffering injury on the premises by reason of any danger due to the state of the premises or to things done or omitted to be done on them'.

liability is confined to dangers created *as an occupier*, that is from one's control over land, and is not due to activity taking place on it. Hence a splinter from the shed might give rise to liability under the 1984 Act, but not the activity of shooting. The result of the case is to render the distinction between the liability arising at common law and under the 1984 Act of little, if any, practical difference in many cases.[47] Or, in the words of Weir, 'having decided on insufficient grounds to ignore the criminal quality of the plaintiff's conduct, to treat him like a toddler who had lost his way'.[48] Weir, you may be relieved to hear, is not advocating that occupiers may freely shoot at burglars. If, he argues, Newbery had deliberately shot the burglar in cold blood (rather than firing blindly through a hole in the shed door) then he would be guilty of trespass to the person, subject to any defence of reasonable force.[49] In the case of negligence, however, Weir argues that the common-sense response is to apply the defence of *ex turpi causa*: 'Many more decisions like this and the Court of Appeal will forfeit the respect of lawyer and layman alike.'[50]

***

Both case notes, almost 30 years apart, address fundamental issues arising in the law of tort: Should the courts award compensation for negligently-incurred pure economic loss, or would this undermine the law of contract? Do criminals ever deserve compensation in the tort of negligence? In both cases, Weir argues in favour of 'self-help' – for the advertising agent to pay for a contractual right to sue and for the householder to be permitted some limited ability to defend his property against burglars. Embattled citizens, he argues, are entitled to question the law when it compensates criminals and fails to encourage businesses to take measures to minimise the risk of financial loss. As David Johnston has commented, a general theme in Weir's work is the importance that law, in the face of competing policy arguments, never lose sight of principle.[51] Here the *arrêtiste* is arguing for a particular vision of tort law. For the lawyer and academic, the issue here is not whether one agrees with this view – indeed Weir is perfectly aware that many will not. Weir forces us to look again at the position of the court and whether it can be defended against such piercing criticism. It is entirely consistent with an adversarial legal tradition to challenge the reasoning of the courts, high and low. Indeed, Weir would argue, it is the role of the academic to do exactly that.

[47] WE Peel and J Goudkamp, *Winfield and Jolowicz on Tort*, 19th edn (London, Sweet & Maxwell, 2014) para 10-041.

[48] Weir, 'Swag for the Injured Burglar' (n 45) 183.

[49] The trial judge had considered whether the action should be regarded as a claim for trespass to the person or a claim in negligence, and had preferred to treat it as a case of negligence on the basis that it had not been argued that the defendant ever intended to hit anyone with the shot either at any time or on this particular occasion.

[50] Weir, 'Swag for the Injured Burglar' (n 45) 184.

[51] Johnston, 'A Case, a Statute, and Some Thoughts on the Proper Role of Policy' (n 22) 888.

III. WEIR AS TRANSLATOR AND COMPARATIVE TORT LAWYER

In terms of comparative law, Weir is perhaps best known today as a translator. His outstanding translation of a key comparative law text, Zweigert and Kötz's *Einführung in die Rechtsvergleichung*[52] (or, more familiarly, *Introduction to Comparative Law*)[53] is well known. Weir captures the tone and style of the original text and some of the translations are joyous – my own favourite is the dismissal of the work of the pandectists on the basis that 'much of what they wrote is hairsplitting pedantry and legal spillikins'.[54] The importance of this translation cannot be underestimated, not least that Weir's translation of Zweigert and Kötz remains in print some 20 years later, retaining its place on comparative law reading lists. Weir, by expressing the authors' argument clearly, and importantly by presenting such an excellent translation to the English-speaking world, brings to a wider audience the scholarship contained in the text and what is widely regarded as the best current account of the functional method of comparative law.[55]

The difficulties of translating across different jurisdictions, particularly when dealing with different legal traditions such as the common and civil law, are well known. The EU itself, with 24 official languages,[56] provides an example of the many issues that can arise in attempting to translate complex legal concepts across the disparate legal traditions found in Member States.[57] Whilst Weir did not have the challenge of producing a translation that would ensure the uniform application of the translated law across common- and civil-law

[52] K Zweigert and H Kötz, *Einführung in die Rechtsvergleichung auf dem Gebiete des Privatrechts*, 3rd edn (Tübingen, Mohr Siebeck, 1996).

[53] Zweigert and Kötz, *Introduction to Comparative Law* (n 4).

[54] ibid 141.

[55] R Michaels, 'The Functional Method of Comparative Law' in M Reimann and R Zimmermann (eds), *The Oxford Handbook of Comparative Law* (Oxford, OUP, 2006), who comments (at 340) that '[t]he functional method has become both the mantra and the *bête noire* of comparative law. For its proponents it is the most, perhaps the only, fruitful method; to its opponents it represents everything bad about mainstream comparative law'. See also M Graziadei, 'The Functional Heritage' in P Legrand and R Munday (eds), *Comparative Legal Studies: Traditions and Transitions* (Cambridge, CUP, 2003) 100; and JM Smits, 'Taking Functionalism Seriously: On the Bright Future of a Contested Method' (2011) 18 *Maastricht Journal of European and Comparative Law* 554.

[56] See the EU's 'Language Policy' at europa.eu/european-union/abouteuropa/language-policy_en. See also T Schilling, 'Beyond Multilingualism: On Different Approaches to the Handling of Diverging Language Versions of a Community Law' (2010) 16 *European Law Journal* 47; S Lindroos-Hovinheimo, 'On the Indeterminacy of Legal Translation' in T Wilhelmsson, E Paunio and A Pohjolainen (eds), *Private Law and the Many Cultures* of Europe (The Hague, Kluwer Law International, 2007) 367; E Paunio, 'The Tower of Babel and the Interpretation of EU Law – Implications for Equality of Languages and Legal Certainty' in T Wilhelmsson, E Paunio and A Pohjolainen (eds), *Private Law and the Many Cultures* of Europe (The Hague, Kluwer Law International, 2007) 385; E Paunio, *Legal Certainty in Multilingual EU Law* (London, Routledge, 2016).

[57] See B Pozzo, 'The Challenges of a Multi-Lingual Approach' in C Twigg-Flesner (ed), *Research Handbook on EU Consumer and Contract Law* (Cheltenham, Edward Elgar, 2016) 138, 141–43.

jurisdictions by creating equally authentic language versions,[58] the literature on translation studies highlights that translations can only be approximations of the original text and that preservation of meaning is not even an objective of translation.[59] At a basic level, then, translating legal terminology raises fundamental contextual difficulties that require the expertise of a linguist-lawyer who is able to understand how the concept in question functions within a particular system of law before finding, where possible, a means of translating it to a new audience. By way of a simple example, if we try to explain the law of contract by simply referring to the terms 'contract', *contrat* and *Vertrag*, we are using hollow terms that give no sense of how these concepts differ in operation[60] (the same applies to 'tort', 'delict' (for our Scottish friends), *responsabilité civile extracontractuelle* and *Deliktsrecht*). Technical terminology is often system-bound. Legal terms get their meaning through legal usage, through communication within the legal system.[61] Where no immediate equivalent concept exists, the skill of the translator is tested to its limits.[62]

In a recent study, Jaakko Husa highlighted the tension that exists between the translator, who traditionally sees the text as static, and the lawyer, who is interested not only in the actual wording of the legal document but also in the contextual surroundings of the text.[63] Legal translation, he argues, requires familiarity with comparative law – its whole point is to linguistically transform the original text so that it becomes operative in the target language.[64] It is Weir's expertise, therefore, as a comparative lawyer that renders his translation of such high quality, opening up new areas of scholarship to a broader audience. For Husa, this is fundamental: 'the flow of information between legal systems takes place through translation'.[65] In Weir's translation of texts, including Franz Wieacker's *A History of Private Law in Europe*,[66] Hein Kötz and Axel Flessner's

[58] See B Pozzo, 'Multilingualism and the Harmonisation of European Private Law: Problems and Perspectives' (2012) 20 *European Review of Private Law* 1185; S Šarčević, 'Legal Translation and Legal Certainty/Uncertainty: From the DCFR to the CESL Proposal' in B Pasa and L Morra (eds), *Translating the DCFR and Drafting the CESL: A Pragmatic Perspective* (Munich, Sellier, 2014).

[59] Lindroos-Hovinheimo, 'On the Indeterminacy of Legal Translation' (n 56) 371.

[60] As ably discussed by Cartwright in his text: J Cartwright, *Contract Law: An Introduction to the English Law of Contract for the Civil Lawyer*, 3rd edn (Oxford, Hart Publishing, 2016).

[61] Lindroos-Hovinheimo, 'On the Indeterminacy of Legal Translation' (n 56) 375.

[62] Consider the example cited by Lindroos-Hovinheimo in relation to translating the concept of the Finnish Consumer Ombudsman into Japanese, where the concept is lacking. She comments perceptively that 'the difficulty of translating the concept of Consumer Ombudsman into Japanese does not lie in the fact that the institution does not exist in Japan. The problem is that *because* the institution does not exist in Japan, it is likely that there is no established way of talking about it or referring to it in Japanese. So the ultimate problem is not that the Japanese legal system lacks something, but that Japanese use of language lacks something': ibid 374–75.

[63] J Husa, 'Translating Legal Language and Comparative Law' (2017) 30 *International Journal for the Semiotics of Law* 261.

[64] ibid 264.

[65] ibid 262.

[66] F Wieacker, *A History of Private Law in Europe, with Particular Reference to Germany*, tr Tony Weir (Oxford, Clarendon Press, 1995).

European Contract Law,[67] Bernhard Grossfeld's *The Strength and Weakness of Comparative Law*[68] and Jean-Louis Halpérin's *The French Civil Code*,[69] Weir has brought French and German scholarship to a global audience and, in so doing, enriched how we think about comparative law and how we address its content.

The esteem in which Weir's fellow comparative lawyers held his translations may be seen in relation to reviews of Weir's translation of Wieacker's work. Alan Watson, one of the world's foremost authorities on Roman law, comparative law, legal history, and law and religion, commented:

> Tony Weir is a brilliant translator of legal German, and here he has surpassed himself. For this we should be all the more grateful, because Franz Wieacker (1908–1994) was one of the great German scholars of the post war world. His range and depth of learning are unsurpassed. His German is remarkably complex and difficult ... Weir has astonishingly managed to convey this complexity, in thought as in language, in English that is nonetheless fluent.[70]

George Gretton, in the *International and Comparative Law Quarterly*, took a similar view:

> Wieacker's *Privatrechtsgeschichte der Neuzeit* has long been a classic, and its appearance in English is a major event. Every serious law library outside German-speaking Europe will purchase a copy ... In the insightful and beautifully written foreword Reinhard Zimmermann remarks that the book 'must have been excruciatingly difficult to translate'. Wieacker's German is hard. Weir has achieved the miracle of a fluent and readable version which at the same time is faithful to the original ... The legal world was already deeply indebted to Weir: this book much increases those obligations, in rendering accessible Wieacker's masterpiece. It is to be hoped that more treasures of German scholarship will also one day be translated by Weir himself or others inspired by him.[71]

Yet the skill of the translator derives not only from linguistic ability, as Husa has indicated, but from an ability to understand the differences between legal systems (in terms of terminology, procedure, methodology, etc) and how to engage with domestic legal discourse (and often the economic institutions to which law is closely coupled) in a manner leading to mutual understanding.[72] Vivian Grosswald Curran summed up the process as attempting 'to steer through the messiness of the foreign by reordering it into the language of the

[67] H Kötz and A Flessner, *European Contract Law*, vol I, tr Tony Weir (Oxford, Clarendon Press, 1998).

[68] B Grossfeld, *The Strength and Weakness of Comparative Law*, tr Tony Weir (Oxford, Clarendon Press, 1990).

[69] JL Halpérin, *The French Civil Code*, tr Tony Weir (London, UCL Press, 2006).

[70] A Watson, 'Book Review' (1997) 102 *American Historical Review* 1147, 1147.

[71] G Gretton, 'Book Review' (1996) 45 *International and Comparative Law Quarterly* 973, 973–74.

[72] See G Teubner, 'Legal Irritants: Good Faith in British Law or How Unifying Law Ends up in New Divergences' (1998) 61 *MLR* 11.

familiar without betraying the original',[73] and it is difficult to put it better than that!

No discussion of Weir as a comparative tort lawyer would be complete, however, without reference to his majestic comparative study of delict and torts, undertaken with Pierre Catala, at the very start of his career and published in four sections in the *Tulane Law Review*.[74] 'In this work', Catala and Weir announce, 'a new systematic approach to the comparative study of law is being tried out' in which the authors juxtapose the law relating to tortious liability for the wrongful act of a person in France and England.[75] Their research covers topics as varied as the nature of tortious liability, the distinction between tortious and criminal liability, the influence of risk theory and strict liability, fault-based liability and the common law duty of care, abuse of rights, the imputability of the wrongful act, actionable damage, causation, *novus actus interveniens*, *force majeure* and remoteness. It is a masterclass of comparison – a dissection of tort law and delictual responsibility step by step by two academics completely conversant with the inner workings of their legal systems and theoretical and practical underpinnings. This is not, however, a conventional description of the English law of tort to an American audience, but a critical dissection of the law, covering themes that would continue to appear in Weir's work throughout his life. For example, Weir recognises at this early stage of his career that

> to try to define 'tort' is to be caught at once in 'a thicket of difficulties' … In truth, then, tort is a bag of nuts and bolts. History can say how they came there, but science is pressed to rationalize their presence.[76]

Weir's anti-theoretical approach to tort law thus began at an early age. Equally, he is alert that there may be differences in relation to key concepts between common- and civil-law systems:

> The effort required to coax the English law of torts into the pleasingly neat categories of French law is particularly obvious when that category is 'damage'. The concept is absent from the digests and indices, and it has never been a central topic of discussion … There are both functional and historical reasons for this.[77]

This is the comparatist speaking, and one who continues to speak even in the final edition of his *Casebook* in which, in its introduction, Weir draws the

[73] VG Curran, 'Comparative Law and Language' in M Reimann and R Zimmermann (eds), *The Oxford Handbook of Comparative Law* (Oxford, OUP, 2006) 704.

[74] P Catala and JA Weir, 'Delict and Torts: A Study in Parallel' (1963) 37 *Tulane Law Review* 573 (Part I); (1964) 38 *Tulane Law Review* 221 (Part II); (1964) 38 *Tulane Law Review* 664 (Part III); (1965) 39 *Tulane Law Review* 701 (Part IV). See also Weir's contribution to the *International Encyclopaedia of Comparative Law*: Weir, 'Complex Liabilities' (n 8).

[75] Catala and Weir, 'Delict and Torts: A Study in Parallel' (Part I) (n 74) 573. The term 'tortious liability' should be taken here to include both the common law of tort and the French law of delict.

[76] Catala and Weir, 'Delict and Torts: A Study in Parallel' (Part I) (n 74) 578–80 (citation omitted).

[77] Catala and Weir, 'Delict and Torts: A Study in Parallel' (Part III) (n 74) 665.

reader's attention to examples from French and German law in the hope that he or she may 'find it instructive'.[78]

Weir concludes:

> It is, of course, in the methods that the systems differ – in style of disposition, treatment of sources and form of judgment … French laws plant a principle, and the judges tend its growth; English statutes prune and lop, and the judges fear the shears.[79]

Here comparison is not black or white – or, to use a cliché, an exercise in comparing apples and oranges[80] – but rather one that engages with similarity and difference to facilitate a deeper understanding of the operation of the law in these jurisdictions. Judicial activism in the law of tort in France (the *Code civil* has famously operated with only five codal provisions since 1804[81]) and England and Wales means that lawyers in each jurisdiction have much to learn from each other. Weir and Catala did not find striking differences – in the great majority of cases the result would be the same – but nevertheless they identified that French law in substance and procedure was generally more favourable to claimants than English law. This is a result that leading French tort scholar Jean-Sébastien Borghetti would confirm is still the case today.[82]

IV. WEIR THE BREXITEER

And yet this learned scholar of European private law systems remained a Eurosceptic, unconvinced, in particular, by EU measures to harmonise private law. Weir, in the tenth (and final) edition of his *Casebook on Tort*, is openly critical that the UK has, in his opinion, 'abandoned our sovereignty' and submitted to 'the unremitting flow of pragmatic and unprincipled mandates from Brussels and the demented proposal of the European Parliament that the entire private law of members states be unified and codified'.[83] It comes as no surprise then that, in 2002, Weir expressed his disapproval of the intervention of the EU into the law relating to defective products (Directive 85/374/EEC) and consumer sales (Directive 1999/44/EC).[84] Noting the copious legislation emanating from

[78] Weir, *A Casebook on Tort* (n 13) 3.

[79] Catala and Weir, 'Delict and Torts: A Study in Parallel' (Part IV) (n 74) 780–81.

[80] See C Valcke, 'Reflections on Comparative Law Methodology – Getting Inside Contract Law' in M Adams and J Bomhoff (eds), *Practice and Theory in Comparative Law* (Cambridge, CUP, 2012) 22.

[81] This number excludes the additions made to implement the Product Liability Directive 85/374/EEC. There are, however, proposals for change: see *Projet de réforme du droit de la responsabilité civile* at www.textes.justice.gouv.fr/textes-soumis-a-concertation-10179/projet-de-reforme-du-droit-de-la-responsabilite-civile-29782.html, presented by the Ministry of Justice on 13 March 2017.

[82] JS Borghetti 'The Culture of Tort Law in France' (2012) 3 *Journal of European Tort Law* 158.

[83] Weir, *A Casebook on Tort* (n 13) 2.

[84] T Weir, 'European Directives Protective of the Individual Consumer' [2002] *Economia e diretto del terziario* 443.

Brussels, Weir argued that the rights it gives individual citizens are either actually dangerous or, less controversially, merely disappointing. In 'Divergent Legal Systems in a Single Member State' in 1998,[85] Weir also targeted proposals from bodies such as the Lando Commission on European Contract Law (which had proposed its *Principles of European Contract Law* as a European response to the United Nations Convention on Contracts for the International Sale of Goods),[86] commenting that

> there are proposals to unify the private law of the different multilingual components of the European Union … [I]t may be useful to consider how very different, after nearly three centuries of political unification in an unquestionably single market, the laws of Scotland and England continue to be.

In 1999, he was equally dismissive of the idea of *Principles of European Tort Law*: 'It is in practice a *voie sans issue*. Still, who ever said that international cooperation should be productive as well as fun?'[87] Here comparative law is being used to highlight diversity. Such a viewpoint contrasts starkly with Zweigert and Kötz's assertion that '[t]here are, therefore, grounds for believing that although the Common Law and the Civil Law started off from opposite positions, they are gradually moving closer together even in their legal methods and techniques'.[88] Their famous *praesumptio similitudinis* (presumption of similarity) takes as its basis the idea that, in practice, the law tends to address roughly the same social problems reaching similar legal solutions across jurisdictions.[89] On this basis, they depict the role of comparative law as going beyond national legal systems to 'provide a comparative basis on which to develop a system of law for all Europe'.[90] In contrast, the insight comparative law provides to Weir is one of understanding difference.[91] He was scathing, therefore, of the attempt of Walter van Gerven, in his 'Ius Commune Casebook' on tort law,[92] to argue that the courts of Europe approach questions of law from a very similar cultural, ethical and legal background: 'Well, if you would believe that, you would believe

[85] T Weir, 'Divergent Legal Systems in a Single Member State' [1998] *Zeitschrift für Europaisches Privatrecht* 564.

[86] O Lando and H Beale (eds), *Principles of European Contract Law*, Part I: *Performance, Non-Performance and Remedies* (Dordrecht, Martinus Nijhoff, 1995). See now O Lando and H Beale (eds), *Principles of European Contract Law Parts I and II* (The Hague, Kluwer Law International, 2000); O Lando et al (eds), *Principles of European Contract Law Part III* (The Hague, Kluwer Law International, 2003).

[87] T Weir, 'Book Review' (1999) 58 *CLJ* 643, 645.

[88] Zweigert and Kötz, *Introduction to Comparative Law* (n 4) 271.

[89] See C Valcke and M Grellette, 'Three Functions of Function in Comparative Legal Studies' in M Adams and D Heirbaut (eds), *The Method and Culture of Comparative Law: Essays in Honour of Mark van Hoecke* (Oxford, Hart Publishing, 2014) 99.

[90] Zweigert and Kötz *Introduction to Comparative Law* (n 4) 29.

[91] Herman comments that Weir 'focused an anthropologist's curiosity upon legal differences stemming from a society's intellectual and cultural preoccupations': Herman, 'Friendship's Bounty' (n 1) 719.

[92] W van Gerven, J Lever and P Larouche, *Cases, Materials and Text on National, Supranational and International Tort Law* (Oxford, Hart Publishing, 2000).

anything, for even if the underlying principles were the same or were required to be the same by Strasbourg [or Luxembourg], the legal techniques are quite different.'[93] Herman, in his tribute to Weir, noted that while Weir relished the finding of legal difference, he was, in turn, dismayed by contemporary tendencies to airbrush legal differences from the lived law.[94] He is not alone in this position. Montesquieu, in his 1748 work, *De l'Esprit des Loix* (*The Spirit of the Laws*),[95] classically highlighted that climatic, geographical, cultural, religious, economic, moral and political factors rendered differences between legal systems inevitable. More recently, the work of Pierre Legrand argues that the differences between common- and civil-law systems signify that European harmonisation projects are doomed to fail.[96] Whilst not all share this view – and indeed some might argue that the EU was created to try and resolve the dangers of conflict arising due to 'difference'[97] and that a presumption of difference can be equally flawed[98] – as Dannemann wryly remarks, there would be little point in comparing identical systems of law.[99] While some similarities are needed to make the comparison worthwhile, the comparatist should be alert to the unknown. The methodology of functionalism should not therefore be permitted to disguise real differences in legal process, structure and reasoning. To quote Dannemann again:

> Studies which see similarity everywhere can appear as pointless or boring as studies which only note differences. While this technique of contrasting similarities with differences produces more attractive results, the researcher would nevertheless be well advised to keep an eye open for differences in an area of perceived similarities, and for similarities in an area of perceived difference.[100]

Inevitably, as Markesinis and Deakin observe, Weir's Euroscepticism did colour his analysis and extended beyond criticism of the EU to include the European Convention on Human Rights (ECHR).[101] In particular, Weir sought to attack human rights lawyers for seeking to 'impose' a rights-based culture based on the ECHR on the common law. We see, therefore, vintage Weir in 1999 commenting, as ever in the *Cambridge Law Journal*, on the Strasbourg ruling

[93] T Weir, 'The Unwanted Child' (2002) 6 *Edinburgh Law Review* 244, 250–51.

[94] Herman, 'Friendship's Bounty' (n 1) 726.

[95] Charles de Secondat, Baron de Montesquieu, *De l'Esprit des Loix* (Geneva, Barrillot et fils, 1748).

[96] P Legrand, 'European Legal Systems Are Not Converging' (1996) 45 *International Comparative Law Quarterly* 52. See also P Legrand, 'The Impossibility of Legal Transplants' (1997) 4 *Maastricht Journal of European and Comparative Law* 111.

[97] Jean Monnet famously stated that his goal was 'building Union among people, not cooperation between States'.

[98] Note Watson's critique, for example, of the work of Pierre Legrand: A Watson, 'Legal Transplants and European Private Law' (2000) 4(4) *Electronic Journal of Comparative Law* at www.ejcl.org/ejcl/44/44-2.html.

[99] G Dannemann, 'Comparative Law: Study of Similarities or Differences?' in M Reimann and R Zimmermann (eds), *The Oxford Handbook of Comparative* Law (Oxford, OUP, 2006) 384.

[100] ibid 406.

[101] S Deakin, A Johnston and B Markesinis, *Markesinis and Deakin's Tort Law*, 7th edn (Oxford, Clarendon Press, 2013) 7.

in *Osman v UK*.[102] While the title highlights his acerbic wit ('Down *Hill* – All the Way?'),[103] in the case note Weir addresses the tensions that exist between the ECtHR and the English courts. Weir was not alone in his criticism of *Osman*. The decision received judicial[104] and academic[105] disapproval, and indeed the ECtHR itself in *Z v UK*[106] came to accept that a misunderstanding had taken place. Weir quite correctly chides the ECtHR for its lack of understanding of the context in which the decision of the English Court of Appeal in *Osman v Ferguson*[107] was made, in particular its failure to appreciate the practical role played by the striking-out procedure in tort law suits:

> One wonders if the judges in Strasbourg were fully aware of quite how expensive in time and trouble litigation in England actually is, involving, as it does, discovery of documents, oral testimony of witnesses and the use of one of a small number of judges (ECHR alone has 39!) or, indeed, of how effective the threat of provoking such as waste of time and trouble can be in eliciting the reluctant settlement of an unmeritorious claim.[108]

Substantively, then, his critique is correct. And yet his conclusion that this was 'a dubious arrogation of power' is clearly indicative of an antagonistic relationship towards the ECtHR. His conclusion – that '[n]ations should decide for themselves whether public funds should be directed to victims of past malfunction in public services'[109] – is consistent with the argument of Brexiteers advocating that the UK leave the EU and take control of the nation's finances. In a later article he is openly critical that a decision of the ECtHR is making 'our judges tremble in their boots'.[110] For Weir, as seen above, understanding the law of another legal system served primarily to highlight difference rather than laying down a basis for identifying commonality between different legal traditions. Deference to Strasbourg and Luxembourg would therefore be problematic for common lawyers and contrary to common law principle, particularly when judges of these courts 'think very differently from ourselves'.[111] Despite his much

[102] *Osman v UK* (1998) 29 EHRR 245.

[103] T Weir, 'Down *Hill* – All the Way?' [1999] *CLJ* 4. The ruling sought to limit the authority of the House of Lords decision in *Hill v Chief Constable of West Yorkshire* [1989] AC 53 (HL).

[104] See, eg, Lord Browne-Wilkinson in *Barrett v Enfield LBC* [2001] 2 AC 550 (HL) and (extra-judicially) Lord Hoffmann, 'Human Rights and the House of Lords' (1999) 62 *MLR* 159, who regarded the judgment as a failure to understand the operation of precedent in the common law, and how the 'fair, just and reasonable' test operates.

[105] CA Gearty, 'Unravelling *Osman*' (2001) 64 *MLR* 159; G Monti, '*Osman v UK* – Transforming English Negligence Law into French Administrative Law?' (1999) 48 *International and Comparative Law Quarterly* 757.

[106] *Z v UK* (2002) 34 EHRR 3.

[107] *Osman v Ferguson* [1993] 4 All ER 344 (CA).

[108] Weir, 'Down *Hill* – All the Way?' (n 103) 6.

[109] ibid 7.

[110] Weir, 'The Unwanted Child' (n 93) 246.

[111] Weir, *An Introduction to Tort Law* (n 10) x. The fear of an arrogation of power by the Strasbourg court has been shared by others: see, eg, Lord Hoffmann, 'The Universality of Human Rights' (2009) 125 *LQR* 416.

celebrated (and indeed treasured by many comparative lawyers) translation of Zweigert and Kötz, Weir's own views of convergence and divergence could not be more different.

In sum, EU and European human rights law for Weir posed a threat to the coherence and integrity of the common law. Using his skills as a comparative lawyer, Weir saw his role to make the nature of this threat as visible as possible in order to defend the common law system he knew so well.

V. CONCLUSION

As this chapter has shown, the contribution of Tony Weir to the law of tort and comparative law was immense. Where would comparative law scholarship be without Weir's excellent translation of Zweigert and Kötz? Where would tort law scholarship be if Weir had not challenged us with his provocative phrase, 'Tort is what is in the tort books, and the only thing holding it together is their binding'[112] – a phrase I continue to hear at common law conferences across the world. He leaves, therefore, a legacy of a distinct approach to tort law. His approach is perhaps now not quite *à la mode*, as he put it in the Preface to his *Introduction*. Weir was no great theorist, and would have no truck with the current heated debates between corrective and distributive justice tort theorists. He would equally have refused to engage in the debates concerning methodology and legal transplants that inform comparative law discourse today, and scoffed at attempts to address global legal pluralism and concepts such as post-secular comparative law. He proudly recounts in *An Introduction to Tort Law* an encounter with the (unnamed) Dean of an American Law School, who asked him to outline his normative theory of tort law. It was, he wrote, 'a rather poor lunch and, I thought, a very stupid question. Tort is what is in the tort books … [I]t is surely [more] desirable to become familiar with what that ragbag actually contains'.[113] His critique from the perspective of principle will remain, providing valuable critical perspectives on leading tort cases such as *Hedley Byrne v Heller* and *White v Jones*. While his textbooks will gradually be placed in storage in library vaults,[114] his case notes, thanks to electronic sources, will remain accessible and continue to enlighten generations of students seeking a pithy response to important common law precedents. His strongest legacy, however, will be his excellent translations, bringing to the English-speaking world key literature from the civil law world. They represent an example both of how to engage in translation of legal texts and of how good legal translations can influence comparative law scholarship across the English-speaking world.

[112] Weir, *An Introduction to Tort Law* (n 10) ix, a phrase described by Richard Mullender as 'bracingly antitheoretical': R Mullender, 'Book Review' (2003) 19 *Professional Negligence* 415, 415.
[113] Weir, *An Introduction to Tort Law* (n 10) ix.
[114] Although the final editions of the *Casebook* and *Introduction* still grace library shelves in 2019.

I end with one last anecdote that, in my view, tells us much about the determination, perspicacity and independence of mind of this distinguished tort law scholar. Tony Weir's last publication was a case note published in the first volume of the 2012 edition of the *Cambridge Law Journal*.[115] The editors wrote:

> Our colleague, Tony Weir, died on 14 December 2011. For forty years, he was a regular contributor to the *Cambridge Law Journal*. He did not want any tributes or memorial. We publish below a long case note which he wrote in 1973 and published privately when it could not be included then in this *Journal*. *Si monumentum requiris, lege*![116]

The circumstances behind the posthumous publication of a case note written in the 1970s in relation to the now largely forgotten 1973 decision of the Court of Appeal in *Morris v Ford Motor Co*,[117] highlight Weir's own idiosyncratic response to academia. The note in question is entitled 'Subrogation and Indemnity', and it is indeed 'long' at 3,290 words. Rumour has it that it was rejected in 1973 on the basis that it was far too long (the word limit for *CLJ* case notes is around 1,500 words) and the editors insisted on its being cut. Weir was, however, convinced of the case's importance, notably in relation to the interaction of tort law and insurance,[118] and, not one to take defeat lightly, had the note privately printed as 'Subrogation and Indemnity: A Note on *Morris v Ford Motor Co* [1973] QB 792'. As Roderick Munday has recounted,[119] to emphasise his sense of grievance, Weir further had a cover printed that exactly resembled the pale blue as well as the fonts of the *Cambridge Law Journal*. In a profession where academic careers now depend on publications in well-respected journals, such a robust response to rejection is notable to say the least. Reading the case commentary today, we see a strong argument, reference in passing to the position in French and German law, and a principled defence of the argument that *Lister v Romford Ice & Cold Storage Co*[120] should be reversed. He ends, however, on a typically caustic note:

> The best way to achieve this result would no doubt be to take the bull by the horns and provide that a person who is entitled and able to recover in respect of any loss or liability from an insurer or other indemnitor should to that extent be unable to recover from any other person, unless, perhaps, that other person is himself entitled

[115] Weir, 'Subrogation and Indemnity' (n 30).

[116] ibid 1.

[117] *Morris v Ford Motor Co* [1973] QB 792 (CA).

[118] In the decision itself, Lord Denning MR controversially blocked a contractual right of indemnity by an insurer on the basis of equity, thereby circumventing the authority of *Lister v Romford Ice & Cold Storage Co Ltd* [1957] AC 555 (HL).

[119] See Obligations Discussion Group (obligations@uwo.ca), posting dated 6 January 2012. Professor Munday further suggests that the incident may also explain the five-year hiatus in Weir's *CLJ* case-note production between 1973 and 1978.

[120] *Lister* (n 118).

> and able to recover from an indemnity insurer. It need hardly be said that there is not the slightest chance of this being done.[121]

Weir was, of course, correct. Yet underlying this statement is the fact that the role of the tort law scholar is not necessarily to 'get things done' – however hard we may try – but to continue to point out the *need* 'to get things done'. It is to be hoped that Weir's example will continue to inspire the tort scholars of the future to do exactly that!

[121] Weir, 'Subrogation and Indemnity' (n 30) 7.

13

Law, Fact and Process in Common Law Tort Scholarship

PETER CANE*

I. INTRODUCTION

IN THIS CHAPTER, I shall try to cast some light on modern, common law tort scholarship by constructing two models of legal scholarship and tracing their historical roots. The two models will be called respectively the 'common law model' and the 'civil law model'. Note that these are only models. Even though they are historically based, they do not purport accurately to represent

* In addition to the works cited elsewhere in this chapter, I have found the following particularly helpful: R Pound, *Law and Morals* (Chapel Hill, NC, University of North Carolina Press, 1926) ch 1; R Pound, *The Formative Era of American Law* (Boston, MA, Little, Brown & Co, 1938); RE Megarry, 'Law as Taught and Law as Practised' (1966) 9 *Journal of the Society of Public Teachers of Law* 176; NM Crystal, 'Codification and the Rise of the Restatement Movement' (1979) 54 *Washington Law Review* 239; HJ Berman, *Law and Revolution: The Formation of the Western Legal Tradition* (Cambridge, MA, Harvard University Press, 1983); PG Stein, 'Judge and Jurist in the Civil Law: A Historical Interpretation' (1985) 46 *Louisiana Law Review* 241; RC Van Caenegam, *Judges, Legislators and Professors: Chapters in European Legal History* (Cambridge, CUP, 1987); A Watson, 'The Structure of Blackstone's Commentaries' (1988) 97 *Yale Law Journal* 795; MH Hoeflich, *Roman and Civil Law and the Development of Anglo-American Jurisprudence in the Nineteenth Century* (Athens, GA, University of Georgia Press, 1997); N Duxbury, *Jurists and Judges: An Essay on Influence* (Oxford, Hart Publishing, 2001); R Zimmermann, *Roman Law, Contemporary Law, European Law: The Civilian Tradition Today* (Oxford, OUP, 2001); N Duxbury, *Frederick Pollock and the English Juristic Tradition* (Oxford, OUP, 2004) ch 5; JH Merryman and R Pérez-Perdomo, *The Civil Law Tradition: An Introduction to the Legal Systems of Europe and Latin America*, 3rd edn (Stanford, CA, Stanford University Press, 2007); M Lobban, 'Common Law Reasoning and the Foundations of Modern Private Law' (2007) 32 *Australian Journal of Legal Philosophy* 39; H Dedek, 'From Norms to Facts: The Realization of Rights in Common and Civil Private Law' (2010) 56 *McGill Law Journal* 77; P Brand, 'Judges and Judging 1176–1307' in P Brand and J Getzler (eds), *Judges and Judging in the History of the Common Law and Civil Law: From Antiquity to Modern Times* (Cambridge, CUP, 2012); J-L Halpérin, 'The Process of Codification Applied to the Law of Delicts' in M Lobban and J Moses (eds), *The Impact of Ideas on Legal Development* (Cambridge, CUP, 2012); H Potter, *Law, Liberty and the Constitution: A Brief History of the Common Law* (Woodbridge, The Boydell Press, 2015); T Herzog, *A Short History of European Law* (Cambridge, MA, Harvard University Press, 2018).

legal scholarship at any particular time or in any particular place. The function of models is not to describe but to interpret and explain. Their value depends on the clarity of the interpretation and the plausibility of the explanation. They are designed to highlight some characteristics of scholarly activity that help us (I argue) to understand better what modern, common law tort scholarship is for and about. At the core of the distinction between the two models respectively lie two different ways of constructing the relationship between law and fact in judicial decision-making. I shall trace a link between the respective roles of judges and jurists in the legal system. At the most basic level, I argue, different ways of constructing the relationship between law and fact reflect different understandings of the nature of law. The story I tell probably fits English tort scholarship best, and I wait to see how well it travels. The history of the interplay of common law and civilian ideas is long and complex, and the pattern is constantly changing. I leave for others the question of how well the story fits areas other than tort law.

In suggesting that the nature and purposes of legal scholarship may be understood in terms of the nature and purposes of judicial process and, ultimately, ideas of law, I am departing from standard accounts of the relationship between jurists and judges, which tend to interpret it in terms of some concept of 'influence'. A major limit of the discussion should be noted: it is concerned with the relative roles of the Bench and the Academy and, to a lesser extent, of Bench and Bar, in law-making. By virtue of (the nature of) the relationship between Bench and Bar, that between the Bar and the Academy is at least of equal significance.

II. LAW, FACT AND PROCESS IN COMMON LAW AND CIVIL LAW

A. Common Law

The story (greatly compressed, simplified and stylised) begins even before the dawn of the English common law in the eleventh and twelfth centuries. The sixth-century compilations of Justinian, later collectively known as the *Corpus Iuris Civilis*, represent the apotheosis of the Imperial Roman legal system. The *Corpus Iuris* has three main parts: the *Codex*, a collection of imperial legislation; the *Digest*, a compilation of juristic writings; and the *Institutes*, a sort of student text modelled on the earlier *Institutes of Gaius*.[1] After the collapse of the Western Empire, the *Corpus Iuris* fell into obscurity in Europe. At the time of the Norman Conquest, law on the Continent was dominated by more-or-less localised regimes.

In the meantime, Canon law – the law of the Roman Church – had been developing as the Church's political power grew. In the middle of the

[1] There is a fourth part, the *Novellae*, consisting of imperial legislation post-dating the *Codex*.

twelfth century, in his *Concordia Discordantium Canonum* (commonly known as the *Decretum*), Gratian did for Canon law what Justinian had done for Roman law in the sixth.[2] The 'rediscovery' of the *Digest* in northern Italy in the late eleventh century may have been associated with early attempts to systematise Canon law. At all events, it led to a flowering of secular legal scholarship and the rise of the first universities, which became centres of legal learning and expertise, both Canon and Roman. As a result, Roman law gradually became a sort of common law (the first '*ius commune*') for Continental Europe. In Patrick Glenn's compelling account,[3] a common law exists and operates relatively to multiple, non-common 'local' laws. Common law, in this 'relational' sense, is necessarily pluralistic. To a greater or lesser extent, it accommodates local laws, allowing and enabling a measure of choice of law by both governors and governed. In this respect, common law can be contrasted with sovereign law. Sovereign law, which is associated most strongly with the nation-state, recognises no competitors. Relativity and sovereignty are both matters of degree. Two factors are salient: the ability of the common legal authority to impose its law on local authorities, and its need to do so. In medieval Europe, Roman law (unlike Canon law) was not backed by the force of a common authority and competed with local laws on its merits. Its champions in the competition were professional lawyers trained in the universities.

Post-Conquest English law started out as a relational common law. The Normans did not bring law with them or attempt to impose law on the Anglo-Saxon English, who already had a sophisticated governmental and legal system, with a dense array of local courts based in counties, hundreds and manors, and local bodies of law.[4] Of course, the Normans used a goodly measure of brute force to build their new state. But by the end of the twelfth century, their successors had developed a centralised, judicial/administrative bureaucracy, which, by virtue of its efficiency and efficacy in resolving legal disputes, was able to outcompete the bulk of its indigenous, local competitors in the 'justice industry'. This was before the development of Parliament, at a time when monarchs made few legislative decrees ('statutes')[5] and the main instrument of royal, central governance was the writ – effectively, a letter of royal instruction to a local, judicial or non-judicial official.[6] Early English monarchs would have wanted not only to control the existing machinery of law and order, but also to mould

[2] Actually, he did rather more by way of systematisation: HJ Berman, 'The Origins of Western Legal Science' (1977) 90 *Harvard Law Review* 894, 921–30.

[3] HP Glenn, *On Common Laws* (Oxford, OUP, 2005).

[4] HP Glenn, *Legal Traditions of the World*, 5th edn (Oxford, OUP, 2014) 246.

[5] RC Van Caenegem, 'Government, Law and Society' in J Burns (ed), *The Cambridge History of Medieval Political Thought* (Cambridge, CUP, 1988) 192–194.

[6] See generally HJ Berman, *Law and Revolution: The Formation of the Western Legal Tradition* (Cambridge, MA, Harvard University Press, 1983) 440–61; RC Van Caenegem, *The Birth of the English Common Law*, 2nd edn (Cambridge, CUP, 1988); P Brand, 'The Formation of the English Legal System' in A Padoa-Schioppa (ed), *Legislation and Justice* (Oxford, Clarendon Press, 1997).

indigenous law in ways that would promote their political, economic, military and social objectives.[7] The category of royal officials who were to become 'the common law judges' of the 'common law courts' were primarily responsible for this process of (re)making pre-Conquest English law on behalf of the new regime. By the thirteenth century, English law[8] was, to a significant extent,[9] no longer a relational common law but had become, effectively, a sovereign law for a new polity. This is not to say that it was comprehensive in its coverage, but only that within its chosen domain, it brooked no competition.

The underlying logic of relationality deserves to be spelled out in a little more detail. Richard and John are both tenants of Lord William. Richard turfs John off one of his fields. William's court finds for Richard, a crony of William. John petitions the King, who instructs the sheriff to bring Richard before the King's court so that (the King's) justice can be done between Richard and John. The main aim of the exercise is not to determine whether Richard has acted unlawfully or whether, in any absolute sense, John has a right against Richard, but rather to help the King make the decision whether to back John with the threat of royal coercion against Richard. The common law begins with such requests for the deployment of royal force. The King's priority is to run the country efficiently and peacefully in accordance with royal policies. There is, however, a very large fly in the King's ointment: the ultimate decision for or against John will not be made by the King or by the King's justices but by God, or Fate, or oath-swearers, or a jury. The only thing the King('s justices) can control is whether Richard will be put to his proof, and on what terms. The resulting law, we might now say, was a law of remedies, not rights.[10] It was only indirectly relevant to the outcome of the case and spoke immediately to the questions of whether there would be a trial, and on what issue.

Another way of putting this is to say that the early English common law originated as a law of action(s):[11] by issuing a writ, the monarch instructs an official to act ('Bring Richard to court!') with a view to informing the monarch what action, if any, should be taken in response to John's complaint about the decision of William's court. Until the end of the twelfth century, this process generated very few surviving records.[12] This is, perhaps, unsurprising so long

[7] This helps to explain why property law developed much earlier than other branches of law, and dominated the medieval common law. Real property was the basis of economic activity.

[8] For a succinct account of the substantive content of English law in the 13th century, see P Brand, 'The English Medieval Common Law (to c 1307) as a System of National Institutions and Legal Rules: Creation and Functioning' in P Dresch and H Skoda (eds), *Legalism: Anthropology and History* (Oxford, OUP, 2012) 180–85.

[9] Glenn, *Legal Traditions of the World* (n 4) 269–72.

[10] ibid 251–52.

[11] FJ Port, *Administrative Law* (London, Longmans, Green and Co, 1929) 24: 'Action was the chief attribute of kingship at first …'.

[12] J Gillingham, 'Bureaucracy, the English State and the Crisis of the Angevin Empire, 1199–1205' in P Crooks and TH Parsons (eds), *Empires and Bureaucracy in World History: From Late Antiquity to the Twentieth Century* (Cambridge, CUP, 2016); P Crooks, 'Before Humpty Dumpty: The First English Empire and the Brittleness of Bureaucracy, 1259–1453' in P Crooks and TH Parsons (eds),

as the ultimate decision can be committed to modes of trial such as ordeal and compurgation; but even when juries take their place, the jurors' role is to apply their own local knowledge and judgment, not anything said by the parties or the judge, whether or not written down.[13] In this relational phase of the common law, the judge presides over the court but is not a judgment-giver. In modern terms, the judge's task is more administrative than judicial.

Even when official written records (registers of writs and plea rolls) begin to be kept, they typically tell us only about the pleadings, which are oral, and little or nothing about the trial (which would address the 'general issue' of 'liable or not', 'guilty or not') or the outcome. The judgment-giving took place inside a black box.[14] What the parties argued about between themselves and with the judge (and what may be recorded) is whether the claim would be put to judgment, and on what issue, not what the outcome should be. The writs, likewise, told claimants what they had to do to get their claim to judgment, not what they had to do to win. The judgment-giver would decide, without explanation, what the facts were and how the relevant law applied to those facts, declaring the result of consideration of these issues in simple binary form: judgment for C or for D.[15]

Writs were (amongst other things) entry tickets to the common law courts, which, by the thirteenth century, were three: Common Pleas, King's Bench and Exchequer.[16] Royal justice was initially exceptional – a favour granted in response to a petition. But even when the common law matured from relationality to sovereignty, and the relationship between the common law courts and others became more complementary and less competitive, the use of entry tickets survived. When Common Pleas settled at Westminster in the first quarter of the thirteenth century, tickets could be purchased to transfer a case from a local to the central registry (as it were) if, for instance, the claimant could not afford to wait until the next local sittings to have the case decided. This set the pattern for the future: an 'original writ' became a universal requirement for entry to a common law court. Inevitably, the function of the writs changed. Instead of providing access to exceptional royal justice, they became determinants of the course of proceedings at common law. Each form of action specified its own procedure; there was

Empires and Bureaucracy in World History: From Late Antiquity to the Twentieth Century (Cambridge, CUP, 2016).

[13] JH Baker, *The Common Law Tradition: Lawyers, Books and the Law* (London, Hambledon Press, 2000) chs 8 and 10.

[14] SFC Milsom, *Historical Foundations of the Common Law*, 2nd edn (London, Butterworths, 1981) 81: 'Rights and wrongs were not made in the first place. They had been there within the ordeal, within the conscience of a defendant swearing with his compurgators, known in the same sense to jurors; and the judge who first directed them was focussing their own minds, not reading from a book which he knew and they did not. There was no book.'

[15] SFC Milsom, 'Law and Fact in Legal Development' (1967) 17 *University of Toronto Law Journal* 1.

[16] Even today, tickets are sometimes needed: to make an application for judicial review, for instance, or to appeal to the Supreme Court.

no uniform set of procedural rules.[17] The common law judges could still not control the trial, but they could now control pre-trial and post-trial procedure: 'managerial judging' as we might say post-Woolf.[18]

Early modes of decision-making were 'irrational'.[19] Right and wrong was in the hands of God or Fate or conscience. Then came the jury. At first, the jurors' job was to apply their understanding of the local community's sense of right and wrong, and their knowledge of the facts, to the general issue. Finding of facts, ascertainment of (local) law and the application of the law to the facts all took place in the black box of the jury. Because members of juries were (unlike God and Fate) human, not super-human, they could not always be trusted. Sometimes appearances might deceive and onlookers – even locals – might get the wrong end of the stick. The increasing centralisation of justice at Westminster aggravated this problem because there, the typical jury was not local. They could not be expected to know the facts or the local law. They had to be told: the box had to be furnished with the facts before the decision mechanism could operate. Jury fallibility and lack of local knowledge might also justify limited judicial regulation of what would happen inside the black box. A party might be permitted (by means of a 'special plea') to focus on some crucial fact of the case that might otherwise be ignored or misunderstood. This development generates decisions by the court about whether the jury is permitted or required, as a matter of 'law', to take account of the pleaded fact. Most of what goes on in the black box remains inaccessible to the litigants and the court; but gradually, fragments escape – the judges and the law begin to be concerned not merely with whether the case gets into the black box, but also with some of what happens inside. Procedure, which allows facts to be presented to the judge in the pleadings, starts to generate 'decisional' law relevant to outcomes rather than process. This development is helped along by a change from oral to written pleadings. The development of the Chancellor's 'equitable' jurisdiction is parallel.[20] At first, complaints about failures of justice in common law courts concern the black box itself or the route to the black box. It is only when the internal workings of the box are opened to external regulation that 'equity' can take a truly outcome-oriented turn.

To summarise: in the development of the common law, finding the facts of the case, identifying the relevant law and applying the law to the facts were

[17] The link between procedure and the writs is emphasised in FW Maitland's classic, *The Forms of Action at Common Law* (Cambridge, CUP, 1909).

[18] See, eg, J Sorabji, *English Civil Justice after the Woolf and Jackson Reforms* (Cambridge, CUP, 2014) 184–87.

[19] One of those modes – wager of law – was not formally abolished until the 19th century.

[20] Milsom, *Historical Foundations of the Common Law* (n 14) ch 4. See also JH Baker, *An Introduction to English Legal History*, 4th edn (Oxford, OUP, 2007) ch 6. Because Chancery did not use juries, from the 16th century onwards (at least) its intervention led to the explicit enunciation of outcome-oriented equitable principles and, eventually, rules of law. However, equity had very little impact on tort law.

originally harnessed together by a process that initially committed all to God, Fate, conscience or a jury. Gradually, certain 'special' facts could be kept out of the black box, allowing the courts and the common law to address outcomes as well as procedure directly.

B. Civil Law

The *Institutes* of Justinian were modelled on the *Institutes* of Gaius, who was a non-practising jurist. The classical Roman legal system bore significant procedural similarities to the early English common law, in the sense that access to adjudication was policed by a ticketing system administered by public officials. Gaius' achievement was to provide a systematic, 'principles-based' statement of the law that separated substance from procedural form. Justinian's *Institutes* (like those of Gaius) are in three distinct parts: the law of persons, the law of things and the law of actions.[21] This arrangement puts substance first and procedure second. If the Western Empire had survived, it is anyone's guess how Roman law, arranged in this way, would have developed in practice in Europe. When it was 'rediscovered' in the eleventh century, it was no longer the law of a working legal system but a scheme of abstract rules and principles embodied in texts. It was, we might say, not a law of action(s) but a 'law of the word', a set of ideas rather than a social practice. The revival of Roman law in the eleventh and twelfth centuries was a scholarly enterprise of textual analysis and ('scholastic') philosophical reflection rather than a political exercise in creating a legal system or building a governmental structure or settling disputes.[22] Nor were the analysis and the speculation based on documents generated by the decision of individual cases by judges. The expert 'oracles'[23] of the new Roman law were not decision-makers but scholarly, applied philosophers whose influence over decision-making arose from their employment as advocates and advisers in royal courts around Europe. Of course, action and word are not mutually exclusive foundations of law; they are two tools of power that can be and are used in various combinations and various degrees. They represent two ingredients of a compound.

[21] Concerning the last see E Metzger, 'Actions' in E Metzger (ed), *A Companion to Justinian's Institutes* (London, Duckworth, 1997). More generally, see also J Gordley, *The Jurists: A Critical History* (Oxford, OUP, 2013) ch 1.

[22] This helps to explain why history of legal scholarship, as opposed to history of legal doctrine, is much more developed in the civil law world than in the common law world. A classic example is F Wieacker, *The History of Private Law in Europe*, tr T Weir (Oxford, Clarendon Press, 1995). For public law see, eg, M Stolleis, *Public Law in Germany: A Historical Introduction from the 16th to the 21st Century*, tr T Dunlop (Oxford, OUP, 2017). In the US, 'elite' legal scholarship has become progressively less rooted in doctrine and practice in the past century, and histories of legal scholarship have become more common. Particularly relevant here is GE White, *Tort Law in America: An Intellectual History*, expanded edn (Oxford, OUP, 2003).

[23] JP Dawson, *The Oracles of the Law* (Ann Arbor, MI, The University of Michigan Press, 1968).

The separation of substance and process resulted in a separation of law and fact.[24] The abolition by the Pope in 1215 of trial by ordeal eventually led (outside England) to the adoption of an 'inquisitorial' process under which fact-finding was a job for the judge (unaided by a jury). In this process, there is no 'trial' in the common law sense but rather a fact-finding exercise followed by recourse to the authoritative documents for the law most appropriate to the facts found. Law was the province of the expert guardians and expositors of the texts. Of course, the texts were concerned not only with 'law' in a narrow sense, but also with abstract fact patterns. However, the fact patterns created by the scholars bore no necessary relationship to the facts of individual cases but were, rather, material manufactured for the generation of legal rules and principles. Concrete application of the law to the facts of the case was the province of the judge. The court found the facts, matched the facts to a pattern identified in the texts, and applied the relevant law as expounded by the scholars of the sacred texts. This distinction between concrete and abstract, actual and hypothetical facts is, I shall later argue, important for understanding modern tort scholarship and, ultimately, ideas of law itself.

The civilian judge did not need to be an expert in ascertaining the inherited law, whether decisional or procedural: he could always ask the jurists. Nor were the earliest royal judges in England experts in the decisional (local) law, which was for the jury (or God or Fate). Some were trained in Roman (as well as Canon) law, and this may have affected their making of the common law; but at first, as we have seen, the common law they were making went to process, not outcome. When the common law courts finally settled permanently at Westminster and the common law became increasingly sovereign, a specialised legal profession of court officials started to develop (responsible for pleading), and the practice arose of recruiting the judges from their ranks, thus eventually concentrating common law expertise in Bench and Bar: there were no inherited sacred texts and scholars were not needed to advise the judge. The common law judges became the counterparts of the civilian jurists. Education in the common law was concentrated in the Inns of Court.[25] It was not until the eighteenth century that attempts were first made to give the universities a role in the study of and training in the common law, and not until 100 years later that these attempts bore significant fruit. But even today, legal scholars in the universities do not enjoy a monopoly of 'academic' legal education.

In summary: whereas the common law developed as a law of actions, civil law began as a law of the word. This contrast between a law of actions and a law of the word provides the foundation for the two models of legal scholarship: the common law model and the civil law model. The rest of the chapter will focus primarily on common law scholarship.

[24] For complexities, see JA Jolowicz, *On Civil Procedure* (Cambridge, CUP, 2000) 195.

[25] Even that petered out in the 16th century, to be replaced by an apprenticeship system until 1852.

III. COMMON LAW LEGAL SCHOLARSHIP

A. Before Blackstone

Ironically, the earliest, significant, surviving English example of what we might call legal scholarship[26] – *Glanvill* – thought to have been written in the late 1180s, pre-dates the first appearance of systematic 'action' (or, as we might say today, 'practitioner') literature of English law: the Registers of Writs and Plea Rolls at the very end of the twelfth century, and the Year Books (the first law reports) in the middle of the thirteenth. The author of *Glanvill* knew of the intellectual ferment on the Continent resulting from the rediscovery of the *Digest*. This knowledge posed a methodological issue that, in one form or another, continues to confront common law legal scholarship to this day. Derek Hall described the challenge as being how to 'put dialectic to work on law':

> [T]he use of dialectic as 'an instrument of discovery, suggesting problems which have not actually occurred in practice ... an internal dialectical research' was the supreme contribution of Roman law embodied in the *Digest*. This difficult, inconsistent and infuriating work stimulated the production of a vast literature of glosses, *summae*, *qaestiones* and *casus*. No lawyer who was conversant with it could ever again accept complacently legal writings which presented the law as a mass of single instances.[27]

In more modern terms, the issue is how to give a dialectical, analytical account, in terms of rights and obligations, of law that is not generated dialectically but as part of a process (a set of actions) of deciding, in individual cases, whether or not a claimant should be awarded a remedy. Putting the point quite crudely, how can a word-based law be generated from action based law?

This issue confronted *Glanvill* in particularly acute form. The author's aim was to give an account of the common law. At this point, apart from a few royal decrees (which *Glanvill* ignores), the only official, authoritative ('primary') literature of the common law consisted of the writs, of which systematic records were not yet kept. The writs laid down conditions for entry into the black box of decision-making in the royal courts. From a Romanist point of view, to the extent that the writs contained law, it was law addressing the wrong question – not a question about the respective rights and obligations of the disputing parties but an essentially practical question of pleading – how to get the claim to the decision-maker. *Glanvill*, says Derek Hall, 'wrote at two levels ... an account of the procedure in the royal court on royal writs ... [and] a new venture into substantive law'.[28] At the first level, *Glanvill* deals

> *seriatim* with specific causes of action. The author's other method is that of the modern legal textbook, which sets out to give a systematic exposition of the subject

[26] On precursors see GDG Hall (ed), *The Treatise on the Laws and Customs of the Realm of England Commonly Called Glanvill* (Oxford, Clarendon Press, 1993) xiii–xv.
[27] ibid xvi (footnote omitted).
[28] ibid xxvii.

> in terms of substantive law and supported with such authorities as may be available and pertinent; authority is subordinate to exposition, and lack of authority no bar to speculation.[29]

Hall thinks that *Glanvill* 'stumbled almost by accident' onto the second, dialectical, substantive level of analysis. By contrast, when writing his '*De Legibus et Consuetudinibus Angliae*' in the early thirteenth century, Bracton 'clearly planned in advance his separation of procedure and substance'.[30] *Glanvill's* 'small page of generalities', says TFT Plucknett, was 'expanded nearly three-hundred-fold' by Bracton,[31] despite the fact that three-quarters of *Bracton* is devoted to writ procedure. Both *Glanvill* and *Bracton* were influenced by the Gaian trichotomy of persons, things and actions. However, because of their focus on the writs, the law of actions ('procedure') gets – from a scholarly perspective – quite disproportionate attention. Moreover, the discussion of procedure is not a dialectical analysis of (procedural) rights and obligations but a practical guide to pleading. The common observation that there was no wholesale 'reception' of Roman law in England directs attention not primarily to substantive law but to the contrast between a law of action(s) and a law of the word. As Plucknett puts it, 'the position of England by the end of the 12th century had already become clear: as Glanvill had perceived, English law was the law of writs'.[32]

The next tall peak in the pre-Blackstonian landscape is Thomas de Lyttleton's *On Tenures*, dating from the late fifteenth century. *Glanvill* and *Bracton* both dealt with (the whole of) 'English law', whereas Lyttleton wrote about what we would now call a legal 'area' or 'subject' – land law; and he did so dialectically and analytically. This early achievement, it is widely believed, reflects the all-pervasive political, economic and social importance of land in medieval England, one result of which was that lawyers started thinking substantively about land law much sooner than about other, less socially significant areas of the law, such as contract and tort. Judges were more willing in this area than in others – notably crime and obligations – to direct juries on both law and fact relevant to outcomes. *On Tenures* was enormously influential but attracted no imitators in the sixteenth and seventeenth centuries. Indeed, Sir Edward Coke's equally famous *Coke on Lyttleton*, the first volume of his *Institutes*, published in 1628, consisted of glosses and comments on the original text rather than a systematic reworking in the manner of subsequent editions of modern texts.[33] The next landmark in the history of the 'Lyttleton genre' was probably Sir William Jones's *Essay on the Law of Bailments*, first published in 1781.

[29] ibid xxix.
[30] ibid lix.
[31] TFT Plucknett, *Early English Legal Literature* (Cambridge, CUP, 1968) 34.
[32] ibid 41.
[33] For a more nuanced account, see AWB Simpson, 'The Rise and Fall of the Legal Treatise' in AWB Simpson, *Legal Theory and Legal History: Essays on the Common Law* (London, Hambledon Press, 1987) 275–79.

By this time, the number of writs in regular use had been much reduced and more law – in the area of contract, anyway – had been kept from the black box of the general issue, making statement and analysis of decisional law perhaps more imaginable and less daunting.

The most common forms of legal literature in the early modern period were 'abridgements' and 'digests' of primary materials, organised without analytical system, often alphabetically.[34] It was not until the eighteenth century that anything like *Glanvill* or *Bracton* appeared again, initially in the form of Sir Matthew Hale's *Analysis of the Laws of England*, published posthumously in 1713. Like its predecessors, Hale's work was much influenced by the *Institutes* of Justinian and, through them, by those of Gaius.

B. Blackstone and Bentham

According to AWB Simpson, Hale's book 'made Blackstone's *Commentaries* possible'.[35] The *Commentaries on the Laws of England* were published between 1765 and 1769, in four volumes dealing respectively with 'The Rights of Persons', 'The Rights of Things', 'Private Wrongs' and 'Public Wrongs'. In Book IV, on 'Public Wrongs', Blackstone discusses criminal law and procedure. Book I, on 'The Rights of Persons', deals with aspects of what we would now call public law, employment law and family law. Book II, on 'The Rights of Things', covers property law. It is here that we find Blackstone's brief discussion of contract, which he treats as a mode of acquiring property. Similarly, to the extent that Book III, 'Of Private Wrongs', deals with what we would now call tort law, it is concerned primarily with injury to property interests. There is only one short chapter on injuries to the person. The bulk of Book III is concerned with procedure.[36]

The accepted wisdom is that Blackstone was an 'institutional writer'.[37] The typical institutional work was civilian. As a literary genre, institutes were a product of the development of nation-states in the seventeenth and eighteenth centuries. They represented attempts to domesticate the Roman inheritance and build national identity by comprehensively (re-)stating the law of a particular nation-state, both its 'indigenous' and Roman elements.

[34] Modern counterparts include *Current Law Monthly Digest* and *Australian Legal Monthly Digest*.

[35] Simpson, 'The Rise and Fall of the Legal Treatise' (n 33) 281. On other antecedents see SFC Milsom, 'The Nature of Blackstone's Achievement' (1981) 1 *OJLS* 1, 7–8.

[36] For modern attempts to reconstruct the pre-Blackstonian law of torts see, eg, SFC Milsom, *Historical Foundations of the Common Law*, 2nd edn (London, Butterworths, 1981) chs 11 and 13; D Ibbetson, *A Historical Introduction to the Law of Obligations* (Oxford, OUP, 1999) chs 3, 4 and 6.

[37] eg JW Cairns, 'Blackstone, An English Institutist: Legal Literature and the Rise of the Nation State' (1984) 4 *OJLS* 318.

In undertaking this institutional task, Blackstone was confronted with the same problem as had faced *Glanvill* and *Bracton*, namely how to accommodate the common law, writ system within the tripartite Gaian analytical framework. *Bracton's* solution had been deliberately to separate substance and process, and devote most of the work to actions. By contrast, Blackstone subsumes the law of actions within a novel understanding of law as being about rights and wrongs rather than persons and things. Persons re-emerge as rights holders and wrong sufferers, and things are transformed into objects of personal rights and wrongs. Actions become the machinery for vindicating rights and remedying wrongs. The result is an idiosyncratic account of English law driven, it seems, partly by Blackstone's desire to communicate English law to educated non-lawyers.[38] Attempting to explain English law to the lay-person through the lens of the labyrinthine writ system would have been pointless and thankless.[39]

The institutional tradition survives today in works such as *Halsbury's Laws of England*, *English Private Law* (the brain-child of Peter Birks, now in its third edition, edited by Andrew Burrows) and *English Public Law* (edited by David Feldman). The *Restatements of the Law* of the American Law Institute are also institutionalist in the sense that they propose a common law for the United States of America in the face the Supreme Court's ruling that there is no such thing as a national common law – each jurisdiction (including the federal) has its own common law.[40] Many US law faculties teach a sort of American *ius commune* instead of or in addition to local law; and in this sense, much pedagogical and scholarly literature in the US is institutist in inspiration.

Blackstone's major achievement was to provide an account of English law as a whole (which – even in his day – was overwhelmingly a product of judicial decision-making framed, and more or less constrained, by the formulary, writ system of pleading and procedure) that subordinated form to substance, procedure to outcome. Besides provoking much technical criticism of the account itself,[41] Blackstone's creative and laudatory re-invention of the flagging common law so infuriated Jeremy Bentham that he launched savage and unremitting attacks on the very idea of adjudicatory, judicial law-making and favoured, instead, legislative 'codification' of the whole law according to the principle of utility. In historical perspective, Bentham's campaign, which gained

[38] Milsom, 'The Nature of Blackstone's Achievement' (n 35) 12.

[39] Almost a century later CG Addison (in *Wrongs and Their Remedies Being a Treatise on the Law of Torts* (London, Stevens & Sons, 1860) vii) called it 'remarkable' that tort law formed 'no part of ordinary education or learning'. His explanation was that the law had 'hitherto been so blended with our artificial system of forms of action, and burthened with so many niceties and subtleties peculiar to our ancient and refined system of legal procedure and pleading, that the study of [it] has been rendered tedious and repulsive to all who do not intend to take to law as a profession'.

[40] *Erie Railroad Co v Tompkins* 304 US 64 (1938); N Jansen, *The Making of Legal Authority: Legislative and Non-Legislative Codification in Historical and Comparative Perspective* (Oxford, OUP, 2010) 50–59.

[41] See, generally, A Page and W Prest (eds), *Blackstone and His Critics* (Oxford, Hart Publishing, 2018).

more traction in the US than in England,[42] was almost bound to fail. The theoretical essence of codification is the establishment of the Code as the exclusive source of law, and the relegation of judges to its application in the settlement of disputes. Codification, in other words, presupposes a sharp, categorial distinction between law and its application to fact. As we have seen, this division between law and fact became entrenched in civilian systems as early as the eleventh century at the same time as the common law's harnessing of law and fact was being established. Civilian codification in the nineteenth century was partly a state-building exercise designed to simplify the law but, more importantly, to replace older, natural-law ideas about the sources of law with new-fangled positivism (in France) or *Volksgeist* (in Germany).[43] In France, it was also a product of suspicion of, and a desire to control, the judiciary.[44] It had nothing to do with changing the way the relationship between law and fact, law-making and law application, was understood. To succeed, Bentham's project would have had to do exactly that.

Still, dissatisfaction with the contemporary state of the legal system, and particularly common law procedure, was widespread and deep by the beginning of the nineteenth century. By 1875 the formulary system of pleading had been scrapped in favour of fact pleading,[45] and the sources of jurisdictional competition that had originally given rise to the writ system had effectively been eliminated. These developments fundamentally changed the relationship between process and substance in English law and laid the foundations of modern legal scholarship.

C. Modern (Tort) Scholarship

By 1875 the formulary, writ system was technically dead, except in the area of public law, where the prerogative writs lived on for another century and where some of the values of the old system still find expression in mechanisms and rules designed to keep claims against the government out of court and away from the judges. Two other developments since 1875 deserve to be noted.

[42] There were two codification movements in the US, one early in the 19th century and the other *fin de siècle*. The former (on which see CM Cook, *The American Codification Movement: A Study of Antebellum Legal Reform* (Westport, CT, Greenwood Press, 1981) was motivated partly by a desire to Americanise the inheritance of English law. The latter was more a reaction to the increasing complexity of the law in a rapidly growing, multi-jurisdictional federation with common law roots.

[43] Gordley, *The Jurists: A Critical History* (n 21) 195–204.

[44] M Lasser, *Judicial Deliberations: A Comparative Analysis of Judicial Transparency and Legitimacy* (Oxford, OUP, 2004) 35.

[45] The formulary system also effectively put the choice of law in the hands of the parties, because each writ specified not only the appropriate procedure but also the 'proper' law: Jolowicz, *On Civil Procedure* (n 24) 186–87. Now, the parties choose the facts, and on the basis of those facts, the judge chooses (or makes) the relevant law: ibid 195.

One is the demise of the civil jury. In the earliest days of the common law the jury of locals addressed the general issue without (judicial) direction as to fact or law. When the jury ceased to have any necessary connection with the relevant locality, responsibility for their knowledge and appreciation of the facts shifted to the parties and the court. Moreover, distrust of the jury (as compared with God or Fate) encouraged the development of procedures to prevent juries exercising unfettered discretion over fact. Special pleas narrowed the scope of the issues left to the jury and generated law relevant to outcomes.[46] Eventually, outcome-related issues were systematically divided between judge and jury: fact (as presented by the litigants and shaped by the judge's direction) for the jury and law for the judge (via direction of the jury). With the abolition of civil juries, full responsibility for both law and fact came to rest with the judge. However, unlike the jury, the judge cannot retire to a black box and, on emerging, simply announce a victory for one party or the other on the general issue. The judge must find the facts, ascertain the relevant law, state both, and explain the court's decision by reference to the facts and the law, issue by issue. This is the logic of the procedural regime in place since 1875. And notice: according to this logic, just as law and the facts of the case were intertwined inside the black box of God, Fate or the jury, they are still intertwined, but now in the public, observable role of the judge. The common law – judge-made law – is still not a law of the word in the civilian sense, identifiable separately from and prior to consideration of the facts of the case. Rather, the procedural matrix of common law adjudication harnesses law to those facts. This explains why one way of side-lining an authoritative precedent is to say that it 'depends solely on its facts': if the facts are unique, the law they generate is singular.

By contrast, under the model civilian process, law does not emerge from but is imposed on the facts of the case at hand. Civil law procedure is primarily designed to prepare the factual groundwork for the application of law developed and determined independently *of those facts* (although not, of course, independently of hypothetical facts, which are integral to the dialectical development of the law). In this sense, substantive common law is a product of the judicial process in a way that civil law is not. In the civil law model, the legal experts are jurists (in a broad sense), not officers of the court. Judges and jurists have different jobs.[47] The judges' task is to resolve disputes by 'applying' the law, which the jurists generate by analysis and systematisation – formerly

[46] See, generally, SFC Milsom, *A Natural History of the Common Law* (New York, Columbia University Press, 2003) esp ch 1; JH Langbein, 'Bifurcation and the Bench: The Influence of the Jury on English Conceptions of the Judiciary' in P Brand and J Getzler (eds), *Judges and Judging in the History of the Common Law and Civil Law: From Antiquity to Modern Times* (Cambridge, CUP, 2012).

[47] Judges may and do moonlight as jurists.

of the inherited texts and now of the Code, parliamentary legislation and case law. This is not to say, on the one side, that civilian judges do not contribute to the development of the law by exercising discretion in its application to individual cases. Nevertheless, their contributions do not 'make' the law in individual cases; instead, they provide grist for the juristic mill. Nor is it to say, on the other side, that jurists have law-making authority in their own right. Under the civil law model (at least in its modern manifestations), the legislature alone has law-making 'authority'. Indeed, it is the very absence of judicial authority to make law that provides space for both judges and jurists to contribute to the development of the law, which is, as it were, a joint enterprise between Bench and Academy.[48]

The other, post-1875 development worth noting is 'globalisation' with its effect on the position of the nation-state. Amongst other things, dispute-settling and law-making are basic tools for building political communities. By this criterion, England was a political community long before any modern European nation-state. As suggested earlier, the codification movement of the nineteenth century in Europe may be understood as part of the process of consolidating the identity of the nation-state, which by then had become the basic unit of political community. It was not long, however, before political communities beyond nation-states started to appear to address new supra-national possibilities and challenges. An example is the Universal Postal Union established in 1874, now a UN agency. In the twentieth century, war was a major catalyst of international community-building – first, the League of Nations, then the United Nations, the Council of Europe, the European Union and so on. Law and law-like phenomena are integral to such developments. The second, information-based industrial revolution has witnessed a proliferation of non-state, transnational organisations, about which textbooks are now written.[49] To the study of the employment-focused, internal administrative law of international entities has been added a topic called 'global administrative law',[50] a premise of which is that in some respects, at least, there are now global political communities of state and non-state actors.

We can now turn to the impact of these various developments on common law tort scholarship.

[48] Regarding France, see Lasser, *Judicial Deliberations: A Comparative Analysis of Judicial Transparency and Legitimacy* (n 44) ch 6. Lasser subtly explores the interaction between Bench, (the French counterpart of the) 'Bar' and Academy. As noted earlier, the present analysis omits express discussion of the relationship between the Bar and the Academy. Lasser's spin on the common law is based on the US: ibid, 337–47.

[49] eg J Klabbers, *An Introduction to International Organizations*, 3rd edn (Cambridge, CUP, 2015).

[50] eg B Kingsbury, 'Global Administrative Law Dimensions of International Organizations Law' (2009) 6 *International Organizations Law Review* 315.

D. Abolition of the Formulary System and Civil Jury

i. The Textbook Tradition

The modern textbook was a product of the institutional and procedural reforms of the nineteenth and twentieth centuries. The demise of the writs cleared the way for more systematic exposition and analysis of decisional law with, at most, only subsidiary reference to the process and procedures that produced it. The first, great tort textbooks included those of Sir Frederick Pollock (1887) and Sir John Salmond (1907). As Pollock said in the first edition of *The Law of Torts*:

> Taking into account the fact that in this country the separation of courts and of forms of action has disappeared, though marks of the separate origin and history of every branch of jurisdiction remain, we may now say this much. A tort is an act or omission giving rise, in virtue of the common law jurisdiction of the Court, to a civil remedy which is not an action of contract. To that extent we know what a tort is not.[51]

As we have seen, a century earlier, Blackstone had great difficulty disentangling tort law from procedural law. In this area (as, even more, in criminal law), there was too little judicial regulation of the operation of the black box to make systematic analysis of decisional tort law at all straightforward. Too much was left to the general issue. The problem was aggravated by the continued existence, side by side, of trespass and case, which ensured that a formulary approach to the increasingly significant social problem of 'accidents' would continue well into the nineteenth century. Together, the demise of the writs and the civil jury enabled the text writers to move beyond the point reached by Blackstone, not merely separating procedure from substance but also effectively ignoring it and treating the whole of the law of torts as a law of substantive rights and wrongs. Pollock, for instance, includes quite a short chapter on remedies but nothing on pleading or process, and his treatment of remedies is analytical rather than practical. In modern terms, the classic tort textbook is concerned with the (substantive) *law of tort* to the almost total neglect of the practical operation of the *tort system*.[52]

[51] F Pollock, *The Law of Torts: A Treatise on the Principles of Obligations Arising from Civil Wrongs in the Common Law* (London, Stevens and Sons, 1887) 4. The transitional nature of the work is shown by the fact that while it grew out of lectures given at the Inns of Court (not Oxford University) (ibid vi), the Preface took the form of an open letter to Oliver Wendell Holmes. On the other hand, Pollock did propose a complex, positive, 'principled' definition of a tort (ibid 19). It rests on two distinctions: one between 'personal wrongs', 'wrongs to property' and 'wrongs to person, estate and property generally' (ibid 6–8); and the other between whether the wrong done is 'wilful', 'apparently unconnected with moral blame' or 'the result of imprudence or omission' (ibid 8–12).

[52] The situation is slightly different in the US, where civil juries still play a significant part in tort litigation. For instance, DB Dobbs, PT Hayden and EM Bublick, *Hornbook on Torts*, 2nd edn, (St Paul, MN, West Academic Publishing, 2016) contains a short chapter entitled 'Tort Law in Practice' dealing with topics such as 'Trials and Appeals', 'Judge, Jury and Community Values', 'The Prima Facie Case and the Burden of Proof', 'Remedies and Attorney's Fees' and 'Liability Insurance'.

Because the separation of substance from procedure was still so recent, the early textbook writers enjoyed very considerable analytical freedom. How did they exercise that freedom? Brian Simpson has argued that the authors of the first English contract textbooks engaged in large-scale plagiarism of Continental, Romanist scholarship and were much less original than is often imagined.[53] By contrast, he says, 'So far as I am aware, there is not the least evidence that … the Continental Pandectists, or even the great Savigny, ever had any effect on the common law of tort … in England'.[54] This judgment is, perhaps, supported by the respective distances that contract and tort writers respectively managed to put between their new analytical schemes and the old writ system. Whereas the contract lawyers settled relatively easily on the idea that contract law was based on a broad principle of conduct (even if there was disagreement about what that principle was), the tort lawyers got little further than translating the procedural forms of action into substantive causes of action.[55] They argued about whether English law recognised a law of *tort* or a law of *torts*.[56] In 1939, Glanville Williams simply assumed that this was a practical question for the courts to answer, not an analytical debate to which scholars could legitimately make a contribution.[57] Since then, what Toby Milsom once called 'the deadly touch of authority' has tightened its grip to the point where 'not just rules but even classifications [and] approaches to problems' are under its sway.[58] The combination of the hardening of the doctrines of precedent and *stare decisis*, large increases in the volume of reported cases and proliferation of secondary literature significantly limit the modern textbook writer's leeway for originality and imagination.

Those of us of a certain age have been privileged to witness the process of the birth of a new substantive area of law during our lifetimes.[59] It is not clear

I have tried to integrate or, at least, combine treatment of tort law and the tort system, substance and form, in P Cane, *Key Ideas in Tort Law* (Oxford, Hart Publishing, 2017), as did Patrick Atiyah in his path-breaking classic, *Accidents, Compensation and the Law*, 1st edn (London, Weidenfeld & Nicolson, 1970).

[53] AWB Simpson, 'Innovation in Nineteenth Century Contract Law' in AWB Simpson, *Legal Theory and Legal History: Essays on the Common Law* (London, Hambledon Press, 1987).

[54] AWB Simpson, 'The Elusive Truth about Holmes' (1997) 95 *Michigan Law Review* 2027, 2032. For different views, see CHS Fifoot, *Judge and Jurist in the Age of Victoria* (London, Stevens & Sons, 1959) 10–12; D Ibbetson, *A Historical Introduction to the Law of Obligations* (Oxford, OUP, 1999) 164–75; Gordley, *The Jurists: A Critical History* (n 21) 205–12, 235–48.

[55] PS Atiyah, *Pragmatism and Theory in English Law* (London, Stevens & Sons, 1987) 170–80.

[56] Fifoot, *Judge and Jurist in the Age of Victoria* (n 54) ch 2. Lord Atkin's neighbour principle, enunciated in 1932, did not end the debate even so far as the 'tort of negligence' was concerned: K Barker, P Cane, M Lunney and F Trindade, *The Law of Torts in Australia*, 5th edn (Melbourne, OUP, 2012) 456–62. In England, the latest round was played out in *Robinson v Chief Constable of West Yorkshire Police* [2018] UKSC 4, [2018] AC 736 and *Commissioner of Police of the Metropolis v DSD* [2018] UKSC 11, [2018] 2 WLR 895.

[57] GL Williams, 'The Foundation of Tortious Liability' (1939) 7 *CLJ* 111.

[58] Milsom, 'The Nature of Blackstone's Achievement' (n 35) 12.

[59] A Goymour, 'Reflections on the Restitution Revolution: 1. England and Wales' in S Worthington, A Robertson and G Virgo (eds), *Revolution and Evolution in Private Law* (Oxford, Hart Publishing, 2018) 177–92. Administrative law in Australia provides another good illustration

why the process did not start much earlier than it did; but one advantage of the delay was a certain self-conscious awareness on the part of the participants of what they were doing and their place in the development of common law scholarship. In 1966, in *The Law of Restitution*, Robert Goff (joined in later editions by Gareth Jones) expounded a loose collection of established heads of recovery that did not neatly fall within the contract/tort universe in much the same way as the early tort writers translated the old, procedurally oriented 'forms of action' into new, outcome-oriented 'torts'. Then, in 1985, in his *Introduction to the Law of Restitution*, Peter Birks began the search for the dialectical principles that he claimed underlay both the old grounds and their successor causes of action. Birks (who rose to be Regius Professor of Civil Law at Oxford) was, first and foremost, a Roman lawyer, steeped in the history and learning of the *Corpus Iuris*. He saw himself as a torch-bearer for the Romanist tradition of dialectical scholarship. In the face of much (mainly constructive) criticism, Birks came to believe that in his first attempt at analysing the English law of 'restitution', he had not gained enough distance from the inheritance of the old system. His second attempt, in the much shorter and more radical *Unjust Enrichment* (2003), effectively abandoned action-based, common law ways of thinking in favour of civilian ideas – a move resisted by the UK Supreme Court.[60] The apotheosis of the evolution of the subject can perhaps be found in Andrew Burrows' recent 'quasi-codification'.[61]

Two other, related factors limit the dialectical freedom of common law scholars compared (in theory, at least) with their civilian counterparts. First, the merger of responsibility for both law and fact in the office of the judge has encouraged the translation of what, under the old system, were matters of fact for lay judgment-givers, into matters of law for legal experts. Secondly, the harnessing of law and fact in common law adjudication makes it risky for scholars to abstract decisional principles too far from the facts to which they initially related. Because the judge may side-line an authority on the basis

of the process, though one driven by courts and the legislature, not scholars. Under s 75(v) of the Australian Constitution, the High Court of Australia has original jurisdiction to award remedies of mandamus, prohibition and injunction against Officers of the Commonwealth. This formulary, remedies-oriented approach was supplemented by a 'grounds of review' scheme by the *Administrative Decisions (Judicial Review) Act 1977* (Cth). Now, the High Court seems to be replacing the grounds of review approach with one based on statutory norms of administrative conduct: P Cane, L McDonald and K Rundle, *Principles of Administrative Law*, 3rd edn (Melbourne, OUP, 2018) 6–7 and ch 4.

[60] Goymour, 'Reflections on the Restitution Revolution: 1. England and Wales' (n 59) 185.

[61] A Burrows, *A Restatement of the English Law of Restitution* (Oxford, OUP, 2013). Despite its adoption of the American Law Institute's flagship brand-name, this is not a restatement in the American sense of an attempt to distil a common law from a plurality of local laws. For earlier history of the relevant law, see JH Baker, 'The History of Quasi-Contract in English Law' in WR Cornish, R Nolan, J O'Sullivan and G Virgo (eds), *Restitution Past, Present and Future: Essays in Honour of Gareth Jones* (Oxford, Hart Publishing, 1998); JH Langbein, 'The Later History of Restitution' in WR Cornish, R Nolan, J O'Sullivan and G Virgo (eds), *Restitution Past, Present and Future: Essays in Honour of Gareth Jones* (Oxford, Hart Publishing, 1998).

purely of its facts, the scholar cannot afford to give any judge-made proposition of law too secure a place in their analytical scheme because law is always subject to fact. At the margin, anyway, the provisionality of common law authority (which can always be discounted or discarded at the point of application) is the enemy of analytical certainty and rigour. The high value given to legal certainty by civil law systems arguably reflects the fact that that under civilian procedure, law is not harnessed to, but imposed on, the facts of the case, and that individual decisions provide material for law creation but do not authoritatively create law.

Such constraints affect the writer of 'practitioner' texts even more than authors of student texts.[62] Despite the predominance of legislation in law-making, it still falls to the courts to work the very large body of disparate legal sources, created by many actors over long periods of time, into a 'coherent' whole.[63] This is the role that Continental jurists marked out for themselves in the late Middle Ages. 'Coherence' was the watchword of the first school of Continental legal scholars, the Glossators, who practised a method that became known as 'scholasticism'.[64] In England, the constitutional upheavals of the seventeenth century gave the common law judges the opportunity, by aligning themselves with Parliament, to assume the role of autonomous guardians of the nation's law against royal encroachment. That common law judges enjoy not only autonomous power to make law but also a constitutional responsibility for keeping the law in reasonable, substantive order gives their activities unique significance. Ultimately, legal practice revolves around judicial practice. Dialectical speculation is of limited value to practitioners. Nor is it of much use in education for practice.[65]

The modern, common law scholar is (we might say) a creature of the procedural reforms of the nineteenth century. Although those reforms radically changed the relationships between procedure and substance, and between law

[62] Early practitioner texts on torts included Addison, *Wrongs and Their Remedies Being a Treatise on the Law of Torts* (n 39), first published in 1860; and the first edition of *Clerk and Lindsell on Torts*, published in 1889. The title of Addison's book reflects Blackstone's treatment of torts. Pollock reversed the order of 'wrong' and 'torts' in his title and described the difference between his book and predecessors in terms of 'selecting rather than collecting authorities' (Pollock, *The Law of Torts: A Treatise on the Principles of Obligations Arising from Civil Wrongs in the Common Law* (n 51) viii, xl).

[63] On the influence of the common law on drafting of statutes, see Atiyah, *Pragmatism and Theory in English Law* (n 55) 31–32.

[64] '[T]he resolution of every legal problem by a text and the explanation of every text by means of another': Gordley, *The Jurists: A Critical History* (n 21) 31.

[65] However, the centrality of judicial practice presupposes a judiciary that is expert in the law and much respected. The higher a court in the judicial hierarchy, the greater the legal significance of its individual decisions. The importance of juristic analysis is also affected by expertise of the judiciary. Lay judges decide most criminal cases tried in England. As a result, practitioner texts play a greater role in criminal law than in civil law. In 2017 the legal press reported a stoush between Bench and criminal Bar over which of two texts should be adopted as the unofficial bible – the venerable *Archbold*, or the upstart (and appropriately titled) *Blackstone's Criminal Practice*. Disappointingly, the proposed shift to *Blackstone* seems to have been a cost-saving expedient rather than a judgment of relative quality.

and fact, they left the pre-eminent role of the judges intact or even strengthened. Doctrinal scholarship is inevitably more closely tied to legal practice under the common law-model than under the civil law model. In the civilian picture, jurist and judge can easily be understood as having distinct roles and responsibilities – the former for the law and its coherence, and the latter for facts and application of the law to facts. It is not so easy to see what, if any, is the distinct function of jurists under common law arrangements. The rapid growth of the academic branch of the legal profession in the latter half of the twentieth century, and invention of law as an 'academic' subject, gave the issue a sharp point.

This was Lord Goff's topic in his 1983 Maccabaean Lecture, 'The Search for Principle'.[66] Goff had personal experience as university law teacher and researcher, barrister and judge, and so might be expected to have well-formed opinions on the topic of 'jurists and judges'. Yet the lecture is curiously ambivalent and, as I read it, much less accommodating of jurists than is often assumed. Goff begins by declaring that while the 'formulation of legal principles is not the primary function of judges',[67] it is 'one of the main functions'[68] of jurists. But in the end, he concludes, in 'the development of legal principles, the dominant power should be ... that of the judge ... because the dominant element in the development of the law should be professional reaction to individual fact-situations,[69] rather than theoretical development of legal principles'.[70] The jurist should not, Goff says, try to 'do the judge's job for him' on the basis of 'preconceived ideas' and 'solitary ruminations ... in the quietness of his study', 'without the benefit of [the judge's] practical experience or the assistance of counsel'.[71] Where, then, in Goff's view, does 'the greatest strength of the jurist'[72] lie? In considering, he says, 'more fundamental questions about the law, whether in terms of jurisprudence, or legal principle, or social desirability'.[73] Ignoring this instance of Lord Goff's profligate over-use of the idea of 'legal principle', the province of the jurist, he seems to think, covers 'jurisprudence' and 'social desirability',[74] neither of which, apparently, need or should divert the judge's gaze from the case at hand. The judicial process is a battle of conflicting interests between litigants and their champions.[75]

[66] R Goff, 'The Search for Principle' (1984) 69 *Proceedings of the British Academy* 169.

[67] ibid 170.

[68] ibid 171.

[69] 'Using facts to develop principles', as he puts it elsewhere (ibid 183). A related phenomenon is the judicial urge to do justice that seems to explain cases, such as *White v Jones* [1995] 2 AC 207 (HL) and *Junior Books Ltd v Veitchi* [1983] 1 AC 520 (HL), that scholars find very difficult to explain in terms of 'principle'.

[70] Goff, 'The Search for Principle' (n 66) 185–86.

[71] ibid 185.

[72] ibid.

[73] ibid.

[74] Fifoot argues that jurists may be able to help judges out of an impasse or untangle a knot created by the force of authority and settled ways of thought: Fifoot, *Judge and Jurist in the Age of Victoria* (n 54) 135. But unlike the legislature, jurists must speak softly because they carry no big stick!

[75] Goff, 'The Search for Principle' (n 66) 182.

The judge's job is to react as trained lawyers to factual situations and to generalise from their reactions; and they should be able to do this 'unencumbered by any such thing as a philosophy'.[76]

ii. Scholarship Beyond the Textbook: Tort Theory

Under the civil law model, jurists are, in a very obvious sense, participants in the legal system.[77] As scholars, they have a publicly recognised responsibility for developing the law independently of the consideration of individual cases, and for making it available to judges, who can use it to decide individual cases. Without such a role, jurists under the common law model are caught in a slightly awkward limbo between the academy and the practising profession. One way of dealing with this situation is for legal scholars to position themselves as observers ('theorists') of, rather than participants in, law-generating legal practices.

Tort 'theory' has a very long history. The Romans distinguished between obligations *ex contractu* and *ex delicto*, apparently on the back of the distinction drawn by Aristotle, in the *Nicomachean Ethics*, between claims for rectification arising out of voluntary transactions and those arising out of non-voluntary transactions. Because of the way the common law developed, this distinction could not easily be mapped onto English law of the nineteenth century. For one thing, contract in the modern sense found no place in the early formulary system, which was in terminal decline by the time concepts of contract started to develop in response to the growth of commerce in the eighteenth century. For another, the two categories are neither mutually exclusive nor comprehensive. Contract, which had grown, via *assumpsit*, out of trespass, was treated by Blackstone as a mode of acquiring property; and he treated breach of contract as a 'wrong'. Trespass and case were understood in remedial rather than transactional terms, as concerned with wrongs rather than rights. For Blackstone, rights to security and safety of the person were part of the law of persons, and rights to security and safety of property belonged to the law of things.[78] Under civilian influence, contract law (on which 'the forms of action had not lain so heavily … as on torts')[79] could be quite easily constructed in terms of creation, protection and discharge of a certain class of rights. Tort law was much more difficult because although it certainly protected rights, it did not create them or regulate their discharge. On the other hand, to the extent that tort law was concerned with redressing wrongs, it was typically treated as part of the law

[76] ibid 187.

[77] Regarding France, see Lasser, *Judicial Deliberations: A Comparative Analysis of Judicial Transparency and Legitimacy* (n 44) 39–46.

[78] All this is excellently explained in TC Grey, 'Accidental Torts' (2001) 54 *Vanderbilt Law Review* 1225.

[79] FH Lawson, 'Doctrinal Writing: A Foreign Element in English Law?' in E von Caemmerer, S Mentschikoff and K Zweigert (eds), *Ius Privatum Gentium: Festschrift für Max Rheinstein* (Tübingen, JCB Mohr, 1969) 199.

of actions rather than as an element of decisional law. Blackstone adopted the Roman contract/delict divide, substituting the word 'tort' for 'delict', as a synonym for 'wrong', to cover 'all actions for trespasses, nusances [*sic*], assaults, defamatory words and the like'.[80]

Confronted with this taxonomical dilemma, in the late nineteenth century Oliver Wendell Holmes proposed that tort law be understood as a law of 'accidents', concerned with striking a reasonable balance between the interests we all share in personal security and safety on the one hand, and freedom of action on the other. He argued that the objective concept of 'negligence' was central to this understanding of tort law, but that, in certain circumstances, tort law also imposed standards of conduct either more or less demanding than negligence. Of course, this theory did not solve the taxonomical problem; it simply ignored it by opting to treat tort law as a law of wrongs and as having nothing to do with rights.[81] For that reason, if for no other, although Holmes's approach has been extremely influential, especially in the US, it could not be, and was not, systematically used to organise a body of law that, for practical and pedagogical purposes, continued to be defined negatively rather than positively: not contract, not trust, not crime and not unjust enrichment. The theory simply did not fit the facts even though, ironically, it was developed in the name and spirit of legal 'science'.

a. Economic Theory

Because he led a double intellectual life as judge and theorist, such cognitive dissonance apparently caused Holmes no special discomfort. His theory of torts was a product of his philosophical inclinations, while his practical bent was satisfied by his work on the Bench. In modern times, Richard Posner apparently also leads a double life as practising judge during the week and an economic theorist (or jurisprudential polymath) at the weekend (or perhaps both all the time). As a theory of (tort) *law*, Posnerian economic analysis suffers from the

[80] W Blackstone, *Commentaries on the Laws of England*, III, xiii, 117.

[81] Pollock, *The Law of Torts: A Treatise on the Principles of Obligations Arising from Civil Wrongs in the Common Law* (n 51) provides a plausible historical explanation for one aspect of the make-up of tort law. Tort law grew out of the writs. The writs (as we have seen) were a feature of litigation in the common law courts. Tort law is, therefore, 'confined by the limits within which those courts exercised their jurisdiction' (ibid 3). By Blackstone's time, the main writs were trespass and trespass on the case, out of which both modern contract law and modern tort law were fashioned. By that time, the writs that had originally been developed to address wrongs to property – in other words, to protect property rights – such as the writ of right and detinue, had, because of 'their cumbrous and archaic points of procedure', been replaced by trespass and case (ibid 14). On this basis, Pollock felt able to conclude (ibid 15–16) that the basic principle of tort law was moral wrongfulness, and that tort liability regardless of moral wrongfulness is exceptional and explicable in terms of the formulary system. Unfortunately, this explanation (as Pollock realised) leaves vicarious liability and strict liability for harm (as opposed to interference with rights) unaccounted for. The formulary, act-based origins of the common law have cast a very long shadow over classification and taxonomy.

disability that it focuses on outcomes, and ignores norms and reasons. It shows neither how law is imposed on facts nor how law arises out of facts. In its positive form, it is facts all the way down; and in its normative form, it is a moral, not a legal, theory. Be that as it may, the relevant point here about both Holmes's and Posner's 'theories of torts' is that neither theorises the subject-matter that the doctrinal jurists include between the covers of their tort textbooks.[82] In that sense, the Holmesian and Posnerian strategy for addressing the challenge of developing a theory of tort law, as a social practice involving legislators, judges and jurists, is avoidance.

b. Corrective Justice Theory

Despite their philosophical sophistication, the same, I would suggest, is true of the approaches of the various species of corrective justice and rights theorists. Unlike the economic theorists, the 'moralists' and 'formalists' take norms seriously. However, the law they take seriously is often of their own invention. As we have seen, under the old common law, the writs of 'trespass', case, detinue and so on were concerned with wrongs and harms, not rights. The point is not that 'trespass' means 'wrong' but that, historically, remedies for harms ended up in the early modern tort books because their authors had no theoretical reason for putting them anywhere else. It is unsurprising that the corrective justice and rights theorists are disciples of Aristotle and Kant. On the one hand, they implicitly subscribe to a civilian concept of law-imposed-on-the-facts rather than a common law understanding of law-growing-out-of-the-facts. This explains why they can so easily, it seems, pronounce particular decisions to be wrong, why (just like the economic theorists) they can be so dismissive of what judges actually say, and why at least one of them would apparently impose on judges a constitutional responsibility to apply the law generated by the theory, regardless of the facts of the case.[83] On the other hand, philosophical theorising represents (I would say) a scholarly reaction to the creeping realisation that under the

[82] Of course, this conclusion raises the question of how 'tort law' is and ought to be defined and demarcated. For an excellent general discussion, see S Waddams, 'Classification of Private Law in Relation to Historical Evidence: Description, Prescription, and Conceptual Analysis' in A Lewis and M Lobban (eds), *Law and History: Current Legal Problems 6/2003* (Oxford, OUP, 2004). It is arguable, I suggest, that the civilian approach to classification and taxonomy, based ultimately on the methodology of the *Institutes of Gaius*, is inextricable from the civilian understanding of the relationship between law and the facts of individual cases, namely that the law pre-exists and is imposed on the facts. This allows law to be developed by reference to hypothetical fact patterns that themselves are moulded to fit the chosen classificatory scheme. Under the common law model, where law arises out of the facts of individual cases, it may be as difficult to create tight conceptual categories as it is comprehensively to classify the indefinitely various messes of social life to which the common law reacts. The problem is not the messiness of life as such but that the common law approach seeks to accommodate the messiness as much as possible, whereas the civilian approach tries to regulate and discipline it. This is part of the meaning of the common law's 'pragmatism'.

[83] R Stevens, *Torts and Rights* (Oxford, OUP, 2007) 314.

common law model, 'jurists' have no distinctive niche in the legal ecosystem. They aspire to a world in which the scholars make the law and the judges apply it. The theorists certainly take norms seriously; but in the face of the marginality of scholars under the common law model, they turn their attention from legal reasoning to the extra-legal normative discourse of moral philosophy, in which they can participate without the external constraint imposed by a canon of authoritative literature.

Typically, too, philosophical theorists of the common law construct courts on a civilian model. Following Aristotle, the law of obligations is the law of interpersonal transactions. Courts are public bodies whose function is to apply that law universally across society – to make it a law for everyone.[84] In the Middle Ages, the 'best' private law of obligations was understood to be contained within 'sacred' texts (the *Corpus Iuris Canonicus* and the *Corpus Iuris Civilis*) interpreted and illuminated by scholarly analysis in the light of 'natural' reason. Courts were executives of that law. Since secularisation, the law is now found in a diverse collection of formal legal literature – constitutions, legislation (codes and statutes) and case law – analysed dialectically. Dialectical analysis of legal literature by non-judicial legal experts still plays a central role in law creation in the civilian scheme of things. At the other extreme, under the common law model, courts make law in individual cases[85] and they bear ultimate responsibility for promoting the coherence of the system as a whole. As a result, the prime location of dialectical analysis is the court, not the schoolroom or the study, and the lead actors are Bench and Bar. The authority of the law of the individual decision presupposes a set of rules of hierarchy and precedent to avoid and eliminate conflicts.

c. Civil Recourse Theory

The US legal system, I would say, falls somewhere between these two poles in the role it assigns to courts. By comparison with practice in England and many other common law systems, courtroom dialogue between judge and counsel is truncated. The individual decision is less important, and the 'weight' or 'trend' of the cases counts for more. This is probably almost inevitable in a system that allows federal pluralism in private law. The Australian federal system does not. Despite the fact that private law is essentially a state matter, the Commonwealth High Court has set itself up as ultimate authority for Australia on matters of private law. The US Supreme Court has refused this function. The American Law Institute stepped in to fill the void. The Restatements have two particularly relevant characteristics. One is that they aggregate judicial decisions, having to

[84] eg E Weinrib, 'Private Law and Public Right' (2011) 61 *University of Toronto Law Journal* 191.

[85] This helps to explain why the phenomenon of the 'great judge' – such as Denning or Reid – is a feature peculiar to the common law.

treat none as authoritative but free to treat all as relevant. Secondly, the Restatements contribute to what one author has called the 'textualization' of precedent.[86] Increasingly, the law is found in textual formulations that distil judicial reasoning rather than in the reasoning itself. Courts cease to be temples of reason(ing) and tradition, and become deputy legislators – a conclusion that Ronald Dworkin spent his career resisting, to the delight and approval of the senior English judiciary. Civil recourse theory attempts to capitalise on such characteristics of American law by interpreting the whole of tort law in terms of the role of courts.[87] Tort law, it is said, is best understood as being not primarily about interpersonal transactions but about social provision for dispute resolution. Civil recourse theory was, I understand, inspired by Blackstone.[88] But Blackstone's problem, I think, was different from that addressed by the civil recourse theorists. In order to produce an account of the laws of England accessible to and useful for the lay reader, Blackstone needed to de-centre the courts, to make a move away from law as action to law as word, at a time when, *faute de mieux*, most of the law of the land was made in courtrooms. Because of the dynamics of presidential systems of government, which tend towards legislative inertia, US courts are – *faute de mieux* once again – sites of political contestation to a much greater extent than their counterparts under parliamentary systems. Civil recourse theory may be understood as a reflection of a system in which courts play a relatively active and prominent role in the governmental system, but one different from that played by courts in the classic common law. The solution, for civil recourse theorists, is to understand tort law not primarily in terms of interpersonal transactions but in terms of public provision for governance.

d. 'Sociological' Theory

The strands of modern tort theory so far discussed are essentially court-focused. Such forms of theorising, I have argued, may be understood as modes of participation in the legal project that (implicitly) respond to the marginal role of scholars, relative to judges and advocates, under the common law model. They are forms of participation in the sense that their main concern is to engage with law as doctrine and a mode of practical reasoning in a similar way to Bench and Bar. Other modes of theorising may also be understood as participatory, but very differently, in that they respond to the marginal role of scholars by seeking for them an active part in forward-looking legislative, as opposed to backward-looking, court-based, legal activity. For instance, it has been argued

[86] PM Tiersma, 'The Textualization of Precedent' (2007) 82 *Notre Dame Law Review* 1187.

[87] eg J Goldberg and B Zipursky, 'Rights and Responsibilities in the Law of Torts' in D Nolan and A Robertson (eds), *Rights and Private Law* (Oxford, Hart Publishing, 2012).

[88] H Dedek, 'Of Rights Superstructural, Inchoate and Triangular: The Role of Rights in Blackstone's *Commentaries*' in D Nolan and A Robertson (eds), *Rights and Private Law* (Oxford, Hart Publishing, 2012).

that US legal realism in the 1930s was motivated by the perception that active participation in radical legislative and regulatory programmes associated with the New Deal provided academics with opportunities to play a central part in public affairs.[89] In this frame of reference, courts and court-focused scholarship represent dysfunctional weddedness to the past and to a conservative understanding of the role of law.

On the other hand, sociological, historical, anthropological and related approaches to law may also be motivated by desire to observe and understand law and legal activity from the outside rather than from within. This is not the place for detailed examination of 'observational legal scholarship'. Suffice it to say that it is typically treated as outside the tradition of Western legal scholarship because, at its crudest (or best, depending on one's commitments), it is underpinned by the idea that talk of norms and oughts, rights and obligations is no (or, at most, little) more than a smokescreen for promotion of interests or satisfaction of desires and needs. Traditional legal scholarship, by contrast, rests on the assumption that normative judgments – of ought, may and ought not – can themselves explain and affect human behaviour.[90] In this light, the challenge for observational legal scholarship is to take law seriously by treating the capacity and propensity to understand the world in terms of values as being an integral part of what it means to be human and a central part of what is being observed.

E. Globalisation

Finally, what about globalisation? I think it is more helpful to focus on the underlying phenomena of legal pluralism and relativity. The eighteenth and nineteenth centuries were the heyday of sovereign law and intolerance of legal pluralism. But recall that English law started out as a relative common law, and that for centuries, Roman law performed that function in Europe. Plurality of laws is a fact of life. It was a characteristic feature of imperialism and colonialism with which the Privy Council long grappled.[91]

Legal sovereignty depends on clear rules and hierarchical structures to manage conflicts of laws. The global arena, and some domestic arenas, lack such rules and structures, allowing pluralism to thrive. One scholarly reaction to plurality of laws is to search amongst the alternatives on offer to find the 'best'

[89] R Shamir, *Managing Legal Uncertainty: Elite Lawyers in the New Deal* (Durham, NC, Duke University Press, 1995) 152–57, 164–74.

[90] This helps to explain why 'doctrinal' legal history is in the mainstream of Western legal scholarship. It is participants' history and the history of participation. In this sense, theories that set themselves against 'formalism' – notably, realism and 'critical' theory – also take norms seriously, in that they are concerned with how to use law to regulate human behaviour more effectively than previously or in new and more desirable ways.

[91] eg, P Mitchell, 'The Privy Council and the Difficulty of Distance' (2016) 36 *OJLS* 26.

or 'most favoured' law. Amongst great modern tort scholars, John Fleming put much energy into this project.[92] Tort theory may be understood as a second reaction, to the extent that it makes claims (however implausibly) to universality and singularity.[93] The 'new *ius commune*' and 'European law of torts' movements represent a third scholarly reaction.[94] These are all attempts to manage plurality without sovereign authority. Judicial pluralism, in the form of willingness to look beyond the laws of the forum for answers, seems more difficult to square with a common law system in which individual decisions can make law, than in a civil law system in which individual judicial decisions carry less weight. To this extent, pluralism seems to leave more space for scholarly participation in moulding the law than does sovereignty.

IV. CONCLUSION

In this chapter, I have offered an alternative to ideas of 'influence' as a tool for understanding the role of (tort) scholars and the purposes of legal (tort) scholarship. The explanation is historical and institutional. It is not necessarily inconsistent or even at odds with analyses in terms of influence. Rather, it offers relatively concrete considerations and factors that can be used to give greater focus and substance to analyses of the relationship between jurists and judges and, more widely, the role of jurists in the legal system.

To conclude, let us readjust the lens slightly to focus on recurring themes of the analysis, shared by both models, namely legal pluralism and competition between laws. Early English law was characterised by competition between royal, 'common' law and non-royal, local laws. The proponents of royal law were the royal justices and the pleaders. Early Continental law was characterised by competition between the law of the *Corpus Iuris Civilis* and local, 'customary' laws. The proponents of the first *ius commune* were scholars ('jurists'). The later development of English law was characterised by competition between equity and common law. The proponent of equity was the Chancellor. This competition technically came to an end in 1875. The common law courts also faced competition from Church courts (applying Canon law) and conciliar courts, notably Star Chamber (particularly in matters of crime and public administration). The importance of Church courts and the Canon law they applied was diminished by the break with Rome in the 1530s; and the conciliar source of competition ended in 1641. One way of understanding modern, theoretical, common law tort scholarship is as a source of competition to judges, not only in their role as law-makers but also in relation to their constitutional responsibility

[92] P Cane, 'Fleming on Torts: A Short Intellectual History' (1998) 6 *Torts Law Journal* 1.

[93] J Goudkamp and J Murphy, 'The Failure of Universal Theories of Tort Law' (2015) 21 *Legal Theory* 47.

[94] eg, C van Dam, *European Tort Law* (Oxford, OUP, 2007) ch 6.

to work the various sources of law into a reasonably coherent system. Viewed in this way, 'theories of tort law' provide external benchmarks against which to assess and evaluate tort law as produced by legislatures and courts. The claim of theory to perform this function in relation to 'positive' law seems to be based on assumptions about the metaphysical status of theory as what we might call 'a new natural law'. In this frame, the legitimacy of positive law depends on its consistency and coherence with natural law. Some theorists are quite explicit about the sources of the new natural law – the canonical texts of Aristotle and Kant, for instance. Others, with greater or lesser plausibility, claim to be undertaking 'immanent critique', requiring the positive law only to be true to itself. Either way, the ideal theory is set up in competition with the actual law. The competition offered is based on the supposed merits of the theory rather than its pedigree: let the better norm win!

The theme of competition is also related to the distinction between law and fact through the tension that every legal system must constantly confront between rules, generality and predictability on the one hand, and discretion, particularity and flexibility on the other.[95] In the common law model, the harnessing of law-making to close consideration of the facts of individual cases provides a means of managing this ineliminable tension. In the civil law model (in Hall's words quoted earlier[96]), '[t]he use of dialectic as "an instrument of discovery, suggesting problems which have not actually occurred in practice"' performs a similar function, allowing rules to be tested against imagined fact scenarios to produce desirable qualifications or modifications ready for application by courts in the future should such scenarios present themselves.

As we saw earlier, the common law started out as a means of providing exceptional relief in individual cases by the creation of a dual system of dispute settlement in which royal courts competed with non-royal courts. The capacity of royal courts to perform this function waned as their *modus operandi* shifted from relationality to sovereignty, from exception to rule. This shift reduced the fact-sensitivity of royal justice in the interests of commonality. The assumption of jurisdiction by the Chancellor reintroduced duality into the system; and, importantly, the Chancellor's jurisdiction (like the Privy Council's foreign jurisdiction) escaped Parliament's 1641 attack on conciliar justice. Just as royal justice had earlier been transformed from exception to rule, so gradually the Chancellor's justice ('equity') shed its competitive exceptionality in favour of complementary rule-ishness. This move undermined the *raison d'être* of duality and led, in the nineteenth century, to 'fusion' of law and equity. However, fusion did not and could not eliminate the tension between generality and particularity,

[95] What follows has been much influenced by E Sherwin, 'Modern Equity' and SL Bray, 'Equity: Notes on the American Reception', both forthcoming in D Klimchuk, I Samet and H Smith (eds), *Philosophical Foundations of the Law of Equity* (Oxford, OUP, 2019).

[96] Text to n 27.

norm and exception. Effective abolition of the civil jury (which is of more relevance to tort law than fusion) aggravated the problem by removing another possible source of exception and particularity.[97]

In the absence of institutional and procedural variegation, the burden of managing the tension fell onto some form of dialectic. This may help to explain the shift that Patrick Atiyah documented in his Oxford inaugural lecture entitled 'From Principles to Pragmatism',[98] including the increasing adoption of open-ended concepts and multi-factorial tests in the framing and application of legal rules.[99] And here, at last, we come back again to modern tort theory. We may hypothesise that unitary, singular theories of tort law are offered, in part, as correctives for what their proponents see as excessive flexibility and particularity in modern tort law, which, in turn, we may understand (from the perspective of the monotheorists) as a dialectical over-reaction to the loss of the institutional variegation that provided sources of fact-sensitivity by exception. Instead of vague, manipulable ideas such as 'policy', 'fairness' and 'reasonableness', the theorists offer supposedly more rigid and hard-edged criteria, such as 'economic rationality' and 'rights', to discipline the judicial urge to 'do justice', spectacularly on show in cases such as *Junior Books Ltd v Veitchi Co Ltd*[100] and *White v Jones*.[101]

The shift from institutional variegation to dialectic as the preferred mode of managing the tension between particularity and generality may also help to explain Lord Goff's insistence (noted earlier)[102] that the law should be forged in the hot crucible of fact-sensitive litigation, not moulded in the cool oases of academic principle. The management task, he thinks, is now the sole responsibility of the judge, without access to the escape valve of the jury or a 'court of exception', and without the interference of meddling jurists. How did we get to this point? By the end of the eighteenth century, Chancery had ceased to function as a court of exception. By the same time, the common law had become highly fact-insensitive, leaving pleaders to force their claims into rigid, inflexible legal

[97] Black-box dispute resolution is the extreme version of case-sensitivity. Perhaps the most famous modern illustration of the (criminal) jury performing this function is the trial of Clive Ponting for breach of the Official Secrets Act: at en.wikipedia.org/wiki/Clive_Ponting. Within the law of tort, the distinction between duty of care (a question of law for the judge) and breach of duty (a question of fact for the jury) survived the abolition of the civil jury as a dialectical mechanism for balancing generality and particularity in the absence of the institutional distinction between judge and jury. In the US, where the civil jury survives, the concept of duty still regulates the role of the jury by helping to define issues that the judge must decide.

[98] PS Atiyah, 'From Principles to Pragmatism: Changes in the Function of the Judicial Process and the Law' (1980) 65 *Iowa Law Review* 1249.

[99] For a somewhat different perspective on such concepts and tests, see Lasser, *Judicial Deliberations: A Comparative Analysis of Judicial Transparency and Legitimacy* (n 43) ch 3.

[100] *Junior Books Ltd v Veitchi Co Ltd* [1983] 1 AC 520 (HL); critically discussed in Stevens, *Torts and Rights* (n 83) 182–84.

[101] *White v Jones* [1995] 2 AC 207 (HL); critically discussed in A Beever, *Rediscovering the Law of Negligence* (Oxford, Hart Publishing, 2007) 260–68; and Stevens, *Torts and Rights* (n 83) 176–82.

[102] See text following n 66.

forms as best they could. Abolition of the forms of action and the introduction of fact pleading were designed, in part, to make the common law more flexible by placing more emphasis on the claimant's position and giving the judge greater discretion to mould the law to the exigencies of the case. Now, say court-focused tort theorists, the process has gone too far. However, the judges (aided and abetted – they would say – by sympathetic but misguided, if not disreputable, jurists)[103] lack the ability or the desire to pull back; and so the theorists have taken upon themselves the necessary task of putting some backbone into the law by weaning judges off their post-modern devotion to particularised fairness and justice. What is needed, they say, is much less pragmatism and a whole lot more principle.

Realists and critical theorists see things very differently. For them, the imperative is that the law should serve changing values, objectives and needs, and shake off the dead hand of established principle. In this respect – ironically – they seem to side with judges who, like Lord Goff, are motivated, above all, to do 'justice', whatever that might mean now and for the future. Of course, if the realists' law reforms are to stick for any period, their proponents must, sooner or later, become law-preserving formalists. The competing attractions and demands of generality and particularity, stability and change, are inherent to the human condition. They can and must be managed but can never be finally resolved.

And so, in the words of the children's song, 'the wheels on the bus go round and round, round and round, round and round'.

[103] The most shocking instance of such criticism of which I am aware is that of A Beever, *Forgotten Justice: The Forms of Justice in the History of Legal and Political Theory* (Oxford, OUP, 2013) 308. Referring to John Fleming, Beever says, 'According to one of the most influential analysts of law in the twentieth century, the law, and here specifically the law of negligence, "in origin contemplating only interpersonal justice, eventually also opened itself to a consideration of personal needs, distributive justice and strict liability. This transformation has been rapidly gaining pace since the individualistic fault dogma began to give ground to the mid-20th century quest for social security" [quoted from J Fleming, *The Law of Torts*, 9th edn (Sydney, LBC Information Services, 1998) 114]. There is only a small similarity between this and the following claim [of Joseph Goebbels] *[square brackets and bracketed words added]*, but it is a similarity worth pondering. "On 30 January [with the coming to power of the Nazis] *[original square brackets]* the era of individualism finally died … The individual will be replaced by the community of people"' *[original footnote omitted]*. The small degree of similarity does not relieve – indeed, it greatly magnifies – the foul stench of the innuendo and its utter inappropriateness to academic discourse, even if one does not know that Fleming's father was killed by the Nazis in 1935, after which Fleming's mother sent him to school in England; that he served in the British armed forces during the Second World War; and that Fleming, a master comparativist, made very little reference to German law in his work, and then only towards the end of his career. The close, extended, critical attention given to Fleming's work in Beever, *Rediscovering the Law of Negligence* (n 101) only serves to intensify the odour.

Index

Note: Alphabetical arrangement is word-by-word, where a group of letters followed by a space is filed before the same group of letters followed by a letter, eg 'civil rights' will appear before 'civilian model'. In determining alphabetical arrangement, initial articles and prepositions are ignored.

Page numbers followed by the letter 'n' refer to footnotes on the quoted pages.